Philippe Barbour

BRITTANY

'Breton culture thrives, right in the
centre of Brittany and right by the shore.
Breton dance, Breton bagpipe music
and the pardons... Go and join in these and
other celebrations, laze on those gorgeous
beaches or feel the wind in your hair as
you sail around the rocky Breton coast.'

CADOGANguides

1 The beach at Sables-d'Or-les-Pins,
Côtes d'Armor

2 Megaliths at Carnac, Morbihan
3 The Ile de Bréhat seen from the Pointe
  de l'Arcouest, Côtes d'Armor

3

4 The view of St-Malo from Dinard, Ille-et-Vilaine
5 Low tide at Port de la Houle, Cancale, Ille-et-Vilaine
6 Rocky Trégastel-Plage, Côtes d'Armor
7 The port at Douarnenez, Finistère

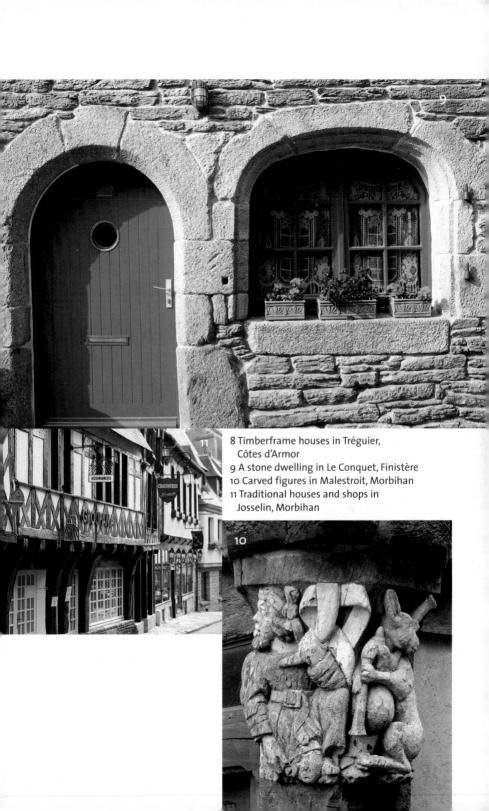

8 Timberframe houses in Tréguier,
  Côtes d'Armor
9 A stone dwelling in Le Conquet, Finistère
10 Carved figures in Malestroit, Morbihan
11 Traditional houses and shops in
  Josselin, Morbihan

12 The Château de Josselin, Morbihan

13 Colourful windowboxes in Malestroit, Morbihan

14 A quayside in Paimpol, Côtes d'Armor

15 The chapel overlooking St-Samson beach, Finistère

16 A gourmet shop window, St-Malo, Ille-et-Vilaine

14

15

17 By the water in Tréguier, Côtes d'Armor

18 An art gallery in Pont-Aven, Finistère

About the author

Philippe Barbour is both Petit Breton and Grand Breton, being half-Breton and half-British. He is passionate about Brittany, and explored virtually every one of its creeks, chapels and boulders to present you with the best of the region in this guide. He has written several other books for Cadogan Guides, including their guides to the Loire and to the Rhône-Alpes, and is the main author of *Flying Visits France*, focusing on French cheap-flight destinations, and of the *Cadogan Guide to France*.

This book is dedicated to Philippe's beloved Breton grandmother, Ninan, who secretively got up before him to make him fresh crêpes before he set out on each day of exploration for the Finistère chapter. It is also dedicated to his Breton aunt and uncle, Dine and René Quiniou, who have always spoilt him in Brittany, and who helped with research. As ever, Philippe's parents have supported his work immensely.

Particular thanks to the press officers around Brittany who helped in the initial research, and to all the guides who presented their sights with such enthusiasm.

About the updater

Robert Harneis is a historian and journalist who lives in France with his French wife. He is on the editorial staff of the English-language newspaper *French News* and is an expert on Général de Gaulle and the military architect Vauban.

Contents

Cadogan Guides
Network House, 1 Ariel Way,
London W12 7SL
info@cadoganguides.co.uk
www.cadoganguides.com

The Globe Pequot Press
246 Goose Lane, PO Box 480, Guilford,
Connecticut 06437–0480

Copyright © Philippe Barbour
1998, 2002, 2005

Cover design: Sarah Gardner
Book design by Andrew Barker
Photographs: John Ferro Sims
Maps © Cadogan Guides,
    drawn by Map Creation Ltd
Managing Editor: Natalie Pomier
Editor: Rhonda Carrier
Editorial Assistant: Nicola Jessop
Proofreader: Alison Copland
Indexing: Isobel McLean

Printed in Italy by Legoprint
A catalogue record for this book is available
    from the British Library
ISBN 1-86011-142-4

Introduction

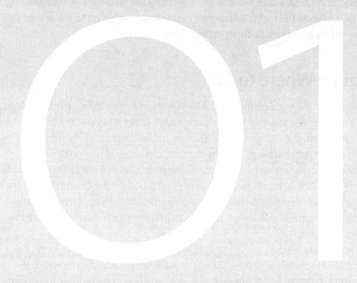

Seagulls bark at you along coastal paths as wind threatens to blow you off a treacherous rocky promontory; sea foam flies against a Breton lighthouse as you sail by, while waves roar into a beach more noisily than motorway traffic; barnacles scratch the soles of your feet as you scramble across rocks; gelatinous algae creepily touch your legs as you swim along, creating mythical sea monsters in your mind. But only translucent sandhoppers or playful children tickle you out of your daydreams as you lie relaxing on warm sands... Brittany's shores can sometimes be calming, but just as often they prove exhilarating.

I have a particularly strong attachment to Brittany and happy memories of holidays on the Breton coast. My mother comes from Brittany and my French family from the most stubbornly Breton, southwestern corner of the region. For me, going to the Pays Bigouden each summer as a child was by far the most important event in the year. I would meet up again with my grandmother, my cousins and my aunts and uncles.

The day we arrived, my uncle René would fetch langoustines fresh from a friend's boat, and my grandmother Ninan would lay them out decoratively next to the pile of crêpes. My aunt Dine would have stocked up on other buttery Breton delicacies. My granny, on her daily walk to the shops in Pont-l'Abbé, would say hello to the old Bigoudènes in their towering *coiffes*. As often as possible we would go to the beach, where the adults would take shelter behind windbreaks and parasols to chat about family friends, and the year's events in the local fishing communities. My grandmother and my uncle, both brought up as Breton-speakers, would sometimes laugh at each other's expressions as they cropped up from time to time in conversation.

We children would be busy digging our own boats in the sand, playing boules, splashing about, later windsurfing, and occasionally dousing the adults with an icy-cold bucket of Atlantic water. Tea was announced by the local fishing fleet heading back to port beyond the rocks. And on fine evenings we would go to the savage Bay of Audierne to watch the sun die its daily death in the sea.

Choosing Where to Go

I have explored the whole length of the Breton shore for this guide, from the deep calm of the bay of the Mont-St-Michel to the rough Atlantic beyond the Loire estuary, . All along the coast, the vestiges of neolithic civilization, the remnants of fortifications, the memories of colonial times, and the scars of Nazi occupation mingle with spectacular Breton beaches, bays and ports. The place names, from St-Malo round to the Pointe de St-Gildas, recall the religious men who crossed the Channel in the Dark Ages to set up communities on this Armorican peninsula, turning it into Brittany. These men were turned into the semi-legendary Breton saints never recognized by the Catholic Church.

An air of mystery remains along the Breton shore, in the endless confusion of its headlands and indented estuaries, and in the drama of reefs and rocks, which in places such as Paimpol and Penmarc'h look as if a shower of meteorites has rained

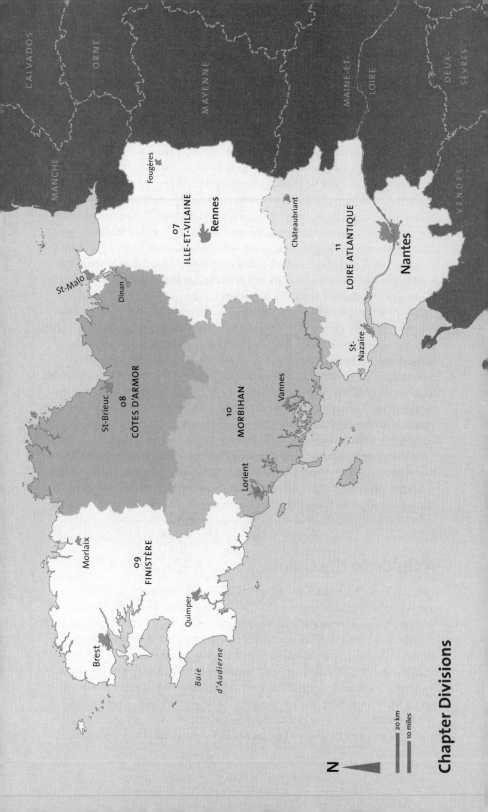

Chapter Divisions

N

20 km
10 miles

down on the sea. Yet much of the Breton coast and all the islands are now fought over by tourists. Such is the high regard in which the Breton resorts are held that, in a recent survey of tour operators asking them which they considered the finest beaches in the world, La Baule in Brittany was voted second. There are numerous more wonderful major resorts to me. Seeking out a quieter corner along the coast in high summer is not easy, but I have tried to pick out places by the sea that are comparatively less well known, such as the staggeringly beautiful bay of St-Brieuc not far east of the fabulous pink rocks of the Côte de Granit Rose.

You really need to head far inland to find truly tranquil corners in the region in high summer. Travel up any of the ever so many crooked, delightful Breton rivers and you quickly leave the pounding ocean for quieter, wooded banks. These estuaries are sometimes known as *abers* or *avens*. The most renowned is that of Pont-Aven, made so famous by the shockingly colourful art of Paul Gauguin and Emile Bernard. Up the estuaries, you come to large historic towns, with their old quays tucked well out of sight from invaders, such as Morlaix, one of the best hide-outs for Breton corsairs, or Quimper, internationally known for its pottery.

After the defensive chain of estuary towns, you can then go in search of peaceful Breton countryside, perhaps following the rivers right up to their sources. You might track the Blavet, for instance, a splendid river that supplies the gorgeous Lac de Guerlédan in the heart of Brittany. Chapels and villages of granite or schist hide among the ridges and boulder-strewn landscapes of the Breton interior. Some of the rocks were turned into neolithic monuments. The chapels most often display naïve statues of the Breton saints. The much-celebrated elaborate calvaries of the province are mainly a feature of the Finistère in the west. In fact, the further west you go in Brittany, the more typically Breton the region looks.

Breton culture thrives, right in the centre of Brittany and right by the shore. Breton dance, Breton bagpipe music and the *pardons*, the pious pilgrimages when the local saints are taken out of their humid churches for an annual airing, are still going strong. Go and join in these and other celebrations, laze on those gorgeous beaches or feel the wind in your hair as you sail around the rocky Breton coast.

A Guide to the Guide

For this book, I have divided Brittany up according to its four official French administrative *départements*: the Ille-et-Vilaine, the Côtes d'Armor, the Finistère and the Morbihan. But I have also included highlights of a fifth, the Loire Atlantique, most of which was traditionally a part of Brittany, with its main town, Nantes, the last capital of the independent medieval duchy. After the general background and practical sections, each *département* is devoted a touring chapter, with descriptions of its historic and tourist sights, practical tourist information, and recommendations on hotels, B&Bs, restaurants and crêperies. This book has been written with a narrative thread you can follow from beginning to end, and to entertain you on the way, the text is peppered with legends of Breton saints, historical titbits and literary tales.

History, Art and Architecture

02

History

Stepping into a Fog of Celtic Romance

Breton history has been dogged by the thickest fog of romance, and it's unlikely this will ever entirely lift. Serious historians are trying to find more trustworthy paths through it, but many don't care to follow. For ages the widely scattered remains of a great neolithic society on the Armorican peninsula were regarded as vestiges of a much later Celtic civilization. Now, at least, Brittany's neolithic society is reckoned to have lasted roughly from around 5000 BC to 2000 BC. Celts, by contrast, are very vaguely estimated to have arrived in Brittany in the latter half of the 1st millennium BC; but some scholars question whether there was a significant influx of Celts as far as Brittany at all – it may have been more a case of Celtic culture from central Europe influencing the native tribes to the west. Armorica, the land of the sea, seems at least to have been the Celtic name adopted for the northwestern region of Gaul before the Romans arrived.

Some nationalistic Bretons think back nostalgically to the ducal Brittany of the Middle Ages as an age of Breton independence. Small matter that in that period the vast majority of rural Bretons had no choices in their subjugated lives. And in the Middle Ages, politics was dominated by aristocratic feudal ties of service and marriage that could jump regional frontiers. The rigid notion of nationhood we know had not developed. Sometimes the Breton dukes allied themselves with France, sometimes with England. As such, the Breton duchy of the medieval period was not strictly independent or united, but Brittany clearly did maintain differences from the rest of France, in identity, cultural influences, and, in part, through language. In fact, although the leading lords of the peninsula spoke French and knew Latin, historically Breton has virtually never, if ever, been spoken across the whole of geographical Brittany. As to Brittany after its union with France under the Ancien Régime, all too little mention is made in general history books of the slave trade in which many Breton merchants were deeply involved. Better known is how the majority of the Breton population has invariably suffered up until the Second World War. A rapid chronological guide follows through the hotly debated history of the Armorican peninsula.

Fiery Prehistory, Neolithic Society and Gaulish Armorica

The vast mountain ranges that towered up many millions of years ago across Brittany are hard to picture now. They were very slowly worn down to reveal the magma turned to granite that had bubbled up underneath them some 300 million years back.

The first remains of human ancestors found on the Armorican peninsula have been dated to the middle of the Paleolithic Age, a dauntingly long and distant period stretching from around 700,000 BC to 10,000 BC. Most excitingly in archaeology, prehistoric finds made at Menez Dregan in the Finistère in 1998 shattered scientists' views on how long ago human ancestors discovered the use of fire, almost doubling estimates from 250,000 years ago to 465,000 years ago, plus or minus 65,000 years for error. These count, to date, as one of the oldest known traces of fire made by human ancestors anywhere in the world. Naturally, various factions are arguing about the validity of the finds.

To discover more about **neolithic** inhabitants in Brittany, visit the museums at Carnac, Vannes and Penmarc'h. After the last ice age some 10,000 or so years ago, as Europe started to warm up again, Mesolithic hunter-gatherers were established on the Armorican peninsula. Just a few traces of them have been discovered, most notably the skeletons covered with shell necklaces and antlers on islands off the Quiberon peninsula. Mesolithic communities appear to have been rapidly supplanted by neolithic agricultural settlers, who acquired or brought over the skills of agriculture developed in the Middle East.

These neolithic people are best known to us from the tombs they left and their mysterious menhirs or standing stones. Their funerary architecture is the greatest legacy of the period, making it easier for researchers to study death in neolithic societies than to guess at what neolithic life may have been like. Two thousand years and more before the great pyramids went up in Egypt, neolithic men in Armorica were already constructing these vast tombs, which are not unique to Brittany but are particularly numerous and spectacular here. The neolithic people cleared land for farming, reared cattle and grew cereals. They also developed stone tools, pottery and weaving. A complex, so far impenetrable system of beliefs evolved, along with hierarchical social structures. It is quite possible that some of the coastal people went some distance to trade.

As a tourist, you will find few remains of civilization dating from between 2000 BC and the Roman conquest of 57 BC in Brittany. Celtic influences only gradually infiltrated a local people with roots established in the area in neolithic times. No traces of large pre-Roman communities have been found in the province, except at Alet, precursor of St-Malo. Towards the end of the pre-Roman period, evidence of strong trading ties with southern Britain do emerge, and Armorican coins from that time have been unearthed in parts of southern Britain, suggesting that the Armorican sailors might have controlled trade in that orbit. The Armorican tribes appear, by the close of the 1st millennium BC, to have been culturally close to many other western European tribes, with a similar mythology and language as well as shared tribal and place names.

Five **tribes** were identified across the Armorican peninsula at the time Caesar conquered Gaul. The Riedones occupied the northeastern corner; the Coriosolitae held sway over a northern slice of territory; the Osismi controlled the largest lands, across northwestern and the whole of the western tip of Armorica; the Veneti occupied the southern side of the peninsula; lastly, around the Loire lay the lands of the Namnetes. Tribal coinage seems to have appeared during the 2nd century BC, the first clear sign of political cohesion in the peninsula.

Caesar and a few other classical writers give us rare glimpses of Celtic Gaulish culture. They identified two privileged groups, the nobles and the druids, who lorded it over a virtually enslaved populace. The druids seem to have been enormously respected, deciding on legal matters, being exempt from military service and taxes, and officiating at religious ceremonies and sacrifices. They passed on learning orally, as their religion prohibited them from committing their knowledge to writing. Caesar claims they also believed in magic and an afterlife.

Roman Conquest and Enslavement, Prosperity and Christianity

Caesar's well-organized troops had little trouble conquering Gaul, including Armorica. But the Armoricans soon took part in revolts, perhaps particularly anxious that the Romans were going to take away their lucrative trade with southern Britain. The Veneti caused Caesar the most problems. Caesar tells in some detail of his campaign to beat and punish them in one of his most famous passages in *The Conquest of Gaul*.

Under the Roman Empire, in the 1st century AD, economic prosperity does appear to have grown substantially, as did the first major Armorican towns, Gallo-Roman tribal centres. But the Romans did not bring only good things; a sad sign that used to stand by a small segment of Roman road by the Vilaine river recalled that: 'The Romans had this road built by their slaves, the Gauls.' The Romanization of Armorica was particularly strong in the urban areas, but pre-Roman Gaulish ways may have remained almost untouched in the countryside. A reasonable number of major Romanized landowners thrived in Armorica, building substantial villas; but the mass of the population probably scraped a simple living through agricultural work. However, prosperity did continue to increase in the 2nd century AD, trade networks extending far and wide.

Christianity seems to have caught on slowly in Armorica. Before the Roman Empire's official adoption of Christianity, Christians were often persecuted. One tale of horror tells of the way Donatien and Rogatien, sons of a governor of Nantes, were tortured and beheaded for their Christian beliefs in AD 304. By the early 4th century however, the Emperor Constantine elevated Christianity to the position of exclusive imperial religion. Early bishoprics seem to have been set up at Nantes and Rennes, under the guidance of the Church at Tours. When Christianity turned from persecuted to persecutor, the rural peoples would put up some resistance to its intolerance of old ways and beliefs.

The Dark Ages and the Creation Myths of Brittany

Swirling mists of particularly disorientating legend obscure any clear view of how the Armorican peninsula turned into Brittany during the Dark Ages. The extremely hazy picture is of a large number of strongly Christian immigrants coming from Ireland and the so-called Celtic fringes of western Britain, particularly south Wales, to impose themselves on the native Armoricans, profoundly influencing the culture of the region.

One popular conception is that these pious Celtic Christian groups felt threatened by the heathen Angles and Saxons taking over Britain, and headed for Armorica as peace-loving, evangelizing heroes. The stories of saintly miracle men leading this exodus (*see* 'Stone Boats and Slain Dragons', p.31) are much more immediately entertaining than what may actually have happened. Credible recent historians have proposed a complex diversity of reasons why Britons settled in Armorica, and have argued that the emigrations took place over several centuries, lasting up to the early 7th century, and probably commenced before the collapse of the Roman Empire in the early 5th century. Some historians have put forward the theory that violent Irish incursions into western Britain in the late 3rd century caused some panic emigration south across the Channel that early. One oft-quoted source on the subject of the Briton immigration, Gildas, wrote poetically in the mid 6th century of Britons being forced away from their lands in the century before by the menacing Angles and Saxons. These Britons, wrote Gildas, 'made for lands beyond the sea... Beneath the swelling sails they loudly wailed, singing a psalm that took the place of a shanty'. Another plausible theory is that in the late Roman Empire, certain native British fighters proved themselves capable warriors, and were asked to cross the Channel to help the Gallo-Romans try to stop the advance there of the hordes from the east.

Zealous Christian leaders looking for new challenges and conquests seem to have played a very important part in the change from Armorica to Brittany. Irish monks may have been the first to try to work their magic on the Armoricans. Charismatic Welsh Christian leaders certainly appear to have travelled across the Channel to spread the word across the Armorican peninsula. Seven of these early evangelizers became known as the so-called **founding saints of Brittany** (*see* 'Stone Boats and Slain Dragons', p.31). Most of this host of Breton saints were probably well educated and able to negotiate a good deal for themselves and their followers when they landed in Armorica, and the communities that they established appear to have included members who could spin a good yarn.

The first known instance of at least some of the Armorican peninsula being referred to as Brittany, or rather Britannia, comes from the Byzantine historian Procopious; writing in the the mid 6th century, he seems to imply that the region was heavily colonized by then. Legends telling of the heroic creation of a British state spanning both sides of the Channel were largely believed up until the 18th century, and were most famously peddled by the 12th-century writer Geoffrey of Monmouth, in his unreliable *History of the Kings of Britain*.

There is a pretty notion that the Dark Ages Celtic immigrants were simply warmly received, without any complications, by their 'cousins' across the seas.
Events were doubtless nowhere near that innocent. What seems likely is that the Gallo-Roman Armoricans, that is the people firmly settled in the peninsula at the end of the Roman Empire, found themselves increasingly pressured by British immigrants establishing themselves in particular in northern and western Armorica, as well as by **Frankish settlers** moving in from the east. The areas around Rennes, Nantes and Vannes, which contained rich agricultural lands and mineral deposits, in fact came under the rule of Frankish nobles in the 6th century.

Tensions, both territorial and religious, between Bretons and Franks ran high. The papal-controlled Church of Rome would eventually impose its authority on western Brittany, but a distinctly different Celtic Christianity did last in the region up until the 9th century and beyond. The Bretons generally seem to have been as bellicose as the rest in these bloody times, but tensions exploded in the second half of the 6th century, involving the Bretons and the Franks in all manner of vicious family intrigues, gruesomely retold by the 6th-century Frankish historian and bishop of Tours, Gregory. The most famed and feared Breton leader to emerge in the period was Waroc, who took on the Franks of the Vannetais and won after a long-drawn-out and cunning campaign; this extended Breton frontiers eastwards.

The Vilaine river, and in the north the Couesnon river, perhaps became a kind of very rough boundary between Bretons and Franks. The Bretons' territory seems to have been divided at some stage in the Dark Ages into three major sections: Dumnonia or Domnonée running west from the bay of the Mont-St-Michel, Cornovia or Cornouaille occupying western Brittany, and Broërec extending across southern Brittany. Several references from the 7th and early 8th centuries to one chief or little king of Dumnonia, Judicaël, seem to indicate that he had to travel east to apologize to the Frankish king Dagobert in AD 635 for warring with his Frankish neighbours. Another reference, from 691, states that the Bretons, who had previously acknowledged the authority of the Merovingian Franks, now found themselves freed from it by Merovingian in-fighting.

The Short-lived 'Kingdom of Brittany'

After the deposition in AD 751 of this Merovingian dynasty by **Pépin le Bref**, the first of the Carolingian Franks, warring flared up on the Breton borders. Possibly in response, Pépin le Bref's troops sacked Vannes in the 750s and created the March of Brittany, a protective border zone covering the areas around Rennes and Nantes, which lasted from approximately the 770s to the 820s. Its most renowned prefect or supervisor was one **Roland**, who became the hero of the most famous epic verse tale in early French, the *Chanson de Roland* (actually recording a harrowing Frankish defeat by the Basques at Roncesvalles way south in the Pyrenees).

The Carolingian Empire failed to establish its authority in Brittany but probably helped to unite it politically through antagonism. Fighting having proved frustrating, the Carolingian emperor and son of Charlemagne, **Louis le Pieux**, tried diplomacy in the 820s. This worked initially, and some talented Breton figures soon rose high in the imperial ranks. **Nomenoë** (or Nominoë), a native Breton, was given the honour of becoming imperial *missus*, which gave him control of military, civil, judicial and, unusually, ecclesiastical power over much of Brittany. This exceptional degree of power, however, was conferred upon him by the Frankish-Carolingian emperor outside Brittany. Louis le Pieux's religious leaders also saw to it that Brittany was brought into the fold of the Roman Church of the Holy Roman Empire.

While Louis le Pieux reigned, Nomenoë remained loyal to the Carolingian Empire. But in the disintegration of the empire that followed Louis's death, Nomenoë and his son **Erispoë** became entangled in vicious local warring, for instance around Nantes. **Charles le Chauve** (the Bald), new king of the Franks, tried to intervene with almost disastrous consequences – his troops were routed by Nomenoë's Bretons at the **battle of Ballon** (near Redon on the Vilaine) in 845, and for a few days some thought that Charles himself had been killed. Nomenoë also had to contend with Viking raids. It seems that he managed to bribe these unwelcome newcomers into going and looking for booty elsewhere. Nomenoë took control of the Church across Brittany, replacing the five bishops at Dol-de-Bretagne, Alet, St-Pol-de-Léon, Quimper and Vannes with Bretons of his own choice. When Nomenoë died in 851, Charles the Bald thought he might be able to defeat Erispoë; but he was again deeply humiliated, this time in 851, at the battle of Jengland-Beslé (also by the Vilaine river).

Erispoë capitalized on Charles the Bald's weak position; he would accept peace only in return for territories on the fringes of Brittany, the counties of Rennes, Nantes and the area of Retz to the south of the Loire. These new territorial gains were named Britannia Nova. Erispoë's acquisitions would profoundly change the Breton boundaries, to last pretty much unchanged through to the 1960s. Erispoë also demanded suitably grand recognition, and became the first non-Carolingian to be given the title of ruler of a *regnum* or kingdom in the Holy Roman Empire. Brittany became the Regnum Britanniae. In 856, the year before he was violently assassinated by his cousin, Erispoë saw his daughter married to Charles le Chauve's eventual successor as king of the Franks, Louis le Bégayeur (the Stammerer).

Salaun (or Salomon), Erispoë's lethal cousin, went on to become the most successful of all Breton leaders in terms of the territories that he acquired. Charles the Bald conceded a piece of Anjou and then handed him the whole Cotentin (or Cherbourg) peninsula in gratitude for helping to defeat a common enemy. In exchange, Salaun seems to have integrated Brittany still more fully into the Carolingian system, both administratively and religiously. He moved the centre of Breton political affairs further to the east, where it has remained ever since.

Breton ecclesiastical and cultural life in the early 9th century shared in the so-called Carolingian Renaissance. But importantly, in Brittany a passion for the great Celtic Christian evangelizing immigrants of earlier centuries was kept alive. These ancient leaders were venerated in a spate of largely invented biographies, which would continue to be churned out in the coming centuries.

Vicious Vikings, Breton Dukes and the Counts Next Door

Vicious **Viking raids** on British and French shores wrought periodic havoc throughout the 9th century. But the strong Breton and Frankish resistance that was mounted around Brittany made the Vikings turn their attentions to weaker foe further north for some time. However, the situation in Brittany got dramatically worse in the early 10th century. While some of the Vikings began settling into cohesive communities, the various counts of Brittany fled to Britain, as did the king of the Franks, the well-named Louis d'Outremer (Overseas Louis). The Breton kingdom effectively ceased to function between 913 and 936. There is only evidence of one count in Brittany staying and successfully resisting the Norman takeover at this period, **Berengar of Rennes**. The Breton hero of the period is **Alain Barbetorte** (Twisted Beard), Count of Cornouaille, who came back from Britain in 936 to take on and oust the unwelcome settlers. After this traumatic break in Breton and Carolingian history, ducal Brittany emerged.

Alain Barbetorte and the leaders of Brittany who followed him were, more modestly than their predecessors, titled '*duces Britonum*'. The **Breton dukes** of this early feudal period proved unable to wield the same power as the leaders of the Regnum Britanniae. For a start, the territorial gains Salaun had made were lost. Over the next few centuries, Brittany's ducal rulers would find themselves more and more pressurized and influenced by the increasing might of the neighbouring regions, first Normandy and then Anjou. These two expanded into substantial European powers for a time, while the Capetian kings of France ruled over a much weakened kingdom based around Paris and Orléans. Particularly because the Breton dukes found it impossible to unite the Breton counts below them, Brittany could not compete with such strongly led neighbours.

Brittany around 950 was divided into **nine dioceses** that would last until the Revolution, with the bishoprics based at Rennes, Dol-de-Bretagne, Alet, St-Brieuc, Tréguier, St-Pol-de-Léon, Quimper, Vannes and Nantes. These religious centres formed the nucleus for Brittany's important early medieval towns. The founding of feudal *castellanies*, based around a castle, with a priory provided nearby, would lead to the establishment of another series of medieval Breton towns, examples being Fougères, Vitré, Dinan and Josselin. **Conan I**, Count of Rennes, and his successors assumed the position of dukes of Brittany between around 970 and 1066. Under **Duke Conan II** (who ruled from 1040 to 1066), the duke's uncle and former guardian, Eudes, started a messy civil war in Brittany. The counts of Cornouaille also acted very independently during this time. In fact, **Hoël of Cornouaille** assumed the title of duke in 1066, as Duke Conan II left no direct heir.

Bretons played a significant part in the Norman conquest of England in 1066 and were rewarded with English estates (*see* 'Strong Bonds Across the Breton Seas', p.28). One Breton and English nobleman, **Raoul de Gaël**, proved to be a particularly rebellious thorn in William the Conqueror's side; the Norman champion arrived to take Dol-de-Bretagne in 1076, but failed, as illustrated on the Bayeux tapestry. Duke Hoël's son and successor **Duke Alain IV** married first into the Normandy ruling family, then into the Angevin one. His second wife, Duchess Ermengarde, greatly influenced the reign of her son, the next Breton duke, **Conan III**.

Religious foundations mushroomed up in Brittany in the 11th and 12th centuries, in particular in the east; they brought greater links with the main ecclesiastical movements in France, but many Bretons clung doggedly to old ways, particularly in the west. Superstition and magic apparently flourished, even among parish priests and monks, and the writing of Breton saints' lives continued as a source of popular inspiration. These strands of alternative belief remained strong in rural Brittany down to modern times. In the western half of the province, the Breton language thrived, but the feudal systems that had been adopted faster in eastern, Gallo-speaking Brittany were gradually reinforced. By the late 12th century, Brittany consisted of around 40 major *castellanies* under which lay another important level of local lordships, *seigneureries*.

Plantagenet and Capetian Intervention and Domination

Angevin **Henri II Plantagenet**, alias King Henry II of England, imposed his will of steel on the Breton peninsula in the second half of the 12th century. He thoroughly controlled **Duke Conan IV**, who was much put upon by the feuding factions within his province. Conan IV formally recognized King Henry II's overlordship at Avranches in 1158 and often attended the Plantagenet court. Duke Conan IV married Marguerite, sister of Malcolm IV of Scotland, in 1160, but although some have interpreted this as an act of defiance, it seems that Conan IV continued as a puppet duke.

In 1166, King Henry II arranged for Constance, daughter of Conan IV and Marguerite, to be betrothed to his fourth son, **Geoffrey**. He then decided he would rule Brittany directly until Geoffrey came of age; Conan IV timidly acquiesced. In this time, new Angevin administration was imposed on Brittany and feudal obligations were much more rigidly defined; these changes were to remain influential down the Middle Ages. King Henry II had no truck with dissenters; the castles at Rennes, Fougères, Bécherel and Léhon were among those destroyed on the king's orders when the nobles there displeased him. Early medieval Brittany had apparently been scarcely involved in sea trade, but thanks to Angevin links with Aquitaine and England, Breton ports developed rapidly. Breton shipping merchants flourished and many Breton vessels carried Bordeaux wine to England.

King Henry II's son and successor, **Richard the Lionheart**, would maintain an iron grip on Brittany, however, causing the frustrated **Duke Geoffrey** to side with the Capetian king, **Philippe Auguste**, whose love for Geoffrey was great. After Geoffrey died from wounds that he had sustained during a chivalric tournament in Paris in 1186, Philippe Auguste tried to throw himself into his friend's open grave. When King Richard died in 1199, **Duke Arthur** of Brittany had a strong claim to the English throne as the grandson of King Henry II, but Richard's brother **John** inherited. In 1199 and 1202, Arthur paid homage to Philippe Auguste and from this time on until the end of the feudal system, the kings of France remained the immediate suzerains of the Breton dukes. The wily King John managed to capture Arthur and is reckoned to have had him killed. Philippe Auguste, however, successfully seized most of King John's lands in France.

The inheritance of the Breton duchy fell to Alix, the half-sister of Duke Arthur; she was married to **Pierre de Dreux**, who was a Capetian relative of Philippe Auguste. Pierre tried to cut his vassals down to size and to diminish the Church's holdings in Brittany (hence his nickname, **Mauclerc**, 'Bad to Clerics'). He swiftly became enormously unpopular but did manage for a time to control many of the warring factions within Brittany, and also fought back opportunist neighbours. He entered into alliances both with other awkward French princes to defy the French king, and with King Henry III of England. In 1230, rebel Breton nobles called on King Louis IX's assistance against Mauclerc, and in 1234 the Breton duke had to yield to the French crown. A coalition of Breton barons forced Mauclerc to give up the dukedom to his son Jean as soon as the latter came of age. This he did in 1237.

Like father, like son. **Duke Jean I** not only angered the king; he also found himself excommunicated by the pope. He did, though, manage to subdue the many Breton lordly families who detested him, and he was to enjoy the longest reign of any Breton duke – an impressive 49 years. **Duke Jean II**, who succeeded in 1286 and ruled until 1305, benefited from his father's successes. All in all, the 13th century saw the position of the Breton dukes much strengthened, but in the early part of the 14th century the French crown put pressure on the duchy, making heavier demands for military service and Church taxes. Brittany would also soon be split in two by a terrible war of succession that followed **Duke Jean III**'s death in 1341 without any legitimate heir.

The Breton War of Succession, 1341 to 1365

The question of Breton succession became another bone of contention between the kingdoms of France and England, and it played out like a subplot to the early Hundred Years War. Breton law stated that Duke Jean III's nearest descendant should inherit, be that person a man or a woman. The most obvious heir was **Jeanne de Penthièvre**, a niece of his. She had been married to a nobleman with French royal connections, **Charles**, son of Guy, **Count of Blois**, and nephew of the French king Philippe VI. **Philippe VI** was the first Valois king of France. He had successfully defended his right to inherit the French throne in 1328 against the claim of King Edward III of England, leading to the outbreak of the Hundred Years War.

Jeanne de Penthièvre and Charles de Blois, however, had a rival for the Breton duchy. He was **Jean de Montfort**, son of Duke Arthur II of Brittany (who had preceded Duke Jean III) by the latter's second marriage; and he was Jeanne de Penthièvre's half-uncle. Rather than plunging straight into conflict, as earlier accounts claim, it seems that both sides waited for a commission appointed by Philippe VI to decide who should inherit. Philippe VI declared in favour of Jeanne de Penthièvre and Charles de Blois. King **Edward III**, in defiance, offered the Honour of Richmond, the English estates that had traditionally been granted to the dukes of Brittany by the English crown, to Jean de Montfort. With such favourable backing, De Montfort called upon supporters to rally round him and the Breton War of Succession began. Some absurdly basic interpretations of this war make it sound as though the English simply arrived as an invading enemy force, the French supporting the Bretons, which was far from the case.

Close family ties bound most of the powerful lords of northern Brittany to the Penthièvre cause. But Jean de Montfort found followers among the disgruntled lesser nobles, notably in the Breton-speaking west. Certain historians argue that these smaller nobles were concerned about defending Brittany against the encroachment of centralizing French monarchical control, although Jean de Montfort had scarcely shown any interest in Breton independence previously. That many Breton towns and port authorities readily supported De Montfort because of the importance of their trading ties with English crown territories seems plausible enough.

Early on, Jean de Montfort was captured. But De Montfort's wife, **Jeanne de Flandres** (daughter of the Count of Flanders), remained free and furious, heading a resistance movement. In response, several English armies arrived in Brittany in the course of 1342, and the English-backed De Montfortists secured the ports of western and southern Brittany. A truce was called in 1343, and Edward III returned to England with Jeanne de Flandres, leaving lieutenants in charge of the section of Brittany under their control. Traitors to the De Penthièvre cause in Vannes allowed the De Montfortists into that city, which became the centre of De Montfortist administration for the remainder of the war.

In 1345, Jean de Montfort, on parole in Paris, ran off to England and payed homage to Edward III; troops were gathered for him there. De Montfort headed off to Brittany, where he promptly died from an old, infected wound. The English lieutenants were then effectively left to run the De Montfortist campaign until 1362, when finally De

Montfort's heir, his son, also called Jean, came of age. Meanwhile, Charles de Blois had tried to beat back the English forces in a series of small battles in the 1340s. But he was captured in 1347 and taken as a prisoner to England; Jeanne de Penthièvre took up the cause. However, with the campaigns of the Hundred Years War spreading into several parts of France, and with the terrifying scourge of the Black Death devastating the country in 1348 and 1349, the action was halted for a time. Fighting would soon resume, and when it did the military leaders spread terror through the countryside. **Bertrand Du Guesclin** is the one most remembered, even lionized in Brittany for his role in the Combat des Trente, a brutal encounter between the best knights on each side of the war, which is often held up as a model of medieval chivalry. The common Breton people suffered terribly through the conflict, and many Breton towns built fortified walls to try to protect themselves during the war.

By March 1353, it appeared that King Edward III might be ready to accept Charles de Blois as the new duke. But the matter was not settled and by 1356 Henry of Lancaster was taking the **young Jean de Montfort** over to Brittany to lay siege to Rennes. Charles de Blois lost the next round of the bout and was forced to pay huge ransoms. The volatile situation continued into the 1360s. Sir John Chandos was besieging Auray in 1364 when a much larger army led by Charles de Blois and Du Guesclin came to meet the Anglo-Breton forces. Blois made a terrible tactical blunder and attacked from an unfavourable position. He was killed and his army defeated; Jeanne de Penthièvre conceded defeat. Du Guesclin was captured. The English sportingly but unwisely let him go. By the **Treaty of Guérande** of 1365, the young Jean de Montfort was declared **Duke Jean IV of Brittany**.

The De Montfort Breton Dukes, 1365 to 1491

The De Montfort dukes and their administrations went on to foster a keen sense of Breton identity at the expense of both the French and the English. But Duke Jean IV's reign got off to an almost disastrous start when he became embroiled in the greater Anglo-French conflict in 1369. The formidable French king **Charles V** attacked Brittany and Duke Jean IV had to flee to England. Briefly it looked as if his duchy would be forcibly joined to France, as Charles V began legal proceedings before the Parlement de Paris to confiscate Brittany. The king missed his opportunity, however, by alienating the aggrieved De Penthièvre party, who felt that one of their number should rightfully succeed the ousted De Montfort. So angered were the De Penthièvres by Charles V that in an extraordinary move they called on Duke Jean IV to return to Brittany, offering him their support. The Breton Du Guesclin had become leader of the French armies at the time and could have stopped Duke Jean IV from landing had he wished. But he made no effort to do so – perhaps his loyalties were divided on that occasion. Duke Jean IV regained his ducal authority, and after King Charles V's death the second Treaty of Guérande of 1381 brought peace between Brittany and France.

In the period of the De Montfortist dukes a kind of semi-independent Breton nationhood was fostered. The Breton ducal administration became a dogged defender of Breton interests, and Breton tax revenues increased, helping to pay for an army that could be called upon at short notice. The ducal household grew in number in the course of the 15th century, as did courtly pomp and entertainments; it was in great contrast to the ascetic, religious Charles de Blois, who had died in a vermin-infested hair shirt.

Cleverly building up its international status, the Breton duchy was represented side by side with sovereign states through much of the 15th century. Even the Breton Church carried on independently from the French one, involved in its own negotiations with the papacy. In 1460, the university of Nantes was founded with papal blessing, an important symbol of intellectual independence for Brittany. Many Breton histories would be written in the period of the Breton dukes, emphasizing Brittany's strong, independent roots. Major opportunities also existed in the 15th century for leading Bretons to find plum positions in French royal circles, with the greater wealth and influence that arena offered. Another Breton, Olivier de Clisson, succeeded Du Guesclin as head of the French army.

Yet all was not quiet and harmonious within Brittany itself. **Duke Jean V** (who ruled from 1399 to 1442), after the humiliation of being held prisoner briefly by Breton cousins, confiscated and redistributed his captors' lands. With the second half of the Hundred Years War in full swing, he first supported the Anglo-Burgundian alliance against the weak King Charles VII of France, but then signed a treaty with him. The Breton duke managed to steer Brittany clear of the worst fighting, however. **Duke François I**, who succeeded Duke Jean V, continued to support the French side, as did the short-lived Breton dukes who followed, Pierre II and Arthur III.

But with the advent of King **Louis XI** in 1461, **Duke François II** of Brittany was faced with a much tougher, expansionist French monarchy. As François had no male heirs, Louis XI made preparations to secure Brittany, enticing Breton courtiers to his side with extravagant rewards. Duke François II's chancellor, **Guillaume Chauvin**, favoured diplomacy with France while the Breton treasurer, **Pierre Landais**, opposed him. Landais managed to win the argument in the early 1480s, but opponents soon staged a coup to oust him; Landais was condemned to death. François, meanwhile, had many of the Breton border towns heavily fortified. But the days of the Breton duchy were numbered.

Marshal Rieux was one powerful Breton who bitterly resented the influence some non-Breton councillors had acquired in Brittany's court under Duke François II. After King Louis XI's death, he allied himself with the regents acting on behalf of the young King **Charles VIII** of France. A French army entered Brittany in 1487 and besieged the ducal capital of Nantes. Rieux actually then changed sides and helped push back the French a first time, but the Valois forces were on the offensive. At the decisive **battle of St-Aubin-du-Cormier** on 28 July 1488, the French defeated the Breton army. The Treaty of Le Verger, a humiliating peace, was signed in neighbouring Anjou. Duke François II died within weeks, and this left his young daughter, **Anne de Bretagne**, as his successor.

Though the 15th century has often been referred to as a golden age for Brittany, a good half of the Breton population are reckoned to have still been living at subsistence level. At least Brittany escaped most of the atrocities of the second half of the Hundred Years War that lasted until 1453 and so devastated some other French regions. Alcoholism, crime, prostitution and leprosy were rife in Breton towns, although such religious figures as **Vincent Ferrier** tried to harangue the populace into leading virtuous lives. Breton textile manufacturing, however, was growing into one of the region's most prosperous enterprises. One particularly rich legacy of the period was numerous Breton Flamboyant Gothic churches, which the textile merchants as well as the local lords would often pay for.

Anne de Bretagne's Hand Unites Brittany with France

After Duke François II's death, a diplomatic skirmish ensued to gain Anne de Bretagne's hand in marriage. In December 1490, the Holy Roman Emperor Maximilian's envoy, Wolfgang von Polheim, even came to Brittany and placed his bare leg on Anne's bed, thus symbolizing a prestigious marriage by proxy. But Anne and her advisers agreed instead that the young duchess should accept the hand of the young King **Charles VIII**. Their marriage in 1491 effectively spelt the end of the semi-independent duchy of Brittany.

Anne de Bretagne is often portrayed in popular Breton history in a quasi-saintly light; you will find her image depicted across Brittany, and her name mentioned in reverential tones on many a guided tour. Actually, she seems to have been an extravagant spender and a stubborn, pragmatic politician intent on defending her own interests. Anne de Bretagne and Charles VIII did not produce a male heir before the king accidentally killed himself in 1498, and as Anne's marriage contract forced her to marry his successor, she was wedded to King **Louis XII** in 1499.

With her new husband, Anne managed to acquire more freedom to run Breton affairs, until her death in 1514. **François d'Angoulême**, Anne's son-in-law, became Louis XII's successor as King François I. He stepped in after Anne's death and appointed his own administrators to run Brittany. From this stage on, Brittany was politically dictated to by central French rule. The **Act of Union between Brittany and France**, signed by the Estates of Brittany and the king in Vannes in 1532, did supposedly grant Brittany some special privileges, although the monarchy could easily ignore them.

Brittany is often portrayed as inward-looking and backward. Yet this was not always the case. Breton fishing fleets set out from the very beginning of the 16th century (some Breton stories even claim before Columbus set sail) for the great cod-fishing banks off Newfoundland. This long-distance, gruelling trade would last for centuries, many of the Breton ports becoming deeply involved in it. The most famous Breton sailor at this time was **Jacques Cartier** (*see* 'The First Croissant in Sumatra', p.36). While the Breton nobles and merchants successfully exploited trading opportunities overseas, the mass of the rural population remained wretched and rooted in its old ways. But even in rural Brittany, the wealth of churches and calvaries commissioned demonstrates that many communities had the money for a good show of piety.

The **Breton Parlement**, an important regional law court run by aristocrats, rather than a parliament with wider-reaching powers, was created in 1554 under King **Henri II**. It would last a little over 200 years, until the Revolution. The French king was represented in Brittany through this period by a powerful, royal-appointed governor or *intendant*.

French Religious Wars and Colonial Wars with Britain

In the second half of the 16th century, tensions between the newly formed Protestant Christians and the Catholics boiled over into the hideous French **Wars of Religion**, and Brittany, as elsewhere, was torn between the warring factions. Protestantism had caught on strongly in eastern and southern Brittany, notably in the territories of the mighty **Rohan family** based at Josselin. The **Duc de Mercœur**, governor of Brittany towards the end of the century, became the savage self-seeking ultra-Catholic leader in the province. Spanish and English troops became involved on opposing sides in the bloody conflict, and in these barbarous times warlords swept round creating hell on earth. King **Henri IV** of France's famed **Edict of Nantes** of 1598 brought most of the fighting to an end, granting religious rights to Huguenots as well as Catholics. In the Counter-Reformation of the 17th century, the Catholic Church and Jesuits in particular took a firm grip of Breton religious life, and in 1685 the Edict of Nantes protecting Protestants was revoked by King Louis XIV. The power of the Catholic Church in Brittany has continued right through to the present.

The largest Breton ports assumed considerable importance in the Ancien Régime's empire-building of the 17th and 18th centuries. Sailors set forth from them on adventures of exploration, colonization and slave trading, as well as on naval expeditions. The great shipbuilders could make the most of the iron-making industry that had taken off in eastern and central Brittany. The very names of certain ports reflected the colonial aspirations of the French monarchy, such as Port-Louis and L'Orient. You can get personal glimpses of Breton life in the late 17th century by reading Mme de Sévigné's vivid letters written during her visits to her provincial château.

The western European battle for colonies was vicious, with endless fighting in the pursuit of colonial riches. St-Malo became a massively wealthy French city at the close of the 17th century, both from international trade and its corsairs. Corsairs were often successful in their raids and added greatly to the tensions at sea.

In the 18th century, the slave trade reached staggering proportions in Brittany. Shipping magnates at Nantes benefited greatly; they organized almost half of all French slaving expeditions. St-Malo and Lorient shipowners were also significant players in the French slave business. In the mid 18th century, colonial conflicts and wars between France and Britain succeeded each other, most significantly the **Seven Years War** of 1756 to 1763. In 1758, the British landed near St-Malo, but the expedition was a failure and the governor of Brittany, the Duc d'Aiguillon, led his troops to crush the stranded rearguard at St-Cast-le-Guildo. The French struck a medal to celebrate the 'battle'. The British referred to it simply as an 'action' or an 'affair'. The next year however, the British navy wiped out a good portion of the French fleet at the **battle of Quiberon Bay**. France soon lost much of its extensive empire to Britain.

The Breton Parlement came increasingly into conflict with the extravagant French monarchy towards the end of the 18th century. In 1762, Breton nobleman Louis-René de Caradeuc de La Chalotais led a move to expel the overpowerful, much-resented Jesuits from Brittany. This brought the regional Parlement into conflict with King Louis XV himself. Such was the level of protest by Breton aristocrats that the king had to climb down. The days of the French monarchy were numbered anyway.

The Chouannerie Fights the French Revolution

Most Bretons were living a pretty wretched existence when the French Revolution exploded. Not that the Revolution was particularly popular in large sections of Brittany; more than three-quarters of the Breton clergy refused to swear the civil oath as the state demanded. Support for the persecuted Church, added to enforced conscription and a strong contingent of angry expatriate noblemen, led to a widespread counter-Revolutionary guerrilla movement in the province, known as the **Chouannerie**. It was not successful.

General Hoche's name is equated with the bloody repression of the Chouannerie by Republican forces. In 1795, an émigré invasion in the Bay of Quiberon turned into a disaster for the Chouannerie, while anti-Revolutionary Vendéens coming up from south of the Loire were crushed at Savenay in the Loire Atlantique. At Nantes, the Republican Jean-Baptiste Carrier organized particularly horrific drownings of anti-Revolutionaries in the Loire. The Chouan leaders are still regarded as heroes by some Bretons; several little museums specifically commemorate them. The Revolutionary authorities came to look upon Brittany, now divided into its five geographical *départements*, as an awkward, counter-revolutionary and deeply reactionary province.

Slow Progress in the 19th Century, Huge Losses in the 20th-Century Wars

A chaos of endlessly changing French governments followed on from the traumatizing Revolution and Napoleonic follies. Brittany was neglected, exploited and denigrated by many 19th-century French governments. However, the armed forces and the navy continued to recruit Bretons in large numbers.

The major Breton canals, one linking the north and south coasts, the other connecting Nantes and Brest, were vast engineering projects for their time, but water transport would rapidly be superseded by rail, tracks being laid from the middle of the century. In the course of the 18th and 19th centuries, the ocean-going ships had grown considerably in size, until many of the large Breton ports that had been built protectively down river estuaries, such as Morlaix, Quimper and Redon, could no longer receive these vessels. St-Nazaire, by the mouth of the Atlantic, would grow out of nothing to become one of the great shipbuilding, industrial ports of France.

Before the end of the 19th century, the Breton population exceeded the 3 million mark. Fish-canning and various other sea-related enterprises took off as mass industrialization developed, for example at Douarnenez, Concarneau and Quiberon. Many people from the poor rural communities moved into the new industrial towns. The railway, and the peace that was achieved in the so-called Belle Epoque between the Franco-Prussian War of 1870–71 and the outbreak of the First World War in 1914, enabled the first Breton resorts to develop. Aristocrats, and even European royalty, flocked to Dinard in particular, while Breton fishermen continued to head out on terrifying expeditions and inland Breton peasant families shared their gruel from a single pot set in the middle of the kitchen table. A growing number of intellectuals and artists were, however, realizing the strengths and the enormous appeal of Breton culture.

French workers were officially allowed to start forming trades unions late in the 19th century; this led the exploited workforce to organize strikes across Brittany, and violent encounters ensued. **Breton nationalism** also began to become popular, and political and cultural groups such as the **Gorsedd**, the **Bleun Brug** and the **Breton Nationalist Party** were formed.

It has often been said that the Breton troops in the **First World War** were exploited by the French military commanders as cannon fodder. Statistics put the number of Bretons who died in the Great War from around 200,000 to 250,000 – a huge proportion of that total population of around 3 million. It is perhaps not surprising, then, that Breton nationalism increased in popularity. The government continued to enforce a policy stopping the speaking of Breton, let alone its teaching, in schools.

Detached from these issues, property developers went ahead with building more glamorous Breton resorts between the two wars. Gritty Douarnenez, by contrast, elected France's first Communist mayor in 1921 and France's first female councillor in 1924, although the law forbade her from serving. Douarnenez also saw some of the biggest Breton strikes in the 1920s.

In the **Second World War**, as France was overrun by the Nazis, some Bretons immediately took up De Gaulle's call to fight to free France from abroad, most memorably the men of the tiny island of Sein. Some Bretons stayed and joined Resistance units in the territory. Many others, however, were forced to work for the Nazis or collaborated with them. Some of the Breton nationalist movements ironically fantasized that through Nazism they would find an opportunity to assert their Breton race. A large number of Bretons, though, were simply downtrodden by occupation; the feelings of division and bitterness from this period still run deep for those who experienced it.

The Germans forced prisoners to help build portions of an Atlantic wall of defences. Most infamously, the Nazis built up huge submarine bases at Brest, Lorient and St-Nazaire. From here, the dreaded U-Boot submarine fleets set out to destroy the vital convoys between North America and Britain in the battle for the Atlantic. While inland Brittany was liberated in summer 1944, pockets of Nazi resistance held out right up until May 1945, notably around the submarine bases and St-Malo. The Allied air forces, in frustration, bombed those cities to smithereens. Several Second World War museums in Brittany, notably that at St-Marcel, recall the war.

Brittany Recovers its Pride

The annihilated Breton ports were swiftly reconstructed, though the countless German blockhouses have been left exposed along Brittany's sides as war scars. A renewed sense of **regionalism** began to develop in France after the Second World War, only this time supported by central government. From the 1950s, the Conseils Généraux of the *départements* were given much greater powers over social and economic affairs, while gradually the Breton language became more accepted in the region's schools, although by then many Bretons had stopped speaking their traditional language even at home. In the shake-up of the French regions, the Loire Atlantique with its capital, Nantes, was removed from administrative Brittany.

Culturally however, the Loire Atlantique remains a part of the old province. The official Région Bretagne today still only numbers some 3 million inhabitants; add the Loire Atlantique and that increases by a million.

Various small **Breton nationalist groups** such as the clandestine ARB (the Breton Revolutionary Army) and the FLB (the Breton Liberation Front) have occasionally performed relatively minor acts of violence, including destroying a television transmission station and statues representing French central authority. There has been little support for such violence or for these groups' visions of independence among the majority of Bretons. Ties between the extremist Breton nationalists, the Basque separatists ETA and the IRA have proved quite strong at times, however, and little outbursts of violence still occur: a nationalist Breton attack in 2000 left one person dead at a McDonald's in Quévert, Côtes d'Armor, and in 2003 police seized arms at Deauville, apparently being delivered by the IRA.

Other Bretons have thrown themselves into working towards the **economic development** of the province. The creation of powerful agricultural cooperatives in postwar Brittany led to commercial success and, thanks to broader thinking, the launch of Brittany Ferries. But with the speed of advances in agriculture, rural Brittany began to empty. *Remembrement*, the government policy of eradicating old field-divides to form more efficient larger plots, has radically altered the look of large parts of the Breton countryside that had remained unaltered for centuries.

Farming has since become an increasingly beleaguered profession. In the 1980s, pictures of angry farmers dumping vast quantities of vegetables they couldn't sell onto the Breton streets caused a storm. Fishing has also been badly affected by recent cuts, as has the navy. In 1994, after a fishermen's protest in Rennes, the historic Breton Parlement building was burnt down by a stray firework. The destruction in the fire of much evidence concerning the murky financial affairs of President Mitterrand led to some suggestions that the event may not have been an accident. The place has now been completely restored.

Tourism has become a hugely successful modern 'industry' in Brittany, though some in this field have disregarded the consequences for their region's **environment** – sections of the coast have been much altered by the holiday industry. Other environmental concerns include the actions of the pig farmers, most noticeably in inland Côtes d'Armor, who have been blamed for polluting the Breton soil, although they are by no means singlehandedly responsible for the problem.

Many Bretons, however, have campaigned against nuclear energy in a country that has otherwise apathetically accepted the French government's enormous reliance on this controversial source of power. Yet they could do little against a series of oil tanker disasters in the 1960s and 1970s, most notoriously that involving the *Amoco Cadiz*, which carried in black tides of oil over long stretches of the north Breton shore. Most recently, the oil tanker *Erika* broke into two south of the Finistère peninsula in 1999, and more than 300,000 birds perished in the muck. The coastline does recover quite rapidly from these man-made catastrophes, luckily, and the French government has now taken vigorous steps to discourage rogue tankers, with huge fines for illegal tank cleaning near the French coast.

Politically, the right-wing French Front National, considered racist by virtually all but itself, has its fair share of supporters in Brittany, but no more than elsewhere, even though its loud-mouthed main leader for so long, Jean-Marie Le Pen, hails from La Trinité-sur-Mer in the region. By contrast, the success of Kofi Yamgnane, black mayor of St-Coulitz and former Socialist minister, was much written about in the French press. And numerous high-flying Bretons have gained high office in Paris. At the same time as the Breton language has fast died out (see 'A Dying Language in Black Dog Shit, p.38), the championing of **Breton culture** has been greatly encouraged at the universities in Rennes and Brest. Breton events have also thrived in the past few decades and a large number of Bretons still derive an enormous amount of joy from their cultural traditions.

Art and Architecture

Breton Building Blocks: from Pink Granite to Mottled Schist

The name of Brittany conjures powerful visual images: neolithic dolmens and menhirs; lichen-covered chapels topped by their openwork steeples; weather-eroded calvary sculptures; towering Breton *coiffes* that look like lighthouses of lace; and brilliant Gauguin paintings from around Pont-Aven.

Gauguin's vibrant blocks of colour stand in strong contrast to the subdued grey tones of the stone mainly associated with Breton architecture – **granite**. This grainy, gritty stone was often used in the building of towns, villages, churches and chapels. Some of the region's granite on the north coast takes on surprisingly bright hues, the rock deeply impregnated millions of years ago with pink and orange elements.

Yet only around a third of the region's surface is made up of this stone. The rest consists mainly of types of **schist** or shale, which also give off surprising dashes of colour, from tinges of browns and oranges to blues and even greens. The castles of eastern Brittany, such as Fougères, Vitré and Châteaubriant, show off schist's distinctive mottled effects, while the architecture around the Fôret de Paimpont has striking patches of purple schist to it. Bright white limestone, associated with Loire Valley architecture, only begins to appear in southern Brittany.

Slate counts among the types of shale found in Brittany, and most Breton houses are roofed with deep blue-black rectangles of it that turn shades of silver and blue in the sunshine. Most of the **thatch** that preceded the slate has disappeared, except in small pockets, notably the Brière, today the most densely thatched part of France. Brittany's **whitewashed houses**, in particular along the coasts and down the river estuaries, help give the region its immediately recognizable and friendly look. In the Breton ports, you will often find brighter scenes, with more diverse colours.

From Numerous Neolithic Remains to Rare Romanesque Ones

You often don't have to venture far from a Breton beach to discover some of the earliest architectural achievements of western Europe. **Neolithic tombs, dolmens** and **menhirs** are scattered around the Breton countryside almost as liberally as Breton churches and chapels. Carnac is far and away the most famous area for Breton neolithic culture. But around the whole of the Golfe du Morbihan you'll find a mass of fascinating neolithic sites, especially those at Erdeven, Locmariaquer, Arzon and Gavrinis. A handful of Breton museums concentrate on the neolithic, notably at Carnac, Vannes and Penmarc'h. Beyond the Golfe du Morbihan, the most imposing vestiges of Armorican neolithic culture are Barnenez, La Roche-aux-Fées and St-Just.

In contrast to the neolithic, few visual signs remain of the cultures of the Armorican peninsula from the end of the neolithic period to the early Middle Ages. That's a gap of some 3,000 years. You may chance upon the odd **Iron Age** promontory fort or grooved column. A few vestiges of **Gallo-Roman** Armorica do remain, such as small sections of ancient walls and seaside villas, while the most moving little vestige of Gallo-Roman art is concealed in a tiny chapel in Langon. Very disappointingly, virtually no traces have been found of the religious foundations and communities established by the Breton immigrants of the Dark Ages, though the excellent Musée Thomas Dobrée in Nantes does include some Dark Ages finds. St-Philbert-de-Grand-Lieu abbey stands apart for the well-preserved remains of its Carolingian church.

After the destruction wrought by the Vikings, **Romanesque** architecture developed in the 11th and 12th centuries. Few Breton Romanesque buildings have survived intact, but many Breton churches have retained portions of Romanesque structures. Churches at Dinan, Daoulas, Landévennec, Loctudy, Quimperlé, St-Gildas-de-Rhuys and Redon count among those with the finest vestiges. Dol-de-Bretagne's main street has the rare distinction of having preserved some Romanesque houses.

Breton Churches – Stern, Colourful and Awkward

If some visitors come to Brittany in search of neolithic remains, many more are in search of Breton countryside churches and calvaries. The further west you travel, the more embedded the Breton look and culture become; it is in the western Breton church enclosures that you come across the elaborate outdoor calvaries, covered with sculptures telling the story of Christ's Passion, while the ossuary, where the bones of the dead were collected, may show a figure of the mocking Breton Grim Reaper, *l'Ankou*, one of the most inescapable and haunting figures in regional culture and folk tales. Calvary, ossuary, a large side porch with statues of the apostles lined up, a gateway for the dead, and a low surrounding stone wall – these make up a typical Breton *enclos paroissial* or parish enclosure.

All nine Breton cathedrals except Rennes show how the **Gothic style** was adopted in the region. One of the first attempts at Gothic in Brittany was carried out in St-Malo's cathedral in the 12th century, and many new monastic establishments or buildings were erected in the God-glorifying, light-filled Gothic style in the 13th century. The most famous is just over the Normandy border, the Merveille of Mont-St-Michel. The Breton cathedrals are, architecturally, rather eccentric. Tréguier's has a nave in which virtually every column is different, while Quimper's has a kink in it, and between its spires, instead of a religious statue rides the figure of legendary Breton king Gradlon. Other significant Gothic buildings, including those at Beauport, Léhon, Boquen and St-Mathieu, have not fared as well, though they remain awe-inspiring.

After the first few decades of the 15th century, a new Gothic style spread across Brittany, **Flamboyant Gothic**, and was stuck to for a long time. The quintessence of Breton church architecture would be a 15th- or 16th-century Flamboyant Gothic granite edifice with open steeple, curvaceous accolade arches above the entrances, and playful patterned Gothic tracery balustrades running round the outside. The decorative joy of window tracery in the shapes of flames, trefoils, quatrefoils, tears or hearts, the ornate brackets of the accolade arches, the wild panoply of stone figures and monsters flying out from gables and corners, all make the style so very appealing. Some of the Breton Gothic openwork church towers rose to vertiginous heights, quite out of proportion with the buildings they soared above.

At approximately the same period as Flamboyant Gothic appeared in Brittany, so did an art form that is pretty well unique to the region, or to western Brittany – the **elaborate Breton calvary**. The most impressive are those of Tronoën, Pleyben, Plougastel-Daoulas, Guimiliau, St-Thégonnec, St-Herbot, Plougonven, Kergrist-Moëlou and Pestivien.

Although the Breton duchy lost its semi-independent powers from 1488, that did not stop the church-building projects. For example, a specific style of church construction was started by **Philippe Beaumanoir** at the turn of the 15th to the 16th century. These Beaumanoir churches stand out for their octagonal steeples bordered by a side stairtower, and for their sharply pointed apses. Breton church building continued to flourish through the 16th and 17th centuries.

Flamboyant Gothic would be tamed across most of France by the rigid, harmonious, symmetrical discipline of the **Renaissance style**, but in Brittany the new form found it hard to establish itself. In Breton religious architecture you will rarely come across a completely Renaissance church or building. Rather, a new addition, such as a tower or porch, might be built in the Renaissance style, with its characteristic decorative motifs derived from antiquity, such as triangular pediments, domes and shells.

Moving into the **Ancien Régime**, after the 16th-century Reformation and through the 17th century, the Catholic Church hit back with the **Counter-Reformation**. Huge new monasteries and convents went up around major towns. In the parishes, to dazzle worshippers, colourful, elaborate decoration was commissioned for the church interiors. Highly carved baptistries, pulpits, set-piece Entombment scenes and the like would proliferate. Showy sacristies were often tacked on to churches, and retables became a particularly common feature of Breton churches; those of eastern Ille-et-Vilaine and of the western Finistère are particularly ornate.

Dark Breton granite and schist can look dour on a dull day, but go inside Breton churches and chapels and you may sometimes be surprised by the highly coloured, perhaps even gaudy-looking pieces of decoration. There, you will most likely find an over-elaborate 17th-century retable, its ornate architectural framework set around an altar, highly carved and smothered with figures of saints. The stringbeams, intricately carved in many cases and once vibrantly painted, may also be worth looking up for. If stained-glass windows are relatively common, few wall paintings have survived. A few Breton churches have retained their naïve 15th-century **painted ceilings**, however, such as Châtelaudren, St-Gonéry, Kermaria-in-Isquit and Kernascléden, and another half dozen or so have preserved their delightful Gothic rood screens, notably Le Folgoët, St-Fiacre, Kerfons, Locmaria and Loc-Envel. Numerous churches hold collections of statues of Breton saints. There may even be the odd ex-voto of a ship donated by sailors thanking the Lord or their patron saint for saving them from drowning at sea. Breton church decoration often has a naïve, almost crude look. Breton art can only rarely be described as refined, and can even have a touch of unintentional comic charm: when you see a statue such as the one of St Thélo at the abbey of Daoulas, where the religious man seems to be squashing the deer he rides on, it's hard to resist a smile.

The best areas for traditional Breton churches and chapels include: in the Finistère, around the Elorn valley, along the Aulne valley and through the Cap Sizun and Pays Bigouden; in the Côtes d'Armor, in the western Goëlo, south and west of Guingamp or around the Lac de Guerlédan; and in the Morbihan, around Pontivy and Le Faouët.

Breton Secular Architecture

Brittany's rural art and architecture have great charm, but its historic towns are deeply appealing too, with plenty of architecture worth visiting. Notable are the **nine cathedral cities** (see p.12). Towns were heavily fortified in the Middle Ages, and awesome fortifications still ring historic Dinan. Guérande has an extraordinarily well-preserved set of ramparts. Other towns that have retained impressive parts of their defensive medieval walls include St-Malo, Quimper, Concarneau, Hennebont and Vannes.

The Breton dukes had several **châteaux** built around their territories. Substantial ones survive at Suscinio, Dinan, Vannes and Nantes, for instance. Fort La Latte is the most spectacular of the coastal castles dating back to medieval times; you can visit further major Breton medieval castles (many in ruins) at Josselin, Combourg, Montmuran, Châteaubriant, La Hunaudaye, Tonquédec and Clisson, among others. At the mighty castles of Fougères and Vitré you get a good lesson in the developing styles of military architecture through the Middle Ages. One of the most glorious and comical examples of the Renaissance in Brittany is the Château de Châteaubriant. The châteaux of Kerjean and La Bourbansais count among further well-known examples, while the Château de Goulaine follows the fashions of the Loire Valley.

The Breton coast continued to be heavily and dramatically fortified during the Ancien Régime. Some other grand châteaux from this period that are worth visiting include Les Rochers-Sévigné, Rosanbo and Caradeuc. You can enter many Ancien Régime **forts** unchallenged; the spiky creations of Port-Louis or Belle-Ile make stunning architecture, and Port-Louis contains a good museum on French colonial history. Vauban's and Garangeau's defensive works, notably around St-Malo, are admirable.

Breton's grandiose, Parisian-looking Parlement went up in Rennes in the first half of the 17th century. As overseas commerce and the slave trade grew in the second half of that century, Breton merchants grew richer. Brittany's major colonial trading cities, St-Malo, Nantes and Lorient, expanded rapidly; exuberant examples of splendid **timberframe mansions** still stand in Morlaix, Quimper, Vannes, Vitré and Rennes. But increasingly wealthy merchants ordered sturdy **granite houses**, even in small country towns such as the gorgeous Locronan, Quintin, Rochefort-en-Terre and Guerlesquin.

Gauguin, Nazis and Le Corbusier – the Past Two Centuries

Perhaps the most remarkable feature of 19th-century architecture in Brittany is the plethora of mighty **lighthouses** built out to sea. The villa of La Garenne Lemot near Clisson and the Palais Briau close to Varades are other interesting buildings of the period, while in the new tourist resorts, sumptuous and eccentric villas sprouted up, most remarkably at Dinard and La Baule.

Yet the 19th century is perhaps most interesting for the **fine arts**. Treasures confiscated at the Revolution plus additional donations led to the opening of substantial museums in Rennes and Nantes. By the second half of the 19th century, Brittany was attracting foreign artists in good number, and Gauguin and Emile Bernard created a new vision in western European art at Pont-Aven (*see* p.335). The main fine arts museums of Brittany, at Rennes, Nantes, Quimper and Brest, all have representative works by the leading lights of the Pont-Aven School, while the Pont-Aven museum puts on some superb exhibitions. There are other fine arts museums at Vannes, and, on a smaller scale, at Le Faouët, Lamballe, Dinan and Fougères. The Quimper pottery museum clearly shows how the Quimper pottery houses began catering for the first tourists' desire for Breton quaintness as early as the 1870s, depicting Breton peasant figures on their wares.

For those who tire of the quaint side of Brittany, Brest, Lorient and St-Nazaire, rebuilt in uncompromisingly modern style after the war bombings, have a gritty attraction that can make a change. Or you can always visit the countless Nazi blockhouses along the coast. There is nothing beautiful in them, but they have been deliberately left standing as testament to Brittany's Second World War suffering. The most famous experiment in modern architecture and modern living in Brittany came with Le Corbusier's design in the 1950s of the Maison Radieuse in Rezé, south of Nantes.

Contemporary art even gets the odd airing in Brittany, in particular in some of the fine arts museums, Nantes's especially. The Château de Kerguéhennec puts on splendid shows, while exhibitions at Ar Vevenn and Le Dourven are more modest. Some chapels north of Pontivy become modern art galleries in summer, while Bazouges-la-Pérouse allows a colony of cutting-edge artists to take over in high season.

The proliferation of museums commemorating local Breton life in the 19th century and the first half of the 20th century are certainly worth visiting, but often with these museums it feels like traditional Breton culture has been tidied up into cluttered old homes that serve as storage cupboards for the Breton past. It is a major problem that much of Breton culture has been reduced to quaint curiosity, but at least since the 1960s Breton music and dance have undergone a revival. Traditional Breton bands, called *bagadou*, fight it out in numerous musical competitions, while anyone can join in the dancing at the traditional *festou noz*, lively evening festivals. And bagpipes fill the air each year in the first fortnight in August, for the largest gathering of modern-day Celts at the Festival Interceltique in Lorient (*see* 'Festivals', p.63).

Topics

03

Strong Bonds Across the Breton Seas

The best-known Breton links across the seas are with Wales, southwest England and Ireland, the popularly termed Celtic fringes of Europe. In the course of the Dark Ages, waves of religious leaders and communities emigrated from those places to the Armorican peninsula and turned it into Brittany. Their influence on the language, culture, spirituality and place names of the region was immense and has lasted in many ways down to the present. Read the history chapter in this book and the topic on saints (*see* p.31) to learn more about these immigrants and their Celtic Christianity and Celtic mythologies.

However, the very name of Brittany derives from that of Britain, not Wales or Ireland. Brittany, it turns out, has extremely strong bonds through history with many parts of England, which go way back into the mists of time. In fact, some experts have claimed that Stonehenge may have been built for a neolithic élite that travelled across from the Armorican peninsula to Britain.

There are clear signs that Englanders and Bretons co-operated before the Norman conquest in response to the Viking invasions of the 9th century, and the Anglo-Saxon King Athelstan appears to have received manuscripts from the abbey of Landévennec by way of thanks for his support. Most interestingly, Bretons greatly helped William of Normandy conquer England in 1066, which gave Breton nobles who took part in the conquest substantial estates across England. Some historians have estimated that 10 per cent of English lands were in Breton noblemen's hands by 1086. The most notable English estates held by Bretons through the Middle Ages were those of the Honour of Richmond, handed down to a string of Breton dukes.

Several significant Breton nobles found refuge at various English courts, and one, Arthur Duke of Brittany, almost became king of England in place of bad King John. The latter, living up to his reputation, had his young rival murdered, it is said. The English went on to become deeply involved in the 14th-century Breton War of Succession. Often in Brittany, the English are portrayed as the enemy in that war, whereas they put into power the most successful line of Breton dukes, the ones who proved most able to assert their independence from France, the De Montforts.

One war after another between the English and French monarchs over the centuries, as well as daring raids by rival corsairs either side of the Breton Sea, as the Channel was traditionally known in Brittany, did however lead to increasingly general animosity between England and Brittany. The English appear as villains in many old Breton songs. Along with the theme of death at sea, another obsession in Breton shanties is of Breton girls being snatched away from their families by English sailors.

Looking across more distant seas, significant historical ties exist between Brittany and North America too. They go back to the very earliest major recorded European discoveries of the contours of the New World in the first half of the 16th century. The cod found teeming in the Newfoundland banks at that time caused many Breton fishermen to go off on long expeditions to those dangerous but lucrative waters for many centuries to come. The most famous cod fisherman of the lot was the Breton Jacques Cartier. On his exploratory voyages, he discovered the great estuary of the

St Lawrence river. Or rather, he was shown it by Native American Indians. After Cartier, the path was open for the French colonization of Canada and other vast portions of North America.

Back with English links, the late Princess Diana was descended from a Breton aristocratic woman of extraordinary character who caused a storm in her day with her meteoric rise to favour at the British royal court in the 1670s. Louise de Kéroual, or Kéroualle, travelled to England accompanying Henrietta-Anne, Duchess of Orléans and King Charles II of England's beloved sister. It seems that Louise had actually been sent on a mission to persuade the English king to come down in favour of alliance with France and the Sun King, Louis XIV. Charles II took Louise as his mistress. He showered her with gifts, including the duchy of Portsmouth, and bestowed the duchy of Richmond on their illegitimate son. Unpopular at the English court, 'Madame Carwell', as she was known, returned to France after Charles II's death, where she continued to lead a colourful life.

At this time, the relationship between Britain and Brittany became particularly sour due to colonial warring between France and England through the French Ancien Régime of the 17th and 18th centuries. In the 18th century, France lost great chunks of its North American territories to the British. The island of Belle-Ile off the southern Breton coast is populated in large part by descendants of French settlers in Canada's Acadia, sent packing by the British. In contrast, an Irish immigrant named Walsh became one of the most accomplished slave traders of mid-18th-century Nantes.

French naval vessels would set sail from Brest to support the Americans in their War of Independence from Britain. By contrast, at the Revolution, a number of nobles and clergy fled Brittany and became involved in some pathetically unsuccessful attempts mounted from across the Channel to try to reinstate French royalty. As to France's greatest Romantic figure, the Breton writer and diplomat Chateaubriand, he sailed off to America to flee his family's slaughter in the Terror. His fiction also crossed the Atlantic; read the luscious, morally challenging *Atala* and *René* to find out more.

Connections between Britain and France, and hence Brittany, have happily become much more positive since Napoleon's demise. Johnny onion-sellers got on boats from Roscoff to cross the Breton sea and travelled round Britain on their bikes to sell their produce door to door from the mid-19th century through to the Second World War and beyond. Starting out at roughly the same time, wealthy British and American visitors helped set in motion the Breton tourist industry, most notably creating from scratch the great resort of Dinard. A colony of Americans was regularly visiting Pont-Aven well before Gauguin got there. In contrast, some poor Bretons in search of a better life emigrated to America in the course of the 19th century. The Breton American descendants from the little inland town of Gourin, for example, have kept strong ties with their past, and there's a thriving Breton-New Yorker community.

The 20th century's two world wars also bound many Britons, North Americans and Bretons. In the First World War, tens of thousands of North American troops landed at the port of St-Nazaire before they headed off to the front. At the start of the Nazi occupation of France in the Second World War, the sailors of the island of Sein immediately answered De Gaulle's call to take to the seas and head for Britain to fight for a free France. Some daring rescue operations were mounted from Brittany to repatriate Allied soldiers caught behind enemy lines, and several hundred pilots saved by Resistance networks were taken to Breton beaches, especially the Plage Bonaparte in the Côtes d'Armor, where the British navy came to pick them up. There is even a tiny portion of US territory in Brest, with a war memorial. Bretons who experienced the war will never forget the liberation of their province by Allied soldiers.

Brittany remains a favourite French destination for British people today. However, the most powerful bond across the seas continues to be that between Bretons and the modern-day Celts of Ireland, Wales and Cornwall. Similarities in mythology, in language, in music, even in temperament, some argue, means that they feel a special solidarity, most joyously expressed at the annual Festival Interceltique at Lorient.

Nutty Theories on the Neolithic

You never know when you might need a menhir.
Obélix

The odd plausible attempt has been made to try to explain the purpose of the neolithic alignments and very many single menhirs or standing stones of Brittany. One of the more seemingly sensible lines of enquiry speculates as to whether those rows of standing stones were erected as some kind of seasonal solar calendar connected with religious rites. Although the precise meanings of the alignments and menhirs remain a mystery, they have inspired some very entertaining and ludicrous notions, especially the most famous alignments of all – those of Carnac. Nutty theories advanced about Carnac's lines of menhirs include claims that the structures were built for a massive fish-drying enterprise; or that these standing stones were the basic columns for a vast marketplace. Lawyers might favour the suggestion that the rows of standing stones are vast symbolic legal documents. One further potty argument says that the lines of menhirs were solid posts erected by a Roman army to set up camp below. As to the Celtic Christian legend of St Cornély, it suggests a different role for the Romans regarding these standing stones – when the legionnaires tried to capture and persecute the religious Cornély, the story goes, he literally petrified them, or turned them to stone.

Some have argued that the stone rows recognize heroes who fell in prehistoric battles. A certain Hirmenech even claimed that it was heroes from Homer's Trojan Wars who were brought here for burial. Another suggestion is that the alignments were built as an elaborate device to guard against invaders from the sea. It was also claimed, tongue in cheek, that after the end of the last war, when the Americans arrived to liberate this part of Brittany, some of them thought the menhirs had been planted by the Nazis as an anti-tank defence. Those with a futuristic bent might prefer to explore the explanation that the alignments are landing signals for extraterrestrials.

A few people have wondered whether it was the Egyptians or the Phoenicians who erected the menhirs of Brittany. Breton legends have concocted a few other stories about the neolithic monuments. The two traditional favourites were that they were put up by Breton fairies, the *korrigans*, or by galumphing giants. Gargantua is even associated with a few of Brittany's standing stones. The Dracontia theory, meanwhile, sees the menhir alignments as the temples of dragons or serpents.

Christian moralizers once spread the rumour that the monuments were wicked people who had been turned to stone by way of punishment by a vengeful God. The Almighty, for example, was apparently angered by a group of girls who went dancing rather than turning up to church on Sunday at Les Demoiselles de Langon, and by a band of debauched monks who indulged in some un-Christian rituals at Le Jardin aux Moines in the forest of Paimpont. As to the alignment on the side of the Montagne St-Michel-de-Brasparts, it is said that evil revellers at a wedding banquet, in their wild state, stopped the priest from going to give the last rites to a dying man and were duly dealt with by God.

The Christian Church certainly did not like these menhirs at all; some resemble uncomfortably that greatly mystifying taboo in Christian societies, the male erection. A fair number of menhirs were Christianized by priests, a simple cross plonked on top of them. Menhirs may well have symbolized fertility originally; although the standing stones of the Breton alignments tend not to be carefully shaped, the isolated menhirs dotted around Brittany are often much more convincingly phallic. It is said that some infertile couples would go to touch a menhir, or to rub themselves against one, or even to slide down one where possible. It is even claimed that desperate couples went to make love in the shadow of a menhir to see if that would bring them joy.

Some people have just been far too frivolous about the possible purposes of the alignments, claiming sporting reasons for planting so many thousands of painfully heavy rocks in the ground. The alignments could, some of these factions argue, have formed solid arenas, or racing tracks, or have constituted the framework for a complex game played out in a labyrinth. And though you may be one of those who leaves Brittany unmoved by the region's neolithic sites, one particularly unobservant physicist by the name of Deslandes was more blasé still – he simply reckoned that the standing stones were a natural phenomenon, not put up by anyone at all.

Stone Boats and Slain Dragons – the Breton Saints

Crossing the seas in stone boats, religious men from Ireland, Wales and Cornwall emigrated to the Armorican peninsula in the Dark Ages, fighting dragons and serpents when they arrived. Or so legends of the Breton saints would have it. Be that as it may, these Celtic Christians who converted the peninsula into Brittany were certainly fired with missionary zeal. How peaceful or not this crusading immigration was, it is hard to say. The simplistic picture is that the new arrivals were warmly received by their Gaulish Celtic cousins from pre-Roman times, the natives of Armorica. Not all seems to have been plain sailing, however.

In several Breton saints' stories, the new Christian evangelizers are not always greeted with open arms. Some of the saints' tales claim that the pinkish rocks of the north Breton shore are tinted that way from the blood of persecuted religious immigrants. And when one Irish religious man known as Ké or Quay landed in Brittany in the bay of St-Brieuc he was supposedly beaten with gorse by the Armorican women who had spotted him arriving. He fell to the ground and was knocked out, but on the very spot where he hit his head a fountain of water sprang up and revived him. Ste Noyale was not so lucky when she ventured across the Channel, on tree leaves supposedly, in the 6th century. She was captured by an evil chieftain Nizall, who had her decapitated for rejecting his advances. She simply picked up her head and continued on her journey. Several other Breton saints wisely began by settling on an uninhabited island first and then progressed on to the mainland.

Legends of Breton saints of the Dark Ages exist all along the Breton coastline. Detailed maps of Brittany reveal just how many places have been named after the Dark Ages Celtic saints, from St-Malo in the northeastern corner of Brittany right round the Breton coast to the Pointe de St-Gildas south of the Loire by Pornic. Some of the names should be distinctly familiar to those living in southwest England and in Wales. The Breton saints also appear to have covered every patch of inland Brittany, leaving no stone unturned in their efforts to convert pagan Armorica to Christianity.

Who were the most important Breton saints? Irish religious figures may have been among the earliest to have arrived in Armorica, perhaps in the 5th century or before. The Breton saints Ronan, Ké, Efflam and Aaron (who beat Malo to St-Malo) count among the best-known Irish religious men to have settled in Armorica, but many of them remain relatively obscure figures.

However, it was a group of particularly influential Welsh religious men of the 6th century who came to be regarded as the founding fathers of Celtic Christian Brittany. The great abbey of Llantwit Major or Llanilltud Fawr in South Glamorgan is said to have supplied a couple of the seven founding fathers of Brittany. Illtud, the creator of Llantwit Major, was not one of them, but several Breton places carry his name and he perhaps visited Brittany to deliver famine supplies. A couple of his disciples did become Breton founding fathers; Samson settled at Dol-de-Bretagne while St Pol Aurelian travelled via Cornwall and Ouessant to create religious foundations at Batz-sur-Mer and, more famously, St-Pol-de-Léon.

Other Welsh founding fathers of Celtic Christian Brittany include Brieuc (or Brioc, or Breock), the patron saint of St-Brieuc, and Tugdual (also known as Tudwal or Tual), the patron saint of Tréguier. Sources say that the latter landed with his numerous family and monks in territory that his cousin already ruled over, but that he was, somewhat surprisingly, given confirmation of his lands by the Frankish King Childebert. St Patern, patron saint of Vannes and another of the Breton founding fathers, also came from Wales, where he had set up the influential abbey of Llanbadarn Fawr in Dyfed.

The other two Breton founding fathers are St Malo and St Corentin. It is pretty obvious where Malo (or Maclou, or MacLow) – very possibly of Scottish origin – settled in Brittany. St Corentin is said in certain British references to have been a religious man from Cornwall who went on to become bishop of Quimper, but Breton sources say that he was the son of immigrants from Britain, born and bred in Brittany. The best-known story ascribed to him is that he fed himself from a single fish, from which he would cut a slice each day. He would then return the fish to the water for it to regenerate. Statues show him, invariably, with a fish in hand. He became the most venerated saint in Breton Cornouaille, and he features in the great Cornouaille legend of King Gradlon and the city of Ys (*see* p.294).

Another particularly important Breton saint who ranks up there with these seven founding fathers is Gildas. He became an extremely influential figure across Celtic Christian circles and corresponded with and visited Irish monasteries. He wrote a famous 6th-century text, *De excidio Britanniae*, portraying the rulers and clergy of Britain as a decadent lot who only had themselves to blame for the victories of the Anglo-Saxons. Later in life he went to Brittany, founding a famous monastery at St-Gildas-de-Rhuys and seemingly influencing a large area of southern Brittany.

These saints' tales were written down on both sides of the Channel, the Welsh ones and the Breton ones elaborating different versions of stories that had been passed down the centuries. For example, Breton saints' legends claim that the man who they call Divy, the great Welsh saint Dewi (known as David in English), was born in far western Brittany after his mother Non or Nonna had moved to the Armorican peninsula. Some Breton saints' lives even tell of religious men going from Brittany to Celtic lands to the north. For example, St Thégonnec and St Nonna (a man not to be confused with Nonna, mother of Dewi) are said to have travelled to Ireland to become bishops of Armagh.

The main sources for the lives of these Breton saints were recorded by monks. The earliest surviving ones date from around the 9th century, but the tradition of writing these Celtic hagiographies lasted several centuries more. They are extremely unreliable. The scribes often resorted to invention, or muddled together several influential figures. Yet the Breton saints remained highly revered, their stories long the best-known ones in the Breton community after those of the Bible. In the 17th century, Albert Le Grand of Morlaix played a crucial role in condensing the Breton saints' stories in his book *La Vie des Saints Bretons*. This became one of the most influential and most widely read books in Brittany, which would have been the staple text along with the Bible in poor country homes until the Second World War.

Go into any Breton church or chapel and there's a good chance that you'll come face to face with a statue of a local Breton saint. Although most of the Breton saints date back to the Dark Ages, the statues you will see were mainly carved in the late medieval period or later. These statues remain venerated by many confirmed Breton Catholics to this day, particularly in the *pardons*, the Breton local pilgrimage processions, when the statues of the Breton saints are given a good airing, carried around the countryside, pilgrims chanting Catholic prayers behind them.

Each saint has a more or less murky history linking him or her with miracles and healing powers. There's a long tradition of *saints guerisseurs*, healing saints. St Cado, for example, was supposed to help the hard of hearing. St Jacut was among the many invoked for epilepsy or any behaviour considered mad or possessed. A large number of saints were prayed to by young women hoping for a good marriage. The tradition at Perros-Guirec was for young hopefuls to stick a pin in Guirec's nose. Not only was the statue's nose deformed by this superstition, it disappeared completely.

Many Breton saints are closely linked with particular animals. Cattle were thought particularly important in Breton rural communities. St Cornély is represented along with cows at Carnac. At St-Herbot, locks of animal hair were laid out on a special altar at the annual *pardon*, and in the deeply rural chapel of Notre-Dame de Restudo in the Côtes d'Armor, horse hooves still cover one of the walls of a side chapel. A number of saints are linked with deer, such as Elorn, Edern and Thélo. As to St Hervé, he was born blind, all the better to see into men's characters, the story goes, and went through Brittany guided by a tamed wolf. Innumerable saints are linked with springs in the countryside. Strong saintly ties with water, fertility, cattle and deer are all thought to have links with pre-Christian Armorican and Celtic beliefs, and some of the *pardons*, such as that at Locronan, may follow sacred tracks laid out before Christian times.

The Breton saints of the Dark Ages are not recognized by the Catholic Church of Rome; they have not been canonized. The Church viewed these saints as part of the traditions of the Celtic Christian Church, which it wanted to suppress. Despite this, a few major medieval religious figures in Brittany did receive approval from the Church of Rome. A 13th-century bishop of St-Brieuc, Guillaume Pinchon, was the first officially recognized by the papacy, canonized in 1247 by Pope Innocent IV. Another exceptional 13th-century Breton religious figure, St Yves, defender of the poor, is much better remembered and revered. Yves was canonized soon after his death, and you will often see him portrayed in churches across Brittany. Surprisingly, the Christian warrior Charles de Blois, who unsuccessfully fought for the Penthièvres in the Breton War of Succession in the 14th century, was made into a saint, though his canonization only dates from very recently. Vincent Ferrier, a 15th-century Spanish preacher who went on an important mission through Brittany, also made the grade for the Church of Rome.

Many mainstream Catholic saints such as St Michael and his dragon are popular in Brittany. So too are St Roch and St Sebastian, who were frequently invoked in times of plague. But most popular of the lot are the Virgin and her mother, St Anne. This Marial tradition was strong across France but thrived in the region — St Anne is regarded as the patron saint of Brittany. However, the story that claims she spent some of her life at Ste-Anne-la-Palud in the Finistère is exceptionally far-fetched. Arguably the most venerated religious site in modern Brittany is Ste-Anne-d'Auray, in the Morbihan. It was one of the few places that Pope John-Paul II visited on his trip to France in 1996.

The Web of Breton Arthurian Legend

The main centre of Breton Arthurian action is the legendary Forêt de Brocéliande, also known as the Forêt de Paimpont, west of Rennes. But how and when did the link between Brocéliande in particular and Arthurian romance start? No one seems sure. Talk is of roots in a cross-Channel resistance campaign against Dark Ages invaders, or even of much older links with pre-Roman Celtic ritual. The passion for Arthurian legends certainly flowered in early medieval times. A claim made at the Château de Comper and in the French *Guide Bleu* suggests that Raoul I de Gaël Montfort, one of the proprietors of the Forêt de Paimpont in the 11th century, took part in the Norman conquest of England and that during this time he became deeply enthusiastic about the Arthurian tales he heard there. Once back in Brittany, he may have started encouraging storytellers to set Arthurian episodes in his Brocéliande. There is much discord, however, among devotees of Arthurian legends as to the precise locations of Arthurian sites. The biggest killjoys even claim that Paimpont forest is not Brocéliande.

The Breton Arthurian plots in Brocéliande revolve around four main figures. Merlin the magician comes first. Then there is Viviane, with whom he falls passionately and fatefully in love. Morgane la Fée, the bitter half-sister of King Arthur, also features frighteningly large, while Lancelot du Lac is said to have been brought up at Comper in Brittany. King Arthur and the knights of his Round Table tend to stay on the periphery, though various tales talk of him and his knights coming to end their lives in Brittany. The Breton word for apples, *avalou*, still sounds remarkably close to Avalon, the mythical island where Arthur goes to die, or at least to sleep until he and his men should be called upon to rescue the two Bretagnes (Britain and Brittany) once again. Brittany's Ile d'Aval is a contender for Avalon.

King Arthur is supposed to have learnt of the existence of the Holy Grail preserving drops of blood from Christ's crucifixion from Merlin. But before that, in Breton Arthurian tales, Merlin supposedly travels to Brittany to ask the Breton chiefs to join Arthur in fighting the Anglo-Saxons. On his way back he passes through the forest of Brocéliande, the name thought to derive from Barc'h Hélan, meaning the empire of the druids. In the forest, Merlin meets Viviane at the Fontaine de Barenton on 21 June, date of the summer solstice, and falls madly for her. Despite the fate he foresees for himself, he can do nothing to resist his feelings for her. The beautiful lady is sometimes described as the daughter of the local lord Dyonas, owner of half the forest of Brocéliande, who had his castle at Kon-Per (Comper today). On one of the Fontaine de Barenton's stones known as the *perron de Merlin*, Merlin's step, the enchanter is himself enchanted. He cannot leave Viviane until she has promised him her love; in exchange she demands that Merlin pass on to her his knowledge and his powers.

Merlin returns to Britain, where Arthur's great Christian army has gathered to fight the enemy who have advanced to Salisbury Plain. The Arthurian troops win a hard-fought battle and Arthur is declared *roi des deux Bretagnes*, king of the two Britains. Arthur and Guinevere tie the knot, and after the wedding Merlin returns to Brocéliande, where the bright Viviane cajoles him into revealing more and more of his secrets to her. Viviane's aim is to learn such mastery of magic from Merlin that she will eventually be able to force him to stay with her forever. Merlin, through his magical powers, conjures up the most beautiful castle for Viviane, not *by* the lake of Comper, but *in* it. Viviane finds a baby by the waters, the child of Ban of Brittany and Queen Helen in Breton Arthurian tales. The boy is named Lancelot, and Viviane takes him to live in her underwater, invisible palace. From this time on, she calls herself the Lady of the Lake and the boy becomes known as Lancelot du Lac.

Merlin has work to do elsewhere, notably in setting up the quest for the Holy Grail. Returning to Arthur's court, Merlin appears in several playful guises before announcing the quest. He explains that only one man will find the Holy Grail, but that the name of this knight will remain undisclosed until the chalice is recovered, leaving all to strive for it. The son of Lancelot du Lac, Galahad, proves to be the chosen one.

Several important Arthurian side-stories involving Lancelot and Morgane la Fée are set in Brocéliande. Lancelot is portrayed as the most noble of the knights of the Round Table. When Guinevere is kidnapped by the 'king of the country from which no one returns', Lancelot manages to defy the impossible-sounding odds. Having released Guinevere, the two become lovers. Guinevere tells Lancelot of her love for him on the Bridge of Secrets, which one tourist leaflet in Brocéliande rather unromantically situates 'on the road from Plélan to Ploërmel'. Morgane la Fée, in Breton Mor Guen (White Sea), is a wicked magician who resorts to terrible action when her lover Guyomart proves unfaithful to her. She imprisons him in her hide-out in the forest of Brocéliande, the Val Sans Retour, or Valley of No Return. This valley becomes a trap for all unfaithful knights, but Lancelot, in his unshakeable love for Guinevere, proves capable of overcoming Morgane's wiles.

Arthur, meanwhile, has been mortally wounded in battle due to the treachery of one of his own sons, Mordret. The dying king goes off to the island of Avalon. But it does not seem that he actually dies. Rather, fairies heal his wounds and keep him in a deep sleep to await his resurrection for when Britain should again be in dire trouble. As to Merlin, he will be trapped by Viviane in the forest of Brocéliande, forever ensnared in the Tombeau de Merlin. But there is a story that says that Arthur will in time come to Merlin's rescue, then the Celts of Wales, Cornwall and Brittany will unite and rise up to find new glory after a desolate period of servitude. In the meantime, Arthurian legends have grown into a vast, confusing literary labyrinth and have provided countless tourist trails through the forest of Brocéliande.

The First Croissant in Sumatra

Bretons were certainly at the forefront of French exploration by sea. In fact, there is a story which claims that Bretons discovered the New World before Columbus. Jehan Coatanlem, banished from the Breton duchy in the second half of the 15th century, went to serve the Portuguese monarchy. While in Lisbon, he met Columbus and is said to have given him wind of certain adventurous Breton sailors who had already found new lands across the Atlantic.

The greatest port from which Breton explorers set forth was undoubtedly St-Malo – the inhabitants of which are known as Malouins. These Malouins and other French explorers wanted to make their fortunes in new trade and were called upon to claim new territories they 'discovered' for king and country. Most famously, the Malouin Jacques Cartier was taken to the mouth of the river he christened the St Lawrence in the 1530s. The daring of such adventures is hard to imagine today, when the limits of the world are so much more familiar to us. It wasn't easy to find a willing crew in those days. Donald S. Johnson describes the departure of Cartier's third expedition across the Atlantic in his book *Phantom Islands of the Atlantic* as an 'expedition of five ships filled with mariners, convicted criminals of both sexes, horses, cattle, swine, sheep, goats, poultry, and twenty-five "persons of quality"...' Conditions on board the ships were appalling; illnesses often decimated the crews, and death at sea and shipwrecks were all too common.

Several other notable Malouin seafaring achievements and milestones stand out beyond Cartier's. The *Croissant* from St-Malo became the first French ship to return from a successful commercial trip to Asia, completing a voyage to Sumatra to collect spices in 1601. In 1698, Gouin de Beauchêne spotted a little archipelago in the midst of the South Atlantic; the islands were baptized the Iles Malouines, later to become the Falklands. In 1701, De Beauchêne again distinguished himself, becoming the first French captain to round Cape Horn from east to west. Over 20 years, numerous vessels from St-Malo rounded Cape Horn without a single loss. They transported merchandise to barter for copper, silver and gold from Chile, Peru and Mexico.

The ship the *Grand Dauphin* left St-Malo in January 1712 on a journey that would make it the first French vessel to circumnavigate the globe. In 1715, Guillaume Dufresne d'Arzel baptized a deserted island in the Indian Ocean the Ile de France for King Louis XIV – now it is better known as Mauritius. Bouvet du Lozier stumbled across an Antarctic island that was subsequently named after him, and Marion Dufresne discovered the Marion and Crozet islands and landed on a piece of land that he called France Australe. Unfortunately he was killed by the natives, Maoris of New Zealand.

The profits made on the back of successful expeditions could be fabulous. Some estimate that between 1705 and 1715 the St-Malo ships brought back to France precious metals worth a quarter of the coinage in the whole country. King Louis XIV exploited the situation to feed his monstrously overspending monarchy. He borrowed 30 million *livres* from the big Malouin merchants, on which he was meant to pay 10 per cent interest; the money was never recovered. There would be more direct disastrous losses too: in 1708, the *Philippe* V sank off Cape Verde with a cargo estimated at a value of 1,200,000 *livres*.

St-Malo continued to produce an extraordinary number of notable French adventurers through the 18th century. The brilliant mathematician Pierre-Louis de Maupertuis headed off to Lapland in 1736 at the head of a group of French intellectuals who would measure the shape of the globe. He was only 25, but was able to calculate the precise length of one degree and to confirm that the earth flattened around the poles. François Mahé de la Bourdonnais was another precocious Malouin. In 1734, at the age of 35, he was made governor of the Ile de France and Ile de Bourbon (the latter now La Réunion). He was also sent off in 1745 to help defend French possessions in India. He took Madras back from the British, and then accepted 10 million *livres* for the British to buy it back. For this, he was accused of treason and imprisoned for four years in the Bastille before being acquitted.

Several Breton explorers were feeling their way around the Pacific at the same time as James Cook. Parts of Australia as well as New Zealand narrowly missed becoming French colonies. A naval officer from Quimper, Yves Joseph de Kerguélen, unsuccessfully set out to find Terra Australis. As consolation, a group of islands in the South Indian Ocean were named after him in 1772. During his exploratory trips, he lost his friend

Louis de St-Allouarn, but it now appears that though this Breton adventurer died in the attempt, he may have discovered part of the Australian shore. Another famous French explorer closely linked to St-Malo, Commander Jean-Baptiste Charcot, led two Antarctic expeditions in the early 1900s, and later organized hydrographic expeditions to chart the oceans around Greenland. But the disappearance of his over-optimistically named vessel, the *Pourquoi Pas?*, off Iceland in 1936 caused a national trauma.

Brittany has produced its fair share of world-famous yachtsmen since the war, including Eric Tabarly, winner of the first Transatlantic race in 1964, and Olivier de Kersauzon, as well as Gérard d'Aboville, who recently rowed across the Atlantic and Pacific singlehanded. With Brittany's adventurous spirit in mind, it is only fitting that St-Malo now hosts an annual travel-writing festival (*see* p.131).

A Dying Language in Black Dog Shit

Breton died out rapidly in the 20th century. Small groups are still trying to keep it alive, but while it once had to be defended against persecution, now the battle is with indifference. If the future of the language looks doubtful, its origins remain extremely obscure. It seems that in the immediate pre-Roman period, the Late Iron Age, Armoricans spoke a kind of Celtic. It would have been shared with other Celtic-influenced communities, or a closely related dialect. This would probably have been spoken over large portions of Europe, including across the precursor of France, the Roman Gaul. Shared tribal and place names either side of the Channel in that period are taken to indicate how close the languages and cultures were. Some scholars have suggested that the so-called Celtic dialects in western Europe grew out of an Indo-European language, the structures of which had been brought across with agricultural settlers arriving from the west as far back as the neolithic period. Some Breton river names, such as the Ille, the Oust and the Odet, may originate in that pre-Celtic language.

With the Roman conquest of Gaul came the Roman language. But in far-flung corners of the Roman Empire such as Armorica, while Latin was probably largely adopted in the new towns, the learning of the language of the conquerors may well have been extremely slow and faltering in the countryside. By the time of the emigration of Irish and British people to the Armorican peninsula in the Dark Ages, it seems that Vulgar Latin or its Romance development had taken hold in significant parts of Armorica. However, one of the major effects the waves of emigration from the north is supposed to have had is to have revived the Celtic dialects.

The Breton language is associated with western Brittany, or Basse Bretagne. Eastern Brittany, or Haute Bretagne, was much less affected by it. Neither historic capital of Brittany, Nantes or Rennes, was ever a mainly Breton-speaking city. The boundaries of the language probably spread to their widest limits under the so-called Breton kings of the second half of the 9th century. This seems to be reflected in the spread of Breton place names, which are packed particularly densely along the northern and western coastal strips of Brittany. There is, though, a pocket of Breton names as far southeast as Guérande, close to the Loire.

The Ligne Loth, or Loth Line, is the name that is sometimes given to the historically shifting language divide cutting north to south across Brittany, showing the frontier of the Breton-speaking communities changing through time. From its most easterly position in the 9th century, the Ligne Loth regressed westwards until the mid 17th century, when the language divide roughly cut down through the middle of the Côtes d'Armor and the Morbihan, passing to the west of St-Brieuc and to the east of Vannes.

The leading Breton lords of the Middle Ages may well have been trilingual, speaking French in their connections with foreign courts, being familiar with Latin in official and religious circles, and understanding the Breton used in their home territories. Although Breton was widely spoken in western Brittany, it was not written down all that often; it was more an oral than a literary language. Fragments of texts written in Breton have survived from the Middle Ages, but the remains are meagre. One of the first printed books in Brittany was the *Catholicon*, a trilingual dictionary dealing with French, Latin and Breton.

Among ordinary western Bretons, Breton was the common language through the Middle Ages and the Ancien Régime, but the Revolutionary authorities had little time for the practical fact that in Brittany many ordinary people spoke Breton as their first or only language. French was the sole language this *liberté* allowed. It would take further concerted efforts from the centralizing French governments of the 19th century and first half of the 20th century to suppress the Breton language. Schooling became compulsory in France, but only in French. The use of a regional language, even if it was your mother tongue, was made to appear shameful and backward through the educational system. French, by contrast, was championed as the language of civilization and progress. It was compulsory in the civil service and the armed forces. Breton parents, increasingly ashamed of Breton, encouraged their children to learn French, which they felt would give them more opportunities in life.

Through the 19th century, Breton language and culture did find their defenders. In 1805 an Académie Celtique was founded, one of whose members, Jean-François Le Gonidec, worked at establishing a Breton grammar and preparing a new Breton dictionary. In the 1830s, Hersart de la Villemarqué published his first edition of the *Barzaz Breiz*, an influential collection of Breton songs. The next decade saw the founding of the Association Bretonne, with economic and historical goals, while the bishop of Quimper of the time, Monsigneur Graverand, started up an influential missionary periodical in Breton, the *Lizeri Breurriez ar Feiz*. Leading Church figures continued to act as defenders of the region's language. Although the teaching of Breton language and history was pushed aside in schools, and the Association Bretonne was suspended through the 1860s, an increasing number of Celtic magazines came into existence. And in the late 19th century, academic chairs were created in Celtic culture.

The late 19th century also saw further efforts to write down traditional Breton tales and legends, to record the long Breton oral tradition. It is probable, given the large Breton population at the end of the 19th century and in the early 20th century, that that was actually the period in history in which there were the most Breton speakers.

Tensions grew again between central government and defenders of Breton language and culture at the start of the 20th century, as the Combes government was both against the clergy and against the Breton language. Not content with Breton being forbidden in schools, it wanted to forbid Breton in the churches. This was a surefire way of creating animosity in deeply religious Brittany. One Abbot Perrot led the founding of *Bleun Brug*, a Breton Catholic organization to defend Breton language and religion. The Parti Nationaliste Breton came into existence in 1911; this new party called for Brittany's total separation from France and for Breton to become the sole national language of Brittany.

The First World War had a strong impact on the Breton language, not just in causing the death of so many young Breton men – it also spread the use of French across the province. After the war, Breton was suppressed in schools with renewed vigour. The shaming of pupils caught speaking Breton became institutionalized. The first child heard using their mother tongue might even be handed a symbolic object, possibly a cow, to indicate their shame; when the next child was caught speaking Breton, the symbol of shame would be passed on.

The Breton nationalist movements that had grown up in the first half of the 20th century became closely associated with the growth of Fascism. Such was the paranoia about this in central government that the Breton language came to be seen as a potential danger, and the speaking of Breton on the telephone was banned in the Finistère in 1939. After the Second World War, spoken Breton continued to decline at an alarming rate. Yet most Bretons seemed uninterested, and practical action to protect the language took a long time coming. Breton has not survived the 20th century like Welsh or Irish Gaelic, and was never made compulsory in Breton schools.

It is only a hardcore of Bretons that has continued to show interest in the Breton language, but central French government has become increasingly sensitive to the issue, if rather late in the day. The 1951 Loi Deixonne allowed the optional teaching of minority languages in French schools, although no measures were taken to train teachers in such specialist language instruction. Despite Breton becoming an official school subject right to final exams in 1965, very few Bretons took up the opportunity.

In the 1970s though, the creation of private Breton-speaking schools, the Diwan establishments, was a big step forward. Most of them were set up in the Finistère. They have struggled to stay alive, so small are the numbers that attend, but government support put them on a firmer financial footing. In state schools in Brittany, pupils can opt to learn Breton, but this initiative has proved only mildly popular. Since 1983, pupils have been allowed to take their *baccalauréat* (the exams at the end of secondary schooling) in Breton. No accurate census of Breton-speakers has ever been carried out, but one 2004 estimate reckoned there were 665,000 passive Breton speakers left, and that maybe only around one third of those were also active Breton speakers. The typical Breton speaker today is a farmer or retired person, over 40, living in the Côtes d'Armor or Finistère.

Language is, of course, much more than just a language. It expresses and defines ways of thinking, and is intimately linked with the history of communities and with their imaginations. The death of a language also means the death of a significant

Breton Sayings

On growing up obediently: *Al lestr na zent ked ouz ar stur/Ouz ar garreg a zento sur.* (The ship that does not obey the helm/Will surely have to obey the reef.)

On getting in the potential mother-in-law's good books: *A ziwar moue ar gazeg/ E vez paked an eubeulez.* (It's by the mare's mane/That you catch the filly.)

On marriage taming the wilder male elements: *Evid reiza ar bleizi/Ez eo red o dimezi.* (To get wolves to settle down/They have to be married.)

A warming culinary Breton expression on love-making: *Pa'h a ar billig war an tan/Eh a an daou en unan.* (When the crêpe-making pan [the man] is placed on the fire [the woman]/The two become one.)

A traditional comparison between women and the sea: *Evid ar mor beza treitour/ Treitourroh ar merhed.* (The sea may be fickle/Women are much more so.)

On traditional male and female roles: *Er forniou-red, er milinou/E vez kleved ar heloiou/Er poullou hag er zanaillou/E vez kleved ar marvaillou.* (At the ovens and the mills/You hear the news/At the wash place and in the attics/You hear gossip.)

A justification of the social hierarchy and the different expectations of life for rich and poor: *Mad eo lêz dous, mad eo lêz trenk/Ha mad da beb hini goûd chom en e renk.* (Sweet milk is good, bitter milk is good/And it is good for everyone to keep in their rank.)

An apparent warning against speculating that might be extended to life generally: *Ar pez a zeu gand ar mare lano/Gand ar mare a dre er mêz a yelo.* (What the sea brings in at high tide/It takes away at low tide.)

---

part of a culture. Languages are inventive and playful, and with their loss much invention and playfulness disappears. The Bretons have traditionally been caricatured as being terribly dour and stern by French people who could not understand their language. But having a look at traditional Breton idioms, you can see how colourful and humorous Bretons can be.

A cousin and I once asked our grandmother, brought up Breton-speaking, to teach us some Breton. She is a dignified former schoolteacher who would never dream of saying a swearword in French. But she had a little giggle as she told us some of the popular Breton expressions she and her schoolfriends used to enjoy. It was something of a shock when she came up with the first one, *kor ki du*. What did that mean, we innocently asked. 'Black dog shit,' she said calmly in French. 'But you must understand that Breton was much more earthy than French,' she explained. And the phrase did seem particularly appropriate in expressing the present state of the Breton language.

In Breton bookshops you can seek out books of Breton phrases translated into French. *Proverbes et Dictons de Basse Bretagne*, for example, collects sayings in the Breton tongue. Most of the sayings in this book offer familiar words of wisdom, but they often use examples from the immediate natural and animal world. Some have a particularly Breton flavour, and can make an entertaining first introduction to the Breton language. A few sound very much more obscure than they would have done a generation or two ago, and of course some are far from politically correct. In the box above is a small selection of sayings to set you thinking about the Breton language.

A Footnote on Astérix and Bécassine

Internationally, the most famous figures to have emerged from Brittany are Astérix and Obélix. But they are not portrayed as Bretons, being Gauls from well before the time of the Dark Ages emigrations to Armorica from Britain. What comes as a bit of a shock is that their names are derived from the language of their would-be oppressors — the words asterisk and obelisk come from ancient Mediterranean languages. Astérix and Obélix's adventures are supposed to take place in 50 BC, just after the Roman conquest of Gaul. In fact, their encounters with Visigoths, Vikings and the like take them into different time periods. Time is concertinaed in these cartoons. Even feminist issues have put in an appearance, as have modern-day stars, thinly disguised under the make-up of caricatural drawing.

Unfortunately for the real Armorican Gauls, there were no successful pockets of resistance against the Romans, no invincible villagers, and no magic potion – despite the claims by some Breton makers of old-style beer, or *cervoise*, that such beer was the Gauls' secret weapon. One Armorican tribe, the Veneti, did, however, play an important part in a widespread Gaulish uprising against Caesar. Caesar himself gave a classic account of the sea battle that ensued and of how he enslaved the defeated enemy. This story is a far cry from the scenario in Astérix, where the brilliant villagers persecute the much put-upon flabby Roman legions.

A few fanatics have tried to pinpoint the true location of the fictional village of Astérixian legend. It is clear that Astérix's village is on the northern, Channel coast, not on the southern coast of the Veneti; just look at the view you are shown through the magnifying glass in the introduction to each new adventure. The *département* of the Côtes d'Armor puts in strong claims for the magic village. Le Yaudet, with its Iron Age fort overlooking the Léguer estuary, has been suggested, but the place is built on a cramped height, while the cartoon evidence clearly shows Astérix's and Obélix's village on flattish ground, by a wide beach. The bay of Erquy, featured in some Astérix competitions, looks more the part. Perhaps you and your children could seek out your own ideal location for Astérix's village.

Brittany did spawn an earlier cartoon icon. In 1905 the character Bécassine, more correctly known as Annaïk Labornez, was born. A farmer's daughter from a remote corner of Brittany, she goes to Paris to become the *domestique* of the Marquise de Grand'Air. Twenty-three adventures follow of the naïve Breton servant girl faced with the big city. Still a huge favourite with French children, her adventures are now also used as a source by social historians.

Food and Drink

04

Food

... a thin, black buckwheat pancake is the national meal – only the Bretons can comprehend its miserable culinary attractions.

Balzac, *Les Chouans*

How wrong Balzac was. **Breton crêpes** (or *galettes*, as the savoury variety tend to be called in eastern Brittany) are appreciated far and wide now. And the Breton crêpe is without a doubt the aristocrat of the pancake world, not a miserable thing. Extremely thin and delicate, it bears no relation to the thick and stodgy pancake many of us are familiar with at home. There is an art to making a good Breton crêpe, which, along with the choice of fillings and décor, is why some crêperies are much better than others. You will find crêperies in every corner of Brittany and they are generally reliably cheap places to eat.

In the mid 19th century, when Balzac came to Brittany, ordinary Breton cooking would have been truly monotonous. *Bouillie*, or gruel, and potatoes were the mainstay of the peasant diet at the time. Chestnuts, *châtaignes*, were gathered as a poor man's food, and *soupe au lait*, milk soup with bread dunked in it, was a popular dish. Meats, vegetables and fruit would have been seasonal treats. Crêpes might have been made once a week; they would certainly not have come with fancy fillings, but might have been used to dunk in gruel or soups.

Nowadays you can order crêpes stuffed with an increasingly imaginative variety of fillings, for example all manner of Breton meats or seafood. Savoury crêpes were traditionally made with *blé noir* or *sarrasin*, buckwheat. Sweet crêpes are now made with more ordinary wheat called *froment*. In some crêperies you will even be able to see the *crêpière* in action, making her *crêpes*. The traditional drinks to accompany crêpes are cider or a milk drink, either *lait ribot* (the residue from butter-making, which is also sometimes used as a kind of filling – to some tongues sour milk), or *gros lait* (curd, made using rennet from a calf's stomach). Crêpes stalls in town are good places to buy a snack, and for the serious crêpe enthusiast, the town of Gourin in central Morbihan even hosts a crêpe festival (*see* p.355).

The other main types of food visitors immediately associate with Brittany are **fish and seafood**. You'll find a plethora of the stuff on offer in port markets or shops every day of the week except Monday, as the fishermen take a day of rest. Do go to one or two larger Breton ports to see the *criée*, the professionals' fish auction market, or visit a *poissonnerie*, a fishmonger's, in a coastal town.

In restaurants, **shellfish** often feature in Breton starters or *hors-d'œuvres*, and are frequently served still in their shells; the exceptions are the posher places. Otherwise, you will most often be expected to peel your own langoustines or prawns, crack open your own crab, or winkle out your own whelks. You may even have to split open clams with a dangerously sharp knife. If you have problems with any of this, ask for help. Oysters and clams are often served raw, or *cru*, as well as a few other types of shellfish. The most elaborate way in which to try Breton shellfish is by ordering a *plateau de fruits de mer*, a seafood platter. Such a platter tends to be quite expensive and quite enormous. Bretons, however, can be serious gluttons when they go out to a restaurant, and they will often tuck in to such a *plateau* as a mere starter. Beginners are probably best advised to stick to one as a main course.

Different sections of the Breton coastline are associated with different catches. The ports of the Pays Bigouden are renowned for their langoustines (sometimes translated as Dublin Bay prawns), generally simply cooked in saltwater and then served with a rich home-made mayonnaise. Langoustines are widely available in summer. Oysters are especially associated with Cancale in northern Brittany and with the Morbihan coast in southern Brittany, although Belon in the Finistère is synonymous with a particularly fine type. Oysters are generally served raw in Brittany, either with lemon to squeeze over them, or with a vinegar sauce, to which chopped shallots are added. You can eat oysters all year round. Mussels thrive in particular in the waters of the bay of the Mont-St-Michel and the bay of St-Brieuc in northern Brittany and at the mouth of the Vilaine river in southern Brittany. Going out to see the forest of wooden posts, the *bouchots*, on which they grow in the bay of Mont-St-Michel, for example, makes for a memorable outing. The most common way for mussels to be served is *à la marinière*, in a light white wine sauce with plenty of onions and parsley added. *Coquilles St-Jacques*, scallops, flourish in the bay of St-Brieuc, and the Rade de Brest also provides good conditions for them. They are fished during the winter months. *Pétoncles* are baby scallops, which are often known as queen scallops.

Crabs are commonplace in Brittany. You can try several different varieties, such as *araignées* (spider crabs), *dormeurs* or *tourteaux* (common crabs), and *étrilles* or *crabes cerises* — the last have a velvety texture, hence the English name of velvet crabs. Although most people in North America and Britain may not be familiar with these as edible crabs, they are considered to have a deliciously subtle taste in Brittany. Shrimps, though relatively pricey, make another popular starter, either *crevettes roses* or the smaller *crevettes grises*; the latter can be eaten whole. The *grises* also have a certain spiciness and can be used to make a *bisque*, a shellfish soup. Lobster, which can feature in a *bisque* too, is expensive, but restaurants across Brittany serve it and it is still regarded as the most refined of seafoods. *Homard* is the blue-black, enormous-pincered variety. *Langouste* is spiny lobster or rock lobster.

Other shells you may find served up regularly include *palourdes* or *praires* (clams), often stuffed with garlic butter but perhaps the finest sea shells to eat raw, with their natural nutty and citrus flavours. *Coques* are cockles, *bigorneaux* winkles and *bulots* whelks, the last being large and fatty, and once considered the poor man's shellfish. *Oursins* (sea urchins) are much rarer, and *ormeaux*, the magnificent-tasting ormers or abalones, are virtually never seen any more.

On to **fish** in Brittany. *Cotriade*, which is the Breton answer to the Mediterranean *bouillabaisse*, is a good place to start. It is a Breton sailors' soup, traditionally made from the left-overs of the catch. It might include whiting, cod, haddock, hake, richer mackerel and eel, even some mussels or other shellfish; potatoes add substance to the soup. As Breton cuisine has become more refined, chefs have tried all manner of combinations in their *nouvelles cotriades*.

There are some 30 types of fish commonly sold from Breton ports. Certain ones are highly prized, such as *St-Pierre* (John Dory), *bar* (sea bass), *daurade* (sea bream), *rouget* (red mullet), turbot and sole. Other fish such as sardines, mackerel, whiting, pollock, coley, lemon sole and tuna are quite common. Eel can be delicate, although conger eel is definitely not for the faint-stomached. *Cabillaud*, fresh cod, is distinguished from *morue*, salt cod. In the second half of the 19th century, tinned fish became a speciality in Brittany, and a major industry. There are still canning factories in ports such as Douarnenez, Concarneau and Quiberon, where fish is prepared using traditional methods. Often the fish are canned in a white wine and shallot sauce, although the manufacturers are experimenting more these days, even adding whisky to some sauces. Breton canned fish soups have a good reputation. The use of *algues*, seaweed, in Breton cuisine is a more recent affair, and *salicornes*, or samphire, which are grown in the Breton salt pans, are another speciality being experimented with in cuisine.

In terms of **meat**, Brittany is known in France for its pork. You can try all manner of Breton *saucissons* (the French equivalent of salami), some with garlic, some covered in pepper. Breton *andouille* uses all manner of unmentionable bits of pork to form a special sausage much appreciated in the province, Guéméné-sur-Scorff being the capital of this delicacy. *Boudin noir*, black pudding, is popular, as are hams and pork pâtés. Cattle are numerous in eastern Brittany, and the town of Châteaubriant is famed for the thick grilled fillet steak named after it. The lambs that graze in the salty fields of Ouessant or the bay of Mont-St-Michel are regarded as being especially tasty but will only feature on a menu in the places where they are reared. It may come as a relief to some of you that Breton horse meat is no longer so popular. The Brière and Nantes are known for duck; Canard Nantais is a classic of the former Breton capital, served with *petits pois*. Free-range chickens are reared in good number around Janzé, also in eastern Brittany. One very traditional dish that has come back into fashion in restaurants is *kig-ar-farz*, which simply means meat and pudding in Breton. Here the many elements are cooked together, the meat, vegetables and pudding added to the broth. The pudding is savoury, made from buckwheat or wheat, sometimes with raisins, and is dropped in a tight bag into the broth to cook.

Breton butter, quite strongly salty, is considered to be a gastronomic treat in itself. It is used both in the preparation of meats and of cakes. Guérande is strongly associated with **Breton salt**, as the salt pans there still produce the stuff. Crossing the Marais Salants of Guérande on a bright summer day you will probably see packets of salt piled on kitchen chairs in front of homes, on sale to passers-by. The *fleur de sel* is the best type of salt.

The sandy Breton soil has proved excellent for growing a wide variety of **vegetables**. The north shore is renowned for its artichokes, cauliflowers and onions. It was from Roscoff that the Johnny onion-sellers set off to conquer the British market. Brittany also produces fine potatoes, shallots, leeks and chicory. Dried beans were once a staple in the province; now green beans are produced in large quantity. Garlic stalls are common around the bay of the Mont-St-Michel. The sauce *à l'armoricaine* so popular across Brittany is made with garlic, tomatoes and olive oil. You will see large quantities of maize being grown, but the vast majority is destined for animal feed.

Moving on to sweet matters, the main **fruit** associated with Brittany is the apple. Brittany is serious cider-drinking territory (*see* below). Fouesnant is particularly reputed for its cherries, while the farmers of Plougastel-Daoulas, a peninsula just south of Brest, have built their fortunes on fine strawberries. In the Nantes region, melons grow well.

Butter is the main ingredient in **Breton cakes and biscuits**. In fact, the most traditional of Breton cakes, *kouign aman*, is served dripping with the stuff, which explains its Breton name, meaning 'cake-butter'. *Gâteau breton* is another highly buttery recipe, producing a denser, heavier Breton butter cake that should melt in the mouth. Some towns, notably Pleyben and Pont-Aven, are well known for their *galettes*, here meaning butter biscuits, not a type of crêpe. In fact Pont-Aven is almost as famous in France for its biscuits as for its artists. Nantes developed into a major biscuit producer in the 18th century, when biscuits formed an important part of ships' provisions. The town is now closely associated with the major Breton biscuit manufacturer Lu. *Crêpes dentelles* were invented in Quimper in the late 19th century. These are superbly crunchy but frustratingly friable wafer biscuits made of ultra-thin layers wrapped round and round. Returning to old-style Breton puddings, you will find *far*, a heavy eggy pudding with dried fruit in the batter, served up in most places. Apples feature in many a Breton pudding too.

Drink

Cider, Apple Alcohols, Muscadet and Other Breton Brews

Cider has long been the traditional Breton alcoholic drink. Some cider-producing areas of the province are even pressing for their own *appellation d'origine contrôlée* (AOC), a label that guarantees authentic, high-quality local production, as with French wines. The Cornouaille has, for example, been awarded a distinguishing *appellation* for its high-quality cider. Look out too for the terms *cidre fermier or cidre traditionnel*, signs that the cider has been made either on smallholdings or traditionally. Cider is produced across most of the province; you will find several cider-themed museums dotted around Brittany. If you are offered a *kir breton* it will be cider mixed with a little blackberry or blackcurrant liqueur.

Lambig, the Breton equivalent of Normandy Calvados, only much rarer, is an extremely well-kept secret. Its distinctive appley dryness varies according to the distiller. Lambig is a *digestif*, to be tasted at the end of a meal. Fine de Bretagne is a Lambig that has been aged for six years or more. Brittany also produces an alcoholic apple apéritif, *pommeau*, worth trying.

Vines did used to be cultivated around Brittany in medieval times, before cider took over. Now wine is only made in any quantity in the Loire Atlantique. The famous wine name of that *département* is **Muscadet**, which is, appropriately enough, the most common wine served with Breton fish and seafood. Its zingy, crisp, fresh taste can stand up to the strong flavours of the sea. The best wine-making area of Muscadet lies just to the southeast of Nantes, the Muscadet de Sèvre et Maine (*see* p.448).

Muscadet-sur-Lie is a class above your average Muscadet. The Loire Atlantique produces other white wines, such as the rather lesser Gros Plant and the rare Malvoisie of the Coteaux d'Ancenis. Otherwise, the Coteaux d'Ancenis produce a range of largely red wines.

A couple of small-scale breweries keep up the tradition of Breton **cervoise**, the beer that was drunk by the Gauls – it's what Astérix and his friends order in the French version of the comic. **Chouchen** is mead, a sweet alcoholic drink made from honey. Producers also make sparkling chouchen, and claim it to be the oldest alcoholic drink in Brittany.

Soft Drinks and Water

Mineral water (*eau minérale*) comes either sparkling (*gazeuse* or *pétillante*) or still (*non-gazeuse* or *plate*). The usual international corporate soft drinks are available as well as a variety of bottled **fruit juices** (*jus de fruits*). Some bars also do the refreshing freshly squeezed lemon and orange juices known as *citron pressé* or *orange pressée*, served with plenty of chilled water. Some French people are fond of sweet fruit syrups, for example red *grenadine*, milky-coloured *sirop d'orgeat*, or ghastly green *menthe*. If lemonade is mixed with them, they become *diabolos*. Many Bretons dislike their **tap water**, and buy bottled water to drink at home. *Eau potable* means drinkable water in French; **non potable** means it is not fit for consumption. Beer (*bière*) is often run-of-the-mill big brands from Alsace, Belgium or Germany; draft beer (*pression*) is cheaper than bottled beer. Ask if there are any local beers on offer.

Restaurant Basics

Eating Hours

The Bretons tend to eat quite early in restaurants, at 12 noon or 12.30 for lunch, and generally starting their evening meal between 7 and 8pm. Breton meals can go on for a very long time, especially if you're beginning with the challenge of a large seafood platter (*see* p.44). Many restaurants do a good-value lunchtime menu. Call at least a day in advance to book a table at restaurants that have a well-established reputation, or that are well located; out of season, phone ahead to check whether or not a restaurant is open. With *fermes-auberges* (*see* p.71) and other specialist types of restaurant, you *have* to call in advance to be served.

Restaurant Menus and Wine

Restaurants should post their menus outside the entrance, but you may want to check that they accept credit cards at the start of the meal – a surprising number of them don't take plastic. Most restaurants, unless they're very small, will normally offer a choice of set-price menus with two to five or even more courses.

A full French restaurant meal normally begins with an apéritif that is served with some little savoury snacks known as *amuses-gueule* (*gueule* is a rather vulgar word for a mouth). The *hors-d'œuvre* are the starters; the *entrées* or *plats/pièces de résistance* or *plats principaux* are the main courses. (Note that if you order a side salad, it will normally come before or after the main course.) *Les fromages*, cheeses, in France are served prior to the *desserts*, the puddings. You could finish a meal with a *digestif* or a cup of coffee, or tea. Drinks to end a meal are often accompanied by *petits fours* or chocolates.

More ordinary meals consist of a starter, a main course and either cheese or pudding. A *plat du jour*, sometimes also referred to as the *plat du marché*, is the day's special, which could be eaten by itself. A *menu dégustation* is a selection of the chef's or the region's specialities. Eating *à la carte* will always be much more expensive than opting for a set menu.

Menus in cheaper restaurants sometimes include a bottle or a carafe of house wine in the price (denoted by the words *vin compris*). Wine in French restaurants tends to be on the expensive side, though the house wine can be good value. French families often splash out on a reasonable bottle when eating out; however, some places now serve *le vin au verre*, wine by the glass. By law, service should be automatically included in the price of set menus nowadays, but you may wish to add a small tip if you're happy with your meal.

Markets and Picnic Food

In small towns, the market day is *the* event of the week, though most of them finish up by around noon. Once you've sorted the parking problem, you should be able to find all sorts of local farm produce, the freshest fish, and piles of seafood. In big towns you can also find more established daily covered markets, *les Halles*. Other good sources for picnic food are *boulangeries* (selling bread, but also tarts and pastries often), *charcuteries* (selling meat specialities, especially pork), *traiteurs* (delicatessens, selling a diversity of elaborate prepared dishes) and *pâtisseries*.

Cafés and Bars

The French café isn't only a place to drink but for many people also a home from home; you can sit for hours over one coffee and shouldn't feel hurried by the staff. Prices for drinks are listed on the *tarif des consommations*; they go up according to whether you're served at the bar (*le comptoir*), at a table inside the café (in the *salle*) or outside (*en terrasse*). Cafés should serve baguettes, croissants and other French pastries, and can make for an atmospheric and cheap setting for the first meal of the day, or for lunch.

French coffee is strong and black, and if you order *un café* you'll get a very small *express*. For more than these few drops of caffeine, ask for *un grand café*; coffee with milk is *un café crème*. The French tend to order *café au lait*, a small amount of coffee topped up with a large quantity of hot milk, at breakfast. Decaffeinated coffee is usually abbreviated to *déca*. *Un thé* is most likely a teabag in a cup of hot water; you'll probably have to specify *thé au lait* (tea with milk) or *thé au citron* (tea with lemon) to get any frills. *Chocolat chaud*, hot chocolate, is popular among children. Popular *infusions* or *tisanes*, that is, herbal teas, include: *camomille*, *menthe* (mint), *tilleul* (lime or linden blossom) and *verveine* (verbena).

French Menu Vocabulary

Starters/Soups
(Hors-d'œuvre/Soupes)

assiette assortie plate of mixed cold hors-d'œuvre
bisque shellfish soup
bouillon broth
charcuterie mixed cold meats
cotriade Breton mixed fish soup
crudités raw vegetable platter
potage thick vegetable soup
velouté thick smooth soup

Fish/Shellfish
(Poissons/Coquillages)

aiglefin little haddock
alose shad
anchois anchovy
anguille eel
araignée spider crab
bar sea bass
barbue brill
baudroie anglerfish
belon flat oyster
beurre blanc sauce of shallots and wine vinegar whisked with butter
bigorneau winkle
blanchailles whitebait
brème bream
brochet pike
bulot whelk
cabillaud cod
calmar squid
carrelet plaice
colin hake
congre conger eel
coque cockle
coquillages shellfish
coquille St-Jacques scallop
crabe cerise velvet crab
crevette grise shrimp
crevette rose prawn
darne slice or steak of fish
daurade sea bream
dormeur common crab
écrevisse freshwater crayfish
éperlan smelt
escabèche fish fried, marinated and served cold
escargot snail
espadon swordfish

esturgeon sturgeon
étrille velvet crab
flétan halibut
friture deep-fried fish
fruits de mer seafood
gambas giant prawn
gigot de mer a large fish cooked whole
grondin red gurnard
hareng herring
homard Atlantic (Norway) lobster
huître oyster
lamproie lamprey
langouste spiny Mediterranean lobster
langoustine Dublin Bay prawn or scampi
lieu pollack or coley
limande lemon sole
lotte monkfish
loup (de mer) sea bass
maquereau mackerel
matelote d'anguilles eels in a wine sauce
merlan whiting
merlus hake
morue salt cod
moule mussel
omble chevalier char
ormeau ormer or abalone
oursin sea urchin
palourde clam
pêche du jour catch of the day
pétoncle queen scallop or baby scallop
poulpe octopus
praire small clam
raie skate
rouget red mullet
roussette dogfish
St-Pierre John Dory
sandre zander or pikeperch
saumon salmon
sole (meunière) sole (with butter, lemon and parsley)
telline tiny clam
thon tuna
tourteau common crab
truite trout
truite saumonée salmon trout
vieille wrasse

Meat and Poultry
(Viandes et Volailles)

agneau (de pré-salé) lamb (grazed in fields by the sea)
aileron chicken wing

andouille pigs' intestine sausage
andouillette chitterling (tripe) sausage
autruche ostrich
bifteck beefsteak
blanc breast or white meat
blanquette stew of white meat, thickened
   with egg yolk
bœuf beef
boudin blanc sausage of white meat
boudin noir black pudding
brochette meat (or fish) on a skewer
caille quail
canard, caneton duck, duckling
carré crown roast
cassoulet haricot bean stew with sausage,
   duck, goose, etc.
cervelle brains
chapon capon
Châteaubriant porterhouse steak
cheval horsemeat
chevreau kid
chevreuil venison
civet meat (usually game) stew, in wine
   and blood sauce
cœur heart
confit meat cooked and preserved in its
   own fat
contre-filet sirloin steak
côte, côtelette chop, cutlet
cou d'oie farci goose neck stuffed with pork,
   foie gras and truffles
crépinette small sausage
cuisse thigh or leg
cuisses de grenouilles frogs' legs
dinde, dindon turkey
entrecôte ribsteak
épaule shoulder
estouffade a meat stew marinated,
   fried and then braised
faisan pheasant
faux-filet sirloin
foie liver
foie gras fattened goose or duck liver
frais de veau calf testicles
fricadelle meatball
gésier gizzard
gibier game
gigot leg of lamb
graisse, gras fat
grillade grilled meat, often a mixed grill
jambon ham
jarret knuckle

langue tongue
lapereau young rabbit
lapin rabbit
lard (lardons) bacon (diced bacon)
lièvre hare
maigret/magret (de canard)
   breast (of duck)
manchon duck or goose wing
marcassin young wild boar
merguez spicy red sausage of North African
   origin
mouton mutton
museau muzzle
navarin lamb stew with root vegetables
noix de veau (agneau) topside of veal (lamb)
oie goose
os bone
perdreau, perdrix partridge
petit gris little grey snail
petit salé salt pork
pieds trotters
pintade guinea fowl
plat-de-côtes short ribs or rib chops
porc pork
pot au feu meat and vegetables cooked
   in stock
poulet chicken
poussin baby chicken
quenelle very light poached dumplings
   made of fish, fowl or meat and bound
   with egg
queue de bœuf oxtail
rillettes a coarse type of pâté
ris (de veau) sweetbreads (veal)
rognon kidney
rosbif roast beef
rôti roast
sanglier wild boar
saucisse sausage
saucisson salami-like sausage
selle (d'agneau) saddle (of lamb)
steak tartare raw minced beef, often topped
   with a raw egg yolk
suprême de volaille fillet of chicken breast
   and wing
taureau bull's meat
tête (de veau) (calf's) head, brawn
tournedos thick round slices of beef fillet
travers de porc spare ribs
tripes tripe
veau veal
venaison venison

Vegetables, Herbs, etc. (*Légumes, Herbes, etc.*)

ail garlic
aneth dill
anis anis
artichaut artichoke
asperge asparagus
aubergine aubergine (eggplant)
avocat avocado
basilic basil
betterave beetroot
blé noir buckwheat
blette Swiss chard
cannelle cinnamon
céleri (-rave) celery (celeriac)
cèpe ceps, wild boletus mushroom
champignon mushroom
chanterelle wild yellow mushroom
chicorée curly endive
chou cabbage
chou-fleur cauliflower
choucroute sauerkraut
ciboulette chive
citrouille pumpkin
cœur de palmier heart of palm
concombre cucumber
cornichon gherkin
cresson watercress
échalote shallot
endive chicory (endive)
épinards spinach
estragon tarragon
fenouil fennel
fève broad (fava) bean
flageolet white bean
fleur de courgette courgette blossom
frites chips (French fries)
froment type of wheat used for sweet crêpes
galipette large round mushroom
genièvre juniper
gingembre ginger
haricot (rouge, blanc) (kidney, white) bean
haricot vert green (French) bean
jardinière mixed vegetables
laitue lettuce
laurier bay leaf
macédoine diced vegetables
(épis de) maïs sweetcorn (on the cob)
marjolaine marjoram
menthe mint
mesclun salad of various leaves
morille morel mushroom

navet turnip
oignon onion
oseille sorrel
panais parsnip
persil parsley
petits pois small peas
pied bleu wood blewits (type of mushroom)
piment pimento
pissenlits dandelion greens
poireau leek
pois chiche chickpea
pois mange-tout sugar pea, mangetout
poivron sweet pepper (capsicum)
pomme de terre potato
potiron pumpkin
primeurs young vegetables
radis radish
romarin rosemary
roquette rocket
safran saffron
salade verte green salad
salicorne samphire (small, fleshy plant that thrives in salt pans)
salsifis salsify
sarriette savory
sarrasin buckwheat
sauge sage
seigle rye
serpolet wild thyme
truffe truffle

Fruit and Nuts (*Fruits et Noix*)

abricot apricot
amande almond
ananas pineapple
banane banana
bigarreau red and yellow cherry
brugnon nectarine
cacahouète peanut
cassis blackcurrant
cerise cherry
citron lemon
citron vert lime
(noix de) coco coconut
coing quince
datte date
fraise (des bois) (wild) strawberry
framboise raspberry
fruit de la passion passion fruit
grenade pomegranate
griotte morello cherry
groseille redcurrant

mandarine tangerine
mangue mango
marron chestnut
mirabelle mirabelle plum
mûre (sauvage) mulberry, blackberry
myrtille bilberry
noisette hazelnut
noix walnut
noix de cajou cashew
pamplemousse grapefruit
pastèque watermelon
pêche (blanche) (white) peach
pignon pinenut
pistache pistachio
poire pear
pomme apple
prune plum
pruneau prune
raisin/raisin sec grape/raisin
reine-claude greengage plum

Desserts

Bavarois mousse or custard in a mould
bombe ice-cream dessert in a round mould
brioche light sweet yeast bread
charlotte sponge fingers and custard
   cream dessert
chausson turnover
clafoutis batter fruit cake
compote stewed fruit
corbeille de fruits basket of fruit
coupe ice cream: a scoop or in cup
crème anglaise thin egg custard
crème caramel vanilla custard with
   caramel sauce
crème Chantilly sweet whipped cream
crème fraîche slightly sour cream
crème pâtissière thick egg custard
crêpe dentelle thin, crunchy Breton biscuit
far filling Breton eggy flan of batter and
   dried fruit
galette butter biscuit or pancake
gâteau cake
gâteau Breton dense Breton butter cake
gaufre waffle
génoise rich sponge cake
glace ice cream
kouign aman crisp Breton pudding dripping
   with butter
macaron macaroon
madeleine sponge cake
miel honey

mignardise petits fours (*see below*)
œufs à la neige floating island/meringue
   on a bed of custard
pain d'épice gingerbread
parfait rich frozen mousse
petits fours tiny cakes and pastries
profiteroles choux pastry balls, often filled
   with cream, *crème pâtissière* or ice cream,
   and covered with chocolate
sablé shortbread
savarin a filled cake, shaped like a ring
tarte, tartelette tart, little tart
truffe chocolate truffle

Cheese (*Fromage*)

(fromage de) brebis sheep's cheese
chèvre goat's cheese
doux mild
(plateau de) fromage (board) cheese
fromage blanc yoghurty cream cheese
fromage frais a bit like sour cream
fromage sec general name for hard cheeses
fort strong

Cooking Terms and Sauces

à point medium (steak)
aigre-doux sweet and sour
aiguillette thin slice
à l'anglaise boiled
à l'armoricaine sauce with brandy, white
   wine, shallots, tomatoes, garlic and
   cayenne pepper
à la marinière light white wine sauce with
   onions and parsley
au feu de bois cooked over a wood fire
au four baked
barquette pastry boat
beignet fritter
béarnaise sauce of egg yolks, shallots and
   white wine
bien cuit well-done (steak)
bleu very rare (steak)
bordelaise red wine, bone marrow and
   shallot sauce
broche roasted on a spit
chaud hot
cru raw
cuit cooked
émincé thinly sliced
en croûte cooked in a pastry crust
en papillote baked in buttered paper
épice spice

farci stuffed
feuilleté flaky pastry
flambé set aflame with alcohol
fleur de sel the finest salt crystals
fourré stuffed
frais, fraîche fresh
frappé with crushed ice
frit fried
froid cold
fumé smoked
galantine cooked food served in cold jelly
galette savoury pancake
garni with vegetables
(au) gratin topped with melted cheese and breadcrumbs
haché minced
marmite casserole
médaillon round piece
mijoté simmered
pané breaded
pâte pastry or pasta
pâte brisée shortcrust pastry
pâte à chou choux pastry
pâte feuilletée flaky or puff pastry
paupiette rolled and filled thin slices of fish or meat
pavé slab
poché poached
salé salted, spicy
saignant rare (steak)
sucré sweet
timbale pie cooked in a dome-shaped mould
tranche slice
vapeur steamed
vinaigrette oil and vinegar dressing

Miscellaneous
addition bill (check)
baguette long loaf of bread
beurre butter
carte menu
confiture jam
couteau knife
crème cream
cuillère spoon
formule/menu set menu
fouace (or fouée) dough ball that puffs up when cooked
fourchette fork
huile (d'olive) oil (olive)

lait milk
menu set menu
moutarde mustard
nouilles noodles
pain bread
œuf egg
poivre pepper
riz rice
sel salt
service compris/non compris service included/not included
sucre sugar
vinaigre vinegar

Drinks (*Boissons*)
bière (pression) (draught) beer
(demi) bouteille (half) bottle
brut very dry
café coffee
café au lait white coffee
café express espresso coffee
café filtre filter coffee
chocolat chaud hot chocolate
chouchen mead
cidre cider
citron pressé fresh lemon juice
demi a third of a litre
doux sweet (wine)
eau water
  gazeuse sparkling
  minérale mineral
  plate still
eau-de-vie brandy
eau potable drinking water
glaçon ice cube
infusion/tisane herbal tea
  camomille camomile
  menthe mint
  tilleul linden blossom
  verveine verbena
jus juice
lait milk
moelleux semi-dry
mousseux sparkling (wine)
orange pressée fresh orange juice
pichet pitcher
pression draught
sec dry
thé tea
verre glass
vin (blanc/mousseux/rosé/rouge) (white/sparkling/rosé/red) wine

Travel

Getting There

By Air

From the UK, Ireland and Paris

The 3 major **airports** in Brittany are Rennes-St-Jacques, Nantes-Atlantique and Brest-Guipavas. Air France operates daily **Brit Air** services from London Gatwick (North Terminal) to all 3. From mid May to early Oct, **Aer Lingus** flies between Dublin and Rennes, stopping at Cork. **Ryanair** also runs low-cost flights between London Stansted and London Luton and the small airport at Dinard. **Flybe** operates low-fare flights linking Exeter, Birmingham and Southampton with Brest. There is also a Southampton-Cherbourg route.

From the Channel Islands, **Rockhopper** runs flights to St-Brieuc. There are also small airports at Morlaix-Ploujean and St-Nazaire.

To fly to Brittany from elsewhere, including the USA and Canada, you have to change at one of the Paris airports. Most flights from Paris to Brittany (about 1hr), are by **Air France**, t 0820 820 820. Flights go either from Orly-Ouest or Roissy-Charles-de-Gaulle, to Rennes, Nantes, Brest, Quimper-Pluguffan and Lorient-Lann-Bihoué-en-Ploemeur.

From North America

During off-peak periods, you should be able to get a scheduled economy flight to Paris from the USA for around $370–$460. Tickets can be booked through **Air France**, **British Airways**, **Northwest Airlines**, or **Delta Air Lines**. For discounted flights to Paris, try **Nouvelles Frontières**. Check the Sunday-paper travel sections for the latest deals, or look up US cheap-flight websites such as *www.priceline. com* (to bid on flights), or *www.expedia.com*.

By Coach

Eurolines, t 08705 143219, has coach services from the UK to St-Malo, Roscoff and Nantes.

Across the Channel

St-Malo and Roscoff are the main ferry ports in northern Brittany. From the UK, **Brittany Ferries** run between Portsmouth and St-Malo (9hrs) and Plymouth and Roscoff (6hrs). **Condor Ferries** run daily high-speed ferries from Weymouth and Poole to St-Malo from May to September, crossing in 4hrs 15mins, plus a Poole–Cherbourg fast service. Alternatively, cross to a northern French port or take your car on the **Eurotunnel** and drive to your destination.

Travelling from Ireland, **Brittany Ferries**, t 0214 277801, *www.brittanyferries.com*, runs between Cork and Roscoff. **Irish Ferries**, t 0818 300 400, *www.irishferries.com*, serves Roscoff and Cherbourg from Rosslare.

Airline Carriers

Air France/Brit Air, UK t 0845 0845 111, US t 800 237 2747, Canada t 800 667 2747, *www.airfrance.com*.
Aer Lingus, t 0818 365 000, *www.aerlingus.com*.
British Airways, t 0870 850 9850, *www.ba.com*.
Delta Airlines, US t 800 221 1212, *www.delta.com*.
Flybe, t 0871 700 0535, *www.flybe.com*.
Northwest Airlines, US t 800 225 2525, *www.nwa.com*.
Nouvelles Frontières, US t 800 677 0720, Canada t (212) 986 3343.
Rockhopper, t (01481) 824567, *www.rockhopper.aero*.
Ryanair, t 0871 246 0000, *www.ryanair.com*.

Channel Crossings

Brittany Ferries, t 08703 665333, *www. brittanyferries.com*. The best choice of ferries to all parts of the Brittany coast: Plymouth–Roscoff, Poole–Cherbourg, Portsmouth–Cherbourg, St-Malo or Caen.
Condor Ferries, t 0845 345 2000, *www. condorferries.com*. High-speed ferries (Weymouth and Poole to St-Malo, Poole to Cherbourg).
Hoverspeed, t 0870 240 8070, *www. hoverspeed.co.uk*. Dover–Calais, Dover–Ostend and Newhaven–Dieppe.
P&O, t 08705 202020, *www.poferries.com*. Services between Dover and Calais.
SeaFrance, t 08705 711711, *www.seafrance.com*. Dover–Calais ferries.
SpeedFerries, t 0871 222 7456, *www. speedferries.com*. New, low-cost, fast ferry service between Dover and Boulogne.
Eurotunnel, t 08705 353535, *www.eurotunnel. com*. Trains travelling from near Folkestone to near Calais.

By Train

To get quickly from Britain to Brittany by train and avoid changing in Paris, take the **Eurostar, t** 08705 186 186, to Lille in northern France, roughly a 1hr 40min journey from London. From Lille, you can reach the following Breton destinations: Rennes (*c.* 4hrs); Nantes (*c.* 4hrs); Redon (*c.* 4½hrs); Vannes (*c.* 5hrs); Auray (a little over 5hrs); Lorient (*c.* 5½hrs); Quimperlé (*c.* 5¾hrs); Rosporden (*c.* 6hrs); Quimper (*c.* 6¼hrs). Check with Eurostar about connections/ waiting times at Lille.

French trains are run by the nationalized SNCF company. From Paris, the SNCF's excellent **TGVs** (*trains à grande vitesse* – French high-speed trains) leave the capital for Brittany from the Gare Montparnasse. (The Eurostar from London arrives in Paris at the Gare du Nord.) There are three main TGV lines through Brittany. The northern line goes to Brest via Rennes, a southern line serves Quimper via Rennes, and the yet more southerly service goes as far as Le Croisic, via Nantes. The TGV journeys from Paris to Rennes last a little over 2hrs. Those to Nantes likewise. The TGVs to Brest take around 4hrs 20mins, those to Quimper a minimum of 4hrs 10mins. Le Croisic is only some 3hrs away from the French capital by TGV. St-Brieuc, Guingamp and Morlaix in northern Brittany, and Vannes, Auray and Lorient in southern Brittany, are well served by the TGVs along the way to Brest or Quimper. The occasional TGV stops at Lamballe, Plouaret-Trégor and Landerneau in northern Brittany, and at Redon, Quimperlé and Rosporden in southern Brittany. Other Breton stops include Ancenis, St-Nazaire and La Baule.

If you are starting your train journey in France, you *have* to **stamp your ticket** yourself in one of the orange machines by the platform entrances or you may be fined. The word you need for this essential procedure is *composter*.

For details and advance reservations of train travel in France, contact **Rail Europe** at: 179 Piccadilly, London W1V 0BA, **t** 0870 584 8848, *www.raileurope.co.uk*, or 226 Westchester Avenue, White Plains, NY 10064, **t** 1-800 438 7245, *www.raileurope.com*.

By Car

In France, you must always have your driving licence and the relevant registration and insurance papers in the car with you. Make sure you are properly insured for driving in France and think about taking out special roadside rescue. Drivers with a valid licence from an EU country, the USA, Canada or Australia don't need an international licence. If you're coming from the UK or Ireland, the dip of the headlights must be adjusted to the right. All cars in France are required to have rear seat belts and these must be worn by rear seat passengers. Carrying a warning triangle is mandatory if you don't have hazard lights and advisable even if you do; in a breakdown the triangle should be placed 50m behind the car. To **hire a car**, look into holiday package deals to save money. Check the fine print for charges.

There are three particular important points to note when driving in France. First, drive on the right-hand side of the road. Second, watch out for *priorité à droite*, an archaic and cunning system whereby traffic coming from streets to your right, unless halted by a stop sign and/or a thick white line, automatically has right of way over you. Third, French motorists rarely respect pedestrian crossings.

If you're involved in an **accident**, consult your insurance papers. The procedure is to fill out and sign a *constat amiable*. If your French isn't sufficient, try to find someone to translate, so you don't accidentally incriminate yourself.

A strong campaign against **drink-driving** and **speeding** has been going for some time in France, and police traps are often set up after French Sunday lunch. Try not to drink any alcohol if you're driving; the permissible levels of alcohol in the blood correspond to only a very small amount of alcohol at a meal. **Fines** for drink-driving can be huge, and like the fines for speeding are payable on the spot. Often, French drivers warn about the presence of police traps by flashing their lights. It is illegal to use a mobile phone while driving; French police enforce their law much more rigorously than their UK counterparts.

Petrol (*essence*) is expensive in France, especially on motorways. Stations can be few and far between in rural areas, and they often shut at lunchtimes, during the night and on

Sunday afternoons. Unleaded is called *sans plomb*, and diesel is often referred to as *gazole* or *gasoil*. If an attendant helps you, they may expect a small tip.

In Brittany, there are no motorways as such, only **dual carriageways** (divided highways) which do not have tolls. They are frequently referred to as *voies express*. The **speed limits** are: 110km/69mph on dual carriageways; 90km/55mph on other roads; 50km/30mph in urban areas.

The word for a **breakdown** is *une panne*. To break down is *tomber en panne*. If you break down on major roads or motorways, use the orange emergency phones to contact rescue services or the police. If you're a member of a motoring club affiliated to the Touring Club de France, ring them; if not, ring the police, **t** 17.

Entry Formalities

Holders of EU, US, Canadian and New Zealand passports don't need a visa to enter France for stays of up to three months, but everyone else should check the requirements. Apply for a visa at the nearest French consulate in your home country. The most convenient visa to get is the *visa de circulation*, allowing for multiple stays of three months over a three-year period. If you plan to stay longer than three months in France (and this includes people who come from a country whose citizens don't need to get a visa to enter France for shorter stays) French law states that you must get a *carte de séjour*. For information, contact the nearest French consulate in your home country.

Getting Around

By Air

You can fly to the island of Belle-Ile from Lorient or Nantes, **Air France**, **t** 0820 820 820, or fly to the island of Ouessant from Brest-Guipavas, **Finist'Air**, **t** 02 98 84 64 87.

By Bus

The extent of services on the French bus network varies between *départements*, though it can take you to many more rural spots than the trains. In larger towns, buses normally leave from the *gare routière* ('road station') as opposed to the *gare* (railway station). The timetable options for anything but travel between major towns is not extensive, and aren't to be entirely trusted. The tourist office or shopkeepers near the bus stop may have more accurate local knowledge.

By Car

See 'Getting There By Car', p.57. The main Breton roads, all crossing the region east–west, are the following: along the **northern coastal strip**, the N176 followed by the N12, taking you from near the Mont-St-Michel to Brest; along the **southern coastal strip**, the N165 linking Nantes and Quimper – the busiest road in Brittany during the summer holidays; for the **centre** of Brittany, the N164, which is joined to Rennes by the N12, and ending up near the Crozon peninsula.

By Train

The TGV lines from Paris (*see* 'Getting There By Train', p.57) are generally excellent. Beyond that, Brittany has a network of much slower trains serving further destinations, especially towns on the coast. The train service does not serve inland Brittany well. (The local bus network is more extensive; *see* above.) Prices on the SNCF are reasonable, and discounts are available (*see* box, opposite). The central number for enquiries about timetables and services is **t** 08 36 35 35 35; or ask at a station.

Make sure to *composter votre billet*, or date-stamp your ticket, in one of the orange machines located by the platform entrances, otherwise you will be liable to a fine. Not all stations have left luggage facilities – check before you travel.

By Bicycle

Before taking your bike by air to France, check whether the bike needs to be boxed and whether it is included as part of your

Discount Rail Fares

The earlier you book the more likely you are to get a cheap ticket, but you can't book more than 60 days before your return date or the date of your journey if it is single. If you are travelling on Eurostar you can book 90 days ahead. For booking from abroad, *see* p.57.

Discount schemes change all the time. If you buy a return or circular ticket and travel at least 200km within 2 months, you get a 25% discount. You have to depart in a *période bleue* (off-peak: Monday 10am to Friday noon, Friday midnight to Sunday 3pm, and outside holidays).

Carte 12–25 Young people aged 12–25, travelling frequently by train, can purchase this card; it's good for a year and gives 50% discount on travel begun in blue periods.

Carte Découverte 12–25 Young people are eligible for a 25% discount if they buy their ticket in advance and begin travel in a *période bleue*.

Carte Enfant+ This is issued in the name of a child aged 4–12, and allows the child and up to 4 people a 50% discount on TGVs and other trains when starting in a *période bleue*. It is valid for 1 year and allows a discount on Avis car hire.

Carte Senior People over 60 can purchase a *carte senior*, valid for a year, offering 50% off blue period travel and 25% at other times. It allows a discount on Avis car hire.

Découverte à Deux If 2 people (related or not) are making a return trip together, they are eligible for a 25% discount in 1st or 2nd class for journeys begun in blue periods. It also entitles you to a discount if you hire an Avis car from a station.

Découverte Enfant+ This is free, issued in the name of a child aged 4–12, and allows a 25% discount for up to 4 others on trains departing in a *période bleue*. Again, there's a discount on Avis car hire.

Senior Découverte Eligibility for 25% off the journey for those over 60, travelling in a *période bleue*. Discount on Avis car hire.

---

total baggage weight. Certain trains (with a bicycle symbol indicated on the timetable) carry bikes for free; otherwise you have to send them as registered luggage and pay a fee for delivery guaranteed within 5 days.

The main towns always seem to have at least one shop that hires out bikes – local tourist offices have lists. You can also hire bikes from most SNCF stations in larger towns, and then drop the bike back off at a different station, as long as you specify where you'll drop it when you hire the bike. *Vélo* is the common colloquial word for a *bicyclette* and a *vélo tout terrain*, or *VTT*, is a mountain bike. Be prepared to pay a fairly hefty deposit on a good bike and/or to supply your credit card number. You may want to enquire about insurance against theft.

Get special maps and cycling information from the **Fédération Française de Cyclotourisme**, 8 rue Jean-Marie Jégo, 75013 Paris, **t** 01 45 80 30 21, or in Britain from the **Cyclists Touring Club**, Cotterell House, 69 Meadrow, Godalming, Surrey GU7 3HS, **t** (01483) 687217. *See also* the list of specialist tour operators on p.60.

On Foot

You can walk almost all the way round the Breton coast by following the region's coastal paths. Breton coastal paths are most commonly and unromantically known as *Sentiers des Douaniers*, or Customs Officers' Paths. The main coastal path is also known as the Sentier Côtier, the Sentier du Littoral, or the Grande Randonnée (GR) 34.

The **Grandes Randonnées** are a national network of walking paths through France. Apart from GR34, many other Grandes Randonnées go through Brittany: GR3, GR341, GR342, GR37, GR38 and GR39. They are marked with white and red signs. *Gîtes d'étapes* are simple, cheap shelters with bunk beds and rudimentary kitchen facilities set along the GRs. You can buy detailed but expensive guides, *Topoguides*, to the individual Grande Randonnée tracks; contact the **Comité National des Sentiers de Grande Randonnée**, 8 Avenue Marceau, 75008 Paris, **t** 01 47 23 62 32. Smaller walking paths known as GRPs are marked with yellow and red signs, and are planned to offer a week of walking. PRs are even smaller, marked in yellow, or sometimes with

Specialist Tour Operators

In the UK

Brittany Direct, t (020) 8335 1810, *www. directtravel.co.uk*. Four-star coastal camp sites, premier mobile homes and self-catering villas and cottages.

Canvas Holidays, t (01383) 629000, *www.canvasholidays.com*. Camping and mobile home holidays.

Cycle Rides – Bike Tours and Events, t (01225) 428452, *www.cycle-rides.co.uk*. Cycling holidays.

Crown Blue Line, 8 Ber Street, Norwich NR1 3EJ, t 0870 160 5634, *www.crownblueline.com*. Canal holidays from Messac in eastern Brittany up to Dinan and down to Nantes, or west along the Canal de Nantes à Brest.

French Golf Holidays, The Green, Blackmore, Essex, CM4 0RT, t (01277) 824100, *www. frenchgolfholidays.com*. Golf breaks.

In the USA

Abercrombie & Kent, 1520 Kensington Road, Suite 212, Oak Brook, IL 60523, t 800 554 7016, *www.abercrombiekent.com*. Fourteen-day trips from the Mont-St-Michel to the Riviera.

Backroads, 801 Cedar Street, Berkeley, CA 94710-1800, t (510) 527 1555, *www.backroads.com*. Five- to 9-day bicycling and walking holidays.

Brooks Country Cycling Tours, P.O. Box 20792, New York, NY 10025, t (917) 834 5340, *www. brookscountrycycling.com*. Cycling tours.

Self-catering

In the UK

See also p.72.

Allez France, 27–31 West Street, Storrington, West Sussex RH20 4DZ, t 0845 330 2048, *www.allezfrance.com*.

Bridge Travel Service, 55–9 High Road, Broxbourne, Herts EN10 7DT, t 0870 191 7140, *www.bridgetravel.co.uk*.

Brittany Ferries Holidays, Millbay Docks, Plymouth PL1 3EW, t 08703 665333, *www. brittanyferries.com*.

Chez Nous, Spring Mill, Earby, Barnoldswick, Lancs BB94 0AA, t 0870 336 7679, *www. cheznous.com*.

The Individual Travellers Company, Manor Court Yard, Bignor, Pulborough RH20 1QD, t 08700 780189, *www.indiv-travellers.com*.

Interhome, 383 Richmond Road, Twickenham TW1 2EF, t (020) 8891 1294, *www.interhome.co.uk*.

VFB Holidays, Normandy House, High Street, Cheltenham GL50 3FB, t (01242) 240340, *www.vfbholidays.co.uk*.

In the USA

Drawbridge to Europe, 98 Granite Street, Ashland, OR 97520, t 888 268 1148, *www. drawbridgetoeurope.com*.

Overseas Connection, Long Wharf Promenade, PO Box 2600, Sag Harbor, NY 11963, t (516) 725 9308, *www.overseasvillas.com*.

thematic symbols, and are meant to last anything from an hour up to a day. Signposts along these French walking paths rather curiously mark destinations in terms of time rather than distance.

Specialist books on Breton walking paths do exist in English, for example those published by Bartholomews, Cicerone Guides, IGN or Robertson McCarta.

There are two other special walking paths that are worth pointing out. The **E5 European path** leaves from the Pointe du Raz, which is one of the westernmost tips of the Finistère, to take you on foot to Venice. The revived 500km **Tro Breizh** or Tro Breiz ('Tour of Brittany' in Breton) was the traditional Breton medieval pilgrimage; it stops at the seven cathedrals dedicated to the Breton saints who are regarded as the founders of the Celtic Christian Brittany of the Dark Ages (*see* p.32). Editions Ouest-France and the regional tourist board have published a cultural guide to this path, *Les Chemins du Tro Breiz*.

Practical A–Z

Beaches

The Breton coastline measures more than 1,000km. You can visit virtually any beach in Brittany; by law, the French coast up to 3m in from the highest tidal point remains public property. Only one or two sections of the Breton coastline are inaccessible, as they lie within military zones or form part of protected bird reserves.

The north Breton (Channel) shore tends to have slightly calmer beaches than the western and southern coasts exposed to the Atlantic, though an indented shoreline with countless protected bays makes for notable exceptions. On the north side of Brittany, the deep, flat bays are greatly affected by the tides. The sea can disappear into the distance for quite some time and then rush back in surprisingly fast – be careful not to be caught out. Local tourist offices and the local press have the times of the daily tides. The southern coast has ever so slightly warmer sea water, although even in the height of summer the Atlantic remains exhilaratingly fresh. The south coast also wins by a margin in terms of hours of sunshine per year.

Some Breton beaches are dangerous for swimming. *Baignade interdite* means bathing is forbidden. The French term indicating that a beach has a lifeguard is *baignade surveillée*. Flags indicate instructions on bathing: green flags mean that swimming is permitted and that a lifeguard is watching the shore (*Baignade autorisée et surveillée*); orange flags mean that swimming is not advised, but that there is a lifeguard on duty (*Baignade surveillée mais déconseillée*); red flags mean that swimming is forbidden and that there is no lifeguard on duty (*Baignade interdite*).

Generally, the Breton beaches get a clean bill of health. For up-to-date info, look out for the annual leaflet, *L'Etat des plages*, published by the state and regional environmental authorities. Tourist offices should keep copies. The quality of the water is divided into 4 categories, from A (good) to D (poor).

Topless bathing is accepted everywhere, though naturism or nudism is only allowed on specific beaches. French Government tourist offices can supply information on specialist naturist holidays in France, and you can contact local tourist offices to find out where the naturist beaches are situated. Most such beaches are gay-friendly.

Climate and When to Go

Breton weather is not reliable, but it is generally mild. It very rarely snows, and it doesn't tend to get too hot even in the height of summer. The coast is often windy; enormous white clouds like rococo whipped cream rush across the Breton skies on many a day of the year. Although Brittany is not as rainy as the cliché would have you believe, always bring a raincoat and something to keep your head dry and warm.

Mid-July to mid-August is the most consistent period for Breton sunshine, but also the high point of the Breton tourist season, when you'll be packed like sardines on the beaches of the most popular resorts. The first half of July and the last half of August can be almost as warm and sunny, and tend to be rather less crowded. May and June, and September and October, can be delightful or disappointing, depending on your luck with the weather. May can be surprisingly busy, as the French have a series of long weekends off in that month, but the countryside looks at its best then. In September, kids will be back in class and you can have large stretches of the coast to yourself. November to March is the best time to see fierce waves crashing against cliffs or jumping over jetties. In autumn and winter, fog and mist will obscure your sea views from time to time. The granite and schist of Breton architecture can look particularly dark in the winter months, but the popular whitewashed houses keep up their bright appearance from afar. April is often particularly cheerful because of the Easter holidays and the colours and foliage returning to the countryside.

Average Temperature chart in °C

Jan	Feb	Mar	April	May	June	July	Aug	Sept	Oct	Nov	Dec
9.3	8.6	11.1	17.1	16.0	22.7	25.1	24.1	21.2	16.5	12.1	9.3

Outside the main holiday seasons, many of the houses in the Breton resorts are closed up, though more recently hotels have been encouraged to stay open for at least ten months of the year.

Consulates or Embassies

UK: 16 Rue d'Anjou, 75008 Paris,
t 01 44 51 31 00.
Ireland: 4 Rue Rude, 75016 Paris,
t 01 44 17 67 00.
USA: 2 Rue St-Florentin, 75001 Paris,
t 01 43 12 22 22.
Canada: 35 Avenue Montaigne, 75008 Paris,
t 01 44 43 29 00.
Australia: 4 Rue Jean Rey, 75015 Paris,
t 01 40 59 33 00.
New Zealand: 7 Rue Léonard de Vinci,
75116 Paris, t 01 45 01 43 43.
South Africa: 59 Quai d'Orsay, 75007 Paris,
t 01 53 59 23 23.

Crime and the Police

Outside cities, the term for a policeman in France is *gendarme*; a *gendarmerie* is a police station. Within city structures, it's *agents de police/poste de police*. Report thefts to *gendarmeries* or *postes de police*. Be warned that this can be a frustrating bureaucratic exercise, particularly if you don't speak French – be patient but very firm. Theft from tourists' cars is a problem across France. Try not to leave valuables in your car, not even in the boot. If your passport is stolen, contact the police and your relevant consulate for emergency travel documents. Holiday homes, as anywhere in France, are particular targets for burglary. You need to get an official piece of paper from the *gendarmerie* to put in an insurance claim.

By law, the police in France can stop anyone anywhere and demand presentation of official identification. There's a feeling that the French police tend to pick on obvious ethnic minorities when making such spot checks. If you are stopped on the road, you're expected to be carrying your official car documents. Speeding fines have to be paid on the spot and breathalyser tests are common.

Disabled Travellers

The **APF** (Association des Paralysés de France), 17 Boulevard Auguste Blanqui, 75013 Paris, t 01 40 78 69 00, has a branch in every French *département*. It publishes *Où Ferons-Nous Etape?* (Where Shall We Stay?). The French railway company, the **SNCF**, publishes a pamphlet, *Guide Pratique du Voyageur à Mobilité Réduite*, covering travel by train for disabled people – contact Rail Europe (*see* p.57). The **Gîtes de France** organization issues a brochure, *Gîtes Accessibles aux Personnes Handicapées*, for special self-catering stays in France.

RADAR (Royal Association for Disability and Rehabilitation), 12 City Forum, 250 City Road, London EC1V 8AF, t (020) 7250 3222, *www.radar.org.uk*, publishes *Holidays and Travel Abroad: A Guide for Disabled People.* In the USA, **Mobility International USA**, PO Box 10767, Eugene, OR 97403, t (503) 343 1248, provides information on exchange programmes and volunteer service. The **Society for the Advancement of Travel for the Handicapped**, 347 Fifth Avenue, Suite 610, New York, NY 10016, t (212) 447 7284, *www.sath.org*, provides travel and access information. The Travel Information Service of the **MossRehab Hospital**, Philadelphia, offers advice for disabled travellers, t (215) 456 9900, *www.mossresourcenet.org*.

Festivals

Major Breton Festivals and *Pardons*

In summer, countless Breton communities organize a *fest noz*, a traditional night festival involving Breton music and dancing, and usually a lot of cider or other alcohol. *Bagadou*, when traditional Breton bands lock in lively musical competition, are fairly numerous too. *Pardons*, by contrast, are serious, sober religious ceremonies, held during the course of the day; they are local pilgrimages, when the saint or saints and the banners of the local church are taken out for a walk with the pilgrims. Virtually every community church and chapel has its *pardon*. Tourists are welcome to join in but must be respectful.

Calendar of Events

May
3rd Sun Tréguier *Pardon de St Yves*
Trinity Sun Rumengol *Pardon*

June
late June/early July Nantes *Quinzaine Celtique* music festival

July
1st ten days Rennes *Tombées de la Nuit* open-air entertainments
Nantes *Festival International d'Eté* culture festival/*Musiques sur l'Île*
1st Sun Quimper *Pardon de Ty Mamm Doué*
mid-July Dinan *Fête des Remparts* historic street festival
Landerneau *Festival Kann al Loar* music festival
2nd week Pont-l'Abbé *Fête des Brodeuses* folk festival
Quimperlé *Festival Musiques Mosaïques*
Vannes *Journées Historiques*
2nd Sun Locronan *Pardon de la Troménie*
last Sun Paimpol *Fête des Terre-Neuvas et des Islandais* folklore festival
3rd week Quimper *Festival de Cornouaille* culture festival
Vannes *Fêtes Historiques*
Fouesnant *Fête des Pommiers* local cider festival
25–26 July Ste-Anne d'Auray *Pardon*

late July–early Aug Concarneau *Festival International de la Baie* world music and dance festival
Vannes *Festival de Jazz*

August
through Aug Quimper *Semaines Musicales*
early Aug Lamballe *Fête Folklorique des Ajoncs d'Or*
Pont-Aven *Fête des Fleurs d'Ajonc*
St-Malo *Festival de Jazz*
1st fortnight Lorient *Festival Interceltique*
Plomodiern *Festival Folklorique du Ménez-Hom*
St-Lyphard *Fête de la Tourbe* local culture festival
Vannes *Fêtes d'Arvor* history festival
Lizio *Fête des Artisans d'Art* craft festival
15 Aug Ste-Marie-du-Ménez-Hom *Pardon*
2nd fortnight Guingamp *Festival de la Danse Bretonne et la Fête de la St-Loup*
Moncontour *Fête Médiévale*
Perros-Guirec *Fête des Hortensias* Celtic music festival
2nd Sun after 15 Aug Ste-Anne-la-Palud *Pardon*

September–December
1st Sun Le Folgoët *Pardon*
Sun nearest 29 Sept Mont-St-Michel *Festival de St-Michel*
Early Dec Rennes *Les Transmusicales* international rock festival

Food and Drink

By law, **service** should be included in the price of set menus, marked by *service compris* or *s.c.* Many people still leave a tip if they are happy with their meal and the service. If you eat *à la carte*, you might add a tip of around 10%.

The **restaurants recommended in this guide** almost exclusively serve typical French or Breton food. In towns especially, you'll find a growing number of fast-food chains and a fair number of ethnic restaurants, including Moroccan, Tunisian, Algerian, Vietnamese and Italian establishments.

Crêpes are relatively cheap, unless you eat a dozen, and the more exotic the filling, the more expensive the crêpe. **Vegetarians** will find crêperies one of the best options in Brittany.

Restaurant Price Categories
Prices quoted throughout the book are for an average two-course à la carte meal without wine, for one person.
luxury more than €60
expensive €30–60
moderate €15–30
inexpensive less than €15

Health, Emergencies and Insurance

Emergencies
ambulance (SAMU national emergency organization), t 15;
police and an ambulance, t 17;
fire brigade (pompiers), t 18.

In a medical emergency (*un cas d'urgence médicale*), take the person concerned to the local hospital – note that *hôtel-dieu* is sometimes used in place of the word *hôpital*, or the phrase *centre hospitalier*. You can also call the local **SOS Médecins**. If you can't consult a phone book, the internet or Minitel, dial **t** 12 for directory enquiries to ask for help.

Local doctors take turns to cover night duty. Local newspapers should give details of doctors on call (*de service*) and should also give the addresses of chemists (*pharmacies*) open for night duty. In a minor emergency in a rural area, go straight to the closest chemist – pharmacists are trained in first aid.

Doctors' Appointments and Prescriptions

Pharmacists should have details on local doctors (*docteurs* or *médecins*) who speak English, if that's necessary.

If you're an EU citizen, take an **E111 form** to get reimbursed for a visit to a doctor, for which you pay on the spot. You can get one from your local social security or post office. At the end of a consultation, make sure the doctor gives you the relevant medical form, filled out as evidence of your visit and of your payment, before you leave. With prescriptions, have the pharmacist complete his or her sections on the medical form the doctor gave you, as you'll need their labels to be reimbursed for medicines. The E111 explains how to reclaim the money. The French health service will only reimburse up to 75–80% of costs, so even with an E111 consider taking out private medical insurance.

If you have private medical insurance, check that you're clear about conditions and procedures to follow before you leave home. Canadians are usually covered in France, though Americans and others should verify the situation with their individual policies.

General Insurance

Consider taking out a **general travel insurance policy**, covering theft and losses and offering a 100% medical refund. Check it covers repatriation for the worst cases. Make sure you have **extra cover for sporting accidents** if you feel that's necessary. You might also verify cover in the case of strikes, increasingly frequent and disruptive in French services .

Internet Facilities

As you would expect, public internet and email facilities are usually limited to the larger towns. Generally, you pay a charge at internet bars or Médiacap centres. The local library sometimes offers a free service, although you may have to book in advance. The tourist office will point you in the right direction, or may have an access point of its own that you can use for a small fee.

Leisure and Sports

The best way to get information on special activities and sports before you go on holiday is either by contacting the CDT for the relevant *département* (*see* 'Tourist Information', p.69) or, if you have already decided where you are going to stay, by contacting the local tourist office (*see* contact details in the relevant touring chapters). The useful general French term used for leisure activities is *loisirs*.

Breton Traditions

The Finistère is the most obvious *département* in which to learn something about Breton culture, including **Breton language**, **dancing**, **music**, **embroidery** and **crêpe-making**; try Ti Ar Vro in Quimper, **t** 02 98 90 69 20, In the Morbihan, but on the border with the Ille-et-Vilaine and the Loire Atlantique, Ti Kendalc'h, Centre Culturel Breton, 56350 St-Vincent-sur-Oust, **t** 02 99 91 28 55, *www.tikendalch.perroy.ano.fr*, is well known for offering a wide variety of Breton cultural courses. In the Loire Atlantique, for all manner of Breton cultural courses, contact the Agence Culturelle Bretonne, **t** 02 51 84 16 07, *www.a.b.c.free.fr*.

Water Sports, Sailing, Boat Trips

Active water sports: You can get lists with contact details from the Breton CDTs or local tourist offices on the following: diving (*la plongée*), sailing (*la voile*), sand yachting (*char à voile*), canoeing (sometimes on the sea), and windsurfing (*la planche à voile*). *Centres/ bases/clubs/cercles nautiques* or *écoles de mer* will generally offer courses in sailing and other water sports. The term for a yacht harbour or marina is a *port de plaisance*.

Major Breton coastal and estuary marinas include, in alphabetical order: Arzal-Camoël, t 02 99 90 05 86; Bénodet, t 02 98 57 05 78; Binic, t 02 96 73 61 86; Brest Moulin Blanc, t 02 98 02 20 02; Camaret-sur-Mer, t 02 98 27 95 99; Concarneau, t 02 98 97 57 96; Crozon-Morgat, t 02 98 27 01 97; Le Daouët by Pléneuf-Val-André, t 02 96 72 82 85; Douarnenez Tréboul, t 02 98 74 02 56; La Trinité-sur-Mer, t 02 97 55 71 49; Le Croisic, t 02 40 23 10 95; Le Pouliguen, t 02 40 60 37 40; Loctudy, t 02 98 87 51 36; Lorient Bassin à Flot, t 02 97 21 10 14; Lorient Kernével, t 02 97 65 48 25; Paimpol, t 02 96 20 47 65; Perros-Guirec, t 02 96 49 80 50; Pornic, t 02 40 82 05 40; Pornichet, t 02 40 61 03 20; Le Crouesty, t 02 97 53 73 33; Port La Forêt-Fouesnant, t 02 98 56 98 45; Quiberon Port Haliguen, t 02 97 50 20 56; St-Malo Bas-Sablons, t 02 99 81 71 34; St-Malo Port Vauban, t 02 99 56 51 91; St-Quay-Portrieux, t 02 96 70 49 51; Ste-Marine, t 02 98 56 38 72; Tréguier, t 02 92 92 42 37; Vannes, t 02 97 54 16 08.

Boat trips out to sea, to Breton islands, or along Breton estuaries: a large number of Breton ports now offer such trips, either in old-style boats (generically known as *vieux gréements*) or in modern vessels. The CDTs and local tourist offices should have listings. Boat trips are also organized along a good number of the beautiful Breton river estuaries.

Major Breton islands you can visit by boat and stay on include: on the northern Breton coast, the Ile de Bréhat and the Ile de Batz; on the western coast, Molène, Ouessant (Ushant) and Sein; on the southern coast, Les Glénans, Groix, Belle-Ile, Houat and Hoëdic. You can enjoy calmer boat trips around the Golfe du Morbihan, landing on the Ile d'Arz, the Ile aux Moines or the Ile de Gavrinis. You can visit but not stay on many other smaller Breton islands.

Thalassotherapy

The term covers a wide variety of often expensive seawater treatments, which are for relaxation, beauty or medical purposes. Increasingly promoted as beauty retreats for the winter and spring, these centres have done something to revive an off-season life in traditionally 'summertime' tourist resorts. The CDTs and local tourist offices will have listings.

General Sports

You can get lists with contact details from the Breton CDTs or local tourist offices on canoeing, cycling (*le vélo*), fishing (*la pêche*), golf, horse-riding (*l'équitation*), swimming in public pools, tennis, walking (*la randonnée*) and more. In some cases, the CDTs produce a separate annual brochure on several or all of these sports, or they may advise you to contact directly the relevant sporting body in the *département*.

Regional Parks

There are two French natural regional parks in Brittany: the Parc Régional Naturel d'Armorique, covering a large swathe of central Finistère (*see* p.227); and the much smaller peat marshes of the Parc Régional Naturel de la Brière in the Loire Atlantique (*see* p.427).

Environment and Ornithology

Centres that concentrate on presenting Brittany's natural environment in a serious and interesting manner include the Centre d'Animation de la Baie du Mont-St-Michel at Le Vivier-sur-Mer (*see* p.121), the Maison de la Baie de St-Brieuc at Hillion (*see* p.176), and the Maison de la Baie d'Audierne west of Pont-l'Abbé (*see* p.315). The guided walks they organize are particularly good. There are a few other Maisons du Littoral around the Breton coast, for example on the Côte de Granit Rose.

Bird reserves are dotted around the coast, notably at the Baie du Mont-St-Michel, the islands off Cancale, the Cap Fréhel, the Sept-Iles off Perros-Guirec, the Baie de Morlaix, the Molène or Ouessant archipelago, the Cap Sizun, the Glénan islands, the eastern Golfe du Morbihan and Belle-Ile.

Other important places for bird-watching in Brittany are the Baie d'Audierne (guided tours organized by the Maison de la Baie d'Audierne; *see* p.315), the Brière and the Lac de Grand-Lieu. Some Breton bird reserves are situated on inaccessible islands. An exciting way to appreciate bird life in Brittany is to go on the boat tour around the Sept-Iles from Perros-Guirec (*see* p.211).

Gardens

Lists are available from the CDTs.

Art

For those of you profoundly interested in Quimper pottery, a course in **décoration sur faïence** might appeal. Contact either M et Mme Taburet, **t** 02 98 95 08 83, or the Musée de la Faïence, **t** 02 98 90 12 72, *www. quimper-faiences.com*. If you are interested in **fresco painting**, courses are run at the Château de la Groulais, Blain, **t** 02 40 79 07 81, *www.chateaudelagroulais.com*, to the north of Nantes.

Casinos and Leisure Parks

Contact local tourist authorities. A few of the big Breton resorts have a casino.

Money and Banks

To check on the latest euro exchange rates, log on to *www.xe.com/ucc*.

It's always a good idea to try to remember to purchase some euros before you go. You can take as much currency as you like into France, but by law you're only allowed to take out €750 in cash.

Traveller's cheques and Eurocheques, though a safe way of carrying money, aren't always accepted, as French banks charge an absurdly high fee to cash them, so don't rely entirely on them.

The major **credit cards** are widely accepted throughout France, but you should verify whether this is the case in rural areas. A fair number of restaurants don't accept payment by credit cards. Most shops and restaurants don't accept payment by credit cards for amounts below €15–20. Before leaving home, find out from your bank which bank tellers (*guichets automatiques*) to use in France if you want to get out money in that way. International Giro cheques are exchangeable at any French post office.

Banks are generally open 8.30–12.30 and 1.30–4. Most close on Saturday or Monday as well as on Sunday. They are closed on national holidays.

Exchange rates vary and nearly all banks take a commission. *Bureaux de change* that do nothing but exchange money and hotels and train stations usually have the worst rates or charge the heftiest commission.

National Holidays

On French **national holidays**, known as *jours fériés*, banks, shops and businesses close, plus most museums, but most hotels and restaurants stay open. The French national holidays are: 1 Jan (*le jour de l'an*, New Year's Day), Easter Sunday (*le dimanche de Pâques*), Easter Monday (*le lundi de Pâques*), 1 May (*la Fête du Travail*, Labour Day), 8 May (*la Fête de la Libération*, Victory in Europe Day in the Second World War), Ascension Day (*l'Ascension*), Whitsun or Pentecost and the following Monday (*la Pentecôte* and *le lundi de Pentecôte*), 14 July (Bastille Day celebrating the start of the French Revolution), 15 Aug (*l'Assomption*, Assumption), 1 Nov (*Toussaint*, All Saints'), 11 Nov (*l'Armistice*, First World War Armistice Day) and Christmas Day (*Noël*).

French school holidays are staggered by region across France. The main holiday periods, apart from around Christmas and Easter, are in summer between mid-June and early September, and in mid-winter some time in February. The May national holidays are also very popular times for families to take short breaks. If a national holiday falls on a Thursday or a Tuesday, many French people take an extra day to *faire le pont* (to bridge the gap).

Religion

Times of Catholic mass, *la messe*, can be found at tourist offices or on a board at the entrance to the smaller towns and villages. Protestant churches are referred to as *temples*. For times for visiting religious buildings as a tourist, *see* 'Visiting Museums, Sights and Towns', p.69.

Shopping

Shops in France normally open at 9 or 10am. Many shops in smaller towns and in villages close for lunch, normally between 12 noon and 2pm or later. Closing time at the end of the day is generally 7pm. In many towns, Sunday morning is a busy shopping period. However, most shops close on Sunday afternoons and all of Monday, though some grocers and supermarkets do open on Mondays.

Breton specialities to look out for:

Clothes: stripy fishermen's jumpers (also in children's sizes); fishermen's hats (*casquettes*); lace shawls; embroidered aprons or waistcoats; clogs, called *sabots*.

Food: fish soups and traditional canned fish; *saucisson* (salami) or *andouille* (pigs' intestine sausage); biscuits, cakes and crêpes; cider and lambig (*see* p.47).

Luxury goods: Quimper pottery; Breton lace, which is known as *picot*.

VAT is TVA in French. Value added tax on many goods in France is 20.6%. If you are from outside the EU and are making major purchases to take home, it is worth asking whether TVA is deductible for export.

Students

Students with the relevant international student card can benefit from considerable reductions on flights, trains and admissions to museums, concerts and more. Agencies specializing in student and youth travel can help you apply for a card if you are entitled to one, as well as advise you on the best deals. Try STA, which has branches worldwide (for your nearest, see *www.statravel.com*). Note that *tarifs jeunes* (for the under-25s, student or otherwise) are generally available on most means of public transport.

Telephones and Post

Telephones and Faxes

Virtually all French telephone and fax numbers now have 10 digits, the first being a 0. If you are telephoning or faxing France from abroad, first dial the international code, t 00 33, then remove the 0 from the front of the regional number and dial the nine digits that follow it.

If you telephone from a hotel room you may be charged a greatly inflated unit price. To telephone from a public telephone booth, you often need a **telephone card**, or *télécarte*, available at newspaper kiosks or tobacconists as well as at the post office, or you may be able to use your credit card. You can telephone from a metered booth in a good number of post offices and then pay at the counter.

For **international calls** out of France, dial t 00, then the country code (UK 44; USA and Canada 1; Ireland 353; Australia 61; New Zealand 64; South Africa 27), followed by the local or area code (generally minus the 0 if there is one in front of the number) and the rest of the number.

For French directory enquiries, dial t 12. For international directory enquiries, dial t 19 33 12, followed by the code for the country in question; once you have given the name and address for the number you want, you can put down the receiver – the company will phone back once it has found the number. On the internet, *www.pagesjaunes.fr* is the French *Yellow Pages*, *www.pagesblanches.fr* is the residential equivalent. To look up a number at a post office you may have to use the Minitel electronic directory. Ask for help if you don't understand the instructions.

Postal Services

French post boxes are yellow, marked with a stylized blue bird. Post offices are called La Poste, Le Bureau de Poste or the PTT. The offices in cities are open Mon–Fri 8am–7pm, and Sat 8am–12 noon. In smaller towns and in villages, the post offices may only open at 9am, are likely to close for lunch from 12 noon to 2pm, and may close as early as 4.30 or 5pm.

Stamps can be bought at newspaper kiosks and tobacconists as well as at post offices. You can receive mail *poste restante* at any French post office if you bring some form of official identification.

Toilets or Rest Rooms

Public toilets in Brittany are generally appalling, although there are signs of improvements. Visitors should be warned that the hole-in-the-ground lavatory is still surprisingly common.

On Breton main roads it makes sense to head straight for the (free) service station facilities, and it's wise to keep a stock of emergency toilet paper on you at all times. There are some public toilets for which you have to pay, either to get into – those funky modern oval-shaped street facilities – or to get out of, when there's a toilet caretaker (you should leave a small tip).

Tourist Information

France is divided up geographically and administratively into *départements*, each with its central tourist information service, the **Comité Départemental du Tourisme** or **CDT**. These are a mine of information, as are local tourist offices. Larger local tourist offices are Offices du Tourisme; smaller ones are misleadingly known as Syndicats d'Initiative.

Another level of official tourist information providers between the CDTs and the local tourist offices, the **Pays d'Accueil Touristique**, often offer excellent tourist booklets and information for their area. You can call or write to Pays d'Accueil, but they don't have offices. Addresses for the Pays d'Accueil Touristique and many local tourist offices are given in the relevant grey boxes in the touring chapters. In many cases, their websites are worth checking out for links to local services and hotels, *chambres d'hôte*, etc.

There is also an official regional tourist service based in Rennes, the Comité Régional du Tourisme de Bretagne (CRT Bretagne), as well as the CRT Loire Atlantique in Nantes, although this cannot provide as useful and specific information as the CDTs, the Pays d'Accueil Touristique or the local tourist offices. It does however, help make interesting guidebooks to Brittany, in French, often published by Ouest-France.

CRT and CDTs

Comité Régional du Tourisme de Bretagne:
1 Rue Raoul Ponchon, 35069 Rennes Cedex, 02 99 28 44 40, www.tourismebretagne.com.
CDT Ille-et-Vilaine: 4 Rue Jean Jaurès, B.P. 6046, 35060 Rennes Cedex 3, t 02 99 78 47 47, www.bretagne35.com.
CDT Côtes d'Armor: 7 Rue St-Benoît, B.P. 4620, 22046 St-Brieuc Cedex 2, t 02 96 62 72 00, www.cotesdarmor.com.
CDT Finistère: 11 Rue Théodore Le Hars, B.P. 1419, 29104 Quimper Cedex, t 02 98 76 20 70, finistere.tourisme@wanadoo.fr.
CDT Morbihan: PIBS, Allée Baco, BP 408, 56010 Vannes Cedex, t 02 97 54 06 56, www.morbihan.com.
CDT Loire Atlantique: 2 Allée Baco, BP 20502, 44001 Nantes, Cedex 1, t 02 51 72 95 30, www.cdt44.com.

French Government Tourist Offices

UK: 178 Piccadilly, London W1V 0AL, t 0906 824 4123 (calls charged at 60p per minute), http://uk.franceguide.com/.
Ireland: 30 Upper Merion Street, Dublin 2, (01) 662 9330, http://ie.franceguide.com.
USA: 444 Madison Avenue, 16th Floor, New York, NY 10022, t (212) 838 7800; 676 North Michigan Avenue, Suite 3360, Chicago, IL 60611; 9454 Wilshire Boulevard, Suite 715, Beverly Hills, CA 90212; nationwide information, t (900) 990 0040, http://us.franceguide.com.
Canada: 1981 Avenue McGill College, No. 490, Montreal, Quebec H3A 2W9, t (514) 288 4264, http://ca.franceguide.com; 1 Dundas Street West, No. 2405 Box 8, Toronto, Ontario M5G 1Z3, http://ca-uk.franceguide.com.
Australia: Level 20, 25 Bligh Street, Sydney, NSW 2000, t (2) 9231 5244, http://au.franceguide.com.
South Africa: PO Box 41022, 2024 Craighall, t (11) 880 8062, http://za.franceguide.com.

For general tourist information on France in your own country, contact the relevant French Government tourist office, though it will not be able to supply you with anything like the detailed information you get from the *département* and local tourist bodies in France. French Government tourist offices are listed above.

Visiting Museums, Sights and Towns

The opening times for museums and sights are included in the text where possible, though these can change (if just the month is given, the place is open the whole of that month). Almost all museums and sights charge an admission fee.

Please note that the opening times for many French museums and sights are quite restricted. The majority are reliably open between 10am and 12 noon and between 2pm and 5 or 6pm, but bear in mind that these times are somewhat deceptive: it's advisable to arrive a good hour before any closing time stated to avoid being disappointed. Guided tours, where they're available or compulsory, normally start on the hour. A growing number of museums and sights are starting to become more flexible about their opening hours, many even doing away with the sacred provincial 2-hour lunch break. The further you get away from the main tourist season, the more restricted opening times tend to be. Virtually all French sights are closed on Christmas Day and New Year's Day, and many close on 1 May and All Saints' at the beginning of November (*see* 'National Holidays', p.67). All publicly owned museums close on Tuesdays.

Breton churches in the countryside are not always easy to visit. Rural communities are particularly concerned about theft these days, so they tend to keep their churches locked. Local tourist offices should be able to tell you at what times local churches are open, and opening times are also often posted on church doors. In some rural areas, there may be a notice telling you where you can get the key from. Don't hesitate to go and ask for *la clef*, though occasionally you may have to leave your own car keys or some official document in exchange. It's a good idea to take binoculars to look at some of the ornate stringbeams and stained-glass windows. Tourist offices should have details on special guided tours of rural Breton chapels by local experts.

Cultural tours of historic Breton towns are also organized regularly in holiday times via the tourist offices. Depending on the guide, they can be fascinating. Many Breton towns have a *petit train touristique* that takes you round some of the highlights (if you can cope with the naffness of it all).

Where to Stay

If you decide well in advance to stay in one particular area of Brittany, you could write to the relevant tourist offices given in the text for complete lists of self-catering accommodation, hotels and camp sites in their area. They're very unlikely to give you any recommendations, however.

The recommendations given in this guide are for hotels and a limited number of B&B addresses that, for the most part, have a good deal of charm. Chain hotels have not been listed, except where other options are limited.

Hotels

Please note that in high season many hotels will only offer half board or full board, not the room by itself. This may suit you for a day or two, but you may find such an imposition a bit restrictive for a longer period.

The French authorities star-grade hotels by their facilities rather than by charm or location, as in most countries in Europe. Stars go from the luxurious 4 (sometimes with an L added to underline exceptional luxuriousness) to a basic single star. There are even some hotels without any stars at all. Most of these are bottom of the range and cheap, but a few may simply not have registered and may be quite smart.

Rooms in 4-star hotels should always be luxurious. In the countryside, many of them will be set in historic houses. Three-star hotels should be very comfortable, with good facilities; many will be charming, but others, in the large towns, may be upmarket chain hotels. In the 2-star range, charm can vary enormously. However, most 2-star hotel rooms have their own WC and bathroom or shower, as well as a television. One-star hotel rooms are pretty basic and may not have their own WC, bathroom or television, but some offer the occasional pleasant surprise.

Single rooms are relatively rare and usually two-thirds the price of a double. If there are a few of you travelling together and looking for a cheap option, some basic hotels have triples or quads that can be good value. Hotel breakfasts can be expensive, so check on the price and ask whether it's optional. If it seems too much, a local bar may be a better bet.

In July and August, around Easter, and over the French May bank holidays, it's best to book well in advance as Brittany is extremely popular. Hotels may well insist on partial payment up front – the easiest way to deal

---

Hotel Price Ranges

Note: all prices listed here and elsewhere in this book are for a double room with bath/shower in high season.

luxury €230 euros and over
very expensive €150–230
expensive €100–150
moderate €60–100
inexpensive less than €60

with this is to give a credit card number. If you are going to Brittany out of season and want to stay in specific hotels, it's always worth ringing in advance to check that they are open. A rough indication of prices for hotel rooms and restaurants has been stated in this guide, but remember that prices change from year to year.

Don't confuse **umbrella organizations** such as **Relais & Châteaux, Châteaux et Hôtels de France, Château Accueil & Bienvenue au Château/La Vie de Château** and **Logis de France** with the chain hotels. Such organizations gather together generally independent hotels to promote themselves more effectively and to maintain standards. Relais & Châteaux hotels are top of the range, generally extremely beautiful and luxurious, with gourmet cuisine. Châteaux et Hôtels de France have a greater variety of hotels full of character, some expensive, some surprisingly good value. Their guidebook includes a number of private châteaux receiving guests, which is the speciality of Château Accueil & Bienvenue au Château/La Vie de Château. While the latter offers wonderful characterful, historic places in which to stay, these addresses tend to be very expensive, and while many are extremely well run, others are not quite so well geared to tourists. That said, the welcome is often delightfully personal, and most owners are not only charming but clearly in love with their home. Logis de France is a much larger organization, its averagely priced hotels signalled by a green and yellow sign with a fireplace depicted in the middle. Some Logis de France are really good value, a few are excellent, and some are dowdy, run-down and unpleasant, so the sign shouldn't be taken as a guarantee of quality. Take a look inside first if unsure. You can get a copy of their free guide at member hotels, which are rated 1, 2 or 3 chimneys, or see *www.logis.de.france.fr.*

Bed and Breakfast and *Fermes-auberges*

Bed and breakfast is known as *chambre d'hôte* in France. B&Bs vary in quality and are officially graded accordingly. By choosing a *chambre d'hôte*, as well as avoiding too many other tourists, you may get the chance to chat with your hosts. Generally, a *chambre d'hôte*

offers good value for money, especially as breakfast is included in the prices stated. Guests do not get the same facilities and services as in a hotel, but B&Bs tend to be much more peaceful and personal. Bear in mind when planning your trip that some prohibit single-night bookings over the busy summer period. Most tourist offices can provide you with a handy-sized directory of *chambres d'hôtes* in the Brittany region.

Table d'hôte is when a *chambre d'hôte* address offers the possibility of an evening meal, which is generally shared with the proprietors, who may in some cases speak some English. You have to let your hosts know in advance if you want to eat with them. *Table d'hôte* is relatively expensive in the more characterful B&Bs, but it is a very good way to meet French people.

Fermes-auberges, farms-turned-inns, are also good value. Accommodation in these can be fairly basic, but they are often atmospheric. Good traditional country cooking using almost nothing but local farm produce is their strong point.

Local tourist offices have lists of *chambres d'hôtes* and *fermes-auberges* in their area.

Youth Hostels and *Gîtes d'Etape*

Most large towns have a youth hostel (*auberge de jeunesse*) offering simple dormitory accommodation and breakfast to people of any age for around €8–12 a night.

To get into a youth hostel you need a Youth Hostel Association membership card. The regulations say that you should get this in your home country (in the UK see *www.yha.org.uk*; in the USA *www.hiusa.org*; in Canada *www.hihostels.ca*; in Australia *www.yha.com.au*), but you can almost always buy one on the spot, or buy international Welcome Stamps. Many youth hostels have kitchen facilities, or can provide a cheap meal.

Youth hostels are the best deal going for people who are travelling on their own. For people travelling together, however, a 1-star hotel can be as cheap. One negative side to youth hostels is that they're often out of the centre of town, and in summer you need to arrive early in the day to be sure of getting a room. It's worth calling ahead to see if you can reserve a place in advance.

A *gîte d'étape* is a simple shelter with bunk beds (no bedding) and a basic self-catering kitchen, set up by a village along walking paths or scenic bike routes. Such accommodation should cost €7 a night.

Camping

Camping is a very popular way to travel, especially among the French themselves, and there's at least one *camping municipal* in every French parish; it is often an inexpensive, no-frills site. Other camp sites are graded with stars like hotels, from 4-star luxury to 1-star basics. At the top of the range you can expect lots of trees and grass, maybe an individually hedged plot, hot showers, a pool, sports facilities, a grocer's, a bar and/or a restaurant. Prices for the top of the range are similar to 1-star hotels. The tourist bodies for the individual *départements* can send you a full list of their camp sites, while local tourist offices should be able to supply you with details on those in their specific area. Camp sites by beaches are numerous in Brittany, but they get very busy in the height of summer. If you want to camp in the countryside, it's imperative to ask permission from the landowner first, or risk a furious farmer, his dog, his gun and perhaps even the police. There are some specialist guides to camping in France, such as the Michelin green camping guide, in which the camp sites are graded.

Gîtes de France and Other Self-Catering Accommodation

Brittany offers a huge range of self-catering options, from inexpensive farm cottages to history-laden châteaux and fancy villas, or even canal boats. If you want a place near the beaches in the holiday season, book early. The Fédération Nationale des Gîtes de France is a French Government service that gives out information on inexpensive accommodation by the week. Lists with photos covering *gîtes* by *département* are available from French Government tourist offices and most local tourist offices. Prices range from €150 to €460 a week, depending on the time of year you go as well as facilities. Nearly always, you'll have to begin your stay on a Saturday. The tourist bodies for the individual French *départements*, the CDTs, also have listings specifically for their county – contact the relevant CDT in the Tourist Information section on p.69.

The UK Sunday papers are full of self-catering accommodation direct from private owners, as are websites such as *www.frenchconnections. co.uk*. Or contact one of the specialist firms listed in the Sunday papers or on p.60. The accommodation the latter offer is nearly always more comfortable and costly than a *gîte*, but the discounts that holiday firms get you on ferries, plane tickets or car rentals can make up for the price difference. For *gîtes* for disabled people, *see* p.63.

Ille-et-Vilaine

07

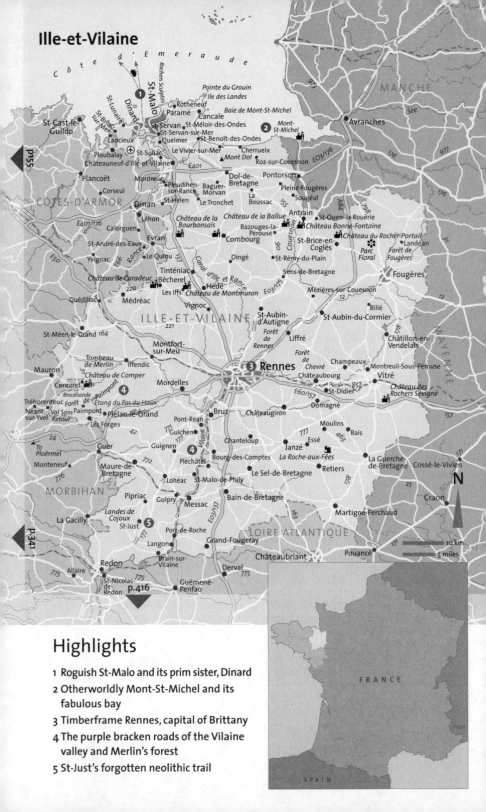

Ille-et-Vilaine

Côte d'Emeraude

Rochers Sculptés

St-Malo
Dinard

Pointe du Grouin
Île des Landes
Baie de Mont-St-Michel

MANCHE

Avranches

St-Lunaire
St-Briac-sur-Mer
Rothéneuf
Paramé
Cancale

② Mont-St-Michel

St-Cast-le-Guildo

Lancieux

St-Servan
St-Servan-sur-Mer
Quelmer

St-Méloir-des-Ondes

St-Benoît-des-Ondes

Pontorson

Ploubalay
St-Suliac

Le Vivier-sur-Mer
Cherrueix
Roz-sur-Couesnon

Châteauneuf-d'Ille-et-Vilaine

Mont Dol

Plancoët

Mordreuc

Dol-de-Bretagne

Pleine-Fougères

St-Quen-la-Rouërie

Corseul

Pleudihen-sur-Rance
St-Hélen

Baguer-Morvan
Le Tronchet

La Boussac

Antrain

Sougéal

CÔTES-D'ARMOR

Dinan

Château de la Ballue

St-Brice-en-Coglès

Château Bonne-Fontaine

Château du Rocher-Portail

Léhon

Château de la Bourbansais

Bazouges-la-Pérouse

Landéan
Forêt de Fougères

Calorguen

Evran

Combourg

St-Rémy-du-Plain

Parc Floral

St-André-des-Eaux

Le Quiou

Dingé

Sens-de-Bretagne

Fougères

Yvignac

Tinténiac

Château de Caradeuc
Bécherel
Hédé

Canal d'Ille et Rance

Mézières-sur-Couesnon

Billé

Quédillac
Médréac

Les Iffs
Château de Montmuran

Vignoc

St-Aubin-d'Aubigné

St-Aubin-du-Cormier

Châtillon-en-Vendelais

St-Méen-le-Grand

ILLE-ET-VILAINE

Forêt de Rennes

Liffré

MAYENNE

Montfort-sur-Meu

Forêt de Chevré

Champeaux

Montreuil-Sous-Pérouse

Tombeau de Merlin
Iffendic

③ Rennes

Château des Rochers Sévigné

Mauron

Château de Comper

Mordelles

Châteaubourg

St-Didier

Vitré

Concoret
Brocéliande

④

Étang du Pas du Haut

Bruz

Domagné

Tréhorenteuc
Néant-sur-Yvel

Forêt de Paimpont
Val Sans Retour
Paimpont

Plélan-le-Grand

Pont-Réan

Châteaugiron

Moulins

Bais

Les Forges

Guichen

Chanteloup

Janzé

Essé

La Guerche-de-Bretagne

Cossé-le-Vivien

Guer

Guignen

④

Bourg-des-Comptes

La Roche-aux-Fées

Retiers

Montenou

Maure-de-Bretagne

Pléchâtel

Le Sel-de-Bretagne

Craon

MORBIHAN

Lohéac

St-Malo-de-Phily

Pipriac

Guipry

Bain-de-Bretagne

La Gacilly

Landes de Cojoux
St-Just

⑤

Messac

Martigné-Ferchaud

Port-de-Roche

Grand-Fougeray

LOIRE ATLANTIQUE

Langon

Allaire

Redon
St-Nicolas-de-Redon
p.416

Brain-sur-Vilaine

Guémené-Penfao

Derval

Châteaubriant

Pouancé

N

10 km
5 miles

Highlights

1 Roguish St-Malo and its prim sister, Dinard

2 Otherworldly Mont-St-Michel and its fabulous bay

3 Timberframe Rennes, capital of Brittany

4 The purple bracken roads of the Vilaine valley and Merlin's forest

5 St-Just's forgotten neolithic trail

FRANCE

ITALY

SPAIN

The Ille-et-Vilaine is scarcely Breton at all, some western Bretons argue. It was only Breton-speaking for a short period; much of the architecture and most of the churches don't look typically Breton; Rennes, though Brittany's capital, was built in good part for aristocratic provincial parliamentarians hardly in touch with the majority of the poor Breton people; and the St-Malo merchants who made a killing through sea voyages remained aloof and independent. Yet the Vilaine valley crossing the *département* did serve as a border between ancient Brittany and the Franks to the east. And it was close to Redon on the Vilaine that Nomenoë grabbed Breton independence in the 9th century. Even if the Breton language has receded westwards, Breton place names at least have stuck up to the Vilaine, and Breton-style legends linger.

The Ille-et-Vilaine may only have a very short stretch of Brittany's vast seashore, but what a staggering one. Its fragment runs from just west of the holy mount of the Mont-St-Michel to a little way west of St-Malo, the great and gritty Breton sea adventurers' city. This section of the Côte d'Emeraude (the Emerald Coast), as the shore is called here, is enviably beautiful.

The daytime mirages and evening sunsets across the bay of the Mont-St-Michel make for some of the most mesmerizing images by which to remember Brittany. Though the holy mount officially stands in Normandy, much of the spectacular flat bay out of which it rises lies behind the Breton border. The regional divide between Normandy and Brittany has traditionally been the Couesnon river. As the popular saying goes:

The Couesnon in a moment of folly
Put the Mont-St-Michel in Normandy.

We've been generous and found a place for the magical sight in this chapter. Between the coast and Rennes, châteaux liberally dot the countryside. Combourg, Ille-et-Vilaine's most famous castle, is linked with gushing French Romantic writer, François-René de Chateaubriand. Born in St-Malo, he travelled extensively around Ille-et-Vilaine. The Route Chateaubriand is an association of sites with connections to the figure that will help take you to the interior of the *département*. By far the most internationally famous literary location in the area is Merlin's forest, officially called Paimpont, better known in legend as Brocéliande. In its landscapes of curious purple schist covered with moorland and woods, little neolithic sites have been turned into fantasy locations for Arthurian legend. The most famous example of neolithic architecture in the Ille-et-Vilaine is La Roche-aux-Fées. St-Just, down the quietly gorgeous Vilaine valley from Rennes, counts among the most unspoilt prehistoric sites in Brittany. But we start our touring with vast medieval castles on the forgotten Breton border.

The Northern Marches of Brittany

Fougères and Vitré boast a couple of the country's mightiest medieval forts. The Breton Marches they stand in form Brittany's frontier with France. Breton boundaries changed a fair degree through history, but maps show an arc of defensive eastern towns of importance through many centuries, from Dinan and Dol-de-Bretagne in the north, via Fougères, Vitré, La Guerche-de-Bretagne and Châteaubriant in the centre, down to Ancenis, Clisson and Guérande on or not that far from the Loire.

Getting There and Around

The D178 is the main road through the Breton Marches from Fougères to Nantes. Vitré is the best-connected town for **rail** travel. It lies on the line from Paris to Rennes, and TGV rapid trains from Paris very occasionally stop at Vitré, taking under 2 hours.

Tourist Information

Pays d'Accueil Touristique de Fougères, 1 Place Aristide Briand, BP 558, 35305 Fougères, **t** 02 99 94 60 30, *www.bretagne-fougeres.com*.

Fougères: 2 Rue Nationale, **t** 02 99 94 12 20, *www.ot-fougeres.fr*.

Pays d'Accueil Touristique des Portes de Bretagne, 1 Rue de la Seiche, 35150 Essé, **t** 02 99 44 58 44, *www.pays-des-portes-de-bretagne.com*.

Vitré: Place St-Yves, **t** 02 99 75 04 46, *www.ot-vitre.fr*.

La Guerche-de-Bretagne: Place de la Mairie, **t** 02 99 96 30 78, *otsi.laguerche@wanadoo.fr*.

Market Days

Fougères: Saturday.
Vitré: Monday and Saturday.
St-Aubin-du-Cormier: Thursday.
Châteaugiron: Thursday.
La Guerche-de-Bretagne: Tuesday (since 1121).
Marché de l'Aumaillerie, La Selle-en-Luitré: Friday (one of the biggest cattle markets in Europe).

Where to Stay and Eat

Fougères ✉ 35300

★★Les Voyageurs, 10 Place Gambetta, **t** 02 99 99 08 20, *hotel-voyageurs-fougeres@wanadoo.fr* (*moderate*). A recently refurbished choice, with an adjoining *haute cuisine* restaurant (*moderate–expensive; closed Sat and Sun eves*) serving excellent traditional French fare such as *tournedos de thon* and offering an old-fashioned *chariot de desserts*. The location leaves something to be desired, however, and the rooms come as a bit of a disappointment after the cooking. *Closed Christmas*.

★★Le Balzac, 15 Rue Nationale, **t** 02 99 99 42 46, *www.balzachotel.com* (*inexpensive*). A simple but charming option well placed in the upper town. Balzac wrote his famous novel *Les Chouans* here (*see* p.78).

Le Bretagne, 7 Place de la République, **t** 02 99 99 31 68 (*inexpensive*). A basic but clean and welcoming place by the station, open 24 hours.

St Léonard, 20 Rue Nationale, **t** 02 99 94 36 23 (*moderate*). Meat-heavy menus close to the castle. *Closed Sun eve, Mon and Sat lunch, and 3wks in Sept*.

Les Vins et une Fourchette, 1 Rue de la Fourchette, **t** 02 99 94 55 88 (*moderate*). A little old butcher's shop very close to the castle entrance, with delightfully decorated, spacious rooms. Many of the excellent, good-value dishes are grilled within view, and the wine list has been lovingly chosen. *Closed Sun and Tues eves*.

Le Buffet, 53 bis Rue Nationale, **t** 02 99 94 35 76 (*inexpensive–moderate*). An appealing option with a full buffet ideal for those who agonize between the *hors d'oeuvre* and dessert paths in a 2-course *formule*. *Closed Sun and Tues even*.

Crêperie des Remparts, 102 Rue de la Pinterie, **t** 02 99 94 53 53 (*inexpensive*). A welcoming choice with a pleasant terrace. *Closed Tues*.

Le Haute-Sève, 37 Boulevard Jean Jaurès, **t** 02 99 94 23 39 (*inexpensive*). An excellent-value, gastronomic choice. *Closed Sun eve and Mon, first 2wks Jan and 15 July–15 Aug*.

St-Brice-en-Coglès ✉ 35460

★★Le Lion d'Or, 6-8 Rue Chateaubriand, **t** 02 99 98 61 44, *leliondor3@wanadoo.fr* (*inexpensive*). A simple but reliable option loctated in a village approximately 15km northwest of Fougères.

La Totinais, La Selle-en-Coglès, a few km north of St-Brice, **t** 02 99 98 64 69 (*inexpensive*). Warm, tasteful, characterful B&B rooms.

Chauvigné ✉ 35490

Maison-Neuve, t 02 99 95 05 64, *www.auberge-lamaisoneuve.com* (*inexpensive*). A good *ferme-auberge* situated about 25km from Fougères. The culinary specialities on offer include cider chicken and nettle soup.

Billé ✉ 35133
Ferme de Mésauboin, Mésauboin, a little way outside Billé, **t** 02 99 97 61 57, *steph.mesauboin@wanadoo.fr* (*inexpensive*). Accommodation in a manor house about 10km southwest of Fougères. The food (*moderate; advance booking required*) includes *gratin fougerais* with leeks, potatoes and cider. *Closed 2wks in Oct.*

Vitré ✉ 35500
This is perhaps a better town to eat at than to stay in, but there are several reasonably priced options.

Le Minotel, 47 Rue Poterie, **t 02 99 75 11 11 (*inexpensive*). A beautiful renovated building well situated in the historic centre, signposted alongside the tourist sites. The modernized rooms, in 'golf club chic' style, are not to every taste though.

*Duguesclin, 27 Rue Duguesclin, **t** 02 99 75 02 96 (*inexpensive*). A decent basic option.

Fauchers, 2 Chemin des Tertres Noirs, **t** 02 99 75 08 69 (*inexpensive*). A welcoming B&B in a characterful old house down the hill near to the Musée St-Nicolas.

Hôtel du Château, 5 Rue Rallon, **t** 02 99 74 58 59 (*inexpensive*). A pleasant basic hotel with TVs and bathrooms in all rooms. Ask for one on the upper floors for a view of the castle ramparts.

Taverne de l'Ecu, 12 Rue de la Baudrairie, **t** 02 99 75 11 09 (*moderate–expensive*). A 15th-century inn where a variety of seafood specialities are served in a medieval-style room. *Closed low season Sun and Tues eves and Wed.*

Le Petit Pressoir, 20 Rue de Paris, **t** 02 99 74 79 79 (*moderate*). A good choice for wine lovers. Food includes a lovingly prepared *crabe millefeuille*. *Closed Sun eve and Mon.*

Le Pichet, 17 Boulevard de Laval, **t** 02 99 75 24 09 (*moderate*). A venue for 'creative' modern Breton cuisine a little way to the east of the town centre.

Auberge de Saint Louis, 31 Rue Notre Dame, **t** 02 99 75 28 28 (*inexpensive–moderate*). A well-regarded traditional choice with a remarkable *fleur-de-lys* façade, in a good location. There's classical music, proper napkins, and deferential service. *Closed Mon and Tues.*

Auberge du Château, 34 Rue d'Embas, (*moderate*). An inn at the base of the castle, offering a choice of seasonal menus, a kids' menu, and a thoughtfully included 1/2/3 *assiette* plan.

La Soupe aux Choux, 32 Rue Notre Dame, **t** 02 99 75 10 86 (*inexpensive*). A family favourite that attracts aficionados of simple French classics. *Closed Sat lunch and Sun in low season.*

Au Vieux Vitré, 1 Rue d'Embas,, **t** 02 99 75 02 52 (*inexpensive*). An atmospheric crêperie set inside a picturesque old building next to Le Minotel hotel.

St-Didier ✉ 35220
***Pen'Roc, La Peinière, just north of St-Didier, **t** 02 99 00 33 02, *www.penroc.fr* (*expensive*). A good upper-range choice with the benefits of a swimming pool, an exercise room and a sauna. Stylish seafood dishes are served either in the modern dining room or on the pretty patio.

La Garde, **t** 02 99 00 90 09 (*moderate*). A *ferme-auberge* that specializes in rustic local fare.

Châteaubourg ✉ 35220
***Ar Milin, 30 Rue de Paris, **t** 02 99 00 30 91, *www.armilin.com* (*moderate*). Pretty little rooms, some of which are set in a former flour mill on the river Vilaine. There's also an elegant dining room, with grilled meats among the chef's specialities.

Châteaugiron ✉ 35410
Auberge du Cheval Blanc, 9 Rue de la Madeleine, **t** 02 99 37 40 27 (*inexpensive*). A former coaching inn on the very attractive main street winding up round the château, serving family cooking (*moderate*).

L'Aubergade, 2 Boulevard Pierre et Julien Gourdel, **t** 02 99 37 41 35 (*moderate*). Carefully prepared Breton dishes here. *Closed Sun and Mon eves.*

La Guerche-de-Bretagne ✉ 35130
La Calèche, 16 Avenue du Général Leclerc, **t 02 99 96 21 63 (*inexpensive*). Spacious, comfortable rooms and a bright dining room where you can enjoy good food (*inexpensive–moderate*).

Fougères and its Forests

In a rather wooden description, Victor Hugo once compared Fougères to a great big spoon. The castle he saw as the spoon itself, the steep old ramp of a street leading up the hill from the castle as the spoon's handle. Unusually, Fougères's massive fort does not dominate the town. In fact, for the best view of it on its mound down in the Nançon valley, you need to climb to the rather grand upper town, or even up the church of St-Léonard's tower. Visitors often miss Fougères's upper town, or Bourg Neuf, but it has sober, elegant 18th-century façades, some fine streets and shops, two museums – one dedicated to the late-Impressionist-style works of Emmanuel de la Villéon and one to the history of time-pieces – as well as the oldest free-standing belfry in Brittany.

History

Fougères castle was the centre of feudal power games through the Middle Ages. But in the town members of the successful tanning and weaving corporations built up their own prosperity. In fact, the traders' belfry, built in 1387, is the earliest of its type in Brittany and is a symbol of the early independence they achieved.

The Duc de Mercoeur, the fanatical Catholic leader in Brittany during the 16th-century French Wars of Religion, caused chaos and bloodshed in the region by occupying Fougères until King Henri IV had renounced Protestantism. Linen- and sail-making continued to bring wealth to Fougères merchants through the Ancien Régime period, and fine cut glass became another town speciality; some leading perfume brands still have their bottles made here. A series of fires swept through the Fougères streets in the 18th century, wiping out many medieval buildings, so the great architect Jacques Gabriel, among others, helped redesign the town.

Fougères and its area became one of the most significant centres of the Chouannerie, the violently anti-Republican, pro-Catholic and pro-royalist uprising in which so many Bretons fought against the French Revolution. Hugo, whose great muse, Juliette Drouet, was born in the town, set the less well-known *Quatre-Vingt-Treize* largely in Fougères. The truly memorable novel describing in detail the anti-Revolutionary uprising in and around Fougères is Balzac's *Les Chouans* (*see* box, below). Chateaubriand, whose family was decimated by the Revolution,

Balzac's Vision of a Brutal Breton Uprising

'Nous sommes diables contre diables (We are devils fighting devils)', one of the leading Chouans declares in *Les Chouans, ou la Bretagne en 1799*, published in 1829 and regarded by many critics as Balzac's first major work. It gives a dramatic and damning picture of French society scarred by the Revolution and the Napoleonic era. The terrible turmoil in the Marches of Brittany at the close of the 18th century is the main subject of the novel, though the serious topic is somewhat undermined by a love story that develops at the same time. A clog filled with the hot blood of a Breton traitor who has had his head chopped off like an animal by former comrades counts among the most savage acts described in this rip-roaring, filmic read.

wrote of an extraordinarily terrible Revolutionary incident that occurred at Fougères involving his sister; this was not fiction, this was the real thing. A **promenade en littérature** rather proudly lets you retrace the Fougères steps of the not inconsiderable collection of French writers who were both inspired by the town and engaged enough to write about it.

A Tour of Fougères

Begin a tour of Fougères up among the well-planned streets and squares of the **Bourg Neuf**, on the **Place Aristide Briand**. It is rather surprising to find a connection with the American War of Independence up here, but on the square stands the house that belonged to Armand Tuffin, Marquis de la Rouërie, who fought for George Washington before coming back to wage war against the French Revolution. The house where he was born was transformed into the *tribunal d'instance* (magistrates' court) in the 19th century.

Above the Place Aristide Briand lies the sweet **Place du Théâtre** with its ornate late-19th-century town theatre. From here, the Rue de la Pinterie could take you swiftly and extremely steeply down the hillside to the castle, but you might like to stay up in the Bourg Neuf to explore its sites or to shop. Head along the grandiose, mainly 18th-century **Rue Nationale**, off which you can easily spot the 14th-century **belfry**, which also served as a watchtower. Back on the Rue Nationale, a medallion marks the façade of the house where Chateaubriand came frequently in order to visit one of his sisters.

Along the Rue Nationale you'll also find the **Musée Emmanuel de la Villéon** (*open daily June–Sept, rest of year Sat, Sun and school hols*). The house stands out clearly – it is the only remaining *maison à porche* in central Fougères, its wooden structure and protruding covered walk typical of late Gothic houses. It makes a charming setting for a quite beautiful little collection of paintings. Their artist, Emmanuel de la Villéon, was born in Fougères in 1858. He subsequently spent little time here, but he did paint many scenes of Breton peasants and Breton landscapes. The museum contains his first recognized painting and his very last Parisian pieces – sad wintery scenes done in the midst of the Second World War. Down the road the **Atelier Musée de l'Horlogerie** (*open May–Oct Tues–Sun 9–7; rest of year Tues–Sat 9–6.30*) traces the evolution of time measurement. In the spirit of a modern museum, it also functions as a workshop, allowing you to watch the watchmaker in action.

The **church of St-Léonard** at the end of the Rue Nationale is a substantial Gothic building with big dragon gargoyles spitting down on passers-by. You can climb the 17th-century **belltower** for views down onto all sides of the town, including Fougères's castle, with scarred, quarried cliffs beyond it. Back in the church, you can find some fine 12th-century stained glass, with one medallion depicting scenes from the life of St Benedict. This turns out to be the oldest piece of stained glass in Brittany, though it was originally made outside of Paris for the royal abbey of St-Denis.

Beside the church, the **Place aux Arbres public garden** meanders towards the château; this is the most picturesque way down to the old town and the fort. The winding paths lead precipitously to the **Bourg Vieil**, where the tanners and dyers

La Fée Mélusine de Lusignan

Unreligious legend crops up frequently in Breton churches. The fairy Mélusine's sad story was apparently transported here from the Poitou region in the 13th century. The tale goes that she killed her father, an unstable and violent king, to stop him battering her mother. As punishment, she was transformed every Saturday night into a fearful creature – part-woman, part-serpent. To keep her shameful secret, she hid underground in the caves of her castle every time the miserable metamorphosis occurred. Unfortunately, one weekend her husband discovered her hiding place and her terrible secret, at which Mélusine let out a horrendous scream and vanished.

The legend of Mélusine was kept alive in Fougères, where it was said that her cry could be heard on the eve of major disasters. But the legend takes many forms in France; some even view her as a beneficent figure encouraging family prosperity and fecundity, and protecting the forests.

once made use of the waters to prepare their animal hides. Washhouses still line the fast-flowing stream, its bright green watergrasses combed by the current. The atmosphere of this old quarter comes in part from the timberframe houses that have survived. Off Rue des Tanneurs, the oldest house to have survived in Fougères, the **Maison de Savigny**, hosts a variety of exhibitions during the summer months. **Place du Marchix**, the old market square, looks particularly colourful. Off the Rue Lusignan, a path leads up the wooded **Butte de Bigot** from which you can get another good view down onto the castle.

Down by the castle, you might care to cast an eye over the **church of St-Sulpice**, if not go to pray to the once much-revered statue of Notre-Dame des Marais within. This probably dates from the 14th century (though it now sports an 18th-century head), but the story goes that it was irreligiously thrown into the castle moat by King Henry II Plantagenet's troops, only to be dredged up again around 1300, miraculously saved. The legendary Fée Mélusine (*see* box, above) features outside the south choir door.

Fougères Castle

Open daily mid-June–mid-Sept 9–7, April–mid-June 9.30–12 and 2–6, Oct–Dec and Feb–April 10–12 and 2–5. Guided tours in English June–Aug at certain times of day.

This magnificent debris of the Middle Ages... adorned with its square and rounded towers, each one large enough to put up a whole regiment.

Balzac, Les Chouans

The castle of Fougères is an immense empty shell. Once across the moat with its row of watermill wheels, you have to penetrate several protective layers to reach the heart of this massive medieval fortification. The 13 surviving towers are bare, but the great lengths of walls, made of mottled schist, with bands of granite separating the storeys, look mighty enough. Machicolations and loopholes and conical slate roofs make the place look a perfect picture of medieval defence, although many of the inner buildings have disappeared.

An initial fortification was constructed on this site early in the 11th century. In the struggle for supremacy between regional feudal lords, Duke Conan IV of Brittany submitted to the mighty Angevin who became King Henry II Plantagenet of England. But one Breton vassal of Conan's, Raoul II de Fougères, defied Plantagenet power here. Henry II's troops destroyed Fougères's castle in 1166; Raoul II later set about rebuilding it on a huge scale.

The castle serves as an excellent illustration of advances in military fortifications across the centuries of the medieval period. The square towers date from the late 12th or the early 13th century the round ones (which allowed better views of the enemy on all sides and could apparently resist projectiles better) are generally from the 13th or 14th centuries, while the horseshoe-shaped ones went up in the 15th century, built to resist new artillery fire. The Tour de la Haye St-Hilaire leads you into the first restricted trap of a courtyard, l'Avancée. Then the Tour de Coëtlogon takes you through a second line of ramparts into the main *basse cour*, where daily château life would have taken place. Only traces of the chapel and the lord's quarters remain. Up on a hillock within the fort, a third ring of defences protected the *réduit*; this was the last refuge against invaders. You can walk along long stretches of the ramparts.

Although it was often described as a Breton frontier castle, for much of the medieval period the Château de Fougères was a pawn in the much more complex and local power games of feudal times. For such an impregnable-looking military structure, the fort has a pretty ignominious track record. Sometimes sieges, sometimes ruses caused the castle to be taken. The various lords of the castle frequently showed conflicting loyalties as to which overlord to support.

Then, in the later stages of the Hundred Years War, Surienne, a Spaniard working for the English, swiped the château by stealth one night in 1449, and he and his men pillaged Fougères as well as killing inhabitants. Duke François II of Brittany had to come and lay siege to the rebellious Spaniard, who gave up when plague struck in the castle. After this, the duke had the two anti-artillery towers called Françoise and Tourasse erected. To little avail. Soon La Trémouille was attacking Fougères in the name of the French king. He took the castle within a week, just before the Battle of St-Aubin-du-Cormier, which sealed the fate of an independent Breton duchy. The enormous castle served little over the following centuries. Now temporary sculpture exhibitions are often displayed within the fortifications.

Parc Floral de Haute Bretagne, Château de la Foltière

Open 14 July–15 Aug daily 10.30–6; 20 Mar–11 Nov Sun and public hols 10–6, Mon–Sat 2–5.30.

Set in a countryside of gorgeous towering beeches a dozen kilometres northwest of Fougères (take the D798 then branch off for Le Châtellier), this floral park was created from nothing, virtually overnight. The magic was wrought by Alain Jouno, an engineer who fell in love with the place when he saw it in an abandoned state and bought it in 1995. He did phenomenal work, executed with considerable intelligence. The series of separately inspired gardens are set in a 19th-century landscaped park, by a 19th-century country house rather in the style of a *malouinière* (*see* p.147). The various gardens each have a clear theme reflected in their names, such as the Persian Garden, the City of Antiquity, the Valley of the Kings, the Vale of Poets, the Blue Lagoon.... These titles might make the place sound a bit clichéd, but the care and the work that went into creating each set piece are admirable.

For an alternate excursion into the countryside, the **Ferme de Chênedet** (**t** 02 99 97 35 46), located northeast of Fougères and the Forêt de Fougères, at Landéan, offers a programme of outdoor activities all year round.

Along the Couesnon to St-Aubin-du-Cormier

If you head straight to Rennes from Fougères, the N12 passes through the town of **St-Aubin-du-Cormier**. You can also follow the more picturesque **Couesnon valley** to this town, known in Brittany as the site of the battle in 1488 in which the last duke of Brittany's troops were defeated for the final time. Six thousand Bretons died in the fight. English, German and Spanish mercenaries had fought alongside the Bretons, and all were expelled after this defeat. The duke's heiress Anne would have to ask King Charles VIII of France's permission to marry; he himself would soon insist that she marry him. The French dismantled the ducal castle here, and only a few sad fragments remain as a symbol of the disaster.

Vitré and its Pays

Its fabulously turreted triangular castle makes Vitré easily memorable, but the town's 15th- and 16th-century houses may leave almost as much of an impression on you. The later importance of Vitré town was built on the cloth trade.

History

Vitré lies provocatively far east on the Breton border, like an outpost to protect Rennes. This beautiful old town was once the centre of one of the nine counties into which early feudal Brittany was divided. The history of its major ruling family illustrates just how divided loyalties were for many noble families living on feudal frontiers. In this case they had to decide whether to support the Breton duke or to back the French king.

The first fort went up in the mid 11th century, the count of Rennes calling upon a loyal family to help him establish firm defences for his border and for Breton autonomy. The triangular château took shape in the 13th century, and the town found itself surrounded by walls. However, 1251 saw a vital change in the ownership of Vitré. The baron of the time passed away, leaving Vitré to his daughter, who married the baron of Laval in the neighbouring province of Maine. For many centuries to come, Vitré was ruled over by a line of Lavals, who owed allegiance to the French king. Fruitful marriages added estates to the family's possessions, so that the Lavals became just about the most powerful family in Haute Bretagne, as the eastern half of Brittany is known.

Brittany's independence was fast drawing to an end by the second half of the 15th century. But one famous Vitréen, Pierre Landais, served the last independent duke, François II, in memorable fashion. The most powerful merchant the town ever knew, Landais became treasurer of Brittany and the duke's principal counsellor, but his politicking led to serious ducal displeasure, and he was executed in Nantes in 1485. Though further massive fortifications had been added to Vitré in the last duke's time, in the final campaign by the French, Vitré put up no serious resistance.

Through much of the 15th and 16th centuries, a fair number of Vitré merchants managed to make their fortunes with the help of the farmers and workers involved in local cloth manufacturing. These merchants were extraordinarily successful in exporting their wares. In 1472, an official trading body, the Marchands d'Outremer ('Overseas Merchants'), was formed in Vitré, the very title reflecting the scale of its ambitions. The merchants went as far as the ports of the Hanseatic League and to the Iberian peninsula, and later even as far as South America, to build their fortunes. The wealth of Vitré from that period, still evident today in the extravagant old townhouses, owed much to them.

Refined Italian influences certainly reached the lords' dwelling in the first part of the 16th century, as a fraction of the architecture in the castle courtyard shows. In the second half, the town was rocked by the French Wars of Religion. By inheritance, the town had come into a branch of the Coligny family, staunch supporters of the reformation of the Church. Catholic troops came to lay siege to the Protestant stronghold for five months one year, but were unsuccessful. In the 17th century, Vitré became the property of another mighty French family, that of La Trémouïlle, but they neglected the castle, which fell into disrepair.

Inside the Château de Vitré

Open July–Sept daily 10–6; April–June daily 10–12 and 2–5.30; Oct–March Wed–Fri 10–12 and 2–5.30, Sat–Mon 2–5.30.

A tour of the town museum within the château, clambering up and down bits of ramparts, is mildly enjoyable, but the main interest of the Château de Vitré lies in its architecture. The Tour St-Laurent tower contains fine fragments of old stone carving and old lead finials from Vitré houses, while along the ramparts the Tour de l'Argenterie has a bizarre collection of preserved animals. A further room in the Tour de l'Oratoire displays religious objects, including liturgical costumes and Limoges enamel panels painted with grizzly grey-faced figures.

To appreciate the architecture of the Renaissance oratory, go back down into the gravel-covered castle courtyard. From below, you can spot the detailed carving of rows of Renaissance motifs including eggs, faces on pedestals, and one row of breasts.

A Tour of Old Vitré

Vitré has retained its medieval street plan, with just a few 19th-century arteries added, and many of the solid town ramparts have remained in good shape. Leaving the **Place du Château**, head up to the **Place Notre-Dame**. At the top of this sloping square, the broad façade of the church dominates the scene. With Gothic pinnacles looking sparkling new, it boasts some richly carved Renaissance doors. Inside, the furnishings are neo-Gothic. Down in one of the bottom corners of the *place*, a little passageway takes you under two townhouses-cum-bridges and leads out to the **town ramparts**. The **Rue du Bas Val** descends sharply past the château's foundations and leads to the St-Nicolas quarter (*see* below).

Back up by the church of Notre Dame, heading up along the **Rue Notre Dame**, you pass some delightful timberframe houses and the magnificent Hôtel Ringues de la Troussannais, a 16th-century mansion set back in its little courtyard with some delightful French Renaissance decoration, including putti standing on top of the windows. You then come to a string of pretty squares; from here you can head back into the old town from the Place de la République via a different route. **Rue de la Borderie** is a main shopping street that leads in the right direction. The arcaded **Rue Poterie** and the **Rue Sévigné** are worth seeking out. The **Rue Baudrairie** (*baudroyeurs* were leather workers) has the best display of timberframe houses in town, and the most highly decorated façades of Vitré. The **Rue d'En Bas** leads off the Rue Baudrairie and vies for attention with it.

The **Musée St-Nicolas** (*open same times as Château de Vitré*) celebrating sacred art lies in the lower town, past the *lavoirs* (washhouses) on the Vilaine river. The museum took over the enormous former chapel of the hospital, built in the 15th and 16th centuries; a few very worn frescoes can still be made out on its tall walls: Christ shows his wounds to doubting Thomas, St George rescues a princess, and a giant St Christopher helps travellers, including Jesus, across a river. But this is nothing compared with the display of Church wealth next door – reliquary crosses, chalices, ciboria (goblets to hold the consecrated wafers for Holy Communion), patens (plates for the wafers) and monstrances (in which the consecrated Host is shown to be adored) fill the side room. One of the oldest pieces is a 15th-century reliquary box covered with semi-cut precious stones.

Sights around Vitré

Well signposted north out of Vitré, the **Musée de la Faucillonnaie** (*open same hours as Château de Vitré*) at **Montreuil-sous-Pérouse** recalls the more comfortable side of country life in centuries past. This is not one of those desperately cluttered country museums that attempts to demonstrate with 1,001 objects just how desperately poor and unmaterialistic previous times were; only a small but carefully chosen number of items is displayed in the rooms of this plain-fronted manor. Evocative paintings of the area of Vitré and some of its people add to the atmosphere.

The little village of **Champeaux** in light, mottled stone, its houses set around a green, lies less than 10 kilometres northwest of Vitré, a short way north of the D857 to Rennes. Before turning into village houses, the buildings were the homes of canons serving the collegiate **church of St Mary Magdalene**, set up and paid for by the wealthy local Espinay family from 1432. The main attraction is the decoration in the choir end; the Renaissance stained glass shows remarkable finesse.

Château des Rochers Sévigné

Open same hours as Château de Vitré.

I go for a wander along these pleasant alleys. I have a lackey who follows me. I have books. I move from one spot to another and vary the course of my walks. A book of devotion, another on history, one switches – that makes things entertaining. One dreams a little of God, of providence, of the soul, of the future. Finally, at 8 o'clock I hear a bell. It is supper time.

Madame de Sévigné writing to her daughter in 1689

The prettily freckled Château des Rochers Sévigné less than 10 kilometres south of Vitré was the Breton country retreat of the 17th-century society figure Mme de Sévigné, whose private correspondence, published by her family in the early 18th century, reveals much about her times and her temperament. Her Breton country house still hides coyly behind a walled garden, just the odd tower emerging as you arrive. Mme de Sévigné's spirit wafts over the place, much more telling than the few badly aged physical mementoes of her you are shown in the château.

Hot Chocolate and Politics from the Perceptive Mme de Sévigné

Marie de Rabutin-Chantal was 18 when she married Henri de Sévigné in 1644. Les Rochers had been in her husband's family since the early 15th century and had been reconstructed in the 17th century – only a few elements were retained from the earlier building. The couple spent some happy times here at the beginning of their marriage, but after only six years of wedlock the roguish husband was killed in a duel over 'la belle Lolo', described as a lady of easy virtue. Mme de Sévigné came to mourn here. She never remarried and lived until 1696.

Mme de Sévigné did not spend huge amounts of time at Les Rochers, but the place meant a great deal to her. She found solitude here away from a hectic social life, and she also came to collect the rents from her estates to help pay for her partying and her trips. Her correspondence was mainly with her beloved daughter, who had married a Provençal lord, and whose letters she seemed to live for more than for anything else at times. In her depictions, political events were treated as swiftly as her social life, her state of mind and her health, and even ranked alongside such weighty matters as her up-and-down relationship with drinking chocolate.

Mme de Sévigné paid some attention to the fabric of Les Rochers, notably seeing to the addition of the octagonal chapel. This is one of the small number of rooms you are shown on the swift guided tour. Mme de Sévigné planned the symmetrical chapel with her uncle, a kindly religious man. The inside would have been very plain in their day. But the family that bought the château from Mme de Sévigné's granddaughter embellished it. Tubby cherubs and garlands are carved round the boxed staircase to the belltower, while symbolic *fleurs de lys* and stylized ermine tails put in an aristocratic appearance. Plush wide red chairs set out in front of the altar make this look like a confused mix between a chapel and a salon. The retable painting of an exquisite Annunciation to the Virgin is attributed to Guido Reni.

You are then shown the more secretive, private façade of the château. The ground floor displays in the main building include various published editions of the letters, and a few battered personal possessions of the *marquise*. The letters were only published for the first time in 1725. Among several portraits on the first floor, the full-length one of Mme de Sévigné at the time of her marriage stands out. Pale-skinned, coiled curls tumbling down, wearing a richly patterned wrap around her bejewelled dress, she certainly looks graceful and intelligent, and dauntingly mature for her age. Her granddaughter Pauline de Grignan, Marquise de Simiane, is portrayed as more of a vacuous, rosy-cheeked stereotype of her era. This granddaughter is the person who decided to have her grandmother's correspondence published, though she burned some letters that she considered too uncomplimentary to the family.

Towards Rennes from Vitré

West of Les Rochers Sévigné towards Rennes, at **Domagné**, the **Musée Louis Raison** (*open Mon–Fri 9–12 and 2–6, Sat and Sun 2–6*) recalls how cider was made, in this, one of the biggest cider-apple growing corners left in Brittany. Opened by Louis Raison, who has one of the largest cider-making businesses in Brittany, it offers free tastings.

West of Domagné, the village of **Châteaugiron** has bulging, dark-schist old château towers that make an impressive picture, as well as a charming main street curving up to this darkly speckled castle on its esplanade. There is very little to see inside the château, but the enormous separate 13th-century keep, isolated to one side, houses a tourist office and local exhibitions. Its sheer size gives an indication of Châteaugiron's former importance. Its barons were once powerful in the Breton duchy, several receiving the title of chamberlain to the duke through inheritance. In 1472, the duke of Brittany signed a joint treaty with the English king at Châteaugiron in a vain attempt to keep out the French.

La Guerche-de-Bretagne

This small Marches town (south of Vitré along the D178) has managed to retain its lovely arcaded streets, although its château has long gone. The dukes of Brittany placed one of their vassals here from around the year 1000 to oversee this frontier territory. Du Guesclin bought the lordship of these parts in 1379, taking it briefly out of their hands. Then it fell into neglect under the dukes of Alençon, who had married into the Breton ducal family.

The town was given ramparts in the 13th century, the same period that the **collegiate church of Notre-Dame** first went up. Only the choir remains from that time, with a defensive-looking, stocky slate tower above it. A neo-Gothic spire in a style popular in Brittany in the 19th century towers over town at the west front. The nave and south aisle date from the 16th century, with a row of rich stained-glass windows, some partly mutilated in the Wars of Religion but still showing vivid figures. However, the most striking art is reserved for the shocking choir stalls, carved in part with Gothic monstrosities, in part with Renaissance grotesques.

Dolmen de la Roche-aux-Fées

The fairies did fabulously good work at the **dolmen of La Roche-aux-Fées** (west of La Guerche-de-Bretagne just past Retiers, then north up the D341 to Essé), if you believe the legend. These supernaturally strong creatures are credited with flying the vast blocks, which weigh anything between five and 40 tonnes, from their original site, (thought to be some four kilometres south, in the Fôret de Theil) to here, spinning all the while as they went.

This is one of the most famous and largest neolithic dolmens in Brittany, thought to date very vaguely from between 3000 BC and 2500 BC. It differs a good deal from the styles of dolmens that are found further west in Brittany. In fact, this kind of neolithic architecture is more linked with the Loire's earlier inhabitants. The opening, which leads into a sort of antechamber, is aligned with the rising sun of the winter solstice. The scale is so large that you can stand up quite comfortably in the main gallery. This structure would have been covered with a mound of stones and earth, which has completely disappeared. On many Wednesday evenings in July and August, there's an atmospheric guided walk, **La Balade des Fées**, taking you through the local legends.

Rennes

The capital city of Brittany never lacks vitality – not surprisingly, with up to 50,000 students and researchers milling around its wonderful old streets, with its masses of bookshops, bars and bistrots. Rennes also hosts a couple of major festivals. In 1994, the highly symbolic and sumptuously decorated Parlement de Bretagne, built in 1618–1706, burned down in the wake of a fishermen's demonstration that got out of control, but it has now been restored to its magnificent original state and is open for guided tours on weekdays (**t** 02 99 67 11 11). The Musée de Bretagne, set up as a showcase of Breton culture, is being wound down and moved to swanky new premises in the Nouvel Equipement Culturel on the Esplanade du Général de Gaulle (due to open in 2005/6), but it is still hosting temporary exhibitions. That leaves the Musée des Beaux-Arts and the delightfully Gothic Chapelle St-Yves, where you'll find the tourist office and an exhibition on the history of the city. The city centre has both grand vistas leading to planned squares and secret corners crammed with timberframe houses, while the Place des Lices, the former jousting arena in medieval times, boasts some of the most spectacular and high-rise timberframe houses in France. Old Rennes lies north of the Vilaine, though the most interesting modern quarters have gone up on the southern side.

History

Rennes was built at a crossing of trading routes in the Celtic era, where the Ille river meets the Vilaine. The Riedones, who were one of five main tribes in Armorica (Celtic Brittany), settled here. Under Roman rule, the main city of the Riedones became known as Condate, meaning confluence. There's virtually nothing visible in

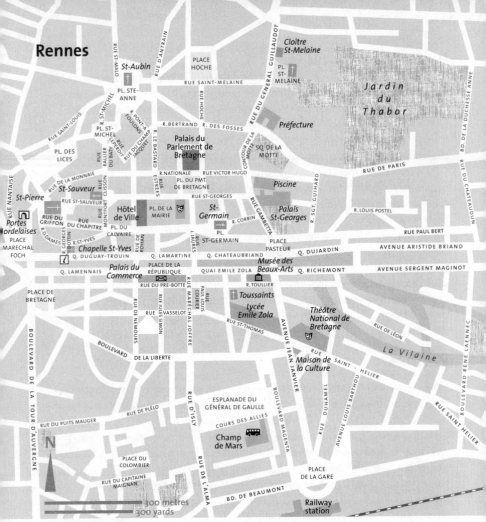

Rennes of Gallo-Roman times, let alone Celtic ones, but in the Musée de Bretagne you used to be able to see a few highly interesting fragments of these civilizations. A huge number of Roman coins were discovered in the Vilaine at Rennes, thought to have accumulated here as offerings to appease the water gods. Rennes' agricultural area was already relatively densely populated in Gallo-Roman times. The town became the seat of a bishopric with the arrival of Christianity in the peninsula, but again virtually no traces remain of this period. In Carolingian times, perhaps in response to Breton incursions across the Vilaine, the Franks formally instituted the Breton Marches, the county of Rennes part of their buffer zone. But in the 9th century, successful Breton leaders won back the county of Rennes. From as early as the 9th century, religious institutions multiplied in the area; in the 11th and 12th centuries, they mushroomed considerably. St Melaine played a major role in helping to spread Benedictine monasticism across the duchy. St-Georges de Rennes became the first significant nunnery in Brittany. Links between Brittany and England were strengthened by the

Getting There and Around

Rennes is 2 hours from Paris by TGV **train** (t 08 36 35 35 35). The **bus** station (t 02 99 30 87 80) is close to the rail station. For info on bus services within Rennes, go to the Place de la Mairie or call t 02 99 79 37 37.

Tourist Information

Rennes: 11 Rue St-Yves, t 02 99 67 11 11, *www.ville-rennes.fr.*

Market Days

Place des Lices: Saturday. One of the best markets in northern France.
Boulevard de la Liberté (a few streets south of the Palais du Commerce). Rennes's bustling permanent covered market, with attractive stalls and 1920s architecture.

Festivals

Tombées de la Nuit (t 02 99 67 11 11 for information and reservations) cultural festival practically takes over the whole of the centre of Rennes at the start of July.
Les Transmusicales is a major French rock festival held in the first or second week of December. Many successful French artists have launched their careers here.
Folies Rennaises, end May–early June. A more left-of-field contemporary music festival.
Jazz en Terrasse, a yearly programme of jazz in the Villejean university district northwest of the centre, in the first 2 weeks of October. Information from the **Ferme de la Harpe**, Avenue Charles-Tillon, t 02 99 59 45 38.
Le Grand Soufflet, mid-October, t 02 99 22 27 30. An annual accordion festival with music concerts and informal performances in bars.
Le Bon Accueil, 74 Canal St-Martin (north of city), t 02 99 59 22 76, *S-E-P-A@wanadoo.fr.* An 'artistic laboratory' opened in 1998 to provide a work and resource space for gifted young local artists. You can view their work Fri–Sun 2–7.

In July and August there's a programme of free organ concerts in the main churches in the centre of town.

Where to Stay

Rennes ✉ 35000

Very Expensive

****Lecoq Gadby, 156 Rue d'Antrain, t 02 99 38 05 55, *www.lecoq-gadby.com.* North of the centre, this is something of an institution, renowned for catering for large family gatherings in its countless dining rooms. It also has a small number of rooms, a tennis court and a garden.

Expensive

***Mercure Pré Botté, Rue Paul Louis Courrier, t 02 99 78 82 20, *www.accor.fr.* This is part of a hotel chain, but it's situated within an intriguingly converted industrial building, the former print works of *Ouest-Eclair*, later to become *Ouest-France*. Though centrally located, it has the benefit of being on the quieter, southern side of the Vilaine quays.

Moderate

***Relais Mercure, 6 Rue Lanjuinais, t 02 99 79 12 36, *relaismercure.rennes@tiscali.fr.* A mid-range option with a bit of 19th-century character down a small street parallel to Quai Lamennais.

Inexpensive

**Garden, 3 Rue Duhamel, by the railway station, t 02 99 65 45 06, *gardenhotel@wanadoo.fr.* Modern rooms with charm, plus a bar and patio.
**Hôtel des Lices, 7 Place des Lices, t 02 99 79 14 81, *www.hotel-des-lices.com.* A hotel with some rooms looking over the spectacular square.
**Hôtel M.S. Nemours, 5 Rue de Nemours, t 02 99 78 26 26, *www.hotelnemours.com.* A reasonable option within close proximity of the Place de la République.
**Le Victor Hugo, 14 Rue Victor Hugo, t 02 99 38 85 33. A friendly hotel on a street full of antiques dealers near the Parlement.
*Hôtel d'Angleterre, 19 Rue Maréchal Joffre, t 02 99 79 38 61. A central bargain with some large, comfy old rooms with good bathrooms.
*Hôtel de Léon, 15 Rue de Léon (east along the Vilaine quays, down from Quai Richemont),

t 02 99 30 55 28. A characterful little address with rooms decorated by the artist owner. *Closed Aug.*

Hôtel de la Tour d'Auvergne, 20 Boulevard de la Tour d'Auvergne, **t** 02 99 30 84 16. A reliable and sizeable establishment, with plain but clean rooms with showers.

Le Rocher de Cancale, 10 Rue St-Michel, **t** 02 99 79 20 83. An old posting inn with 4 lovely rooms above one of the busiest streets in town, best known for its restaurant. *Closed Aug.*

Auberge de Jeunesse, 10 Canal St-Martin, **t** 02 99 33 22 33, *www.fuaj.org*. A friendly hostel where Rue St-Malo meets the canal in the north of the city 2km from the train station. A café and laundry facilities are on hand.

Eating Out

Expensive–Very Expensive

L'Escu de Runfao, 11 Rue du Chapitre, **t** 02 99 79 13 10. Daring cuisine served up in a beautiful 16th-century house, including coquilles St-Jacques with caramelized endives in ginger sauce. *Closed Sat and Sun eves.*

Expensive

Auberge St-Sauveur, 6 Rue St-Sauveur, **t** 02 99 79 32 56. A restaurant in one of the original timberframe houses that just escaped the 1720 fire. The cuisine and décor are classic, and there's a lobster tank. *Closed Mon and Sat lunch, Sun, and 3wks Aug–Sept.*

La Coquerie, 156 Rue d'Antrain. The restaurant of Lecoq Gadby hotel (*see* p.89).

Le Corsaire, 52 Rue d'Antrain, **t** 02 99 36 33 69. Excellent seafood north of the town centre. *Closed Sun eve and Tue.*

La Fontaine aux Perles, Manoir de la Poterie, 96 Rue de la Poterie, **t** 02 99 53 90 90. A manor house southeast of the centre, with a French-style garden. *Closed Sun eve and Mon.*

Moderate

Au Four à Ban, 4 Rue Sainte-Mélaine, **t** 02 99 38 72 85. A restaurant serving a unique and excellent blend of Mediterranean and Breton cuisine. *Closed Sat lunch, Sun, Mon eve, and 3wks July.*

Auberge du Chat Pitre, 18 Rue du Chapitre, **t** 02 99 30 36 36. A 15th-century timberframe house with waiters in medieval costume. *Closed Sun eve.*

Café Breton, 14 Rue Nantaise, **t** 02 99 30 74 95. Refined food in an atmosphere reminiscent of a Parisian bistrot. *Closed Sat and Sun eve.*

Chez Kub, 20 Rue du Chapitre, **t** 02 99 31 19 31. A restaurant with a warm, wood-panelled interior, in the old part of town. Many of the meat and fish dishes here cooked in a wood-fired oven. *Closed part of Aug.*

Chouin, 12 Rue d'Isly, **t** 02 99 30 89 86. A popular address, inauspiciously located opposite the enormous Champ de Mars but offering generous seafood platters. *Closed Sun, Mon and 2wks in Aug.*

Piccadilly Tavern, 15 GalerieThéâtre, **t** 02 99 78 17 17. A reliable, lively brasserie in the heart of town.

Inexpensive

There's an excellent choice of inexpensive ethnic restaurants along Rue St-Malo, up from the Place Ste-Anne.

Ar Pillig, 10 Rue d'Argentré (near Quai Lamennais), **t** 02 99 79 53 89. Outstanding central crêperie with decor by Breton artists.

Le Bocal-Pty Resto, 6 Rue d'Argentré, **t** 02 99 78 34 10. A beautifully decorated *resto* in the informal style, near the Quai Lamennais. The young and hip, and the old and hungry, flock here for 2-course lunch *formules* featuring unctuous tarts and salads, or the full menu, which might include home-smoked salmon.

Crêperie des Portes Mordelaises, 6 Rue des Portes Mordelaises (leading up from Place Maréchal Foch), **t** 02 99 30 57 40. A decent crêperie in the heart of old Rennes.

Crêperie Ste-Anne, Place Ste-Anne, **t** 02 99 79 22 72. Western Breton specialities on a lively square. *Closed Sun.*

Au Marché des Lices, 3 Place du Bas-des-Lices (off Place des Lices), **t** 02 99 30 42 95. A warm, family-friendly place offering sturdy Breton crêpes, including a variety of specialities and a *galette du mois*, plus good cider. Well sited between the clamourous Rue St-Malo and the calmer south *Centre Ville*. *Closed Sun and 2wks Aug.*

Bretons' part in the Norman conquest. Conan IV of Rennes, for example, was confirmed in his succession to the earldom of Richmond by Angevin King Henry II of England. Henry II later came to tear down castles in the Breton Marches, including Rennes' château. But in the ensuing centuries, the city retained its pre-eminent position in the Breton duchy.

Du Guesclin Jousts His Way Into His Father's Heart

The best-known story in Rennes from the period of the Breton War of Succession and the Hundred Years War is of the warrior Bertrand Du Guesclin's appearance on the scene. Shunned by his family as an ugly misfit, at 17 he supposedly came to a Rennes tournament to prove himself. At the Place des Lices he is said to have demonstrated his unmatched skill in jousting. An anonymous contender, he proved himself unbeatable, and only when he was about to face his father did he bow out and reveal his true identity. His proud dad was finally able to accept his odd son with pride. Du Guesclin became the most important knight on the French side in the first part of the Hundred Years War. In 1356, he played an instrumental part in the seizing of Rennes for the French (*see* pp.108–9).

The Era of the Breton Parlement

Thirteen provincial Parlements were set up around France in the Ancien Régime, and a royal decision was taken in 1561 that the Parlement of Brittany should settle in Rennes. The mainly noble Breton parliamentarians, who met twice a year, benefited from their position, as did Rennes, where they built sumptuous townhouses. In the course of the 17th century, a grand parliament house was also built. This Parlement incorporated the highest court in Brittany and became a provincial body increasingly at odds with the royal authorities and their representatives, the governors.

La Révolte du Papier Timbré

Among the most traumatic times for Rennes, and Brittany, in the Ancien Régime period was when the royal administration attempted in 1675 to impose a crippling tax on officially required documents. This led to the Révolte du Papier Timbré across Brittany. The uprising, on a large scale, was violently crushed by the royal troops. Mme de Sévigné wrote of 5,000 soldiers arriving to impose the royal will: 'A tax of 100,000 écus has been levied on the merchants; and if this money is not raised within 24 hours the amount will be doubled and the soldiers will be able to go into action to demand it. The families in one of the main streets in town have been chased out of their houses and banished, while others have been forbidden from taking them in on punishment of death. So you could see all these wretched people, among them the elderly, and women with newly born children, wandering in tears through the outskirts of town, not knowing where to go, without food or a place to sleep. A violin player who had started up a dance mocking the stamped paper tax was broken on the wheel the day before yesterday. He was quartered after his death, and the four pieces of his body were displayed around the town... Sixty merchants have been arrested. Tomorrow the hangings begin. This province offers a good example to the others, above all that governors should be respected, not insulted, and that it is dangerous to throw stones into their gardens.' As part of its punishment for its involvement, Rennes saw the Parlement moved to Vannes for 15 years – a major blow to the city.

A New Town Emerges After the 1720 Fire

In towns packed with timberframe houses, fire was always a major risk. In 1720, a drunken carpenter started one off that destroyed much of the old centre of town. The terrible conflagration lasted a week, and hundreds of the finest houses went up in smoke. It was decided that the new town centre would be built almost entirely using stone façades. A much more carefully planned city structure emerged, with wider streets and grand vistas. Rennes also gained a university in the 18th century. You can see many important 19th-century additions to the fabric of the town on a tour of Rennes, including the Lycée Emile Zola, where the Jewish scapegoat Alfred Dreyfus underwent his second trial. Hi-tech industries requiring high-level researchers have settled in the city since the war, making Rennes a cutting-edge provincial capital.

Musée des Beaux-Arts

Open Wed–Sun 10–12 and 2–6.

It's thanks to the plunderings of private and foreign collections during the Revolution and the Napoleonic Empire that Rennes so rapidly acquired a fine arts collection. Due to the enlightened passions of Christophe-Paul, Marquis de Robien, one Rennes family found itself in possession of a phenomenal art collection at the end of the Ancien Régime. When Christophe-Paul's son ran off at the Revolution, the city was free to 'adopt' the Robien treasures, almost all 17th-century works, more than half from northern European schools. This Robien collection was then added to early in the 19th century by a handout from all the Revolutionary and foreign booty gathered at the Louvre. The most cited individual painting in the museum is Georges de La Tour's *Le Nouveau-né*, depicting the glow of a newborn baby. The 20th century brought numerous interesting acquisitions. Violence appears as an extremely frequent theme in the collections, although one or two pre-17th-century paintings do stand out for their gentler or lighter tone, such as the Venetian-school rendering of St John the Baptist crowning the lamb with flowers by Paris Bordone, showing a much tenderer John than is sometimes the case.

The major French schools of the 19th century are represented, such as Orientalism. You only come to paintings with more Breton subject matter much later in the collection. Evariste-Vital Luminais painted pseudo-historical or legendary Breton scenes. *La Chevauchée de St-Guénolé et du roi Gradlon* interprets the legend of the Ville d'Ys (*see* p.294) in tacky melodramatic fashion. Among the post-Impressionists, look out for a couple of Pont-Aven School pictures here – Paul Sérusier's *Solitude*, which depicts a deeply unhappy-looking coiffed girl in a countryside of Breton boulders, and Emile Bernard's strikingly beautiful *L'Arbre jaune*. Intriguing Breton pieces by Lacombe, Loiseau, Maufra and Moret also stand out. Picasso's *Baigneuse*, which was apparently painted at the Breton resort of Dinard, can still shock with the distorted geometry of the woman's body and the bold, deliberate simplicity of its forms. Probing still deeper into the subconscious is *L'Inspiration*, an aqueous work by the surrealist Yves Tanguy.

A Tour of Rennes

South of the River

The beautiful streets and squares of old Rennes lie just north of the quays along which the Musée des Beaux-Arts stands. But one or two interesting spots are worth picking out south of the Vilaine. Cultural events programmed throughout the year may take you down to the curvaceous modern building of the **Maison de la Culture**, which cuts its figure of eight along the Rue Saint-Hélier. The **Théâtre National de Bretagne** is also based down here.

Back behind the museum, the **Rue Toullier** and **Rue du Pré-Botté** run parallel to the quays on the south side. Behind Rue Toullier and the church of Toussaints lies the **Lycée Emile Zola**, a school complex designed in the 19th century by the town architect Jean-Baptiste Martenot; this school is famous for hosting the second trial of Alfred Dreyfus, the Jewish French army officer falsely accused of spying in the mid-1890s. It took Major Henry's admission of forgery and a third, civilian trial in 1906 to clear Dreyfus's name.

Along **Rue du Pré-Botté**, the successful newspaper *Ouest-France* and its predecessor *Ouest-Eclair* used to be produced in the impressive printworks. *Ouest-France*, the largest regional daily in France, also publishes a very extensive book list, specializing in titles on French culture and tourism. The company's head office has a **Ouest-France bookshop** with a wide choice of titles on Brittany and a spot where you can consult the local paper. **Rue Vasselot**, one parallel further south, has a clutch of lively bars and the odd old house, most notably No.34, with a spectacular wooden staircase in what was once a **Carmelite convent**. Modern quarters lie behind the Rue Vasselot, including the cultural arts centre **Le Colombier**.

Back on the **quays**, the Vilaine river has been hidden underground since the 19th century. Because the townhouses are set so far apart, though, you sense its presence. Shops, restaurants and bars line these quays. One of the most striking and grandiose post offices in France, the **Palais du Commerce**, lies on Place de la République.

Rennes's Oldest Quarters

On the north side of the quays, turn up the **Rue Georges Dottin** and enter the **oldest quarter** to have survived the 1720 fire, full of timberframed atmosphere and multicoloured cobblestones. Several of the grand houses have carved beams or charming little courtyards. At the corner of the **Rue St-Yves** is the **Chapelle St-Yves**, a delightful, light Gothic chapel, now a tourist office and exhibition space. The chapel's architecture shows the influence of the Loire Valley courts. The **Rue des Dames's** curve reveals where part of the former town ramparts used to lie. **Rue Griffon** and **Rue du Chapitre** are lined with many fine 16th-century houses, some revived to their original shockingly bright colours. Set back from the street, the **Hôtel de Blossac** looks more sober and grand than the rest.

St-Sauveur and the Cathedral

At the eastern end of the Rue du Chapitre, the straight line of the **Rue Montfort, Rue Clisson** and **Rallier du Baty** forms one of the grand shopping axes in Rennes, leading up from the Place du Calvaire to the vibrant Place St-Michel. Go up as far as the **church of St-Sauveur**, soberly classical on the outside. Within, it contains a dark and absurdly ornate baldaquin over the choir and some vulgar modern stained-glass windows. Along the side of the church, the **Rue St-Sauveur** heads towards the back of the cathedral. Rue St-Sauveur leads you into **Rue de la Psalette**, which conceals a secretive series of wonderful timberframe façades, ending with the gilded, scrolled monsters on the house on the corner with the **Rue du Chapitre**.

The **Cathédrale St-Pierre** was built on the site of a Gallo-Roman temple, but the oldest part of the cathedral now standing only goes back as far as 1560. The edifice took more than a century to complete. The architecture behind the façade was started in the late 18th century on the plans of architect Mathurin Crucy. Two colonnades of brown-veined stone glisten along the nave. The side aisles take the form of spacious walks. Decoration overwhelms the interior; much of the wall painting and the gilding was added in the course of the 19th century. The wall paintings depict the saints most revered in the different parts of Brittany, their names usefully written below them. Look out for the even more ornate gilded 15th-century reredos from Flanders in one side chapel; the wealth of Gothic detail, from the finely carved niches to the chimera, overwhelms at first glance. The monumental piece actually depicts the life of the Virgin.

A Tour of Rennes's Grand Squares

West of the cathedral front, a neglected side street (off the Rue de la Monnaie) leads to the **Portes Mordelaises**, once the grandest town entrance, now sadly sidelined. The **Place des Lices**, Rennes's most spectacular square, stands just north of the Rue de la Monnaie. Its soaring, beam-patterned buildings actually date from the mid 17th century, providing a contrast with the sober classical style more in vogue at the time. Two stylish steel and brick 19th-century market halls occupy the centre of the square, their design by Jean-Baptiste Martenot, the most influential Rennes architect of the 19th century.

Leave the square by the northeast corner and you soon come to the restaurant- and bar-crowded **Place St-Michel**, one of the liveliest and prettiest meeting places in town. Another quirky little square, the **Place du Champ Jacquet**, lies tucked away just east of Place St-Michel (reach it via Rue Leperdit). The timberframe houses here look down on a statue of Leperdit, portrayed as a heroic mayor of Rennes during the Revolution. The **Place Ste-Anne** counts among the busiest social hubs of old Rennes, teeming with students and tourists in the evenings. The church of St-Aubin towers over the square. To the left of the church, the **Rue St-Malo** is the magnet for the trendy and the slightly alternative. All sorts of ethnic restaurants line the way.

Return to the corner watchtower at the meeting of Rue du Champ Jacquet and **Rue Le Bastard**. This last street actually turns out to be one of the most respectable and chic avenues in town, leading down to the most central of the town squares, the **Place de la Mairie**. The central section of the town hall, topped by an ornate belfry, is concave, while opposite this 18th-century building, the 19th-century theatre was given a convex auditorium. This playful architecture gives a light touch to the spacious square. Much more sober and serious, the **Place du Parlement de Bretagne** is dominated on one side by the former home of the parliament of Brittany and of the law courts. This is the building that went up in flames in 1994, but its restoration is now complete. On the corner of the **Rue St-Georges**, look out for the gorgeous carving at the entrance to the Maison de la Coiffure, including, comically enough, an amazing figure in a wig. Art galleries and antique shops are the specialities along this charming street, as they are along the **Rue Victor Hugo**, north and parallel to the Rue St-Georges.

South from the Rue St-Georges, you come to the **Place St-Germain** around the **Eglise St-Germain**. This towering Flamboyant Gothic church was built for the wealthy town haberdashers, its façade completed in the mid 16th century. It's a bit of a botched building, with a few charming features. At the back of the church, the Rue Corbin leads east to the **Rue Gambetta**. It's hard to miss the bulk of the **Palais Abbatial St-Georges** with its formal gardens sloping towards the river; the 17th-century palace gives a good notion of the former wealth of this religious institution. Most irreverently, the site of the former abbey church up the Rue Gambetta is now occupied by a colourfully ornamented 1920s swimming pool, a cheerful piece of architecture.

St-Melaine and the Jardin du Thabor

A string of streets climb north from the Rue Gambetta to the Thabor gardens. Some substantial old townhouses and grand civic buildings line the way via the Contour de la Motte and the Rue du Général Guillaudot. A statue of the Virgin lords it over the **church of St-Melaine**, standing proud on her copper tower. The façade drips with Baroque decoration; look out for a whole row of fine, full putti faces. The founder of the monastery is represented facing St Benedict. The simple Romanesque interior contrasts surprisingly with this elaborate exterior. To the north of the church, the abbot's palace, with its cloister, displays more 17th-century grandeur.

The Benedictine garden was long ago transformed into Rennes's elegant **public garden**, the **Jardin du Thabor**. Some of Rennes's most exclusive 19th-century townhouses lie around the extensive gardens. With shaded alleys of trees, formal French parterres, statues and topiary, a bandstand and a children's carousel, and even an outdoor table-football that you can play on if you bring your own ball, this garden is where many Rennais come for a stroll or to play. North and east of the Jardin du Thabor, the modern university buildings and campuses stretch out.

On the Outskirts of Rennes

The Ecomusée du Pays de Rennes, La Bintinais

Open April–Sept Tue–Fri and Sun 9–6, Sat 2–6; Oct–Mar Tue–Fri and Sun 9–12 and 2–6, Sat 12–2.

The towerblocks almost come up to touch this substantial showcase of a Rennes farm-turned-museum of rural life on the southern outskirts of the city. The place sells honey from its bees, cider-apple trees grow here, and several rare breeds of cattle are kept in very clean conditions. Interesting temporary exhibitions are held in the converted farm buildings.

The Purple Vilaine Valley: Rennes to Redon

If you've wandered around Rennes's old streets, you may well have noticed the variety of colours of the cobblestones beneath your feet. Many are shades of purple. This distinct purple stone, purple schist, gives a particular look to a fair section of western Ille-et-Vilaine, including the Vilaine valley that stretches southwest from the Breton capital.

Purple **Pont-Réan** on the river, with restaurants and hotels by the 18th-century bridge, attracts crowds from Rennes at weekends, so don't expect to find tranquillity. The still prettier river scene at the **Moulin de Boël** a few kilometres outside the town sometimes proves irresistible for the hordes too. South of Pont-Réan, the road climbs steeply out of the Rennes basin to Guichen. Below the town of Bourg-des-Comptes (on the river's east bank), look out for the little streets leading to the tiny, unspoilt old **Port de la Courbe**, weeping willows on its banks, prunus on the old village square with its old village bar, the 18th-century château of Gai-Lieu nearby.

Cross the river at Pléchâtel-Plage, a few kilometres away, and in the distance you get dramatic views of the massive spire of St-Malo-en-Phily rising above a scarred cliff. **St-Malo-de-Phily,** an unspoilt village up from its separate little port of Bruère, exudes charm. The monks of Alet, by the town of St-Malo, brought the saint Malo's relics back from the Saintonge (north of Bordeaux), where he had been buried, through here to their monastery. The local lord, supposedly cured of an illness when the relics passed by, gave the monks a piece of land. Regnault's early-20th-century church, in mixed neo-Byzantine-Romanesque-Gothic style, looks absurdly, even spectacularly, oversized for such a little community. Black and white stone effects add decorative impact to the façade's arches and the rose window. You can walk out a few hundred metres from the village to a chapel in contrasting, delightful old Breton style.

The riverside at the combined ports of **Guipry and Messac** looks surprisingly industrial after the rural idyll above. This is the main centre for hiring boats for this stretch of the Vilaine. At Lohéac, a handful of kilometres northwest of Guipry along the D772, cars are lined up row upon row in the **Manoir de l'Automobile** (*open Tue–Sun 10–12 and 2–7*). This vast collection of chassis and bodies was amassed by automobile press baron Michel Hommell.

Getting Around

By **road**, the D177 links Rennes with Redon, but try to follow smaller country lanes. Redon and Guipry-Messac have regular **train** links with Rennes. Bruz, Guichen, Pléchâtel and Grand-Fougeray also have **railway** stations.

To hire a **boat** on the Vilaine, contact Crown Blue Lines, Port de Plaisance, Messac, **t** 02 99 34 60 11; Bretagne Plaisance, 12 Quai Jean Bart, Redon, **t** 02 99 72 15 80, or Comptoir Nautique, 2 Quai Surcouf, Redon, **t** 02 99 71 46 03. To canoe, ask at Messac tourist office.

Tourist Information

Pays d'Accueil Touristique de Vilaine, Place de la République, 35600 Redon, **t** 02 99 72 72 11, *www.rivieres-oceanes.com*. For information from St-Malo-en-Phily to the Atlantic.

Guipry-Messac: 90 Avenue du Port, **t** 02 99 34 61 60, *syndicat.initiative.guipry.messac@ wanadoo.fr*.

Langon: 7 Grande Rue, **t** 02 99 08 76 55, *www.langon.fr*.

Redon: Place de la République, **t** 02 99 71 06 04, *www.ville-redon.fr*.

Market Days

Guipry: Thursday.
Grand-Fougeray: Saturday.
Pipriac: Tuesday.
Redon: Monday.

Where to Stay and Eat

Pont-Réan ✉ 35580
Le Grand Hôtel, **t 02 99 42 21 72 (*inexpensive*). A hotel next to the bridge, with pretty, modern rooms and a riverside restaurant.

Bourg-des-Comptes ✉ 35580
Auberge du Relais de la Place, 16 Place de l'Eglise, **t** 02 99 57 41 12 (*moderate*). Hearty, delicious country dishes served in a cheerful dining room or shaded garden. *Closed Sun, and Mon and Tues eves.*

Guignen
Ferme-auberge France, off the D42 about 3km west of Guignen (on the D177 between Guichen and Lohéac), **t** 02 99 92 05 56 (*moderate*). A welcoming historic manor where you can sample local produce. Advance booking required.

Grand-Fougeray ✉ 35390
La Tour Duguesclin, Rue du Château, **t** 02 99 08 31 30 (*moderate–expensive*). A place serving imaginative dishes, set in a park and affording a view onto the historic keep. *Closed Sun eve and Mon.*

Redon ✉ 35600
Chandouineau, 1 Rue Thiers, **t 02 99 71 02 04 (*inexpensive–moderate*). A pleasant townhouse near the railway station, with soundproofed modern rooms. The dining room is warm and spacious; the chef cooks up a variety of interesting local dishes (*moderate–expensive*) using Redon chestnuts and eels in season. *Closed Sat, Sun eve and 1wk Aug.*

Hôtel Asther, 14 Rue des Douves, **t** 02 99 71 10 91 (*inexpensive*). Corporate-style rooms just across from the tourist office. The brasserie provides Alsatian specialities.

La Bogue, 3 Rue des Etats, **t** 02 99 71 12 95 (*moderate–expensive*). A quaint setting for meat and fish dishes, near the huge Mairie building. *Closed Sun eve and Thurs.*

L'Île aux Grillades, 9 Rue de l'Enfer, **t** 02 99 72 20 40 (*inexpensive–moderate*). Wood-fire grills and a 3-course *formule*. *Closed Sun, Mon and 2wks end Aug.*

L'Akène, 10 Rue du Jeu de Paume, **t** 02 99 71 25 15 (*inexpensive*). A port-side crêperie with a garden terrace.

Around Redon
Le Moulin de Via, Route de Gacilly (D873), **t** 02 99 71 05 16 (*moderate–expensive*). Refined cuisine with home-produced ingredients, opposite a lake. *Closed 1wk end Aug.*

La Morinais, Bains-sur-Oust, **t** 02 99 72 12 17, *guerin-nicolas@wanadoo.fr* (*moderate*). A *ferme-auberge* in a lovely rural setting 4km north of Redon, with excellent food. Advance booking essential.

Auberge du Poteau Vert, St-Nicolas-de-Redon (just southeast of Redon), **t** 02 99 71 13 12 (*inexpensive–moderate*). A popular place with locals. *Closed 3wks Aug.*

The Neolithic Monuments of St-Just

Continue a few kilometres south from Pipriac to visit the monuments of St-Just (*guided 3hr tours in French 15 July–31 Aug Sun 3pm from the Point Information*), one of the most atmospheric neolithic sites in Brittany. The monuments stretch across several kilometres of heath, visited by few tourists.

Among the series of monoliths along the moorland ridge, the **Landes de Cojoux alignments** include small lines of quartz standing stones. Different groups seem to have been erected at different periods, one lot perhaps around 4500 BC, another through 4000 BC to 3500 BC. There are also schist megaliths, the dark tones of which contrast with the quartz. Between some of these menhirs, holes have been discovered that may have been made to hold wooden posts. A Bronze Age coffin was found in the top line of megaliths, dated to around 1500 BC.

A further set of megaliths lie close together at the Croix St-Pierre. The *tertre tumulaire* is marked by a rectangle of stones, with quartz used on the southern side, and schist on the northern one. It is reckoned to date from approximately 3000 BC. Some rather unorthodox archaeologists have been at work in this area – a colony of rabbits digging their warrens in this tumulus brought a polished axehead to the surface!

Next comes a half-restored dolmen, dated to around 5000 BC and used as a collective burial site. Experts have particularly admired the floor, which is described by the guide as 'the Versailles parquet flooring of its period'. By contrast, the Dambiau tomb was constructed around 4000 BC for an important individual – a sign of how hierarchies were evolving in neolithic communities in this period. Le Tribunal (Law Court) is the name given to the monument that follows because its semicircle of stones reminded researchers of a court. An isolated stone stands some 20 metres away from the hemicycle of stones that may have served as a calendar marking special days.

The Vilaine via Langon

Back by the Vilaine, the country lanes from Guipry-Messac to Redon are about as beautiful as those up to Rennes. At the **sites de La Corbinière et de l'Ermitage,** the river runs through another of its dramatic little gorges, where you can take one of the prettiest Vilaine towpath walks. At **Port-de-Roche** the Vilaine is crossed by a metallic bridge constructed for the Paris Universal Exhibition of 1867, moved here in 1868.

Frescoes form a little theme at the village of **Langon**. The viciously pointed and slate-covered tower of the **Eglise St-Pierre** stands out as you arrive. Inside it, a 12th-century mural of Christ blesses all comers. But the more extraordinary patch of frescoes lies hidden in the tiny **Chapelle Ste-Agathe** (*guided 1hr visits only, 3pm, meet 2.45 at the Syndicat d'Initiative, daily July and Aug, rest of year Sun only*). This building's fine and colourful masonry consists of little cubes of purple schist divided up by layers of orange tiles; this is Gallo-Roman architecture in part.

It is rare enough to see remnants of architecture from such a distant period, and rarer still to view frescoes dating from so far back in time. Inside the chapel, you'll see that the diminutive apse is covered with fish swimming around a figure of Venus, the

Roman goddess of love. The goddess's features have been wiped out, but it is still possible to distinguish her elegant hair by the meagre torchlight that the guide allows you.

What are the frescoes doing here? After their rediscovery in 1839, they were thought to have been made to adorn a temple to Venus, a mausoleum, or Roman baths. Recent archaeological excavations proved the baths hypothesis to be correct. It is thought that the frescoes were painted some time between AD 180 and 230, to decorate part of a substantial private villa.

Above the village you can find more megaliths, the **Demoiselles**. The now comical-seeming Christian legend claimed that a bunch of young girls, instead of going to vespers, went to dance on the heath. By way of punishment, they were literally petrified by God. Medieval chronicles and bishops' archives do mention pagan cults taking place on neolithic sites, but it is hard to judge how much truly went on, and how much was Church propaganda or paranoia.

East of Langon, **Grand-Fougeray** has retained a solid keep, the **Tour Du Guesclin**, a once substantial 13th-century fort. The keep by its lake hosts exhibitions in summer. On the way from Langon to Brain-sur-Vilaine, a panel indicates a small stretch of Gallo-Roman way preserved under trees by the river. Apparently, a bitter sign used to read: 'The Romans had this way built by their slaves, the Gauls'. **Brain-sur-Vilaine** is both a little port and a pretty old village; the locals keep their punts along the river. Around the village, you can see some of the traditional architecture incorporating *palis*, thin schist slabs used in place of wooden fencing.

From Langon to Redon, the Vilaine forms a piece of the Ille-et-Vilaine's southern border with the Loire Atlantique and the river banks give way to wide marshlands and flood plains. Seek out the ramshackle, atmospheric hamlet of **Gànnedel** here.

Redon

Redon stands trapped in the fork where the Vilaine and the Oust converge, in the southwestern corner of the Ille-et-Vilaine, surrounded by boundaries and water. The Loire Atlantique *département* lies to the south, the Morbihan *département* to the west. The Canal de Nantes à Brest passes through the centre of town, as does a major railway line. The surrounding countryside is regularly flooded by winter waters.

Redon is known in Brittany above all for its **Romanesque abbey church of St-Sauveur**, part of the abbey to which the town owes its existence. Redon's abbey is closely linked with the story of Brittany's independence. In the Breton territorial expansion eastwards during the 9th century, the Breton monk St Conwoïon, protected by the power of Nomenoë, set up a religious community at Redon. He appears to have encouraged Nomenoë to fight for Breton emancipation from the Carolingian kingdom. Some 10 kilometres north of Redon, on the D67 passing to the east of Bains-sur-Oust, a cross commemorates the Battle of Ballon in which Nomenoë effectively achieved Breton independence. Conwoïon's persuasive role is acknowledged there in the nationalistically pro-Breton text.

Through the Middle Ages, the abbey of Redon was one of the most influential religious institutions in Brittany. It benefited from a privileged position, not just with dukes of Brittany, but even with the Vatican, and it saw to the foundation of several other abbeys in southern Brittany. It was also an important place of pilgrimage for the journey to Santiago de Compostela, and held many relics.

The expertly built Romanesque tower, with its three levels of arches and its specially rounded corners, marks the exterior. Inside, the Romanesque-style nave has a mere six of its original 11 arches. Inside the transept, covered by an octagonal cupola, is a remarkable achievement of the 12th century, with the outlines of worn frescoes to pick out. A high, light Gothic choir held up by flying buttresses was added to the church in the 13th century, but its light was partly obscured by the enormous Lavallois-style retable added in the 17th century.

To Redon's Port

Redon's **Grande Rue**, the main shopping street, boasts an interesting mix of façades, some of them timberframe and some in stone, including elements in light tufa that was brought from the Loire. The street leads down to where the Canal de Nantes à Brest crosses town. The Vilaine flows by just to the east. Along it, the name of the Quai St-Jacques is a reminder of the fact that pilgrims for Compostela left from here by ship.

Redon was for centuries a thriving inland port, acting as a stocking place for imports that were waiting to be carried up to Rennes. The Compagnie des Indes, which was the official French trading company with the Indies, even had some offices here. The extension of the Quai St-Jacques south along the Vilaine, the Quai Duguay-Trouin, has slightly wonky but grand stone houses complete with wrought-iron balconies that once belonged to wealthy merchants.

The yachting harbour lies to the west. Down the Quai Jean Bart, the **Musée de la Batellerie de l'Ouest** (*open 15 June–15 Sept daily 10–12 and 3–6; rest of year Mon, Wed, Sat and Sun 2–6*) explains the importance that the inland waterways and Redon once had in Breton trading. A former Redon riverman is often on hand to talk about his experiences of the life.

The Forêt de Paimpont, or Merlin's Forest of Brocéliande

The forest of Paimpont, or Brocéliande as Arthurian aficionados should call it, is one of those places where the imagination gets much the better of the real or even the religious. To read about Arthurian legend in Brittany, *see* **Topics**, p.34.

The best place to get your bearings in the forest is Paimpont, a purple-coloured village by a typically atmospheric lake, one of many in the forest. After visiting Paimpont, you can go on walks from various car parks leading to the 'Arthurian' sites. You can pick up a map of the itineraries from the tourist office in Paimpont.

Getting Around

The N24 main road linking Rennes and Ploërmel passes just to the south of the forest of Paimpont. To find out about catching a bus to the forest from Rennes, contact TIV, t 02 99 31 34 31. There is an infrequent train service that runs from Rennes to Montfort-sur-Meu.

The Grande Randonnée 37 hikers' path comes down from Montfort-sur-Meu and crosses along the southern edge of the forest of Paimpont.

Tourist Information

Pays d'Accueil de Brocéliande,
37 Avenue de la Libération,
35380 Plélan-le-Grand, t 02 99 06 86 07,
www.broceliande-tourisme.info.
Paimpont:abbey, t 02 99 07 84 23,
syndicat-dinitiativepaimpont@wanadoo.fr.
It's here that you can find out about the times of French-language guided tours of the forest's legendary sites (*July and Aug Thurs and Sat; Sept Sat*).
Tréhorenteuc: church, t 02 97 93 05 12.
Montfort-sur-Meu: 2 Rue du Château,
t 02 99 09 31 81, *ecomusee@club-internet.fr.*

Market Days
Montfort-sur-Meu: Friday.

Where to Stay and Eat

Paimpont and Around ✉ 35380

Visiting a rural area such as Paimpont is an ideal time to experience the homely charms of a B&B (*chambre d'hôte*). Around Paimpont you'll see a proliferation of signs directing you off the road and into people's homes.
Ferme-auberge de Trudeau, Trudeau, a short way east of Paimpont along the D40, t 02 99 07 81 40 (*inexpensive–moderate*). An inn in a pretty setting, with wonderful food (*moderate; advance booking essential*) cooked in an old bread oven. There is also a *gîte* for walkers with about 30 places.
**Relais de Brocéliande, Le Bourg, t 02 99 07 81 07 (*inexpensive*). A typical,

very pleasant French country address situated practically opposite the archway leading into the village.
La Corne de Cerf, at Le Cannée, a short way to the east of Paimpont, t 02 99 07 84 19 (*inexpensive*). A truly beautiful B&B, with rooms that have been gorgeously done up by the Morvans, the artistic couple who own the place.
Château du Bois, Paimpont, t 02 99 07 83 58 (*inexpensive*). A misleadingly named B&B in a simple modern home.
La Ruisselée, just outside Paimpont on the road to Plélan-le-Grand, t 02 99 06 85 94 (*inexpensive*). Three vast, modern and scrupulously clean bedrooms in a converted 17th-century house, run by one Mme Hermenier. The bathrooms are wonderful, and there is a family room with sleeping facilities for up to 4 people. In the summer months, breakfast is served on tables out in the garden.
Les Forges de Paimpont, t 02 99 06 81 07 (*inexpensive–moderate*). A restaurant set in the pretty village of Les Forges situated to the southeast of Paimpont, providing a range of traditional French meals. *Closed Mon eves and 2wks Sept.*
Aux Berges de l'Aff, La Lande, Beignon, t 02 97 75 74 25 (*inexpensive*). A healthy crêperie where you can try out *crêpes biologiques* (organic pancakes). *Closed Tues eve and Wed lunch.*

Concoret ✉ 56430
Chez Maxime, Place de l'Eglise, t 02 97 22 63 04 (*inexpensive*). A tranquilly located and attractive inn offering extremely simple rooms and a variety of tasty local dishes. *Closed Wed in winter.*
Auberge de Jeunesse , t 02 97 22 76 75, *www.fuaj.org* (*inexpensive*). The youth hostel, set in an area of pretty moorland close to Concoret.

Montfort-sur-Meu ✉ 35360
**Le Relais de la Cane, 2 Rue de la Gare, t 02 99 09 00 07 (*inexpensive*). A very pleasant and comfortable little country town hotel run by a dedicated young couple who do their utmost to make their guests feel at home.

The Forêt de Paimpont

The woodland of the Fôret de Paimpont, alias Brocéliande, only covers 7,000 hectares now. Along with the traditional oak and beech, willow adds a touch of lightness to the mix of foliage, while pines were planted from the 19th century. However, much of the higher land of the so-called forest is covered with heathery moors.

A Few Historical Facts to Cling to in the Legendary Forest

Here are a few solid stepping stones across the thick swamp of legend. As in so many parts of Brittany, signs of neolithic civilization can be found, including dolmens, menhirs and gallery chambers. Iron production also appears to have been going strong here when the Roman Empire ruled over Gaul. A significant historic figure connected with Paimpont is St Judicaël, a king or chief of Domnonia during the 7th century, credited with founding the priory of Paimpont around 640. Breton continued to be spoken in the Paimpont area up until the 12th century. Rarely for the Ille-et-Vilaine, the place names here still show the influence of the Celtic language.

Religious authorities held sway over the forest for a good many centuries, the abbey of Paimpont being a foundation of some standing. The bishop of Alet (St-Malo) had to intervene, though, when Eon, a hermit in these woods, went mad and claimed that he was the Christ of the Last Judgement. Iron production here continued to thrive down the centuries, as you can see in the 18th-century village of Les Forges in a quaint lakeside spot. The forges were highly productive in their day, supplying the major Breton arsenals of Rennes, Nantes, Lorient and Brest with arms. Since the 19th century, interest in Arthurian legend has brought the forest international renown and an international following.

Paimpont

Paimpont is a one-street village, entered by an archway at one end, finished by a large **abbey** next to a grand mirror of a lake. The abbey's roots go back to Judicaël's time, around AD 645. The monks first followed the order of St Colomban, before the place became a Benedictine priory in the 9th century. At the end of the 12th century, the monks switched to the rule of the Augustinians, and early in the 13th century the priory became an abbey, having fought for its independence from the abbey of St-Méen. The church dates mostly from the 13th and 15th centuries, and the main wing of the abbey now houses the tourist office and the town hall.

You enter via the west side, through a Gothic door graced by a statue of the Virgin and Child. The nave is covered with a quite plain wooden ceiling. Below the big Gothic windows, the Baroque woodwork is much more ornate, with putti, grape bunches, birds and busts among the garlands. Compare the refinement of this work with the wood carving in the round of Notre Dame de Paimpont, also in the nave, a blushing robed and painted 15th-century Virgin holding her vacuously grinning Christ-child under a baldaquin. The guide says that the transept rose window is the oldest in Brittany, dating from the beginning of the 13th century. Overdecorated retables show more signs of the Counter-Reformation imposing itself in the Ancien Régime.

The sacristy, which stored and safeguarded the ornate objects of the Catholic mass, has preserved many of its treasures and much of its decoration. The most amazing reliquary takes the shape of a silver arm (its pieces joined together by gold nails) holding a book encrusted with precious stones. The arm, with a little window incorporated in it, is meant to contain a finger of St Judicaël, the Paimpont lord who came to be regarded as a saint by the local population. This significant piece of Breton reliquary art was donated to the abbey by one of the wives of the last duke of Brittany, François II. Another exceptional piece on display is a 17th-century ivory carving of Christ, said to be the work of a monk at the abbey.

A Tour of the Forest of Brocéliande

Take the D71 northeast from Paimpont and branch off to look at the **Etang du Pas du Houx**, the largest of the forest lakes, beautiful but private. A 20th-century castle in the Norman style named the Château de Brocéliande lies on the lake's edge.

Continue up the D71 and look out for a turning left for the **Tombeau de Merlin**. Viviane is supposed to have imprisoned Merlin for good in nine magic but invisible circles, so don't be surprised if you don't see much here. You'll need to use your imagination too, if you go down the lane from Merlin's tomb to the **Fontaine de Jouvence**, the Fountain of Youth, a basic watering hole but one with legendary waters supposed to have rejuvenating powers.

Get onto the D31 to Concoret and you come to the **Château de Comper**, home to the **Centre de l'Imaginaire Arthurien** (*open Thurs–Mon July and Aug 10–7, March–June and Sept–mid-Oct 10–5.30*). Inside, the annual exhibitions delve into old Celtic legends, using waxworks scenes and textual explanations. The château also has the advantage of being right next to the **lake of Comper**, along with the Val Sans Retour (*see* p.104) the most atmospheric spot in the forest. It is actually within this lake that Merlin is supposed to have built Viviane her magical home.

It's quite tricky finding your way to nearby **Folle Pensée** ('Mad Thought'). There may have been an asylum for the mentally ill here, and they may have been taken to the **Fontaine de Barenton** – with its legendary power to unleash terrible storms – to drink from it in the hope that it might cure them. To get to the fountain, you pass through the red schist village of Barenton; it's a three-kilometre walk to and from the car park to see the fountain. During July and August, the Paimpont tourist office conducts guided forest tours.

In the parish of **Néant-sur-Yvel** some way west, **Le Jardin aux Moines** is a neolithic rectangle of stones that appears to have avoided being touched by Arthurian legend. The mysterious low blocks, a mix of schist and quartz, are estimated to have been erected between 3000 BC and 2500 BC, and the story here goes that a group of orgy-loving monks were turned to stone by way of punishment.

Tréhorenteuc, a little village tucked in below the purple moorland slopes leading to the Vale of No Return, boasts a **church** where Arthurian legend shares the limelight with Christian stories. Once you have paid a small fee to enter, you can see a sparkling mosaic showing flaming red and haloed wolf-like lions surrounding a white hart carrying a cross on its necklace. Panels illustrate scenes of Arthurian legend, while the stained-glass windows represent both Joseph of Arimathea, the man who saved several of the crucified Christ's drops of blood in the Holy Grail, and St Onenne, sister of King Judicaël. She chose a life of chastity and retired to Tréhorenteuc, where she kept a flock of geese; apparently they warned her of the approach of soldiers with sordid intentions and fought off her assailants.

Just south of the village of Tréhorenteuc, a purple schist road leads up to the **Val Sans Retour**. This is the vale where the bitter Morgane le Faye, sister of King Arthur, supposedly trapped unfaithful knights, turning them into her puppets. If they tried to escape from the valley, terrifying visions created by Morgane would stop them in their tracks. These knights were eventually liberated from their prison of pleasure by fellow knight Lancelot, who, despite having an adulterous relationship with Arthur's Queen Guinevere, remained faithful to her.

Nowadays it's none too easy to get down into the Val Sans Retour. Ask the way at the tourist office, open seven days a week opposite the church. First, you need to find the track down to a gilded old tree that stands out like golden stag's antlers. This is the Arbre d'Or, a monument designed after the forest fires of 1990. The gilded tree is surrounded by a handful of charred, stumpy trees and stands in a patch of sharply planted slices of local rock, like a crop of thin stalagmites growing out of the earth. Then follow the valley along the pond's side. The atmospheric pools, the purple sides to the valley, and the willow, pine and gorse, give character to this secretive vale. After a while you come to a three-way fork with signposts signalling the different walks that you can take.

Going south by road, you have to take a long loop to reach the **Château de Trécesson**, a beautiful castle of purple schist. You cannot visit the moat-surrounded property, but you can walk up the hillside above it. Dramatic views open out over the countryside, but at the top of the crest you reach the boundaries of the enormous military camp of Coëtquidan stretching eastwards. The **Ecole de St-Cyr-Coëtquidan** is France's equivalent to the British Sandhurst or the US Westpoint. You can visit the interesting **military museum** within the camp (*open Tues–Sun 10–12 and 2–6; you will need to show your passport at the entrance*). It commemorates 17,000 graduate officers killed in battle.

To see the once workaday but still gorgeously picturesque side of the forest, visit **Les Forges de Paimpont**, a purpose-built 18th-century village by a lake that was once entirely devoted to iron production.

To Montfort-sur-Meu

On the way to this little town 20 kilometres northeast of the Fôret de Paimpont, those interested in finding out about traditional Breton games should contact **La Jaupître** (*t 02 99 07 47 02*) at Monterfil to organize an outing. **Montfort** is still in purple schist country, and its **Ecomusée** (*open Mon–Fri 8.30–12 and 2–6, Sat, Sun and public hols 2–6*) continues to pay homage to the Arthurian theme. The tower is virtually all that remains of a massive medieval fort. The museum has interesting displays on local costumes and on simple rural childhood toys of the past, cleverly fashioned out of basic country materials. The Fôret de Montfort south of the town is rather beautiful.

Romantic Châteaux and Artistic Villages North of Rennes

Northwest and north of Rennes, there are two easily drawn lines of sights through the Ille-et-Vilaine countryside you might follow, with interesting châteaux and little villages along the way. The first goes along the D220 and D221, from St-Méen-le-Grand to Hédé close to the Canal de l'Ille et Rance. The second lies east of the canal, starting at the Château de la Bourbansais and continuing to the area around Antrain.

St-Méen-le-Grand to Caradeuc

St-Méen's most celebrated son, **Louison Bobet**, has a small **museum** devoted to him here (*open Oct–June Wed–Mon 2–5*). Bobet was the Breton cyclist who became the first man to win the Tour de France three times in a row. The son of a local *boulanger*,

Getting Around

A **bus** links St-Méen-le-Grand with Rennes. Transports Armor Express, **t** 02 99 26 16 00, runs buses from Rennes to Dinard, via Bécherel. Combourg lies on a **train** line linking Rennes with Dol-de-Bretagne, St-Malo and Dinard.

Tourist Information

Pays d'Accueil Touristique de la Baie du Mont-St-Michel–Bretagne Romantique, 3 bis Grande Rue des Stuarts, 35120 Dol-de-Bretagne, **t** 02 99 48 34 53, *git.pays.de.la.baie@wanadoo.fr.*
Tinténiac: Espace Cour Frémur, 17 Rue de la Libération, **t** 02 99 68 09 62, *tinteniac.tourisme@free.fr.*
Combourg: Place Albert Parent, **t** 02 99 73 13 93, out of season **t** 02 99 73 00 18, *www.combourg.org.*
Bécherel: 8 Place Alexandre Jéhanin, **t** 02 99 66 75 23, out of season **t** 02 99 66 80 55, *www.becherel.com.*
Bazouges-la-Pérouse: Mairie, **t** 02 99 97 40 94, *www.bazouges.com.*

Market Days

Bécherel: Saturday.
Hédé: Tuesday.
Tinténiac: Wednesday.
Combourg: Monday.
Bazouges-la-Pérouse: Thursday.
Antrain: Tuesday.

Where to Stay and Eat

Quédillac ✉ 35290
★★Relais de la Rance, 6 Rue de Rennes, **t** 02 99 06 20 20 (*inexpensive–moderate*). A well-reputed establishment in typical 19th-century buildings in the middle of this village between St-Méen and Médréac.

Bécherel and Around ✉ 35190

Château de Montmuran, near Les Iffs, **t** 02 99 45 88 88, *www.montmuran.com* (*moderate*). B&B with splendid views (*see also p.108*).
Mme Goar, 1 Porte Bertault, Bécherel, **t** 02 99 66 71 10, *guillemette.goar@free.fr* (*moderate*). An 18th-century B&B.
Hôtel du Commerce, 11 Rue de la Libération, Bécherel, **t** 02 99 66 81 26 (*inexpensive*). A no-frills, old-fashioned inn.
Le Logis de la Filanderie, 3 Rue de la Filanderie, Bécherel, **t** 02 99 66 73 17 (*inexpensive*). A B&B with a friendly English-speaking host.

Hédé ✉ 35630

★★Le Vieux Moulin, Ancienne Route de St-Malo, **t** 02 99 45 45 70 (*inexpensive*). An ivy-fronted building with a comical belltower. Some of the renovated rooms give on to the garden. There's lots of fish on the menu.
La Vieille Auberge, Ancienne N137, Le Perray, Bazouges-sous-Hédé, **t** 02 99 45 46 25 (*expensive*). A largely 17th-century restaurant, with a cosy dining room and a lake. *Closed Sun eve, Mon and 2wks Aug–Sept.*

he was sent out to deliver fresh *baguettes* at breakneck speed from an early age – the perfect training. Newspaper cuttings, photographs, diplomas, old trophies and old shirts build up a picture of his path to success. His first important victory came at the age of 18, when he won the 1943 Grand Prix de Lamballe (in Brittany). He went on to victory in the Tour de France in 1953, 1954 and 1955, and in 1954 he was also crowned world champion. Louison Bobet is doubly famous for having brought *thalassothérapie* to Brittany; he ran the first such seawater therapy centre in Quiberon from 1963.

Continue to the **abbey of St-Méen,**where you can learn about the town's other saint, Méen or Mewen. He came over from Britain in the 6th century, and at one point was sent into the Breton interior to settle a dispute between two rival lords. On the way, he met Kaduon, who offered him land. Returning from sorting out the dispute, he took up Kaduon's offer and started a monastery here. In the side chapel, very worn frescoes, thought to date from the 14th century, recall the saint's life.

Le Genty-Home, Vallée de Hédé, **t** 02 99 45 46 07 (*moderate–expensive*). Good country cooking in an old stone house on the edge of woods. *Closed Sun and Tues eves and Wed.*

Vignoc ✉ 35630
Château de la Villouyère, just south of Vignoc (a few km south of Hédé along the N137), **t** 02 99 69 80 69 (*moderate*). Lodgings in the former home of Admiral Jean Toussaint de la Motte Picquet, with elegant, symmetrical forms dating from the 18th century.

Pleugueneuc ✉ 35720
Château de la Bourbansais, t 02 99 69 40 07, *www.labourbansais.com* (*inexpensive*). Luxury B&B rooms at bargain prices (*see* also p.110).
Le Lézard Tranquille, Les Cours Verdiers, at entrance to the Château de la Bourbansais park, **t** 02 99 69 40 36 (*inexpensive*). Spacious B&B rooms and a summer terrace.

Le Tronchet ✉ 35540
★★★**Hostellerie Abbatiale,** down from the Abbey of Le Tronchet, **t** 02 99 58 98 21, *abbatiale.letronchet@wanadoo.fr* (*moderate*). An attractive, sprawling hotel in former abbey buildings in the countryside.

Combourg ✉ 35270
★★★**Le Château,** 1 Place Chateaubriand, **t** 02 99 73 00 38 (*moderate–expensive*). A grand, well-positioned townhouse of character, with a terrace that looks down to the lake.

★★**Hôtel du Lac,** 2 Place Chateaubriand, **t** 02 99 73 05 65 (*moderate*). Comfortable, modern rooms by the atmospheric lake. There's an airy dining room and a garden for barbecues on summer evenings.
L'Ecrivain, Place de l'Eglise, **t** 02 99 73 01 61 (*inexpensive*). Refined food. *Closed Thurs, Sun, and Wed eves in low season.*
Chez Moustache, 11 Place Albert Parent, **t** 02 99 73 06 54 (*inexpensive*). A wonderfully named and well-regarded crêperie.

Bazouges-la-Pérouse ✉ 35560
Château de la Ballue, t 02 99 97 47 86, *www. laballue.com* (*very expensive*). An idyllically located B&B with spacious rooms and comical ensuite bathrooms. There's quirky modern art on the ground floor and in the lovely formal gardens. *Table d'hôte* is available.

St-Rémy-du-Plain ✉ 35560
Château de la Haye d'Irée, 15km south of Bazouges-la-Pérouse down the D90, **t** 02 99 73 62 07, *www.chateaubreton.com* (*moderate–expensive*). An elegant 18th-century granite Breton manor with views of the surrounding countryside, a heated pool and grounds.

St-Ouen-la-Rouërie ✉ 35460
Château des Blosses, t 02 99 98 36 16 (*expensive*). A little 19th-century château set in spacious grounds, with a swing-golf course, comfortable rooms, hunting trophies on the walls, and *table d'hôte* on reservation.

To the west of Bécherel are the gardens of the **Château de Caradeuc** (*open Easter–mid-Sept daily 12–6; 16 Sept–Oct daily 2–6; rest of year Sun 2–6*), which was built in 1723 for Anne-Nicolas de Caradeuc, a member of the Breton parliament. Anne-Nicolas's son Louis-René, Marquis de Caradeuc de la Chalotais, became procurator general of the Breton Parlement and famously stood up to the royal-appointed governor of Brittany, the Duc d'Aiguillon, in the 1760s. The Breton parliament wanted to expel the powerful religious and teaching order of the Jesuits from Brittany and voted for their removal from the province, against royal policy. King Louis XV called the leaders of this insubordination to Versailles and exiled three of them. The whole Breton parliament then resigned and Louis XV had Caradeuc arrested and imprisoned. He spent time in various gaols, from which he wrote a moving defence of his actions. The Paris Parlement gave its backing to the Breton one. The royal authorities felt forced to climb down in this significant blow to royal authority. Although Caradeuc was forced to live in exile from 1766 to 1774, King Louis XVI did make up to some extent for his royal mistreatment, conferring the title of marquis on the Breton protester in 1776. Surprisingly, given the clash with the monarchy, a huge white statue of Louis XVI stands out among the outrageous garden ornaments.

Bécherel

Bécherel was a fortified spot as far back as Gallo-Roman times. Its location overlooking the surrounding countryside was chosen as an obvious site for a fort by Alain de Dinan in the 12th century. The Plantagenets grabbed hold of it later in the century, and King Henry II Plantagenet had the village fortified. His son, Geoffrey, subsequently besieged it and burnt it down. In the Breton War of Succession, English troops supporting the claim of Jean de Montfort took control of Bécherel. The place was repeatedly attacked and it is said that one siege lasted 18 months.

A few traces remain of the castle, plus small portions of five out of nine towers that once enclosed the village. You can get a fine sense of the fortified position from the garden at the top of the village, which is reached by navigating a labyrinthine little network of alleyways. The grand village houses are explained by the success of the linen made here and exported to various parts of Europe from the 16th to the 18th centuries.

Trade in **second-hand books** has grown at an extraordinary rate here since 1989. You can get a full list of the dozen and more relevant shops from the tourist office. This village has become a small but significant eastern outpost of the dwindling Breton-speaking culture. The Bécherel **book festival** takes place on Easter weekend, and there's a **book market** on the first Sunday of every month.

Les Iffs and the Château de Montmuran

The village of **Les Iffs** to the east may seem a bucolic backwater, but it has a richly decorated **church of St-Ouen** that dates from the 14th century. Keys are available from the wary lady behind the village bar, who will demand a car key or passport in return. The stained glass is the main attraction inside. Nine windows date from the Renaissance, with glass executed by the workshop of Michel Bayonne of Rennes.

Outside the village, the **Fontaine St-Fiacre** is apparently the only such covered fountain, which are so typical in western Brittany, to be found in Ille-et-Vilaine. Dating from the 15th century, the fountain used to be called upon to provide miraculous rain in periods of drought – the local priest would lead a procession to the fountain and dip his cross in the waters here, and if the locals' prayers were heard, a storm would soon follow.

At the **Château de Montmuran** (*open June–Sept Sun–Fri 2–7*), the château-keeper himself acts as tour guide. Du Guesclin, the viciously ambitious Breton medieval warrior who became leader of the French armies in the 14th century (*see* box below), plays the starring role in the guide's tales. The high ridge on which the château was built, with its glorious views northwards, has been fortified since at least the 11th century. The oldest parts of the castle that now stands date back to the 12th and 13th centuries. As to the splendid entrance *châtelet*, one tower is 14th century, the other 15th. On either side of the drawbridge you can spot a couple of comical hump-backed medieval figures in stone who are shown struggling to hold up the massive weight. Once you reach the courtyard, the splendid views are offset by the massed banks of outstanding 200-year-old lime trees. One of the most peculiar features of the architecture is the chapel, placed above the vaulted passageway into the courtyard.

Bertrand Du Guesclin, Brittany's Most Famous Warrior

Bertrand Du Guesclin came into the world in 1321 at the Château de la Motte-Broons near Dinan, the first child of a minor noble Breton family. Something of a runt, portraits show him to have been notably ugly. With nine siblings born after him, he seems to have had to learn how to fend for himself from an early age, and is said to have had an army at the age of 12. The popular tale goes that he became an uncontrollable delinquent, leading a band of local peasants into terrible mischief. At the age of 17, he entered a jousting tournament in Rennes, where he distinguished himself memorably (*see* p.91).

In the Breton War of Succession, Du Guesclin decided to fight for Charles de Blois, the contender backed by the French monarchy. With the private army he amassed, he terrorized the enemy lines. He is supposed to have come to the Château de Montmuran in 1354 for a grand feast, while the English troops lay close by at Bécherel. Suspecting that the enemy might attack during the festivities, he posted archers on the road to the castle, and was able to surprise the assailants with an unexpected reception party. The tale goes that he was immediately honoured for his actions by being knighted at the château.

One romantic strand to his story tells of how a bright young woman of Dinan, Tiphaine Raguenel, was so impressed by Du Guesclin's famed performance in Dinan that she was easily wooed by him and they got married. In 1360, Du Guesclin was made governor of Pontorson, just to the south of the Mont-St-Michel. On the holy mount itself he built a safe home for Tiphaine while he went off warring around France and Europe.

You only see a few rooms inside but they are full of curiosities, including a model of the full medieval fort and a 15th-century hot water and hot air system. Most unexpected of all is the carving from a chest that is said to date back to Carolingian times. In the chapel, Du Guesclin is remembered in 19th-century stained glass, and in a painting. The tour of Montmuran finishes with a climb up the *châtelet*, but those who suffer from vertigo should not go up.

Hédé and Tinténiac

Hédé, some 20 kilometres to the north of Rennes, stands along the D221, high above the valley through which the **Canal d'Ille et Rance** runs. The Rance flows up from the centre of Brittany to Dinan, and out into the Channel between St-Malo and Dinard; the Vilaine goes down to the Atlantic. In an extraordinary 19th-century engineering project, the two rivers, and hence the Breton Channel coast and the Breton Atlantic coasts, were joined almost at the widest point in the province.

Hédé itself is a quietly attractive place, with its ruined castle and its Romanesque church. The stretch of canal that runs below Hédé is well known for its close-packed **11 locks**. You can appreciate them most fully by going for a stroll along the towpath, which is well maintained. The **Maison du Canal d'Ille et Rance** (*open July and Aug daily 10.30–12.30 and 1.30–6; April–June, Sept and Oct Wed–Mon 2–6; rest of year Wed*

In western Brittany during campaigning in 1363, Du Guesclin took many Breton strongholds, but also organized an abortive expedition across the Channel, the ships departing from St-Pol-de-Léon. His run of success would end in 1364, when Charles de Blois's army met with disaster at the battle of Auray. Although the troops were led by Du Guesclin, some say that he had been against the fight. Charles de Blois was killed, thus bringing an end to the Breton War of Succession. Du Guesclin was imprisoned, and the French side purportedly payed 100,000 crowns for his release.

He then went off to war for the French king on a much wider scale, becoming a major player in the Hundred Years War. Captured by the English in a battle in Spain in 1367, he was taken as a prisoner to Bordeaux, but another ransom payment freed him in early 1369. He headed off back to Spain, and that same year was declared king of Granada. Such was Du Guesclin's success that he reached the very pinnacle of the French military hierarchy, being appointed Connétable de France (basically, commander in chief of the French armies) in 1370.

After Tiphaine's death, Du Guesclin married his second wife at the Château de Montmuran in 1374. Jeanne de Laval was a mere 17, her husband 53. An idealized version of them can be seen in the 19th-century windows of the Château de Montmuran's chapel. Du Guesclin battled on to the very end of his life. He was still out warring when he died, in 1380, having taken Châteauneuf-de-Randon in the Massif Central. His will stated that he wished to be buried at Dinan. His heart was taken there, but his entrails were left in Châteauneuf-de-Randon. In a rare honour, his skeleton was buried with the Capetian kings of France, in their family mausoleum at St-Denis outside Paris.

and Sun 2–6) was opened at the road bridge just by the locks both to commemorate the construction of the canal and remember the trading boats that once employed this waterway.

At **Tinténiac**, which lies six or so kilometres to the north of Hédé along the canal, another little museum, the **Musée de l'Outil et des Métiers** (*open July–Sept Mon–Sat 10–12 and 2.30–6, Sun 2.30–6*) recalls the old crafts that were so important before the age of the tractor.

Château de la Bourbansais

Open daily May–Sept 10–7, rest of year 2–6.

The park of La Bourbansais (outside the village of Pleugueneuc up the N137 between Rennes and St-Malo) looks elegant enough, but the château is much more beautiful still in its speckled schist. The perspective to the main façade has a carefully planned symmetry, with two dovecotes, followed by two mansarded outbuildings, then two side wings to the castle leading in to two corner towers, each topped by a delightfully domed bell-shaped roof. All this symmetry is a sure sign that this château dates from after the arrival of Renaissance architecture in France. It was started in the late 16th century for the Breton parliamentarian Jean du Breil. An architect famed for his bird's-eye drawings of the period's royal châteaux, Jacques Androuet du Cerceau, apparently designed the main façade. Descendants of the same family have lived here since its completion.

You can visit a series of small *salons* on the ground floor. Originally, these spaces simply served as cellars and as a buffer against the dampness of the marshy location. But then windows were pierced in the walls and the rooms were kitted out with gorgeous Ancien Régime panelling, tapestries and decoration. The panelling counts as the masterpiece of the carpenter Mancelle, done in refined Louis XVI style. Republican troops apparently passed this way in 1793, intent on setting fire to the château. But Mancelle's son had become the château-keeper while the proprietors were away. He could not bear to see the pride of his father's life destroyed, so he appeased the revolutionary vandals by offering them a drink from the château cellars; he got them so merry that they left without harming the interiors. In the little **zoo** attached to the château, deer are protected; somewhat ironically, on the other side of the château, you can also admire a pack of hunting hounds.

If you are staying a while in the area, a little detour to the neolithic Allée Couverte de Tressé and the remains of the Abbaye du Tronchet makes for an atmospheric excursion. They lie a dozen or so kilometres up the N137 from Pleugueneuc and along the D9 going east. The **Forêt du Mesnil** makes for a deeply shaded, dark setting for the **Allée Couverte de la Maison-es-Feins or Tressé**, whose existence is attributed to fairies. Apparently, one fairy's lot of cows caused damage to the fields of a local farmer, so the fairy offered him a loaf that would never run out and never go stale, as long as he told no one how he got it. After enjoying the advantages of this magic bread for many years, the farmer let slip the secret, and the loaf turned to stone. Some loaf it would have been! The tomb, around 11 metres long, is covered by seven weighty stones, and was probably built around 2500 BC. Pairs of breasts, a sign that an Earth Mother was worshipped here, were carved in relief in the granite chamber at the entrance, although many were mutilated in the 1960s.

East along the D9 from Tressé, the **Abbaye du Tronchet** presents a bucolic picture of 17th-century monasticism, but the place is now in large part a hotel (*see* p.106).

Château de Combourg

Park open Wed–Mon 10–6 (daily July and Aug). Guided tours of château Easter–Oct Wed–Mon 2–5.30 (daily July and Aug).

... secret passages and stairs, prison cells and dungeons, a labyrinth of galleries, some covered, others open, walled-up underground tunnels which disappeared off no one knew where; all around, silence, darkness and the stony appearance of the place...

François-René de Chateaubriand's description of the château in *Mémoires d'outre-tombe*

To appreciate a visit to the Château de Combourg, you need to know something of the life of its most famous inhabitant, the great French Romantic, Chateaubriand (*see* box, p.112). The first fortification at the château goes back to the 11th century, when Ginguené, a bishop of Dol-de-Bretagne, decided to strengthen control of his lands. The château then passed into military hands. Through to the 13th century, it was periodically besieged and battered due to warring between Brittany and neighbouring Normandy. So the castle you now see dates in the main from the 14th and 15th centuries. The look is forbiddingly military still. During the Breton War of Succession, the lords here supported the French claimant to the dukedom, Charles de Blois. Jean de Coetquen, of Combourg, fought against the fanatical Catholic side of the Ligue during the French Wars of Religion, and his descendants remained powerful military figures into the 18th century. The Maréchal de Duras became lord of the castle in the mid 18th century and decided to sell it. In 1761, it was bought, along with the title, by René-Auguste de Chateaubriand, father of the great writer.

The tall, sheer castle walls rise up in hostility as you approach, a defensive tower on each corner. Above the main entrance, the coat of arms with lots of *fleurs de lys* recalls a medieval lord of Châteaubriant (a stronghold in southern Brittany) who went off to serve the French king in the crusades. 'My blood colours the banner of France', the motto proudly reads in French.

The neo-Gothic interiors date from after Chateaubriand's time. Chateaubriand's eldest brother, Jean-Baptiste, inherited the castle from his father in 1786 but was guillotined in 1794. Eventually the property was handed back to Jean-Baptiste's son, but the fort was left to fall into ruin. The memory of Chateaubriand the writer is preserved inside. The chapel witnessed the double marriage of two of Chateaubriand's beloved sisters, and this is where his mother is said to have spent much of her time in the house, trying to pray away some of her unhappiness caused by her husband's terrifying moods.

France's Most Miserable Romantic

Chateaubriand, France's most famous Romantic writer and prime contender as the nation's most miserable memorialist, described in brilliant detail the dark and dour Château de Combourg, where he spent a little of his deeply unhappy childhood. Were you to read the first sections of Chateaubriand's cheerfully titled autobiography, *Mémoires d'outre-tombe* (Memoirs from Beyond the Grave), you would get a vivid visual depiction of Combourg, as well as of St-Malo, where the writer was born in 1768.

Chateaubriand is a nationally known figure in France, seen by some as a Romantic hero in his own right, loathed by many for his misery and his political and Christian posturing. Few readers today have the patience to plough through the hundreds of pages charting his depressions, but his style can sweep you away like a whirlwind. He had a fascinating life, surviving the Revolution, going on a great journey through the USA in the course of that turmoil, becoming a political journalist and ambassador, and writing heady, emotive fiction that tests the limits of Christian morality. His most famous works of fiction, *Atala* and *René* (mercifully much shorter than his memoirs, more the length of short stories), are set along the Mississippi. They drip with descriptions of nature and details of Native American Indians eating bear ham and sacred dog, but they also reflect upon the moral and religious outlooks separating the civilizations of Europe and America.

After America, Chateaubriand went to live in exile in London for a period, suffering bitter poverty while there. He went on to champion the cause of Christianity, which had suffered such persecution, censorship and denigration during the French Revolution. In his *Génie du Christianisme*, he put forward his reasons for continuing to believe, and his Christian ideals pervade his fiction. He also had grandiose political aspirations, which were never fully fulfilled, although he held some important posts, including several as French ambassador.

A huge staircase in wood was placed in what was once an interior courtyard; before this was built, château dwellers had to go to one of the corner stairtowers to find a way up to the other floors. Along with a massive tapestry on the central staircase, you can see a Venetian chest portraying battle scenes, apparently a wedding gift when Chateaubriand married Céleste Buisson de la Vigne. The *salle des gardes* so eerily depicted by the Romantic writer was converted into two rather brighter rooms later in the 19th century. The salon walls were covered with rich wall paintings of lions, palms and crusaders. A portrait of Malesherbes, a major liberal Ancien Régime politician who supported Chateaubriand, and a couple of 15th-century paintings are to be admired.

Up via one tower, you can view the Romantic's deathbed, his desk and some other battered pieces related to his life. There's also a copy of Girodet's famous moody portrait of him and an engraving portraying Juliette Récamier, whose passionate friendship was so important to Chateaubriand in later life. The guide claims that in the 14th century there was a tradition of placing a live black cat or a stillborn child in castle walls to keep away evil spirits. The screaming cat skeleton on display was supposedly found in one of the castle's walls during 19th-century restoration work.

The château lies in what the French call an English-style park, which you can walk round. You might also wander along the prettyish main street of the little town of Combourg. The best views of the castle are from the far side of the lake below it.

To Bazouges-la-Pérouse

The steeple of wacky **Bazouges-la-Pérouse** is visible for many miles around. Simple houses snail up the village hillside towards it. On the flat top of the hill, the streets are set out in a grid pattern. **Avant-garde artists** have moved in and taken over here: the traditional houses have been turned into galleries, the former little private school into a summer exhibition space. Several of the painters who base themselves here in summer are well known in Paris for their trendy, trenchant and risqué contributions, largely to the thriving French cartoon magazine scene. Schwartz is particularly well known as he frequently draws cartoons for the big-selling *Ouest-France* newspaper. The old people, the main year-round inhabitants of Bazouges-la-Pérouse, often help out these seasonal artists by keeping the galleries open when they go off travelling.

Amidst the less permanent art in Bazouges-la-Pérouse stands the very substantial **church**, apparently the result of two medieval churches being rolled into one in the 19th century. Inside, the most notable features include the carved baptismal fonts from the 13th century, one engraved with gorgeous animals symbolizing the evangelists, and the 16th-century stained glass near the entrance, depicting the life of Christ. The past wealth of the village came from linen-making and woodwork.

The **Château de la Ballue** (*open 1–5.30 Fri–Sun and public hols, daily July and Aug*), just a few kilometres northeast of Bazouges-la-Pérouse, also now hosts **modern art exhibitions**. The château was one of three built in the Ille-et-Vilaine for Gilles Ruellan, a self-made 17th-century man from the nearby town of Antrain. Born to innkeepers there, after a career as a carrier, he joined the Protestant forces supporting Henri de Navarre against the fanatical Catholics in the French Wars of Religion. Such was his success that he was richly rewarded by Henri, who had become king of France. As tax collector, Gilles Ruellan amassed considerable wealth to build his string of châteaux. This pretty little 17th-century château has delightfully playful, small, Baroque-inspired formal gardens with glorious views. The Mont-St-Michel lies within striking distance.

Mont-St-Michel

One of Christianity's Most Sensational Symbols

Slip across the Breton frontier to visit the breathtaking Mont-St-Michel in Normandy. A visit can be uplifting or nightmarish, depending on when you go, but what a glorious piece of beautiful Christian power propaganda the Mont is. You can read so many symbols into its very appearance. From a distance even its triangular shape evokes the Holy Trinity. And that human-defying church steeple pointing so sharply to the skies appears like a timeless sign reminding you to think of heaven. The power of the Christian Church could scarcely be more awesomely and appealingly presented.

Tourist Information

Mont St-Michel: t 02 33 60 14 30, *www.ot-montsaintmichel.com*.

Maisons de la Baie Information Centres
The official Maisons de la Baie, at 4 locations around the Baie de Mont-St-Michel, are the best source of information on walks and all other nature- and wildlife-related activities and local ecology. Genêts is the place to find out about walks across the sands to Mont-St-Michel, and Courtils has an excellent interactive exhibition on the history and ecology of the bay. Their joint website is *www.baiedumontstmichel.com*.

Maison de la Baie de Courtils, Route de Roche Torin, **t** 02 33 89 66 00 (south side of bay); **Maison de la Baie de Genêts**, 4 Place des Halles, **t** 02 33 89 64 00 (north side); **Maison de la Baie de Vains**, Route du Grouin du Sud, **t** 02 33 89 06 06 (north side, just west of Avranches); **Maison de la Baie du Mont St-Michel**, 35960 Le Vivier-sur-Mer, **t** 02 99 48 84 38, *www.maison-baie.com* (south side, just inside Brittany).

Walks to Mont-St-Michel, bird-watching and other activities

Several agencies take groups across the sands at low tide, following the old pilgrim routes to the abbey, or to other parts of the bay, such as the Mont's sister island of Tombelaine (uninhabited, but full of birds). Some provide special-interest walks (for bird-watching, for seeing the sunset) and walks for children, and with some it's also possible to cross the bay on horseback. **No one should try any walks in the bay without an expert guide.**

Most guides are based in Genêts, where most walks begin, though some start from the car park at Mont-St-Michel. Walks usually run April–Oct, some all year. The schedule depends on the weather and tides. Groups to the Mont follow the old pilgrim route through the Bec d'Andaine, just north of Genêts. This walk (barefoot, and in shorts) takes about 45mins each way, with 1–2hrs on the mount. Reliable guide organizations include:

Chemins de la Baie, 14 Place des Halles, Genêts, **t** 02 33 89 80 88, *www.cheminsdelabaie.fr*.

Maison de la Baie de Genêts, *see above*. The official *maison* runs excellent, varied walks.

Maison du Guide, 1 Rue Montoise, Genêts, **t** 02 33 70 83 49, *www.decouvertebaie.com*. A big range of walks, and crossings on horseback.

Didier Lavadoux, Genêts, **t** 02 33 70 84 19, mobile 06 75 08 84 69.

Where to Stay and Eat

On the Mount ✉ 50116

It's expensive to stay here, and you need to book ages in advance for high season. These hotels line the street leading from the entrance and also have the best restaurants.

★★★La Mère Poulard, t 02 33 60 14 01, *www.mere-poulard.com* (*expensive–luxury*). The famous name, bolstered by the reported patronage of various celebrities. Although it has some pretty rooms, the prices at the upper end are as high as the Mount itself, so you might be happier sampling its famous fluffy omelette in the restaurant (*expensive*).

★★★Auberge Saint-Pierre, t 02 33 60 14 03, *www.auberge-saint-pierre.fr*. Comfy rooms (*moderate*) and a welcoming restaurant in a classified historic monument with some endearing touches of kitsch: carpet-backed chairs and waitresses in regional dress.

★★★La Croix Blanche, t 02 33 60 14 04 (*moderate*). Good rooms and a restaurant. *Closed 2nd wk Nov–3rd wk Feb*.

★★Hôtel du Mouton Blanc, t 02 33 60 14 08, (*moderate*). Rooms scattered in several houses and two restaurants, one in a 14th-century building.

La Vieille Auberge, t 02 33 60 14 34 (*inexpensive–expensive*). Rooms with terraces and a sea view, and a lunchtime brasserie.

La Sirène, t 02 33 60 08 60 (*inexpensive*). A good, popular option for crêpes.

On the Way to the Causeway ✉ 50116

★★★★Relais St-Michel, t 02 33 89 32 00, *www.relais-st-michel.com* (*expensive–luxury*). An ultra-modern place with some rooms looking out onto the mount.

★★★Hôtel de la Digue, t 02 33 60 14 02, *www.ladigue.com* (*moderate*). Another option with views of the mount.

★★★Le Relais du Roy, t 02 33 60 14 25, *www.le-relais-du-roy.com* (*moderate*). An older hotel with a grand dining room.

The Mont-St-Michel in Peril

The Mont-St-Michel has two major problems. The first is the number of visitors who come each year, reaching around three million now, making the mount the most visited monument in France outside Paris. The second major problem for the mount is only partially man-made: the bay is silting up. This is why only the very big tides actually carry the sea water right up to the ramparts of the mount nowadays. The building of the causeway and the canalization of the Couesnon (the main river flowing out into the bay) in the last century added significantly to the problem. The tide also brings enormous amounts of sand that the rivers of the bay would have difficulty pushing back anyway.

A massive project is underway to re-establish the maritime aspects of the Mont. One main aim is to let natural erosion in the bay take its course once again. But some of the *tangues*, the fine sands that are carried in by the tides, will be artificially removed. One of the most obvious changes will come with the destruction of the causeway. It is to be replaced by a pedestrian and rail bridge and a shuttle service starting two kilometres away. As well as an ultra-modern transport system that pollutes as little as possible, the accent will be on encouraging people to walk over the bridge. You will no longer see the vast car parks at the feet of the mount and the ramparts should come into their own again. This is all very exciting and will be enormously expensive, which is why nothing has happened so far.

As we went to press, work was due to start on a new dam to be built at Couesnon, to increase the flow of the river and help clear away sediment. With any luck, the bulk of the work on the causeway will be done from 2006 to 2009, but as it is to cost 134 million euros, the dates may slip. For full details, with simulated pictures of the effect of the works, see *www.projetmontsaintmichel.fr*. When it is all finished, it will give Mont-St-Michel back to the sea.

History

The colourful explanation of how the mount came to be so isolated in the bay is that it was once surrounded by dense woods, the Forêt de Scissy; in a sudden geological shift, this forest was swallowed by the seas, leaving the mount stranded, only occasionally reconnected to land by a narrow strip of sand revealed at low tide. Neolithic inhabitants possibly erected a monument on top of the rock.

In the 6th century, hermits settled on the island, which was then known as the Mont Tombe. Two chapels were built, one of them to St Etienne and the other to St Symphorien. But then, in the early 8th century, Aubert, who was the bishop of the nearby town of Avranches, had a dream. Or rather, he had a series of dreams, about St Michael, which would give the rock major Christian significance, turning it into one of the greatest pilgrimage destinations in the whole of Europe. One night in 708, so the story goes, St Michael swooped down into Aubert's dreams and instructed him to build a church in his honour on the Mont Tombe. Aubert, who was at first unconvinced by his visionary visitor, received several more messages from the insistent militant saint; he subsequently turned his attention to the mount to do his voice's bidding.

St Aubert commissioned a copy of the grotto on Mount Gargan, a place in Italy where St Michael had also supposedly put in an appearance. Pilgrims started to come to the grotto and the rock became known as the Mont-St-Michel. After his death, Aubert's skull ended up in the church of St-Gervais in Avranches; a hole in his cranium was claimed to have been caused by St Michael rather too forcefully trying to convince Aubert of his message with a prodding finger. St Michael has always appeared as one of the most violent enforcers of the Christian message.

The religious buildings would develop and be added to from the end of the Dark Ages and through the medieval period. From 867 to 933 at least, the Mont-St-Michel was officially the possession of Breton lords. But Duke Richard I of Normandy came to impose Norman ownership on the rock. Why, you might ask, did the Mont-St-Michel celebrate its 1,000 years in 1966? The year 1708, a millennium after Aubert made his dream come true, would seem more like the right date. But in 966, the duke of Normandy called on a band of Benedictine monks from St-Wandrille to go to the mount to take control of St Michael's sanctuary. This became the first Benedictine foundation in western Normandy. The spiritual site grew in importance under the Benedictines and it was decided to replace the pre-Romanesque buildings with a much more substantial monastery.

The Romanesque abbey went up roughly from the start of the 11th century to the mid 12th. Donations of lands from nobles and of money from visiting pilgrims gave the abbey considerable wealth. The place became a celebrated school of learning as well as a renowned centre for producing illuminated manuscripts. Robert de Tombelaine and Anastase the Venetian counted among the most revered scholars of their day, working on the mount in the 11th century. In that period, a first collection of stories of miracles connected with the mount was compiled here. A whole network of pilgrim routes to the holy place evolved, known as the *chemins montais*.

It was in the second half of the 12th century, under Robert de Torigni, abbot from 1154 to 1186, that the abbey knew its greatest period. Under Torigni, who was quite close to King Henry II, the number of monks reached its peak of 60. Such was the prolific production of manuscripts in this period and the size of the collection of the abbey library that the Mont-St-Michel became known as the Cité des Livres, the City of Books. The town of Avranches still conserves many of the abbey's manuscripts.

The Mont also became a strategic and symbolic stronghold in the Middle Ages. At the start of the 13th century, King Philippe Auguste of France decided to win back Normandy from the English. Breton soldiers fighting for his cause set fire to part of the abbey, destroying much of it. After his victories, Philippe Auguste, seemingly repentant, donated a huge sum to build a magnificent new monastery on the north side of the abbey church. This Merveille, or Wonder, as the new monastic block became known, counts as the greatest architectural achievement on the Mont-St-Michel. From the mid-13th century through to the start of the 16th, further administrative and residential buildings went up on the east and south sides of the abbey church.

The impressive ring of ramparts dates in the main part from the 15th century, and was built to defend the rock from English assailants in the Hundred Years War. The English never managed to take the mount, and with the war over, visitors came to thank St Michael for delivering them from the evil scourge of the English. They also gave money to pay for the rebuilding of the choir end of the abbey's church, destroyed during the war.

Practically all the French kings came to the Mont-St-Michel on a pilgrimage. However, abbey life was radically altered during the early 16th century, when the royal administration took over control of the appointment of abbots in France under the system of the *commende*. These posts became lucrative preferments for absentee lords, and some of these *abbés commendataires* scarcely came to the mount at all. Monastic life and scholarship suffered dramatically. During the bloody French Wars of Religion, the iconoclastic Huguenots or Protestants tried to come and deface the abbey, but many of them were massacred in the attempt. With the installation of the Maurist Benedictine order in 1622, religious life improved somewhat on the mount, but only some 10 monks lived in the abbey towards the end of the 18th century. With the Revolution, the situation only got worse. The monks were expelled and replaced by prisoners, which at least kept the abbey buildings from crumbling entirely.

During the course of the 19th century, people interested in protecting French culture, including Victor Hugo, protested at this sacrilegious use of the abbey. Under Napoleon III, in 1863, the place was freed from its demeaning role and 19th-century restorers moved in in force. In 1873, the abbey was declared a French historic monument. The architect Edouard Corroyer, who made some wonderful cross-section drawings of the mount, was one of the principal planners of the repairs, working on the place between 1872 and 1888. The splendid neo-Gothic spire, which was built in 1897, was the work of Victor Petigrand. The statue of St Michael that tops the spire, sparkling in gold, was executed by Emmanuel Frémiet, and the causeway that links the mount to the mainland was also a 19th-century creation. Some members of the Benedictine order were brought back to the abbey in recent times, but they were replaced by the Monastic Fraternity of Jerusalem, who continue receiving guests on religious retreats. UNESCO has included the Mont-St-Michel on its list of world heritage sites, of course.

Up the Mont-St-Michel and a Tour of the Abbey

Daily service in the abbey church at 12.15.

The entrance to this heavenly site proves heavily military. Once you walk through the massive rampart gates, a couple of enormous cannons greet you. These cannons were taken from the English in the course of the Hundred Years War. Look upwards and your gaze will be struck by the extraordinary gilded figure of St Michael flying at vertiginous height way above you. The arduous, crowded climb up the one street to the abbey then begins. Such a gem of architecture to look at from a distance, the abbey stands austere and forbidding close up. Don't expect many decorative frills. The abbey buildings were made from granite quarried locally and on the Iles Chausey, islands out beyond the bay of the Mont-St-Michel.

The Abbey

To go on a guided walk around the mount, contact the Maison de la Baie, t 02 33 89 64 00, or L'Association Découverte, t 02 33 70 83 49. To see the Mont-St-Michel from a plane, call t 02 33 58 02 91, or from a microlight, t 02 33 48 67 48.

You can visit the abbey by yourself or on a guided tour, in English or French. The **tour-conférence** is a splendid, more detailed tour in French, but it involves a gruelling number of steps.

Entering the abbey, at the top of the first impressive flights of steps, you come to a smallish room with some useful **models of the abbey** as it was at different historical periods. You then go out onto the spacious **terrace in front of the abbey church**. You can enjoy spectacular views from this terrace, both of the abbey, with its sheer stone faces plunging down the sides of the rock, and of the great sands that surround the mount. To the north, the other substantial rock stranded in the sands of the bay is the Ile Tombelaine.

The Abbey Church

In 1776, a storm destroyed the western end of the Romanesque nave of this vast church, hence the truncated form fronted by a classical façade. As you walk through the door, all you see for a second is a thin Gothic window in the distance. Then the light of the tall Gothic choir with its lancet shapes draws attention. But most of the church dates from earlier; this was one of the earliest Romanesque edifices to be built in Normandy. Much has been restored in the abbey church, but the south aisle of the nave is original 11th-century Romanesque, with a purplish stone that contrasts with the yellow one on the north side. This construction was of great size, height and daring for its time, with three levels, the top one provided with good-sized windows. The way that this abbey church was built right on the pinnacle of the mount is extraordinary. The crossing of the church was actually placed on the very top of the rock, though much of the rest of the church rests on four supporting lower chapels. The choir is late Gothic, started in the 1440s, with very little decorative sculptural detail, just the odd Renaissance element added on.

Among the Flying Gothic Buttresses

The views from the flying buttresses are exceptional, but you will only get the chance to climb up among them on the **tour-conférence** (*see* above). The soaring figure of the golden St Michael looks a good deal closer, and from this height you can peer down on the Merveille monastery buildings and the cloister. The 'lacework' of a Gothic-tracery balustrade stops you from falling.

The Abbey Crypts

Most of these crypts are only open to those who follow the **tour-conférence**. A dizzying walk takes you down a spiral staircase from the flying buttresses to the **Crypte des Gros Piliers**. This dates from the same Gothic period as the choir above. You reach the second crypt, the **Crypte des 30 Cierges**, via a very narrow corridor. Here you feel that you are really reaching into the rock. This crypt was built as part of the Romanesque foundations, supporting the massive church above. Traditionally, 30 monks would come down here, each carrying a candle, to pray to the Virgin. The statue of the Virgin is not original, but the large, strange figure with its oversized head and timid smirk is one of the rare effigies you will see on a tour of the abbey.

You can follow the **promenoir**, a surviving part of the Romanesque monastery, round its horseshoe shape. This connecting corridor was built during the 11th and 12th centuries and allowed the masons to try more delicate vaulting. The way leads round to **Notre-Dame Sous Terre** (Our Lady Under Ground), a pre-Romanesque building from the mid 10th century that is the oldest part of the abbey. This could also be the spot where Bishop Aubert had the first sanctuary to St Michael built in the 8th century. Beyond this underground chapel is the area where the monks' infirmary used to be. Here, an enormous wheel was used to shift great building blocks of stone up the sharp incline of the rockside. The spectacular machine would have been set in motion and driven by men running within the wheel like hamsters.

The last crypt you can visit is the **Chapelle St-Martin**, the twin of the Crypte des 30 Cierges. It has kept its pleasing 11th-century volumes, with its rounded apse end, known as a *cul de four* ('oven bottom'). Again, it was built to support the church above, but also served as the chapel of the dead. Pilgrims would have been allowed to come and pray here, unlike in the crypt chapel dedicated to the Virgin.

The Merveille

In addition to the church and its crypts, there was the monastery alongside. Most of the Romanesque one was destroyed during fighting, but the new monastery that King Philippe Auguste substantially financed became known as the **Merveille**, the Wonder, because of the staggering brilliance of its architecture. It is open to all visitors. It basically consists of two rooms on each of its three floors and rises on the northern side of the rock. On the top level, the **cloister** lies open to the skies. The delicate columns were made from English stone. You can spot the very few original ones, slightly eaten away by time. The patterned layout of the columns reflects a theme in the architecture of the Merveille; they are staggered diagonally, rather than being aligned.

The long **refectory** of the Merveille, located next to the cloister, is beautifully lit, but there are no direct views out from here. Instead, the diagonal line is used to make the light come in subtly and indirectly. The room would have been colourful during the medieval period, and the acoustics are musical and ringing. Slender columns and capitals attached to the window surrounds repeat themselves down the sides of the room. It is here that the monks would eat, while listening to readings from biblical or saintly works.

On the next level down, the two vast rooms are now known as the *salle des chevaliers* and the *salle des hôtes*. The ***salle des hôtes***, under the refectory, was where noble and prestigious pilgrims would have been received. They would also have eaten and slept here. Guests would first have been led to the side chapel of the great room, then they would take part in prayers of purification.

The room next door, referred to as the *salle des chevaliers*, is thought to have served in its time both as the abbey's chapterhouse and as its scriptorium, known also as a *chauffoir*. The famous Mont-St-Michel abbey manuscripts would have been prepared here. The north-facing windows would have provided a consistent light helpful for the copying and colouring work. The two vast fireplaces would have provided the warmth required not only for the monks' hands but also for heating the ink.

On the lowest level of the Merveille, the ordinary people would be received in the *aumônière*. Next door was the dark and massive **cellar**, used to store the mountains of provisions for the abbey and its pilgrims. A copy of Frémiet's statue of St Michael is displayed here; from so close up, he looks particularly mean and violent.

Other Tourist Sights on the Mount

Most of these sights inevitably lie along the Grande Rue, the main street that snakes up to the abbey entrance. Tucked into the rock to one side of the Grande Rue is the **church of St-Pierre**, the other serious religious stop on the mount. In fact, the rock actually puts in an appearance at the back of the benches. This charming building dates from the 15th and 16th centuries, with many decorative items of religious devotion added in the 19th. Joan of Arc stands at the entrance, and in the side chapel a bejewelled, metal-covered 19th-century St Michael looks stoical as he slays the dragon.

Back outside, take the arch under the apse, up past displayed tombstones, to the quiet cemetery. You can take the high path either to the abbey or round to the west from here, demonstrating that the Mont-St-Michel is not quite a one-street village.

The abbey can seem very cold and empty to children, and a tour of it long. The nearby **Archéoscope** offers them an appealing introduction, using a slick 20-minute presentation to explain how and why the abbey was built. Smoke, lights and videos bombard the senses. The commentary is only in French, but the splendid film footage, taken from a helicopter, can be appreciated by all.

By contrast, the **Musée Historique**, close to the stairs at the entrance to the abbey, is archaic, with a few very amusing elements, the most absurd being a tableau of the mount made of fragments of postage stamps. The tour ends with a short recorded historical commentary in a cavernous room full of waxworks. You come out of the museum to find yourself in the midst of a souvenir shop.

The **Maison de Tiphaine** is claimed to have been built by the Breton and French warrior Bertrand Du Guesclin (*see* p.108) for his wife Tiphaine to stay in while he was off warring. The tall, narrow house has a certain dilapidated charm, and it can sometimes provide a quieter corner in the chaos of the mount. At the four-floor **Musée Maritime** (close to the bottom of the Grande Rue), English-speaking visitors are given a taped commentary to listen to via headphones. Most of the displays are of model ships and boats. The succinct films explain the tides in the bay and its natural habitat, the problem of silting and possible solutions. The place also gives advice on walking across the bay. The museum ends in another souvenir shop.

At night, the Mont-St-Michel is gloriously lit up. In high season the abbey hosts a **son-et-lumière** show, **Les Imaginaires** (*selected nights in early May, and mid-May–Aug 10pm–1am, last adm midnight; Sept 9.30pm–midnight, no adm after 11pm, and verify* *showings for last few days of Sept*). This gives visitors the chance to look round the abbey at night – a deeply atmospheric experience. Within the great and more intimate spaces, artworks and pieces of music, many contemporary, add to the sense of occasion. You take this tour at your own pace, following the signs. Late at night, with fewer people around, the vast abbey can be distinctly eerie and Gothic in feel.

The Bay of Mont-St-Michel

Even without the Mont-St-Michel, the bay in which it stands would be mesmerizing enough. The whole bay is one of those places of rare beauty classified as a world heritage site by UNESCO. It is stunningly flat, which is why the Mont-St-Michel appears all the more imposing, and visible from such long distances. Not many visitors notice or know that the western, Breton side of the bay has its own forest – of wooden posts on which mussels are cultivated. Taking a tractor out onto the muddy sands and then walking through the thick gunge among the hundreds of thousands of wooden pillars makes for an unforgettable experience. You can take this trip from Cherrueix or Le Vivier-sur-Mer.

Inland from these two bayside villages, another mount rises out of the flat countryside. This is the Mont Dol, again affording fantastic views onto the bay. On the ridge behind it stands the severe cathedral of St-Samson at Dol. A few little museums are scattered around Dol, plus one of the very largest menhirs in Brittany. Back on the bay, the north Breton cliffs begin around Cancale. This popular resort is famed for the quality of its locally cultivated oysters.

Cherrueix, the nearest Breton community to the mount along the coast, actually lies some 30 kilometres distant from the magical site by road. But from the village's protective dyke, you can still make out the mount very clearly on good days. The little 17th-century chapel of Ste-Anne stands isolated on the dyke a little way east of the long-drawn-out village. From the chapel, keen walkers can follow the GR34 path across the polders to the mount, passing a row of disused windmills on the western edge of Cherrueix. From Cherrueix you can take an enjoyable tractor ride (**t** 02 99 48 84 88) out into the bay to see the mussels growing on their *bouchots*. But for the best place from which to take a tour of this amazing sandscape, go to the **Centre d'Animation de la Baie du Mont-St-Michel** at **Le Vivier-sur-Mer** (**t** 02 99 48 84 38) and reserve tickets for a trip out on the guided tour. Even if you don't speak French, you should enjoy the extraordinary journey, as well as the walk in the muddy sand of the bay.

The Bay's Measurements, Mussels and Other Vital Statistics

We slid in the warm mud, our feet sinking into it up to our ankles.

Flaubert

Can you see in your mind's eye 50,000 very muddy football pitches laid out side by side? That is apparently how many could be fitted into the 25,000 hectares of the bay of Mont-St-Michel. Geographically, the bay stretches from the Pointe de

Champeaux in Normandy to the Pointe du Grouin above Cancale. The waters withdraw as much as 25 kilometres with big tides, measured from the deepest point of the bay in Brittany. The bay has the fastest-moving tides in Europe, coming in at around nine kilometres an hour. Every year tragedies occur because of people who don't heed the warnings about these treacherous waters. What marine life might you see if you take a tractor trip from Cherrueix? Certainly artificially grown mussels galore. The flat oysters, the *plates*, by contrast, were native to the area, but now the

Getting Around

If you don't have a car, you can use the **bus** services from St-Malo to explore this region (*see* St-Malo, p.131, for coach company details).

Tourist Information

Dol-de-Bretagne: 3 Grande Rue des Stuarts, **t** 02 99 48 15 37, *www.pays-de-dol.com*.
Cancale: 44 Rue du Port, **t** 02 99 89 63 72, *www.ville-cancale.fr*.

Market Days

Dol-de-Bretagne: Saturday.
St-Méloir-des-Ondes: Thursday (also Mon–Fri 9.30–10.30am Sipefel traders' market)
Cancale: Sunday.

Where to Stay and Eat

Roz-sur-Couesnon

Mme Gillet, Val-St-Revert, **t** 02 99 80 27 57 (*inexpensive*). A B&B guesthouse with superb views out on to the bay of Mont-St-Michel.
M. Piel, La Poultière, La Bergerie, **t** 02 99 80 29 68, *www.france-bonjour.com/la-bergerie* (*inexpensive*). A good-quality B&B.

Cherrueix

This is an excellent place for cheap B&Bs.
Manoir La Pichardière, 172 La Pichardière, close to the Chapelle Ste-Anne, **t** 02 99 48 83 82 (*inexpensive*). Neat rooms in a peaceful former farmyard.
Lair Chambre d'Hôte, **t** 02 99 48 01 65 (*inexpensive*). Good-quality B&B rooms.
Les Trois Cheminées, 110 Route de Ste-Anne, **t** 02 99 48 93 54 (*inexpensive*).Basic rooms, some with sea views.

La Hamelinais, **t** 02 99 48 95 26 (*inexpensive*). A lovely farmhouse belonging to a charming couple who administer tea and extras. Rooms are in the main part of the house or at the back through a separate entrance. A family room is available.

Le Vivier-sur-Mer ✉ 35960

★★Beau Rivage, 21 Rue de la Mairie, **t** 02 99 48 90 65, *contact@beau-rivage.fr* (*inexpensive*). A bright place with clean rooms.
★★Hôtel de Bretagne, 23 Rue de la Mairie, **t** 02 99 48 91 74, *bretvivier@wanadoo.fr* (*inexpensive*). A hotel in an excellent location by the bay, with a dining room with great views if fairly ordinary food.

Dol-de-Bretagne ✉ 35120

M. et Mme Rênting, Haute Lande, **t** 02 99 48 07 02, *renting@wanadoo.fr* (*expensive*). A B&B in an old manor house 3km from Dol.
★★Grand Hotel de la Gare, 21 Avenue Aristide Biand, **t** 02 99 48 00 (*inexpensive*). A simple, cheap hotel with refurbished rooms.
La Grabotais, 4 Rue Ceinte, **t** 02 99 48 19 89 (*moderate*). A good 16th-century timberframe restaurant with a characterful interior, serving fish specialities and meats grilled on a wood fire. *Closed Mon.*
Grill-Crêperie Le Plédran, 30 Grand'Rue des Stuarts, **t** 02 99 48 40 80 (*inexpensive*). Delicious crêpes served in one of Dol's splendid old houses, plus a selection of meats grilled over the big fireplace. *Closed Mon and Thur eves.*

Baguer-Morvan ✉ 35120

Ferme-Manoir Halouze, **t** 02 99 48 07 46 (*inexpensive*). Delightful B&B accommodation in a modest 14th-century manor house a few kilometres southwest of Dol-de-Bretagne. *Table d'hôte* is available.

much more viable *creuses* are shipped in from far afield. Cockles, razorshells or razorclams, green crabs (which are inedible), orange sponges, and red and green sea lettuce are all fairly common here. The *crépidules* are all too prolific, causing a big problem in the bay now. You may come across little transparent langoustines wriggling in the mud, or even the tiny beginnings of lobsters. As well as gulls you can spot teal, sandpipers and crested lapwing in the bay; in winter thousands of geese stop here.

Manoir de Launay-Blot, south of Baguer-Morvan, **t** 02 99 48 07 48, *launay-blot@cergiv.cernet.fr* (*inexpensive*). B&B accommodation in a charming if slightly ungroomed 17th-century setting. *Table d'hôte* meals are available with advance booking.

Roz-Landrieux ✉ 35120
Manoir de la Grande-Mettrie, t 02 99 48 29 21 (*inexpensive*). A manor house a short way west of Dol-de-Bretagne offering B&B and *table d'hôte*.

La Boussac ✉ 35120
Moulin du Brégain, t 02 99 80 05 29 (*inexpensive*). A selection of pretty B&B rooms set in an old mill to the southeast of Dol-de-Bretagne.

St-Méloir-des-Ondes ✉ 35350
Mme Boutier, Le Pont-Prin, **t** 02 99 89 13 05 (*inexpensive*). Smart B&B accommodation on a farm.

Cancale ✉ 35260
★★★★Maisons de Bricourt, t 02 99 89 64 76, *www.maisons-de-bricourt.com* (*expensive–luxury*). One of the very best hotels in northern Brittany, owned by one of the finest chefs in the whole of France and divided between three locations: the **Le Relais Gourmand** dining room is set in the 18th-century *malouinière*, where renowned chef Olivier Roellinger conjures up such dishes as spicy John Dory *Retour des Iles*; some of the older hotel rooms are in **La Petite Maison** near the restaurant, with good views from the heights; and the other luxurious rooms are south of town in the **Château de Richeux**, with its smart and more reasonably priced bistro-style restaurant, **Le Bistrot Marin Le Coquillage**.

★★L'Emeraude, 7 Quai Administrateur Thomas, **t** 02 99 89 61 76 (*inexpensive*). Stylish rooms in several locations in town, most on the quayside, plus a chic restaurant.

L'Huîtrière, 14 Quai Gambetta, **t** 02 99 89 75 05 (*inexpensive*). Bright, modern little rooms and good-value menus.

Le Surcouf, 7 Quai Gambetta, **t** 02 99 89 61 75 (*expensive*). Excellent seasonal dishes. *Closed Wed and Thurs exc July and Aug.*

Le St-Cast, Route de la Corniche, **t** 02 99 89 66 08 (*moderate–expensive*). A conservatory dining room with views on to the southern part of Cancale's port, though the delicious seafood specialities and platters will distract you from outside. *Closed low season Tues, Wed and Sun eves, July and Aug Wed.*

Ty Breiz, 13 Quai Gambetta, **t** 02 99 89 60 26 (*moderate*). Good, simple seafood dishes served on a port-side terrace or in the deeply rustic interior. *Closed Tues eve and Wed.*

Around Cancale
★★Hôtel de la Pointe du Grouin, t 02 99 89 60 55, *www.hotelpointedugrouin.com* (*moderate*). A hotel with a location to die for, on the headland looking across Mont-St-Michel bay. It's a bit expensive for a two-star, but it's worth paying a bit extra for a room (and dining room) with such a romantic view.

M. and Mme Dragonne, Grande Randonnée, Lavieuville, **t** 02 23 15 19 30, *dragonne. promotion@wanadoo.fr* (*moderate*). A B&B in an 18th-century building with a pool.

★★Le Châtellier, 1km west of Cancale along the main inland D355 road towards St-Malo, **t** 02 99 89 81 84, *www.hotelchatellier.com* (*inexpensive*). A converted family farm resembling a comfortable modern Breton home, run by a charming couple.

Farmers have been exploiting this environment for a good long time. The first dykes around the bay date as far back as the 12th century. They protected the fishing villages on the bay's edge and the agricultural land behind. Once the tractor journey has taken you out some five kilometres into the bay, you are first shown some of the old fishing methods using fences made out of tressed branches.

Mussel-farming began here in 1954. The descendants of the two families who began this trade have a stranglehold on production and have planted 300 kilometres or so of wooden pillars in the mud. *Moules de bouchot* is a sign you will probably see on many restaurant menus in Brittany, generally taken as a sign of good-quality mussels. A *bouchot* is 110 posts planted in a line along 100 metres. The mussels are brought up first in the Charente-Maritime on France's western Atlantic coast. The *naissins* or spats are transported here after a few months of growth and attach themselves to the oak supports. They dine on phytoplankton and are left to mature undisturbed for 14–22 months. They are only harvested once they have grown to 3.5 centimetres in length or more. Leviathans, part-tractor, part-boat, drive out into the bay to pick the mussels for the insatiable tourists. The monstrous machines' claw is a kind of hydraulic arm that sucks up the creatures. Up to 15,000 tonnes can be harvested each year. The quality of the mussels from the bay is highly regarded and local farmers hope to be granted an *appellation d'origine contrôlée*, a sure indicator of quality.

Le Mont-Dol

South from Le Vivier-sur-Mer, the granite mount emerging from the flat landscape is the Mont-Dol, an island stranded on dry land but once surrounded by sand and sea like the Mont-St-Michel. The landscapes are bucolic, but picnickers and photographers take over in summer. Palaeolithic remains of mammoths, deer and other creatures were found in digs here, and 19th-century Christianity left its mark – a tall white Virgin stands at the top of the narrow-staired tower, which visitors fight to climb up for a marginally better view. The tale goes that St Michael was called upon to fight Satan in this spot. The marks of their legendary struggle can supposedly be seen in some of the rocks, if you have a good imagination: the devil's claws, the devil's seat and the devil's hole are among the evocative names they were given. There's also the imprint of St Michael's foot, left behind when he took an almighty leap back onto the Mont-St-Michel after victory. The chapel on the Mont Dol contains a stained-glass window in honour of survivors of the First World War who made a pilgrimage here.

Dol-de-Bretagne

I dwell among scorpions, surrounded by a double wall of bestiality and perfidy.
Baudry of Bourgueil, Archbishop of Dol from 1107 to 1130

Dol-de-Bretagne looks like an innocent little tourist and shopping town, and it is hard to imagine the debauchery that perturbed Baudry of Bourgueil. It became the seat of one of the early Breton bishoprics when British immigrants came across the Channel in the Dark Ages to settle and spread Celtic Christianity (*see* box, opposite).

Samson and Dol

The seeds were sown, it is said, by a 6th-century Welshman called Samson. Something of his life is known from an 11th-century manuscript that survived down the centuries. According to the story, the young Samson was sent to the great Welsh abbey of Llantwit Major, run by Illtut. Educated in the ways of the Celtic Church, he fast acquired enviable knowledge, to the extent that Illtut's nephews became so jealous of him that he left. Samson went on to become the very model of a Celtic Christian missionary, travelling far and wide to spread the gospel. He first went to Caldey Island in Wales, where he became abbot. Then he crossed to Ireland and reformed a monastery there. After that, he spent a period as a hermit living close to the Severn river, before taking on the position of abbot in a nearby monastery. This restless evangelizer continued on to Cornwall. There he settled for a longer period. His disciples included Austell, Mewan and Winnow – important figures in the Cornish Church. One of the Isles of Scilly is named after Samson.

His ceaseless quest took him on, like many other Welsh evangelizers of the time, to Brittany. The Breton story of Samson has it that he was donated land by the local lord of Dol-de-Bretagne by way of thanks for curing the nobleman's wife of leprosy and exorcizing demons that had been plaguing the man's daughter.

History

Breton tradition holds that it was in Dol that Nomenoë had himself crowned the first Breton king in 850, having replaced all previously appointed Breton bishops with his choices. Serious historians now say there is no firm evidence that this crowning took place, but Nomenoë's election of Breton bishops is attested, and it did secure the Breton Church a good degree of independence, which it kept for some time.

Despite the clearly unhappy words of Baudry de Bourgueil quoted opposite, Dol remained a significant religious centre right up to the Revolution. The cathedral was always an important halt on the **Tro Breizh**, the major pilgrimage route to the cathedrals of the seven founding Celtic Christian saints of Brittany (*see* p.32). At the end of Dol's long line of bishops, Monseigneur de Hercé was shot during the Revolution, and in 1801 the city lost its bishopric for good.

Dol, so close to the border with Normandy, suffered wave after wave of sieges in the Middle Ages. William the Conqueror, Duke of Normandy as well as King of England, had a go at it three times without success, the Bretons backed by the might of the French Carolingians. King John of England's troops burned down the Romanesque cathedral in 1204. Much later, the Catholic, royalist, anti-Revolutionary Chouans put up a fierce resistance to the Republican army in Dol during the Revolution. Victor Hugo imagined the terrible detail of a battle in which thousands died in his book *Quatre-vingt-treize*.

A Tour of Dol

Once situated by the sea, as its cliff edge indicates, the town now overlooks the Marais de Dol, the reclaimed marshlands left when the water retreated. Some historians claim that the waves still lapped at the city's feet as late as the 10th century. Dol's severe, miserable hulk of a cathedral sulks to one side of town, looking out mournfully over the Marais. The **Grande Rue des Stuarts**, however, lined with some surprisingly old and quirky medieval houses, has a cheerful appearance. Some of the townhouses of Dol date back to before the present cathedral was built. The best ones line the main street, which Victor Hugo compared to a wide river fed by the little streams of its sidestreets. Look out for characteristic arches of the Romanesque period. Once this high street would have been lined with arcades, but these have now been glassed off and turned into delightful shopfronts.

The austere **cathedral of St-Samson**, set in rather bleak surrounds, looks so defensive that it doesn't even come as much of a surprise to find what look like crenellations on the north side of the choir. The main façade of the cathedral is unprepossessing, with virtually no decoration. However, one ugly male gargoyle does stand out, said by townspeople to be a likeness of the detested King John, whose men destroyed the previous cathedral. On the south side, a Flamboyant Gothic porch sticks out, covered with some incongruous white panels carved with low-relief sculptures; these were only added in the early 19th century, and are the work of Jean Boucher. The smaller neighbouring porch dates from the 13th and 14th centuries; its central column is decorated with hearts, in a playful pun on the name of one bishop, Etienne Coeuret – *coeur* being the French for heart.

As you enter the cathedral, striking 13th-century stained glass gives colour to the distant apse. The edifice is almost 100 metres in length. The great long nave is held up by columns made up of gathered shafts, and the decoration of the pillars is typical of Norman Gothic style. The choir was completed around 1280. The stained glass of the main window, the oldest such glass to have survived in Brittany, is admirable, if much restored. The medallions running along each lancet tell the story of a saint or biblical figure. Try to see the ornate 14th-century choir stalls with their carved heads. In the transept the tomb of Bishop Thomas James counts as one of the earliest works in French Renaissance style to be found in Brittany. The bishop, who died in 1504, apparently developed a taste for Italian art, and commissioned the Justi brothers, Italian sculptors working in the Loire Valley, to prepare this sumptuous tomb for him.

By the cathedral, the **Cathédralscope** (*open daily May–Sept 10–7, Oct–Dec and Feb–April 10–6; open high season Wed until 11pm*) offers a comprehensive history of cathedrals in Europe, including the symbolic meaning of their architecture and the lives of the men who inhabited them.

Head south down the D795 just out of town and you soon come to the **Menhir de Champ-Dolent**, one of the most impressive neolithic standing stones in Brittany; it is made of pinkish granite and rises to almost 10 metres in height. Legend says that this rock fell from the skies to separate two feuding brothers engaged in a bloody battle. The menhir is slowly sinking into the ground; when the stone disappears altogether, the world will end, so the typical Breton legend goes.

A few kilometres southwest out of Dol, the **Musée de la Paysannerie** to the east of Baguer-Morvan (*open 10–7, May, June and Sept Mon and Thurs, July and Aug daily*) recalls the rural Breton life of the past, with presentations of traditional crafts and old agricultural implements.

To Cancale

The main coast road running from Le Vivier-sur-Mer to Cancale hugs the flat shore, passing a number of abandoned windmills and stalls where you can taste mussels and purchase local garlic. It takes you through **St-Benoît-des-Ondes**, an old village built right by the bay, and busy **St-Méloir-des-Ondes**, which gets packed out with local potatoes and cauliflowers as well as tourists in season, as professionals come to buy the much-vaunted vegetables of these parts. After St-Méloir, the road climbs towards Cancale.

In front of **Cancale's port**, the **Port de la Houle**, oysters packed tight into their bags grow until they're big enough for the tourists, packed tight as sardines in the town's restaurants, to eat them. Cancale is a victim of its own success in the main holiday period. Here, the problem is exacerbated because the portside is simply made up of a narrow strip of houses backing on to cliffs. But sitting among the crowds, looking past the flat-bottomed oyster boats and across the vast expanse of the bay to the Mont-St-Michel, it's hard not to appreciate the glory of the sight.

On the one-way road down to the harbour from the south of Cancale you can visit the **Ferme Marine** (*open mid-June–mid-Sept for daily guided tours: English tour at 2, French tours at 11, 3 and 5; mid-Feb–Oct for French tours only, Mon and Fri at 3; groups by arrangement, t 02 99 89 69 99*). The tour of this oyster farm on the slopes of the Cancale cliffs gives visitors an insight into how the supposedly aphrodisiac shellfish are reared.

In the mid 16th century, Cancale was granted special privileges for supplying the French court with oysters, and until the late 1780s anyone was permitted to drag up the much-sought-after shells from the seabed here. In 1787 a royal edict put a stop to this free-for-all. To protect the oysters' reproduction, catching them was forbidden between April and mid-September. The oyster population continued to dwindle, so that from 1920 the Cancalais had to turn to modern methods and rear them in a carefully controlled manner. The *huîtres plates,* or flat oysters, have been almost completely replaced by the *huîtres creuses,* concave ones.

In the times when the oyster-fishing season was firmly set, the first day of the new season was a time of great excitement in Cancale. The *bisquines* (the type of light Normandy-designed sailing boat that the local fishermen used from the 19th century onwards) would rush out to sea to drag up oysters in their nets. A limited number of visitors can go on trips on a *bisquine, La Cancalaise,* that still operates today. You have to join its association first, which costs around 60 euros (*t 02 99 89 77 87*).

The main livelihood for the men of Cancale came for a long time from joining the fishing fleets that went off for many long months to catch cod off the coast of Newfoundland. The Cancalaises, the women of the port, gained a reputation for being tough creatures, as they had to run their own communities for much of the year and to deal with the all too frequent news of deaths at sea. Jeanne Jugan, who was born into a typical Cancale fishing family, went on to create the charitable order of the Petites Soeurs des Pauvres (Little Sisters of the Poor) to look after the elderly who found themselves without means of support. Her order spread around the world, and in 1982 she was beatified by the pope. The **Maison Natale de Jeanne Jugan** in the upper town has been turned into a small museum to her memory (*open by appointment, t 02 99 89 62 73*).

Many shipowners built their smart houses in the upper town in the 18th century. The church dedicated to St Méen, the possible founder of the original village here, was converted into the **Musée des Arts et Traditions Populaires** (*open July and Aug Mon 2.30–6.30, Tue–Sun 10–12 and 2.30–6.30; June and Sept Fri–Mon 2.30–6.30*). The Romanesque form had already been renovated in the 18th century. Inside the museum, the harrowing fishing expeditions to Newfoundland are recalled in detail, as well as a number of old Cancale customs.

Two rocks lie out to sea just to the north of Cancale, the **Rocher de Cancale** and the **Ile des Rimains**; the latter was fortified after Cancale came under bombardment by the British fleet in 1779. North from Cancale, the pretty little bays before the Pointe du Grouin are worth seeking out. Just before this dramatic headland, **Port-Mer** boasts the first sandy beach along Brittany's north coast. From one of the several bars and restaurants here you can admire the sun setting on the Mont-St-Michel, now a tiny speck of rock in the distance. At Port-Mer you really start to feel you have reached the Breton seaside.

From the rocky **Pointe du Grouin**, you get spectacular views east and west. This headland closes off the bay of Mont-St-Michel on its western side. **L'Ile des Landes**, with its scaly dragon's back, adds its mystery to the foreground as you look across towards Normandy. It was turned into a bird reserve by the Breton Society for the Protection of the Natural Environment (the SEPNB), which adapted a Nazi bunker on the mainland into an information centre on the natural world here. Great cormorants particularly appreciate the Ile des Landes, and you may manage to spot the colony of dolphins that come fishing for mackerel off the Pointe du Grouin in summer. When the tide is out, you can climb down to the grotto that looks out onto the Iles des Landes and the Herpin lighthouse.

Westwards from the Pointe du Grouin, a handful of further dark rocky headlands stretch their rough fingers out into the sea. A number of sandy beaches lie in the protected bays between them. The **Chapelle du Verger**, which overlooks the largest of the beaches in the parish of Cancale, contains a variety of ex-votos of boats hanging from the ceiling; they were donated by fishermen who went off to Newfoundland and managed to make it back from the brink of disaster. From this side of Cancale, their wives would come and watch the fleet heading west on its way off to those dreaded expeditions.

The **Anse Du Guesclin** with its long, fine, sandy beach and its rock pools may look like an idyllic holiday spot now, but the island, cut off by high tides, has been fortified since the early Middle Ages. The ramparts that you see today date from 1757, and were put up to guard against attack by the British. This bay inspired the poet Théophile Briant and the poetic French singer Leo Ferré. The latter even came to live in the Fort Du Guesclin for a time in the 1960s, accompanied by his pet monkey Pépée. The French author Colette particularly loved this stretch of Brittany's Emerald Coast too (*see box, opposite*).

Erotic Orangeade

Colette, one of the most sensual writers in French literature, came frequently to stay on the coast between Cancale and St-Malo, at Roz-Ven east of the Pointe du Meinga. She set one of her most evocative and erotic books here, *Le Blé en herbe* (*Corn on the Blade*), a still shocking tale of a pure childhood summer friendship changing in nature as two adolescents discover their sexuality. Her prose is certainly at its most caressing in *Le Blé en herbe*, and reading this book on a winter's day you will immediately be transported to summer on the north Breton coast, from the very first paragraph when Vinca goes off fishing in rock pools in her 'espadrilles racornies par le sel' ('espadrilles curled by salt').

St-Malo and the Clos Poulet

Le rocher ('the rock') is the surprisingly plain way the inhabitants of St-Malo, the Malouins, refer to their magnificently arrogant walled old city, the *ville intra-muros*. But the city that you see isn't actually old. During the Second World War, the town was reduced almost entirely to rubble by Allied bombing in 1944; it destroyed 80 per cent of the buildings within the old ramparts. In June 1971, a stone cross was placed at the top of the cathedral of St-Vincent to symbolize the completion of St-Malo's long reconstruction. It has re-emerged as one of the great cities in France.

The walled city certainly looks both noble and defensively aloof as you arrive. The many-storeyed mansion blocks in austere grey granite peer haughtily over the stupendous ramparts, while inviting golden-sanded beaches spread at their feet at low tide. The Clos Poulet, the stocky, wider promontory on which St-Malo is located, is full of interesting tourist sights. The great Malouin merchants built their country homes, the *malouinières*, across this area.

History

Aleth Before St-Malo

Ignore St-Malo for a moment. The very early action took place west of the walled rock, at Aleth (or Alet) close by. Aleth has been subsumed by St-Servan in modern times; this town is now joined to St-Malo by urban sprawl. Aleth was formed to guard the entrance to the estuary of the Rance river; the Celtic Coriosolitae built a port here, active by the 1st century BC. These men traded with southern Britain and with the Channel Islands, and erected a substantial promontory fort, one of the very few major pre-Roman urban settlements to have been found in Brittany. With the Roman conquest of Gaul, the main Coriosolitae town became Corseul, inland up the Rance, near Dinan. Towards the end of the Roman Empire, as tribes from the east moved into Gaul, Aleth became an important fortified Gallo-Roman site. Around 350, a *castellum* protected the peninsula with sturdy walls, a few fragments of which remain. Because of its defensive qualities, Aleth gained considerably in importance; an early bishopric was established, and the first cathedral was built possibly around 380. With the subsequent arrival of immigrants from across the Channel, this Christian centre

St-Malo

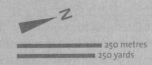

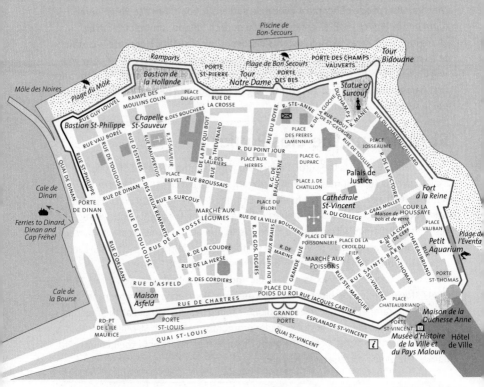

Piscine de Bon-Secours

Ramparts
Môle des Noires
Plage du Môle
PORTE DU MÔLE
Bastion de la Hollande
PORTE ST-PIERRE
Plage de Bon Secours
Tour Notre Dame
PORTE DES BÉS
PORTE DES CHAMPS VAUVERTS
Tour Bidouane
Statue of Surcouf

Bastion St-Philippe
RUE GUY LOUVEL
RAMPE DES MOULINS COLIN
PLACE DU GUET
RUE DE LA CROSSE
R. DES BOUCHERS
Chapelle St-Sauveur
RUE DU BOYER
R. STE-ANNE
R. DE LA CLOCHE
R. DUCHAMPS
RUE GROUT
RUE DE ST-GEORGES
R. MANET
RUE DU CHÂTEAUGUILLARD

RUE VAU BOREL
RUE DE TOULOUSE
R. ST-SAUVEUR
R. DE LA PIE QUI BOIT
R. THEVENARD
R. DU POINT JOUR
PLACE DES FRERES LAMENNAIS
RUE DE TOUILLIES
PLACE JOSSEAUME
RUE DE LA VICTOIRE

Bastion St-Philippe
RUE ST-PHILIPPE
RUE VAU BOREL
RUE D'ESTREES
R. MAUPERTUIS
R. DES LAURIERS
RUE
PLACE AUX HERBES
PLACE G. DUPARC
Palais de Justice
Fort á la Reine

Cale de Dinan
QUAI DE DINAN
PLACE BREVET
RUE BROUSSAIS
R. G. DE BEAUCHESNE
PLACE J. DE CHATILLON

Ferries to Dinard, Dinan and Cap Fréhel
PORTE DE DINAN
R. DES VIEUX REMPARTS
RUE R. SURCOUF
Cathédrale St-Vincent
R. DU COLLEGE
R. GRAS MOLLET
COUR LA HOUSSAYE
Maison de bois et de verre
PLACE VAUBAN
Plage de l'Eventa

RUE DE DINAN
MARCHÉ AUX LÉGUMES
PLACE DU PILORI
R. DE LA CORNE DE CERF
Petit Aquarium

RUE D'ORLEANS
RUE DE TOULOUSE
RUE DE LA FOSSE
R. DE CDS. DEGRES
RUE DE LA VILLE BOUCHERIE
PLACE DE LA POISSONNERIE
PLACE DE LA CROIX DU FIEF
R. DE LA CORNE DE CERF
RUE CHATEAUBRIAND
PORTE ST-THOMAS

Cale de la Bourse
R. DE LA COUDRE
RUE DE LA HERSE
R. DES MARINS
GRANDE RUE
RUE STE-BARBE
RUE ST-THOMAS
MARCHÉ AUX POISSONS
R. DU PUITS AUX BRAIES
RUE SAINTE-MARGUE
RUE S/ST-VINCENT
RUE STE-MARGUER

RUE D'ASFELD
R. DES CORDIERS
PLACE DU POIDS DU ROI
RUE JACQUES CARTIER
PLACE CHATEAUBRIAND

RD-PT DE L'ÎLE MAURICE
Maison Asfeld
PORTE ST-LOUIS
RUE DE CHARTRES
GRANDE PORTE
ESPLANADE ST-VINCENT
PORTE ST-VINCENT
Maison de la Duchesse Anne

QUAI ST-LOUIS
QUAI ST-VINCENT
Musée d'Histoire de la Ville et du Pays Malouin
Hôtel de Ville

250 metres
250 yards

thrived. Although an Irish hermit, Aaron, got here before him, the man who most left his mark was called Malo (or was it Maclou, or MacLow?), who came from Britain in the 6th century. Malo became bishop of Aleth and a miracle worker. Aleth continued to be a lively centre until the Vikings came to lay waste to it. A new cathedral was built early in the 9th century, but a third one had to be constructed after the Norsemen wrought their destruction. The ruins of this 10th-century church are still easily visible and quite impressive.

The Attention Switches to St-Malo

In the ensuing centuries, the urban, commercial attention would move from Aleth to the rock to the north, people perhaps encouraged to move to its safety with the Viking raids. In the 8th century, the remains of St Malo had been brought back to the area where he had served the Church. The island became known as St-Malo-en-l'Isle. It was only joined to the mainland by a *sillon*, a strip of sand.

The man who is considered to be the principal developer of medieval St-Malo is Jean de Chatillon, also known as Jean de la Grille. Elected bishop in 1143, he took on the power of the Benedictines on the rock and sent them packing.

A new cathedral went up in his time, and he also had the rock defended by solid ramparts, which enclosed 16 hectares of ground. Great mastiffs were brought from England, and the tradition of these terrifying guards being let out at night to roam the strands continued up to the 18th century. In 1230, the duke of Brittany gave the

Getting There

Brittany Ferries (local number for enquiries, t 02 99 40 64 41) runs **ferries** between Portsmouth and St-Malo. There are also ships to and from the Channel Isles and Poole by Condor, t 02 99 20 03 00, and Emeraude Jersey Ferries, t 08 25 16 51 80.

The nearest **airport** to St-Malo is Dinard-Pleurtuit, on the western side of the Rance, t 02 99 46 18 46, serviced by flights from London with Ryanair.

St-Malo is slightly awkward to reach by **train** – you have to change at Rennes. The trip from Paris takes around 3hrs, with the change.

Getting Around

The walled city is surrounded by paying (in summer) **car** parks, most of them allowing you to stop for irritatingly short periods of time. In high summer, it's a real fight to find a space. The long avenues heading down to Paramé can be a good place to park, with some stretches of free parking.

For **bus** services, there's a central *gare routière* on the Esplanade St-Vincent outside the Porte St-Vincent. For local bus information, call t 02 99 56 06 06.

If you want to explore the surrounding area by **coach**, Les Courriers Bretons (t 02 99 19 70 80), and the Compagnie Armoricaine de Transport (t 02 96 39 21 05) run services to a variety of destinations.

Tourist Information

St-Malo: Esplanade St-Vincent, t 02 99 56 64 48, *www.ville-saint-malo.fr*.

Market Days
St-Malo intra-muros: Tuesday and Friday.
Paramé: Wednesday and Saturday.
St-Servan: Tuesday.
Rocabey: Monday, Thursday and Saturday.

Festivals

Etonnants Voyageurs is an international travel-writing festival held in May/June.
Folklore du Monde, in mid-July, celebrates folklore from around the world.
Fête du Nautisme held mid-May.
Le Solidor en Peinture is an artists' gathering at the end of June.
Festival de Musique Sacrée is for classical music lovers from mid-July to mid-August.
Promenades Littéraires, a programme of literary walks, takes place in July and Aug.
La Route du Rock is a rock festival that takes place in mid-August.
Quai des Bulles is the second biggest strip cartoon festival in France, held at the end of October.

Where to Stay

St-Malo Intra-Muros
The most exciting place to stay is within the historic walls of the old city. This is the centre of the action – vibrant and characterful, although relatively expensive and, in summer, crowded and often noisy.

Expensive
***Hotel des Abers, 10 Rue de la Corne de Cerf, t 02 99 40 85 60, *www.abershotel.com*. Flash rooms and an Indonesian restaurant where you would least expect one, just north of the Place de la Croix du Fief.
***Hôtel Elizabeth, 2 Rue des Cordiers, t 02 99 56 24 98, *www.st-malo-hotel-elizabeth.com*. A small luxury hotel within the ramparts, with a late-16th-century façade behind which lie stylish little apartments.

Moderate
***Central, 6 Grande Rue, t 02 99 40 87 70, *centralbus@wanadoo.fr*. Part of the reliable Best Western chain, with varied decoration in the rooms, some of which are *expensive*.

port a great number of trading privileges. That same year, troops of King Henry III of England landed in St-Malo, sent on an expedition to Brittany. However, under the French king Louis IX, or Saint Louis, St-Malo crews took part in the defeat of the English fleet down by Bayonne.

★★Anne de Bretagne, 10 Rue St-Thomas, t 02 99 56 18 00. A simple, completely refurbished option with a pleasant bar.

★★Le Bristol Union, 4 Place de la Poissonnerie, t 02 99 40 83 36, *www.hotel-bristol-union. com*. A slightly old-fashioned but reasonably good-value choice.

★★Hôtel France/Chateaubriand, Place Chateaubriand, t 02 99 56 66 52, *www.hotel.fr.chateaubriand.com*.
The most visible hotel in the city, with the crowds milling around it spilling on to its almost irresistible café terrace. The place certainly has character, but it isn't cheap for a two-star hotel.

★★Le Louvre, 2 Rue des Marins, t 02 99 40 86 62, *contact@hoteldulouvre-stmalo.com*.
A stylish family-run hotel located just off the Grande Rue, offering guests a buffet brunch. Some of the bedrooms can sleep up to 7 people, and some of them look out over a courtyard.

★★Univers, 14 Place Chateaubriand, t 02 99 40 89 52, *univershotel@hotmail.com*.
The other obvious hotel on the busiest St-Malo square, with its fair share of character, an excellent restaurant, and the well-known Bar de l'Univers below.

Inexpensive

★★Le Nautilus, 9 Rue de la Corne de Cerf, t 02 99 40 42 27, *www.lenautilus.com*.
A brightly painted option with a loud bar, making it a draw for the younger crowd. Situated off the Rue Sainte-Barbe and just a few steps away from the beach, it has several very cheerful little rooms, but avoid those on the first floor if you want a good night's sleep.

★★Hôtel du Palais, 8 Rue Toullier, t 02 99 40 07 30. A small and characterful hotel set in a quieter area up the hill.

★★Hôtel Porte St-Pierre, 2 Place du Guet, t 02 99 40 91 27, *www.hotel-porte-stpierre.com*.
A popular old-style hotel-cum-restaurant near the beach.

★★Pomme d'Or, 4 Place du Poids du Roi, t 02 99 40 90 24, *lapommedor@wanadoo.fr*.
This hotel, well located by the Grande Porte, will satisfy any hankering you may have for rooms with a vivid floral aesthetic.

You can find a variety of cheap options well outside the ramparts and the city centre close to the railway station, but the area is not particularly charming.

Eating Out

The road beginning with La Duchesse Anne, Rue Jacques Cartier, has a string of very touristy restaurants on the left, all covering the Breton favourites, including seafood, and offering their own specialities.

Brigitte et Didier Delaunay, 6 Rue Sainte-Barbe, t 02 99 40 92 46, (*expensive*). An established family-run restaurant renowned for its very fresh dishes, accompanied in season by fine local vegetables. The décor is fairly formal. *Closed Sun–Mon out of season.*

La Duchesse Anne, Place Guy La Chambre, by the Porte St-Vincent, t 02 99 40 85 33 (*expensive*). A classic Malouin restaurant set within the thick town ramparts. *Closed Wed and Mon eves, and Sun eve out of season.*

Le Chalut, 8 Rue de la Corne de Cerf (near Rue Sainte-Barbe), t 02 99 56 71 58 (*moderate–expensive*). A posh restaurant popular with local fish lovers, offering renderings of treats such as *poêlée de St Pierre filet* with chanterelles and a sauce pressed from langoustines. Reservations are essential. *Closed Mon and Tues lunch, and Tues eve out of season.*

Le Borgnefesse, 10 Rue du Puits aux Braies, t 02 99 40 05 05 (*moderate*). A traditional restaurant run, as its absurd name suggests, by a bit of a character (and local hero), who is full of tales of St-Malo. There's a very warm welcome but this is not a place for the timid. Reservations are essential. *Closed Sun, and Sat and Mon lunch.*

The religious and secular authorities would often take opposing sides in the course of St-Malo's history. A secular council was established in St-Malo from 1308, but the Church would continue to control justice here until 1513. The Breton War of Succession in 1341 split the city; the bishopric supported the French-backed

Crêperie du Corps de Garde, 3 Montée Notre-Dame, t 02 99 40 91 46 (*moderate*). A crêperie set in an old observation post on the ramparts.

Crêperie Brigantine, 13 Rue de Dinan (continuation of Rue Broussais), t 02 99 56 82 82 (*inexpensive*). One of the more charming crêperies in town, with walls covered with photos of classic sailing ships.

Where to Stay and Eat

Towards Paramé and Rothéneuf

There are many excellent hotels looking out onto the great arc of a beach leading east from the walled city.

★★★★**Grand Hôtel des Thermes**, 100 Boulevard Hébert, Courtoisville, t 02 99 40 75 00, *www. thalassotherapie.com* (*moderate–luxury*). The grandest option, with a thalassotherapy centre, swimming pool and gym. Very elaborate dishes are served up in its Art Deco dining room, but the cheapest *menu* is relatively good value.

★★★**Le Beaufort**, 25 Chaussée du Sillon, t 02 99 40 99 99, *www.hotel-beaufort.com* (*expensive–very expensive*). A hotel closer to the old city, with several of its modern-style rooms boasting a private terrace looking out to sea, plus a restaurant with a sea view.

★★★**Hôtel Alba**, 17 Rue des Dunes, Courtoisville, t 02 99 40 37 18, *www.hotelalba.com* (*expensive*). A delightful, neat white villa, with a few rooms with sea terraces.

★★★**La Villefromoy**, 7 Boulevard Hébert, Rochebonne, t 02 99 40 92 20, *www. villefromoy.fr* (*moderate–expensive*). A small hotel, with some rooms with sea views in a refined 19th-century townhouse, and suites in a very comfortable annexe by the garden.

★**Les Charmettes**, 64 Boulevard Hébert, Courtoisville, t 02 99 56 07 31 (*inexpensive*). A clean option with just a few rooms looking out to sea.

Le Neptune, 21 Rue de l'Industrie, t 02 99 56 82 15 (*inexpensive*). A bargain option for student travellers.

Auberge de Jeunesse, 37 Avenue du R. P. Umbricht, t 02 99 40 29 80, *www.fuaj.org* (*inexpensive*). The youth hostel, located to the south of Paramé.

St-Servan

This is the best area if you want to be close to the ferry terminal.

★★★**Hôtel Ascott**, 35 Rue du Chapitre, t 02 99 81 89 93, *www.ascotthotel.com* (*expensive*). A bright, elegant and welcoming choice.

★★★**Hôtel Korrigane**, 39 Rue Le Pomellec, t 02 99 81 65 85, *www.st-malo-hotel-korrigane. com* (*expensive*). Extremely comfortable rooms in a smart 19th-century home with period furniture and its own garden.

★★★**Le Valmarin**, 7 Rue Jean XXIII, t 02 99 81 94 76, *levalmarin@wanadoo.fr* (*moderate–expensive*). An exclusive *malouinière* set its own shaded garden, with stylish rooms.

★★**Hôtel de la Rance**, 15 Quai Sébastopol, t 02 99 81 78 63, *hotel-la-rance@wanadoo.fr* (*inexpensive*). Situated within close proximity of the Tour Solidor, this small, traditional hotel has rooms overlooking the beautiful Rance estuary on the western side of St-Servan.

Restaurant Saint-Placide, 6 Place du Poncel, t 02 99 81 70 73 (*moderate–expensive*). A cosy establishment on a leafy square a few steps from the sea, offering interesting, spiced-up takes on a variety of classic Breton dishes.

Crêperie Solidor, 7 Esplanade du Commandant Menguy, t 02 99 80 64 53 (*inexpensive*). A decent crêperie with a terrace looking on to the port.

Le Repaire des Corsaires, opposite the beach, t 02 99 56 78 22 (*inexpensive*). A place serving seafood straight from the boats, and at bargain prices.

candidate, the town the English-backed one. The latter side eventually won in the bloody conflict when Jean de Montfort became Duke Jean IV of Brittany. But he would incur the wrath of the Malouins.

Ni Français, ni Breton: Malouin suis

'Neither French nor Breton, but Malouin I am' ran a popular motto of the town. St-Malo cultivated its independent streak down the centuries, and became something of a defiant city state. Seeing his ducal treasury depleted, Duke Jean IV tried to cash in on the wealth of the city, and the townsmen revolted. In the 1370s, backed by substantial English troops, he tried to gain control of St-Malo. It held out from June until November. The French king, Charles V, keenly supported the Malouins' uprising, sending the Breton knight, Bertrand Du Guesclin, to dislodge the English.

The French then attempted to impose their authority. King Charles V was foolish enough to try prematurely to declare Brittany's union with the French kingdom in 1379, and many of the Breton lords united to call back Duke Jean IV. But the leader of St-Malo, the bishop Josselin de Rohan, proclaimed that the town recognized no overlord except the Pope. The angry duke laid siege to St-Malo again, seizing Malouin property that lay outside the city walls. He had the sturdy Tour Solidor built on the Rance to the south of Aleth in 1382, to hold one garrison. In the second year of the siege, the bishop called upon the Avignon pope, Clement VII, to intervene. The papal legate persuaded the Malouins to give in to the duke. Two years later, the Malouins simply turfed out the duke's officers. The citizens survived the next siege, and this time took the defiant step of calling on the next king of France, Charles VI, to be their overlord. Charles VI granted the rebel city important privileges, not levying any duties on its commerce.

In the second half of the Hundred Years War, the Malouin merchants did not fare too badly. In part, they prospered from the pillaging of English ships. Such ruthless means of supplementing their business were to become a trademark of the tough Malouins over many centuries. Following English raids on the Breton coasts, in 1403 Malouin forces sacked Plymouth. Two years later they targeted Yarmouth.

The Malouin ships' captains were often daring; in 1425, they defied the English siege of the Mont-St-Michel, managing to take supplies to the island. King Charles VII of France thanked the city by giving its merchants special trading rights with other French ports. Duke Jean V of Brittany had also become close to the French king, and the latter handed over the lordship of St-Malo to the Breton duke. Duke Jean V soon had to submit to the English, though. In 1427, he was forced to make peace with King Henry VI of England, who demanded rights of entry into St-Malo.

Medieval St-Malo presented a very different picture to the St-Malo you now see. The ramparts stood still higher, but there were not nearly as many gateways as punctuate the walls today. The main entry route for merchandise was via the Grande Porte. Ships would moor along the quay outside or simply be pulled up on the sandy shore. The Grande Rue (the name remains) led into town, and was the only street wide enough to take carts in the dense maze of timberframe houses. The bishop's palace at the top of the rock lorded it over the working quarters.

Duke François II succeeded Jean V and continued the building of St-Malo's ducal fortress, adding the massive tower known as La Générale. With the Wars of the Roses raging in England, Henry Tudor (the future King Henry VII) apparently came to take refuge in St-Malo's cathedral, causing the English king to declare war on Duke François II. Then it was the turn of the French king to do likewise. In this conflict, the Malouins supported the Breton duke for once. But French forces under the commander La Trémouille marched on St-Malo, having beaten the Breton troops at St-Aubin-du-Cormier in 1488 (*see* p.16). The French cannon managed to breach the walls and the Malouins gave in quickly to La Trémouille's demand for 12,000 gold *écus*, paid up straight away.

Once Anne de Bretagne, the last Breton duchess, was forced into marriage to the French king, Charles VIII, work began on another enormous tower for the ducal château. The Malouin authorities were displeased and told Anne as much. She firmly dismissed the complaints and the tower became known as the Quic en Groign, after a shortening of a phrase that Anne de Bretagne had engraved on it: *Quic en groign, ainsi sera, c'est mon plaisir* ('Whoever may complain, this is how it will be – it is my pleasure').

According to Anne's marriage contract with Charles VIII, Brittany was supposed to remain largely autonomous, keeping its privileges and freedoms. But Charles VIII couldn't resist the thought of the crown taking command of such a rich corner of Brittany, and he declared himself master of St-Malo. The Malouins don't appear to have complained much this time, as he gave them better terms than the bishop had done, fewer taxes and a larger share of booty from captured enemy ships.

Cartier's Discoveries and St-Malo's Breakaway Republic

Jacques Cartier (*see* p.144) is the most famous 16th-century Malouin and the most famous French explorer of that century. The young Cartier was first sent off fishing in Newfoundland. Later, he suggested exploratory expeditions of his own. He is credited with securing Canada for the French after he found his way up the St Lawrence river.

Cartier died of the plague in 1557, just before the period that was dominated by the terrible French Wars of Religion. The night of the horrific St-Bartholomew's Day massacre in 1572, when some fanatical Catholics butchered Huguenots around France, the Catholic Malouins spared the enemy in their midst, and left the Huguenots in town to flee to England and to Holland. But the city did go on to support the ultra-Catholic *Ligue*. The Malouins themselves could not escape another terrible plague that struck in 1583, and some estimates reckon that it wiped out as much as half of the city's population.

When the French king, Henri III, had Henri Duc de Guise, the leader of the *Ligue*, assassinated in the royal castle at Blois in 1588, the Malouins reacted with anger. The king's representative hid in the castle, while the town elected a council of 12 to rule St-Malo. The king's side proposed talks, but when the city authorities intercepted a message showing the falsity of the king's attempt at reconciliation, they strengthened their resolve to remain independent.

Henri de Navarre, of the Bourbon family, became King Henri IV of France. But he was a Huguenot, an ally of the English, and therefore unacceptable to the Malouin authorities. They kept the king's governor trapped in his castle until he had promised to remove all taxes; and then they declared that they would remain a neutral territory until France had a Catholic monarch at its head. In March 1590, news reached St-Malo that Henri IV was not far away, and the governor said that he would let him into the city. The displeased Malouin leaders stormed the governor's castle, apparently with the aid of an angry Scottish soldier within, whose daughter had been seduced by the governor. The governor was assassinated, and the leader of the attack, Picot de la Gicquelais, led the cry of 'Vive la République' the next day. St-Malo effectively became a republic from March 1590 to December 1594, only relenting after Henri IV had renounced the Huguenot faith.

The Famed Shipowning 'Messieurs de St-Malo'

Whatever the terribly negative moral judgement on St-Malo's rapacious shipowners, ships' captains and corsairs seen from today's perspective, many of the leading Malouins were spectacularly successful through the 17th and 18th centuries, and were often involved in extraordinary expeditions as well as outrageous acts. Some of the Malouins' most significant voyages are charted in the topic 'The First Croissant in Sumatra' (*see* p.36).

Jean-Baptiste Colbert, that tirelessly enterprising great minister under King Louis XIV, took an understandable interest in St-Malo, as he was intent on building up a great fleet for France and on reorganizing the French colonies. In 1655, it was decided that the crew for the king's *flotille du Ponant* (fleet of the west) should be made up entirely of Malouins, because they were such tried and tested sailors. In 1660, Colbert founded an *école d'hydrographie* in town in order to train naval officers, and it is still going strong.

Colbert founded the French Compagnie des Indes trading company in 1664, following previous abortive attempts at organizing French colonial commerce. But with Colbert's death and other difficulties, the company found itself in trouble. The minister Louis de Pontchartrain realized that the Malouin shipowners would be important partners to get on board to rescue the situation. He invited 'the gentlemen of St-Malo, the most capable in the realm of supporting such a grand enterprise as the commerce with the Indies, to take on its running. This they did, and for 15 years all the trade from the French Indies ended up at St-Malo. At the close of the 17th century, St-Malo was the port in France with the largest number of vessels with a capacity of more than 100 tonnes. Some 40 families built hugely successful trading empires in St-Malo and around the world, controlling a large slice of French colonial trade.

Colonial Wars and Corsairs of St-Malo – a Heroic Scourge

Malouin corsairs made a killing in the latter part of the 17th century. Corsairs are not to be confused with plain pirates, although they are humorously known as pirates with a permit. They were officially given *lettres de course* by the royal administration to go 'coursing' after the enemy, hence their name. The mere threat of boarding was often enough to make the enemy capitulate. Between 1688 and 1697, the Malouin corsairs captured a staggering number of commercial vessels, British, Dutch and Iberian.

Angry British and Dutch merchants called upon their governments to attack St-Malo itself. The English mounted violent attacks on the city in the 1690s. After the battle of La Hogue in 1692, 21 French vessels took refuge down the Rance to avoid destruction. The next year, in November, more subtle attacks were thought up by the English. Their vessels came bearing white flags, which the Malouin look-outs took for the French squadron from Brest. It was actually a British force under John Benbow, drawing surreptitiously into St-Malo's waters. The British cannon bombarded the city for three whole days. Although fires broke out in St-Malo, the English eventually appeared to have given up.

But they had one more trick up their sleeve: under cover of night, they launched another unmanned, black-sailed ship towards St-Malo. It was packed with an enormous amount of explosives: an estimated 25 tonnes of gunpowder and some 600 huge bombs. Petrol, sulphur and straw were placed on top. The idea was that this infernal machine should be carried by the tide to hit St-Malo's rock and blow up, destroying much of the city. The English miscalculated, and the black ship hit a rock 400 metres from St-Malo. The explosion was supposedly heard as far away as Granville on the Normandy coast. Bits of metal rained down on the roofs of St-Malo and most of the city's windows were blown out, but the damage was otherwise limited. The British returned two years later, supported by Dutch ships. They launched over 1,500 missiles on the city over three days. But once again the Malouins survived, putting out many of the fires with sand.

During the 1690s, the islands just off St-Malo were strongly fortified. The great military engineer Maréchal Vauban planned the considerable number of military installations involved, but it was a subordinate of his, Siméon de Garengeau, who actually oversaw their construction. La Conchée is a particularly admired feat of engineering, making the most of the natural shape of that particular rock.

Duguay-Trouin, Corsair Extraordinaire

War meant good times for St-Malo. Its inhabitants knew of no more charming festival.
Jules Michelet in his famous 19th-century *Histoire de France*

The most notorious and successful of St-Malo's corsairs during this period was René Duguay-Trouin, originally destined for the priesthood. Equally excited by women as by war, he declared in his memoirs that 'Mars and Venus were my two ruling passions.' By the age of 18, such was Duguay-Trouin's skill in taking enemy vessels that he was given command of his own ship. For three years, he wreaked havoc in the Irish Sea. In 1694, his vessel was caught in a trap by six English ships and he was taken to Portsmouth as a prisoner. The story goes that having seduced an English rose, he managed to escape. His continued triumphs led to his presentation at the royal French court, and at the age of 24 he was elevated to the rank of captain of a frigate in the French navy. In his letters of nobility, Duguay-Trouin's achievements for the navy were lovingly noted: he had taken more than 300 merchant vessels and 20 enemy warships and corsairs' vessels. His most outrageous act, however, was seizing Rio de Janeiro from the Portuguese in 1711 and ruining the enemy fleet there. He was made lieutenant general in 1728, and long afterwards ended up with the posthumous honour of having his remains moved into St-Malo's cathedral.

Treaties, Slaves and Revolution

The very start of the 18th century constituted perhaps the most lucrative period for the big St-Malo merchants all round. But the Treaty of Utrecht of 1713, ending the Spanish War of Succession and punishing France, seriously curbed the Malouins' trading possibilities. Vauban had suggested the idea of constructing protected docks on the mainland side of St-Malo. The Malouins rejected this forward-looking project, but did opt for Garengeau's plans for various enlargements to the town, which were carried out between 1708 and 1736. The 18th century was also the major slave-trading period for France, and St-Malo saw the mounting of 216 slave-trading expeditions across the century. Further 18th-century wars, including the War of Austrian Succession (1740 to 1748) and the Seven Years War (1756 to 1763) made 'honest' trade much harder, and the corsairs would come back into their own. But the Malouin merchants were increasingly crippled by Louis XV's chaos of conflicts. Many went bankrupt and were not able to recover under the reign of Louis XVI.

Come the time of revolutions, St-Malo became one of the French ports where volunteers for the American War of Independence set off to fight the British. Their resources much depleted, the town's merchants even managed to drum up 360,000 francs for the Revolutionary authorities. They did not show enough zeal to satisfy Le Carpentier, however. This fanatical proconsul under the Terror changed the name of the city to Port Malo and had an inventory drawn up of each family's belongings. Protesters were imprisoned. Another of St-Malo's famous sons, François-René de Chateaubriand (see p.112), headed off during the Revolution and travelled through North America. With the fall of Robespierre and Le Carpentier, St-Malo became a stronghold for anti-Revolutionaries. The Napoleonic Empire brought some relief to its fortunes, but enemy blockades made trade extremely hard.

One More Malouin Makes his Fortune out of Misfortune

St-Malo did have one last hero of a corsair at the end of the 18th century and start of the 19th. He was Robert Surcouf, who built up a dazzling career and fortune in very little time, partly through slave-trading, but in the main from the most daring of corsair raids. His first extraordinary feat was typical of the man: in 1795, he captured the British ship *Triton* with its 150-man crew and 30 cannon, while he is said to have been in charge of a mere 19 sailors manning just four cannon. The capture in 1800 of the British ship, the *Kent*, features as his greatest accomplishment – the vessel was returning from Brazil, filled with treasure.

By his late twenties, at the start of the 19th century, Surcouf had made a fortune large enough for him to retire on. The Emperor Napoleon was full of admiration for the man and offered him an important naval post, but Surcouf preferred to keep his independence and accepted a title of baron instead. Surcouf also became the first Malouin captain to receive the Légion d'Honneur, the French order of merit created by Napoleon in 1802. At the start of the first decade of the 19th century, it did seem as though this wayward son of St-Malo would settle down. He married and moved into a sumptuous townhouse, known as the Cadran Solaire. But he would take to the seas for a couple more years of wild adventure from 1807 to 1809.

Cod-fishing Overtakes the Corsairs

Time was up for the corsairs and slave-trading in the 19th century. St-Malo corsairs ceased coursing around 1815, and corsair action would be officially banned in France in 1856. Cod-fishing in far-off waters became the main occupation for the port of St-Malo in the 19th century. The quays were substantially developed, with drying-houses built along them. The railway line came to St-Malo in 1864, while a radical change in Anglo-French relations brought a very different breed of English person to the port of St-Malo than in centuries past – tourists.

But the first half of the 20th century also brought German warfare. The St-Malo cod-fishing fleet was seriously depleted in the First World War. Still, in the period between the wars, the port remained a substantial destination of long-distance fishermen, with around a third of the French cod catch made by Malouin ships. The main story recounted about St-Malo in the Second World War is of the city's destruction as Germans and Allies battled it out to the last. The Nazis surrendered on the mainland on 17 August 1944, but a hardcore of German troops resisted on the Ile Cézembre until 9 September. The city has put this harrowing period behind it and has developed into a thriving holiday spot, but it has also managed to maintain a fair number of its shipbuilding and sea trading activities.

A Tour of the Walled City

That's where I was brought up, companion of the waves and the wind.
Chateaubriand, *Mémoires d'outre-tombe*

A crown of stone placed on the waves.
Flaubert

... a real sea bird's nest ...
Maurice de Guérin

... basically, it's a prison ...
Stendhal

Around the Ramparts

To appreciate the seascapes from the walled city and to peer indiscreetly into grand Malouin apartments, take a walk up on the glorious broad **ramparts**. You can follow these ramparts almost all the way round the old town; they now make a wonderful promenade. Once up on the ramparts above the Porte St-Vincent, you can look out to the *bassins à flot*, the extensive protected inner harbours. The view of St-Malo this side is industrial and quite barren. By contrast, within the walls, the elongated **Place Chateaubriand** at your feet bustles with life. Before the city was enlarged to cover this area in 1708, there used to be a beach here, the Anse de Bonne Mer, and it was from here that Jacques Cartier set sail in 1534.

Continue along the ramparts to the **Grande Porte** above the **Place du Poids du Roi**. Below lies the area in which the corsairs came to find work in times of war. They were drafted in inns with colourful-sounding names such as La Belle Anglaise (The Beautiful Englishwoman), Le Tambour Défoncé (The Broken Drum) and Le Chat Qui Danse (The Dancing Cat). The gate itself is the oldest entrance into the city, with enormous twin drum towers from the 15th century. These house the Association du Cotre Corsaire, which saw to the construction of a replica of Surcouf's ship the *Renard*.

The **southwestern ramparts** are pierced in the centre by the Porte de Dinan. Outside this gate you can see where the little **ferry boats cross to Dinard**, a wonderful short trip over the Rance estuary. The *vedettes* also run longer tours to Dinan and to the Cap Fréhel. The tentacle of the **Môle des Noires**, a long, thin jetty, sticks out into the sea from the southern corner of the city outside the **Bastion St-Philippe**.

St-Malo's fine central beaches start here, but they only reveal themselves when the tide goes out. The **Plage du Môle** lies at the foot of the ramparts between the Bastion St-Philippe and the **Bastion de la Hollande**, where Jacques Cartier's statue is prominent. On one end of the Bastion de la Hollande, the **Porte St-Pierre** allows you to go down the ramp past the sailing school to the **Plage de Bon Secours**, a wonderful urban beach. At low tide it is possible to walk out from the beach on to the island of Grand Bé, the location of Chateaubriand's tomb (*see* p.143). Back by the Bastion de la Hollande you might try to seek out the kennel in which the terrifying night guards of St-Malo were once housed. Twenty-four mastiffs would be let loose to patrol the beaches once the nightly curfew had been sounded. The mastiffs were finally done away with in 1770, after a tragic accident in which a naval officer was mauled to death.

Continuing along towards the Tour Notre Dame, you can get down to the other end of the beach of Bon Secours via the **Porte des Bés**. Up on the triangular **Champs Vauverts** with its **Jardin du Cavalier**, the statue of the corsair Surcouf cuts a very dashing figure. The impressive **Tour Bidouane** dates from the 15th century, and today its thick-walled chambers contain a number of fascinating exhibits from marine archaeological excavations around St-Malo's waters. These include pots and plates but also, more hauntingly, shoes and pipes, plus the skeleton of a ship's monkey. From above, glorious views open out to the east.

The tour of the ramparts ends at the **Porte St-Thomas**, where you can get out on to the rocky beach, the **Plage de l'Eventail**. This is where Chateaubriand most enjoyed playing as a child. The account of his pre-revolutionary boyhood, in his memoirs, reads more like Tom Sawyer than the great romantic. The description of the impoverished aristocratic hooligans brawling on the seashore is entertaining. The great shimmering sands of Paramé stretch away to the east.

Sights and Museums Within the City Walls

Down from the ramparts, the streets within St-Malo's walls can seem quite dark and overbearing; the height of the granite mansion blocks shows this was something of a high-rise city for the 18th century. The builders generally constructed short streets and used curves to break the force of the winds. So instead of vistas, you get the feeling you're entering a disorientating and complex labyrinth. Perhaps the most evocative way to imagine historic St-Malo is to think of the corsairs who brought such wild life to these streets under the Ancien Régime. On their return from successful raids they would be greeted as heroes. Then they would often tour the town, getting appallingly drunk.

There's a discreet but well-signposted and numbered **historical trail** from Place Chateaubriand. It takes you almost immediately to the façade of the house where the Romantic writer was born in 1768, the 17th-century **Hôtel de la Gicquelais**, not surprisingly along the street now known as Rue Chateaubriand. Close to Chateaubriand's first home, the **Maison de la Duchesse Anne** probably never saw the duchess, but it does have a certain 15th-century grandeur, with its stairtower and sculpted corner figures. The trail leads to another distinctive old-styled building, the **Maison de Bois et de Verre**, the House of Wood and Glass, with little glass-pane-panelled additions to the façade. This is also known as the **Maison Internationale des Poètes et des Ecrivains**, a venue for highly popular recitals of poetry and traditional song, small-scale art exhibitions, and lively street theatre evenings in summer.

The trail then takes you to the highest point of the rock, past the grand 17th-century entrance to the posh school of St-Malo, close to the ruined cloister now in the grounds of the Ecole Hydrographique, and on to the plain little chapel to St Aaron.

The Cathédrale St-Vincent

Not all the cathedral was destroyed in the Second World War, but photos in the side entrance show the extent of the devastation. The spire, long a navigational mark for St-Malo's sailors, looked rather different in times past. The nave and its vaulting, with most of the choir, survived the bombs. All the original stained-glass windows fell out, though, and the south side of the building was reduced to rubble. The Romanesque church was begun in the 12th century by Benedictine monks, on the site of an earlier, much more modest building. After the influential bishop Jean de Chatillon had the Benedictines turfed out, work on the nave continued, but the construction of the ceiling shows how a new and different style, early Gothic, was employed, using deep ribbed vaults. The north aisle and one arm of the transept were added by Thomas Poussin from Dinan, who became an official royal architect, late in the 16th century. The 13th-century choir was influenced by Anglo-Norman techniques, and even the stone came from Caen in Normandy. Its quirky end wall contains a fine rose window.

St-Malo's cathedral seems dedicated almost as much to Jacques Cartier's glory as God's; the Malouin explorer is practically sanctified here. Along the central aisle of the nave a plaque in the floor declares: 'Jacques Cartier kneeled here to receive the benediction of the bishop of St-Malo before his departure for the discovery of Canada on 16 May 1535'. Look out too for stained glass representing him, and for his tomb.

Down in the lower parts of town around the cathedral you'll find the main **shopping quarters**, the streets sometimes giving onto little squares whose names, such as Place de la Poissonnerie, Marché aux Légumes and Place aux Herbes, indicate that they were once occupied by specific traders.

Demeure des Magon de la Lande or Maison Asfeld

Open 10–11.30 and 2.30–5.30 Feb–11 Nov Tues–Sun, July and Aug daily.

You'll get the best picture of the life of the wealthy St-Malo merchants of the Ancien Régime by visiting this building, one of the very few original 18th-century mansions to have survived in St-Malo. It stands in the southeastern corner of town, close to the Porte St-Louis. In this house, voyages were planned, exotic produce stored and commercial deals struck. Family life went on here too, that of just one family. François-Auguste Magon, the Malouin for whom this grand townhouse was built, had by the age of 45 amassed an immense fortune and constructed this home. The Magon family was one of the most successful of all St-Malo's trading dynasties. A Magon from Vitré had settled in St-Malo as far back as the 14th century, and different Magon branches had flourished from that time on. 'Shake any bush and a Magon will fall out of it', the Malouins used to joke.

The 70-room building is now divided up into flats, but one of the tenants organizes guided tours round certain rooms. A couple of the reception rooms you pass through stand quite empty except when the odd amateur painting exhibition is put on. There are many hidden passageways behind the walls. The visit ends in the cellars, occupied by a wine merchant – the conditions are excellent for keeping bottles. At the period the house was built, spices and tea could have been stored down here in quantity. The ceilings were built using huge beams recuperated from ships that had been scrapped.

The Magon family probably only spent around three months a year in their townhouse. François-Auguste Magon also owned one of the most delightful *malouinières* in the countryside, La Chipaudière, where he and his family had more space and a decent garden. A branch of the Magon family still owns La Chipaudière, and its gardens can be visited from 1 July to 10 August.

Musée d'Histoire de la Ville et du Pays Malouin

Open 10–12 and 2–6 April–Sept daily, Oct–March Tues–Sun.

Dark, dismal and pretty dead, the Musée d'Histoire de la Ville et du Pays Malouin is locked away in part of the château of St-Malo. The first gloomy chamber evokes the maritime history of St-Malo, with a panel detailing far-flung corners of the earth to which Malouins sailed. Ships' models, guns and the odd colonial object are displayed. One room features a huge wooden prow carved as a corsair's head, the figure with feathered cap and flowing hair dandily sporting medal and scarf. Ecclesiastical mementoes from the area fill a further room, while another reveals the destruction of St-Malo in the Second World War and its reconstruction. An upper room is devoted to 19th-century Malouin writers. Romantic Chateaubriand is depicted in Napoleonic, windswept pose in front of a Roman theatre, in a famous work of 1807 by Girodet.

A massive, rounded adjoining castle tower forms a further part of the museum. There, one level concentrates on the Malouin tradition of fishing in Newfoundland, with maps, icy paintings, and models combining to give a good picture of the trade. On another level of the tower, pipes carved with mermaids or grotesque faces vie for attention with coiffes placed on silly wooden faces and other bits and pieces of past Clos Poulet culture. The top floor displays a mixed bag of paintings of St-Malo, plus Paul Signac's cheering *Le Pardon des Terre-Neuvas* of 1928.

The nearby **Petit Aquarium d'Intra-Muros** (*open daily 10–1 and 2–6 exc school hols; July and Aug 10–8*) has its tanks within the ramparts running westwards along the Place Vauban (close to and just to the north of the Place Chateaubriand). The setting is unusual and practical, although the tanks may be a bit high for many youngsters. It is also rather odd to be looking at such a variety of tropical fish so very close to cold Channel waters.

The Islands around the Ville Intra-Muros

> When the tide goes out it uncovers a beach of the finest sand. Then it is possible to walk all the way round the nest where I was born. Rocks lie scattered around, some close by, some far out to sea, some turned into forts, others uninhabited – Fort-Royal, La Conchée, Cézembre and Le Grand Bé, the latter where my grave will be.
> Chateaubriand, *Mémoires d'outre-tombe*

Ant trails of tourists head out from the ville intra-muros for the islands of Grand Bé and the Fort National. When you look back on the walled city from them, St-Malo is stunning. Many French people go to the **Grand Bé** expressly to see **Chateaubriand's tomb**, a place of Byronic proportions to them. With a simple granite cross on a simple base, it looks out towards the Channel. The **Fort du Petit Bé** can be visited too.

The **Fort National** (*open June–Sept at low tide during the day*) is also splendidly sited, its defences bringing clearly to mind brutal times and military campaigns. You can walk out to the islet at low tide, picking your way through the rocks, to arrive at the sharp layers of the fortification. Before 1689, this islet was known as the Roc d'Islay. It not only served as the location for a lighthouse: during the time the St-Malo authorities had the right to administer justice, it was also where people were executed. In 1689, its conversion into a fort began. The outer ring of defences was added in the 19th century.

In such big forts it's always a bit of a disappointment to see the diminutive size of the building that lies at the heart of so many ramparts; but the layers of fortified walls have the same effect as diminishing Russian dolls. Two water tanks and gunpowder rooms were built into the rock below, and the place was fitted out to hold a reasonably sized garrison. On the tour you are taken down into the dark underground chambers. No natural light can enter these sinister places; an ingenious system of zigzagging air vents provides oxygen. The Fort National has never been taken by force to date.

The **Ile de Cézembre**, a rocky island that seems harshly unshaded on a hot summer's day, lies a boat ride away (from in front of the Porte de Dinan, summer only). Breton monks retreated here from the 6th century. Local legend has it that young women of

St-Malo would go out to Cézembre on a pilgrimage to St Brendan's oratory. There they would pray for his help in finding a lizard with three tails – a sign that they would get married within the year. You're not supposed to wander off from the blindingly white sands, as German mines may still be lurking under the surface.

East of St-Malo: Paramé to Rothéneuf, and Jacques Cartier's Manor

Paramé is St-Malo's seaside resort, stretching east of town behind a glorious arc of beach. It is now very built up and hugely popular in summer, and a great number of hotels line the shore, looking out to sea. The busy road that is hemmed in by suburban clutter behind the coast leads to **Rothéneuf**, with its curious sculpted rocks and Jacques Cartier's manor.

Musée-Manoir Jacques Cartier

Open July and Aug daily 10–11.30 and 2.30–6; June and Sept Mon–Fri 10–11.30 and 2.30–6; rest of year tours Mon–Fri at 10 and 3.

Jacques Cartier, born in the walled city of St-Malo in 1491, bought this little country home on the back of his adventures. There is not a great deal to see inside – lifestyles were relatively simple in the 16th century. But on the guided tour you hear the story of Cartier's life. A rapid commented slide show in the first room also puts his achievements in the context of French exploration and colonial expansion more generally. Only fleeting attention is paid to the Native American Indians who helped Cartier.

Jacques Cartier and the French Connection with Canada

From the age of 11, Cartier had gone on cod-fishing expeditions to Newfoundland. Shortly after getting married to the daughter of the constable of St-Malo, he leapt at the opportunity, in the early 1520s, of joining the navigator Giovanni da Verrazzano on a voyage of discovery. Verrazzano had been commissioned by King François I to find a westerly route from France to Asia via North America, and had come to St-Malo to recruit an able crew. Cartier had many skills for the period: he could read and write, as well as having a detailed knowledge of navigation. Though after a year of sailing up and down the American coast the expedition was a flop, Cartier had been bitten by the bug of exploration.

Gathering funds for a voyage of his own proved no easy matter, and such adventures into uncharted territory clearly carried risks. But the Malouin did show indomitable persistence. His father-in-law's high office and contacts helped his cause. In 1532, François I had gone to the Mont-St-Michel on a pilgrimage. Cartier made the most of the occasion to gain a royal audience, the royal seal of approval for his voyage and 6,000 livres to pay for it. The mission, according to Cartier's own memoirs, was rather vague, but the aim deeply material: 'to discover certain islands where it is said that a large quantity of gold and other rich things are to be found'. He left St-Malo in

1534, and it took him a mere 19 days to reach what he called the Détroit de Belle Ile. Heading into the continent, he met some Iroquois Indians and brought back two sons of their chieftain to present to François I.

The next year he left on another royal-backed trip from the Rance by the Tour Solidor, with three ships. This crossing to the Détroit de Belle Ile lasted 40 days. He took back the two Indians. On 10 August 1535, they reached the estuary of a great river. It was the feast day of St Lawrence – and so the river got its European name. The ships travelled inland down the estuary and Cartier dropped off the Indians at the place that became Quebec City. He planted a cross there and then travelled further upriver, planting another cross on the spot that would develop into Montréal.

The third important Cartier voyage took place in 1541. By this time, François I was intent on securing French royal possession of the land that French sailors discovered. However, Cartier was not noble, and it required an aristocrat to be able to lay claim officially to colonial lands. On this expedition, Cartier was supposed to go as the explorer, Lord Roberval as the colonizer. But the impatient Cartier was ready to set sail 10 months before Roberval and left well before his superior. The Indians he met this time talked of another kingdom and a sea three moons away. Cartier must have thought that he was going to find glory; he reckoned that this was the western way to China and even went as far as naming one turbulent stretch of river the Rapides de la Chine. On top of that, he thought he had discovered diamonds and precious stones. The cold weather coming in and the increasing hostility of the native Indians caused Cartier to return home and on the way back to France he crossed paths with Roberval.

Rather than being greeted triumphantly, Cartier found himself out of favour with the king. He had disobeyed his superior. He had not managed to discover a western route to China. And he had returned with fool's gold and dud diamonds. But he had found what would prove a very important passageway to the Great Lakes and new territories for the French colonizers. He took the Native American Indian word for little village and gave it to the new lands he had come across – Canada.

After his voyages, Cartier settled at Limoëlou. For a person whose life had such an impact on the history of the western world, the interior of his manor is fairly basic. He enlarged it to make it into a comfortable family home with a smart stairtower. In Cartier's day, and for many centuries to come, the house would have been thatched. In the 19th century, a further extension was added. David MacDonald Stewart, a Canadian tobacco tycoon turned philanthropist, bought the farm from a local man in the 1970s, and it was turned into this museum to Cartier's memory.

The rooms inside are furnished to look like the ones Cartier might have known. The whitewashed kitchen has a beaten-earth floor with a large fireplace. Two openings, one to what was the bread oven, the other to what may have been a salt storage space, can be made out. Salt was a highly valued commodity at the time. Upstairs, you see a 'guest room' (the Cartiers had no children), with some simple watercolours of the manor. You can also peer into a loft that served as a young servant's quarters. Then you go into the Cartiers' bedroom, where he died of the plague in 1557. The tour ends with a second slide show explaining Cartier's Canadian voyages. You can also consult a CD-ROM on the French discovery of Canada, which is on sale here.

Rochers Sculptés of Rothéneuf

Open daily Easter–Sept 10–7; rest of year 10–12 and 2–6 exc in bad weather.

These sculpted coastal rocks are very bizarre indeed. The carvings are crude and chaotic, seemingly therapy for a sickness-struck priest, the Abbé Fouré, who worked on them for some 25 years through the late 19th century. They are like stone cartoon figures, representing the deeply confusing story of the legendary Rothéneuf family, their retinue, and their battles. The Rothéneufs are supposed to have taken control of piracy and smuggling along this stretch of the coast. The story's action apparently unfolds between the 16th century, when the family establishes its supremacy, and the Revolution, after which pirates from the Channel Islands wreak havoc on the family and its hangers-on. The carnage attracts sleeping monsters from the bottom of the sea, who rise up to devour the bodies, including that of the last Rothéneuf.

Beyond the Rochers Sculptés, the **Havre de Rothéneuf** provides a haven of calm, with fine, clean beaches.

South of St-Malo: Aleth, St-Servan and the Rance

St-Malo's ferry port lies south of the old town. South beyond that you come to **Aleth-cum-St-Servan**, St-Malo's older sibling. Aleth has plenty of character of its own and a divided opinion on its now bigger sister. On the St-Malo side of Aleth, the **Bas Sablons** has a great, old-fashioned-looking beach. The area also has a big **marina**. The views onto St-Malo *intra-muros* make it worth a visit. On the **tip of Aleth**, the ruined 18th-century fort was built by the English when they briefly occupied this point of land in 1758. This was also the site of the pre-Roman Celtic town. The Nazis turned it into a stronghold and now it is a camp site. The **Mémorial 1939–1945** (*open daily June–Sept 10–12 and 2–6, April–mid-Nov 2–6*), in a German blockhouse actually in the camp site, recalls St-Malo under Nazi occupation, and its liberation. Go for a walk along the Promenade de la Corniche to appreciate the setting. Heading down from the tip of Aleth to the Tour Solidor on the Rance, you can pass by some of the ruins of Christian Aleth, the remnants of the grand 10th-century cathedral.

The Tour Solidor and the Musée International du Long-Cours Cap-Hornier

Open 10–12 and 2–6 April–Sept daily, Oct–March Tue–Sun.

The dramatic story of centuries of perilous voyages round Cape Horn could have been more excitingly conveyed than in this rather old-fashioned museum – the awesome 14th-century architecture of the fortified tower leads you to expect something altogether more grandiose. The museum recalls the history of the Cape Horn sea route, which is charted roughly chronologically floor by floor. On the ground floor, you get an introduction to the limits of the world as it was known to western Europeans from 1400 to 1600, and you can trace the various paths that were taken by the most significant explorers.

Of the great 18th-century navigators to pass the savage cape, you may not be familiar with Louis Antoine de Bougainville. The largest of the Solomon Islands was named after him, as was the bougainvillea plant. He colonized the Falkland Islands for France – for a long time they were the Iles Malouines, hence the Argentinian name for them, Las Malvinas – and subsequently saw to their transfer to Spain. He took part in the American War of Independence against the British, and Napoleon awarded him the Légion d'Honneur. Old texts, old maps, models of boats, photos of natives and the odd exotic object picked up on voyages make up the rather meagre débris meant to help build a picture of further dramatic voyages. On one floor, paintings depict the huge waves that batter the cape, said to suffer 300 days of storm a year.

Out on the battlements of the Tour Solidor, you can take in Dinard and St-Malo in the same glance. At the foot of the tower, you look down on the peaceful Rance, its flow made all the calmer by the hydroelectric dam built across it.

Grand Aquarium

Open daily July 9.30–8 (15–31 until 10pm); Aug 9am–10pm; Sept–June 10–6.

You have to get through offputting layers of mass commercialization to reach the eight rooms of St-Malo's massive out-of-town fish-gazing complex, which are very intelligently presented. They're also air-conditioned and dimly lit, making it an attractive option on blinding hot summer days. The most sensational room is the *anneau*, a large ring of an aquarium – you can stand in the middle, as if you're in the midst of a shoal, and watch the fish turn in endless circles.

Malouinières of the Clos Poulet

The great Malouin merchants of the Ancien Régime grew massively wealthy but kept a restrained, sober appearance to their houses. They had grand town blocks built with many storeys for the storage of goods. They also built country retreats, *malouinières*, between the 1660s and the late 18th century. More than 100 survive, scattered around the Clos Poulet. They were most densely situated nearer to the city, as the merchants wanted to remain within comfortable distance of the port.

In these retreats, granite only served for borders and surrounds, and the main sections of the façades were covered in plaster. Decoration was kept to a minimum on the outside. The *malouinières* look pretty dour at first sight, not showy or flamboyant but neat and practical, and are normally hidden behind a stone wall. The plan of the two-storey buildings is simply rectangular, perhaps with a protruding central bay widening the view onto a garden, plus a row of dormer windows in a steep roof.

Château du Bos

Open July and Aug only; you must be at the chapel entrance for 3.30.

Well separated from the cauliflower fields that provide one of the thriving trades for the Clos Poulet area, this *malouinière*, built in 1715–17, lies behind extensive walls. To reach it from St-Malo, follow signs for Dinard, then branch off for Quelmer. On that road, the way to the château is well signposted. You enter the estate by the chapel.

This is one of the grandest of all the *malouinières*, built for a branch of the Magon family; some of the 40,000 *livres* required for its construction came from corsair expeditions. You are shown round the elegant carved panelled rooms of the ground floor by the charming owners, who talk of the Magons coming here to find peace from the stresses of their harrowing trading, and from the terrible stench of Ancien Régime St-Malo in summer. The delectable grounds dip down to the Rance river.

Recently, several more grand *malouinières* have opened to the public. Ask at St-Malo tourist office about the possibility of visiting **La Chipaudière**, the **Domaine de la Briantais**, **Le Puy Sauvage** and **La Ville Bague**.

Down the Rance into Cauliflower Country

While you are in the area, explore the east bank of the Rance. The indented bays off the wide estuary were once exploited by tidal mills, some of which you can still see. Birds of many species are attracted to the marshy areas, and salt was dried here.

The sloping main street of **St-Suliac** leads down to a long riverside front. A church tower shoots out from the upper part of the village, with its houses of speckled schist. The Breton saint, Suliac, is supposed to have founded a priory here in the 6th century. The church dates in part back to the 13th century, but its façade is 17th century. St Suliac features in a relatively recent statue in the north porch, slaying a three-headed dragon who terrorized the area from the Mont Garrot, a rock sticking out of the promontory south of the village. You can see the saint's tomb and relics within. An oratory overlooks one side of the village, built to the Virgin by Newfoundland fishermen in thanks for bringing them all back from a late-19th-century expedition. In the tourist season, the sailing school teems with life, as the protected estuary is a good place for beginners. Night fishing for sand eels in the Rance apparently remains a popular local pastime.

Close to the village of **Châteauneuf d'Ille-et-Vilaine** lies the semi-ruined **Fort de St-Père-Marc-en-Poulet**. Normally, forts show off their mighty defences to intimidate the enemy, but this huge one (covering roughly the same area as St-Malo *intra-muros*) hides out in the countryside. It was built in 1777 to help protect the Clos Poulet from the English, who had tried to take St-Malo by land, and has remained virtually intact. German POWs were kept here in the First World War and the Nazis stored arms here in the Second. Up to 1985 the French army still used it as a munitions base, until the local parish bought it and tidied it up. Concerts are held here now (**t** 02 99 58 81 06).

Château de Montmarin

Open July and Aug Sun and Mon 2–6; May, June and Sept Sun 2–6.
Special theme days in early May, mid-July, mid-Aug and mid-Oct,
*plus some public hol openings – check with tourist office (**t** 02 99 88 58 79).*

This exceptional *malouinière*, one of the last one to be built, looks much more ornate and fancy than most of the rest of them. It also lies on the western bank of the Rance, just outside the Clos Poulet. Here, you really feel and see the exoticism that the Malouin sea voyages brought home. An impressive steep rockery garden has been laid out down by the river, where you can see the remnants of an old shipbuilding yard.

Dinard and the Coast to St-Briac-sur-Mer

The gorgeous beaches and winding coastal paths watched over by grand villas are the highlights of Dinard and the coast to the west of it. Dinard, St-Lunaire and St-Briac-sur-Mer have practically merged into one now. The rocky islands scattered so picturesquely a short distance out to sea, colourful sails weaving in and out of them, make this one of the most pleasing stretches of coast to contemplate in Brittany. Royalty, aristocracy and artists once flocked to Dinard. The British and American connections are deep rooted and an English-speaking community still thrives here.

Dinard

We have one Mrs Faber to thank for Dinard. She settled here, on a near-virgin coast, in the 1850s, and, joined by a few British and American families, set the fashion for holidays in this beautiful location. By the turn of the century, Dinard was one of the most chic resorts in the world. European royalty swanned around the town, as did the ultra-wealthy from many continents, together with the likes of the home-grown Cognac-Hennessey family. These visitors built palatial villas along the rocky cliffs above the protected beaches. The place attracted artists too, notably Picasso, who painted a few of his most wildly exuberant pictures here over two summers.

A Tour of Dinard

The main tourist promenade and beach is the **Plage de l'Ecluse**, but this is not the finest part of the town. Several of the grand buildings that once lined the beach have been destroyed or truncated. There is action aplenty, though, with the casino, the swimming pools, and the beach itself, backed by lines of changing booths. In summer, fresh blue and white striped changing tents are set up on the sands.

Place M. Joffre is where everything collides, roughly in the middle of the beach. Hotels, restaurants and stalls cluster around the square. A statue paying homage to Alfred Hitchcock blew down recently, but Dinard still holds an annual festival of British cinema. In front of the square, towards the sea, are panels reproducing provocative works by Picasso in some way inspired by this beach. They form part of a trail of 20 panels along the coast to Cap Fréhel, illustrating how artists were inspired by scenes along the shore. Local tourist offices have an English-language brochure, 'Emerald Eyes', showing their locations.

From the Plage de l'Ecluse, you look out onto the splendid and eccentric neo-Gothic villas of the Pointe du Moulinet to the east and the Pointe de la Malouine to the west. Islands lie out to sea, notably the Ile de Cézembre. Whether you walk east or west from the beach, the coastal path is fabulous. Head round the **Pointe du Moulinet** and St-Malo comes stunningly into view. Beyond the **landing stage for the ferry service to St-Malo** is the **Promenade du Clair de Lune**; on summer nights the exotic plants along here are lit up in gaudy colours, and romantic recorded music is piped into the air. The path then leads down to the well-protected **Plage du Prieuré**. Climb the steep Rue Faber behind the aquarium to reach the neo-Gothic **British-American church of St Bartholomew**; with its small palm garden, it is a pretty haven in the summer.

Further back from the beaches, the grand **Villa Eugénie** with its four corner towers was built in 1868 and carries the name of Napoleon III's wife. Rumour had it that the imperial couple were coming to spend the summer here and officially inaugurate the resort of Dinard, but apparently they fell out over a dog the empress wanted to bring with her but that the emperor could not abide. Eugénie never came to Dinard and flounced off to Biarritz instead.

Back at the main Plage de l'Ecluse, the coastal path leading west round the **Pointe de la Malouine** to St-Enogat makes for the most unforgettable of all Dinard's walks. The narrow path takes you under rocks and grand villas to beautiful sandy beaches. The views out to sea, the waters strewn with reefs and sails, are superlative.

Getting There

Dinard has a small airport linked to London Luton and London Stansted by low-cost Ryanair flights (*see* p.56).

Tourist Information

Dinard: 2 Boulevard Féart, **t** 02 99 46 94 12, *www.ville-dinard.fr.*
St-Lunaire: Boulevard du Général de Gaulle, **t** 02 99 46 31 09, *www.saint-lunaire.com.*
St-Briac: Jardin du Béchet, **t** 02 99 88 32 47, *www.saint-briac.com.*

Market Days
Dinard: Tuesday.
St-Enogat: Wednesday in July and Aug.
St-Lunaire: Sunday April–Sept.
St-Briac: Friday all year; Monday July and Aug.

Where to Stay

Dinard ✉ 35800

Expensive–Very Expensive
****Grand Hôtel, 46 Avenue George V, **t** 02 99 88 26 26, *www.lucienbarriere.com.* A distinguished establishment high above the Rance promenade, overlooking St-Malo. The many rooms are elegant, with all mod cons, and there's a swimming pool and a cocktail bar, as well as the restaurant.

Expensive
***Reine Hortense, 19 Rue de la Malouine, **t** 02 99 46 54 31, *reine.hortense@wanadoo.fr.* A grand old Dinard villa on a smaller scale than the Grand. It isn't the prettiest from the outside, but it is stylish within, with refined furnishings. Rooms look out to sea from just above the central beach.
***Novotel Thalassa, Avenue Château Hébert, **t** 02 99 16 78 10, *www.accorthalassa.com.* A monster of a health hotel above the rocks at the west end of the beach of St-Enogat west of Dinard, with splendid sea views. The beach is close by, but an indoor heated seawater swimming pool, saunas, jacuzzis and a gym are all to hand. The restaurant offers both gourmet and dieters' fare.
***Hôtel Roche-Corneille, 4 Rue Georges Clemenceau, **t** 02 99 46 14 47, *www.hotel-dinard-roche-corneille.com.* Elegant and impeccable rooms without sea views in one of Dinard's 400 classified villas. The smart restaurant serves refined classics such as *poêlée de St-Jacques à la bretonne.*

Moderate
***Le Vieux Manoir, 21 Rue Gardiner, **t** 02 99 46 14 69, *www.hotel-levieuxmanoir.com.* A calm, good-value hotel in its own private garden towards the centre of town.
L'Améthyste, 2 Rue des Bains, St-Enogat, **t 02 99 46 61 81, *www.hotel-amethyste.com.* A very comfortable if characterless option a short walk from the beach.

St-Lunaire

Debussy was apparently inspired to write *La Mer* here, which is an indication of the magic of this place. St-Lunaire attracted artists and speculators aplenty in the late 19th century. It was a massively wealthy Haitian, Scylla Laraque, who decided to create this resort, first ordering the building of the grandiose late-19th-century block of the Grand Hôtel that still dominates the main beach.

For the truly smart Belle Epoque set that Laraque wished to attract to St-Lunaire, his architects built a series of extravagant villas by the **Pointe du Décollé**, west of the Grand Hôtel beach. Spot some of these follies by going along the Boulevard du Décollé or the Boulevard des Roches. The rocky point has been marred by modern restaurants, but the views in either direction are worth the detour. The old **church of St-Lunaire** doesn't go back as far as the 6th century when Lunaire hit the shore (*see box, below*) but has preserved its 11th-century Romanesque nave. Look out for St Lunaire's tomb, a Gallo-Roman sarcophagus with a 14th-century effigy on top.

Printania, 5 Avenue Georges V, **t 02 99 46 13 07, *www.printaniahotel.com*. A wonderful old-fashioned hotel lapped by the waves, with rooms with fine views towards St-Malo. The restaurant with its Breton furniture serves traditional fare. *Closed mid-Nov to mid-March.*

Inexpensive

Emeraude Plage, 1 Boulevard Albert 1ᵉʳ, **t 02 99 46 15 79, *www.emeraudeplage.com*. A big hotel close to the central beach, with welcoming, English-speaking staff.
L'Hôtel du Parc, 20 Avenue Edouard VII, **t 02 99 46 11 39. An unglamorous choice with a touch of old-fashioned charm.
*Beauséjour, 2 Place du Calvaire, St-Enogat, **t** 02 99 46 13 61. A well-located budget option.
*Le Prieuré, 1 Place du Général de Gaulle, **t** 02 99 46 13 74. Seven rooms and a restaurant with superb views onto Dinard's eastern beach, the Plage du Prieuré. *Closed Jan.*
Hôtel les Mouettes, 64 Avenue George V, **t** 02 99 46 10 64. A simple, very good, family-run hotel in the posh part of town.

Eating Out

Dinard ✉ 35800

L'Escale à Corto, 12 Avenue George V, **t** 02 99 46 78 57 (*moderate*). An atmospheric seafood restaurant near the sea. *Closed lunch, and Mon eve outside school hols.*

La Salle à Manger, 25 Boulevard Féart, **t** 02 99 16 07 95 (*moderate*). A well-regarded gastronomic restaurant in town. Lobster from its tank is a speciality. *Closed Nov–Feb, and Mon and Tues lunch in low season.*
Des Marins, 12 Avenue George V, **t** 02 99 46 78 56 (*moderate*). A reasonably priced restaurant with nautical décor and a good ambiance. *Closed Mon eve.*
Le Dauphin, 5 Boulevard Féart, **t** 02 99 46 76 83 (*inexpensive*). A simple, good-value crêperie.
Du Roy, 9 Boulevard Féart, **t** 02 99 46 10 57 (*inexpensive*). A busy, large, central crêperie.
Kerguelen, 26 Rue Gougeonnais, La Richardais, **t** 02 99 46 66 76 (*inexpensive*). Crêpes with quite elaborate fillings served in a Breton house in a residential area south of the centre.

The west end of the central Plage de l'Ecluse has some basic but bustling restaurants.

Pleurtuit ✉ 35730

***Le Manoir de la Rance, Château de Jouvente, 7km south of Dinard down the Rance, **t** 02 99 88 53 76, *www.chateauxhotels.com* (*expensive*). A 19th-century manor with beautiful views on to the estuary, private gardens and large rooms.

St-Briac ✉ 35800

Hotel de la Houle, 14 Boulevard de La Houle, **t** 02 99 88 32 17, *hotelde.lahoule@wanadoo.fr* (*inexpensive–moderate*) A cross between a hotel and a *brocante* (secondhand shop), hosting musical evenings in summer.

How a Saint Cuts His Way Through Fog

As the name of the resort of St-Lunaire indicates, a Breton saint got here well before the property developers and holiday villas. The religious man supposedly landed here in the 6th century; being a saint, however, it had to be by slightly unorthodox means. The legend goes that dense fog greeted Lunaire as he approached the Armorican coast with his 70 or so companions from Britain. Impatient to find land on which to settle, he took out his sword and literally cut through the fog; the horizon suddenly opened up before him. You are supposed to be able to make out his sandal marks where he stepped on to dry land among the rocks of the Pointe du Décollé.

St-Lunaire has four beaches in all. The small ones to the east are well sheltered, while the large Plage de Longchamp to the west attracts windsurfers. At the western tip of this beach you come to the **Pointe de la Garde-Guérin**. The moorland here plunges dramatically into the sea, reefs surrounding it. From this spot, in 1758, the local guards witnessed the landing of some 10,000 English troops in the Anse de la Fosse. This army had been sent on an expedition to destroy that *bête noire* city to the British, St-Malo. The campaign ended with the disastrous English defeat at St-Cast.

Dinard golf course, one of the most famous in France, crosses from St-Lunaire into the parish of St-Briac. Created in 1887–92 and spectacularly located, it attracted wealthy Brits and Americans. The Germans mined it in the Second World War. The dunes of the **Plage du Port-Hue** below are protected. The beach looks out on to the islands of Dame-Jouanne and Agot.

St-Briac-sur-Mer

The coast all around St-Briac is cluttered with villas; the village itself looks on to the Frémur estuary. The delightful **estuary beaches** are provided with beach huts, and otherworldly rockscapes emerge at low tide. In the old fishermen's village, you could go in search of the odd stone-carved mackerel on the **church**; look along the north side and in the font. Mackerel, when they came into local waters, announced the arrival of spring and were considered a sign of good fortune. The church's ornate granite belltower displays the arms of a local noble family, the Pontbriands. Inside, the Irish saint Briac, who is said to have founded a religious community here in the Dark Ages, is depicted in the modern stained-glass windows. Painters were attracted to St-Briac when it developed into a resort at the end of the 19th century. In the 1880s, Auguste Renoir, Emile Bernard and Paul Signac all came. The last introduced Henri Rivière to the village; Rivière then executed a series of well-known woodcuts, inspired by Japanese models, showing scenes from this part of the Breton coast.

Côtes d'Armor

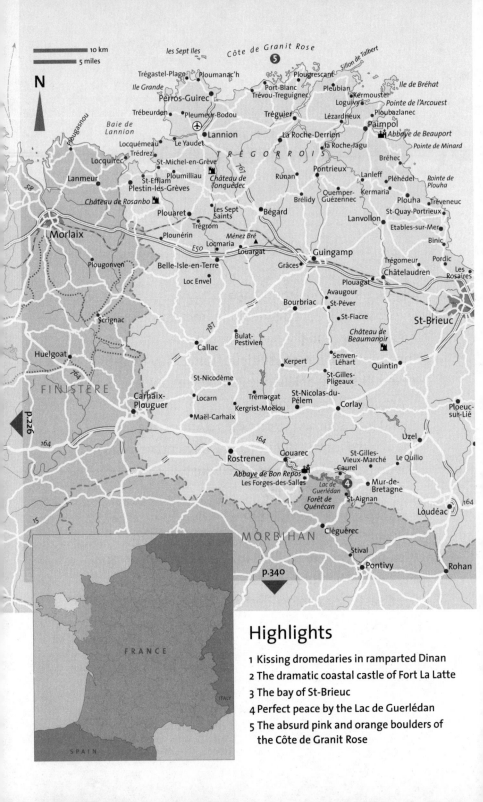

Highlights

1 Kissing dromedaries in ramparted Dinan
2 The dramatic coastal castle of Fort La Latte
3 The bay of St-Brieuc
4 Perfect peace by the Lac de Guerlédan
5 The absurd pink and orange boulders of
   the Côte de Granit Rose

Côtes d'Armor

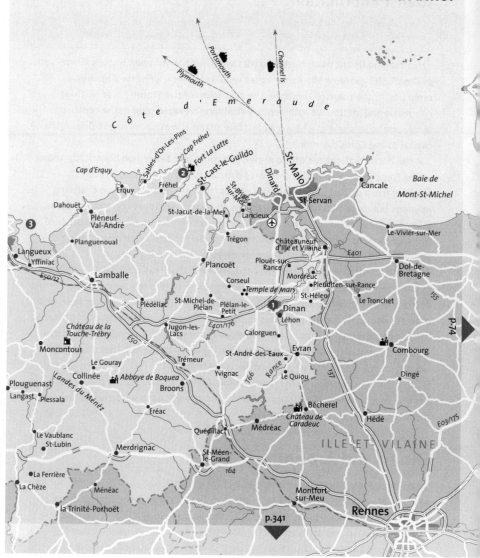

Pink rocks, orange boulders, emerald seas and glorious rocky stretches of coastline follow in quick succession as you travel along the Côtes d'Armor's seashore. The mauve moorlands by the Côte d'Emeraude give way to the gorgeous grey mudflats of the bay of St-Brieuc. Brittany's tallest cliffs rise around Plouha but tumble down into disorienting chaos by the time you reach the bay of St-Brieuc's most romanticized port, Paimpol. The outrageous pink boulders of the Côte de Granit Rose around Perros-Guirec mark this famous stretch. Legends claim that some of the rocks of the Côtes d'Armor were turned red by the blood of persecuted saints.

Tourist Information

Comité Départemental du Tourisme,
in the Maison du Tourisme,

7 Rue Saint-Benoît, B.P. 4620,
22046 St-Brieuc Cedex 2,
t 02 96 62 72 00,
www.cotesdarmor.com.

Head inland up the main river estuaries and you soon hit upon historic towns such as Dinan, still guarding the Rance valley with its superbly preserved medieval ramparts, or the town of Lamballe, the champion of the Breton horse, with its enormous and impressive 19th-century stud farm situated right in the centre of town. Lamballe is one of a string of historic inland towns encircling St-Brieuc, the capital of the Côtes d'Armor.

In the northwest of the Côtes d'Armor, you come into the region historically known as the Trégor, which straddles the Côtes d'Armor and the Finistère. Its capital, Tréguier, has a cathedral that ranks as one of the most interesting and charming religious buildings in Brittany. But perhaps the finest religious legacy of the Côtes d'Armor can be found scattered around villages lost in the southwestern corner of the *département*, down from Guingamp, where Breton folk music and dancing still thrive and where the boulder-strewn countryside is rich in legends.

You can distance yourself from the modern world more easily in these parts than in just about any other corner of Brittany. The ridges of hills reaching into the centre of the province give this area a peculiar wild beauty. The Blavet river rises here, and provides the water for the gorgeous Lac de Guerlédan, right in the heart of Brittany.

In the countryside, the roads sometimes bear the signs of heavy agricultural use, while the smell in the air can all too obviously give away the fact that one of the *département's* most successful industries is pig breeding. In fact, the Côtes d'Armor is the biggest pork producer in France. Unfortunately, as a result, the region has become one of the most polluted of France, though this otherwise enchanting *département* is acting on the problem.

Dinan and Around

A memorable winding street bordered by timberframe houses links the two halves of Dinan, the port down by the Rance, and the upper fortified town. The medieval ramparts, which still virtually encircle the town, are the glory of Dinan. Within these walls, the main monuments to visit include the Eglise St-Sauveur, a mixture of Romanesque and Gothic church architecture, and the Château de Dinan, which contains the town museum. But the main pleasure of Dinan is simply wandering through its picturesque streets and squares. Back down along the Rance sits the house of the 20th-century painter Yvonne Jean-Haffen, now a charming museum.

History

William the Conqueror is depicted in the Bayeux tapestry attacking a simple hilltop castle called Dinan in 1065. Yet the first sure mention of a fort dates from 1123, the year in which Geoffroy I de Dinan split his properties in two to make donations to his two sons. Important religious establishments were founded before the close of the 11th century. Benedictine monks from the great abbey of St-Florent near Saumur on the Loire were called upon to start one institution. They set up mills, organized fishing, and collected dues from boats passing along the Rance. The church dedicated to St Malo was certainly in existence by 1060. The church of St-Sauveur, the most famous monument in Dinan, went up in the 12th century, although an earlier, simpler structure may have predated it.

King Henry II Plantagenet attacked Dinan in 1169. Most history books talk of the dukes then taking control of northern Dinan. It has taken Peter Meazey, a Welshman who fell for Dinan and has adopted it as his own, to rewrite much of the town's early medieval history from this point. He argues convincingly that the Angevin-English

Getting Around

Dinard-Pleurtuit **airport**, t 02 99 46 18 46, not far north of Dinan, has Ryanair flights from London Stansted and London Luton.

Dinan is on a **train** line that links it with Dol-de-Bretagne in the east and St-Brieuc in the west.

As well as enjoying **coach** trips between St-Malo, Dinard and other tourist towns from Dinan, you might consider taking a **boat** up and down the Rance from Dinan's port.

Tourist Information

Pays d'Accueil de Dinan, Le Grand Clos, Quévert, t 02 96 39 62 64.
Dinan: 9 Rue du Château, t 02 96 87 69 76, *www.dinan-tourisme.com.*

Market Days

Dinan: Thursday.

Where to Stay

Dinan ✉ 22100

★★★D'Avaugour, 1 Place du Champ Clos, t 02 96 39 07 49, *www.avaugourhotel.com* (*expensive–very expensive*). Cosy, tastefully decorated rooms in a completely renovated 18th-century building on the largest of Dinan's squares, with a delightful garden looking onto the ramparts.
Le Logis du Jerzual, 25 Rue du Petit Four, t 02 96 85 46 54, *sry.logis@online.fr*

(*inexpensive–moderate*). A very pleasant B&B on the winding old street to the port, constructed between the 15th and the 18th centuries and filled with antique furniture.
★★Arvor, 5 Rue Pavie, t 02 96 39 21 22, *arvor@ destination-bretagne.com* (*inexpensive*). Comfy modern rooms on the site of a former Jacobin monastery, with private parking.
★★Hôtel de la Porte St-Malo, 35 Rue St-Malo, t 02 96 39 19 76, *www.hotelportemalo.com* (*inexpensive*). Extremely pleasant rooms opposite the ramparts, and private parking.
L'Hostellerie du Vieux St-Sauveur, 21 Place St-Sauveur, t 02 96 85 30 20 (*inexpensive*). A basic option on a delightful old square, with rooms above a noisy bar.
Hôtel du Théâtre, 2 Rue Ste-Claire, t 02 96 39 06 91 (*inexpensive*). A historic building with very basic rooms.
Rhona Lockwood's, 53–55 Rue de Coëtquen, t 02 96 85 23 49 (*inexpensive*). A very welcoming B&B near the historic centre, in two terraced houses tastefully converted into one, with good bathrooms.
Auberge de Jeunesse, Le Moulin du Méen, Vallée de la Fontaine des Eaux, t 02 96 39 10 83, *www.fuaj.org* (*inexpensive*). A youth hostel in a former mill wonderfully located north along the west bank of the Rance.

Plouër-sur-Rance ✉ 22490

★★Hôtel-Manoir de Rigourdaine, Route de Langrolay, t 02 96 86 89 96, *www. hotel-rigourdaine.fr* (*inexpensive–moderate*). A tranquil spot with a pretty terrace, looking on to the Rance some 10km north of Dinan, on the west side of the river.

king merely tamed Roland de Dinan, an unruly lord of southern Dinan. After that, under King Henry II and his third son Geoffroy, who became duke of Brittany by marriage, several Dinan aristocrats were given highly important posts in the duchy, and substantial land holdings in England and Wales. Roland de Dinan himself served as *justicier* for Brittany, in charge of fiscal and military matters as well as justice, and as tutor to King Henry's young son Geoffroy. Without heirs of his own, Roland de Dinan adopted his nephew Alain de Vitré, who became *sénéschal* of Brittany, as would the latter's son-in-law, Juhel de Mayenne.

The two lordships into which Dinan had been split were briefly reunited by inheritance and marriage under Alain d'Avaugour in the course of the 13th century. But, in a deal that many historians have regarded as an act of folly, he sold them to

---

Calorguen ✉ 22100

La Tarais, on the west side of the Rance south down the D12 from Dinan, **t** 02 96 83 50 59 (*inexpensive*). A pretty B&B in a converted farm. There's a kitchen for guests' use.

St-Michel-de-Plélan ✉ 22980

La Corbinais, **t** 02 96 27 64 81, *www.corbinais.com* (*inexpensive*). Cute B&B rooms in a typical Breton long house near Corseul, with an adjoining 9-hole golf course. *Table d'hôte* meals are available.

Eating Out

Dinan ✉ 22100

Auberge du Pélican, 3 Rue Haute Voie, **t** 02 96 39 47 05 (*moderate–expensive*). Traditional cuisine in a fine half-timbered building in the old town. *Closed Mon exc July and Aug.*

Chez La Mère Pourcel, 3 Place des Merciers, **t** 02 96 39 03 80 (*moderate–expensive*). Fine food served up in a characterful dining room with an impressive 16th-century wooden staircase, behind a rich timberframe front. *Closed Sun eve, and Mon and Tues in low season.*

La Fleur de Sel, 7 Rue Ste-Claire, **t** 02 96 85 15 14 (*moderate–expensive*). All things gutsy, including roasted brick of Camembert and curried avocado, in a lightly furnished and tasteful *salle*. *Closed Mon eve and Tues.*

Le Restaurant de St Louis, 9–11 Rue de Léhon, **t** 02 96 39 89 50 (*moderate–expensive*). A restaurant that is popular for its *hors d'oeuvre* buffet, where you can load up with

charcuterie, seafood and mixed salads. *Closed Mon and Tues.*

La Courtine, off the Rue de la Croix (no.6), **t** 02 96 39 74 41 (*moderate*). Excellent cooking popular with locals. Grills and fish are a speciality.

Relais des Corsaires, 3 Rue du Quai, **t** 02 96 39 40 17 (*moderate*). A restaurant set behind one of the prettiest old façades of lower Dinan, at the port. The seafood dishes come recommended. *Closed Mon and Tues.*

Le Restaurant Cantorbery, 6 Rue Ste-Claire (*moderate*). A popular place with Brits, and rightly so, offering delicacies such as jugged rabbit with ginger and spices, and a speciality potted fish. *Closed Tues.*

Crêperie Ahna, 7 Rue de la Poissonnerie, **t** 02 96 39 09 13 (*inexpensive*). One of the best crêperies in town, also serving grilled meat.

Crêperie Le Connétable, 1 Rue de l'Apport, **t** 02 96 39 06 74 (*inexpensive*). A popular crêpe house in splendid old town quarters.

Le Léonie, 19 Rue Rolland, **t** 02 96 85 47 47 (*inexpensive*). A quiet restaurant in the centre, small but popular with locals, so book ahead.

Lanvallay ✉ 22100

Le Bistro du Viaduc, 22 Rue du Lion d'Or, **t** 02 96 85 95 00 (*moderate–expensive*). A restaurant situated just outside Dinan past the viaduc, offering a fine view of the Rance valley together with good food – try the pigs' trotters. *Closed Sat lunch, Sun eve and Mon.*

Dinan's Connections with the Earls of Pembroke

The lords of Dinan in the early medieval period had numerous connections with England and Wales through their feudal inheritance. From 1222 to 1234, the lord of Dinan was in theory an 'Englishman', Richard Le Maréchal, a son of Guillaume Le Maréchal, or William the Marshall, Earl of Pembroke, one of the very greatest knights of English medieval history and the loyal servant of several English kings. William the Marshall's eldest son, also William, succeeded him in England. As to Richard, he was actually brought up in Normandy and married into a branch of the Dinan family. But in 1231, on the death of Richard's brother, Richard Le Maréchal inherited hugely valuable estates in Wales, Ireland and England. He would cross the Channel to assert his feudal rights there, which included the inheritance of the position of Marshal of England and numerous castles. King Henry III of England tried to misappropriate his rights and Richard Le Maréchal was forced to defend them against the grasping king.

the duke of Brittany. It was Duke Jean I who ordered the commencement of the construction of Dinan's striking ramparts, though most of the ramparts date from later than that, with extremely important additions being made in the 15th century.

The Breton War of Succession, which began in 1341, turned Dinan into a major theatre of war. Jeanne de Penthièvre, the rightful heir to the duchy, was a direct descendant of Josselin de Dinan, essentially a D'Avaugour. She was backed by the French monarchy, and her Breton cousins included most of the big feudal lords of northern Brittany. In 1342 the English sacked Dinan, stealing treasures from the church of St Sauveur. The walls of Dinan were much strengthened after the first English attack, though in 1357 the English, under the Duke of Lancaster, again laid siege to the town. After some unsuccessful attacks, the English leader called a truce.

In this period Dinan witnessed a celebrated medieval joust between the most famous of all Breton knights in history, Bertrand Du Guesclin (*see* p.108), fighting for Charles de Blois in the French-backed corner, and Thomas of Canterbury in the Jean de Montfort, English corner. The nationalistic notion is that Du Guesclin virtually singlehandedly beat back the English. What happened was that in the course of the period of truce while the English were attacking Dinan, Du Guesclin's brother Olivier was captured by the English knight Thomas of Canterbury. The latter then demanded an unusually high ransom for his release. Not normally one to play precisely by the chivalric book, Du Guesclin objected to Thomas of Canterbury's action, both in taking a prisoner in a time of truce and then in asking for an excessive transfer fee. Du Guesclin came from his post at Pontorson by the Mont-St-Michel to challenge Thomas of Canterbury to a duel. God was supposed to be the arbiter. Du Guesclin comprehensively beat his opponent, who was sent back, dishonoured, to the English army. After the De Monfort side had won the terrible Breton War of Succession, Duke Jean IV of Brittany invested in a wide castle-building programme, which included the construction of a new Château de Dinan. Its towering keep went up in the 1380s.

During the French Wars of Religion that took place at the close of the 16th century, the ultra-Catholic leader in Brittany, the Duc de Mercoeur, made Dinan one of his strongholds. With the triumph of the Counter-Reformation in 17th-century

France, Dinan saw the building of two substantial new religious institutions, and the place would remain one of the most important towns in Brittany right through to the Revolution.

Cloth-making became a speciality here, as in many towns across the Côtes d'Armor and northern Brittany. This cloth was exported very successfully between the 15th and 18th centuries, though evidence for its making goes back to at least the mid 13th century. The 15th-century town belfry, built by and for merchants, was a symbol of their power. Before the Revolution, the textile trade with the French Caribbean colonies and the Iberian peninsula proved particularly fruitful for the Dinannais. In the 18th century, with repeated threats of the colonial wars with Britain spilling over onto dry land in Brittany, the town ramparts were reinforced yet again. On a lighter note, wit and society figure Charles Duclos-Pinot was perhaps the most brilliant figure the town produced under the Ancien Régime; after dazzling the court and intellectuals in Paris, he retired to Dinan to become mayor. During the Revolution, the religious orders that had had such a large share of Dinan were disbanded and some religious buildings damaged. In the 19th century, Dinan produced a highly popular artist who sang the praises of Brittany's traditional provincial ways – Théodore Botrel.

During the Second World War, on 2 August 1944, a terrible rain of 2,000 shells fell on the town when American troops liberated Dinan from the Nazis. Dinan has grown substantially beyond its ramparts since the war, though it flaunts its traditional side for the numerous visiting tourists.

A Tour of Dinan

Old Dinan is densely packed with historic buildings, but it is not dauntingly large, neatly enclosed within its three kilometres of ramparts. Set out from the joint **Place du Champ Clos** and **Place Du Guesclin**, which are lined with elegant 18th-century houses and rows of trees. The Place Du Guesclin, where the famous joust between Du Guesclin and Thomas of Canterbury took place, contains a triumphant equestrian statue of the victor; erected in 1902, it was executed by Emmanuel Frémiet, who made the striking statue of St Michael that crowns the Mont-St-Michel. Head south of these squares and you come out at the castle.

The Château and Musée de Dinan

Open Wed–Mon 1–5.30.

The Château de Dinan looks more like the sturdiest section of the town's ramparts than an independent castle. The separate Tour de Coëtquen and the massive gateway of La Porte du Guichet are generally considered part of the château these days. The museum's highpoints include its soaring architecture and a collection of medieval tomb effigies kept down in an isolated, dank basement.

Go right down to the deep, dark, lowest chamber of the main museum first, to follow the chronological order of the exhibits. The keep was made to be lived in – this you can see in the vaulted kitchen with its massive fireplace fit to roast whole animals. A small display of prehistoric finds starts off the collections. On the way up to the ground floor, look out for the beautiful carved schist plaque showing a marine god fighting a seahorse, a work from the 2nd or 3rd century.

The ground floor of the keep includes the former chapel, with a heated corner, and next to it the *Salle au Duc,* with another colossal fireplace and a collection of engravings, maps, furniture and sculpture haphazardly recalling Dinan's past. Further levels present the textile-making traditions of Dinan and the *coiffes* of the region, as well as paintings of the town. Nineteenth-century works by George Clarkson Stanfield and Isidore Dagnan stand out here, offering dramatic depictions of Dinan.

Head on to the Tour de Coëtquen; its two top floors are used for annual exhibitions, often of modern artists' works. Down the stairs past a statue of St Gilles caressing his pet is the atmospheric, dimly lit **Salle des Gisants**, often with pools of water on its rough floor, holding seven forceful medieval tomb effigies, from that of Roland de Dinan, said to be the oldest armed effigy in western Europe, to big-headed Geoffroi le Voyer, chamberlain to Duke Jean III of Brittany, and his shrivelled, painfully thin second wife.

You can get out of the ramparts under the massive **Porte du Guichet**, a 13th-century mass walled up by the Duc de Mercœur in the 16th century and only pierced through again in 1932. A walk down the **Promenade des Petits Fossés** leads you past two sturdy medieval towers, the **Tour du Connétable** and the **Tour de Beaufort**. Below you'll find the **Jardin des Petits Diables** (Little Devils' Garden).

To the Tour de l'Horloge

The **Rue de Léhon** leads back into the centre of town and the way turns into the **Rue de l'Horloge**. The **Maison de la Harpe** (*open mid May–Sept Tue, Wed, Fri and Sat 3–7, Thur 11–5, otherwise French school hols exc Christmas Wed, Thur and Sat 2–6*) occupies the 16th-century **Hôtel de Kératry**, just one of many exceptional old townhouses in Dinan, although this one is something of a fraud, saved from ruin in a village near St-Brieuc and transported here. The exhibition inside focuses on the history of the Celtic harp. Opposite, a tomb effigy was discovered during restoration work on one house and is now displayed outside it. The towering presence in this street is the **Tour de l'Horloge**, the 15th-century belfry, which you can climb in summer.

The Eglise St-Sauveur and the Historic Centre

Kissing dromedaries are not a common feature of French churches, but they are one of the decorative items that survive from the Romanesque **church** on the delightful lime-tree-lined, cobbled **Place St-Sauveur**. The story goes that a chivalric hero from Dinan, Riallon le Roux, vowed that he would build a church in the town if he got back alive after he had gone out crusading in the 12th century. He returned to Dinan, and seems to have communicated his strong memories to the masons. The few other pieces of this Romanesque church that survived are rather wonderful. The bull and the lion on the outside are the common symbols of the evangelists Luke and Mark. Barbary apes count among the other visible signs of the influence of the crusades. Look out too for the 11th-century baptismal font, with four beheaded figures holding its sides and a couple of stone fish carved inside it.

The bulk of the church is Gothic, the higher part of the nave and the left-hand aisle being built in the 15th century; this left-hand aisle offers a wonderful Gothic-pointed perspective down its length. The transepts and choir were constructed in the early 16th century. The heart of Bertrand Du Guesclin lies in a chest in the north transept. He is also romantically depicted in a 19th-century painting by Antoine Rivoulon; it was offered to the town by the French king, Louis-Philippe. The cemetery has been turned into the pretty **Jardin Anglais**, from where you can walk along stretches of the ramparts.

Just north, on Rue Haute Voie, the **Musée de la Théière** is a tearoom that doubles as a museum dedicated to that most revered of British household objects, the teapot. On **Place des Merciers** the restaurant Chez La Mère Pourcel (*see* p.158) has the most famous of the grand timberframe façades, but this quarter contains all manner of quirky old houses. Carry on along the wide major shopping street of the **Apport** to the **Place des Cordeliers**. You can get a good view here on to the Gothic choir end of the **church of St-Malo**, rebuilt in the 19th century in Flamboyant style.

Rue Comte de la Garaye from the back of the Eglise St-Malo takes you out to some of the most impressive portions of ramparts. Turn right at the end of the street and you can walk along the **Promenade des Grands Fossés** below the Tour Beaumanoir and the Porte St-Malo. Up on the **Tour du Gouverneur** you get a wonderful view of old Dinan and its many church towers. Return to the centre of town via the **Rue de l'Ecole**, lined with grand 18th-century houses. Some were owned by Compagnie des Indes sea captains who retired here with luxuries to adorn the interiors of their sober-faced homes.

To the Port

Rue du Petit Four and **Rue de Jerzual**, packed with fine timberframe houses all the way down to the Rance, are divided by the Porte de Jerzual, the passageway passing through its tower. The river was one of the major trade routes in Brittany. Textiles, wood, leather and cereals would be shipped up to St-Malo and abroad. Fish, salt and wine, and later tea and other luxury goods from abroad, would be hefted up the hill. These steep streets are now the town's main tourist trap. The most famous house is the **Maison du Gouverneur**, with its grand late-15th-century to early-16th-century forms.

Reaching the picturesque riverside, cross the bridge for the **Maison de la Rance** (*open July and Aug daily 10–12.30 and 2–7, April–June and Sept–Nov Tue–Sun 2–6, rest of year Sun 2–6*), which explains the history, ecology and workings of this tidal river with some verve. Guided visits of the Rance are organized from here.

Maison d'Artiste de La Grande Vigne

Open summer afternoons only, call t 02 96 87 90 80 or t 02 96 39 22 43.

Along the quays back on the other side of the river, this sweet little house set in terraced gardens served as home and studio for prolific painter Yvonne Jean-Haffen from 1937 until the early 1990s. A student of that great recorder of daily Breton life, Mathurin Méheut (*see* p.179), Yvonne was introduced to Brittany by him. The artists apparently became lovers in Méheut's later years, though Yvonne was married. Méheut's life is celebrated alongside hers here, but most works are by Jean-Haffen.

Dinan Festivals and Boat Trips

Many of the townspeople of Dinan get decked out in medieval dress to celebrate the **Fête des Remparts**, which takes place every other year in mid-July. To escape Dinan **by boat along the Rance**, contact Corsaire, **t** 08 25 16 80 35 (*tickets also available from tourist office*), or Le Jaman IV, **t** 02 96 39 28 41. You can also hire a boat from Danfleurenn Nautic, **t** 06 07 45 89 97. The **Musée du Rail** (*open daily June–mid-Sept 2–6*) at Dinan's railway station has a large collection of model railways as well as material on rail travel around Brittany. The **Théatre des Jacobins**, in the old town, has good musical programmes year round.

Around Dinan

South along the Rance to Léhon

On the outskirts of Dinan towards Léhon, a collector fascinated by the Second World War has created the **Musée Remember** (*open 10–12.30 and 1.30–6.30 April–Oct daily, Nov–March Sat, Sun, and public and school hols*), a museum that, as well as displaying war vehicles, looks in some detail at the daily life of the soldiers, both Allied and German.

A palm tree grows in the middle of patterned hydrangeas in the calming ruined cloister of the **abbey of Léhon** (*open July and Aug Mon–Sat 10–12 and 3–6; year-round for guided group visits by appointment, call **t** 02 96 39 07 19*), one of several enchanting visions in this old village just to the south of Dinan. Léhon dates back earlier in history than the main town by which it was eclipsed. That rebel against the Carolingians, Nomenoë, gave land here to monks to build the first abbey in the 9th century. These monks are said to have stolen relics of St Magloire for their religious foundation. A fort went up on the hillside above the abbey, while the latter grew into a centre of learning. A manuscript, *The Life of St Magloire of Léhon*, was produced to vindicate the setting up of the abbey. But it would soon suffer from Viking raids, and the whole settlement was ravaged. The monks managed to escape east with their relics, then returned in the 11th century to rebuild the abbey. In the 12th century, the lords of Dinan built a stone castle on the hill beside it and it seemed that Léhon was set to thrive again. However, King Henry II Plantagenet swept through and had his troops sack the castle. An enormous new fort was then erected, which knew its finest hours in the 13th and 14th centuries.

The main doorway leading into the **abbey church** looks Romanesque, but the rest of the vast vessel is plainly 13th-century Gothic. Eight medieval tomb effigies are lined along the walls of the nave. One represents the niece of the warrior Bertrand Du Guesclin, surrounded by coats of arms showing her noble credentials. Several of the tombstones depict lords of the mighty chivalric Beaumanoir family. The 17th-century cloister situated to the north of the church has lost its roof, but it nonetheless retains an exquisite atmosphere of peace. As part of the guided tour, you can visit the splendidly restored 13th- to -14th-century refectory, with its finely wrought Gothic openings.

West to Corseul

A great Gallo-Roman city, capital of the Roman-subjugated Celtic Coriosolitae tribe, arose at Corseul some 10 kilometres northwest of Dinan from around the year 10 BC. It grew to cover some 100 hectares and more, and possibly counted up to 10,000 inhabitants. It thrived for four centuries, gradually being abandoned from around AD 360. The remains of one of the most important monuments from these times, a **Temple to Mars**, stands close to the D794, some three kilometres from the main settlement. The height of the octagonal temple is impressive.

In Corseul itself, the displays of Gallo-Roman finds are slightly disappointing unless you're an expert on the subject. The town hall garden is decorated with the stubs of Gallo-Roman columns found in digs, the evidence of which can be seen in a patch of ground to one side of the *mairie*. The Gallo-Roman town was laid out on a grid plan, with the usual civic provisions such as temples and baths. The **Musée de Corseul** (*open July and Aug Mon–Sat 9–12 and 2–5; rest of year Mon–Fri 9–12 and 2–5, Sat 9–12*) is housed within the town hall. A few little rooms on the top floor display finds from the local excavations, including dice, decorated pottery, statuettes, a phallic amulet and buttons, one amusingly showing the head of a wild boar.

North Along the Rance

On the east side of the Rance river, the village of **St-Hélen** (off the N176 towards Dol) conceals more carved medieval tomb effigies in its church. This place lay at the centre of the fiefdom of the Coëtquens, an important feudal family in the area. The ruins of the Château de Coëtquen also lie close by.

At **Pleudihen-sur-Rance**, you can go and visit the lively, well-laid-out **Musée de la Pomme et du Cidre** (*open June–Aug daily 10–7; April, May and Sept Mon–Sat 2–7*) to learn about traditional Breton farm cider. Nearby, at **Mordreuc**, the views on to the Rance are particularly gorgeous as it widens heading north. You might cross the river at tiny **Lyvet**, where local fishermen still sometimes use their *carrelets*, square fishing nets left suspended above the river bank until they are submerged to catch fish.

The Côte d'Emeraude from Lancieux to Cap d'Erquy

The Côtes d'Armor coast up to the bay of St-Brieuc forms part of the stretch known as the Côte d'Emeraude. Five rough spits stick out into the Channel along the way, making for dramatic views. The first three peninsulas have yielded to the pleasures of beautiful, well-to-do family holiday beaches, dominated by the resorts of Lancieux, St-Jacut-de-la-Mer and St-Cast-le-Guildo. The two western spits, the Cap Fréhel and Cap d'Erquy, have a much wilder, emptier feel, covered as they are with large stretches of heathery moor running to dramatic cliffs. Fort La Latte, a spectacular promontory castle, steals the tourist limelight in the area. The stone is already starting to turn pink here, while the moors change to a bright heathery mauve in season. One more fine beach resort along this stretch is the 1920s Sables-d'Or-les-Pins.

Lancieux

Lovely villas punctuate the shore around Lancieux, the resort on the left bank of the Frémur (see St-Briac-sur-Mer, p.152, for the other bank). In summer time, shoals of fish-sized boats are left stranded on the extensive sands when the tide goes out. As you look out to sea, islands of rocks and pines are periodically joined to the mainland when the low tide reveals their causeways of sand. In the middle distance, the scattering of rocks makes up the Ebihen islands (the name derives from the Breton, An Inizi Bihan – the Little Isles).

Bloody Saint's Rocks

Ruddy streaks of colour stain some of Lancieux's rocks. One legend has it that a St Siog (in Breton) or Cieux (French for skies) was born here and cleared the land to make it fertile. Having gone off to convert the pagans inland, he returned battered and bruised, on the verge of death. The blood he spilt here is supposed to have reddened the local rocks. Another tale about Siog claims that he came from Britain and got his name from a dream he claims to have had, in which he saw himself carried up to heaven, which explains the French name for him.

St-Jacut-de-la-Mer

An Irish saint is credited with founding a community here in the Dark Ages. The abbey of St-Jacut grew into one of the most important ones in Brittany, and ran one of Dinan's large religious establishments. Virtually nothing remains of the abbey except for parts in a family boarding house run by nuns.

Originally, fishermen here lived off mackerel-fishing in particular. But there has also always been an abundance of shellfish. The local women used to go out to collect and sell the shellfish they dug up from the enormous expanses of sand revealed around St-Jacut at low tide. A small and ancient-rooted community does stay on through the winter, when the tourist hordes have left. They even still practise their Jégui together, the local form of Gallo, the dialect of eastern Brittany whose roots go back to Gallo-Roman times.

The Arguenon Estuary and Plancoët

You need to cross the Arguenon estuary to get on to the peninsula of the large resort of St-Cast-le-Guildo. The Arguenon, which flows down from the Méné hills in central Brittany, once served as the medieval frontier between the lordships of Dinan and Penthièvre. You can walk around the substantial ruined walls of the medieval **Château du Guildo**. Built for the lords of Dinan, it guards the eastern entrance to the Arguenon river. The pretty quayside of the village of **Le Guildo** lies nearby.

A detour up the right bank of the Arguenon leads to what apparently became a neolithic centre of some importance, although only scant signs of it remain. Following the Arguenon inland, you come to the old town of **Plancoët**, near which you can enjoy a free glass of the local mineral water; the Perrier group has been in charge of bottling this pure source since 1961.

Côte d'Emeraude

10 km

5 miles

N

To Paimpol

Plouha

St-Quay-Portrieux

Etables-sur-Mer
Les Godelins

Cap d'Erquy
Tu-Es -Roc
Erquy

Caroual

Binic

Pointe de Pordic

Pointe de Pléneuf

Le Val-André

Château de
Bien Assis

Pordic

Trégomeur

Les Rosaires

Baie de
St-Brieuc

Dahouët

Pléneuf-
Val-André

La Bouillie

Pointe du
Roselier

Le Port Morvan

St-Laurent-de-
la-Mer

Le Port Morvan

La Cotentin

St-Alban

To Châtelaudren

Plérin

Anse d'Yffiniac

St-Brieuc

La Grandville

Planguenoual

Hillion

Langueux

Yffiniac

La Poterie

E50/12

Lamballe

CÔTES D'ARMOR

To Moncontour and
La Chèze

To Quintin

St-Cast-le-Guildo

St-Cast-le-Guildo lies on a wider, less insular peninsula than St-Jacut. The two communities used to be rivals over fishing. Now they compete with their holiday beaches; St-Cast boasts seven. St-Cast's name evokes the memory of an important battle between the British and the French in 1758, during the Seven Years War. The story goes that General Bligh led an invasion landing on St-Lunaire, to the east along the coast. His British fleet withdrew to wait at St-Cast. Bligh's campaign failed and he and his many thousands of soldiers headed rapidly to St-Cast. However, the army of the Duc d'Aiguillon, royal governor of Brittany, was waiting for them. In a chaotic battle, the French eventually triumphed, as the chivalric symbolism on top of the St-Cast column reflects, the greyhound vanquishing the English leopard.

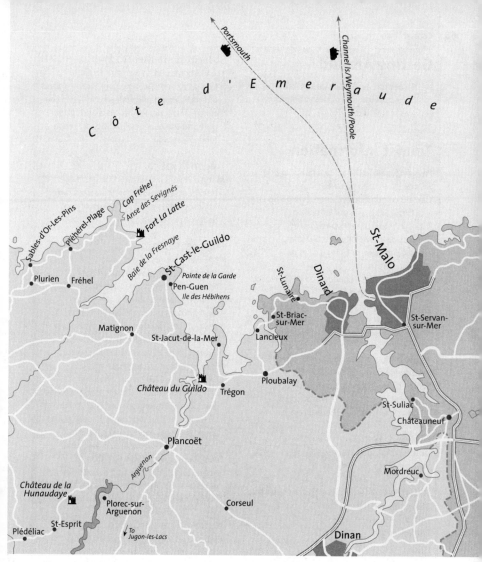

The first beach on the east side of the St-Cast peninsula, the **Plage des Quatre-Vaux**, is a rural delight before the more built-up beaches of the resort itself. The big **beach of Pen-Guen** (White Point) lies south of the main part of town. Wealthy holidaymakers began building spacious villas on the southern tip of the old town, Pointe de la Garde, from the second half of the 19th century. You can enjoy a walk along the *sentier touristique* through these quarters, with their fine trees and views over to St-Jacut and the Ebihen islands. **La Garde**, the main beach of chic St-Cast, stretches some two kilometres below the town. The old fishermen's quarters, **L'Isle**, lie on the tip of the peninsula. A local association organizes trips on old-fashioned fishing boats.

A track leads to the very tip of the peninsula. The bay of La Fresnaye separates the St-Cast peninsula from that of the Cap Fréhel and the Fort La Latte. You can make out the fort's dramatic forms from the top of the Pointe de St-Cast. The way down the

Getting Around

Plancoët has a **railway** station. Ask at local tourist offices for information about **bus** services in the area.

Tourist Information

Pays d'Accueil de Dinan, Le Grand Clos, Quévert, t 02 96 39 62 64.
Lancieux: Square Jean Conan, t 02 96 86 25 37, or t 02 96 86 22 19 out of season, *lancieux.tourisme@wanadoo.fr*.
St-Jacut-de-la-Mer: Rue du Châtelet, t 02 96 27 71 91, or t 02 96 27 71 15 out of season.
Plancoët: Rue des Venelles, t 02 96 84 00 57, *infos@ot-plancoet.fr*.
St-Cast-le-Guildo: Place Charles de Gaulle, t 02 96 41 81 52, *www.ot-st-cast-le-guildo.fr*.
Matignon: Place du Général de Gaulle, t 02 96 41 12 53.
Fréhel: Le Bourg, t 02 96 41 53 81, *otfrehel@wanadoo.fr*.
Sables-d'Or-les-Pins: t 02 96 72 18 52, *otplunen@wanadoo.fr*. (For written enquiries, use the Fréhel address.)

Market Days

Lancieux: Tuesday in season.
St-Jacut-de-la-Mer: Friday.
Plancoët: Saturday.
St-Cast-le-Guildo: Friday; Monday in season.
Matignon: Wednesday.
Fréhel: Tuesday.
Plurien: Friday.

Where to Stay and Eat

Lancieux ✉ 22770

★★★**Les Bains**, 20 Rue du Poncel, t 02 96 86 31 33, *bertrand.mehouse@wanadoo.fr* (*inexpensive*). Comfortable modern rooms and a private garden.
Hôtel de la Mer, 1 Rue de la Plage, t 02 96 86 22 07 (*inexpensive*). A well-located option.
Les Hortensias, Villeneuve, 40 Rue du Moulin, t 02 96 86 31 15 (*inexpensive*). A B&B close to a road but in a pretty, old house with tastefully decorated rooms, lots of books and a warm welcome.

St-Jacut-de-la-Mer ✉ 22750

★**Le Vieux Moulin**, 22 Rue du Moulin, t 02 96 27 71 02 (*inexpensive*). Simple round rooms in an old mill well positioned in the centre of the peninsula, close enough to the port and the beaches. Traditional French food is available.

Trégon ✉ 22650

Maryse Revel, La Hautière, t 02 96 27 25 87 (*inexpensive*). A B&B in restored old farm buildings, plus gîtes, just south of the St-Jacut peninsula.

Plancoët ✉ 22130

★★★**Hôtel l'Ecrin**, 20 Les Quais, t 02 96 84 10 24, *www.crouzil.com* (*expensive*). Smart, spacious rooms furnished with antiques. This place is best known for its 2-Michelin-starred restaurant **Chez Crouzil** (*very expensive*), where the chef adds exotic touches to Breton dishes. The wine list has some 450 vintages. Not one for those on diets.
La Pastourelle B&B, close to St-Lormel, a few km north of Plancoët along the west bank of the Arguenon river, t 02 96 84 03 77 (*inexpensive*). An old country house with small and cosy rooms, and simple but copious food. *Table d'hôte* is available.
Ferme-auberge du Grand Trait, on the road towards Dinard, t 02 96 84 01 23 (*inexpensive*). Farm produce, such as rabbit in cider and apples, in country surroundings.

Notre-Dame-du-Guildo ✉ 22380

Château du Val, t 02 96 41 07 03 (*moderate*). A château on the site of an earlier manor that was apparently destroyed by the British in the battle of St-Cast, though the owners offer even British guests luxury B&B rooms. There's a tennis court in the grounds.
Le Gilles de Bretagne, close to the port, t 02 96 41 07 08 (*moderate*). A reliable restaurant, named after the ill-fortuned brother of a Breton duke who had him murdered.

St-Cast-le-Guildo ✉ 22380

★★★**Les Arcades**, 15 Rue du Duc d'Aiguillon, t 02 96 41 80 50, *hotel.arcades@wanadoo.fr* (*moderate*). Comfortable, quiet rooms, some with sea views, and a brasserie.

Les Dunes, Rue Primauguet, **t 02 96 41 80 31 (*moderate*). An old-fashioned hotel that stands out for its high standards. The beach is close by, and there's a private tennis court available for guests' use.

Hôtel Ker Louis, 15 Rue Du Guesclin, **t 02 96 41 80 77 (*inexpensive*). A reasonably priced option.

Hôtel Les Mielles, 3 Rue du Duc d'Aiguillon, **t 02 96 41 80 95 (*inexpensive*). A hotel situated just 50m or so from the beach; some of the modern bedrooms have views on to it.

Hotel Port Jacquet, 32 Rue du Port, **t 02 96 41 97 18 (*inexpensive*). An excellent hotel with a restaurant, situated right on the seafront. The room prices vary depending on the view.

Alain Pilard, Les Landes, **t** 02 96 41 01 77. (*inexpensive*). B&B accommodation in an attractive old farmhouse located just outside town.

Le Biniou, Plage de Pen Guen, 2km south of town, **t** 02 96 41 94 53 (*moderate*). Interesting seafood dishes served in dining rooms and on terraces with panoramic views over the beach. *Closed Mon.*

Crêperie Le Bretan'or, 8 Place Anatole Le Braz, **t** 02 96 41 92 45 (*inexpensive*). A holidaymakers' favourite. *Closed Wed out of season.*

L'Etoile de Mer, Rue du Port, **t** 02 96 41 92 45 (*inexpensive*). A pleasant crêperie set right by the sea.

Fréhel ✉ 22240

Ushuaïa-Bellevue, Fort La Latte, **t 02 96 41 41 61 (*inexpensive*). A hotel-cum-crêperie that is quite magnificently located fairly close to the most stunning coastal castle in the whole of Brittany.

Le Relais de Fréhel, Route du Cap-Plévenon, **t** 02 96 41 43 02 (*inexpensive*). A little B&B within a family home, with its own wild garden. It's won itself a good reputation for the warmth of its welcome and for the family cooking on offer.

Auberge de Jeunesse, La Ville Hardieux, Kerivet-en-Fréhel, **t** 02 96 41 48 98, *www.fuaj.org* (*inexpensive*). The local youth hostel.

Le Victorine, Place de la Mairie, **t** 02 96 41 55 55 (*moderate–expensive*). A place that prides itself on its fresh seafood, for which you would be well advised to reserve ahead.

Sables-d'Or-les-Pins ✉ 22240

***La Voile d'Or/La Lagune, Allée des Acacias, **t** 02 96 41 42 49, *la-voile-dor@wanadoo.fr* (*moderate–very expensive*). The smartest address in town, though the bedrooms are fairly ordinary (some have sea views, however). The menu has an excellent selection of seafood.

Manoir St-Michel, Le Carquois, Route du Cap Fréhel (north along the coast from Sables-d'Or), **t 02 96 41 48 87, *www.fournel.de* (*inexpensive–expensive*). A real find, with a noble Breton exterior, excellent, spacious rooms complete with antique furniture, and wonderful views onto the sea from the garden, which boasts its own lake.

Le Diane, seafront, **t 02 96 41 42 07, *www.hoteldiane.fr* (*inexpensive–moderate*). An option that has plenty of charm, and a period feel to the rooms that suits the resort. Some of the bedrooms look out on to the beach.

Les Pins, Allée des Acacias, **t 02 96 41 42 20, (*inexpensive*). A place behind the beach, with a pleasant atmosphere.

Restaurant La Duchesse Anne, seafront, **t** 02 96 41 49 05 (*moderate–expensive*). A restaurant offering unfussy and reasonable-value food in a dining room with views out to sea, aquariums and old Breton furniture.

Plurien ✉ 22240

Hôtel-Manoir de la Salle, Rue du Lac, **t 02 96 72 38 29, *www.manoir-de-la-salle.com* (*inexpensive–moderate*). A 16th-century manor on the outside, with bedrooms decked out in a modern style.

Matignon ✉ 22550

Crêperie de Saint-Germain, village square, **t** 02 96 41 08 33 (*inexpensive*). A good place to come to enjoy a wide variety of traditional crêpes made using top-quality local produce.

western side of the St-Cast peninsula along the bay of La Fresnaye is more broken up by cliffs than the beachy eastern side. At low tide, the bay turns into a vast mudflat; mussels and oysters are cultivated here.

Matignon Without the French Prime Minister

Matignon may be the French prime minister's residence in Paris, but it is also a Breton village inland from St-Cast-le-Guildo. The name derives from the fact that Jacques Goyon-Matignon, of the local lordly family, once owned the Parisian house that is now the French prime minister's residence. Another Goyon-Matignon, François, Comte de Thorigny, married the heiress of the Grimaldi family, becoming Prince of Monaco. A Matignon lord also ordered the building of the stupendous Fort La Latte.

The Cap Fréhel Peninsula

What a change, after all the family resorts from St-Malo to St-Cast-le-Guildo, to come to the wild heaths of this peninsula.

Fort La Latte

Open daily April–June and Sept 10–12.30 and 2.30–6.30; July and Aug 10–7.

Isolated on its rocky promontory, stung by winter storms, this fort has all the drama you would expect to inspire Romantic artists and Hollywood 'historical' films. Indeed, Kirk Douglas and Tony Curtis came here in 1957 to play at Dark Ages fighters in *Vikings*. It was also used as a set in the 1980s filming of Balzac's Breton novel, *Les Chouans* (*see* p.78). It's the most sensational and attractive Breton coastal castle.

The fort was built in the course of the 14th century for Etienne III Goyon-Matignon, and was first known as La Roche-Goyon. Battered by warring and later the victim of neglect, it has lost many of its original features. Several original elements do stand out, though, from as far back as the 14th century: the first of the two drawbridge defences dates from medieval times, as do four of the rampart towers with their distinctive shapes, funnelling out towards the bottom. The most spectacular piece of the whole fort, the keep, also dates from the 14th century. There are virtually no windows here, just arrow slits the height of a man, plus little loopholes in the bottom slits to take *couleuvrines*, the first miniature cannons. A ring of machicolations runs round the top of the keep. This donjon, although sober looking, does have its own very discreet decoration – symbols of the four evangelists placed on the outer walls, marking the cardinal points.

Brittany was rocked by the War of Succession in the mid 14th century. Then the king of France, Charles V, tried to claim Brittany for himself. His Breton-born army leader, Bertrand Du Guesclin, took this stronghold in 1379, but the treaty of Guérande in 1381 rapidly restored the property to the Goyon-Matignons. Though placed in such a splendid lookout's position, the fort scarcely served in military terms in the 15th–16th centuries. It was left in ruins through the 17th century, still the neglected property of the Goyon-Matignons, who continued to appoint governors to oversee it.

Simon Garengeau, the man mainly responsible for fortifying St-Malo, was given charge of the conversion of Fort La Latte's ruins in the late 17th century, when France and Britain were at war. Although the Goyon-Matignons were to remain in possession of the place until 1720, when the French military finally bought it from them, these transformations were paid for by the state. The guards continued to be recruited locally, while the governors stopped living at the fort, preferring to take more comfortable lodgings nearby. However, one famous guest did stay at Fort La Latte in 1715 – none other than the pretender to the English throne, James Stuart. He was forced to take refuge here on a stormy evening and wrote of the fort being one of the grimmest, most godforsaken spots in which a man could spend a night. He complained that there was not even wood to cook with, and no comforts whatsoever.

After so much effort spent adapting Fort La Latte, the 18th-century military action took place along other stretches of the Breton coast. Even during the battle of St-Cast so close by, the fort did not play any role. During the Revolutionary period, a comical addition was made to the fort. The French naval command had ordered that cannonball ovens be built along the north Breton coast, in order to help react swiftly to any passing enemy vessels, the aim being to set their ships on fire. Unfortunately it took two and a half hours to 'cook' a cannonball to the desired heat, which was hardly swift enough to surprise the foe, who would be warned by smoke from the oven. You can still see the cannonball oven at Fort La Latte.

By 1886, the military presence had been reduced to one castle-keeper. The estate was put up for sale, and Frédéric Joüon des Longrais, who had been passionate about the place since his childhood, bought the fort in 1931. With the assistance of the Historic Monuments of France, he set about restoring the dilapidated buildings. Armies of tourists come to visit this spectacular site each summer now. The fort can seem rather empty within, but one of the most exhilarating parts of the visit is climbing onto the roof of the keep, which is covered with slabs of stone by way of tiles – they are unlikely to blow away even in the strongest gale.

To the Cap Fréhel

The energetic among you could walk from Fort La Latte, across the heathery coastal moors above the cliffs of the Anse des Sévignés and its fairy grotto of La Teignouse, to the Cap Fréhel. The path offers a spectacular but dangerous way to appreciate the varied colours of the cliffs and islets, made of schist and pinkish sandstone, with porphyry thrown in. This peninsula's roads are marred by traffic in summer, but virtually no houses grow on the purple moorlands. A German blockhouse is now a centre explaining the history of the location, as well as its rich botanical and ornithological interest.

Guillemots, petrels and the odd couple of gannets count among the rare species of birds that nest on the islets off the coast. You may also spot the *petit pingouin* (*alca torda*) and the rare raven. The largest colony of crested cormorants in France nests at the Cap Fréhel. At certain times of year, the Breton society for the protection of nature organizes local ornithological walks. To appreciate the soaring cliffs from a different angle, take a **boat trip** round the Cap Fréhel from Dinard or St-Malo.

You can climb up the **Phare de Fréhel**, which takes you almost 100 metres above the sea. From here, you can look down not just to Fort La Latte, but also along the whole Côte d'Emeraude, past the city of St-Malo to Normandy's Cotentin peninsula on the finest days. Occasionally, you can also glimpse the bay of St-Brieuc and the Ile de Bréhat to the west. The corniche road from the cape heads towards the resort of Sables-d'Or-les-Pins. Again, there are virtually no houses here, just moors and cliffs and the odd stretch of sand down steep paths. The waters can be dangerous along this area. **Pléhérel-Plage** looks like a friendly family resort though, with a wonderfully situated village church overlooking the sea.

Sables-d'Or-les-Pins

You then come to the surprise of the failed utopian resort of **Sables-d'Or-les-Pins**. The name, which was invented by two dreaming 1920s developers, highlights the attractions here: the glorious stretch of beach, and the pines that are planted in profusion on the dunes behind it. Launay and Brouard called in architects and landscape gardeners to create some Norman-style villas, the odd Art Deco building and a chic ambiance. The first villas were snapped up, and the social scene grew lively, but the great crash, together with mismanagement, brought a swift halt to development in the early 1930s. The resort has never been finished, leaving a curious atmosphere to the place.

To the Erquy Peninsula

East of Sables-d'Or-les-Pins, the coastal path follows the cliffs of the Erquy peninsula. At low tide, you can walk to the islet of St-Michel with its chapel. The GR34 continues along the northern coast to the Cap d'Erquy, with its gently rolling moorlands. Splendid views give out to sea and across the bay of St-Brieuc.

The Bay of St-Brieuc from Erquy to St-Brieuc

The views across this immense bay are staggering – they really do almost match those across the bay of Mont-St-Michel. But whereas the coast along the bottom of the bay of Mont-St-Michel is flat as a pancake, cliffs line the shore of the whole of the bay of St-Brieuc. The old fishing ports around it have been turned into modern resorts with varying degrees of success.

The Peninsula and Port of Erquy

Archaeologists say that Celts and Gallo-Romans once guarded the coastline from the vantage point of the **Cap d'Erquy** above the port of Erquy. Heather and bracken dominate, with just a scattering of pines, allowing open views all round. The local pink rocks of Erquy apparently went into the building of Paris' Arc de Triomphe. The area has been ravaged by tourist hordes recently, and visitors are now herded along precise tracks.

Well-marked paths lead from Tu-Es-Roc around the peninsula. Beaches of varied character lie around the sides of this block of land. On the east edge, from the Plage du Guen, backed by pine woods, you can walk right over to Sables-d'Or-les-Pins when the tide is out. The beach of Portuais has impressive rocks as a backdrop. Closer to the western tip of the cape, the fine Plage du Lourtuais is a favourite with nudists.

Erquy

The port is the best part of this seaside town on the eastern end of the bay, with great chunks of pink Erquy rock protecting the harbour. Erquy still employs many people in scallop-dredging; it is the largest port in France for this catch. The ridge of houses around the bay may not be the most inspiring in Brittany, but this is a popular family resort. Turn the corner of the Pointe de la Heussaye on the western end of Erquy's bay and you come to the spacious Plage de Caroual, reputed for its fine sands.

Getting Around

St-Brieuc (*see* p.188) is the place to go to in search of public transport along this section of coast.

Yffiniac has a **train** station on the line between St-Brieuc and Rennes.

Tourist Information

Erquy: Boulevard de la Mer, t 02 96 72 30 12, *www.erquy-tourisme.com*.
Pléneuf-Val-André: Cours Winston Churchill, t 02 96 72 20 55, *www.val-andre.org*.
Hillion: t 02 96 32 21 53, or t 02 96 32 21 04 out of season.
Yffiniac: t 02 96 72 59 81 (high season only).

Market Days

Erquy: Saturday.
Pléneuf: Tuesday.
Le Val-André: Friday in summer.

Where to Stay and Eat

Erquy ✉ 22430

★★Beauséjour, 21 Rue de la Corniche, t 02 96 72 30 39, *hotel.beausejour@ wanadoo.fr* (*inexpensive*). A hotel that watches over the bay with its two glassy eyeballs – one is the reception, the other is the restaurant. Rhubarb crêpes are a speciality of the latter.

★★Hôtel de la Plage, 21 Boulevard de la Mer, t 02 96 72 30 09 (*inexpensive*). A modern option by the beach.

★★Le Relais, 60 Rue du Port, t 02 96 72 32 60 (*inexpensive*). Rooms with lovely views on the eastern end of town, and a popular seafood restaurant.

La Cassolette, 6 Rue de la Saline, t 02 96 72 13 08 (*moderate–expensive*). A great-value choice offering *cassolettes* such as crayfish with orange, plus other dishes based on the 'pick-of-the-sea'. *Closed mid-Nov–Feb, and Wed, Thurs, and Fri lunch in low season.*

L'Escurial, seafront, t 02 96 72 31 56 (*moderate*). Carefully prepared and imaginative dishes.

Le Reflet de la Mer, 18 Rue du Port, t 02 96 72 00 95 (*inexpensive*). Simple galettes and even simpler rooms opposite the beach. Wonderful value. *Closed Nov–March.*

St-Aubin ✉ 22430

Le Relais St-Aubin, Route de la Bouillie, t 02 96 72 13 22 (*moderate–expensive*). A 17th-century priory with a leafy garden, 3km inland from Erquy. Seafood is a speciality, and meats are grilled in a monumental fireplace. *Closed Mon.*

La Bouillie ✉ 22400

Auberge La Bonnaie, t 02 96 31 51 71 (*inexpensive*). A simple B&B offering traditional Breton meals (*moderate*) for residents and others on reservation. A good taste of rural Brittany.

Château de Bien Assis

Open mid-June–mid-Sept for guided visits, Mon–Sat 10.30–12.30 and 2–6.30, Sun and public hols 2–6.30.

Inland from Erquy, this converted medieval château lurks behind an impressively solid wall. A sign warning of *Douves!* reminds you as you arrive not to drive right into the well-concealed moat. Little remains of the 15th-century castle that was ordered by the Quélénec family, except for a mighty tower at the back. If you look carefully at the façade you will see a dividing line running down the middle of the building – the Château de Bien Assis turns out to be something of a semi-detached castle. One half was commissioned by Gilles Visdelou in the 1620s and the second half was added in the late 18th century by François-Hyacinthe Visdelou. Before the Revolution, the château became the property of the Comte de La Ville-Théart, who was the founder of a series of Breton stud farms. As the Terror raged in 1792, the count found himself

Pléneuf-Val-André ✉ 22370
★★Grand Hôtel, 80 Rue Amiral Charner, **t** 02 96 72 20 56, *www.grand-hotel-val-andre.fr* (*inexpensive–moderate*). A hotel with a grand façade, looking out to sea. The bedrooms are modern and comfortable.
★★Hotel de France, 4 Rue Pasteur, **t** 02 96 72 22 52 (*inexpensive*). An establishment run by the same family since 1906. *Closed Sun eve and Mon out of season.*
Au Biniou, 121 Rue Clemenceau, **t** 02 96 72 24 35 (*moderate*). Succulent seafood, including delicious fish stews. *Closed Tues eve and Wed.*
Restaurant Le Haut-Guen, above the Plage des Vallées, **t** 02 96 72 25 07 (*moderate*). A fully non-smoking restaurant right by the sea, offering fricassee of prawns in whisky as a speciality. *Closed eves May–Sept.*

St-Alban ✉ 22400
Ferme de Malido, **t** 02 96 32 94 74 (*inexpensive*). A charming Breton farm with simple B&B rooms, a basic kitchen you can use, and a barbecue corner.
Auberge du Poirier, Poirier roundabout, **t** 02 96 32 96 21 (*moderate–expensive*). A restaurant with a strong local reputation, and seasonal menus. *Closed Sun, Mon and Tues eves.*

Planguenoual ✉ 22400
★★★Domaine du Val, **t** 02 96 32 75 40, *www.chateauxhotels.com* (*expensive–*

very expensive). A luxurious hotel incorporated in a medieval castle and outbuildings, offering all the modern comforts you'd expect for the price. You pay more to stay in the château itself. The grounds, situated less than 1km from the sea, are listed, and there's also a covered sports complex containing an indoor tennis court, two squash courts and a heated swimming pool.
Le Manoir de la Hazaie, Lamballe, **t** 02 96 32 73 71 (*expensive–very expensive*). Ultra-grand B&B accommodation luxury in a beautiful 16th-century house. The bedrooms are extremely spacious, with antiques and often with four-poster beds and/or monumental old fireplaces, and the bathrooms are a dream.

Hillion ✉ 22120
Château de Bonabry, **t** 02 96 32 21 06 (*expensive*). Luxury B&B rooms inside a stern-faced little castle situated close to the dunes of Bon Abri. The bedrooms are sumptuously decorated and boast their own private salons. Guests are free to wander round the grounds, which include a chapel and old stables.

Langueux ✉ 22360
Crêperie des Grèves, Rue des Grèves, **t** 02 96 72 56 96 (*inexpensive*). A reasonably priced place using excellent local produce in its range of crêpes.

by coincidence in Britain 'buying thoroughbreds'. Denounced as an émigré, he had his property ransacked. The château served briefly as a prison and then was the property of a Napoleonic general. The Kerjégus bought and rescued it in the 1880s. The architecture contains some clever references to the sea, as you will learn during the guided tour.

To Pléneuf-Val-André and Dahouët

If you're a keen walker, you could take on the superb coastal path from Erquy to the resort of Le Val-André. The way leads you past the excellent beaches of Ville-Berneuf and the Grève des Vallées. But first a word or two on the **Ile Verdelet**, the bay of St-Brieuc's answer to the Mont-St-Michel rock. This dramatic, triangular-looking island draws the attention from right round the bay. It is now a bird reserve, home to great cormorants, crested cormorants and all manner of gulls. At low tide, a causeway of pebbles and sand is revealed, making it possible to walk out to the island. Normally though, access is forbidden, to leave the birds in peace.

With the dramatic presence of the Ile Verdelet adding to the obvious attraction of its long sandy beach, **Le Val-André** was chosen as the site for a brand new Breton resort in the 1880s. The sands are excellent for children, and, as they widen with the outgoing tide, sand-yachts make the most of the space provided. On the eastern end of the resort you'll find the sailing school, next to the small port.

Dahouët is the port hidden away behind the Pointe de la Guette. It has much older and deeper roots than the resort of Le Val-André, and is said to have been used by Viking raiders. It is certainly cleverly concealed down the narrowest of rock-lined estuaries, out of harm from lashing waves – a fact modern marina developers have unearthed too. The ports around the bay of St-Brieuc are historically renowned for their great long-distance, perilous fishing expeditions to the waters off North America and Iceland. Dahouët claims to have been one of the first French ports from which boats left for gruelling cod-fishing journeys off Newfoundland, as early as the start of the 16th century. Colourful fishing boats still draw up by the quayside houses and bring in scallops part of the year, overlooked by a protective Virgin Mary. You can go out on trips in the *Pauline*, a reconstruction of a local boat from the 1900s. In summer, hundreds of yachts are crammed together in the shiny new marina.

Secretive Spots Along the Cliff-lined Coast to St-Brieuc

A breach in a cement wall leads on to the **beach of Le Port Morvan**; this cove is often particularly warm thanks to the high sides of the cliffs protecting it. When you walk out towards the sea at low tide, St-Brieuc comes into view. The tarmac track ends before you get to the **Grèves du Vauglin**, a splendid little sandy cove enclosed by rocky points, a little island adding interest to the middle distance. Follow the winding village road through attractive **La Cotentin** to the cliffs.

After the next creek at Jospinet, head down to **L'Hermot d'en Bas** and the **Chapelle St-Maurice**. The little chapel on its hillock beyond the Nazi blockhouse stamps its character on this short stretch of the bay's coastline. A curious low cliff of orange earth forms the back wall to the beach of **St-Maurice**. Beyond, the Gouessant river snakes its way through the mudflats to the sea at low tide. Panels warn of the Gouessant's channel here, treacherously disguised when the tide comes up. Above the **Plage de Béliard** you can get an excellent view of the incoming tide arriving to cover up the lines of wooden posts on which mussels grow out in the bay.

At the splendid expanse of the **Plage de la Grandville**, more warning panels alert you to the speed of the incoming tides. This is one of the most spectacular beaches along the north coast of Brittany. The **Dunes de Bon Abri** are gorgeous, hidden out of sight from St-Brieuc by the Pointe de Guette. Mussel-farming tractors work by these dunes, dogs are left to race joyfully across the great tracts of sands at low tide, and the odd trotter-horse racers come out in their comical chariots to practise their skills. As you walk across the beach, mussels crunch underfoot.

Hillion and the Maison de la Baie de St-Brieuc

West of the Pointe de Guette, the **Anse d'Yffiniac**, the deep, sharp inland point of the bay of St-Brieuc, turns into one vast mudflat when the tide goes out, so this is not a place to come swimming. However, many of the residents of **Hillion** keep a little boat by the shore. The suburban quarters of Hillion have grown in recent years, but its coastal path along the Anse d'Yffiniac remains unspoilt and provides for a magical walk. You might like to visit the **Maison de la Baie de St-Brieuc** on Rue de l'Etoile (*open all year, t 02 96 32 27 98*) first, and then join the coastal path that lies just beyond it. The Maison explains the environment of the bay, which is affected by the fifth largest tidal movements in the world; the difference between low tide and high tide can be 12 metres, and the sea can withdraw seven kilometres at low tide, revealing a staggering 3,000 hectares of mudflats. The *marinarium*, or marine aquarium, presents the diversity of marine life to be found in the bay.

In nearby Langueux, the new **La Briqueterie** (*open 2–7 July and Aug Wed–Mon, Sept–June Fri–Sun*) museum depicts life in the bay, particularly the brick-making trade.

The Ring of Historic Penthièvre Towns Around St-Brieuc

A fine trio of historic towns, Lamballe, Moncontour and Quintin, are within easy reach of the coast but also make good bases for exploring inland, rural Côtes d'Armor.

Lamballe

Once capital of the quarrelsome Breton county of Penthièvre, which stretched south from the Côte d'Emeraude and the bay of St-Brieuc, Lamballe is now capital of the Breton horse, as well as one of the most overlooked of Brittany's characterful market towns, set in its hollow in the Gouessant valley. Virtually nothing remains of the medieval fortified town, although the semi-fortified church of Notre-Dame de Grande Puissance on its hillside hints at its defensive importance.

History

A Gallo-Roman settlement in the area was followed by a Christian one founded by Pal, or Pol, who converted many in the area in the 6th century. In the 10th century, the Vikings destroyed the hilltop fort that existed here. Lamballe acquired particular political significance when Duke Alain III of Brittany gave the lordship of Penthièvre as an apanage to his brother Eudes in 1034. From this time to 1420, the counts of Penthièvre were frequently a thorn in the side of the Breton dukes.

Lamballe inevitably became embroiled in the vicious Breton War of Succession of the mid 14th century; after all, the French-backed contender for the Breton dukedom, Charles de Blois, was none other than the husband of Jeanne de Penthièvre. In 1420, well after the war had finished, the victorious Duke Jean V of Brittany had Lamballe's town ramparts torn down.

King Charles IX elevated the county of Penthièvre to a duchy in the 16th century. The Duc de Mercoeur, the feared ultra-Catholic leader in Brittany during the French Wars of Religion at the end of that century, was also duke of Penthièvre. One of his greatest enemies, the Calvinist La Nouë, nicknamed Bras-de-Fer ('Iron Arm') because of an artificial limb he wore, came to attack Lamballe in 1591. He was seriously wounded in the siege, much to the chagrin of King Henri IV for whose cause he had been fighting. 'He was worth a whole army on his own', the king is supposed to have

Getting Around

Lamballe is on the TGV rapid **train** line linking Paris with Brest, but few TGV trains actually stop at the station. The journey from Paris takes a little under 3hrs. Lamballe is served by more regular trains between St-Brieuc (15mins away) and Rennes (c. 1hr away). You can also travel by train from Lamballe to Dinan and Dol-de-Bretagne.

Tourist Information

Lamballe: Maison du Bourreau, Place du Martray, **t** 02 96 31 05 38, *www.lamballe-communaute.com*.
Jugon-les-Lacs: t 02 96 31 70 75, *tourisme.jugon.les.lacs@wanadoo.fr*.
Moncontour: 4 Place de la Carrière, **t** 02 96 73 50 50, or **t** 02 96 73 41 05 out of season, *www.pays-moncontour.com*.
La Chèze: t 02 96 26 70 99, *www.centrebretagne.com*.
Loudéac: Place du Général de Gaulle, **t** 02 96 28 25 17, or **t** 02 96 66 85 00 out of season, *www.centrebretagne.com*.
Quintin: Place 1830, **t** 02 96 74 01 51, *otsi.pays-de-quintin@wanadoo.fr*.

Market Days

Lamballe: Thursday.
Jugon-les-Lacs: Friday.
Moncontour: Monday.
Loudéac: Saturday.
Quintin: Tuesday.

Where to Stay and Eat

Lamballe ✉ **22400**
Hôtel Kyrial, 29 Rue Jobert, **t 02 96 31 00 16, *www.hotel-lamballe.com* (*moderate*). A refurbished option near the station, formerly the Hôtel d'Angleterre.
La Tour d'Argent, 2 Rue du Docteur Lavergne, **t 02 96 31 01 37, *latourdargent@ wanadoo.fr* (*inexpensive*). An old townhouse with a garden and a restaurant, situated right in the centre.
Hôtel du Lion d'Or, Rue du Lion d'Or, **t** 02 96 31 20 36 (*inexpensive*). A hotel on a quiet street, with *chambres mansardées*, and tables and chairs out in its garden.
Le Teno, 14 Rue Notre-Dame, **t** 02 96 31 00 41 (*inexpensive*). The birthplace of the artist Mathurin Méheut, with very good-value and spacious B&B rooms.

remarked regretfully. After the Wars of Religion had been settled, King Henri IV donated the Penthièvre to his illegitimate son, César de Vendôme, whose mother was Gabrielle d'Estrées, Henri IV's renowned mistress. Under the rule of King Louis XIII, his half-brother César plotted against Richelieu. The cardinal had Lamballe's castle destroyed in 1626 by way of retaliation; only the chapel was left standing. The titles bestowed on the rulers of the Penthièvre became ever more extravagant through time, however. By the Revolution, they styled themselves as princes. The last one proved to be particularly dissolute; he died as a result of his debauchery three months after his arranged marriage to a young princess from Piedmont. The widowed princess, later known as Mme de Lamballe, went on to serve Marie Antoinette as a lady-in-waiting for some 20 years until she lost her head in the French Revolutionary Terror of 1792 – it was infamously paraded through the Paris streets on a pike.

A Tour of Lamballe

Although Mme de Lamballe was so savagely butchered in the Revolution, the **town hall** of Lamballe preserves a splendid painting of her from 1780 by Jean-Laurent Mosnier; it is a fine vision of the last years of Ancien Régime noble grandeur. One of Lamballe's most interesting present-day attractions, by contrast, is its collection of simple paintings and drawings of everyday Brittany and Bretons made in the first half

Crêperie Ty Coz, 35 Place du Champ de Foire, t 02 96 31 03 58 (*inexpensive*). A popular local restaurant.

La Poterie ✉ 22400
★★Manoir des Portes, t 02 96 31 13 62 (*moderate*). Extremely comfortable rooms set around the courtyard of a 16th-century manor, plus high-quality cuisine.

Plédéliac ✉ 22270
Manoir-Auberge Belouze, t 02 96 34 14 55 (*inexpensive*). A restaurant and café serving medieval-style food in an old Breton house. The dynamic hostess has a medieval herb garden, runs exhibitions and events during the summer, and also offers B&B accommodation (mostly for groups).

Plorec-sur-Arguenon ✉ 22130
★★★Château Le Windsor, Le Bois Billy, on the bank of the Arguenon opposite the medieval ruins of the Château de la Hunaudaye, t 02 96 83 04 83, www.chateau-le-windsor.fr (*moderate–luxury*). A clean, straight-lined 18th-century château with luxurious rooms. Guests can enjoy the splendid outdoor swimming pool to its rear.

Moncontour ✉ 22510
A La Garde Ducale, 10 Place Penthièvre, t 02 96 73 52 18 (*inexpensive*). A B&B on the central square, with quaint wood-panelled rooms and slightly twee furnishings. *Table d'hôte* meals are available.
Chaudron Magique, Place de la Carrière, t 02 96 73 40 34 (*inexpensive–moderate*). A restaurant where waiters serve you in medieval costume in the evenings (if you order the medieval menu, you dress up too!).
Crêperie Au Coin du Feu, Place Penthièvre, t 02 96 73 50 56 (*inexpensive*). A crêpe-house with a good atmosphere.

Quintin ✉ 22800
Le Clos du Prince, 10 Rue Croix-Jarrots, t 02 96 74 93 03 (*moderate*). An unforgettable, excellent-value B&B with a cavernous fireplace in the reception, a granite staircase leading to 18th-century panelled rooms, and hydrangea borders and ancient trees in the garden. Rooms are decorated with style and touches of humour. *Table d'hôte* is available when everything else is shut.
★★Hôtel du Commerce, 2 Rue Rochenen, t 02 96 74 94 67 (*inexpensive*). Peaceful rooms, a characterful old dining room, and great food.

of the 20th century, by the Lamballe-born artist Mathurin Méheut (1882–1958). The **Musée Mathurin Méheut** (*open June–Sept Mon–Sat 10–12 and 2.30–6*) shows how the artist painted obsessively, daily. The works are displayed in one of Lamballe's grandest old townhouses, the timberframe **Maison du Bourreau** ('Hangman's House'), which also contains the tourist office and the little museum of local history, the **Musée du Pays de Lamballe et du Penthièvre** (*open July and Aug Mon–Sat 9.30–6.30, Sun and public hols 10–12; April–June and Sept Mon–Sat 10–12.30 and 2–6; Oct–Mar Mon–Sat 10–12.30 and 2–5*). The Maison du Bourreau is tucked away in a corner off the main historic square of Lamballe, the picturesque sloping rectangle of the **Place du Marché**. The tower of the church of St John peers over one end of the square. Back down at the Place du Marché, the Rue Villedeneuf leads north to the vast **Place du Champ de Foire**, on one side of which lies the stud farm, very much in the centre of town.

Lamballe Haras or Stud Farm

Open 15 June–15 Sept daily 10–12 and 2–5.30, guided tours on the half hour; 16 Sept–Dec and mid-Feb–14 June Wed, Sat and Sun 10–12 and 2–5.30, guided tours on the hour in the afternoon. Most tours conducted in French; call t 02 96 50 06 98.

It is in good part thanks to the French predilection for eating horse meat that the stocky breeds of Breton horses survived the 20th century. Developed for strength, these squat, square-built steeds are the rugby men of the horse world. You can go and see some of the thick-necked, massive-rumped creatures in Lamballe's magnificent 19th-century stables. Founded in 1825, by the start of the 20th century the Lamballe stud was the biggest in France, with accommodation for 400 stallions. Now it houses up to 70 stallions at any time. The bulk of these are either *chevaux de trait bretons*, Breton cart or draft horses, or Breton *postiers*, which are a mix between the traditional Breton *trait* and Hackney and Norfolk horses from England.

Across to the Arguenon Valley

East from Lamballe, the D52 leads to Plédéliac. From there it's a short way along the D55 to **La Ferme d'Antan at St-Esprit**, a re-creation of a Breton farm as it would have been at the start of the 20th century. Animals occupy the farm buildings, and the smell of horses comes right into the single room where the family would have lived.

Signs from St-Esprit lead you to the **Château de la Hunaudaye** (*being restored but visits possible, call t 02 96 34 82 10*), an impressive pentagon of a ruined medieval castle in a dip in marshy land not far from the Arguenon. Five great towers make the ramparts look very impressive. The château was owned for much of its history by the Tournemine family, related to the Plantagenets. It was built in 1360 and damaged in the Wars of Religion, though it was the Chouannerie terrorist warfare of the 1790s that put paid to it. You can wander up and down spiral staircases in the towers and go into ruined vaulted rooms within the ramparts. A medieval play, staged in summer within the ruins, brings a bit of life and comedy to this stern ruin.

A little way north, enjoy the French-style gardens around the solid **Manoir de Vaumadeuc** (*open Easter–Oct Thur–Tue 12–6*).

Moncontour

Set on a rocky hilltop, surrounded by medieval fortifications, Moncontour looks more like a picture postcard village from the southwest of France than a typically Breton one. Long a stronghold of the lords of Penthièvre, it guarded the road between Lamballe and Pontivy, sited above two small valleys.

In the Breton War of Succession, when Moncontour was frequently besieged, the place even gained the right to mint money. In the last independent years of the Breton duchy in the late 15th century, French troops managed to seize Moncontour and Duc François II himself tried, unsuccessfully, to liberate the place in 1487. The administration of the French king, Charles VIII, allowed Moncontour to rebuild its much put-upon ramparts. In the late 16th century, the Huguenots and the ultra-Catholics battled over the site. A little museum above the tourist office, the **Maison de la Chouannerie et de la Révolution** (*open 14 July–Aug daily 10–6.30; rest of period mid-June–mid-Sept 10–12.30 and 2.30–6.30*), concentrates on local history and the civil war here through the Revolutionary period.

The legacy of the wealthy linen merchants of Moncontour is the fine 17th- and 18th-century houses, particularly those around the village church, the **Eglise St-Mathurin**. Its impressive 18th-century Baroque façade looks outsized for what is a small community. An unusual 20th-century belfry rises from the building, though the bulky rest of the church dates from the early 16th century. The bright old stained-glass windows are the highlight within; they were inspired by Flemish Renaissance models. The **Pardon de St-Mathurin** counts as one of the two most important religious processions in the Côtes d'Armor, taking place at Whitsun. A silver reliquary bust of St Mathurin stands out among the statues; he was reputed to help cure the mentally ill.

To the Abbaye de Boquen

Go in search of the Abbaye de Boquen lost in its forest east of Moncontour. To get there you might take the D6 then the D25 past the **Château de la Touche-Trébry**, a noble-looking Breton moated château in granite, dating mainly from the 16th century, with its shapely roofs rising out of flat scrubland. The proprietors open a few rooms for a short period in summer (*July and Aug Mon–Sat 2–6*).

Or you can meander towards the abbey via the heights of **Bel-Air**, one of the highest points in Brittany. Bel-Air lies in the **Méné range of hills**, also known as the Landes de Menez. They traditionally separated the Breton counties of Penthièvre and Le Porhouët. Streams to the north head for the Channel, those to the south for the Atlantic. You really feel that you're starting to explore the deserted centre of Brittany around here. Signs point to the **Site de Croquelin** (west of Le Gouray), a small scattering of boulders lost on a high Méné ridge typical of the area.

The **Abbaye de Boquen** (a few kilometres east of the village of Le Gouray) counts as one of the most peaceful religious sites you can visit in Brittany. Originally built in the 12th century, it is home to a group of nuns who have been here since the mid-1970s. The sisters sell gifts in the shop at the entrance to the abbey grounds. The abbey was actually restored by a passionate local priest, Mathurin Presse, alias Dom Alexis, who roped in much help to bring the ruined structure back to life from 1936 onwards. His main aim was to see religious life restored to Boquen. The touching story of Dom Alexis's almost superhuman efforts to revive the abbey are told in a room you can visit before heading down the track to the well-hidden, vast abbey church, in which you could hear a pin drop, while the mill house on the way explains the role of the present-day Sisters of Bethlehem.

South From Moncontour

Take the D1 south from Moncontour to head deep into the Côtes d'Armor. You could stop at the wonky **church of Langast**. Some of the Romanesque arches within look as though they are about to tumble over. Other arches date from the Gothic period. Brilliantly stylized, frog-eyed figures were painted on the older arches, possibly as early as the 10th century. Beautiful stained glass fills the apse window and one retable has been turned into the frame for a memorial to the parish's war dead.

The D1 continues down through the gorgeous once-industrial village of **Le Vaublanc**, purpose-built for iron production from the 1670s. The little **church of St-Lubin** south of Le Vaublanc conceals a few charming details under its Romanesque helmet of a slate steeple. Old stained-glass windows present a striking depiction of Christ being crucified, while angels and dragons run along the carved stringbeams. Look out also for the painted statue of St Lubin with blue hands in one of the two wood-carved retables. The **church of La Ferrière** on the D14A off the D1 displays a fine collection of stained-glass windows and old Breton statues. The best-known grouping, in the left transept, shows the Annunciation. Although much of the architecture is 14th and 15th century, three sets of stained-glass windows date from the 16th century, the period of the French Renaissance.

La Chèze, further on along the D14A from La Ferrière, lies quite prettily by the Lié river. It has the ruins of a medieval castle that you can walk around, and a cluttered **Musée Régional des Métiers** (*open July and Aug daily 10–12 and 2–6; May, June and Sept daily 2–6, March and Oct Sun–Fri 2–6*), the objects divided up according to the old trades. **Loudéac**, the main town of central inland Côtes d'Armor, situated 10 kilometres west of La Chèze, is best known for its Easter horse races, its Lent passion play and its flies, for fishing.

Quintin

As at Moncontour, the hill at Quintin seemed an excellent site for the lords of Penthièvre to fortify in medieval times. A first castle went up at the start of the 13th century, guarding what was a major inland route from St-Malo to Carhaix. Subsequent châteaux followed through the centuries, each either devastated by war or left incomplete through lack of resources. Their bits and pieces dominate one side of town; a soaring 19th-century church stands in the background. The splendid old streets in the centre of Quintin date back in good part to the 17th and 18th centuries, when the local merchants made their fortunes out of manufacturing linen for export. The church supposedly owns a segment of a much older and more exceptional piece of cloth – a fragment of the Virgin's girdle.

The Château de Quintin

Open July and Aug daily 10–7; June and Sept daily 10.30–12.30 and 1.30–6.30; April, May and Oct Wed–Mon 2–6; Nov–March Sat and Sun 2–6.

A discreet gateway off Quintin's main market square leads you into the spacious, quiet, lawn-covered castle courtyard. The wings of the main château consist of the 17th-century stables, converted into the main lord's lodgings, and a low 18th-century wing now holding the dining room and kitchen. The remains of the unfinished 17th-century château lie derelict to one side, above the Gouët lake.

Though this château looks scrappy, it has the rare distinction of having kept most of its old archives, and the Bagneux family that own the place love to tell its story, their enthusiasm compensating for the often amateurish displays inside. The first 12th-century fort was destroyed by the bellicose Olivier de Clisson in 1394, rebuilt in the next century, and destroyed by the troops of the then Prince of Orange in 1488, only to be quickly reconstructed once again. At the end of the 16th century, in the Wars of Religion, the Quintin lord took the Protestant side. The ultra-Catholics came to lay siege to the castle and caused a great deal of damage. In 1638, the dejected proprietor sold to his brother-in-law, Amaury Goyon, Marquis de la Moussaye. His influential family keenly supported Protestant reform of the Christian Church; he wanted to make Quintin into a centre for Protestants, as well as building himself a grand new château. Quintin became a Protestant stronghold. However, after De la Moussaye's death, his successor was unable to finance further construction work on the new château or support the Protestant community as it required. In 1681, the castle was sold to a rich cousin of the family, Guy de Durfort, Maréchal de Lorge. One Dufort girl married into the Choiseul family, and their descendants own the château.

A Tour of the Old Town

The **Place 1830** has all the timberframe charm that you could wish for in a Breton provincial market town. From one corner, the **Rue Notre-Dame**, with its finely carved doorways and a Breton fountain to one side, leads down to the very 19th-century neo-Gothic **Basilique Notre-Dame**. The copy of the supposed piece of the Virgin's girdle has been stolen, however. Leaving the Place 1830 by the sloping **Rue Emile Nau**, at the crossroads in the dip you come to the **Maison du Tisserand**, where you can see traditional looms at work.

Back at the Place 1830, the **Grand'Rue**, the principal shopping street, leads to the elegant cobbled **Place du Martray**, where medieval English prisoners were apparently brought after a battle at La Roche-Derrien to the west. The commander had promised that their lives would be spared. But as they were led through town to the castle, nothing could stop the fury of the local butchers of Quintin, who are said to have savagely slaughtered the English prisoners.

Inland into Southwestern Côtes d'Armor

Were you to try to locate the geographical heart of Brittany, the gorgeous lake of Guerlédan might fit the bill nicely. This lake only dates from early in the 20th century, but there's nothing artificial about some of the sights that surround it: Mur-de-Bretagne's chapel to St Suzanne; the ruins of the Abbaye de Bon Repos; and Les Forges-des-Salles, possibly the most beautiful ironworks in the world.

From Quintin to the Lac de Guerlédan

The D790 from Quintin leads into deeply rural southwestern Côtes d'Armor. At **Corlay**, you come to the border between traditionally Gallo-speaking Brittany to the east and Breton-speaking Brittany to the west. Corlay, a small market town known for horse breeding, has a small **Maison du Cheval** (*open mid-June–mid–Sept daily 10–12 and 2–4; otherwise Easter–June and Sept 10–12 and 2–4 for guided tours Sun 3–6*) on the history of local horses, in the remains of Corlay castle. One story has it that members of the lordly family brought back Arab thoroughbreds from the crusades, which were gradually mixed with local stock. Nowadays Corlay is known across Brittany for its horse races, held between spring and autumn at the local Petit Paris track.

As you approach the Lac de Guerlédan from Loudéac to the east, at **St-Thélo** on the Oust, **La Maison des Toiles** (*open July–Sept daily 10.30–6.30, Oct–Dec and Feb–June Sun and public hols 2–6*) tells of how flax and the linen made from it deeply affected these parts of inland Brittany from the time of the Ancien Régime.

Mur-de-Bretagne and the Chapelle Ste-Suzanne

With a mix of white and schist houses on its slope, Mur-de-Bretagne is a pretty little central Breton town. Its main attraction is the 18th-century paintings covering the ceiling of the **Chapelle Ste-Suzanne** in the upper part of the town. The classical tower makes for an unusually refined entrance to a Breton church. It has a lovely double doorway and a decorative motif of shells repeated up its façade. This tower is framed by an alley of splendid oaks that inspired the great French 19th-century landscape artist Jean-Baptiste-Camille Corot. The chapel boasts its own paintings, albeit in typically naïve Breton style, the work of Roch F. Delaporte from 1723. The scenes depict the story of St Susan, falsely accused of adultery.

St-Aignan

This is an adorable old village, a mix of stone and whitewashed houses. Its medieval **church** has a few treasures, including a remarkable Tree of Jesse carved in wood and crammed with figures; it may have been made for the Abbaye de Bon Repos (*see p.185*).

Old St-Aignan is an extremely surprising location for the **Musée du Pays et de l'Electricité** (*open July–15 Sept daily 10–12 and 2–6; May and June Mon–Fri 2–6, Sat and Sun 10–12 and 2–6; 16 Sept–Oct Sat and Sun 2–6*), a delightful museum of electricity that includes a substantial old electric train set. The **hydroelectric dam** (*free guided*

Getting Around

Getting around by public transport is not an easy matter in this area. The centres to seek **buses** from are the town of Loudéac, which lies 20km to the east of Mur-de-Bretagne, and the town of Pontivy, which is roughly the same distance to the south, in the Morbihan.

For walkers, there are some wonderful Grande Randonnée **hiking paths** around the Lac de Guerlédan.

Tourist Information

Pays d'Accueil de Guerlédan et de Korong, Gouarec, **t** 02 96 24 85 83.
Corlay: t 02 96 29 42 90.
St-Nicolas-du-Pélem: Place Kreisker, **t** 02 96 29 71 47, or **t** 02 96 29 51 27 out of season.
Mur-de-Bretagne: Place de l'Eglise, **t** 02 96 28 51 41, *otsi.guerledan@ wanadoo.fr*.
Rostrenen: 4 Place de la République, **t** 02 96 29 02 72, or **t** 02 96 29 00 35 out of season, *tourismekb@wanadoo.fr*.

Market Days

Mur-de-Bretagne: Friday during the summer months.
Rostrenen: Tuesday.

Where to Stay and Eat

Mur-de-Bretagne ✉ 22530

★★★Auberge Grand'Maison, 1 Rue Léon le Cerf, **t** 02 96 28 51 10 (*inexpensive–expensive*). A place offering charming bedrooms and superlative *à la carte* food, such as profiteroles filled with foie gras with a truffle sauce.
M. Le Bouldec, Le Pont Guern, **t** 02 96 28 54 52 (*inexpensive*). A pretty, flower-decked cottage by the Canal de Nantes à Brest. Guests can breakfast on farm produce and home-made jam.

Caurel ✉ 22530

★★Beau Rivage, t 02 96 28 52 15 (*inexpensive*). A reasonably priced option set on the lakeside by the Beau Rivage beach. It gets pretty lively in the height of summer, but otherwise it's a calm place to spend some time.
★★Le Relais du Lac, t 02 96 28 56 93, (*inexpensive*). A former posting inn that's been converted into a comfortable hotel with its own restaurant. Guests can hire mountain bikes.

St-Gilles-Vieux-Marché ✉ 22530

Up from Mur-de-Bretagne in the atmospheric enclosed valley of Poulancre , this village makes for a pleasant stop.
★Hôtel de la Vallée, Le Bourg, **t** 02 96 28 53 32 (*inexpensive*). A family-friendly place offering cheap rooms.

St-Guen ✉ 22530

Auberge de Jeunesse, on the D35 towards Le Quilio, **t** 02 96 28 54 34, *www.fuaj.org* (*inexpensive*). A highly recommended and exemplary youth hostel – clean, bright and friendly. Guests must show a youth hostelling membership card to stay. *Closed Oct–March.*

St-Gelven/ Abbaye de Bon Repos ✉ 22570

Les Jardins de l'Abbaye de Bon Repos, **t** 02 96 24 95 77, *lesjardinsdelabbaye@ wanadoo.fr* (*inexpensive*). Accommodation in a glorious setting right by the abbey ruins. Inside, the newly renovated rooms have old beams.
Café de l'Abbaye, Bon-Repos, Perret, **t** 02 96 24 91 06 (*inexpensive*). An atmospheric bar situated in an old lockkeeper's cottage near the abbey.
Crêperie-bar Bon-Repos, Bon-Repos, **t** 02 96 24 86 56 (*inexpensive*). A basic option just by the abbey. *Closed Mon and mid-Sept–mid-Oct.*

Gouarec

★★Le Blavet, RN 164, **t** 02 96 24 90 03 (*inexpensive*). A characterful and friendly hotel tucked into the corner of the Blavet river, with comfortable, old-fashioned rooms and good bathrooms. It also has a large restaurant overlooking the river together with a convivial, cosy bar where you can relax in the evening.

tour by Electricité de France Tues–Fri 10.30, 3 and 4.30, Sat 3 and 4.30 – check with the Mur-de-Bretagne tourist office for meeting place), the reason for the museum, was a massive 1920s engineering project. The guides explain how the system works and how the dam is kept waterproof. Normally the lake is emptied every 10 years, but this did not occur in 1995. The next emptying is scheduled for 2005.

To follow an itinerary up the beautiful Blavet river from its estuary in the Morbihan back to the Lac de Guerlédan, *see* the section beginning on p.355.

Resorts on the Lac de Guerlédan

The main resort lies on the north side of this serpent of a lake. You reach it by going down via **Caurel**, with its little row of attractive bars, to **Beau Rivage**, with its lively summer beach. You can try your hand at all sorts of watersports here, or take a boat trip round the lake.

On the southern shore of the lake, at the **Anse de Sordan**, you will find a smaller resort with a little artificial beach in its wood-surrounded inlet, as well as some boats and a bar. The D15B road leading from St-Aignan and the Anse de Sordan to Les Forges-des-Salles is exceptionally beautiful, shaded by pine trees.

Les Forges-des-Salles

Open July and Aug daily 2–6; Sat, Sun and bank hols afternoons out of season but check to confirm on **t** *02 96 24 90 12.*

It is hard to imagine an industrial site more beautiful than Les Forges-des-Salles, a purpose-built 17th- and 18th-century iron-making village set by a lake and tucked into its own little valley. Actually, Les Forges-des-Salles looks more like a château with delightful outbuildings than a foundry these days. Iron production is an often forgotten part of Brittany's industrial past, but small-scale production had been going on in these parts from the Middle Ages until the early 17th century. Then the powerful duke of Rohan decided to start up larger-scale ironworks; slabs of cast iron were made here and transported via the canal to the naval yards of Brest.

The Abbaye de Bon Repos

The ruins of this abbey lie just a few kilometres north of Les Forges-des-Salles. They too are picturesquely set by water, the Blavet meandering below. A beautiful stone bridge crosses the river at this spot. Make for the ruins via the information centre with a gigantic slate chair set in the front of it. The abbey's charming former outbuildings, in mottled schist, almost eclipse the grey, sober abbey walls. A couple of craft shops and a hotel and restaurant were opened in this renovated section. The abbey itself is being much more slowly restored, to create a cultural centre on research into monastic life and art, and on Breton history.

An abbey was first built on the site in the 12th century, after Alain III de Rohan had seen the Virgin in a dream. He and his wife Constance de Bretagne wanted to make this the place for family burials. Cistercian monks came to occupy the buildings, and for centuries the abbey exercised its influence over much of central Brittany. But the place was wrecked in the 16th-century French Wars of Religion. From 1683, the Abbé de St-Genies set about restoring the abbey and ordered the building of the palatial wing looking across to the wooded meander in the Blavet. But the establishment deteriorated once again, and the last monks were thrown out at the Revolution. The abbey now serves as the dramatic backdrop for occasional *son-ét-lumière* evenings.

The D44 heads north from the Abbaye via the **Gorges du Daoulas**. In the narrow, curious Daoulas valley, blocks of stone rise up above you, and they are strewn in the stream below. You can walk up from there to the **Landes de Liscuis** with their unspoilt, almost prehistoric-looking landscape and neolithic gallery chambers, or *allées couvertes*. The path is fiendishly steep, however; go up towards Laniscat for an easier path.

West of the Lac de Guerlédan

The main N164 road across the south of the Côtes d'Armor leads you to the market town of **Rostrenen**, known in Brittany for its traditional Breton singing and dancing. Fishermen will appreciate the rivers and lakes around Rostrenen, and we recommend getting lost in the depths of the Breton countryside north of there, with its bizarre boulder-strewn landscapes and rural tranquillity. Head for Kergrist-Moëlou.

Kergrist-Moëlou

Christ has lost his arms at the top of the exceptional **calvary of Kergrist-Moëlou**. He stands dying in isolation on his column, while around the octagonal structure below, the story of his life unfolds. The calvary dates from the 16th century, the church from the 15th. The church's outer gables feature many figures from the medieval bestiary, while here and there carved angels bear heavy coats of arms. Inside the church, your attention will be drawn immediately to the painted ceiling, executed by a local artist recording in 1871 the members of the Vatican One council. The nave also contains the extraordinary sight of a large fireplace, apparently provided to heat the place for baptisms on cold days. If the Café Bonhomme is open, you can warm yourselves there while admiring their collection of traditional Breton furniture.

Rustic Routes from Kergrist

East of Kergrist, follow the **road to Trémargat**, with its extraordinary rock-strewn countryside; granite is excavated at Trémargat. You can then walk in the atmospheric **Gorges de Toul Goulic**; you'll need to leave your car in the car park to descend into this boulder-filled valley of the Blavet, where mythical Breton creatures are supposed to guard hidden treasure. But it has served as a hideout to others in history, notably the Chouan Cadoudal, fleeing from Revolutionary troops. Head west on the D20 to the **Menez** and **Menhir Guellec**, to walk on the moors. You pass a gorse-defended, hulking menhir overlooking a vast unspoilt section of inland Brittany. Archaeologists believe neolithic inhabitants dug for gold here, due to the presence of neolithic stone bassins near the menhir. North of the Menez Guellec explore the mysterious **Gorges du Corong**, with further extraordinary rock formations.

From St-Brieuc to St-Quay-Portrieux

Founded by the Welshman Brieuc, one of the seven saints to create the first Celtic bishoprics of Brittany, the town of St-Brieuc has only the odd trace of history left, notably its forbidding medieval cathedral. From its Port du Légué, you can set off up and down the rollercoaster cliffs of the Côte du Goëlo. This Goëlo coast forms the western side of the bay of St-Brieuc, stretching from the Côtes d'Armor's capital city to the port of Paimpol and the sensational pink and orange rocks of the Ile de Bréhat.

St-Brieuc

St-Brieuc, administrative capital of the Côtes d'Armor, sprawls across several deep valleys, roads straddling them on tall bridges. It has strong literary connections. Louis Guilloux, one of the most respected Breton authors, was from St-Brieuc and set his most famous work, *Le Sang noir*, here. The absurdist Alfred Jarry (he of the zany *Ubu roi*), the defeatist Tristan Corbière, and the unsettlingly idealistic Villiers de L'Isle-Adam, all major French literary figures, were either born or went to school in St-Brieuc. The recent arrival of university faculties has brought in more bright young people.

The Historic Centre of St-Brieuc

The **Cathédrale St-Etienne** is one of those stern Breton cathedrals that seem to have been built almost as much for defence as for worship. In fact, look at the towers on the entrance façade and you can spot arrow slits and machicolations. Guillaume Pinchon, a 13th-century bishop of St-Brieuc, is reputed for having become the first Breton to be canonized by the papacy. In 1346, during the Breton War of Succession, English troops ruined the cathedral Guillaume would have known. During the Revolution, the massive edifice was turned into an arms depot and stables, almost all the furnishings demolished. But one altarpiece, the curvaceous Baroque masterpiece of Yves Corlay, was supposedly saved by being hidden under a great pile of straw.

Off the cathedral square, past the 19th-century covered market, the sloping **Rue Fardel** counts among the prettiest and most colourful streets in the town. Just adjoining the other side of the cathedral square, you'll find an uncompromisingly modern shopping square, the **Place du Chai**, with café terraces squashed in. The **Place de la Résistance** close by includes the main cultural centre here, La Passerelle, with a theatre, a gallery and a cinema within its walls. The **Musée d'Histoire des Côtes d'Armor** (*open Tues–Sat 9.30–11.45 and 1.30–5.45, Sun 1.30–5.45*) lies a short walk to the south. The museum focuses on local art and history, as well as the traditional trades of the Côtes d'Armor. Along the **Rue de Rohan** just up from the museum, the shop Prenaye Lin sells traditional Breton linen. The **Rue St-Guillaume**, east of the Place de la Résistance, is the main shopping artery.

Make sure that you keep your eyes peeled for signs to St-Brieuc's port on the banks of the Gouët estuary; get onto the north side of the port unless you want to end up among the kaolin and fertilizer warehouses. The **Port du Légué** lies in a typically deep and narrow St-Brieuc valley, the legs of a great bridge crossing it. On the north side of the river, the yacht harbour is followed by the fishing harbour. Tucked so discreetly away, the port turns out to be one of the biggest in Brittany, with an atmosphere all of its own.

Up the Gallo Part of the Goëlo Coast

The urban barrage that St-Brieuc forms in front of the western side of the Anse d'Yffiniac shouldn't put off the more adventurous among our readership from going along to explore the coast here. The social pecking order seems to be reflected on the cliff of **St-Laurent-de-la-Mer**, the resort just to the north and around the corner from St-Brieuc's Port du Légué. There you'll find a line of swanky modern villas topping the steep cliff, while down below you are treated to a characterful array of shacks.

Getting Around

St-Brieuc has a small **airport**, t 02 96 94 95 00; Rockhopper flies there from Jersey in the Channel Islands (*see* p.56).

The town is linked to Paris by the TGV fast **train**, which takes around 3hrs.

The main **bus** station for the area is located by St-Brieuc's train station.

Tourist Information

St-Brieuc: 7 Rue St-Gouéno, t 02 96 33 32 50, *www.baiedesaintbrieuc.com*.
Plérin/St-Laurent-de-la-Mer: t 02 96 74 68 79.
Châtelaudren: 2 Rue des Sapeurs Pompiers, t 02 96 74 12 02.
Binic: t 02 96 73 60 12, *www.ville-binic.fr*.
Etables-sur-Mer: t 02 96 70 65 41, *otsi.etablessurmer@wanadoo.fr*.
St-Quay-Portrieux: t 02 96 70 40 64, *www.stquayportrieux.com*.

Market Days

St-Brieuc: Wednesday, Saturday and Sunday (Sunday at Cesson and Croix St-Lambert).
Plérin: Sunday.
Pordic: Friday.
Châtelaudren: Monday.
Binic: Thursday.
Etables-sur-Mer: Tuesday.
St-Quay-Portrieux: Monday and Friday.

Where to Stay and Eat

St-Brieuc ✉ 22000
★★★**Hôtel de Clisson**, 36–38 Rue de Gouët, t 02 96 62 19 29, *www.hoteldeclisson.com* (*moderate*). The smartest address in town, with a garden and warmly decorated modern rooms.
★★**Le Duguesclin**, 2 Place Duguesclin, t 02 96 33 11 58 (*inexpensive*). A hotel with a reliable restaurant specializing in smoked fish.
★★**Hôtel du Champ de Mars**, 13 Rue du Général Leclerc, t 02 96 33 60 99, *hoteldemars@wanadoo.fr* (*inexpensive*). Ultra-modern rooms and a well-known brasserie with good dishes.
★★**Le Ker Izel**, 20 Rue de Gouët, t 02 96 33 46 29 (*inexpensive*). Comfortable rooms in a cosy old house in the historic part of the town.
Auberge de Jeunesse, Manoir de la Ville-Guyomard, Les Villages, t 02 96 78 70 70, *www.fuaj.org* (*inexpensive*). A youth hostel situated in a splendid Breton manor. You must present your youth-hostelling card to stay here. It is small, so reservations are essential.
La Croix Blanche, 61 Rue de Genève, Cesson, on the spit of land south of the Port of Légué, t 02 96 33 16 97 (*moderate–very expensive*). Highly original *haute cuisine*. *Closed Sun eve, Mon and Sat lunch, and 3wks Aug–Sept*.

Follow the coast northwards to the **Pointe du Roselier** and you emerge from the urban fray of St-Brieuc's outskirts to some of the most sensational views of the bay of St-Brieuc. A 1980s granite monument remembers those from the area who have died at sea. You can go walking along the cliffs, passing a cannonball oven and a coastguard's cottage. Heading steeply down from the point, you come to the little grey pebble beach of **Martin-Plage**. Tides and currents can be deceptive here.

Les Rosaires, by contrast, is welcoming and relaxing, a chic resort that feels rather cosmopolitan. The seafront appears very 'clean' as the French sometimes say. A wide pedestrian promenade parallels much of the two-kilometre beach. Wealthy Briochins go on their dog-jog along it on weekend mornings. The place has a mix of villa styles, some pre-war, in mottled stone, some more experimental and modern.

The next tiny resort to the north, **Tournemine**, is a much more private little place than Les Rosaires, difficult to get to and with a pebbly beach. Then you reach the **Pointe de Pordic**, with more fabulous views across the bay.

L'Amadéus, 22 Rue de Gouët, t 02 96 33 92 44 (*expensive*). A smart restaurant offering quirky dishes mixing seafood with Breton meat specialities. *Closed Sat, Sun, Mon lunch and 2wks Aug.*

Aux Pesked, 59 Rue du Légué, t 02 96 33 34 65 (*moderate–expensive*). Delicious, refined cooking on the way down to the port, looking across to a typical St-Brieuc valley. *Closed Sat lunch, Sun eve, Mon, 1wk May and 1wk Sept.*

La Vieille Tour, 75 Rue de la Tour, Plérin, north of the centre, t 02 96 33 10 30 (*moderate–expensive*). Seafood specialities served in an elegant dining room that hosts changing exhibitions of local artists' work.

Le Petit Bouchon, 10 Rue Jules Ferry, t 02 96 94 05 34 (*inexpensive–expensive*). A decent choice offering a range of seafood dishes. *Closed Sat lunch and Sun.*

Crêperie-Saladerie Le Ribault, 8–10 Rue Fardel, t 02 96 33 44 79 (*inexpensive*). A good option for those in search of low-priced crêpes, salads and potato dishes. *Closed Sun out of season and school hols.*

Pordic ✉ 22570
Le Pré Péan, t 02 96 79 00 32 (*inexpensive*). A pretty Breton farm converted to a B&B.

Plélo ✉ 22170
Ferme-auberge au Char à Bancs/La Ferme des Aïeux, t 02 96 74 13 63 (*moderate*). Luxuriously furnished B&B rooms by the village of Plélo, 3km north of Châtelaudren. The food, served in a bulky converted watermill, is traditionally Breton. The whole Lamour family plays an enthusiastic part; sometimes Monsieur does guided tours of the old farm on the hill, now a museum illustrating old Breton ways.

Ferme-auberge de la Ville-Andon, t 02 96 74 21 77 or t 02 96 74 12 75 (*moderate*). Traditional cuisine served up in a delightful rustic dining room. *Closed Thurs.*

Binic ✉ 22520
★★Le Neptune, Place de l'Eglise, t 02 96 73 61 02 (*inexpensive*). A modest hotel in an unpretentious resort, with sea views.

La Mascotte, Quai de Courcy, t 02 96 73 30 77 (*inexpensive*). A restaurant with one dining room on the port and one on a boat, used in good weather.

St-Quay-Portrieux ✉ 22410
★★★Ker Moor, 13 Rue du Président Le Sénécal, t 02 96 70 52 22, www.ker-moor.com (*expensive*). A well-located neo-Arabic hotel with onion-shaped domes. The rooms with sea views are more expensive than those giving on to the pretty garden.

★★Le Gerbot d'Avoine, 2 Boulevard du Littoral, t 02 96 70 40 09, www.gerbotdavoine.com (*inexpensive*). A traditional French hotel, with some of the 20 bedrooms boasting sea views, plus a restaurant, a bar, a billiards room and a reading room.

Inland to Trégomeur and Châtelaudren

Inland from the Pointe de Pordic, the **Zoo de Trégomeur** or **Jardin Zoologique de Bretagne** (*closed for improvements at time of writing; due to reopen summer 2005, for opening times call* **t** *02 96 79 01 07*) lies down a steep valley north of the village of Trégomeur. Once you've negotiated the little shop at the entrance (with latest news on newly born animals posted on the board) you can wander past animals kept in slightly barren fields, including laboratory-freed macaques. The playful lemurs are the passion of Monsieur Arnoux, the devoted founder of this zoo.

Head westwards another 10 kilometres or so inland from Trégomeur to arrive at **Châtelaudren**, historic capital of the Goëlo. In the centre, it has a few attractive streets of 18th-century stone houses and an old, abandoned printworks by the Leff river. It may look like a slightly dull village at first glance, but the place has an outstanding chapel that eclipses any other attractions. You'll be absorbed by the colourful detail of the painted ceiling of the **Chapelle Notre-Dame-du-Tertre** (*open Mon–Sat 10–12 and 4–7*), not to be confused with the church in Châtelaudren's main square; it lies on the other side of the river, up the slope.

Almost 100 biblical scenes adorn the wooden planks of the choir ceiling. Another 36 scenes in the side chapel, the Chapelle Ste-Marguerite, tell the stories of St Marguerite and St Fiacre. The paintings were executed between 1450 and 1480, by a team of craftsmen, it would appear. But no one is sure as yet who commissioned these works, or precisely when, or who exactly executed them. The wealth of detail make the ensemble look overwhelming at first sight, but a guide is normally on hand to explain the order of the scenes, in French at least.

Beginning with the story of the creation, God is portrayed as a rather noble oriental king going about his duties. A striped serpent with a woman's head tempts Adam and Eve, then bleak scenes help recount the story of Cain and Abel. Moving swiftly on to Noah, the artist depicts the ark but not the animals. There follows Abraham's attempted sacrifice of Isaac, Jacob's dream of an angels' ladder to heaven, and Moses receiving the Ten Commandments. Twelve prophets take up the next row, prefiguring the arrival of the son of God on earth. And so we move on to the New Testament, starting with Gabriel's Annunciation to the Virgin, then Christ's circumcision, by a man wearing a bishop's hat! Jesus quickly grows up. The story of his betrayal is told as though it were some courtly tale, Pilate like a medieval lord, a jester sometimes in tow.

The stories of St Marguerite and St Fiacre may be less familiar to you. Marguerite is supposedly based on a 3rd-century figure hailing from Antioch in the Middle East. Her nanny taught her Christianity, which she refused to renounce in front of her pagan priest of a father. Rejected by him, she became a shepherdess. The governor Olibrius fell for her, but she fought off his advances. In response, he subjected her to a series of horrendous tortures. She was eventually beheaded, but before she died she found the time to ask God to protect women who were going through the agonies of child labour, hence her veneration by pregnant women in particular during the Middle Ages.

Fiacre is said to have been a 7th-century Irish saint, born of royal parents, who became a monk and sailed to France, where he performed saintly deeds but was also harassed by a trouble-making woman, La Becnaude. The artist has used his noble background to show a colourful medieval joust and a medieval war scene. Yet more painted scenes in the side chapel concentrate on the life of Mary Magdalene.

Back on the Goëlo Gallo

Back on the Goëlo coast, the port of **Binic** boasted one of the most important long-distance cod-fishing fleets in 19th-century Brittany. A few old houses and streets recall those major fishing days, but Binic has long been converted to tourism – part of its port is a yacht harbour. There's a sandy beach either end of the port. **Binic Museum** (*open April–Sept Wed–Mon 2.30–6*) is appropriately set in a disused fish-canning factory, although it doesn't make for the most inspiring of settings. Coiffes are comically displayed in what look like disused butchers' showcases.

Etables-sur-Mer, the next resort, has steep roads leading down to its pair of dramatic beaches. To get to the **Plage des Godelins** at the foot of steep cliffs, you pass a neo-Gothic horror of a mansion. A bit north, the **Plage du Moulin**, also set between cliffs, has lovely fine sand.

St-Quay-Portrieux

This place is part port, part resort, the latter slightly suburban-looking. The port area lies to the south, its first **marina** now superseded by a large 1990s development, surrounded by crude walls made from piled up blocks of rock. This was built to make sure that the harbour was provided with deep water at all times rather than being at the mercy of the tides.

To the north, you come to the **Plage de la Comtesse**. The **Ile de la Comtesse**, joined to the mainland at low tide, was bought by the town in the 1970s, and now you can go walking round it when the sea has withdrawn. The coastal path leads up to the third and prettiest part of St-Quay-Portrieux. A white-balustraded path provided with brightly coloured benches looks down on a series of delightful beaches. The **Plage du Châtelet** and the **Plage du Casino** are the two main stretches of sand below. Two pretty seawater pools, as well as a casino, add to the attractions on this side of town.

St-Quay-Portrieux's history as a beach resort goes back to the mid 19th century. Two wealthy women from the nearby inland town of Guingamp were told by their doctor back in 1841 to come and take the sea air. They stayed with nuns of the Sacrés-Cœurs de Jésus et Marie, and so the fashion for seaside stays was launched here. However, Quay, or Ké, got here long before them, in the Dark Ages. Unfortunately, he was not as well received as the ladies of Guingamp. Exhausted from his trip crossing the seas from Ireland in a stone boat, the story claims that he was beaten with gorse by local women when he landed on Brittany's shores. Knocked out, he fell to the ground; where he fell, a spring rose up and revived him. Unfazed, he went on to found a religious community in the area.

The Northern Goëlo Coast: Plouha to Paimpol

You arrive at the Breton-speaking part of the Côtes d'Armor coast here and it immediately feels more typically Breton. Some of the highest cliffs in Brittany plunge to the sea here, while just inland from Paimpol lie several curious religious sights.

The Coast Around Plouha

The cliffs grow taller heading north from St-Quay-Portrieux, and the area has been left almost untouched by modern housing. Roads shaded by tall trees run steeply down narrow valleys to flat stretches of sand or makeshift, tiny harbours. There are no more proper ports after St-Quay-Portrieux until you reach Paimpol.

The dramatic clifftop coastal path seems a world apart from the beaches below. If you follow this path on foot you could still be tempted down a precipitous descent to the odd beautiful beach from time to time. You could seek out **Port Goret** with its lovely beach, east of Plouha and a short drive from Tréveneuc. Just a bit north, the spectacular location of the **Plage des Palus** has attracted a pleasant little group of simple restaurants behind the long curve of its pebble bank.

Back up on the clifftop path, the views from the **Pointe de Plouha** are stunning. Rocky cliffs melt into the distance and St-Quay-Portrieux is reduced to model size. These cliffs are said to be the highest in Brittany, rising more than 100 metres above sea level.

Up until Paimpol, the same pattern of steep cliffs and sandy coves repeats itself. The makeshift port of **Gwin Zégal** is exceptional, however. Protected by the Ilot de Gwin Zégal, little boats are simply tied up to five rows of tall thin wooden posts planted in the waters. This antiquated, quirky, but utterly picturesque port has been listed as a European Maritime Heritage site.

Port Moguer to the north is a tiny harbour better sheltered than Gwin Zégal, with a pink granite wall to help protect it against the elements. The nearby **Plage Bonaparte** was a beach used by the French Resistance in the Second World War to evacuate Allied soldiers hiding behind enemy lines. At high tide its glorious expanse of sands disappears.

On the cliff tops above the Plage Bonaparte stands a major **Second World War memorial** looking out to sea. Stone plaques donated by Allied troops salute the efforts of the French Resistance here. In the course of the war, 135 Allied aviators and agents who had been shot down across France and subsequently rescued by Resistance members were secretly brought to this location, where on dangerous night operations they were transferred onto Royal Navy gunboats that came in close to the shore to pick them up. The beach was codenamed Bonaparte, hence the curious name. Eight successful rescue trips were carried out here between January and August 1944. Jane Birkin's father was one of the British sailors involved.

Skeletons in the Chapel of Kermaria-in-Isquit

Skeletons dancing with the rich and powerful illustrate the vulnerability of life for all at the chapel of Kermaria-in-Isquit a few kilometres west of Plouha village. This *danse macabre*, a popular theme in art and writing that became familiar all over

Europe in the Middle Ages, counts among the most striking of church paintings in Brittany. The frieze of the dance runs along both sides of the nave, above some lovely pointed Gothic arches. The paintings are thought to date from between 1488 and around 1500; the humans represented are dressed in period costume, in descending social rank.

Continue a few kilometres west of Kermaria and you come to Lanleff and its medieval Romanesque **Temple de Lanleff**, long thought to have been a Gallo-Roman temple. Much of the church has fallen into ruin, but the central arcade and the ambulatory encircling it are still in a reasonable state of repair, the capitals carved with some engrossing period motifs.

We return to the coastal cliffs and beaches north of Plouha and head on towards Paimpol. At **Bréhec**, with its wide, long, unspoilt beach below the cliffs, the boats are simply pulled in on to the sand behind the jetty. A couple of further spectacular clifftop points, the **Pointe Berjule** and the **Pointe de Minard**, look out onto the bay of St-Brieuc. It is at the **Pointe de Bilfot** that Paimpol and its bay finally come into view. The granite looks purple here. From the Pointe de Bilfot you can go down to the steep-sided **Port Lazo** below St-Riom.

Abbaye de Beauport

Open daily 15 June–15 Sept 10–7, rest of year 10–12 and 2–5. Guided tours in summer months.

After failed attempts to create a monastery on the island of Riom out in the bay of Paimpol in the 12th century, Count Alain de Penthièvre et de Goëlo paid for a new foundation on the coast early in the 13th century, giving charge of it to monks from a Norman abbey, Lucerne, near Avranches and the Mont-St-Michel. Much of the abbey was constructed by the middle of the century, except for the refectory, completed in the 14th century. The ruins are therefore mainly Gothic in style.

The abbey quickly assumed an important role in north Breton religious affairs. It was placed under direct authority of the papacy and its abbot was allowed to don a mitre, symbol of his high status, the towering religious hat normally associated with the title of bishop. Substantial new abbot's lodgings went up in the 14th century and the cloisters were redrawn in the 15th. Under the Ancien Régime, the abbey fell more and more into decline, however; it was sold off at the Revolution and its substantial library was shipped to St-Brieuc, although most of the books and manuscripts were ruined on the way. The Gothic chapterhouse with its splendid period vaulting, the *salle au duc* and the *salle aux hôtes* have survived most impressively, but you can also see the vestiges of various other rooms. Now, concerts and cultural events take place within its walls in summer, on Thursday evenings.

Beyond the beaches around the Anse de Beauport, which is also known as the Anse de Poulafret, you can walk to the end of the curious spit named the **Pointe de Guilben**, where a kind of black basalt rock mingles with the pink granite. The mild climate on the peninsula encourages relatively exotic flora, and also attracts birds in large numbers.

Getting Around

Paimpol is on a slow **train** line linking it to Guingamp, where you can pick up the fast TGV service.

For information on **bus** services eastwards from Paimpol, contact CAT, **t** 02 96 33 36 60. For bus services westwards, contact Voyages Guégan, **t** 02 96 22 37 05.

Tourist Information

Plouha: **t** 02 96 20 24 73, *www.plouha.com*.
Paimpol: **t** 02 96 20 83 16,
   www.paimpol-goelo.com.

Market Days

Plouha: Wednesday.
Paimpol: Tuesday.

Where to Stay and Eat

Plouha ✉ 22580

Plage des Palus has beachside places to eat.
★★Le Relais d'Armor, Place de la Bretagne, **t** 02 96 22 44 88 (*inexpensive*). A little village hotel near the sea, with simple, clean rooms.

Pléhédel ✉ 22290

Château-Hôtel de Coatguelen, **t** 02 96 22 37 67 (*moderate*). A delightful 19th-century château with exquisite furniture, a golf course, a swimming pool and a tennis court. B&B is offered, and there's a brasserie.

Paimpol ✉ 22500

★★★Hotel K'Loys, 21 Quai Morand, **t** 02 96 20 40 01, *www.k-loys.com* (*moderate–expensive*). Eleven spacious and immaculate rooms.
★★★Le Repaire de Kerroc'h, 29 Quai Morand, **t** 02 96 20 50 13, *repairekerroch@aol.com* (*moderate*). One of the few old shipowners' houses left standing on the quays by the port (the original owner made his fortune as a corsair), with stylish rooms and good food.
★★Hôtel de la Marne, 30 Rue de la Marne, **t** 02 96 20 82 16 (*inexpensive*). Simple Breton architecture, tastefully done rooms and delicately spiced food.
★★L'Origano, 7 bis Rue du Quai, **t** 02 96 22 05 49 (*inexpensive*). Curiously shaped, bare rooms in a characterful old house just behind the Quai Morand.
★Hôtel Berthelot, 1 Rue du Port, **t** 02 96 20 88 66 (*inexpensive*). A simple option.
La Ferme de Kerroc'h, Route de Bréhat, **t** 02 96 55 81 75 (*moderate–expensive*).

Paimpol

Paimpol drowning under a tidal wave of sea-widows' tears – such is the popular image of this port, symbolic victim of the cruel centuries-long trade of long-distance cod-fishing. But expectations are somewhat disappointed at first sight. Rather than facing ever so bravely out to sea, Paimpol hides like a coward down an inlet, which drains to a black marsh when the tide goes out. And the quays of Paimpol are no longer lined with granite shipowners' mansions. Instead, a modern quayside has been built, with all the character of a modern shopping arcade, which is basically what it is. To add insult to injury, the national school of the merchant navy based in Paimpol closed down only to be replaced by a catering college. Tough cod-fishing has been replaced by delicate cod cuisine.

Yet a whiff of an atmosphere lingers in the air. Behind the quayside you can find old squares and winding, cobbled streets to wander through, especially around the **Place du Martray** and the **Place de l'Eglise**. By the shattered old church, of which only the steeple remains, a monument pays its respect to Théodore Botrel. This early-20th-century Breton crooner, popular across France, had a big hit with a song called *La Paimpolaise*, about fishermen from the port wistfully remembering their beautiful women back home, here depicted in stone.

A restored Breton farmhouse where you can come to tuck into some good homemade cooking. *Closed Sun eve, Mon, and Tues lunch.*

Le Restaurant du Port, 17 Quai Morand, t 02 96 20 82 76 *(moderate–expensive)*. A restaurant with a first-floor dining room looking out over the port, offering good seafood platters.

La Vieille Tour, 13 Rue de l'Eglise, t 02 96 20 83 18 *(moderate–expensive)*. A reliable place for excellent, inventive Breton fare, served up in a warm dining room that's curtained off from the outside world. *Closed Sun eve and Tues.*

L'Islandais, 19 Quai Morand *(moderate)*. A restaurant serving a well-respected menu to a consistently packed *salle*.

Crêperie L'Agapanthe, 12 Quai Duguay Trouin, t 02 96 20 42 09 *(inexpensive)*. A cosy place that's worth seeking out for its *Paimpolaise* with artichoke.

Crêperie Alizés, Rue de la Poissonnerie, t 02 96 22 03 90 *(inexpensive)*. A large and lively crêperie.

Morel, 11 Place du Martray, t 02 96 20 86 34 *(inexpensive)*. An authentic Breton crêpe joint with a variety of specialities, including a Guémené sausage filling.

Porz-Even, Ploubazlanec ✉ 22620

★★Pension Boucher, 44 Rue Pierre Loti, t 02 96 55 84 16 *(inexpensive)*. A pleasant, traditional home offering rooms and good seafood.

Pointe de l'Arcouest ✉ 22620

★★★Hôtel Le Barbu, t 02 96 55 86 98, *hotel. lebarbu@wanadoo.fr (moderate–expensive)*. The place to stay if you want to be in pole position to catch the ferry to the island of Bréhat. Most of the rooms have a sea view, but you pay for the good location. There's a swimming pool and a restaurant serving a wide range of seafood specialities.

Loguivy ✉ 22620

★★Le Grand Large, Le Port, t 02 96 20 90 18 *(inexpensive–moderate)*. A superbly situated choice with views of the sea and the Bréhat archipelago. Some bedrooms have sea views.

Kergrist ✉ 22500

Le Relais Brenner, overlooking the Trieux river by the bridge over to Lézardrieux, t 02 96 22 29 95 *(moderate–expensive)*. A plush option with very refined decoration in the rooms. The large, well-kept gardens lead down to a private beach, but there's also a heated indoor swimming pool.

Two very little museums give you a frozen image of Paimpol's past. The **Musée du Costume** *(open in high season daily 10.30–12.30 and 2.30–6)*, which is located in a typical little fisherman's cottage, has a collection of traditional furniture on the ground floor and on the first floor a display of local costumes. Meanwhile, the **Musée de la Mer** *(open daily mid-June–Aug 10.30–12.30 and 2.30–6, at other times call t 02 96 22 02 19 for an appointment)* pays its respects to Paimpol's maritime past. Appropriately enough, this museum's collections are housed in a former cod-drying building. They concentrate on the fishing expeditions to Iceland.

It seems that fishermen from these parts may have gone cod-fishing on the lucrative banks off Newfoundland as early as the 16th century. They would head off at the end of February for gruelling, long stints in the terrible waters of the Atlantic. Before they went, a religious *pardon* was held, with the boats decked out for the occasion. In the 19th century, sailors switched their attention from Newfoundland to the seas off Iceland. Each boat had a crew of around 20 men and boys; the catch was collected in larger vessels that could return frequently to France in a season, but the fishermen themselves stayed half the year out at sea. The Icelandic fishing came to an end in 1935. It has been estimated that about 2,000 men died on the Paimpol expeditions in one 80-year period alone.

Reduced to Tears by Cod's Emotional Wallop

The camp naval officer and romantic writer Pierre Loti saw his tear-jerker *Pêcheurs d'Islande* published in 1886. This tale of tragic romance set in Paimpol and the Icelandic seas rapidly became a hugely popular work across France. Loti himself never went on a cod-fishing expedition, but he did have the solid background of his career, during which he had crossed the oceans, to help him write about this environment. And he befriended many fishermen from Paimpol when he visited the area.

Loti's real name was Julien Viaud; during a stay on Tahiti he was nicknamed Loti after a Pacific flower. He was an exotic figure, with his finely curled moustaches and his love of flamboyant clothes. He did view life on board the Breton fishing boats as extremely harsh, but he tried to emphasize the simple camaraderie on board, and the heroism of the fishermen. *Mon Frère Yves*, Loti's other highly popular Breton fishing novel, tackles the painful fact that many Breton fishermen were driven to drink by their desperate lives at sea.

The Paimpolais and Paimpol still feel strongly attached to their fishing past. And the attachment to Breton culture generally is particularly evident. There's a Breton-speaking Diwan school in the town and plenty of Breton activities. Contact the tourist office about special Breton dancing lessons for tourists. You can also go out in the boat *Le Vieux Copain* for a half-day or full-day outing at sea, or for fishing tuition (*from one day to a week; call t 02 96 20 59 30*). Alternatively, try the *Néluleuse* (*t 02 96 55 44 33*) or the *Eulalic* (*t 02 96 55 95 99*). From June to September you can take a trip on a **steam train** between Paimpol and Poutrieux in the Trieux valley (*bookings a day in advance on t 08 92 39 14 27*).

The Paimpol Peninsula

Heading north along the coast around the bay of Paimpol, you can climb the **Tour Kerroc'h**, a 19th-century tower, to take in wide views of the peninsula. The village of **Ploubazlanec** that follows contains an extremely moving reminder of just how many local men lost their lives in the cod-fishing expeditions between 1853 and 1935; black plaques along the **cemetery wall** are inscribed with the names of the sailors who disappeared at sea.

Fishing still goes on from the two little ports, **Porz Even** and **Loguivy**. Between these two, you'll find the **Pointe de l'Arcouest** and its little terminal for boat trips to the splendid Ile de Bréhat or down the Trieux estuary. Because of the massive popularity of Bréhat, the roads above Paimpol get clogged up in season.

Ile de Bréhat

The Ile de Bréhat is like a beautiful object that has shattered into a thousand little pieces; just the odd larger fragment remains. The magical archipelago boasts rocks of a rare beauty, even by Brittany's standards, with their many gradations of pinks and oranges.

Bréhat, the main island, is actually two large pieces of rock joined together by a diminutive bridge. The south island is very different from the north, much more lush and densely populated. The north island is more barren, tranquil and wild, and much more exposed to the wind. Bréhat's miniature ecosystem is in danger of being killed by tourism, so avoid high season if possible.

History

There are no obvious signs of the neolithic and Gallo-Roman settlements that are said to have existed on Bréhat. Nor can you see anything to prove that St Budoc came here in the 5th century. Actually, he is supposed to have founded one of the oldest Breton monasteries on the island of Lavrec just to the east of the main island, around AD 470. This monastery is thought to have exercised an important Christian influence over a good portion of Brittany in the early period of Dark Ages immigration from Britain.

Bréhat was fortified in the medieval period. A château was built facing the island of Lavrec. The original church in the main village dates back to the 12th century. As to St-Riom, it was constructed in the northeastern corner of the island to serve as a small lepers' colony, provided with its own tiny chapel. In the 15th century, Duke Jean V of Brittany called on the English for help; they landed on Bréhat and ransacked the place, although the admiral in charge did lose his life in the incident. At the end of the 16th century, the ultra-Catholic leader, the Duc de Mercœur, had the battered castle repaired. But in 1591, Englishman General Norris came to Bréhat in support of Protestant King Henri IV of France. Norris had several of the Ligueurs hanged from the sails of the windmill of Crec'h Tarek; Mercœur then sent Spanish allies to wreak his revenge on the island. Finally, it is said that King Henri IV ordered the destruction of Bréhat's castle.

Under King Louis XIV's warring reign, Vauban apparently came to see about fortifying the island, but a meagre causeway seems to have been the only result. Many of the island's menfolk were drafted into the navy in that period. A tidal mill was added in the 17th century, located by the bay of La Corderie, between the island's two halves, the wide inlet there serving as the port for the local fishermen for centuries. Some Bréhat men became corsairs, notably the captains Corouge and Lambert. Port-Clos, built in 1770, gave the island a safer harbour.

Practical new buildings went up on the island in the 19th century in order to improve its safety. Two lighthouses were constructed, as was a naval watchtower. The southwestern tip of Bréhat was fortified with a Second Empire citadel, and the chapel of St-Michel rebuilt on top of the highest point of the island, serving as a seamark for sailors as well as a symbolically high-perched place of worship.

Artists came from afar, attracted by the otherworldly beauty of the place. Bréhat gradually turned chic and chichi after the Second World War. It used to be local fishermen who would retire here, buying a small plot of land to cultivate, but it became increasingly fashionable, in particular for the wealthy intellectual set. It was in this period that exotic flowers were brought in large number on to the southern island – until then, potatoes were what the islanders nurtured.

A Tour of the Island

You land in the protected **Port-Clos**, where you can hire bikes. The pine-wooded, cliff-sided point to the west is the site of the 19th-century citadel. Extraordinary views open out from the **Bois de la Citadelle** on that side.

The point to the east of Port-Clos leads to the **Grève du Guerzido**, the best-known beach on Bréhat. According to the season, you can see flowering four-seasons mimosas, whole alleys of agapanthus and fuchsias the size of small trees, as well as the occasional flash of a pink neiris, known here as *belles toutes nues* ('beautiful women completely naked'), among many other plants. Spanish broom brings splashes of yellow; fig trees, eucalyptus and palm trees also prosper here.

Le Bourg, up the eastern side of the south island, is the unimaginatively named main village, but it is quite an attractive place, centred around a cheerful circular square shaded by plane trees. You might cast an eye inside the church, in very small part dating back to the 12th century, but mostly a mid-17th-century edifice. Just up from Le Bourg along the eastern side lie the vague ruins of the castle.

Continue to the western side of the south island, taking the track past the ruins of the windmill on its hill. Then head up to the **Chapelle St-Michel**, the high point of Bréhat, which is clearly visible from afar with its deliberately colourful and un-Breton orange roof tiles. This hillock probably served as a religious site for prehistoric settlers. Up by the basic whitewashed chapel you get sensational views across the archipelago.

Getting There and Around

Ferries to the island of Bréhat depart from the Pointe de l'Arcouest to the north of Paimpol; be aware that you need to book well in advance during the high season (contact Les Vedettes de Bréhat, **t** 02 96 55 86 99). No **cars** are allowed on the ferries, so make sure that you leave time to find a parking space and walk to the ticket office. You may have to use a different jetty from the one you arrive at to get back to the mainland, depending on the state of the tides, so leave time for that potential surprise.

You can go for magnificent **walks** or **cycle rides** round the island; it's roughly 12km round the whole of Bréhat. Take a **boat** tour of the entire island if you don't want to use your own two feet.

Tourist Information

Ile de Bréhat: t 02 96 20 04 15, *syndicatinitiative.brehat@wanadoo.fr*.

Market Days

Daily in July and August.

Where to Stay and Eat

Ile de Bréhat ✉ 22870

B&B rooms on the island are few and far between, and you'll need to book in advance. Contact the tourist office for details.

Hôtel Bellevue, Port-Clos, **t 02 96 20 00 05, *www.hotel-bellevue.com* (*moderate*). A pretty if standard and overpriced portside hotel. Some rooms have sea views. The restaurant terraces are invaded by visitors with each boat that arrives.

La Vieille Auberge, Le Bourg, **t 02 96 20 00 24, *www.ihotels.com* (*moderate*). A small hotel situated in the main village, almost as overpriced as the Bellevue. It also has its own restaurant.

La Brazérade, main street, **t** 02 96 20 06 30 (*inexpensive*). A simple option for *moules frites*. Closed Nov–March.

From the mound, you can look down on to the very pretty 17th-century **tidal mill**. It has been restored to working order and is occasionally open to the public. In olden days, at high tide, boats could come right up to a handy window in the building and deliver the grain to be milled. Another great viewing point on Bréhat is from the **Croix de Maudez**, a cross erected on the most westerly tip of the island in 1788.

Crossing the Pont ar Prat, you come onto the wilder **northern half of the island**. This part of Bréhat contains far fewer houses. Moors rather than carefully tended gardens dominate here. You could head up the western side to the whitewashed naval watchtower and lighthouse of Le Rosédo, passing the 19th-century granite **chapel of Keranroux** with its little spire and whitewashed interior. Next, head for the northernmost tip of the island and the Phare du Paon.

Several legends revolve around the utterly pink rocks of the **Phare du Paon**, or peacock lighthouse, and its chasm in which the waves roar. The hackneyed story concerns young women wanting to know if they would get married in the year. They were supposed to throw a stone into the abyss; if the stone plopped straight into the water, then they would supposedly be married in the year. If the pebble hit the sides of the chasm, then they would have to wait as many years as the stone bounced against the rocks.

A much more gruesome story about the place tells of an evil pair of young siblings whose father, Mériadec, was a wealthy lord of Goëlo. Greedy to get hold of his riches, they decided to kill him. But Mériadec got wind of their plans and fled to Bréhat. His diabolical children tracked him down to the northern end of the island and murdered him there. As they were about to dispose of his body, they were transformed into the cruelly lacerated rocks you now see, stained with their father's blood.

From Pontrieux into Inland Trégor

Pontrieux, an inland port not too surprisingly located by the Trieux river, serves as an outer harbour for the town of Guingamp further inland. A trip around Guingamp takes you away from the tourist hordes to a place of rural tranquillity.

Pontrieux

At Pontrieux, a pretty, quiet little historic river town, the squares and streets almost mirror each other either side of the Trieux. The two halves have seemingly lived almost as separate communities through time. Each had its own *coiffeur* and café, and even its own church. In centuries past, Pontrieux served as a trading junction on the border between the Goëlo and the Trégor, as well as acting as a port for Guingamp inland. Here, the Trieux is still quite narrow, its banks lined with boathouses and former washhouses that the townspeople now smother with flowers. They have also placed models of washerwomen in traditional costume along the way, although these figures are not exactly convincing. Mid-August sees a big celebration along the river, **the Fête des Lavandières**, or festival of the washerwomen.

Pontrieux merchants grew wealthy from their mills (both to make flour and paper) and from the linen trade at one time, as houses such as the towering timberframe **Maison d'Eiffel** (now home to the tourist office) prove. A large number of craftspeople have set up shop here. On the northern side of town you will find the Pontrieux yacht harbour. From the railway station nearby, you can take the **tourist train** along a dramatic track above the Trieux river to Paimpol.

The impressive castle that you can spot high north along the west bank of the Trieux is the **Château de la Roche-Jagu** (*open daily July and Aug 10–7, rest of year 10.30–12.30 and 2–6*), a defensive block built in the 15th century and now looking like a severe fortification of a house. The ornate chimney stacks add a decorative touch. An annual exhibition (*mid-June–11 Nov*) on a Côtes d'Armor theme is held in the otherwise rather empty chambers within, with their vast fireplaces and beams. The gardens are currently being carefully restored.

Runan

In the Middle Ages, the dukes of Brittany had a castle, Châteaulin-sur-Trieux, in the area. This has disappeared. The dukes also used to attend the local **church at Runan** (just west of Pontrieux via the D21), as did the lords of the Château de La Roche-Jagu. With such wealthy local patronage, it is perhaps not wholly surprising that it should have been so richly decorated, but it is slightly startling to see so much adornment added on to this basic Breton Gothic edifice. The south porch, exceptionally for a little Breton church, has been given unexpected grandeur, the archivolts packed with finely sculpted figures. Above the porch, a stone panel represents a couple of major scenes from the New Testament. A dozen coats of arms, elaborately carved in stone, have been encrusted into the church's south side. The wild decoration continues inside.

Guingamp

Guingamp is a strongly traditional small Breton market town. **La Fête de la St-Loup**, the week-long celebration of Breton dancing held here, starts the Sunday following 15 August, and *La Dérobée de Guingamp* is known as one of the liveliest Breton dances, although it may have been brought over by Napoleonic soldiers fighting in Italy.

The main church in town is dedicated to the Black Virgin known as **Notre-Dame de Bon Secours**. Her *pardon* counts as a major event for Catholics in this part of Brittany, taking place on the first Saturday in July. But in this instance the pilgrims wait until nightfall to start processing by torchlight. At any time of year in Guingamp, however, you will find believers coming to light candles to the Black Virgin sheltering in one of the church's porches. The whole sturdy edifice mixes several periods of architecture. In 1535, the right-hand side of the Gothic church fell down. That section was rebuilt without any attempt to match the old style, using swanky new Renaissance forms.

Inside, the church is darkly spectacular, with the main ceiling held up by Gothic vaulting. The contrast between the aisle on the left, resting on Gothic arches, and that on the right, which is supported by Renaissance ones, could hardly be more marked, providing a good lesson in the differences between the two styles. The design of the gallery above the Renaissance arches is wild, turning Baroque with its extravagant curves. The heavier, earlier Romanesque period makes its weighty presence felt in the crossing, where the solid arches almost separate off this part of the church from the rest of it. Beyond the crossing, the choir looks lightly Gothic. Normally, flying buttresses are added to the outside of Gothic churches to help support the walls, but here internal buttresses hold up the ambulatory. In the choir, keep an eye out for the carved panels of Christ's Passion, which are crowded with carved detail.

Down from the church, the triangular square, the **Place du Centre**, is the focal point of the town. Bordered by grand houses, some in stone, some in timberframe, its charm is added to by the **Fontaine de la Plomée**, distinctly uncharacteristic of Brittany in its finesse. This Renaissance fountain from the 1580s is decorated with wild figures, including spectacularly winged griffins, naked, winged women hiding their breasts, and winged putti heads. Two of the three vases of the fountain are made from lead – *plomb* in French, hence the name *Plomée*.

Getting Around

Guingamp, the main centre of travel in the area, is conveniently served by the TGV fast train between Paris and Brest. Pontrieux is on a local train line that heads along the side of the Trieux river and up to Paimpol.

Tourist Information

Pays d'Accueil d'Argoat, Vallée des Forges, 22390 Bourbriac, **t** 02 96 43 44 43.
Pontrieux: Maison Eiffel, **t** 02 96 95 14 03, or **t** 02 96 95 60 31 out of season, *www.ulys.com/pontrieux.*
Guingamp: Place du Champ au Roy, **t** 02 96 43 73 89, *www.ot-guingamp.org.*
Bourbriac: 12 Place du Centre, **t** 02 96 43 46 03, or **t** 02 96 43 40 21 out of season.
Callac: Place du Centre, **t** 02 96 45 59 34, or **t** 02 96 45 50 19 out of season.
Belle-Isle-en-Terre: Place de la Mairie, **t** 02 96 43 01 71, *officebelleisle@qualite-info.fr.*

Market Days

Pontrieux: Monday.
Guingamp: Friday and Saturday.
Bourbriac: Tuesday.
Callac: Wednesday.
Louargat: Thursday.
Belle-Isle-en-Terre: Wednesday.

Where to Stay and Eat

Guingamp ✉ 22200
★★★**Le Relais du Roi**, 42 Place du Centre, **t** 02 96 43 76 62 (*expensive*). A 16th-century house with elegant interiors and refined cuisine.
★★**Hôtel d'Armor**, 44 Boulevard Clemenceau, **t** 02 96 43 76 16, *www.armor-hotel.com* (*inexpensive*). A modern hotel near the station.
La Boissière, 90 Rue de l'Yser, **t** 02 96 21 06 35 (*moderate–expensive*). A characterful place with picturesque grounds, serving grills and *fruits de mer*. Reservations are advised.
Crêperie St-Yves, Rue St-Yves, **t** 02 96 44 31 18 (*inexpensive*). A tiny, very popular crêperie.

Louargat ✉ 22540
★★**Manoir du Cleuziou**, 4km along the D33A from Louargat, **t** 02 96 43 14 90 (*inexpensive–moderate*). Excellent-value, stylish rooms in a lovely old manor, plus a pool and tennis court.

Belle-Isle-en-Terre ✉ 22810
★★**Le Relais de l'Argoat**, 9 Rue du Guic, **t** 02 96 43 00 34 (*inexpensive*). A classic French rural town hotel with reliable food.

Loc-Envel ✉ 22810
L'Air du Temps, **t** 02 96 43 04 03 (*inexpensive*). A well-known local *café littéraire* with a B&B. Call ahead to make sure it's open.

The Church of Grâces and Charles de Blois's Resting Place

Jeanne de Penthièvre's husband, Charles de Blois or Charles de Chastillon, defended her interests during the Breton War of Succession, supported by the king of France. A deeply religious man, De Blois also made donations to many religious foundations in northern Brittany, for instance in Guingamp. But he would lose the war, dying at the battle of Auray in 1364. His remains lie in a reliquary box in the church at Grâces, a village just west of Guingamp. After his death, a cult grew up around him, and the religious warrior was in fact eventually declared a saint.

The grand Gothic village church of Grâces only dates from the late 15th century, but it was funded by the last Breton duchess, Anne, also countess of Penthièvre – hence the presence of the Breton ducal insignia in various parts of the building. The whole edifice is rich in all manner of decorative details; a pair of baboonish-looking rampant lions hold up a coat of arms on one of the gabled sides of the church, and a Breton bagpipe player is carved over the door to the belltower. Still funnier animals are represented inside, haring along the stringbeams in hunting scenes and various cautionary tales.

South of Guingamp

For a near-forgotten corner of Breton villages and chapels, head for the area around St-Péver. Some of the sights along this route have a desolate beauty; some are badly neglected. To visit a couple of run-down, almost windowless chapels here, you need to get the keys from local houses (details are posted on the chapel doors). At the basic, severe-looking **Chapelle Notre-Dame d'Avaugour** (a little north of St-Péver), the architecture is strikingly ascetic. The Breton statues prove the main wealth within what is a crumbling edifice. The most touching sculpture, in the choir end, depicts a crudely carved crucified Christ resting on God, his father's, knees for once. The Virgin appears with the baby Jesus in the most beautiful of the chapel statues.

The virtually windowless **Notre-Dame de Restudo** seems still more detached from the modern world. Some very worn frescoes have just about survived, painted on the Gothic arch dividing up the nave. Beyond the dividing arch, look at the side-chapel, its wall covered with horseshoes – the place is dedicated to St Eloi, patron saint of farriers. In the **chapel of St-Fiacre** nearby, boxes containing the bones of the dead were still displayed in the ossuary not that long ago.

Follow the steep country road on south to **Senven-Léhart** and you will come to a chapel there containing one of the most easterly sited of the Breton calvaries, the 16th-century work of the studios of Roland Doré. The neat drapery folds look like the furrows of seashells.

Just to the south of Senven-Léhart, the rock-strewn **village of St-Connan** looks particularly pretty. The tiny D4 road then leads you a little further south down to **St-Gilles-Pligeaux**, a village with a photogenic ensemble of church and chapel. The two fountains below them are lovely. Venture west to the **vestiges of the abbey of Coat-Mallouen at Kerpert** to view these attractive but rather dangerous ruins.

Back west of St-Péver, **Bourbriac** boasts a vaingloriously large and slightly neglected church on its big barren square. The crypt goes back to the 11th century or even earlier, and the church contains a Merovingian tomb, said to be that of the Breton saint Briac, supposed to be able to cure epilepsy.

West along the D24 some 15 kilometres, Pestivien and Bulat-Pestivien have an exceptionally interesting religious legacy. The **Chapelle St-Blaise** and its **calvary at Pestivien** were made from light grey stone, now covered with grey lichen and set in a green-grassed enclosure. On the calvary, peculiarly elongated figures look down on the dead Christ. The chapel also contains interesting carvings. Two memorable *pardons* were traditionally held here, the *pardon au beurre* (the butter *pardon*) on Trinity Sunday, when butter used to be offered to St Blaise, and the *pardon du coq*, the first Sunday of February, when the tradition was for a slaughtered cockerel to be thrown down from the tower onto the congregation.

The **Eglise Notre-Dame de Bulat** in **Bulat-Pestivien** is a much more substantial affair than the St-Blaise chapel. It towers above the village, out of all proportion with it. Bulat-Pestivien became a particularly revered spot in Brittany because the 12th-century Breton lawyer-saint, St Yves (*see* p.205), came to pray to Notre-Dame de Bulat on numerous occasions. As to the local lordly Pestivien family, it played a significant part in the 14th-century Breton War of Succession.

The church dates mainly from the 14th and 15th centuries. The soaring church tower has a typical curving Gothic accolade arch on its front, but 16th-century French Renaissance details have been carved around it, while Renaissance-style windows appear above. A stone couple in Renaissance attire even greet you on either side of the main doorway. To the right of the main entrance, a mocking series of lively skeletons act as a chilling reminder of the frailty of human life. One of these figures of the grim reaper, *l'Ankou* in Breton, is shown preaching, brandishing bones.

Enter the church via the porch with its severe statues of the apostles. The conspicuous lord's loggia inside was built so that the local nobles could sit comfortably apart from the rest of the congregation. Curious sculptures include Charles de Blois, portrayed in mock-chivalric style, and a Breton in clogs holding up the lectern.

The area around Bulat-Pestivien and Callac to the west are known for breeding the Breton spaniel, a much-appreciated hunting dog in France.

West of Guingamp Around the Menez-Bré

The N12 dual carriageway rushes west through the countryside from Guingamp to Morlaix, passing below the **Ménez-Bré**, once a sacred hill, sometimes known as the Good Giant to Bretons from this area. From up on its heights, you can get views of the western Côtes d'Armor stretching in all directions.

The Ménez-Bré is associated with the blind 6th-century Breton saint, Hervé, who went around guided by a wolf. His blindness was considered a gift from God, to stop him from being deceived by appearances. Hervé is said to have had powers of healing and exorcism; he is also credited with discovering the spring on the side of the hill.

West along the N12 is **Belle-Isle-en-Terre**, a picturesque village slightly disturbed by the dual carriageway passing close by. **Traditional Breton wrestling** brings particular life to the place on the third Sunday in July. The life story is often told here of Maï Manac'h, born in 1869, the daughter of a local miller and his wife. She went up to Paris where she married a market porter who took her to live in London. After he died, she became the lover of Prince Antoine d'Orléans, grandson of King Louis Philippe of France, before marrying British industrialist Robert Mond, nicknamed the King of Nickel and knighted by King George V. Lady Mond, as she became known, remained generous to her home village, donating her château, now turned into a school.

Lord and Lady Mond's mausoleum, with its massive plain pink granite tomb, lies by the pretty **chapel of Locmaria** on a hillside a couple of kilometres to the north of Belle-Isle-en-Terre. The chapel is best known for its rood screen. On one side of this, the 12 flat-faced, bearded apostles all look like they were made to the same model.

Southwest from Belle-Isle-en-Terre the charming slope-side **church of Loc Envel** is set in a forest-bordered village and boasts an accomplished rood screen. Many decorative features stand out inside, such as the 18th-century clock, or the figure of a praying, kneeling lord. Look out too for the host of angels floating above your head.

The Presqu'île Sauvage and Tréguier

The Trégor stretches along the coast, from the Trieux estuary in the Côtes d'Armor to the Morlaix river in northeastern Finistère. One of the four distinct dialects of Breton developed in the Trégor. Arriving in the area, we come to the Presqu'île Sauvage, an unkempt peninsula. Then we move on to Tréguier, capital of the Trégor, renowned for its cathedral and cloister, and its religious son, 13th-century Yves, defender of the poor.

The Presqu'île Sauvage

Lézardrieux makes the most of its position overlooking the beautiful Trieux estuary. It has a successful fleet of oyster boats and an outrageously sized yachting harbour for such a small place. The **moulin à mer de Traou-Meur-en-Pleudaniel**, a 17th-century tidal mill just south of Lézardieux, can only be visited on the *journée du patrimoine* in mid September each year. If you're in search of coastal walks without the hordes of the Côte de Granit Rose, the Presqu'île Sauvage fits the bill. If you book in advance, you could go on a guided canoe trip into the rocky seas around here from the Club Nautique de Trieux (**t** *02 96 20 92 80*).

Curious spits of land stick out into the sea north of here. On **Pen Lan**, the **Centre d'Etude et de Valorisation des Algues** (*open for visits July and Aug Mon–Fri at 2.30 and 4, Sun at 3; 2nd half June and 1st half Sept Mon–Fri 2.30*) presents algae and its varied uses in a suitable setting, looking across the rock-strewn waters to Bréhat.

The **Sillon de Talbert** needs to be seen to be believed. How come this narrow strip of sand and pebbles hasn't been washed away by the tides, you may well wonder? You can go for a magical walk right along its mysterious length. The **Phare des Héaux** stands out in the distance out to sea, at 45 metres the highest sea lighthouse off the French coast. Two warnings about walking along the Sillon de Talbert – it is extremely dangerous to try to wander out beyond the end of the *sillon* at low tide, as you may well get caught out by the incoming sea; and when the terns are nesting, the *sillon* is closed to visitors.

Behind, at **Pleubian**, you might like to go in search of the richly carved and weather-worn round granite **outdoor pulpit**, a variation on the theme of the stone calvaries so numerous further west in the Finistère. The unusual circular form of the frieze dates back to the 15th century.

Tréguier

My son, live in a way that will make you a saint.
Purported words of Azou de Quinquis to her son Yves Helory de Kermartin.
(He did become a saint – talk about living up to parental expectations.)

Tréguier is the deeply serious religious capital of the Trégor. The soaring steeple of its remarkable cathedral makes it very clear who was boss in centuries past. The city lays claim to being one of the original seats of Christian power in Brittany.

History

Tugdual or Tugwall, described as a Welsh monk of the 6th century, became the first bishop of Tréguier in 540. The town grew into one of the most important spiritual centres in Brittany. A few records have survived showing how the bishops of Tréguier carried through far-reaching Church reforms in the early Middle Ages. For example, in 1221, Pope Honorius III's administration allowed the new bishop of Tréguier to absolve priests in his bishopric who had been excommunicated for having concubines or for wearing unsuitable attire.

In 1253, Yves Helory de Kermartin was born near the city, at Minihy-Tréguier. From a noble family, he grew up to become a talented Church lawyer, training in Paris. He took on a position as an ecclesiastical judge in Brittany, serving at Rennes and Tréguier, and became particularly respected by the common people for his fairness and his concern for the poor. Yves then changed career to serve as a priest, and with incredible energy he went around Brittany preaching. It is said that he sometimes delivered four or five sermons a day. He also turned part of his family home at Kermartin into a hospital for the poor and the sick.

Yves was considered to have performed many miracles during his lifetime. He died on 19 May 1303, and was buried in Tréguier cathedral. A cult subsequently grew up around his memory and relics. He became the only Breton parish priest to be canonized in the Middle Ages.

The Gothic cathedral of Tréguier was embarked upon in 1339. From 1347, the tomb of St Yves was installed there and for a small sum pilgrims were even allowed to touch his skull. Pilgrims came in large numbers during the second half of the Middle Ages

Getting Around

Lannion **airport** is not far from Tréguier. The **bus** service along this coastal area is run by Voyages Guégan, **t** 02 96 20 59 50.

Tourist Information

Pays du Trégor-Goëlo, 9 Place de l'Eglise, 22450 La Roche-Derrien, **t** 02 96 91 50 22, *www.tregorgoelo.com.*
Tréguier: **t** 02 96 92 22 33, *www.paysdetreguier.com.*

Market Days
Lézardrieux: Friday.
Pleubian: Saturday.
Tréguier: Wednesday.

Where to Stay and Eat

Quemper-Guézennec ✉ 22260
Ferme-auberge Le Marlec, a few km east of Pontrieux, **t** 02 96 95 66 47 (*inexpensive*). Pleasant, simple B&B rooms in a granite farmhouse surrounded by flowers and known locally for its hearty country cooking.

Lézardrieux ✉ 22740
★★Hôtel Le Littoral, Rue St-Christophe, **t** 02 96 20 10 59 (*inexpensive*). A pleasant Breton family hotel close to the Trieux estuary and the centre of the village.

Brélidy ✉ 22140
★★★Château de Brélidy, **t** 02 96 95 69 38, *www.chateau-brelidy.com* (*moderate*). A small, much-restored 16th-century castle, with luxurious bedrooms in which great attention has been paid to detail. Two rivers flow through the grounds, where you can go fishing in season. You'll also find a jacuzzi under an arbour in the garden. The ruins of a 10th-century castle hidden in the park and a billiards room back in the younger castle add to the fun.

Pommerit-Jaudy ✉ 22450
Château de Kermezen, **t** 02 96 91 35 75 (*moderate*). A splendid little Breton castle just to the south of La Roche-Derrien, offering the most luxurious type of B&B experience. The family that greets you has roots here going back some 500 years. A couple of the rooms have useful galleries where children can sleep.

on the Tro Breizh, the religious tour of the seven Breton cathedrals. Trade prospered during this time, and Tréguier became an important Breton centre for printing from the late 15th century.

After suffering in the nightmare of the French Wars of Religion, when Tréguier briefly supported the Protestant side and as a result was severely damaged by Catholic attacks, the city centre up on the hillside became largely dominated by its Catholic religious establishments. But, with the French Revolution and the demise of the Church, Tréguier lost much of its importance. However, the fertile vegetable fields of this stretch of the north Breton coast brought some prosperity in the 19th century, until tourism also helped to revive Tréguier's fortunes. The powerful attraction of its religious legacy has also meant that the pilgrims have never stopped coming.

Tréguier Cathedral

This is definitely the heart and soul of Tréguier. It is wonderfully eccentric, and arguably the most interesting and appealing of all Brittany's cathedrals. It also recalls much of the town's history. From the cloisters, you can see the three distinctively different towers rising in a dramatic row. The outrageously tall spire over the south porch (63 metres in height) is cut with simple patterns like a child's toy. By contrast, another of the crossing towers is a squat, sober Romanesque construction. You may

Tréguier ✉ 22220

★★★Aigue Marine, 5 Rue Marcellin Berthelot, Port de Plaisance, **t** 02 96 92 97 00, *www.aiguemarine.fr* (*moderate*). A large hotel by the yachting harbour, with comfortable traditional rooms, a heated swimming pool, a jacuzzi, a gym, a sauna and good food.

★★★Kastell Dinec'h, Route de Lannion, just west of Tréguier, **t** 02 96 92 49 39, *kastell@club-internet.fr* (*moderate*). A converted Breton manor in the countryside, with ornately decorated, romantic little rooms, an excellent, stylish restaurant offering wonderful seafood specialities, and delightful gardens with a swimming pool. Half-board is preferred in the high season (15 July–15 Aug).

★★Hôtel des Roches Douvres, 17 Rue Marcellin Berthelot, **t** 02 96 92 27 27 (*inexpensive*). A clean, modern hotel overlooking the marina.

Le St-Bernard, 3 Rue Marcellin Berthelot, **t** 02 96 92 20 77 (*moderate*). A restaurant down by the marina, offering a choice of good-value menus.

Crêperie-Grill Les Archers, 4 Rue de St-Yves, **t** 02 96 92 33 54 (*inexpensive*). A popular place for crêpes and regular *formules*, in a pretty building.

La Poissonnerie du Trégor, 2 Rue Renan, **t** 02 96 92 30 27 (*inexpensive*). A fishmonger's situated just behind the cathedral, with a first-floor dining room where you can try Breton seafood, and a takeaway service.

Plougrescant ✉ 22170

Manoir de Kergrec'h, **t** 02 96 92 59 13 or **t** 02 96 92 56 06 (*moderate–expensive*). Gorgeous luxury B&B rooms in a solid 17th-century manor by the coast.

Mme Janviers, Route du Gouffre, **t** 02 96 92 52 67 (*inexpensive*). A friendly B&B with simple, pleasant rooms.

Auberge de Pen-Ar-Feunteun, Route de Penvénan, **t** 02 96 92 51 02 (*inexpensive*). A simple rustic restaurant that should fit the bill if you're on a tight budget.

Porz Hir ✉ 22820

Chambre d'hôte de Pors-Hir, Hent-Pors, just north of Plougrescant, **t** 02 96 92 52 14 (*inexpensive*). A B&B looking out over a delightful tiny port, with extremely basic bedrooms. It is run by a former fisherman, so it comes as no surprise that the seafood is excellent.

be tempted, or forced, to enter the church by the south porch, the **Porche des Cloches**, sticking out from under the soaring steeple. This porch's delicate Gothic tracery, held up in the centre by one slender column, shows just how seductive Gothic architecture can be. Entering the cathedral this way, you come immediately to a traditional Breton carving showing St Yves. You may, though, enter the cathedral via the west door, known as the **Porche des Ladres**, or the Lepers' Door. Apparently lepers were not allowed into the cathedral during services but could listen from here.

Much of the interior decoration was axed to pieces in just one day of Revolutionary fury. The feared Bataillon d'Etampes swept through on 4 May 1794, destroying tombs, furnishings and stained-glass windows. Off the nave, inside the **Chapelle au Duc**, you will find the tombs of St Yves and Duke Jean V of Brittany, but both are modern works – replacements. Duke Jean V had his chapel added in the mid 15th century; imprisoned by Marguerite de Clisson, he made a vow to build it if he regained his freedom, which he did. He donated his weight in silver, a reasonably healthy 95 kilos, to the cathedral to have it built. Unfortunately, the reworked 1945 tomb of Duke Jean V is relatively plain.

The tomb of St Yves, much venerated, is a copy of the medieval one that Duke Jean V ordered. It is in the neo-Gothic chivalric style. A further monument in the chapel also recalls the last bishop of Tréguier, who fled to England at the Revolution. Lawyers from around the western world attend the annual **Pardon de St Yves**. One of the stained-glass windows in his chapel was donated by the US bar; another, donated by the French *barreaux*, displays the national cockerel of France. A third was the gift of the Belgian bar. The Pardon de St Yves is often presided over by a high Catholic Church official. Recent ex votos here show how many Bretons still put their trust in St Yves.

Towering arches spring up from the **cathedral crossing**. Up in the heights of the ceiling you can make out paintings of angels. They carry flowing banners made to contain quotes from the Bible. The **south transept** off the crossing is lit by a tall window divided up by sensational Flamboyant Gothic tracery. Reaching the **choir**, you come to a much more harmonious piece of Gothic architecture, built in the late 14th and early 15th centuries. In the centre of the choir, the stalls from the early 16th century have delightfully carved misericords displaying the usual Gothic bestiary; the carpenters apparently came from Flanders and the Rhine.

In the **north transept**, much of the Romanesque architecture has survived. A huge wooden Christ with an even bigger wooden head looks down on this transept. From here, you can go out into the peaceful 15th-century cloister and to the treasury (you have to pay a small fee). Behind the lacy Gothic tracery, the covered walkways serve as something of a museum for a collection of fine **medieval tomb effigies** collected from churches and abbeys around the Côtes d'Armor that were destroyed in the Revolution; several come from the abbeys of Bonrepos, Bégard and Beaulieu.

In the cathedral **treasury**, you can pay your respects to the skull of St Yves. This prized relic was hidden under one of the cathedral's flagstones during the Revolution. Among other curiosities still held in the treasury is a 17th-century revolving *chasublier*, an original piece of furniture to hold all the bishop's finery in an easily accessible manner – a godsend for your dandy bishop.

Nearby, the **Musée Renan** pays homage to a widely respected 19th-century son of Tréguier, the theological intellectual Ernest Renan. Trained to join the Church, he then embarked upon a series of monumental histories that controversially questioned the origins of Christianity. In his lifetime, the powerful, pious bigots of Tréguier reviled him.

Chapelle St-Gonéry, Plougrescant

This curious chapel, north of Tréguier just past the little oyster port of La Roche Jaune, has one end as crooked as a building from a fairytale, topped by a leaning, barbed little lead tower that looks like an instrument of medieval torture. Monstrous gargoyles drool down from this sinister steeple, but it turns out that this strange prong was only added in the 17th century. The crooked chapel below dates back to the Romanesque period.

Local people will show you round the interior for a paltry sum, though the commentary may be delivered as emotionlessly as the Massacre of the Innocents is depicted on the ceiling. The chapel's glory is the striking series of Biblical paintings daubed on the wooden planks of the vault. In the main panels, the chosen few Old Testament stories are told against a red and flowery background, while Adam and Eve are memorably depicted being expelled from Eden clad in a wonderful pattern of leaves. Selected New Testament scenes are represented below them.

There are other elements of decorative wealth inside the chapel. The Romanesque tower contains a couple of tombs for St Gonéry. At the opposite end, in the choir, Guillaume du Halgouët, a 16th-century bishop of Tréguier, ordered a grand mausoleum for himself. In the south transept, the rather splendid piece of Flamboyant Gothic furniture was built to store the parish archives and to keep the relics of St Gonéry. The skull on display, supposedly his, is brown as a berry.

The mother of St Gonéry, the splendidly named Ste Eliboubane, was venerated on the **Ile Loaven** just north up the coast from Plougrescant. Beyond that lie the **Iles d'Er**, adding greatly to the picturesque views out to sea. At very low tides, these islands become accessible by foot. West from here, the Côte de Granit Rose begins in earnest. At the top of the Plougrescant peninsula, a wonderful coast road leads you past the minuscule boulder-surrounded port of **Porz Hir** to the Pointe du Château.

The Côte de Granit Rose

The Côte de Granit Rose covers roughly 20 kilometres of some of the most gorgeous granite on the Breton coast, and counts among the most famous stretches of shore in the whole of France. It's not just that the rocks are pink along the Côte de Granit Rose; they have also been carved by the elements into some of the most bizarre shapes. This has led to many of the rocks being named after the objects they resemble, such as the *Upturned Foot*, the *Bottle* or *Napoleon's Hat*. From the well-to-do resort of Perros-Guirec, boats leave for the ornithological reserve of the archipelago of Les Sept Iles, where puffins, gannets and seals can be seen in spring and early summer.

From Porz Hir to Perros-Guirec

At Porz Hir, you already come across houses set among vast boulders. The **Pointe du Château**, better known as **Castel Meur**, has one of the most famous houses in Brittany trapped amongst its rocks. This house right on the sea, backed by a lagoon, looks as though two enormous boulders have been dropped at either end of it, imprisoning it in their stony embrace. It is so unusual that it has featured in all manner of advertising campaigns and magazine articles on Brittany. To divert attention from the house between the rocks (there are many more such houses caught among the boulders along this pink coastline), the Conservatoire du Littoral, the national body set up to protect the French coastline, has a **Maison d'Accueil** to teach the public about the natural environment. Continuing westwards along the coast, you come to the **Pointe du Gouffre**, with a great split between two rocks into which the sea can come raging.

The magical rockscapes continue around **Pors Scarff**, again with sonorous pebble slopes running down from the boulders. The **Plage de Ralevy** follows. At the **Anse de Gouermel**, you come to a bay with wider views. Around **Buguélès**, houses mingle in greater number with the boulders. They all make a truly fantastic sight. The small islands that are visible just off the mainland from here are known as the **Penvénan archipelago**. From Buguélès, it's amusing to try and reach Port-Blanc by car or by foot by the shortcut across the **Anse de Pellinec**, which is only passable at low tide when the causeway is revealed. Fertile fields surround the bay, producing crops of artichokes and cauliflowers.

Port-Blanc itself is absolutely stunning, though not very white. However, some white seamarks do stand out like sugarloaves on the rocks. The pink rockscapes are more tranquil than those to the east, and the waters look temptingly blue. The **Plage de Rohanic** is particularly splendid. Port-Blanc's most noticeable feature on the seafront is a tower sticking out from on top of one of the tallest boulders.

You can follow the coast westwards on foot, but a glorious high road leads from Port-Blanc to **Trévou-Tréguignec**. Two spectacular rock-protected beaches lie down from the village, **Les Dunes** and **Royau**. Big rectangular blocks of quarried pink granite, patterned with the cuts of the drills, act as sea walls. Out to sea, you can make out the barren Ile Tomé and the Sept-Iles. The coast around the tiny **Port Royau** is so strewn with rocks that it seems like an act of folly to have placed a port here.

Port l'Epine just further west, has more beautiful rocky creeks, low rockscapes and pebbly beaches. On the west side of the scrub-covered spit, the most popular resort of the Côte de Granit Rose, Perros-Guirec, comes into view.

Perros-Guirec

Perros-Guirec is a beautiful Breton resort with a modern marina. Grand villas and hotels climb the coastal slopes. Perros-Guirec's **port** lies on the eastern side of town. There are a couple of beaches this way too, the **Plage des Arcades** and the **Plage du Château**. The busy town shopping centre lies up on the hilltop. Perros-Guirec's **two large beaches**, **Trestrignel** and **Trestraou**, lie to the west of the Pointe du Château. With their fine sands and very gentle inclines, they make excellent stretches for toddlers to play on. Trestraou has the luxury thalassotherapy centre, the **Thermes Marins de Perros-Guirec** (*t 02 96 23 28 97*), a casino and nightclubs. From a jetty to one side of the beach, boats leave for trips around the ornithological reserve of the Sept Iles, one of the richest in France for rare marine birds (*see* opposite).

In such a glamorous seaside resort as Perros-Guirec, it comes as a slight surprise to find a museum by the port commemorating a painful time in Breton history. The **Musée de Cire** (*open daily June–Aug 9.30–6.30; April–end May, Sept and school hols 10–12.15 and 2–6*) is a museum on the Chouannerie (the anti-Revolutionary, pro-Catholic movement in northwest France), with waxwork scenes re-creating the bloody events that took place in the vicinity. Respects are also paid to Ernest Renan (*see* p.208) and to Maurice Denis, one of the greatest painters to have been seduced by Brittany, who bought a villa here and put some of the pink rocks of this coast on canvas in the late 19th and early 20th centuries.

At the **Eglise St-Jacques** in the old part of Perros, masons put some of these deep pink rocks into building the church. As a result, the dome looks as though it's suffering from a bad case of sunburn. Inside, the nave is clearly divided between the 12th-century Romanesque half and the 14th-century half, separated by an arch.

Getting Around

Lannion has a **train** station and an **airport** with regular flights to and from Paris.
The **bus** service along this coastal area is run by CAT, **t** 02 96 37 02 40.

Tourist Information

Trévou-Tréguignec: **t** 02 96 23 71 92.
Perros-Guirec: 21 Place de l'Hôtel de Ville, **t** 02 96 23 21 15, *www.perros-guirec.com*.
Trégastel: Place Ste-Anne, **t** 02 96 15 38 38, *www.ville-tregastel.fr*.

Market Days

Perros-Guirec: Friday.
Trégastel: Monday.

Where to Stay and Eat

Port-Blanc ✉ 22710

★★Grand Hôtel, Boulevard de la Mer, **t** 02 96 92 66 52 (*inexpensive*). A hotel by Port-Blanc's main landmark, overlooking the rocky bay. In high season you may be obliged to take half-board, although the food here is pretty unexceptional.
★★Le Rocher, Rue de la Sentinelle, **t** 02 96 92 64 97 (*inexpensive*). Pleasant, simple hotel with a cheerful feel, a street from the sea.

Louannec ✉ 22700

Demeure de Rosmapamon, just east of Perros-Guirec along the coast, **t** 02 96 23 00 87 (*moderate–expensive*). The former house of writer Renan (*see* p.208), offering simple, peaceful B&B rooms in a wooded park .

Le Colombier, Coat Gourhant, **t** 02 96 23 29 30 (*inexpensive*). A simple renovated farm not that far from the coast, with loft rooms.

Perros-Guirec ✉ 22700

This is one of the most popular resorts in Brittany, so there's a wide choice of accommodation, and many hotels boast restaurants with sea views.
★★★L'Agapa, 12 Rue des Bons Enfants, **t** 02 96 49 01 10 (*expensive*). A classic 1930s hotel set among pine trees, with bright rooms and sea views. At the time of writing it was closed for full renovation, due to reopen in 2005.
★★★Les Feux des Iles, 53 Boulevard Clemenceau, **t** 02 96 23 22 94, *www. feux-des-iles.com* (*moderate–expensive*). A hotel with wonderful views over to the Sept Iles, characterful rooms, a pretty garden, a tennis court and a restaurant serving, alongside other specialities, *foie gras* with figs.
★★★Le Grand Hôtel, 45 Boulevard Joseph Le Bihan, **t** 02 96 49 84 84, *www.grand-hotel-trestraou.com* (*moderate*). A large hotel in an early-20th-century building above the Plage de Trestraou, with an enormous restaurant.
★★★Le Manoir du Sphinx, 67 Chemin de la Messe, **t** 02 96 23 25 42, *lemanoirdusphinx@ wanadoo.fr* (*moderate*). A villa typical of this early-20th-century resort, in its own gardens lording it over the Plage de Trestrignel, with delightful sea views. The good restaurant offers spit-roasted turbot.
La Bonne Auberge, Place de la Chapelle, La Clarté, **t** 02 96 91 46 05 (*moderate*). A warm, charming hotel outside the centre, serving local fare such as poultry with basil and Breton chutney. Half-board is required.

A Boat Trip Around les Sept Iles

*Reserve seats on **t** 02 96 91 10 00. Tickets are about €13–16 but worth it.*

Even in the height of summer, one of the islands of the Sept Iles appears to be covered in snow: the gannet colony turns the north side of the Ile Rouzic completely white with the sheer number of nesting birds. The gannets, with their distinctive black-tipped wings, yellow heads and piercing blue eyes, stay from spring until roughly late September. They do not fly to the mainland, keeping well away from people; the Ile Rouzic is the only place in France where they come to reproduce.

Le Gulf Stream, 26 Rue des Sept Iles, **t** 02 96 23 21 86 (*moderate*). An extremely warm and welcoming option enjoying a wonderful location high up on the Perros-Guirec hillside, and offering high-quality cuisine in a dining room with sea views. Those foregoing a room with ensuite bathroom will be rewarded with an unparallelled vista on to the ocean from the shared showers.

★★Hôtel Morgane, Plage de Trestraou, **t** 02 96 23 22 80, *www.hotel-morgane.com* (*moderate*). A hotel in an old-style house, with plain modern rooms and a covered, heated pool.

★★Au Bon Accueil, 11 Rue de Landerval, **t** 02 96 23 25 77 (*inexpensive*). Hotel with comfortable, modern rooms, most with views of the port.

★Les Violettes, 19 Rue du Calvaire, **t** 02 96 23 21 33 (*inexpensive*). A friendly choice with cheerful rooms and a restaurant offering good-value menus.

Digor Kalon, 89 Rue du Maréchal Joffre, **t** 02 96 49 03 63 (*inexpensive*). A tranquil haven of a café-restaurant, with eclectically furnished rooms, affording the perfect antidote to the monotony of much hotel dining. The food consists of a variety of Breton and seasonal *délices*, offered on tapas-style menus, and is outstanding value. There are also delicious desserts (including rice pudding cooked in the oven for 5hrs) and Trégorien & Morlaix beer and cider.

Hamon, Rue de la Salle, **t** 02 96 23 28 82 (*inexpensive*). An establishment that has become well known in the area for the breathtaking crêpe-throwing skills of its chef. You may need to book a table ahead to watch her in action (she only performs in the evenings).

Les Vieux Gréements, **t** 02 96 91 14 99 (*inexpensive*). A decent crêperie with nautical decor.

Ploumanac'h ✉ 22700

★★Hôtel du Parc, Parking St-Guirec, **t** 02 96 91 40 80 (*moderate*). A hotel in a simple stone house opposite one of the main car parks, close to the beach and the amazing rock formations, offering half-board only. The seafood restaurant is permanently packed out with tourists.

★★Les Rochers, Chemin de la Pointe, **t** 02 96 91 44 49 (*moderate*). High-quality rooms by the beach, and a dining room looking on to the pink rockscapes.

Trégastel-Plage ✉ 22730

★★★Belle Vue, 20 Rue des Calculots, **t** 02 96 23 88 18, *www.hotelbellevuetregastel.com* (*moderate*). A reasonably priced option with many rooms giving on to the spacious garden and out to sea.

★★Beau Séjour, Plage du Coz Pors, **t** 02 96 23 88 02 (*moderate*). A fine option, with a restaurant terrace looking out on to the rocks.

★★★Armoric, Plage du Coz Pors, **t** 02 96 23 88 16, *www.hotels-bretagne.com/armoric* (*inexpensive*). A large, well-kept and traditional seaside hotel with the benefit of a reliable restaurant.

Hôtel des Bains, Boulevard du Coz Pors, **t** 02 96 23 88 09 (*inexpensive*). A hotel offering a number of simple rooms in whitewashed buildings.

Crêperie L'Iroise, 29 Rue Charles Le Goffic, **t** 02 96 15 93 23 (*inexpensive*). Good crêperie.

Crêperie Ty Maï, 21 Place Ste-Anne, **t** 02 96 23 41 95 (*inexpensive*). A decent basic option.

The mascot of Perros-Guirec is a puffin; from spring to around mid to late July you can spot them on the Sept Iles. This colony of 'sea parrots' almost died out because of men coming to hunt them until early in the 20th century. It was due to this danger that the Ligue pour la Protection des Oiseaux (LPO) fought to have the Sept Iles declared an ornithological reserve, which it has been since 1912. Spring is the best time to come if you're a keen ornithologist. Then you can also spot cormorants, razorbills, guillemots, manx shearwaters, fulmars and kittiwakes, among others. The other major attraction around this archipelago are the grey seals. The baby grey seals are in fact white; they grow darker in colour with age.

On calm days, the tour includes a stop on the Ile aux Moines, the name of this steep barren rock recalling the fact that monks tried valiantly and ascetically to colonize the place at one time. The boat trip lasts around 90 minutes if it isn't possible to land on the Ile aux Moines, but if landing is possible, count another hour for the round trip.

To Ploumanac'h via the Pink Coast or the Pink Quarries of La Clarté

If you feel full of energy, you could go from Perros-Guirec to Ploumanac'h along the beautiful coastal path, which becomes increasingly cluttered with a chaos of pink rocks. The view of the Sept Iles out to sea accompanies you all the way on clear days. Sculptors like to try their hand at exploiting the rare local rock, and a mixed bag of works has been left on display in a slightly unkempt public park on the road from Perros-Guirec to Ploumanac'h.

It's a bit dangerous going to see the dramatic **quarries** that are still in operation in the hillsides behind La Clarté. Mammoth lorries thunder up and down the valleys, carrying away enormous pieces of pink granite of up to 40 tonnes in weight, which are piled up in the quarry craters like huge building blocks destined for some vast, camp pyramid.

You might care to take a look at the **church of Notre-Dame de Clarté** instead. Like the church of St-Jacques, its ruddy stone makes it a rarity. The story goes that the church was constructed thanks to a vow made by the Seigneur du Barac'h, a nobleman from these parts who once found himself stuck in fog in the treacherous seas around the Sept Iles. He prayed for the Virgin's assistance to get him out of the soup. The Virgin appeared to have answered the local lord's prayer when the fog suddenly, if not miraculously, lifted. From its height, the church looks down towards the sea in the distance. The south porch is decorated with some low relief carvings. The stations of the cross illustrated within are said to have been designed by Maurice Denis.

Some tourists make the pilgrimage to the cemetery nearby to see the grave of Thierry Le Luron, one of France's most popular postwar comedians, who died of AIDS and wished to be laid to rest here, buried in the pink hills – the pink stone of the area is very much in demand for tombstones.

Ploumanac'h

To see the funniest, craziest rocks in Brittany, the peninsula of Ploumanac'h is the place to go. First have a look at the **Plage St-Guirec**, one of the most dramatic beaches in the whole of Brittany, tucked away on the western side of the Ploumanac'h peninsula. The little oratory perched on a rock is dedicated to St Guirec, said to have landed here in the 6th century. A statue of the saint has stood protected on this rock most of the time since the 12th century. Traditionally, young women anxious to get married would come to stick a hairpin in the wooden statue's nose, now completely worn off. Outside the walls of the enclosure of **St-Guirec's chapel** set back from the beach, the religious man's 'bed' turns out to be a stone basin; water from it was said to have miraculous properties.

A dream of a mock castle stands out on the **Îlot de Costarès** a little way out to sea from the beach. Built in the 1890s for a Polish engineer, Bruno Abdank, who then lived there, it has seen several famous visitors and further owners. Abdank's most famous guest was the author Henryk Sienkiewicz, who supposedly completed his best-known story, *Quo Vadis*, at the castle.

The **coastal walk** around the **Parc Municipal** guides you past Ploumanac'h's absurd geological formations in pink granite. They turn a particularly fiery colour in the setting sun. Because of the damage that was being caused to this extraordinary coastal strip by the hundreds of thousands of tourists who were traipsing all too freely over the rocks, you are now sensibly restricted to marked paths. They take you from the Plage de St-Guirec round the **Pointe de Squewel**. The names that have been given to some of the rocks give you a good indication of just how fanciful some of them look, for example the *Rocher des Amoureux* (the Lovers' Rock), *La Tête de Mort* (the Skull), *La Bouteille* (the Bottle), and even the extremely easily recognizable *Pied Renversé* (the Upturned Foot).

Behind the lighthouse (in pink granite too, of course – it was rebuilt after it was destroyed in the Second World War), you come to the **Maison du Littoral**. The story starts with the formation of the earth, which apparently occurred some 4,600 million years ago. As to the pink granite here, it was formed across the same period as the other Breton granite, some 300,000 million years ago, when great veins of magma bubbled up beneath enormous mountains that then covered the region, reaching higher than the Alps. The magma cooled and turned to granite, while the mountains were slowly eroded by the elements. Eventually, after an inconceivably long time, the granite was exposed on the surface. Apparently, the vein on the Côte de Granit Rose seems to have remained open and active for approximately 10 million years, giving more diverse types of magma the time to reach this level. It all sounds as unbelievable as the Breton legends. Explanations are also given here on the various local flora and fauna.

Some of the postcards displayed in the Maison du Littoral show that the very poor used to make shelters under the rocks and live there in their makeshift caves. Today, the pink granite is used as much for art as for shelter. To appreciate absurdly shaped rocks in the shade, you could go walking in the deep **Vallée des Traouïero**, the path heading inland from Ploumanac'h to Trégastel (as opposed to the resort of Trégastel-Plage). Small exhibitions are held in the tidal mill along the way.

Trégastel-Plage

Trégastel-Plage boasts the most absurd pink rocks of the lot. Head up to the **aquarium** (*open daily July and Aug 10–2, May, June and Sept 10–12 and 2–6, school hols 2–5*). Its chambers are set under a pile of the most enormous pink slabs. The phenomenon is purely natural though. Underneath the enormous boulders there are just three rocky rooms to wander round. Representative fish from the Breton coast are given just a little more space in their fishtanks than the visitors in these caverns.

The sea deserts the resort of Trégastel-Plage at low tide. Then you can go on a voyage of discovery on foot among all the rocky piles and isles. At any time, the walk onto the Ile Renote takes you past some particularly spectacular rock formations, including the *Skull*, the *Pile of Crêpes*, the *Die* and the *Great Chasm*. The views from here along the coast are staggering.

Actually, at any time of year you can also go swimming at Trégastel-Plage, at the Forum, an indoor sports complex built overlooking the spectacular **beach of Coz-Porz**. Its design caused a scandal, but it has been relatively sensitively landscaped, and it has kept low to the ground. From inside, you can enjoy excellent views out onto the rockscapes and swim in warm surrounds even in mid-winter. The facilities are luxurious and up to the minute, with jet sprays and jacuzzis around the pool. Entrance is expensive, however. West of here are further wacky rocks towards the Grève Blanche, such as the *Tirebouchon* (the Corkscrew).

Trégastel to Plestin-les-Grèves

After Trégastel, the pinkness goes out of the rocks and the crowds gradually thin out. As to the Ile Grande, now home to an important ornithological centre, it is in fact no longer an island. Inland, a satellite centre dominates the landscape, with a telecommunications museum, a planetarium and a fake Gaulish village established below it. Nearby Lannion has grown slightly out of control on the back of its hi-tech industries.

But travel down the Léguer valley and you soon come into a pretty unspoilt valley with typical castles and chapels, including the Chapelle de Kerfons and the ruins of the Château de Tonquédec. The coast to the southwest of Lannion turns wilder, with spectacular, high coastal cliffs. The final stretch of the Côtes d'Armor leads you to the Lieue de Grève, a stunning wood-fringed bay that has served as the setting for many a legend.

Ile Grande

The Ile Grande is now permanently joined to the mainland by a bridge. The granite here has blueish-grey tinges, and much of the island is covered with a scrubland of gorse and bracken. Past the neolithic gallery chamber near the top of the island, you can scramble up to the rocks marking the highest point. Among the islets to the east, the wooded one puts in its claim to being the Avalon of Arthurian legend, where King Arthur went off to die, or at least to rest until he should be brought back to life to fight once more. Various versions exist of Arthur's end on this island of Aval (*see* p.34).

The Ile Grande is best known now for its reputable bird hospital and ornithological centre, run by the Ligue Pour la Protection des Oiseaux (LPO), the official French bird protection agency. The **Station Ornithologique de l'Ile Grande** (*open July and Aug Mon–Fri 10–1 and 2.30–7, Sat and Sun 2.30–7; rest of year daily during French school hols Mon–Fri 10–12 and 2–6, Sat and Sun 2.30–7, outside school hols Sat and Sun 2–6)* opened in 1984, in good part to deal with the effects of oil slicks on birds. The information centre for the ornithological reserve of the Sept Iles (*see* p.211) is also to be found here.

Pleumeur-Bodou and Around

The **Centre de Télécommunications par Satellite** at **Pleumeur-Bodou** is dominated by the **Radôme**, which looks like an outrageous new golfing complex built in the shape of the most enormous golf ball, but the massive structure was actually a pioneering satellite centre. The first satellite broadcast between America and Europe took place here. The national telecommunications company, **France Télécom**, has a **hi-tech museum**, inside the Radôme, which tells the story of the development of French telecommunications over the past century and a half (*open July and Aug daily 11–7; May and June daily 11–6; April and Sept Mon–Fri 11–6, Sat and Sun 2–6; school hols Sun–Fri 2–6*).

The **Planétarium du Trégor**, close to the telecommunications museum, runs a regular programme of shows on the sky and the stars. Although the **Gaulish village of Meem** opposite the planetarium is fake, with reconstructions of Celtic huts, this is run by a humanitarian organization trying to raise money for community schools in the bush in Togo, Africa, hence the reconstruction of some Togo huts alongside Gaulish ones.

The one genuinely old monument around Pleumeur-Bodou is the **Menhir de St-Uzec**. However, the neolithic standing stone was vandalized by overzealous Christians in the 17th century, who carved primitive Christian symbols on it. On the slope above the menhir, you can get a hilarious view of the crudely Christianized monument with the Radôme appearing in the background like a huge miraculous moon.

To Trébeurden

Back with the coast from Pleumeur-Bodou and north of Trébeurden, among the wide landscapes of the **beach of Groas Trez**, lie the **marshlands of Quellen**, where ornithologists can make the most of three observatories. You can also spot the odd Camargue white horse brought in to graze.

Trébeurden brings you back into major beach holiday country after the little nature break to the north. The bulk of the **Ile Millau** close to the shore marks the sea views from Trébeurden and shelters some of the resort's beaches. When the tides are particularly low you can actually walk out to this island and discover its contrasting sides, the windswept west and the more protected east, rich in flora.

At the northern end of the resort, a couple of upmarket hotels stand high above the first beach. Then you come to the **Plage de Pors-Termen** with a modern marina that caused a local stir. It is made from big, chaotic piles of granite. The money to finance this project came from those responsible for the environmental disaster of the oil tanker *Amoco Cadiz*, which badly affected the area. **Le Castel** is the natural fort of rock that towers above the port.

Getting Around

Lannion has an **airport** with regular flights to and from Paris. It also has a **railway** station. For local **bus** services contact CAT on **t** 02 96 37 02 40.

Tourist Information

Pleumeur-Bodou: t 02 96 23 91 47, *pleumeur.office@leradome.com.*
Trébeurden: Place de Crech-Héry, **t** 02 96 23 51 64, *tourisme.trebeurden@wanadoo.fr.*
Lannion: Quai d'Aiguillon, **t** 02 96 46 41 00, *www.ot-lannion.fr.*
St-Michel-en-Grève: t 02 96 35 74 87, or **t** 02 96 35 74 17 out of season.
Plestin-les-Grèves: t 02 96 35 61 93, *officetourismeplestin@wanadoo.fr.*

Market Days

Ile Grande: Thursday.
Trébeurden: Tuesday.
Lannion: Thursday.
St-Michel-en-Grève: Monday.
Ploumilliau: Saturday.
Plestin-les-Grèves: Sunday.

Where to Stay and Eat

Le Toëno ✉ 22560
Auberge de Jeunesse, 2km north of Trébeurden, **t** 02 96 23 52 22, *www.fuaj.org* (*inexpensive*). A well-located if ugly hostel right by the sea.

Trébeurden ✉ 22560
***Manoir de Lan Kérellec, t 02 96 23 50 09, *www.lankerellec.com* (*moderate–luxury*). A 19th-century building on the heights, with luxurious rooms with sea views and bathrooms with maritime touches. The dining room resembles the interior of a ship, and the delicate Breton dishes, such as turbot steaks with artichokes, suit the atmosphere. The grounds include a tennis court and a plush terrace.
***Ti al Lannec, 14 Allée de Mezo Guen, **t** 02 96 15 01 01, *www.tiallannec.com* (*expensive–very expensive*). A hotel lording it over the sea, with terraces set among pretty garden borders, characterful rooms and high-quality food.
Les Ajoncs d'Or, 13 Rue Trozoul, **t 02 96 23 50 40 (*inexpensive*). A small, peaceful option a few hundred metres from the beach.
Ker An Nod, 2 Rue de Pors Termen, **t 02 96 23 50 21, *www.kerannod.com* (*inexpensive*). A hotel in a perfect location to enjoy the perfect sunsets, with a restaurant with wide bay windows. The rooms are small but neatly presented, and many of them have sea views.

Servel ✉ 22300
Manoir de Crec'h Goulifern, Route de Beg Léguer, **t** 02 96 47 26 17 (*inexpensive–moderate*). Cosy rooms in a typical Breton home just southeast of Pleumeur-Bodou, about 3km from the beach, with menhirs and tennis courts to hand.

On the southern side of Le Castel lies the principal beach of Trébeurden, the kilometre-long **Plage de Tresmeur**, set in its own well-protected bay. The **Pointe de Bihit**, the headland to the south, takes you out of the sprawling resort. From here you get glorious views of the last coastal stretch of the Côtes d'Armor, and on good days you can see as far as Roscoff and the island of Batz in the Finistère. Under the tip of the Pointe de Bihit, **Porz Mabo** has a gorgeous long stretch of beach looking out onto the large bay of Lannion.

There are some more intimate beaches along the bay towards the Léguer estuary. You might go in search of the **Crique de Mez-an-Aod**, with its wonderful sandy shore, particularly appreciated by nudists who favour the northern end, or settle for the delightful **Plage de Goalagon**. At the headland of **Beg Léguer** you get enchanting views down onto the Léguer estuary. The town of Lannion lies inland on its banks.

Lannion ✉ 22300
★★Le Graal, 30 Avenue du Général de Gaulle, **t** 02 96 37 03 67 (*moderate*). A reasonably priced option with comfortable rooms.
Auberge Le Léguer, 13 Rue Georges Pompidou, **t** 02 96 37 04 44 (*moderate*). A cosy setting for seasonal dishes. Book ahead.
Le Serpolet, 1 Rue Félix Le Dantec, **t** 02 96 46 50 23 (*moderate*). Good-value dishes served in a quirky dining room with a fireplace. *Closed Sat lunch, Sun eve and Mon.*
Auberge de Jeunesse, 6 Rue du 73e Territorial, **t** 02 96 37 91 28, *www.fuaj.org* (*inexpensive*). A hostel full of life and activity.
Le Fournil d'Hubert, 6 Place du Général Leclerc (*inexpensive*). Good snacks, including Breton bread cooked in a woodfire oven.

Rospez ✉ 22300
La Ville Blanche, **t** 02 96 37 04 28 (*expensive–very expensive*). Delicious, classic fine French cuisine, plus a herb garden, just to the east of Lannion. *Closed Sun eve, Mon, Wed and 1wk in June.*

Ploubezre ✉ 22300
Manoir de Kerguéréon, **t** 02 96 38 91 46 (*moderate*). Two luxurious rooms in a delightful Breton buliding.

Tonquédec ✉ 22140
Le Queffiou, **t** 02 96 35 84 50 (*inexpensive–moderate*). Large B&B rooms and bathrooms in a slate-roofed house. Rooms are done out in different styles and there's a large garden.

Au Coin Fleuri, 4 Rue du Général de Gaulle, Cavan (east of Tonquédec), **t** 02 96 35 86 16 (*moderate*). A rustic restaurant serving good food in an ivy-covered old house.

Trégrom ✉ 22420
L'Ancien Presbytère B&B, **t** 02 96 47 94 15 (*inexpensive*). An enchanting B&B opposite the church just east of Plouaret and Le Vieux Marché, with extremely comfortable rooms with beautiful antiques and wallpaper. *Table d'hôte* is available on request.

Le Yaudet ✉ 22300
★★Ar Vro, **t** 02 96 46 48 80 (*inexpensive*). A simple, well-kept, rural hotel.

Trédrez ✉ 22300
Auberge St-Erwan, **t** 02 96 35 72 51 (*inexpensive–moderate*). A wonderfully rustic inn serving crêpes and grilled meats.

St-Michel-en-Grève ✉ 22300
★★Hôtel de la Plage, Place de l'Eglise, **t** 02 96 35 74 43 (*inexpensive*). Good-value rooms with wonderful views across the bay. The attached restaurant does summer BBQs.
Au Bon Accueil, **t** 02 96 35 74 11 (*inexpensive*). Simple rooms and excellent seafood.

Plestin-les-Grèves ✉ 22310
★★Les Côtes d'Armor, Route de la Corniche, **t** 02 96 35 63 11, *www.residencedescotesdarmor.com* (*inexpensive*). A modern, purpose-built holiday hotel with studios for short lets.

Lannion and Around

Lannion's merchants became prosperous on trade generated by this inland port in centuries past, and it's thanks to them that the place has such a rich legacy of grand townhouses on the slopes above the Léguer. Many of these merchants' homes have been turned into chic shops. The concentration of fine houses-turned-boutiques is around the main rectangle of a square, the highly picturesque **Place du Général Leclerc**. Some are tall timberframe numbers, others have been clothed in tight-fitting slate, while still more were built in chunky granite. An impressively clichéd picture of a 19th-century French town hall marks one corner of the square. Below it you'll find the typical 19th-century covered market, still in active use. The main market square, the **Place du Marchallac'h**, is a short walk up the hill from the Place du Général Leclerc, and is similarly surrounded by old townhouses. Air trips are possible via the Aéroclub de Lannion (**t** 02 96 48 47 42).

The main cultural attractions lie outside Lannion centre – two beautiful churches set in a couple of old outlying villages now caught in the sprawling suburbs of the place. You could climb the 143 steps from Lannion centre to the **church of Brélévenez** on its hilltop, apparently fortified by a branch of the crusading-rich Knights Templar. The church dates in part from the 12th century, with fine Romanesque details. Two very narrow stairs lead down to the crypt.

To see the **chapel and fountains of Loguivy-lès-Lannion**, you need to cross to the west bank of the Léguer. Here, you escape the modern shopping streets of Lannion to discover a much quieter atmosphere. The double-fountained chapel in 15th-century Breton Flamboyant Gothic style is delightful.

From Lannion into Rural Côtes d'Armor

Head south out of Lannion down the D11 and the Léguer valley to get into the rural, inland Côtes d'Armor that so contrasts with the crowded coastal strip. A few surprising chapels and châteaux lie along the way.

The **Chapelle de Kerfons**, discreetly hidden away on its chestnut-covered slope above the Léguer just to the southeast of Ploubezre, is one of those rural Breton chapels full of delightful ornamental detail. The structure is in the main Breton Flamboyant Gothic. The most striking aspect inside the chapel is its late 15th-century rood screen, still in place dividing the nave from the choir, decorated with swooping angels and cheeky monkeys as well as the apostles. The choir end is full of decorative surprises. Some of the original 15th-century stained glass remains, gracefully illustrating the early life of Jesus. Below, a rococo altar from the 17th century drips with little caryatid figures, pomegranates and pears. The pulpit too is extravagant. The tombs of the Marquise de Goulaine, who once owned the lands round and about, and her daughter, are to be found here. (Goulaine is a famous château in Muscadet country, see p.452.)

The **Château de Tonquédec** a short way south off the D11 presents a spectacularly sturdy image of a medieval castle, its walls strengthened by enormous towers. These towers have lost their roofs and the walls had to be much restored. A first château went up in the 13th century but was destroyed. The second, constructed for Guy de Coetmen, viscount of Tonquédec, was brought down by order of Duke Jean IV of Brittany in 1395. So the fort you see dates mainly from the 15th century; it was built for Roland IV de Coetmen, who went off to die fighting in the crusades. In the early 17th century, supporters of Marie de' Médicis, mother of the young King Louis XIII and rebellious figure against Cardinal Richelieu, took the castle. Once they had been defeated, Tonquédec was in good part demolished again.

The **Château de Kergrist** a little further south still, down off the D11, is sometimes open too. In contrast with the Château de Tonquédec, this hides timidly behind its wall, only a handful of pepperpot towers sticking out. The architecture is actually rather grand, the original 16th-century form much added to in the 18th and 19th centuries, though visits focus on the grand gardens and tearoom.

Further down the D11, the sleepy hamlet of **Les Sept Saints** lies a bit further from the main road than the three previous sites. Its early-18th-century **chapel** contains a crypt made from a prehistoric dolmen. The images of seven saints were found here; they have been reproduced as typical Breton statues above the altar. The originals may have represented the seven saintly sleepers of Ephesus, persecuted by the Roman Empire in the 3rd century for their belief in Christ and eventually walled up alive.

A Legendary Coast from Le Yaudet to St-Efflam

La Côte de Bruyère ('Heather Coast'), the tourist name given to this stretch, gives an indication that here nature still has the upper hand, and indeed the stunning series of dramatic, high promontories has proved unsuitable for holiday developments.

Le Yaudet

The village of Le Yaudet, set high above the southern bank of the estuary of the Léguer, would be delightful enough without the additional fantasy that this might be the site of Astérix's and Obélix's village. However, such a steep and awkward location goes totally against the cartoon evidence – close observation of Uderzo's drawings over the years suggests that the village of the indestructible Gauls was set down close to a beach, not on a promontory.

A panel in the village tries to point you to the exact spots where you can in fact find signs of previous civilizations. You can also walk down and around the promontory. The path isn't particularly easy, but the effort is rewarded by fine views. The port, really not much more than a jetty, is located on the eastern side of the promontory, most of the boats being left at anchor down the unspoilt Léguer estuary.

A walk to the chapel up in the village is much easier than trying out the coastal path. Virtually nothing remains of the 15th-century edifice that once stood here; this church dates almost entirely from the 19th century and is in the neo-Gothic style. It contains some admirably tacky Catholic kitsch, a Virgin with her baby Jesus, tucked in a bed covered with lace. Eccentric literature in the chapel claims Celtic roots for this image of the recumbent Mary, saying that the druids taught their people to expect the arrival of a miraculous virgin who would give birth to a child.

To the Pointe du Dourven

Leave Le Yaudet following the extremely steep street west and it takes you down to **Port Roux**, very prettily tucked behind a small sandy cove. Unless you're walking, you then have to leave the coast for a short distance to get to Locquémeau. Here, head for the **Pointe** and **Domaine du Dourven**. An atmospheric path of boulders and trees leads to a modern house where **contemporary art exhibitions** are often held. Following the coastal track around the spit, to the east you can see down the Léguer estuary, to the north you can look up the rocky coast towards the Ile Millau in front of Trébeurden, while to the west you can make out the curious flat spit of land of the Pointe de Séhar and the beaches near it.

Locquémeau to the Lieue de Grève

Locquémeau still has an active fishing port and a couple of sandy beaches, Notigou and Kiriou, which give it a great deal of appeal. At the western end, you reach the **Pointe de Séhar**. This extraordinary barren, flat peninsula is made up almost entirely of pebbles and boulders. The place has a messy charm, a little port, a fish market and a few shops and cafés bringing life to it. The houses are a hotchpotch, their gardens mostly just piles of stones.

The coastal path heads due south, along the **cliffs of Trédrez**, among the most impressively unspoilt in Brittany. If you're in your car, you can only rejoin the coastal path again around five kilometres to the south, beyond the **village of Trédrez**. The place feels lost in the Breton countryside and in time. This was where the great Breton religious lawyer Yves served as priest for a time in the 13th century. The pretty church only dates from the late 15th century to early 16th century, built in typical Beaumanoir Gothic gabled style.

The point of land beyond Trédrez is the glorious **Beg ar Forn**. Cars have to be left well away from the coastal path high above the foaming sea. Once on the coastguards' track, you can watch the waves sweeping in to crash against the cliffs stretching up to the Pointe de Séhar. Westwards, you can see across to the Locquirec peninsula in the Finistère. Turn the southern corner of the headland and the splendid protected bay of the Lieue de Grève comes into view.

The Lieue de Grève

Extremely steep country roads lead down to **St-Michel-en-Grève**, which is beautifully situated on the eastern end of the Lieue de Grève. The village cemetery sticks out from the side of the church into this sensational bay. Although the silhouette of the Eglise St-Michel looks striking, the building has been spoilt by restoration work. There are apparently traces of the masonry of a couple of Roman baths in the cemetery wall. Rich Gallo-Romans appear to have appreciated this corner of Armorica, given the number of finds from the period that have been discovered along the coast. St-Michel-en-Grève today is a good place to sit and admire the landscape. The seawaters withdraw some two kilometres at low tide, and the views stretch between four and five kilometres to the other side of the beach and the village of St-Efflam.

As a pilgrim or traveller arriving at the Lieue de Grève by foot or on horseback centuries ago, you had to cross the sands at low tide. Horror stories are still told of those who were caught out by the rising tide and its currents. For centuries, the **Croix de Mi-Lieue**, a cross planted in the middle of the bay, served as a marker to show voyagers when they could start out over the sands – if, when you arrived at the bay, the cross's base was clear of the water, it was fine to continue. As one expression had it, the journey would be safe as long as *la croix nous voit* ('the cross can see us').

Nowadays, you can follow the coast road along the back of the Lieue de Grève. A large rock, the **Grand Rocher**, protrudes from the hills roughly in the middle of the curve. A dragon once lived within this great rock, local legend has it, a creature King

Legends around the Lieue de Grève

St Efflam was heroically linked with legend, even Arthurian legend, in these parts. Different versions of the story tell how the Irishman helped Arthur to slay the evil dragon causing terror around here. One rather begrudging account gives only a small part of the action to Efflam. Arthur and the dragon had been engaged in violent combat for some time. The British king was exhausted by his efforts and felt his energy giving up on him. Efflam came to the rescue, discovering a source of water to refresh Arthur. The noble warrior was able to take up the fight again and triumph, killing the dragon. Other local tales give Efflam more of the glory.

For much of the Middle Ages, priors from the Mont-St-Michel were given lands and rights around the Lieue de Grève. The local priests were incensed at this gift to the powerful Norman abbey, and waged a long campaign against the Norman presence. Some local historians have argued that it was to rival the story of St Michael slaying the dragon that the local legend of St Efflam taking on his own beast grew in importance. The great 17th-century recorder of Breton saints' lives, Albert Le Grand, wrote that Efflam simply ordered the dragon to drown itself in the sea, and the mesmerized monster obeyed. But a popular song claims that Efflam enchanted the beast by making it play regularly to itself, morning, noon and night, music that would keep it forever quiet and captivated.

Some of the local tales relate that the dragon lived in the Grand Rocher, guarding a great treasure. This rock was supposed to open up just twice a year, in the time the bells rang for midnight signalling Christmas and Pentecost. As the bells fell silent, the rock closed up again. None of the men foolhardy enough to have ventured inside the rock ever escaped to say what lay inside.

Arthur himself came to fight (*see* box, above). After the Grand Rocher, a longish line of villas signals the start of the village of **St-Efflam**, a resort that has known more fashionable days, as you can tell by some of the slightly dilapidated but smart buildings. Look out into the bay from here, and you can clearly make out the dragon form of the Rocher Rouge with its spiky spine and tail.

On the façade of the modest whitewashed **chapel** tucked into the western side of the bay, statues in granite represent St Efflam and his virginal wife, Ste Enora. The Irish Efflam is said to have left just after they had got married to go abroad and proselytize; Enora apparently demonstrated saintly chastity in his absence. He and his followers apparently landed in this bay in the late 4th or early 5th century. The elaborately domed fountain down from the chapel used to be said to have a power often associated with Breton springs – of telling girls when they were going to get married.

It is sobering to stop and remember how the Lieue de Grève was affected by the Second World War. The Nazis mined the beach, destroyed many of the villas along the coast and built a great number of defensive blockhouses along the hills; these monstrosities are now thankfully quite well hidden by vegetation. The Germans were anxious that the bay might provide a favourable spot for an enemy landing. In the event, this did become the only place along the north Breton coast where an Allied landing took place in 1944.

There is one major modern-day problem with the Lieue de Grève that cannot go unmentioned. Since the 1970s, it has suffered appallingly at certain periods from attacks of green algae that come to die on the beach and that cause the most diabolical stench. This most splendid of beaches is actually one of the most polluted in the whole of Brittany. The algae are said not to be dangerous for humans, but their smell can mar a visit.

Inland behind the Lieue de Grève, the village of **Ploumilliau** has strong links with sinister Breton legend. It is renowned for its wooden statue of the grim reaper, *l'Ankou* in Breton (*see* box, p.224). This typically Breton figure is to be found in the Flamboyant Gothic church, built by the Beaumanoir school.

Château de Rosanbo

The Château de Rosanbo (*open July and Aug daily 11–6; April–June daily 2–5; Sept and Oct Sun 2–5*) sits aloof and alone above the calm Bo valley. A great driveway leads you to the enormous round dovecot in front of the walls of the property. This building acts as a powerful reminder of the grandeur of the owners of the château under the Ancien Régime. In fact, the family line can be traced back some 1,000 years by the present owners, the Marquis and Marquise de Rosanbo.

Little remains of the original castle, which was built for the Coskaërs around 1500 on the base of earlier medieval fortifications. The buildings you now see date mainly from the 17th, 18th and 19th centuries. In the late 17th century, the heir to Rosanbo, Geneviève de Coskaër, married into the powerful Le Peletier family, several of whose members became head of the Paris parliament under King Louis XIV. Geneviève's father-in-law succeeded Colbert as finance minister to the French king. She gave birth to a son, Louis, but died a few years later. Her husband took on the title of Rosanbo, and Louis XIV elevated him to the rank of marquis. He had the dovecot of Rosanbo built in 1697.

Before the Revolution, the heir to the Rosanbo title had married into the illustrious Malesherbes family. The great statesman Malesherbes was to defend the deposed King Louis XVI during the Revolution. He lost his head for his troubles, as did his daughter and son-in-law, the Marquise and Marquis de Rosanbo. At the same time as these three, Aline de Rosanbo and her husband went to the guillotine. Aline was a granddaughter of Malesherbes and married to the brother of the great Breton Romantic writer Chateaubriand, who retells the bloody tale of their deaths in his autobiography *Mémoires d'outre-tombe* (*see* p.112).

In 1910, the landscape designer Achille Duchêne was called upon to redesign the gardens, and you can go and enjoy their shaded alleys and many hundreds of metres of romantic arbours before seeing inside the castle's neo-Gothic rooms. These gardens are nostalgic *jardins à la française*, with no flowers, but playing on space with neatly cut hedges and paths. Along the way, you come across the usual sculptures of animals you would expect to have found in an Ancien Régime garden.

An autumn organ festival of Baroque music is held at **Lanvellec**, the village closest to the château, to show off the restored mid-17th-century instrument in the church. It was made by Robert Dallam and is a copy of the one in King's College, Cambridge.

The Legends of *l'Ankou* and Anatole le Braz

Anatole Le Braz was one of the major figures in the late 19th century to write down many of the legends previously passed down by word of mouth in Brittany. His father came to teach at Ploumilliau in the 1860s, and the young Anatole's imagination seems to have been fired by tales he heard. The *Légende de la Mort*, a book in which he collected Breton legends associated with death and in particular *l'Ankou*, the grim reaper who pays his chilling visit on those about to die, is a classic.

One of the stories in the *Légende de la Mort* is set in Ploumilliau itself. One Christmas Eve, the blacksmith Fanch ar Floc'h was still busy at work. He preferred to carry on working rather than go to midnight mass. He told his wife and children to go without him. His wife asked him to show some respect, and to at least stop working by the time the Host was lifted in the church for the congregation's adoration. But Fanch forgot. Before the service was over, there was a knock at his workshop door. A tall man in a wide-brimmed hat stood in the doorway. 'I have the most urgent of services to ask of you,' the man declared. He showed Fanch his scythe, whose blade was turned outwards. 'It just needs a nail put in it,' the stranger explained. Fanch obliged, repairing the scythe. 'I will not pay you for your trouble', the tall stranger said by way of thanks, 'but I will only give you a warning. Go to bed right now, and when your wife returns, tell her to go and get the priest. The work you have just done for me is the last you will do in your life.' Fanch's wife returned home with the children to find her husband in agony. As the cock crowed at dawn, Fanch passed away.

Around Plestin-les-Grèves

Back close to the Lieue de Grève, Plestin-les-Grèves is the market and shopping town connected with the bay. Due north of it, the coast road follows the fairly built-up peninsula of Plestin round to the Côtes d'Armor's border with the Finistère. On the end of the point lies a little port and a beach. In the 1980s, remnants of a Gallo-Roman baths were dug up from the sands on the eastern side of the peninsula; the **Thermes du Hogolo** have been dated to around AD 50.

The views here are beautiful, looking on to the very sandy shores leading to the Finistère resort of Locquirec and to the protected Douron estuary, which divides the Finistère and the Côtes d'Armor.

Finistère

09

Finistère

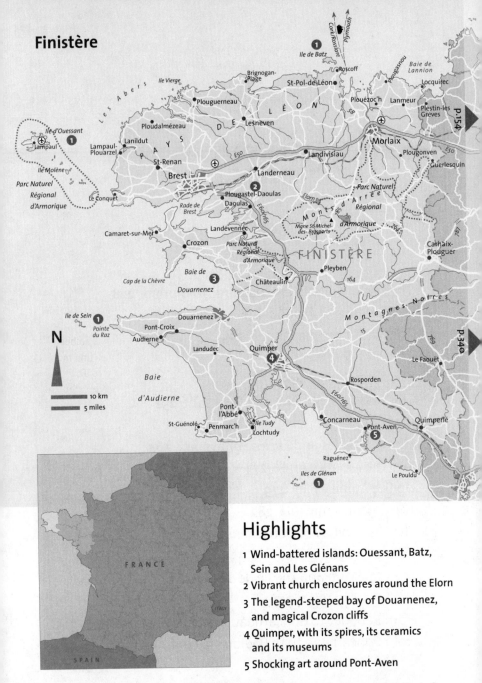

Highlights

1 Wind-battered islands: Ouessant, Batz, Sein and Les Glénans
2 Vibrant church enclosures around the Elorn
3 The legend-steeped bay of Douarnenez, and magical Crozon cliffs
4 Quimper, with its spires, its ceramics and its museums
5 Shocking art around Pont-Aven

The most Breton of Brittany's *départements*, the Finistère (or Penn ar Bed, 'End of the Earth') spans the western tip of the region. The Finistère looks unrelentingly Breton, with countless kilometres of sandy and rocky coasts guarded by some of the tallest lighthouses in Europe along three of its four sides. Inland, innumerable Breton openwork steeples mark the countryside with their silhouettes. The majority of the elaborate Breton calvaries are to be found here, while in Pont-l'Abbé some women still don the towering Bigoudène coiffe. The Finistère is also where the Breton language has clung on the most tenaciously, and where Breton winds blow hardest.

Roscoff is the major modern port of the eastern Léon (northern Finistère), well known because of its ferry terminal. Its neighbour, St-Pol-de-Léon, is pretty well unmissable thanks to its collection of soaring church towers. The Léon coast round from Roscoff to Brest is sometimes known as the Côte des Légendes. After that comes the stretch officially known as the Côte des Abers, with the deep river estuaries of the Aber Wrac'h, the Aber Benoît and the Aber Ildut following each other in quick succession. The archipelago of Ouessant (Ushant in English), one of the most feared obstacles to shipping in Europe, comes into view at the French entrance to the Channel. Brest, in its almost cowardly location – protected from the enemy and the rough Atlantic by a splendidly calm bay known as the Rade de Brest – is home to the French Atlantic fleet and to the best aquarium in Brittany, as well as to a splendid, secretive semi-tropical garden.

Inland Léon is flatter and duller than central and southern Finistère. Cloth-making, however, brought a certain prosperity to these parts for several centuries, and so the churchyards or *enclos paroissiaux* of the area were given elaborate entrance arches, calvaries, ossuaries, sacristies and porches. Head on to the Monts d'Arrée to find more unspoilt villages and churches set on the rugged slopes of these barren hills. The Monts d'Arrée form part of the long swathe of central Finistère specially protected as the Parc Naturel Régional d'Armorique. This exceptionally beautiful park stretches westwards, covering the Crozon peninsula and Ouessant. The Monts d'Arrée separates the Léon, northern Finistère, from Cornouaille, basically southern Finistère.

The Aulne river meanders its way very prettily from central Finistère to the Crozon peninsula, the most sensational portion of the Parc d'Armorique. You can quickly find calm away from these dramatic cliffs along the bay of Douarnenez, the poetic backdrop for the legend of the drowned city of Ys. South of the Pointe du Raz you then sweep down round the inspiringly inhospitable curve of the Baie d'Audierne. The southwestern tip of Cornouaille is guarded by notoriously savage rocks, yet a whole string of fishing ports have tucked themselves into the coast here.

Past Loctudy, the southern Finistère coast becomes much more gentle, the protected wooded river estuaries, here known as *avens* rather than *abers*, offering yachts safe havens. Even the major fishing port of Concarneau is prettified by the most picturesque of walled old towns. Pont-Aven, however, can be the victim of its artistic success in high summer. Most of Cornouaille away from the coast tends to look cheery, a land of cider and cherries. Quimper, the capital of Cornouaille, counts among the prettiest of all the big Breton towns, the soaring twin spires of its cathedral dominating the Odet river.

Tourist Information

Comité Départmental du Tourisme,
11 Rue Théodore Le Hars,
B.P. 1419, 29104 Quimper Cedex,
t 02 98 76 20 70,
www.finisteretourism.com.

Northern Finistère

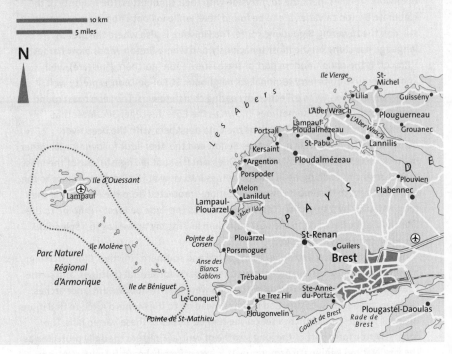

10 km
5 miles

N

Ile Vierge • St-Michel
• Lilia Guissény •
L'Aber Wrac'h • Plouguerneau
Lampaul-Ploudalmézeau L'Aber Wrac'h Grouanec
Portsall • St-Pabu Lannilis
Kersaint •
• Argenton Ploudalmézeau
Porspoder
Melon • • Lanildut • Plouvien
Lampaul-Plouarzel • L'Aber Ildut Plabennec •
Pointe de Corsen Plouarzel St-Renan
Porsmoguer • • Guilers
Parc Naturel Anse des Blancs Sablons **Brest**
Régional • Trébabu
d'Armorique Ile de Béniguet
Ile de Molène Le Conquet Le Trez Hir Ste-Anne-du-Portzic
Pointe de St-Mathieu Plougonvelin • Plougastel-Daoulas •
Goulet de Brest Rade de Brest

Ile d'Ouessant
Lampaul

Les Abers
PAYS D E S

The Trégor Finistérien: Locquirec to Morlaix

Locquirec has the typical Breton elements that might make you want to stay a few days. The compact resort takes up a whole little spit of land, with nine beaches; follow the coastal path round the headland to discover them. The east side is well protected, but as you come to the point, the landscape becomes wilder. With its port and hotels, Locquirec is full of bustle in summer, but there isn't much to see in the village itself beyond the harbour and 17th-century church with its typical Beaumanoir bell-tower.

Just west of Locquirec along the coast, the **beach of Poul-Rodou** with the delightful surprise of its café-cum-bookshop is worth seeking out. A couple of other sandy creeks lie hidden below the splendid coastal path taking you past the **Beg ar Fri headland,** the Chaises (Chairs) de Primel the evocative name of the rocks out to sea.

Inland, by **Lanmeur,** the **chapel of Notre-Dame de Kernitron** reveals its Romanesque roots with a typical doorway decorated with the carved symbols of the Evangelists surrounding Christ. A possibly even older piece of Christian architecture lies below the mainly reconstructed village church, disturbing, fat serpentine forms in stone writhing round the pillars of the crypt where the saintly 6th-century nobleman Mélor may have been buried after being hounded to death by his evil uncle Rivod.

The 15th-century **church of St-Jean-du-Doigt,** located in a dip a short distance inland from the coast just to the east of Plougasnou, is famous for its fabulous finger (*doigt*). This is supposedly no mere local hero's digit, but a piece from John the

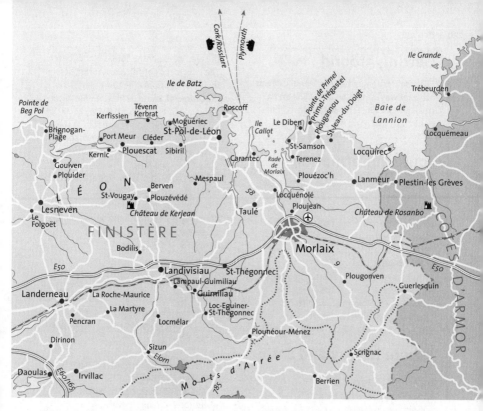

Baptist himself, brought back by a crusading lord in the Middle Ages. The miraculous healing properties of the finger long drew droves of sick pilgrims to the *pardon*, held here on 23 and 24 June.

Head northwards through the village of **Plougasnou** to reach the slightly unkempt little resort of **Primel-Trégastel**. You can go diving, canoeing or even sand-yachting here. It's quite a demanding walk just clambering over the small but dramatic headland of the **Pointe de Primel** with its granite rock formations. You might make it up to the customs cottage at the top, which was constructed during Napoleonic times in order to survey the coast. In the Bronze and Iron Ages, men had already enhanced the natural fortifications, turning the headland into an *éperon barré* (a barricaded spur).

To the Grand Cairn de Barnenez

Following the coast road you pass by a series of little ports. At delightful **Le Diben**, with its point hidden among rocks, lobsters are left to stew in tanks along the quayside until they're snapped up by French restaurateurs. You can join a guided tour to discover more about the big-clawed critters at this, one of their largest prison camps in Brittany.

The large beach of **St-Samson** is overlooked by a pretty chapel. Well-protected **Terenez** has superb views on to Barnenez's spit of land and the spectacular fortifications of the Château du Taureau (*see* p.232) out on an island.

Getting Around

The nearest major town is Morlaix, which has a **railway** station on a TGV line and a small **airport**. The **ferry port** of Roscoff lies quite close by.

Tourist Information

Pays de Trégor, 41 Avenue des Frères Le Gall, 22310 Plestin-les-Grèves, **t** 02 96 35 03 04, *www.paysdetregorgoplo.com*.
Locquirec: Place du Port, **t** 02 98 67 40 83, *www.locquirec.com*.

Market Days

Locquirec: Wednesday in summer; there's also a *marché à la ferme* at the farm of Pen ar Roz by Plouégat-Moysan on Wednesday morning during the summer holidays.

Where to Stay and Eat

Locquirec ✉ 29241

★★★**Le Grand Hôtel des Bains**, 15 bis Rue de l'Eglise, **t** 02 98 67 41 02, *www.grand-hotel-des-bains.com* (*expensive*). A joy of a hotel with a lovely indoor swimming pool and good cuisine. Some bedrooms have wide terraces, and the garden with its quirky trees and little follies overlooks a beautiful bay. It's half-board only in high season.

L'Hôtel du Port, 5 Place du Port, **t** 02 98 67 42 10 (*inexpensive*). An ivy-sided hotel in a prime location giving directly onto the port. Its restaurant terrace (*moderate*) gives you a ringside seat on the summer bustle.

Les Sables Blancs, 15 Rue des Sables Blancs, **t** 02 98 67 42 07 (*inexpensive*). A hotel in a stunning semi-isolated location overlooking the wild waves of the Sables Blancs beach. The informal, light-filled restaurant serving tasty crêpes affords the same views.

Le St-Quirec, 56 Route de Plestin, east of the resort towards Plestin, **t** 02 98 67 41 07 (*moderate*). A restaurant situated at the end of the Locquirec bay, offering enchanting views and serving seafood specialities. *Closed Mon and Tues.*

Caplan & Co., west of Locquirec at Poul-Rodou beach, **t** 02 98 67 58 98 (*inexpensive*). A café serving light salads and the like, doubling as a second-hand bookshop for students or enthusiasts of French literature. *Closed Sun–Fri in winter.*

St-Jean-du-Doigt ✉ 29630

★★**Hôtel Le Ty Pont**, Le Bourg, **t** 02 98 67 34 06 (*inexpensive–moderate*). A hotel with reasonable rooms, some very cheap, within view of the church. Meals can be arranged. *Closed Dec–Easter.*

Le Diben and St-Samson ✉ 29630

★★**Hôtel Au Temps des Voiles**, 20 Rue de l'Abbesse, **t** 02 98 72 32 43, *www.hotel-autempsdesvoiles.com* (*inexpensive*). A hotel at the back of a little bay, boasting a swimming pool supplied with seawater, plus a fine view over the rocks in the distance.

★★**Roc'h Velen**, **t** 02 98 72 30 58, *www.hotelrochvelen.fr* (*inexpensive*). A good-value option.

Plouézoc'h ✉ 29252

Résidence Hôtelière Chez Michette, **t** 02 98 79 51 80 (*inexpensive*). A very cheap option with a kitchen, bar and salon.

Café du Port, on Le Dourduff's port (*inexpensive*). A place with a terrace where you can enjoy local oysters and mussels.

The Cairn of Barnenez

Open for guided visits daily at 10.15 and 11.15, and between 2.15 and 5.45.

Neolithic builders appear to have had an aesthetic eye when it came to positioning their burial sites. The cairn of Barnenez, one of the best located in Brittany, is possibly the largest neolithic barrow in Europe, a vast, step-layered, dry-stone structure of impressive proportions, constructed with infinite care. It's hard to believe that this massive tumulus was only rediscovered in the 1950s, and by accident. The stones amassed here proved a welcome find to an entrepreneur with a contract to build the local road in the 1950s. The story goes that it was only when he had failed to pay some of his workers, who then went to complain to the local authorities, that the nature of the ancient mound that he was wrecking came to light. By that point a sizeable bite had been taken out of one side of the cairn.

But this highly significant neolithic site was then left to the experts, including respected archaeologist P. R. Giot, who worked on excavations and restoration at Barnenez from 1955 to 1968. From the pottery found in the tombs, archaeologists date the earlier part of the cairn (to the east and in local dolerite stone) to around 4500 BC. The later part, to the west, on more of a slope, and in granite that had to be transported here, has been estimated to have gone up around 4000 BC.

To Morlaix

On the way down the **Rade de Morlaix**, views of the oyster parks and the Château du Taureau add to the natural beauty. The prettiest route takes you through Plouézoc'h and past the lovely little port of **Le Dourduff**. This spot, next to the excellent natural harbour in front of Morlaix, is where Duchess Anne de Bretagne had her famous ship, *La Cordelière*, built. At low tide, the bay of Morlaix can be an excellent place for bird-watching, and there's an observatory along the coastal path.

Inland to Morlaix and Around

Morlaix

Morlaix bridges the medieval counties of the Trégor and the Léon. Its extraordinary theatricality comes from the massive arches of the 19th-century viaduct that dominate the centre. Tucked out of sight down its deep river estuary, the town became one of the great havens for Breton corsairs, as well as a major trading port.

History

English alliances and enmities have profoundly marked the history of Morlaix. In the Breton War of Succession, Morlaix supported the French claimant Charles de Blois. But the English-backed De Montforts won the battle for the duchy and most unpopularly stationed English troops in town, leading to a period of conflict and revolt. From the 14th to the 17th centuries Morlaix grew into one of the major ports in the western Channel. It thrived on the cloth trade, its market the focus not just for local production but also for export. Trade with the Iberian peninsula was particularly lucrative, and it may be that Morlaix's distinctive *maisons à lanterne* derived some features from the Spanish type of house built around a patio.

The Morlaix corsair Jean Coatanlem created havoc among the Bristol fleet at the end of the 15th century and even plundered the city once. A few decades later, the English under King Henry VIII were the villains; English sailors mounted a surprise attack on Morlaix in 1522, only to be punished for their greed, slaughtered as they became slowed down by all the booty they were carrying. It was after this unhappy incident that the town decided to build the advanced and spectacular defence of the Château du Taureau on an island to the north.

In the terrible 16th-century French Wars of Religion, Morlaix became one of the last strongholds of the ultra-Catholic Ligueurs under the Breton leader Mercoeur. King Henri IV's Marshal d'Aumont, supported by English troops, laid siege to the Ligueurs, who had eventually to give in, the Spanish support they had hoped for failing to materialize. The castle of Morlaix was then destroyed.

In the mid 18th century, Charles Cornic of Morlaix became one of the great scourges of the British at sea. Less reprehensibly perhaps, Tristan Corbière, the son of a local 19th-century ship's captain, became a notorious avant-garde poet. His father had tried his hand at writing sea adventures, but Tristan, embittered in his youth by a painful combination of arthritis and frustrated love, took to writing provocative, anti-Romantic poetry that, along with his eccentric behaviour, shocked many. He published some of his black but partly humorous works in 1873 under the title *Les Amours jaunes*. The Morlaix fishermen of his day nicknamed him *l'Ankou*, the Grim Reaper.

Getting Around

Fast TGV **trains** between Paris and Brest stop regularly at Morlaix, which also has a small **airport**.

The **ferry** port of Roscoff lies less than 30km away and is easily reached by train or **bus**.

Tourist Information

Morlaix: Place des Otages, **t** 02 98 62 14 94, *www.morlaixtourisme.fr*.

Market Days

Morlaix: Saturday.
Plougonven: Tuesday.
Guerlesquin: Monday.

Where to Stay and Eat

Morlaix ✉ 29600

The **Auberge de Jeunesse** (youth hostel) is set to reopen in 2006; ask for details at the tourist office.

★★**Hôtel de l'Europe**, 1 Rue d'Aiguillon, **t** 02 98 62 11 99, *www.hotel-europe-com.fr* (*moderate–expensive*). The most stylish option in the centre, with excellent food (*moderate*) served in an extravagant dining room and more sober-looking bedrooms. The hotel's **Brasserie de l'Europe** next door has a modern split-level design and a teak-tinted basement bar; the cuisine here is modern and good.

Le Port, 3 Quai de Léon, **t** 02 98 88 07 54 (*inexpensive*). A comfortable modern choice, although the road on which it is set can be a bit noisy.

Le St-Melaine, 75 Rue Ange de Guernisac, **t** 02 98 88 08 79 (*inexpensive*). The closest hotel to the viaduct, a friendly, family-run little place with typically quirky French interior decoration and a simple dining room where you can enjoy good old-fashioned French fare.

La Marée Bleue, 3 Rampe St-Melaine, **t** 02 98 63 24 21 (*moderate–expensive*). A warm, cosy and tranquil option offering well-prepared seafood in refined surroundings with more than a hint of the marine. *Closed Sun eve and Mon*.

L'Agadir, Rue Ange de Guernisac, near Place de Viarmes (*moderate*). A fresh-looking place where you can experience a selection of Moroccan specialities in a brightly painted atmosphere. *Closed Wed*.

Les Bains Douches, 45 Allée du Poan Ben, **t** 02 98 63 83 83 (*moderate*). A restaurant eccentrically located in the former public baths, with décor dating from c.1900, and a footbridge over the water to the door. Inside,

The year 1863 saw the building of the impressive viaduct. It survived attempts by RAF bombers to cut off the Nazi route to the west during the Second World War. Central Morlaix looks so bourgeois today that it is hard to associate it with some of the most violent farmers' demonstrations in Brittany of the past decades. Most memorably, in 1961, Alexis Gourvennec, fiery leader of the Breton farmers, led the occupation of the *département's* administrative buildings in the town.

A Tour of Morlaix

Start a tour of Morlaix in the shadow of the great **viaduct**. Under it you'll find car parks and the tourist office. Climb up either side of the valley and you can get on to a path leading through its monumental arches. From on high you can enjoy the drama of the architecture and the views down on to the centre of town and the port.

Come down off the viaduct onto the **Rue Ange de Guernisac**, which passes the Flamboyant Gothic **church of St-Melaine**. The slate-covered and timberframe sides of the houses give the street great appeal. Picturesque alleyways known as *venelles* lead up the slopes from here. Continuing along Rue Ange de Guernisac you come to the Place des Viarmes. Turn down Rue Carnot for the **Grand'Rue**. As you look upwards you

---

it is large and pleasant with a rather redundant-looking piano and leather banquettes. The kitchen offers a selection of typical French bistro fare. *Closed Sun, Mon and Sat eves.*

Brocéliande, 5 Rue des Bouchers, t 02 98 88 73 78 (*moderate*). Refined food and décor in a restaurant that looks a little like a porcelain museum. *Closed lunch, and Mon and Tues.*

Crêperie du Kiosque, 11 Place des Otages, t 02 98 88 41 40 (*inexpensive*). A quite sophisticated and very central place that prepares crêpes the old-fashioned way.

L'Hermine, 35 Rue Ange de Guernisac, t 02 98 88 10 91 (*inexpensive*). A rustic and very pretty place offering a range of traditionally made crêpes.

Tempo, Quai de Tréguier, t 02 98 63 29 11 (*inexpensive*). The trendiest restaurant in town, despite its rather basic food, with the benefit of a terrace overlooking the port. *Closed Sat and Sun.*

Ploujean ✉ 29600

Manoir de Roch Ar Brini, t 02 98 72 01 44, *www.brittanyguesthouse.com* (*inexpensive*). An exceptional *chambre d'hôte*, set in a grand stone villa located 3km from the town centre, built in the 1840s by Edouard Corbière, father of poet and local celebrity Tristan Corbière.

Plougonven ✉ 29640

La Grange de Coatélan, t 02 98 72 60 16 (*inexpensive*). A former cloth-producing farm that has been lovingly converted into a small inn offering a few attractive rooms on a B&B basis.

Mme Le Fer, t 02 98 79 22 80 (*inexpensive*). A charming B&B address offering good food. Book ahead.

Plounéour-Ménez 29410

Domaine de Lanheric, just past Pleyber-Christ, coming from Morlaix, t 02 98 78 01 53 or t 02 98 78 06 30 (*inexpensive*). A hotel offering several rooms in a handsome 18th-century house that is located by a flower-filled courtyard on the side of the Monts d'Arrée.

Guerlesquin ✉ 29650

Les Monts d'Arrée, 14 Rue du Docteur Quéré, t 02 98 72 80 44 (*inexpensive*). A hotel-restaurant that looks a wonderful picture of granite architecture and flowers from the outside. The bedrooms are simple, the menus (*inexpensive–moderate*) on the imaginative side.

Crêperie du Martray, t 02 98 72 83 21 (*inexpensive*). A place that draws in people from round and about with its selection of tasty crêpes.

can see the old houses leaning in towards one another. Number 9, the **Maison de Pondalez**, is a 16th-century house open to visitors year round. By the covered market was the drawbridge through which Mary Queen of Scots was carried when she passed through Morlaix as a girl in 1548, on her way to join the French court on the Loire.

Head for the **Eglise et Musée des Jacobins** (*open July and Aug daily 10–12.30 and 2–6.30; Easter–June, Sept and Oct daily 10–12 and 2–6; rest of year Mon and Wed–Fri 10–12 and 2–5, Sat 10–12*). These 13th- and 14th-century religious buildings have been much abused since the Revolution, when they were turned into stables. Before that, as well as serving the Dominicans, the place welcomed Anne de Bretagne and Mary Queen of Scots. Of great consequence for Breton culture, the monk Albert Le Grand studied here in the early 17th century. He went on to write a book on the life of the Breton saints, *La vie des saints en Bretagne*, a Breton bestseller for centuries.

Inside, the Gothic arches are put to good use, providing elegant separations between the various collections, which range from items on the history of Morlaix, old paintings of the town, and religious statuary from the town's lost religious establishments, to modern art. The stained-glass rose window of the church's apse counts as one of the most beautiful and original exhibits in this museum.

Cross back via the market squares of the centre of town to reach the **Maison de la Duchesse Anne** (*open April–Sept Mon–Sat; call* **t** *02 98 88 23 26 for times*) overlooking the sizeable **Place Allende**. This famous Breton 'lantern house' is sadly grimy on the outside, but spare a few minutes to take a closer look, as the architecture and carvings provide several entertaining surprises. You can make out numerous figures on the façade, including saints and archetypal Gothic figures. The cavernous central room within stretches way up to the roof. This is really like a covered patio provided with a monumental fireplace and is the characteristic feature of Morlaix's *maisons à lanterne* — the inner courtyard was traditionally covered by an opaque roofing from which a lantern was hung to give light to the silo-sized room, hence the name. There are many intriguing artistic curiosities to admire at the **Eglise St-Mathieu** nearby.

Wander back north in the direction of the viaduct, maybe stopping at a café to sample Coreff, the locally brewed bitter. North, at the **port** and quays, the splendid 18th-century **Manufacture de Tabac**, designed by the king's architect, Jacques François Blondel, manufactured cigars up to the end of the 20th century.

Les Jardins de Suscinio (*call* **t** *02 98 72 05 85 for times*), a botanical garden set round a 17th-century château in the Suscinio area a few kilometres from the centre, on the Ploujean hillside, presents plants that 'follow the trail' of the famous corsair Cornic.

East of Morlaix: Plougonven and Guerlesquin

Head southeast out of Morlaix down the D9 to Plougonven, and the Monts d'Arrée hills come into view as a backdrop. The **church at Plougonven** is relatively unknown, though it has a major **calvary** on which scenes from Christ's Passion are dramatically sculpted. Plougonven's calvary dates from 1554. The church itself is from earlier in the century, topped by a Beaumanoir steeple.

Directly east, **Guerlesquin**, categorized as a *petite cité de caractère*, consists of one large, elongated, dipping square, divided up by various important buildings. The top section, the Place de la Liberté, has retained its gibbet. The elegant building at the other end, euphemistically called the *présidial*, was surely one of France's prettiest prisons.

The Haut-Léon via Roscoff

Coming to Brittany from Ireland or southwest England, you may well land in the Haut-Léon, at lively Roscoff, protected by the unspoilt island of Batz. The great religious figure of the area, St Pol Aurélien (St Paul Aurelian), came from Wales in the 6th century to spread the gospel to these parts. The name Léon is thought to derive from Caerleon in south Wales. It's religion, not commerce, that most marks the look of St-Pol-de-Léon, spiritual capital of the Léon, with its soaring spires.

The Carantec Peninsula

The village of **Locquénolé**, full of charm, with a little *enclos paroissial* to go with its Romanesque church, looks out over the natural harbour north of Morlaix and on to the small port of Le Dourduff on the other side.

Getting There and Around

Ferries from Cork, Rosslare and Plymouth arrive at Roscoff.

Roscoff and St-Pol-de-Léon have railway stations and frequent **trains** to Morlaix, where you can join the fast TGV network.

Buses run regularly between Roscoff, St-Pol-de-Léon and Morlaix.

Tourist Information

Pays d'Accueil Touristique du Haut-Léon, Place de l'Evêché, 29250 St-Pol-de-Léon, t 02 98 29 09 09.
Carantec: 4 Rue Pasteur, t 02 98 67 00 43, *www.ville-carantec.com*.
St-Pol-de-Léon: Place de l'Evêché, t 02 98 69 05 69, *www.stpoldeleon.com*.
Roscoff: 46 Rue Gambetta, t 02 98 61 12 13, *www.roscoff-tourisme.com*.
Ile de Batz, 25 Rue de la Plage, t 02 98 61 75 85, *www.iledebatz.com*.

Market Days

Carantec: Thursday.
St-Pol-de-Léon: Tuesday.
Roscoff: Wednesday.
Plouescat: Saturday.

Where to Stay and Eat

Carantec ✉ 29660
★★★Hôtel de Carantec, Rue du Kelenn, t 02 98 67 00 47, *www.hoteldecarantec.com* (*expensive–very expensive*). A hotel next to the beach at Kelenn, with 12 very good rooms, 5 with terraces. The view over the bay of Morlaix from the rear is stunning. There's a garden, a nearby 9-hole golf course, a restaurant offering *mariages malicieux* such as red mullet cake with Léon raspberries, and a salon where you can enjoy snack dishes of warm oysters with cider vinegar.
Chambres d'Hôtes Ker Annise, 22 Rue de la Chaise du Curé, t 02 98 78 32 62 (*inexpensive*). A pleasant 1930s house, very Art Deco in look, offering a warm welcome.
Manoir de Kervezec, Kervezec, about 1.5km from Carantec, t 02 98 67 00 26, *gerardbohic@hotmail.com* (*inexpensive*). B&B accommodation with a personal touch, set in a grand 19th-century villa. Some of the bedrooms are relatively simple and sober. The grounds, which are home to llamas as well as horses, look out over the bay of Roscoff.
Le Relais, 17 Rue Albert Louppe, t 02 98 67 00 42 (*inexpensive*). A very cheap option.

Carantec was 'discovered' by posh tourists at the start of the 20th century and has remained one of the most exclusive resorts on the Finistère's north coast. It has a certain glamour and splendid beaches, notably that of Kelenn. One of the delights of staying at Carantec is walking over to the **Ile Callot** at low tide, when the causeway reveals itself. The island, with its sandy creeks and little chapel, has secretive corners but is not an undiscovered delight.

Carantec has a small **Musée Maritime** (*open daily 17 June–July and school hols 2.30–6, July and Aug 10.30–12 and 2.30–6*). Across the road is an exhibition on the work of Ernest Sibiril, a local shipbuilder who, during the Occupation, risked his life operating a number of dreadfully difficult passages for French volunteers and Allied pilots.

St-Pol-de-Léon

... it can't fail to bring to mind the Breton artichoke
Quote from *Guides Bleus: Bretagne*

St-Pol-de-Léon, long the religious pole for this area of Brittany, is now champion of the Breton vegetable, not just the artichoke. However, its religious architecture still dramatically dominates the flat fertile plain for miles around. The staggering spire of

Le Cabestan, t 02 98 67 01 87 (*expensive*). A romantic spot in which to try the local seafood, situated by the port. *Closed Tues, and Mon out of season.*

La Cambuse, t 02 98 67 08 92 (*moderate*). The sister brasserie of Le Cabestan, catering to a younger, louder crowd.

La Chaise du Curé, 3 Place de la République, **t** 02 98 78 33 27 (*moderate*). A restaurant located right in the centre, offering a selection of traditional Breton food in a family atmosphere.

Aux Délices de la Mer, 9 Rue du Pilote Trémintin, **t** 02 98 78 31 78 (*moderate*). A good place to come for splendid seafood platters – the owner sets his own fishing baskets in the sea close by. *Closed Sun eve and Mon.*

Cléder ✉ 29233

Ferme de Kernévez, t 02 98 69 43 01 (*inexpensive*). A traditional family farmhouse 8km from St-Pol de Léon, offering authentic home comforts against a backdrop of fields.

Kerliviry, t 02 98 61 99 37 (*inexpensive*). Reliable B&B accommodation in the home of M and Mme Xavier Ponthieux, a renovated manor house that's surrounded by woodland.

Berven-Plouzvédévé ✉ 29440

Hôtel des Voyageurs, 1 Rue de St-Sol, **t** 02 98 69 96 84, *voyageurs.berven@wanadoo.fr* (*inexpensive*) A good, reasonably priced family hotel offering meals (*moderate*).

St-Pol-de-Léon ✉ 29250

France, 29 Rue des Minimes, **t 02 98 29 14 14, *www.hoteldefrancebretagne.com* (*inexpensive*). An enjoyable place to stay, set in a historic building, with well-priced, comfortable and often spacious bedrooms giving either on to the courtyard or the pretty shaded garden. The cuisine in the restaurant (*moderate*) is well prepared.

Le Passiflore, 28 Rue Pen ar Pont, **t** 02 98 69 00 52 (*inexpensive*). A pleasant option by the station, with bargain menus at the adjoining Routier workers' restaurant.

La Pomme d'Api, 49 Rue Verderel, **t** 02 98 69 04 36 (*moderate–expensive*). A restaurant in an old Breton house, with very refined décor and excellent food – the melting artichoke hearts are particularly recommended.

Crêperie Les Fromentines, 18 Rue Cadiou, **t** 02 98 69 23 52 (*inexpensive*). A place serving good crêpes close to the Kreisker's soaring steeple.

Notre-Dame du Kreisker, commonly abbreviated to the Kreisker (city centre), is the tallest in Brittany. It was apparently commissioned out of pride by Léonard merchants, not the Church.

During the Middle Ages the town became one of the major stops on the Tro Breizh, the great Breton pilgrimage route. Only with the Revolution did St-Pol-de-Léon lose its important religious status as the centre of a diocese. The last bishop, Jean-François de la Marche, also happened to be the last count of Léon. St-Pol's harbour of Pempoul was extremely active down the centuries, until it silted up and the port had to be moved north.

The two main churches in St-Pol-de-Léon contrast quite markedly in style, although both were inspired by Norman buildings. The Gothic **cathedral** was strongly influenced by the cathedral of Coutances on the Cherbourg peninsula. It went up painfully slowly, building work on the nave and aisles lasting through the 13th and 14th centuries, the side chapels and choir completed in the course of the 15th and 16th centuries. The long nave with its pointed Gothic arches and Gothic decoration has a sober simplicity to it. Surprisingly, the stone employed within came from Caen in Normandy, in contrast to the Breton granite employed on the outside. Saint Pol's tomb (*see* p.239) lies in front of the main altar, while you can seek out his supposed

---

Roscoff ✉ 29680

Old Roscoff makes a lovely introduction to Brittany; there are plenty of pleasant hotels with sea views here.

★★★**Hôtel Le Temps de Vivre**, Place de l'Eglise, t 02 98 61 27 28, *www.letempsdevivre.net* (*expensive–luxury*). A spectacularly good hotel and restaurant in an old corsair's house. You'll find many luxurious, inventive dishes on the menus, including spider crab *galette* with fresh vegetables and foie gras.

★★★**Le Brittany**, 22 Boulevard Ste-Barbe, t 02 98 69 70 78, *www.hotel-brittany.com* (*moderate–expensive*). A wonderfully located hotel by the old port, with very comfortable rooms, though those in the annexe are less interesting than the ones in the old part. The cuisine can be quite adventurous – try John Dory served in a blue cheese sauce. Guests can make use of a heated, covered swimming pool with jet streams.

★★★**Le Gulf Stream**, 400 Rue Marquise de Kergariou, t 02 98 69 73 19, *www.hotelroscoff. com* (*moderate–expensive*). A modern hotel with sea views, a heated pool in its flowery garden running down to the beach, and excellent seafood (*moderate*). The *Institut Marin* offering seawater treatments is just a few hundred metres away.

★★**Talabardon**, Place Lacaze, t 02 98 61 24 95, *www.talabardon.fr* (*moderate–expensive*). A typically comfortable Best Western hotel, set in an imposing 19th-century stone building, with some rooms looking onto the sea, others on to the church square, plus a restaurant with panoramic views.

★★**Les Chardons Bleus**, 4 Rue Amiral Réveillère, t 02 98 69 72 03, *www.chardonsbleus.fr.st* (*inexpensive*). A well-kept hotel in a Renaissance house in the centre of town, with tastefully decorated rooms.

★★**Les Tamaris**, 49 Rue Edouard Corbière, t 02 98 61 22 99 (*inexpensive*). A welcoming address well located by the sea, with some of its bright rooms looking out to the island of Batz.

Hôtel des Arcades, 15 Rue Amiral Réveillère, t 02 98 69 70 45, *web@acdev.com* (*inexpensive*). A good-value option, with some rooms with sea views, and a dining room (*inexpensive–moderate*) looking out on to the Channel.

L'Ecume des Jours, Quai d'Auxerre, t 02 98 61 22 83 (*moderate–expensive*). An utterly delightful restaurant serving fine food in a 16th-century house looking out to sea. The menus are good value. *Closed Sept–June, Wed lunch, and Wed eve out of season.*

skull in a reliquary in one of the aisles, plus a miraculous bell that legend says a fish slipped away with from King Marc'h's court in Cornwall. The great organ was the work of Robert Dallam, who also made the one in King's College, Cambridge.

D'une légèreté inquiétante ('of a worrying lightness') wrote Breton art historian Victor-Henry Debidour of the steeple of the **Chapelle Notre-Dame du Kreisker**. This steeple definitely tries to steal the show from the cathedral. From a distance, its defiant arrow, more than 75 metres high, does eclipse the bishops' church. For some time the town council used to meet here. Not surprisingly, Notre-Dame du Kreisker looks rather top-heavy from closer up. Some of it was built in the 14th century, but the flamboyance of 15th-century Gothic triumphs. The tower was added between 1439 and 1472, following the model of that at St-Pierre de Caen. It rockets up from the centre of the building, held in place by the massive pillars of the crossing. You can climb nearly 170 steps up to the viewing gallery.

Several of the streets around these dominating religious buildings contain some splendid houses, many from the 16th and 17th centuries. Except on market days, however, the calm little city of St-Pol-de-Léon can sometimes seem, rather ironically, to lack soul, or at least the bustling spiritual and commercial activity it must have once enjoyed. The life of the area is today concentrated in Roscoff.

Le Surcouf, 14 Rue de l'Amiral Réveilière, **t** 02 98 69 71 89 (*inexpensive–moderate*). A restaurant that's worth visiting for its good-value seafood menus. *Closed Tues, and Wed Oct–June.*

Crêperie de la Poste, 12 Rue Gambetta, **t** 02 98 69 72 81 (*inexpensive*). A decent crêpe house with appealing rustic décor.

Crêperie Ti Saozon, 30 Rue Gambetta, **t** 02 98 69 70 89 (*inexpensive*). A very small place offering crêpes a cut above the average, with interesting fillings such as artichoke hearts with cream of seaweed. Book ahead to make sure of a place. *Closed lunch.*

Ile de Batz ✉ 29253

Grand Hôtel, **t** 02 98 61 78 06 (*inexpensive*). A simple place at the port.

Roch Armor, **t** 02 98 61 78 28 (*inexpensive*). A cheerful option with bargain-priced rooms with views on to the sea.

Ty Va Zadou, Le Bourg (right just before the church), **t** 02 98 61 76 91 (*inexpensive*). The most delightful place to stay on the island, with lovely views from the fresh first-floor bedrooms, and little reception rooms filled with typical Breton furniture. The B&B's owner, Mme Prigent, tells entertaining tales about Batz. Book well in advance.

Auberge de Jeunesse, **t** 02 98 61 77 69, *www. fuaj.org* (*inexpensive*). A splendidly located hostel at Creac'h ar Bolloc'h, with sea views.

La Pussonade, **t** 02 98 61 75 25 (*inexpensive*). Organic pancakes, and mussels with chips.

Morguériec ✉ 29250

La Marine, **t** 02 98 29 99 52 (*inexpensive*). A basic little hotel looking onto this quiet port, with a seafood restaurant (*moderate*).

Mespaul ✉ 29420

La Garenne, **t** 02 98 61 59 72 (*moderate*). A charming B&B with spacious, comfy rooms.

Plouescat ✉ 29430

La Caravelle, 20 Rue du Calvaire, **t 02 98 69 61 75 (*inexpensive*). A family-run hotel with a good reputation, popular for local events.

St-Vougay ✉ 29225

Crêperie du Château, Kerfao, **t** 02 98 69 93 09 (*inexpensive*). Excellent crêpes in a restored farmhouse near the Château de Kerjean.

Porz Meur ✉ 29430

Roc'h-ar-Mor, **t** 02 98 69 63 01 (*moderate*). A hotel well sited for catching the glorious sunsets. Half-board is obligatory.

St Pol, One of the Seven Founders of Celtic Christian Brittany

St Pol is considered to have been one of the seven founding saints of Christian Brittany in the Dark Ages. The legend goes that he was born in Wales in the late 5th century. He is supposed to have been the pupil of St Ildut and then gone on to serve King Marc'h at his Cornish court in Tintagel. But he felt the compulsion to head off and convert non-believers abroad to Celtic Christianity.

He set sail for Armorica around 512, landing first on the Island of Ouessant (Ushant). There he met with strong resistance from the inhabitants. He quickly left, going off to found a monastery on the island of Batz, where he triumphed over the local dragon. On the invitation of the local lord Withur, he then crossed to the mainland to help the people there – the place had just been devastated by raiders. Pol gave the community the impetus to rebuild their settlement and Kastell-Paol soon flourished. It became the seat of Pol's bishopric, the diocese seemingly founded at the end of the 520s.

Roscoff

trou de flibustiers, vieux nid de corsaires (buccaneers' hideout, corsairs' den)
Tristan Corbière, 19th-century local poet

Don't confuse the ferry port just to the east with the old harbour town. Old Roscoff is a delight, although it's somewhat chaotic at the best of times and gets extremely busy during the summer months. It makes rather too much play of its pirating past to be healthy, you might think. But on the more sensible, hard-working side, it also pays homage to its cross-Channel onion sellers in a little museum honouring its Breton 'Johnnies'.

History

The silver sailing ships crossing blue waters depicted on the arms of Roscoff recall the times before ferries became the main shipping interest of this port. The shipowners, corsairs and smugglers of Roscoff were engaged in a centuries-long struggle with the English. In the course of medieval conflicts, one lord of Arundel came and destroyed much of the town in the 14th century. In the early 15th century, the Amiral de Penhouët set out from here to fight the English navy. Through the Ancien Régime, Roscoff corsairs sailed off to join in the battle for control of the seas that raged between France and England. England wasn't the only party Roscoff regularly feuded with – its merchants often entered into conflict with the bishops of St-Pol-de-Léon, who tried to impose their authority over the port.

On a more positive diplomatic note, Roscoff is where Mary Queen of Scots landed in 1548, coming over as a child bride to the French court. And many of Roscoff's merchants prospered on honest trade for centuries, dealing with the Hanseatic League, Flanders and the Iberian peninsula in particular. Tragi-comically, in 1746 Bonnie Prince Charlie, Young Pretender to the English throne, landed here, having escaped from England disguised as 'Betty Burke', supposedly Flora Macdonald's maid.

The serious onion-selling in Britain began relatively early in the 19th century, and local men continued to head across the Channel to sell door-to-door from their bikes until well after the Second World War. Since the setting up of the European Union, the Breton vegetable producers have become much more highly organized. They created a cooperative to market their produce, and after that it was in large part due to them that Brittany Ferries was established in 1972 and became a successful shipping enterprise. The deep-water port to the east of old Roscoff came into existence in 1973, leaving the historic Roscoff to the fishing fleet and to yachts.

A Tour of Roscoff

The merry steeple of **Notre-Dame de Kroaz Batz** looks as if it was built up out of stone bells. The graceful openwork forms of the many levels of Renaissance lanterns mark the Roscoff skyline. The rest of the church's architecture, completed in 1548, is in Flamboyant Gothic style. Roscoff shipowners contributed considerable amounts to the construction, which probably explains why carvings of sailing vessels were permitted in the stone. These were executed as ex votos, to thank God for sparing a ship. Around the church, the grand granite houses of the 16th and 17th centuries, often with stylish dormer windows, reflect the prosperity of some of Roscoff's merchants.

Just west of the church, **Roscoff aquarium** (*closed indefinitely for renovation*) is the public part of the marine biology research centre based here. While it is closed for much-needed modernization, head for **Thalado** at 5 Rue Victor Hugo, where you learn all about Brittany's 800 different types of algae (*open Mon–Sat 9–12 and 2–7*).

One of the joys of visiting Roscoff is promenading up and down the quays of the **old port**, which are always full of bustle – from the boats setting out for the island of Batz, from the fishing fleet, and from holiday yachts. The protective sea walls stick out at odd angles into the port, like tentacles. The **Pointe de Bloscon**, with its tiny Chapelle Ste-Barbe, is whitewashed to serve as a seamark for boats. The seawater in the giant **tanks** (*visits working weekdays 9.30–12 and 2–5*) beyond the chapel is regularly replaced by the tide for the benefit of the lobsters, crayfish and crabs that are reared there. Ask at the tourist office for details on visiting the Criée, the fish auctions.

The **Maison des Johnnies** (*open 15 June–15 Sept Wed–Mon 10–12 and 3–6; if closed ask at tourist office*) is at the entrance to the town centre, on Rue Brizeux. It tells in detail the story of the Breton onion sellers who went forth to make a living purveying their vegetables on British doorsteps. Since this is a happpy tale of Breton-British cooperation, you'll find plenty of elements in English at the museum.

As you approach the ferry terminal, you'll come to **Algoplus** (*open shop hours*), a manufacturer of algae products offering a guided tour during which you learn about how algae are harvested and transformed, plus tastings.

Roscoff, like the island of Batz, has its own exotic garden making the most of the mild climate. The **Jardin Exotique de Roscoff** (*open July and Aug daily 10–7; April–June Sept and Oct daily 10.30–12.30 and 2–6; Nov and March Wed–Sun and Mon 2–5*) is situated to the east of town, near the ferry terminal, and looks out over the spectacular bay of Morlaix. Palm trees, cacti and plants from the southern hemisphere prosper here.

Ile de Batz

As Breton islands go, Batz has remained mainly agricultural and relatively unspoilt by tourism, with a semi-tropical garden on its east end restored to splendid condition. The north coast takes you away from civilization to wildly rocky scenes. The whole island is less than four kilometres long and around a kilometre and a half wide, so you can walk around the coastal path in three to four hours.

While Christian teaching may have thrived for some time on the island, frequent Viking attacks seem to have put paid to the monastery. Fishing, farming and especially the production of seaweed fertilizer were the main activities for the islanders for countless centuries. The lighthouse that marks the western end of the island went up in the middle of the 19th century, in a period when Batz port became relatively busy. Electricity came quite early to the island, in 1938, but the inhabitants had to wait as late as 1970 to receive fresh piped water.

A Tour of the Island

The main **village** stretches round the large **Baie de Kernoc'h**. Plots of vegetables still keep their place among the houses. There are some lovely gardens here, with such exotic plants as cacti, agapanthus and echium in profusion, and a fair number of surprising trees, including tamarisks and palms. The 19th-century church contains a statue of St Pol, as well as a piece of cloth once claimed to have been Pol's stole.

It's a pretty walk to the eastern tip of the island and the **Jardin Delaselle** (*open April–Nov daily 2–6*). After he had fallen in love with the spot and decided to convert it into a garden in the late 1890s, Georges Delaselle had an artificial string of dunes dug to protect it. In the process, many mysterious old tombs were discovered. Then Delaselle imported all manner of exotic plants, palms in particular, from the colonies. More than 40 species of palms are nurtured here; it's the largest outdoor collection in Brittany. It seems extraordinary that in such a windy, salty environment so many exotic plants survive, but this part of the Breton coast remains fairly mild year round.

Batz's best-known **beaches**, the Grève Blanche and the Porz Mellok, lie nearby, their sand sometimes likened to flour, such is its colour and texture. The ruins of the **Chapelle Ste-Anne**, also in the east, are the remains of a Romanesque building from around the 10th century. They may stand on the site of Pol's original monastery.

Up towards the **north side** of Batz, the reefs stick out sharply. In the smallish vegetable plots, traditional crops such as potatoes and cauliflowers have been supplemented by chicory, parsley and tomatoes. Tractors just about outnumber the cars on Batz, and the odd Breton carthorse still works here. The **western side** of the island is dominated by the **lighthouse**.

Getting There

The trip to Batz is serviced by two **ferry** companies, Compagnies associées, **t** 02 98 61 79 66 and **t** 02 98 61 78 87, and Vedettes CFATM, **t** 02 98 61 79 66. The walk across the spectacular crescent footbridge to the embarkation point alone is worth the trip, which costs around €6 and takes *c.* 15mins.

Pol the Dragon-Slayer

When Pol arrived on the island of Batz from Ouessant, he was quickly adopted by the islanders. If the claims are to be believed, he immediately set about miraculously curing three blind people, two mutes and one paralytic. The legend goes that the local lord also asked Pol if he could help fight off the dragon on Batz, which was devouring both livestock and people. Donning his religious ceremonial clothes and accompanied by an armed warrior, Pol went off to see what he could do. The dragon was perhaps simply mesmerized by the glorious religious finery, immediately submitting to Pol's will; one version of the story goes that the holy man then tied his stole like a lead around the dragon's neck, took it to the rocky shore and ordered it to jump into the foaming waters. The dragon obediently followed Christian orders and plunged to its death. Pol then set about establishing his monastery on the island, where he is said to have died in AD 573.

Along the Artichoke Coast

Westwards of Roscoff, you come to the **beach of Le Dossen**, which is a favourite among sand-yachters. At low tides, a causeway makes it possible to walk out to the private **island of Siek**.

Across the Quillec river, you can go for a curious trip along the **artichoke coast** up from Sibiril and round to Plouescat. Vegetables grow almost right up to the sea, among strange rocks. Further bizarre rock formations stand out to sea. The grounds of the **Château de Kérouzeré-en-Sibiril**, a picturesque medieval fort, are often open.

The tiny port of **Moguériec** is beautifully situated on the western side of the Quillec estuary. Continue along the coast to the enticing beach of **Tévenn Kerbrat**, as well as **Kerfissien**, with a series of creeks along the way. More beaches have found a spot among the rocks along the coast between Poulfoen and the **bay of Kernic**, those to the west at **Porz Meur and Porz Guen** the most attractive. On the other side of the Baie de Kernic, the strand is a favourite with volleyball players. All these beaches lie a short distance from the little resort of **Plouescat**, with its 16th-century covered market.

On the coast to the west of Plouescat, wild sandy dunes stretch to the Grève de Goulven, strewn with huge dollops of granite. A section of them was donated to the French Conservatoire du Littoral, official guardian of the French coasts, which has a **Maison des Dunes at Keremma** (*open July–Sept*), organizing nature walks.

Château de Kerjean

Open July and Aug daily 10–7; June and Sept Wed–Mon 10–6; May and Oct Wed–Mon 2–6; April Mon, Wed–Fri and Sun 2–5; rest of year Wed and Sun 2–6.

Heading inland from Plouescat, the D30 leads you to the grandest pre-Revolutionary castle of the Léon. Superb alleys of towering beeches surround it. A bulging dovecot gives you some notion of the former importance of the Kerjean lords' estates. A gibbet still stands in one corner of the much-reduced lands. The château has suffered considerably since it was built in the second half of the 16th century, the century of the French Renaissance. It was commissioned by Louis Barbier to replace a 15th-century manor on the spot. Early in the 18th century, a fire destroyed part of the castle, while during the Revolution the place was pillaged and the widowed owner, Mme de Coëtanscourt, sent to Brest to be guillotined.

Although the Renaissance brought refinement to French architecture, Kerjean was clearly built with an eye to defence. The French Wars of Religion would, after all, be raging through the period of its construction. The courtyard is on an impressive scale, two of its sides graced with galleries. The main lord's quarters was, unfortunately, the section partly destroyed by fire, and it still looks skeletal in parts, with just the frames of aristocratic windows reaching out above the walls.

The château contains a permanent collection of Léonard furniture from down the centuries, although the items were gathered from local farms and so lack the grandeur you might expect in a castle. You can wander round the massive, cold, stone rooms looking at the snug box beds that remained popular across Brittany for so long, or at the chests in which Bretons stored linen and provisions. Wardrobes became fashionable around the mid 17th century, and a tradition arose for rich families to give prettily carved ones to newlyweds.

Apparently the ordinary people of the parish were allowed to attend services in the ornate chapel before the Revolution, but the lord's family had its private oratory. The beams are carved with angels, dragons and protruding figures of the Evangelists.

The château hosts interesting annual exhibitions, including one on modern art and one on a theme from local history. There are also son-et-lumière nights in summer.

The Pays des Abers

This particularly vicious, rocky strip of coast occupies the most northwesterly corner of the province and is known for its strong Breton roots, its legends, and its seaweed. Towering lighthouses try to warn off stray ships from the reefs on which algae thrive, but they have not always been successful: the sinking of oil tanker the *Amoco Cadiz* here was one of the greatest ecological disasters in Europe in the 20th century. The *abers* are the river estuaries along this shore, making deep little cuts into the land.

The Meteorite Coast of the Pays Pagan and Brignogan

Before you hit the more exposed coasts, seek out a couple of sheltered corners in the east of the Pays des Abers. **Goulven** is a little village hidden away behind a vast bay, but there is nothing modest about its **church's** massive Flamboyant Gothic steeple. This contrasts comically with the building's second steeple, over the crossing. The major one, erected over the entrance porch, is a towering achievement from 1593, completely out of proportion to the building below it. The 15th-century steeple over the crossing can only be described as piddling by comparison.

At the western end of the **Baie de Goulven**, vast stretches of firm sand are left stranded at low tide, allowing the sand-yachts to come out to play, flitting around at breakneck speed. The beach of **Plounéour-Trez** is particularly renowned for the sport.

As you continue westwards along the coast from here, the atmosphere becomes increasingly otherworldly, with a fantastical array of massive rocks that seem to have landed in the countryside. The resort of **Brignogan-Plages** curves round a great horseshoe-shaped bay full of unruly boulders. Further formations come out at low tide as the seawater retreats. A few too many rather characterless buildings have gone up at Brignogan itself.

To the north and west of Brignogan, the splendid beaches of **Les Chardons Bleus** and **Ménéham** are particularly worth seeking out. Between these two, you can also take a look at the massive **Menhir Men Marz** (the Miracle Stone), which has been abandoned by the roadside. It looks like some monumental nose that has slipped off the face of a colossal statue.

Nearby, the **Chapelle Pol** is swamped by the enormous boulders that surround it. From here, there are marked coastal paths that take you past the **Pontusval** and its lighthouse, also surrounded by a ring of grim-looking rocks.

Getting Around

The only public transport in the area appears to be the **bus** service. Several lines connect this coastal strip with Brest. One goes from Brignogan-Plages to Brest, via Goulven, Lesneven and Le Folgoët. Another goes via Guissény, and yet another heads down from Plouguerneau.

Tourist Information

Pays des Abers-Côte des Légendes: B.P. 35, 29830 Ploudalmézeau, t 02 98 89 78 44.
Brignogan-Plages: t 02 98 83 41 08, *www.ot-brignogan-plage.fr*.
Guissény: t 02 98 25 67 99, *ot.guisseny@cotesdeslegendes.com*.
Lesneven/Le Folgoët: t 02 98 83 01 47, *ot.lesneven@cotedeslegendes.com*.
Plouguerneau: Place de l'Europe, t 02 98 04 70 93, *ot.plouguerneau@wanadoo.fr*.
Ploudalmézeau: t 02 98 48 12 88.

Market Days
Goulven: Sunday in July and August.
Brignogan-Plages: Friday in July and August.
Lesneven: Monday.
Plouguerneau: Thursday.
Lilia: Tuesday 5–7pm in summer holidays.
Ploudalmézeau: Friday.

Where to Stay and Eat

Plouider ✉ 29260
★★★La Butte, 10 Rue de la Mer, t 02 98 25 40 54, *labutte@club-internet.fr* (*moderate*). A hotel offering spacious, comfortable rooms, and, best of all, views on to the bay of Goulven in the distance. It can be a lively place in which to eat.

Brignogan-Plages ✉ 29890
★★Castel Régis, Plage du Garo, t 02 98 83 40 22 (*moderate*). A hotel set in its own grounds on a wonderful promontory very close to the sea. It has slightly uninspiring, if comfortable, modern rooms, and the added attractions of a heated seawater swimming pool, a tennis court and saunas. Half-board is obligatory in high season.
Café du Port, corner of the port. A pretty place to grab snacks and ice-creams.

Guissény ✉ 29249
Ferme-auberge de Keralloret, t 02 98 25 60 37 (*moderate*). Pleasant B&B accommodation in a farmhouse, together with copious,

Ménéham itself, a hamlet that has long been abandoned by its fishermen, retains great character, even if the thatched cottage roofs have caved in. A coastguard's house is squeezed between two massive boulders. There are plans to restore this extraordinary site. Yet more boulders stack up along the coast round to **Guisseny**.

Lesneven and Le Folgoët

Lesneven inland is not a tourist town, but it is proud of its history as administrative capital of the Léon and houses a fairly interesting historical museum, the **Musée du Léon** (*open May–Sept Mon 2–7, Tue–Sun 10–12 and 2–7; Oct–April Mon 2–7, Tue–Fri 10–12 and 2–7*) in a former Ursuline convent. The main magnet for visitors to the area, though, is the imposing **Basilique du Folgoët**, which looks out of place on the southwestern outskirts of Lesneven, lording it over a plain, modest village set round a wide green. The Flamboyant Gothic monster of a pilgrimage church was constructed roughly from the 1420s to the 1460s in honour of the Virgin Mary and the piety of a local village idiot (Folgoët means Madman of the Wood in Breton) – *see* box p.246.

good-value home-made Breton dishes (*inexpensive*) served in the evenings only. Advance booking is required.

Plouguerneau ✉ 29880
**Castel Ac'h, on the coast at Lilia, t 02 98 04 70 11 (*inexpensive*). A wonderfully located choice by the rockscapes of Lilia, with many of its rooms looking out to sea. The restaurant is extremely popular for its excellent fresh seafood, with many dishes served with touches of local algae. There's also a tennis court.
Trouz ar Mor, Le Correjou (north of town, off the road to the Chapelle St-Michel), t 02 98 04 71 61 (*moderate*). A pleasant restaurant that looks rather basic from the outside but has a surprisingly smart and bright interior, as well as a terrace by the sands for sunny days.

L'Aber Wrac'h ✉ 29870
***La Baie des Anges, t 02 98 04 90 04, *www.baie-des-anges.com* (*moderate*). A hotel up by the side of the estuary road, with lovely views from all the rooms down on to the river.
Le Brennig, St-Antoine, by the port, t 02 98 04 81 12 (*moderate–expensive*). A restaurant that stands out for its

elegant, modern marine décor and its inventive cuisine mixing the likes of queen scallops with goats' cheese. It's good value. *Closed Tues and Oct.*

Plouvien ✉ 29870
Crêperie la Salamandre, Place Général de Gaulle, t 02 98 48 14 00 (*inexpensive*). A reasonable crêperie. *Closed outside public hols, Sat–Sun in winter.*

St-Pabu ✉ 29830
Crêperie de l'Aber Benoît, Pors ar Viln, t 02 98 89 86 26 (*inexpensive*). A delightful Breton crêpe joint.

Ploudalmézeau ✉ 29830
Crêperie/Restaurant Panoramique du Château d'Eau, Route de Brest, t 02 98 48 15 88 (*inexpensive*). A memorable place in which to eat, more than 50m up in a Breton watertower (take the lift, or, to work up an appetite, the 278 stairs). The food is basic.

Portsall ✉ 29830
La Demeure Océane, 20 Rue de Bar al Lan, t 02 98 48 77 42 (*moderate*). A charming B&B with characterful rooms in a substantial old house set in its own garden. *Table d'hôte* (*inexpensive*) is available on reservation.

An Extraordinary Horticultural Happening Gives Birth to a Church

The simpleton Salaun lived in these parts in the middle of the 14th century, while the Breton War of Succession was bringing misery to Brittany. He is supposed only ever to have learnt to speak a few words, but he became obsessed by the Virgin and singing her praises. He went around proclaiming her name all the time, all over the place – while he ate his bread, while he bathed in the fountain, even when he climbed trees (a favourite pastime of his). The villagers merely looked on him as a madman. But after his death a curious lily arose where he was buried, and the sweet-smelling plant supposedly grew to spell out the name of the Virgin. This was taken to be a miracle of considerable significance, and news of the extraordinary horticultural happening travelled across Brittany faster than a bramble spreads its roots. Local churchmen decided to try to track down the source of the mysterious plant, and discovered that it had grown from the dead Salaun's mouth, which they took as a sign of God's joy in the madman's naïve piety.

The main portion of the church is on a very large scale, indicating the popularity the pilgrimage site assumed. The two west towers contrast markedly with each other, the shorter one simply topped by a slate hat of a roof, the other one given a typically soaring Léon spire. The plentiful details around the outside of the church are absorbing, especially the statues. One of the most notable artistic features of Le Folgoët is that it was here, for one of the first times in the province, that Breton stone sculptors started to use the peculiarly dark granite of Kersanton for their works.

Look around the ornate Flamboyant Gothic doorways to appreciate the wealth of sculptural decoration. Over the main entrance you can make out scenes from Christ's Nativity, including the lively arrival of the Three Kings. The Virgin is shown naked-breasted, which seems a surprisingly unprudish representation for the Catholic Church. In the Pietà scene of the calvary, Christ had his head chopped off just like so many French nobles. Look out for the image of the Breton St Yves, typically shown standing between the rich man with his spurs and the poor man with his ragged clothes, or for the depiction of a medieval warrior holding a sceptre and a book. He may be meant to portray Duke Jean V (a Latin inscription on the west porch recognizes him as the founder of Le Folgoët). The most moving figure of all at Le Folgoët is that of the *Mater dolorosa* – the mother of Christ shown in her grief, her thick tears carved in stone.

The interior has been heavily restored – the place served as a barracks and for pigsties at the Revolution. Some of the decorative features stand out, most notably the rood screen. Most Breton rood screens were carved out of wood; this one is made from stone, but it looks remarkably light and elegant, and is a model of Flamboyant Gothic style. The choir, virtually cut off from the rest of the church, is graced by the elegant tracery of a rose window.

On the green outside the basilica, some picturesque old buildings stand to one side. One of them, a former hostel for pilgrims, contains the little **Maison du Patrimoine** (*open mid-June–mid-Sept Mon–Sat 10–12.30 and 2.30–6.30, Sun 2.30–6.30*), with its collection of Breton statues and furniture. One room recreates the kind of chamber Duchess Anne de Bretagne might have stayed in when she came on pilgrimage here. Her visit of 1505 was a notable event. During it, she was presented with live ermines, the animals being the symbol of Breton ducal authority, their tails represented in highly stylized form on the Breton ducal coat of arms from early in the 14th century. The *pardon* at Le Folgoët remains one of the best-attended in Brittany. It takes place on the first Sunday in September.

To Plouguerneau

The local Michel Le Nobletz became one of the most fervent preachers in the region in the 17th century, trying to reinforce Catholic belief among the poorly educated masses across the province. He used specially made illustrated maps to help explain the Christian message simply. These cartoon-like missionary paintings, often executed on sheepskins, sometimes on wood, became known as *taolennou* in Breton. The tradition of painting these *taolennou* continued right into the 20th century, although the main period in which they were made lasted between 1613 and 1639.

Plouguerneau is a popular village with a good choice of beaches to the north of it. It is also a bastion of Breton culture. The place contains an unusual local museum, the **Musée des Goémoniers** (*open July and Aug Tues–Sun 2–6; April–June Sat and Sun 2.30–5; rest of year Sun 2–6*), dedicated to the local seaweed-gathering trade.

The main attractions of this stretch of coast for visitors are the **beaches** around St-Michel and Lilia north of Plouguerneau. Head up to the built-up St-Michel peninsula and on the way you can stop to stare down at the extraordinary engraved tombstones of Tremenac'h.

Iliz-Koz, or the Buried Church of Tremenac'h

Open 15 June–15 Sept Tues–Sun 2.30–6.30; rest of year Sun and bank hols 2.30–5.

The legend claims that the church of Tremenac'h was buried under the sands by way of punishment for the evil deeds of a band of youths from the parish. Led astray by that great evil, boredom, one day they captured the devil's cat and brought it to the blind parish priest to be baptized. When the innocent priest threw water over the puss, it gave out a blood-curdling cry and the blind man saw a ball of fire shoot out in front of him. The evil boys' act brought down the punishment of God. At midnight, a wind whipped the sand dunes into a frenzy and they swirled over the village, burying it. The punishment sounds a bit harsh for such a prank. The legend doesn't quite stop there, however. The pure of heart are supposed to be able to witness the uplifting sight of three suns rising on the anniversary of the burial of Tremenac'h – presumably a symbol of the Trinity.

The lost village of Tremenac'h lay forgotten under the sands for some time. As the land settled, new buildings started to go up. In the 1960s, a bulldozer was shifting earth and sand to start on the foundations of another house when it hit upon the old cemetery. The parish bought the site and cleared it. A dense patchwork of medieval and early modern tombs, around 100 in number, were revealed, both outside the church ruin and within it. The most exciting aspect was that many of the tombstones were engraved – the swords and the gloves were symbols of high social standing, but other details such as caravels and scissors probably represent specific trades.

The Coast Above Plouguerneau

Moving to the beaches around Plouguerneau, close to Tremenac'h you could go to admire the beautifully coloured waters around the little port of **Le Correjou** (or Le Korejou) situated on the peninsula of Penn Enez, with its sandy bay. In 1345 Jean de Montfort, one of the contenders for the duchy of Brittany in the Breton War of Succession, was forced to sail off from here to England, having lost one of the bouts in that long conflict.

If you head east along the coast from here you come to the splendid **dunes of Zorn and Vougot**. You might wander along to some of the other picturesque tips to the west of Le Correjou, on the many-pronged peninsula that lies above Plouguerneau. The small **Chapelle St-Michel** sits on one spit, with an even smaller oratory next to it, built in honour of Michel Le Nobletz (*see* p.247). A cross out on one of the rocks was erected in memory of those who died when the British liner, the *Kurdistan*, sank off the coast here in the early 20th century.

West of St-Michel with its *goémoniers'* village you'll find the sands of **La Grève Blanche**. Beyond them, views open up on to the towering spectacle of the **Ile Vierge (Virgin Island) lighthouse**, the tallest lighthouse in Europe, reaching some 80 metres above sea level. Built at the very end of the 19th century, it dwarfs the previous lighthouse, which looks childlike by its side, at a mere 33 metres in height. Big lumps of rock prostrate themselves at the feet of these giants.

Round a further bay you come to **Lilia** and the magical rockscapes located around its port, where you can often see seaweed being unloaded. To the southwest of Lilia, the lighthouse on the **Ile Vrac'h** looks like a modest house that has suddenly sprouted up like a straight beanstalk into the sky. Its steep little sloping roof is perched far above the ground.

Around L'Aber Wrac'h and the Aber Benoît

The Ile Vrac'h lies out to one side of the mouth of **L'Aber Wrac'h**. Various other islands remain stranded in the estuary as the tide goes out. The legendary settlement of Tolente supposedly lies somewhere out in the waters. The best way to appreciate the natural setting of L'Aber Wrac'h, the Fairy's Estuary, is to go to **Paluden** and the south side of the bridge to take a boat trip or a canoe out on to its waters. A corniche road takes you to the little **port of L'Aber Wrac'h**. Beyond it, the Fort Cézon out on its island was ordered by the great military architect Sebastien de Vauban in the late 17th century. The estuary road leads via the **Baie des Anges** and the ruins of a religious foundation to the dunes of the peninsula of **Ste-Marguerite**. The **Aber Benoît** estuary comes out into the Channel just south of L'Aber Wrac'h. Various bird observatories have been posted along the way. One route leads to the little port of **St-Pabu**.

To Portsall

Following the coast west from the Aber Benoît, wide stretches of splendid dunes lie to the north of Lampaul-Ploudalmézeau. From the point above the dunes and beach of **Tréompan**, the spit of land looks out to the island of **Carne**. At low tide you can walk out to see the prehistoric tumulus on the island, the impressive stone structure concealing three dolmens.

Piles of rocks lie on the dunes and out to sea on the way to the port of **Portsall**. This village had the misfortune of being all too closely linked with the environmental disaster of the *Amoco Cadiz*. The port recovered some time ago from the effects of the oil pollution. However, it has kept the vessel's massive anchor as a kind of memorial. The little resort of **Kersaint** is tucked into the bottom of Portsall's bay.

Along the Coast to L'Aber Ildut

The low coastal strip down to L'Aber Ildut looks more than a touch melancholic, with wild grasses and heather growing on the rocky ground that slopes down to the water. Out to sea lie the vicious rocks of Argenton, the enormous **Phare du Four** lighthouse warning ships off them. Further out still, the island of Ouessant (Ushant) comes into view in the distance on clear days. The port of **Argenton**, enclosed in its little bay, looks reasonably picturesque. But go out on to the **Presqu'île de St-Laurent** to get the most sensational views of the Phare du Four on windy days, when the waves fly at the lighthouse.

The little harbours of **Porspoder** and **Melon** that follow are somewhat dominated by rocks. The tiny port of Melon is particularly atmospheric, and is protected from the worst of the waves by the island that lies in front of it.

After Melon you come to the estuary of **L'Aber Ildut**, the southernmost and smallest of the three *abers*, its entrance marked by the Rocher du Crapaud, 'Toad Rock'. Tucked into the estuary you'll find the fine new marina of **Lanildut**. The place also boasts the distinction of being the largest seaweed-gathering port in France. You can go and see the action down on the quays between mid-May and mid-October. The village itself, with flower-covered houses, has some charm, as the granite in this area has attractive pinkish tinges.

The Pays d'Iroise

The Mer d'Iroise is the name for the stretch of sea linking the Channel with the Atlantic here. The Pointe du Corsen in the Pays d'Iroise is the closest point in mainland France to North America. The viewing table at this headland tells you that New York lies a mere 5,080 kilometres away. This *pays* is best known for the port of Le Conquet and the ferries that leave from there for the wild and virtually treeless archipelago of Molène and Ouessant. Directly south of Le Conquet, the Pointe de St-Mathieu counts among the most famous of the innumerable westerly peninsulas in Brittany. It marks the northern entrance to the bay concealing the superbly situated port of Brest. St-Renan is the little historic capital of the Pays d'Iroise, though.

St-Renan

St-Renan is best visited for its Saturday morning market, when it regains some of the vibrant life it knew in centuries past. In 1681, the court and administration of the area were moved to Brest and the previously prosperous merchants' town declined. Some splendid old houses around the sloping hillside **Place du Marché** give you an indication of the past wealth of some of the local traders. The **Musée d'Histoire Locale** (*open July and Aug Tues–Sat 10–12 and 2–6, Sept–June Sat 10.30–12*) off the square has a classic collection of Léon furniture and *coiffes* and recalls the history of the town, including its once thriving pewter industry. St-Renan is said to have been founded by an Irish religious man, Ronan, who crossed the seas to settle here in the late 5th century (*see p.297*).

From L'Aber Ildut to Le Conquet

You can best appreciate the southern bank of L'Aber Ildut by taking the hikers' path from Port Reun. Back on the Atlantic, the first stretch of coast south of the estuary is relatively built up. The port of **Porscave** and the **Grève de Gouérou**, the latter with its algae ovens, are followed by the popular **beach of Lampaul-Plouarzel** and the pretty port of **Porspaul**. The last, in its rounded bay, has the distinct advantage of being protected by the headland of the Beg ar Vir. Dunes shifting with the winds have frequently been a bit of a problem in these parts, even swallowing up a ruined church. Selling sand to Brest in fact became a local industry for some time.

The area around the Pointe de Corsen stands out for its lighthouses. The **Phare de Trézien** looks as though it has gone off duty and strayed inland into the countryside. It's possible to climb the 200 steps to the top on a tour (*contact Plouarzel tourist information on t 02 98 89 69 46 for details*). For a demanding walk along the coast, go in search of the wild creeks of **Ruscumunoc**. To reach the **Pointe de Corsen** by road, turn towards the ruined house at the funky radar base. Maritime traffic along this dangerous coast is regulated from here. Out on the headland you can view the cliffs and creeks along the coast.

A dramatic stretch of the Breton coastal path links the Corsen headland to the protected bay of **Porsmoguer** to the south. Further south, the **Anse des Blancs Sablons** boasts an extremely well-known beach, wild and wonderful, with around a kilometre and a half of sand curving round the bay. There's a nudist section. You can make out the island of Molène from here, but views of the whole archipelago reveal themselves more spectacularly if you walk round the headland of the **Pointe de Kermorvan**.

Le Conquet

Most visitors come to Le Conquet to take the ferry out to the Molène archipelago, especially to Ouessant, the wildest and most westerly island off the French mainland. Le Conquet's harbour is quite charming. The fishermen specialize in catching shellfish now, but in earlier centuries wine and salt from southwest France was shipped via here. However, in 1558 the old houses of Le Conquet were destroyed by an invading English force, apparently avenging a defeat off the Pointe de St-Mathieu at the hands of the Breton admiral Jean de Penhoët. The oratory of **Notre-Dame de Bon Secours**

Getting Around

Buses are the only form of public transport in this area. You can reach the coast at Lampaul-Plouarzel from Brest, via St-Renan. Another bus service from Brest will take you to Le Conquet and the Pointe St-Mathieu.

Tourist Information

St-Renan: Place du Vieux Marché, **t** 02 98 84 23 78, *www.tourisme-saintrenan.com*.
Le Conquet: Parc de Beauséjour, **t** 02 98 89 11 31, *www.leconquet.fr*.

Market Days

St-Renan: Saturday.
Lampaul-Plouarzel: Thursday.
Le Conquet: Tuesday.

Where to Stay and Eat

Trébabu ✉ 29217

Le Grand Keruzou, **t** 02 98 89 11 92 (*inexpensive*). The very picture of a tough yet loveable old Breton manor, offering B&B in charming if relatively sober rooms decorated with a mix of antiques and modern furnishings. *Table d'hôte* is available by reservation only.

Le Conquet ✉ 29217

La Pointe Ste-Barbe, up from the ferry jetty, **t 02 98 89 00 26, *www.hotelpointesaintebarbe. com* (*inexpensive–expensive*). A hotel with a pleasant traditional entrance and a concrete rear extension that's a bit of an eyesore but has rooms with tremendous views out to sea. The décor in the rooms is pretty minimal. The vast restaurant (*moderate–expensive*) shares the views and serves good seafood. Le Conquet beach lies below.

Le Relais du Vieux Port, 1 Quai du Drellach, **t** 02 98 89 15 91 (*inexpensive–moderate*). A B&B resembling a small hotel. The 7 rooms, which are outstanding value, are beautifully appointed, with wooden floors, vast beds and big bathrooms. The more expensive ones have a great harbour view. Booking ahead is advisable. The excellent ground-floor crêperie has port-side tables for summer dining.

Crêperie des Boucaniers, 3 Rue Poncelin, **t** 02 98 89 06 25 (*inexpensive*). Tasty crêpes served in a characterful old house.

Pointe de St-Mathieu ✉ 29217

***Hostellerie de la Pointe St-Mathieu, **t** 02 98 89 00 19, *www.pointe-st-mathieu.com* (*moderate*). A well-reputed choice on this popular headland, with a dining room (*moderate–expensive*) in a charming Breton stone house, serving highly elaborate cuisine. The rooms, in a modern building, are cosily attractive but don't have sea views. The place suffers somewhat from tourist crowds in high summer.

Le Trez Hir ✉ 29217

La Maison Lyre, 5 Allée Verte, Locmaria–Plouzané, **t** 02 98 48 53 50 (*inexpensive*). An interesting B&B full of books and travel mementoes, situated to the east of Le Trez Hir on the D789 towards Trégana.

looks down on the port. Michel Le Nobletz, that 17th-century Breton missionary (*see* p.247), is buried inside. Copies of some of the *taolennou*, the simple Breton Catholic cartoons he used to help spread the Christian message across the province, are displayed within. Le Conquet does have its own little beach, but a few kilometres to the south the **Plage de Porz Liogan** is a very appealing alternative.

The Pointe de St-Mathieu

The Pointe de St-Mathieu, one of several contenders for Brittany's Land's End, looks a frightful architectural mess when you arrive, with its abbey ruins, its radio transmitters, its inconsequential village and its towering lighthouse. The place often looks more sinister than charming, especially on stormy days, the dark ruins of the huge abbey church looming up by the lighthouse.

This **abbey church of St-Mathieu**, an enormous Benedictine construction from the Middle Ages, was abandoned at the Revolution. Many of its stones were subsequently sold off to builders. The ruins reveal an austere architecture, with little decoration except for some rudimentary designs on some of the capitals of the stocky aisle columns. Although this location is said to have been the site of a religious establishment as early as the 6th century, the place was not dedicated to a local saint from across the Breton seas, but to a Biblical one – it is said that local sailors journeyed all the way to Ethiopia to collect St Matthew's skull and bring it back here.

To the northwest, you see the scattered islands and rocks of the Molène archipelago. The closest island, the **Ile de Béniguet** (a transformation of Benedict), derived its name from the fact that the Benedictines of St-Mathieu also owned it. To the west, on clear days, the red and white of the solid Pierres Noires lighthouse may be visible far out into the ocean, indicating another of those daring 19th-century feats of engineering built to make the Breton seas safer.

The Coast from the Pointe de St-Mathieu to Brest

The rocky cliff path eastwards leads to the daunting **Fort de Bertheaume** (*open July and Aug daily 10–7, April–June and Sept Tue–Sun 2–6.30*) on its island, only just attached to the mainland by a flimsy bridge. This fort guarding the northern approach to Brest was designed by the great military architect Vauban in the late 17th century. It belonged to the French military until just a few years ago. Some spectacular *son-et-lumière* shows take place here in summer.

Plougonvelin and **Le Trez Hir** became popular among wealthy Brest families early in the 20th century, as some of the grand villas testify. Now the people of Brest flock here at weekends as soon as there's the slightest sign of good weather. It's a long walk home along the coastal path from Le Trez Hir to Brest, but the path is by far the best way to appreciate the spectacular **Goulet de Brest**, the Narrows or Bottleneck of Brest. This is the very tight waterway through which all vessels have to pass to make it into the glorious natural bay of the Rade de Brest. This strategic channel has been heavily fortified for centuries. In the waters of the Goulet de Brest, you can see oil tankers, container ships, naval vessels and yachts of all descriptions passing in and out.

The Islands of Molène and Ouessant

Qui voit Molène voit sa peine.
Qui voit Ouessant voit son sang.

This alarming rhyme warns those sailing by the archipelago that they will know grief if they set eyes on Molène, and shed blood if they see Ouessant. Innumerable ships have been wrecked on the devilish rocks that are strewn all around. While the main islands you can visit off the north Breton coast nestle close in to the shore, protected enough to allow semi-tropical gardens to thrive on their meagre soils, the exposed islands off western Brittany are flayed by the winds. Virtually no trees grow on them at all.

Ouessant, known in English as Ushant, is the largest and most westerly fragment of the so-called Molène archipelago. It is an exhilarating island to visit and has two interesting museums. You can also stop off at Molène island. UNESCO has recognized the Molène archipelago as a sea environment of unique significance and as such it is protected as a UNESCO Réserve de la Biosphère.

Molène

This island is both vertically and follicly challenged – some claim its name comes from the Breton *moal enez*, 'bald island', and it has been nicknamed L'Ile Chauve in French. Molène is also minuscule. A local joke went that a cow on Molène could simultaneously stand in one field, graze in a second, and deliver a cowpat in the third.

A British cemetery by the church was made for those who drowned in the sinking of the *Drummond Castle* in 1886. The **Musée du Drummond Castle** (*open daily July–Sept 2.30–6, Oct–June 3–5*) behind the village hall recalls this accident. Moving centenary memorial services were held on the archipelago for the 250 or so passengers and crew, mainly British, who died when the great liner sank in the night, on its way from Cape Town to London. It struck the Pierres Vertes (the Green Rocks between Molène and Ouessant) as most of the passengers were attending the captain's final celebratory ball. The islanders spent several days recovering bodies washed on to the shores and gave them as dignified a burial as was possible. Queen Victoria thanked them by paying for the church clock and donating a chalice made out of gold and precious stones. Various objects recovered from the wreck by divers, are on display.

Ouessant, or Ushant

Ouessant's Maison du Niou Uhella Ecomusée (*see* p.256) crams a lot of information on the island's history and on life on Ushant into two small houses. The island was apparently only isolated from the mainland after the end of the last Ice Age, some 10,000 or so years ago. Small signs of neolithic inhabitants have been found here. And at Mez Notariou in the centre of the island, the ruins of an Iron Age village were unearthed. Moving swiftly from the prehistoric period, Pytheas of Marseille, the Greek navigator and geographer, made a celebrated journey in 330 BC to mark out a new trade route to the tin and amber producers of northern Europe. In his notes, he recorded one island off Armorica that he named Ouxisame, which might have been Ouessant. *Uxisama* is said to have been a Celtic word meaning 'the most elevated'.

In the Dark Ages, the Welsh evangelizer Pol supposedly first put a foot on land across the Channel here. He founded a monastery on the island, possibly in the late 5th century or early 6th century. Lampaul and Pors Paul on Ouessant are both named in memory of this man considered the great Celtic apostle of the Léon (*see* p.239).

From the 13th century to 1589, the island became the property of the bishops of Léon. The Léon bishopric then sold the place to the powerful René de Rieux de Souréac, governor of Brest. He fortified the island. Later, in 1764, Ouessant was bought by the

Crown. Numerous naval battles between French and English ships were fought off Ouessant until the end of the 18th century. The population remained extremely poor down the centuries. Fishing was difficult given the lack of natural harbours, the extremes of the weather and the dangers of the rocky reefs all around. With the discovery over time of great banks of fish to be exploited far from French shores, many of the men of Ouessant would join long-haul fishing expeditions. With Brest so close by, many others also joined the navy.

With their men far away or dead, the women of Ouessant had to tend the land, which was divided up into tiny walled allotments that they hoed, planted and harvested. They took turns too in collecting seaweed, used as fertilizer. Such was the singular position the women of Ouessant held that they even took on the right to propose to men rather than having to wait to be asked.

Major shipwrecks have occurred down the centuries around Ouessant. Towering lighthouses were built in the 19th century to try to improve the warnings to ships. The great Créac'h lighthouse went up in 1862. Today, the food-growing allotments of Ouessant have been abandoned. The other traditional mainstay of the community, sheep, remain, although the tiny Ouessant blackish-brown variety peculiar to the island is very rare. Since the major oil tanker disasters off this coast in the 1960s and 1970s, more measures have been put in place to survey shipping traffic. The radar tower by the Phare du Stiff, 140 metres high, helps in this job. Only about 700 people live on the island year round now, but numbers swell to some 3,000 in summer.

Touring Ouessant

You land on the eastern side of the island, in the protected **Baie du Stiff**. The enormous Phare du Stiff marks the highest point on the island. If you head south from the Baie du Stiff you come to the hamlet of **Penn Alarn**. Some ruins to the east of the village may indicate where the governor's castle once stood; now migrating birds favour this spot. You can take the steep path down to the little port of **Porz Arlan**. To the south you should be able to spot the **Kéréon lighthouse** out on a rock towards Molène. There's a little sandy beach on the Pointe de Penn Alarn, much more tranquil than the beaches on the western side of the island, though the water is supposed to be that much colder.

The advantage of the south coast of Ouessant is that it is much less well known and quieter than the northern one, if less spectacular. However, particularly stirring views open up at the **Penn ar Roc'h** headland. As you reach the southern tip of Ouessant and the **Pointe de Roc'h Hir**, the **Jument lighthouse** dramatically comes into view out to sea. After the Pointe de Roc'h Hir, the coastal path turns to head into the bay of Lampaul, and you come to the main beaches on Ouessant, the **Plage de Prat** and the **Plage de Corz**.

The bustling village of **Lampaul** opens out on to a surprisingly friendly bay. The hotels, restaurants and bike hire shops are clustered close together by the church. In the atmospheric graveyard, you can see how few different family names crop up on a little isolated island such as this – Malgorn seems to be the commonest family name. There's also the monument for the *proëlla* crosses (*see* box, p.256).

Getting There

Make sure always to book **ferry** tickets well in advance, especially during the school holidays, when the demand for places is extremely high.

You can go from Le Conquet and Brest all year round, and from various other nearby resorts in the main tourist season. From Le Conquet, the journey lasts around 30mins to Molène and 1hr 15mins to Ouessant. Times from Brest are roughly 1hr 45mins and 2hrs 30mins respectively. The boats from Brest leave from the Port de Commerce. You can book tickets to go from Le Conquet or Brest with the Compagnie Penn ar Bed (**t** 02 98 80 80 80), which operates all year round. Alternatively, Finist'Mer runs services from April to Oct and also operates from Camaret-sur-Mer (**t** 02 98 27 88 44) and Lanildut (**t** 02 98 04 40 72).

You can also fly from Brest to Ouessant using Finist'Air from Brest-Guipavas **airport** (**t** 02 98 84 64 87).

The easiest way to travel around Ouessant is by **taxi** or **minibus**. Hiring a **bike** is also extremely popular, although **walking** is the only way to appreciate the coast to the full.

Tourist Information

Ouessant: Place de l'Eglise, Lampaul, **t** 02 98 48 85 83, *www.ot-ouessant.fr*.

Market Days

Ouessant: Tuesday, Thursday and Friday.

Where to Stay and Eat

Molène ✉ 29259

For details of B&B accommodation on the island, telephone the village hall on **t** 02 98 07 39 05.

★★Kastell an Daol, quayside, **t** 02 98 07 39 11 (*inexpensive*). A neat and welcoming option, with some bedrooms looking out over the

harbour. The restaurant is the obvious place to eat on Molène (there isn't a wide choice of places), with lobster stew the speciality, while the bar is the social hub of the island. Ask here about boat trips to the rarely discovered, otherworldly little islands of the archipelago, Banneg and Balaneg to the north, and Trielen, Quéménès and Beniguet to the south.

Ouessant ✉ 29242

All of the hotels on the island are situated in the busy village of Lampaul. Accommodation is not luxurious here, but it is generally pleasant enough.

To really get away from the summer crowds, you are advised to try to get a room at one of the B&Bs listed below.

Roch Ar Mor, **t** 02 98 48 80 19, *www.rockarmor. com* (*inexpensive–moderate*). Probably the most attractive of the hotels in Lampaul, well situated and more open than the other options, with views out to sea.

★★Le Fromveur, **t** 02 98 48 81 30 (*inexpensive*). A hotel that distinguishes itself from the crowd by the fact of having achieved 2-star status. The rooms are clean and simple. Half-board is obligatory in season.

La Duchesse Anne, **t** 02 98 48 80 25 (*inexpensive*). A reasonable choice a short distance from the major bustle, looking down on the port.

Hôtel de l'Océan, **t** 02 98 48 80 03 (*inexpensive*). A budget option squeezed into a wedge of a building in the thick of the action. A few of the bedrooms have views on to the sea.

Mme Triolet, Porsguen, **t** 02 98 48 84 06 (*inexpensive*). B&B rooms in a characterful house south of Lampaul.

Mme Dulieu, Route du Créac'h, **t** 02 98 48 86 90 (*inexpensive*). B&B accommodation in a typical house just 50m from the sea.

Crêperie du Stang, Route du Stiff leading out of Lampaul, **t** 02 98 48 80 94 (*inexpensive*). A good alternative to the hotel restaurants, with excellent filled crêpes.

Ouessant's two museums are to be found in the northwestern corner of the island, the busiest part of Ushant after Lampaul, with lots of low stone walls. The little pointed shelters that you can see were for the sheep.

Ouessant's *Proëlla* Ceremony for Sailors Lost at Sea

The *proëlla*, a ceremony unique to Ouessant, held for the bereaved families of those lost at sea, came into existence to help people to somehow come to terms with the pain of having to carry out a funeral without a body. The meaning or root of the word is uncertain. When a Ouessant sailor died on the oceans, the godfather or uncle of the man would generally be told first of the tragedy. He would then go off to fetch a special cross fashioned out of wax and the size of a man's hand. Once night had fallen, the bearer of the cross would go to the house of the wife or parents of the deceased, reciting prayers along the way. He would then solemnly announce that the ceremony of *proëlla* would take place in the house that night. The grieving family would gather around the wax cross, laid like a symbol of the dead man on the table. The cross would be taken to the church the next day, where, after the religious ceremony, it would be kept in a box at the foot of the statue of St Joseph. A priest apparently put a stop to the practice of the *proëlla* in the 1960s.

The Maison du Niou Uhella, the Ecomusée d'Ouessant

Open June–Sept and school hols Tues–Sun 10.30–6.30 (mid-July–Aug also 9pm–11), Oct–May Tues–Sun 2–6.

Conditions were cramped in traditional Ouessant cottages; experience something of their claustrophobia in two that have been turned into this, the first *ecomusée* created in France, celebrating local life. One cottage presents the history of Ouessant, as well as details on the everyday life of the women on the island and the men out to sea. The women's costumes and their agricultural tools are displayed and explained. The more charming cottage retains traditional Ouessant furniture, compactly functional and full of hidden surprises. While there may be nothing radically different from your average mainland Breton peasant family's home of the past centuries, the place has the distinct feel of a ship's cabin, of a family boat moored on the island. Virtually everything shuts tight, as though to guard against the wind that might attack at any moment. The cottage basically consists of one room, the separations formed by the pieces of furniture. But the blue and white paint makes the interior look surprisingly bright and gay. The colours were apparently associated with the Virgin Mary. Much of the furniture was made from wood gathered from shipwrecks. The layout inside the cottage follows a formal pattern, with two distinct sides. To the right lies the *penn lous*, the 'end of the ashes', with fireplace and cooking corner. The *penn brao* is the other, 'beautiful end' of the house, for display.

Centre d'Interprétation des Phares et Balises

Open same hrs as Ecomusée

On the way from the Ecomusée to this unusual lighthouse museum by the massive Créac'h lighthouse, painted with its black and white stripes, you can pass a restored windmill. The island used to be covered with them, practically enough, but most have been left to fall into ruin.

Flashing green and red harbour lights greet you as you enter this substantial museum, dedicated to some of the world's most powerful light beams. The place may blind you a little with its technical explanations of lighthouses, beacons, buoys and other sea markers; take comfort in the aesthetic wonder of many of the objects, displayed in what were the huge electricity-generating rooms required for the lighthouse above.

Just south of here is an **ornithological centre** (*for visits, contact tourist office*). Head on to the enormous bristling mounds of rocks of the **Pointe de Pern**, the island's most westerly point. Another lighthouse, the **Phare de Nividic**, stands out to sea from here.

It's along the **northern coast of the island** that you'll find the most spectacular rock formations of Ouessant. The **Ile de Keller** makes a particularly sensational feature, just detached from the island. On stormy days, Brittany doesn't get more dramatic than this. Beyond is where the seals feel most at home.

Brest

Brest overlooks one of the most beautiful great natural bays in France, the Rade de Brest. For centuries France's main naval harbour, the town has a fascinating history. Taken over by the Nazis in the Second World War, it became one of the Germans' main naval bases, and was consequently smashed to smithereens by Allied bombing.

So Brest's architecture is mainly modern, set on an American-looking grid-plan of streets sloping down to its string of ports. The naval harbour now counts as the second most important such base in France, after Toulon on the Med, but there are still some 17,000 sailors stationed here. Brest is roughly divided in two by the Penfeld river, the naval town stretching to the west, civilian and student Brest to the east. Many tourists are only tempted to venture into the eastern outskirts of town, either to visit Océanopolis, the best aquarium in Brittany, or to take a boat trip around the gorgeous Rade de Brest from the marina nearby. The more daring should venture further west to the museums and harbours in the centre of Brest.

Océanopolis and the Vallon du Stang Alar

Océanopolis (*open daily June–Sept 9–7, Oct–May 9–6*) is an outstanding and entertainingly educational aquarium gently encouraging a little more understanding of marine life and clarifying Brittany's sometimes murky waters. You can follow three main themes: scientists' knowledge of the world's oceans and their latest research into them; navigation and security at sea; and the sea life of the Breton coasts. There is also a kind of tour of the world's water life via the Tropical Pavilion, the Temperate Pavilion (here the Brittany sea is recreated inside a mock-up marine base), and the Polar Pavilion (or the ice of the Arctic and Antarctic).

To get away from the hordes of Océanopolis, head for the peaceful **Conservatoire National de Brest** in the Vallon du Stang Alar (*open daily summer 9–8, rest of year 9–6; greenhouses open July–15 Sept Sun–Thurs 2–5.30, rest of year Sun 9–4.30; guided tours by appointment Mon–Fri year round, call t 02 98 02 46 00*), a gorgeous public garden, set apart from the town in its long, deep valley, and free to visit.

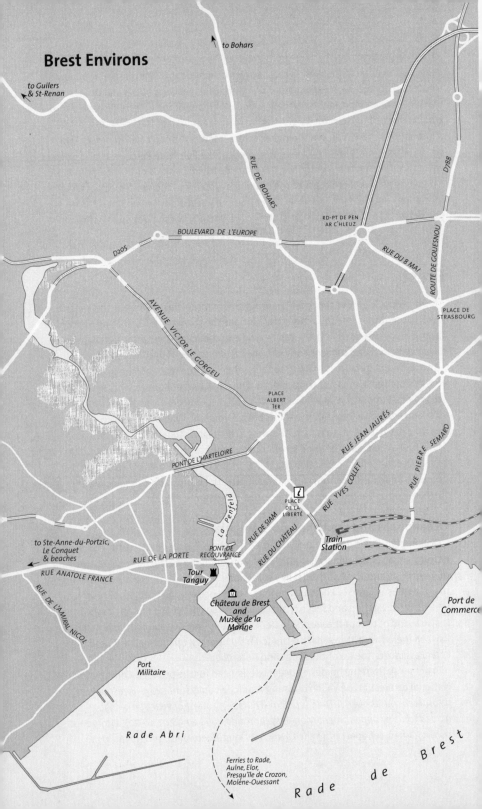

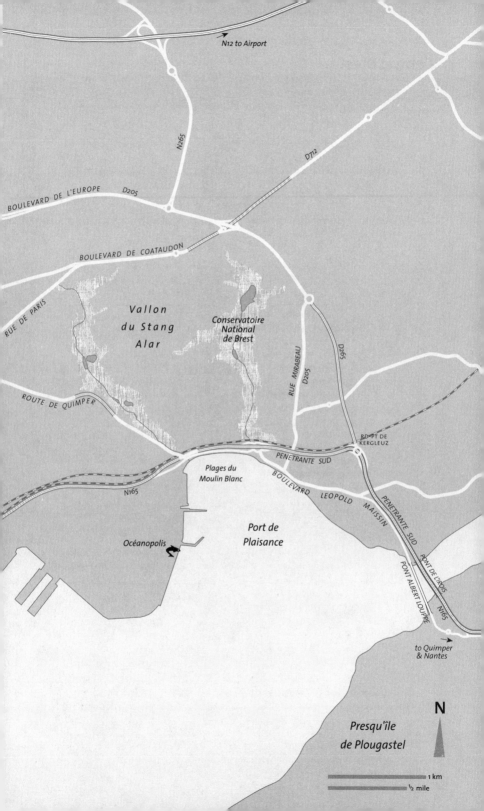

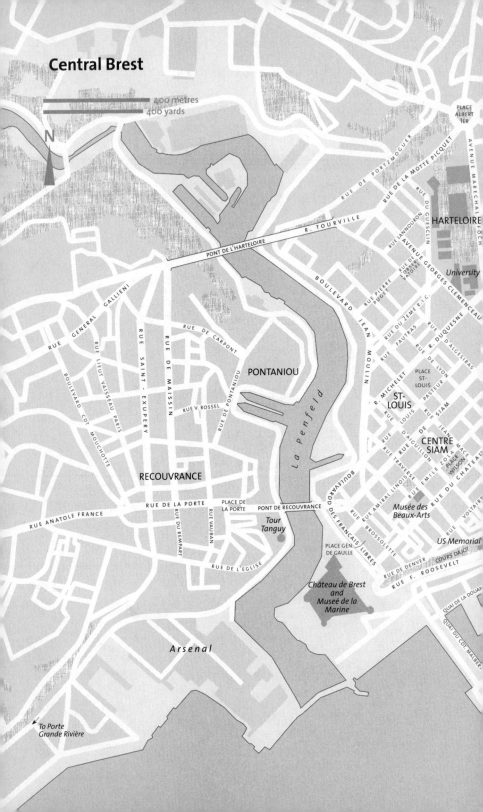

Central Brest

400 mètres
400 yards

N

PLACE
ALBERT
1ER

AVENUE MARECHAL FOCH

RUE DE PORTZMOGUER

RUE DE LA MOTTE PICQUET

RUE DU GUESCLIN

HARTELOIRE

RUE DE PORTZMOGUER

R. TOURVILLE

PONT DE L'HARTELOIRE

RUE LANNOURON

AVENUE GEORGES CLEMENCEAU

University

RUE PIERRE PUGET

RUE DE VOLTAIRE

BOULEVARD JEAN MOULIN

RUE DU 2EME R.I.C.

RUE FAUTRAS

RUE R. DUQUESNE

RUE D'ALGESIRAS

RUE GENERAL GALLIENI

RUE DE CARPONT

PONTANIOU

La Penfeld

RUE MICHELET

PLACE
ST-LOUIS

RUE DE LYON

PASTEUR

RUE LIEUT VAISSEAU PARIS

RUE SAINT - EXUPERY

RUE DE MAISSIN

RUE DE PONTANIOU

RUE SIAM

RUE LOUIS

ST-
LOUIS

RUE V. ROSSEL

RUE D'AIGUILLON

DE

CENTRE
SIAM

RUE JEAN MACE

RUE TRAVERSE

PLACE
WILSON

RUE DU CHATEAU

BOULEVARD COT MOUCHOTTE

RECOUVRANCE

RUE DE LA PORTE

PLACE DE
LA PORTE

BOULEVARD DES FRANCAIS LIBRES

RUE AMIRAL LINOIS

Musée des
Beaux-Arts

RUE EMILE ZOLA

RUE VOLTAIRE

RUE ANATOLE FRANCE

RUE DU REMPART

RUE VAUBAN

PONT DE RECOUVRANCE

Tour
Tanguy

RUE BROSSOLETTE

US Memorial

RUE DE DENVER

COURS DAJOT

RUE F. ROOSEVELT

RUE DE L'EGLISE

PLACE GÉN.
DE GAULLE

Château de Brest
and
Museé de la
Marine

QUAI DE LA DOUANE

Arsenal

QUAI DU COT MALBER

To Porte
Grande Rivière

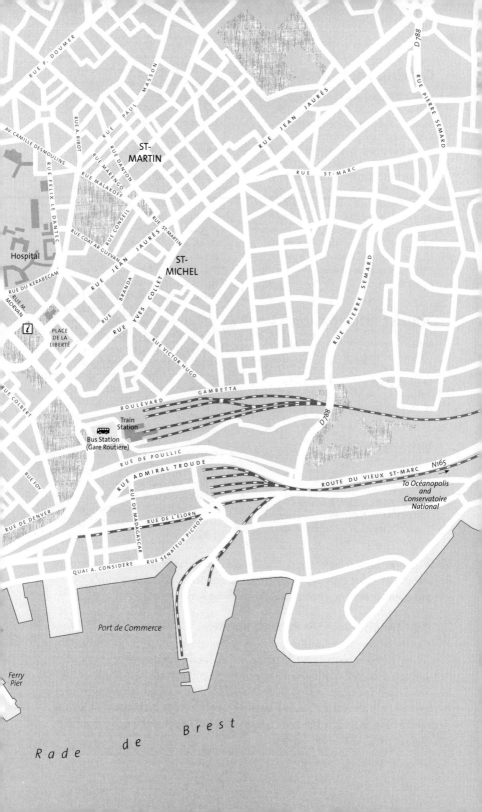

RUE P. DOUMER

AV. CAMILLE DESMOULINS

RUE A. RIBOT

RUE FÉLIX LE DANTEC

RUE MALAKOFF

RUE COAT AR GUEVAN

RUE MARENGO

RUE CONSEIL

RUE PAUL MASSON

RUE DANTON

RUE ST-MARTIN

ST-MARTIN

RUE JEAN JAURÈS

RUE PIERRE SEMARD

D 788

RUE ST-MARC

Hospital

RUE DU KERABECAM

RUE M MORVAN

i

PLACE DE LA LIBERTÉ

RUE COLBERT

RUE JEAN JAURÈS

RUE BRANDA

RUE YVES COLLET

ST-MICHEL

RUE VICTOR HUGO

RUE PIERRE SEMARD

BOULEVARD GAMBETTA

Train Station

Bus Station (Gare Routière)

RUE DE POULLIC

D 788

RUE ADMIRAL TROUDE

RUE FOY

RUE DE MADAGASCAR

RUE DE L'ELORN

RUE SENATEUR PICHON

ROUTE DU VIEUX ST-MARC

N165

To Océanopolis and Conservatoire National

RUE DE DENVER

QUAI A. CONSIDERE

Port de Commerce

Ferry Pier

Rade   de   Brest

Getting There and Around

Brest-Bretagne airport is 11km east of the centre. There are Air France **flights** from London Gatwick. For general airport info in Brittany, call **t** 02 98 32 01 00, for Air France flights, call **t** 0820 820820. Flybe, **t** 0871 700 0535, *www.flybe.com*, flies to Brest from Birmingham, Exeter and Southampton.

Roscoff's **ferry** port, served by Brittany Ferries from Plymouth and Cork and by Irish Ferries from Rosslare (*see* p.56), is 65km north of Brest.

Brest is linked to other major north Breton towns and to Paris by fast TGV **trains**. The journey time from Paris is *c.* 4hrs 20mins.

Buses head off in all directions from the *gare routière*.

Tourist Information

Brest: Place de la Liberté, **t** 02 98 44 24 96, *www.mairie-brest.fr*.

Market Days

There's a Sunday-morning market around the Rue de Lyon, and other markets daily.

Where to Stay

Brest ✉ 29200

***Holiday Inn Garden Court**, 41 Rue Branda, **t** 02 98 80 84 00, *www.holiday-inn.com* (*expensive*). A big chain-owned hotel with spacious rooms in the centre of town.

***Le Belvédère**, 380 Rue Pierre Rivoalon, Le Vernis, Technopôle Brest-Iroise, Ste-Anne-du-Portzic, **t** 02 98 31 86 00, *www.belvedere.brest.com* (*moderate–expensive*). A modern building west of the centre, with spectacular views over the Rade de Brest from its promontory. The rooms are bright and comfortable, the food reliably traditional.

***Océania**, 82 Rue de Siam, **t** 02 98 80 66 66, *www.hotel-sofibra.com* (*moderate–expensive*). A chain hotel with some spacious rooms looking out on to Brest's most famous street, and some surprising decorative details. The cuisine is good.

***La Corniche**, 1 Rue d'Amiral Nicol, Porte Grande Rivière, **t** 02 98 45 12 42, *www.hotel-la-corniche.com* (*moderate*). Very comfortable rooms in an old Breton house north of the Port Militaire. There's a tennis court and a garden with a terrace.

Abalys, 7 Avenue Georges Clemenceau, **t 02 98 44 21 86, *www.abalys.com* (*inexpensive–moderate*). A reasonably priced option with good sea views.

Astoria, 9 Rue Traverse, **t 02 98 80 19 10, *www.hotel-astoria-brest.com* (*inexpensive*). A central choice near the Rue de Siam and close to the harbour, welcoming and clean.

B&B City, 45 Route du Vieux St-Marc, **t 02 98 42 62 62 (*inexpensive*). A hotel by the quay for tours of the Rade de Brest and Ouessant.

Citotel de la Gare, 4 Boulevard Gambetta, **t 02 98 44 47 01, *www.hotelgare.com* (*inexpensive*). A good choice with sea views, handy for the station.

A stream runs through it, supplying a whole chain of small lakes and ponds full of water lilies. Great clumps of elephant-eared gunnera and bamboos, clusters of palms and even of cacti and agaves make for an exotic atmosphere.

Boat Trips out into the Rade de Brest

From the port of Moulin Blanc close to Océanopolis, you can choose between several different boats to get on to the waters of the Rade de Brest. *La Recouvrance*, which is a schooner dating from the early 19th century, is the best-known of the various old-fashioned vessels that carry visitors, but it works out pretty expensive for a day trip aboard it. To book a boat trip, contact An Test, **t** 02 98 33 95 40. Trips up the Rade de Brest in modern-style vessels can be booked through the Société Maritime Azénor, **t** 02 98 41 46 23.

*Hôtel Pasteur, 29 Rue Louis Pasteur,
t 02 98 46 08 73 (*inexpensive*). A decent
budget option – probably the best of the
one-star hotels.

*St-Louis, 6 Rue d'Algésiras, t 02 98 44 23 91
(*inexpensive*). A centrally located option for
the budget-conscious.

Auberge de Jeunesse, Rue de Kerbriant,
Moulin Blanc, by Océanopolis, t 02 98 41 90
41, *www.fuaj.org* (*inexpensive*). First-rate
accommodation for hostellers, set within
a wooded park close to the beaches of
Moulin Blanc.

Eating Out

Le Nouveau Rossini, 22 Rue du Commandant
Drogou, t 02 98 47 90 00 (*expensive*).
One of the finest restaurants in the city,
set in its own quiet grounds to the north
of Place Albert 1er. *Closed 1wk end Aug,
Sun eve and Mon.*

Le Frère Jacques, 15 bis Rue de Lyon, t 02 98 44
38 65 (*moderate–expensive*). A restaurant
with an Art Deco feel and an excellent
reputation. The fish is recommended.

Le Vatel, 23 Rue Fautras, t 02 98 44 51 02
(*moderate–expensive*). An *haute cuisine*
restaurant between the Rue de Lyon
and Rue d'Algésiras. *Closed Sun eve,
Mon and Sat lunch.*

Le Ruffé, 1 bis Rue Yves Collet, t 02 98 46 07 70
(*moderate*). A pleasant, reliable restaurant in
the centre of town, serving French seafood
dishes. *Closed Sun eve.*

La Maison de l'Océan, 2 Quai de la Douane,
down by the Port de Commerce, t 02 98 80
44 84 (*moderate*). A buzzing, popular fresh
seafood restaurant. Come here early to get
an outdoor table on warm days. *Closed Sun
and 2wks Sept.*

La Chaumière, 25 Rue Emile Zola, t 02 98 44
18 60 (*moderate*). A central restaurant
offering simple, good-value dishes.

L'Amour de Pomme de Terre, 23 Rue des Halles,
t 02 98 43 48 51 (*inexpensive–moderate*).
A welcoming place specializing in potato
dishes, by the Place St-Louis.

Ma Petite Folie, t 02 98 42 44 42, Port de
Plaisance du Moulin Blanc (*inexpensive*).
One of the most delightful restaurants in
Brest, set in a former lobster fishing boat not
far from Océanopolis and offering a variety
of excellent seafood dishes. *Closed Sun and
2wks Sept.*

Blé Noir, Vallon du Stang Alar, t 02 98 41 84 66
(*inexpensive*). The best-located crêperie in
the city, east of the centre, at the northern
end of the public gardens,.

Blé Noir Crêperie, Bois de Kéroual, t 02 98 07
57 40 (*inexpensive*). A picturesque crêperie
northwest of city centre towards Guilers.

Crêperie Moderne, 34 Rue Algésiras,
t 02 98 44 44 36 (*inexpensive*). The oldest
crêperie in town, despite the name.

Aux Trois Viandes, 48 Rue Robespierre,
t 02 98 03 55 11 (*inexpensive*). A vegetarian's
nightmare, serving just meat with a
selection of good cheap wine, north of
Place Albert 1er in the Quartier Kerinou.
Closed Mon eve and Sun lunch.

Port de Commerce

West along the shore from Océanopolis, you can drive through the huge docks of
the **commercial port**, some of its vast berths built for supertankers. The port side with
its bars and restaurants is popular with locals in the evening. In July and August, the
Jeudis du Port are free music concerts every Thursday evening. Up behind the port is a
minute portion of US territory, 424 square metres, with a pink granite US war memorial.

Château de Brest and Musée de la Marine

Open Wed–Mon April–Sept 10–6.30, Oct–mid-Dec, Feb and March 10–12 and 2–6.

The architecture of the Château de Brest has been greatly altered since the famed
chronicler Jean Froissart, writing in the 14th century, claimed that it was one of the
largest castles in the world, but this fort is still daunting. Most of it is occupied by the

French maritime authorities, but the front section houses Brest's maritime museum, mainly devoted to the great shipbuilding tradition here, though certain major events in the history of the castle and the town are told along the way, as you go from tower to tower and along the ramparts. Astonishingly, the bottom of the walls formed part of an impressive defensive castrum built here as far back as the 3rd century.

Musée des Beaux-Arts

Open Mon and Wed–Sat 10–12 and 2–6, Sun 2–6.

Some of the fabulously detailed old school paintings of Brest at this museum of fine arts give you further fine views of how the town looked in its heyday. But this museum is best known for its Symbolist collection, notably works by the Pont-Aven School. The lush greens and yellows of Paul Sérusier's *Les Blés verts au Pouldu*, painted in 1890, make it one of his most appealing works. Emile Bernard's depiction of the pink rocks of St-Briac show off the typical *cloisonné* effects of the school. The painting adopted as the symbol of the museum is Georges Lacombe's view of the cliffs at Camaret-sur-Mer. These take on vaguely human shapes against a bilious yellow sea. Striking as this work may be, it is rather harder to stomach than the canvases of the Pont-Aven artists. You will also find quite an engrossing collection of paintings here showing Breton religious processions.

Up the Rue de Siam and Across the Penfeld into Naval Brest

Walk up the **Rue de Siam**, Brest's most famous street, with its big modern black granite fountains streaming with water. In 1686 the town witnessed the arrival of one of the earliest exotic foreign visits to France, when ambassadors sent by the king of Siam (now Thailand) to visit King Louis XIV's court landed here. They carried with them the most precious of letters, engraved on gold. The name of the Rue de Siam commemorates the visit. The way leads up to the **Place de la Liberté** with the town hall. Here you really feel as if you've arrived in 1950s urban America. Behind the Hôtel de Ville, the Rue Jean Jaurès leads up to the **Quartier St-Martin**, where you can go in search of a few traces of pre-war Brest.

Cross the river by the massive Pont de Recouvrance back at the start of the Rue de Siam and you look at the **Tour Tanguy**, which has been turned into a little museum on Brest's mainly vanished history. Further west, the shore down from the centre of town is dominated by the military quarters and military boats, which you won't be allowed to go and see unless you can show a French passport. France's nuclear aircraft carrier, the *Charles de Gaulle*, has a home in the water here.

Elorn Calvaries and *Enclos Paroissiaux*

The most distinctive and well-known art of Brittany, the religious art of the *enclos paroissiaux*, or parish church enclosures, flowered particularly finely in the stretch of land between Brest and Morlaix in the 16th and 17th centuries. A distinct sense of rivalry became evident between the parishes around the Elorn valley.

The Traditional Breton Calvary Scenes

The Breton calvary scenes generally concentrate on the best-known stories of the gospels. They often begin with the Annunciation of the virgin birth to Mary. The Visitation might follow, when Mary goes to see her cousin Elizabeth, also expecting a divinely inspired birth, that of John the Baptist. Sometimes Mary's marriage to Joseph is added in. Following the highly picturesque scenes of the Nativity, the Adoration of the Magi, and the flight to Egypt (occasionally Jesus's circumcision is also shown), Jesus grows up fast.

The main focus of the calvaries is on the harrowing stages of Christ's crucifixion following his entry into Jerusalem. The Last Supper is always a central theme, with Christ's washing of the apostles' feet. His praying in the garden of Gethsemane often features too. Then comes his arrest, maybe his appearance, bound, before the high priest Annas, his encounter with the Roman Pilate, and his flagellation. The painful way of the cross is dwelt on in great detail. Crowned with thorns, Christ is helped along with his burden. The veil of Saint Veronica, which she offered Christ on the way to his crucifixion and which retains the imprint of his face, carved in low relief on the calvary stone cloths, makes for a striking additional scene.

Christ's crucifixion always occupies the high point of the central cross. Generally the two thieves are also represented, much more contorted figures on neighbouring calvaries. The Pietà, or grieving mother of Christ mourning her dead son slumped on her lap, conveys the most powerful emotion along with the entombment scene, Christ's body laid out in front of a group of mourners, the tears of the onlookers sometimes actually thickly carved on the faces. Christ may descend into limbo before the image of hope ends the story, the resurrected Christ stepping out of his tomb.

Why did the Elorn communities build some of the most sumptuous and showy of Breton churches? The main reason was apparently their commercial success, notably in selling cloth to England. This was shipped out from the river ports, such as Landerneau down the Elorn, or Morlaix just northeast of it. This trade really took off after the end of the Hundred Years War. Trade also prospered with Flanders, whose artists particularly influenced stained glass in the region, and the Iberian countries, whose merchants shipped Breton cloth to South America in large quantities.

There's a well-trodden Breton art history pilgrimage you can make to a series of *enclos paroissiaux* along the Elorn. The path goes from Plougastel-Daoulas south of Brest to St-Thégonnec, close to Morlaix (or vice versa). The journey described below takes you to some smaller art-packed Elorn churches as well as to the best known.

Plougastel-Daoulas and its Strawberry Peninsula

The peninsula of Plougastel-Daoulas is by far the most attractive natural area along this religious route, though the town of **Plougastel-Daoulas** was badly damaged by Allied bombing in the Second World War. Its church had largely to be rebuilt, hence the funky neo-Gothic steeple aping the old Breton style but made out of cement.

The famous **calvary** to one side of the church is the main attraction. Covered with 181 sculpted figures, it too was damaged by the bombs, notably its three crosses. The calvary was restored, thanks in good part to the concern of a US officer with a strong interest in art history, John D. Skilton. The calvary of Plougastel-Daoulas counts among the most substantial in Brittany. It was built between 1602 and 1604, after the parish had suffered terribly from the plague in 1598. Some say that this is a *kroaziou ar vossen* (a plague calvary), as indicated by the bubo-like protrusions on the crosses. It is certainly one of the most engrossing calvaries in Brittany. The light colour of the platform, of yellowish limestone from Logonna (the peninsula south of that of Plougastel-Daoulas) contrasts with the dark grain of the Kersanton stone used for the sculptures; the human figures are rather stiltedly refined but sport elaborate costumes; the donkeys and horses are delightful. The base is a relatively complex structure, with four arches that you can walk under sticking out diagonally from the main platform. A staircase leads to the top of the calvary platform, from where preachers could give their sermons.

Other Attractions of the Plougastel-Daoulas Peninsula

There's a small, modern **Musée de la Fraise** (*open Easter–Sept daily 2–6*) in the town for those who would like to know more about the reputed strawberries of Plougastel-Daoulas. The museum also has displays on the little chapels across the peninsula and the various healing powers of their fountains, as well as local costumes and local traditions. This peninsula has often been compared to a hand reaching into the waters of the Rade de Brest; have a look at a regional map to see what you think. Most tourists bypass it because it doesn't have any beaches or resorts, but its maze of badly signposted country lanes are a joy to get lost in.

Patron Saint of Wales Born to Ste Nonne in Brittany?

The 6th-century Melarie, nicknamed Nonnita (the little nun) or Nonne when she took the veil, was the daughter of Brecan, a Welsh chieftain, and of Dinam, an Irish princess. The Breton version of the story has it that one day, as Nonne was crossing a Welsh forest, she encountered a northern Welsh prince. This evil man supposedly raped her and made her pregnant. The shamed Nonne sailed off to Brittany to give birth to her son, Divy (Dewi in Welsh, David in English). She came to Dirinon, the place now named after her. The rock by which she gave birth to her baby softened to form a cradle for the newborn child. A fountain also sprang up, enabling Nonne to baptize her son. She remained here for the rest of her life as a recluse. Divy, the Breton story continues, went back to Wales, where he was taken in by his father. Divy became a great defender of the Christian faith, a celebrated Celtic evangelizer. Canonized in 1120, he was made patron saint of Wales.

Welsh versions of the life of Ste Nonna differ somewhat. Rhygyfarch, writing in the 11th century, wrote that Nonna was a nun at Ty Gwyn near Whitesand Bay in Dyfed. She was seduced by a prince called Sant and as a consequence gave birth to Dewi or David. She went off to settle at Altarnon in Cornwall for a time, where a church and well would be built in her honour. She then travelled to Brittany where she died.

Getting Around

Local **trains** running between Brest and Morlaix make stops at Landerneau, La Roche-Maurice, Landivisiau, Guimiliau and St-Thégonnec. A few of the fast TGV trains from Paris to Brest stop at Landivisiau and Landerneau.

To get to some of the lesser-known *enclos* by public transport you'll need to ask at the tourist office about the **bus** services from Brest or Morlaix.

Tourist Information

Antenne de Plougastel-Daoulas:
Place du Calvaire, **t** 02 98 40 34 98.
Landerneau: Pont de Rohan, **t** 02 98 85 13 09, *www.tourisme-landerneau-daoulas.fr.*
Landivisiau: 14 Avenue Foch, **t** 02 98 68 33 33, *www.otpaysdelandivisiau.com.*

Market Days

Plougastel-Daoulas: second and last Thursdays in the month; there's also a small Saturday market.
Daoulas: Sunday.
Landerneau: Tuesday, Friday and Saturday.
Landivisiau: Wednesday.

Where to Stay and Eat

Plougastel-Daoulas ✉ **29470**
Le Chevalier de Lauberlac'h,
5 Rue Mathurin Thomas, **t** 02 98 40 54 56 *(moderate–expensive)*. A charming restaurant with wood panelling, a coffered ceiling and a little garden where you can take an apéritif. The cuisine is quite refined.
La Belle Epoque, 18 Rue de l'Eglise, **t** 02 98 40 23 14 *(moderate)*. Good, simple fare.
An Ty Coz, Pointe de l'Armorique, **t** 02 98 40 56 47 *(inexpensive)*. A locals' bar-cum-crêperie in a pretty granite house on the way down to the little port of Ty Floc'h.

Daoulas ✉ **29460**
La Ferme du Cloître, Hameau du Cras, **t** 02 98 25 80 56 *(inexpensive)*. A lovely place to come for a relaxing meal of crêpes or for a Breton tea after a strenuous tour of the abbey.

Hôpital-Camfrout ✉ **29460**
Moulin de Poulhanol, on the D770 out of the village towards Le Faou, **t** 02 98 20 02 10 *(inexpensive)*. A delight for those on tight budgets, with basic rooms set in a mill by the bay of Kérouse. The place is run by friendly young people and has a crêperie.

A Welsh Detour to Dirinon

Head up the Elorn along the south bank, taking the D29 from Plougastel-Daoulas to Landerneau. On the way you could branch off to Dirinon, which is set on a height and boasts lovely views around. The charming church is topped by one of those Breton steeples that looks absurdly top-heavy. Above a Gothic accolade arch you will see a statue of Ste Nonne, a figure of vital importance in Welsh history and much venerated in Brittany, said to have died here in the 6th century (*see* box, opposite). The Dirinon church interior is highly decorated. Ceiling paintings along the nave, dating from the Ancien Régime, depict male saints to one side and female saints to the other. Ste Nonne has pride of place in the procession. Her tomb effigy lies in a chapel in the cemetery.

The Abbey and Village of Daoulas

Wend your way a short distance south from Dirinon to the famous abbey of Daoulas, set in a slopeside village full of religious edifices. This village lies up the deep estuary of the Daoulas river, which flows into the Rade de Brest. *Daoulas* became a name given to a reputed, particularly fine Breton cloth produced here, which merchants came to buy from far and wide.

Landerneau ✉ 29800

★★Le Clos du Pontic, Rue du Pontic (outside the centre, up on the southern slope of the Elorn), t 02 98 21 50 91, *www.clos-pontic.com* (*moderate*). A hotel charmingly hidden behind old walls, with modern rooms and a lovely garden.

L'Amandier, 55 Rue de Brest, t 02 98 83 10 89 (*moderate*). A stylish leather-clad bar decorated in discreet mushroom tones, located 500m from the centre of town on the road to Brest and serving classic Breton food such as warm fish terrine with a langoustine coulis.

Restaurant de la Mairie, 9 Rue de la Tour d'Auvergne, t 02 98 85 01 83 (*inexpensive–moderate*). A quayside restaurant opposite the town hall, offering good-value, reliable menus aimed at a family market. *Closed Tues eve.*

Hostellerie du Bon Conseil, Rue des Déportés, t 02 98 85 07 90 (*inexpensive*). A basic eating option for bargain hunters.

La Roche-Maurice ✉ 29800

Auberge du Vieux Château, 4 Grand-Place, t 02 98 20 40 52 (*inexpensive–moderate*). A good-value country inn. Advance booking is essential. *Closed lunch.*

Crêperie-Grill Milin an Elorn, Kerigeant, along the D712 from Landerneau to Landivisiau, t 02 98 20 41 46 (*inexpensive*). Good crêpes by an old watermill on the river Elorn.

Lampaul-Guimiliau ✉ 29400

★★Hôtel de l'Enclos, t 02 98 68 77 08 (*inexpensive*). A functional modern hotel by the church.

Ty-Dreux, near Loc-Eguiner-St-Thégonnec ✉ 29410

Ty-Dreux, t 02 98 78 08 21 (*inexpensive*). Delightful rural B&B rooms in a former weaver's village.

St-Thégonnec ✉ 29410

★★★Auberge St-Thégonnec, 6 Place de la Mairie, t 02 98 79 61 18, *www.aubergesaintthegonnec. com* (*moderate*). An unexciting option from the outside, with comfortable rooms and a plush restaurant with high-quality cooking.

Ar Prespital Coz, 18 Rue Lividic, t 02 98 79 45 62 (*inexpensive*). Six spacious B&B rooms in a former priest's house.

Moulin de Kerlaviou, outside the village towards Landivisiau, t 02 98 79 60 57 (*inexpensive*). B&B rooms in a little farm set by a watermill on a river.

The **abbey church** still retains some of its lovely Romanesque lines, although it has been much altered through time. The west front and the nave look typical of the grand religious architecture of the late 12th century, and the rounded ends of the apse also date from the Romanesque period.

In 1985 most of the abbey buildings were bought by the *département* of the Finistère. A major Breton cultural centre was created, and since then important annual ethnic exhibitions have been held here. Enter the **former abbey** to see the exhibitions and cloisters (*open daily June–6 Oct 10–7, rest of year 10–12 and 1.30–5.30*). The exhibitions, which are organized with the help of internationally reputed archaeologists and ethnographers, have won wide acclaim.

The small **Romanesque cloister** is unique in Brittany, the only one to have survived from its period, although it was much restored during the 19th century. The stone, from Kersanton, is made to look quite delicate, single and double columns holding up the arches, the capitals decorated with foliage. The square tops of these capitals are carved with a pleasing variety of Romanesque geometrical patterns. These patterns appear again on the rare **Romanesque wash basin**. A medicinal **herb garden** has been laid out above the cloister, the neat squares planted with both aesthetics and health in mind.

Wander down into the village to see the 16th-century **oratory of Notre-Dame des Fontaines** and the **Breton fountain**. Several statues adorn the interior of the oratory with its openwork façade. The fountain, with three basins perhaps recalling the Trinity, is watched over by a statue of the Virgin and St Catherine of Siena offering her heart to the Lord. The waters were supposed to cure illnesses of the eye and sterility.

Just a few kilometres inland from Daoulas you might go in search of the strangest of Breton calvaries, by the chapel of **Notre-Dame-de-Lorette**, southeast of Irvillac. This experimental piece was made in 1644, seemingly copying the curved forms more commonly adopted by goldsmiths. Also of interest at the chapel is a most touching naïve low relief carving of Christ's Entombment.

Ignored Peninsulas West of Daoulas

These peninsulas provided Breton sculptors with their precious **Kersanton stone**, a dark granite that was relatively easy to carve and that also resisted the elements better than others. It became the favoured medium of Breton stone sculptors from the mid 15th to the mid 17th centuries.

It's quite easy to get lost on the peninsula of **Logonna-Daoulas** with its tiny lanes. Views open up on to the Rade de Brest. Moulin-Mer, just south of the pretty village of Logonna-Daoulas, is a particularly enchanting spot with its tidal mill. This area actually provided masons not with Kersanton granite but with the distinctive Logonna yellow stone to be seen in the local architecture and at Daoulas.

The unappealingly named but prettily located **Hôpital-Camfrout** lies at the bottom of another river estuary and just within the Parc Régional Naturel d'Armorique. A little detour from Hôpital-Camfrout takes you to the picturesque **Ile Tibidy**, which hasn't been an island for a good long time now. It looks out south to the site of Landévennec on the Crozon peninsula, where the most famous Breton abbey of the Dark Ages was constructed (*see* p.282).

Pencran

Back close to the Elorn, the church route leads from Dirinon to Landerneau via Pencran. Again on a height, the church of Pencran is set in a pretty *enclos paroissial*, mostly built in the 16th century. A simple calvary with various branches shows a little figure, arms raised, above Christ; it acts as a symbol of his departing soul.

The church steeple rises in Renaissance fashion, but the main doorway is Gothic in style. Wonderfully elaborate carvings decorate the outside of it. In the archivolts, you can make out scenes from the Old Testament, from the temptation of Adam and Eve to Noah gathering grapes and then falling into his shameful drunken sleep. A wealth of beam carvings give interest to the interior, the characterful heads of strange men looking down from between foliage motifs.

Landerneau

Before continuing on the rural religious trail of *enclos paroissiaux*, you might like to head down to the Elorn and the historic town of Landerneau. The place became a prosperous river port in centuries past, as you can see from a visit to the centre. All manner of produce could be shipped in and out of this protected inland harbour just 10 kilometres from the Rade de Brest by river. During the Revolution, Landerneau was briefly made capital of the newly formed *département* of Finistère. In the 20th century, Edouard Leclerc, nicknamed the Grocer of Landerneau, created one of the largest supermarket chains in France, becoming a household name.

Historic Landerneau has preserved a few lovely houses, most obviously some of those built on the spectacular **Rohan bridge**. It was Jean de Rohan who had the bridge built in 1510, sturdily enough to carry the weight of the beautiful chaos of houses constructed upon it. They are still lived in – a rarity in Europe. Some further grand blocks line the Quai de Léon on the north bank and the Quai de Cornouaille to the south. Yachts moor along the banks. On the south side you might like to go and pay your respects to Thomas of Canterbury, to whom the Renaissance-style Eglise St-Thomas is dedicated.

Welsh visitors to Brittany might like to make a special detour a few kilometres west to **St-Divy**, dedicated to the Breton version of Dewi or David. His life story was painted on the church ceiling in the 17th century, and one of the statues in the church represents him. The 1552 calvary outside bears the arms of the Rohan family.

La Roche-Maurice

Continue inland up the wooded Elorn valley from Landerneau and you soon come to the pretty site of La Roche-Maurice. The **ruins of a medieval fort** stand out on a bald spur here. You can clamber up to them to get fine views down on to the valley. The 16th-century **church of St-Yves** below is best known for its rood screen. The barrel vault is also heavily painted. Much more elegantly, 16th-century stained glass lights up the choir end, showing scenes from Christ's Passion and his resurrection. The Rohans financed both the church and the windows.

Outside in the parish enclosure, the ossuary of 1639 was built in Renaissance style. Look out, above an outer font, for *l'Ankou*, the Breton Grim Reaper, shown here as a mockery of Cupid with his arrow of love; here you know that the arrow is deadly. The revered St Yves puts in a more reassuring appearance on the exterior of the ossuary. As ever, he is settling a dispute between a rich man and a pauper.

La Martyre

The *enclos paroissial* of La Martyre (located to the south of La Roche-Maurice) reserves a memorable welcome for you along a lovely old village street. This little place gained enough riches to pay for such a magnificent church through its popular annual textile fair, to which English, Irish and Flemish traders once came. The church feels almost walled in here. You enter the parish enclosure under an elaborate triumphal arch. The delightful crooked Flamboyant Gothic church porch beyond is one of the oldest of its type in Brittany, dating from the late 15th century. The best piece of sculpture on it represents the Nativity, although unfortunately Mary's baby Jesus has disappeared from the scene. The accolade arch is covered with a mass of Gothic sculptures. Under the porch, the statues of the apostles you can see were added in the 16th century.

A Renaissance ossuary stands next to the porch. Here the elaborate warning that death awaits us all is inscribed in Breton. The sinister caryatid figure on this little building certainly shows foreign influences; this naked-breasted, emaciated woman has a stiff skirt wrapped around her legs like the bandages of an Egyptian mummy.

The stained glass in the main window is sumptuous, showing the crucifixion of Christ. The influence of an elegant northern European style shines through. The wooden arch carrying a crucifixion scene, the carved stringbeams in the north chapel (in particular the ploughing scene and that of a funeral procession), and the carved panels set around the apse count among the sculptural riches inside the church.

The *enclos paroissial* of Sizun a short distance southeast of La Martyre is covered in the section on the Monts d'Arrée (*see* p.273).

To the East of the Elorn Valley

The *enclos paroissiaux* to the east of the Elorn valley around Landivisiau and St-Thégonnec do not stand in such picturesque locations as those along the Elorn. Here you need to concentrate on the religious art to appreciate these places.

Lampaul-Guimiliau

Lampaul-Guimiliau, with its houses built of thin layers of schist, has all the charm that nearby Landivisiau lacks. In Lampaul-Guimiliau, the **Maison du Patrimoine** (*open July and Aug daily 10–1 and 2.30–6.30, Sept–June Mon–Fri 2.30–6.30*) contains a collection of Breton costumes and furniture. But once again it's the *enclos paroissial* that is the focus of attention. It isn't a rival to the more exuberant Guimiliau, but inside the church shows off an extraordinarily rich series of six 17th-century **retables**. The most famous one depicts stages in the life of St John the Baptist below some tender 16th-century stained-glass figures caught in the tracery of a Gothic window.

Looking down the Gothic nave, you'll be struck by the organ perched on stilts and the remarkable *poutre de gloire*, the main crossbeam, with a polychrome crucifixion scene rising from it. As to the baldaquin-covered baptismal font, it looks rustically entertaining, almost vulgarly bright. Among the many other artistic features of the interior, one of the most famous is the Entombment scene. The Italianate figures were carved from Loire limestone, the fine work of Antoine Chavagnac, from 1676.

The ossuary too contains a retable, covered with saints associated with the plague. The plague of commercialization has struck here, however, with the ossuary now serving as a shop, selling some particularly ugly statues.

Guimiliau

Two naïve riders greet you at the arch leading into Guimiliau's *enclos paroissial*, perhaps the most charming of the major Léon ones, with some of the most intriguing, lively and confusing **calvary** scenes. The calvary figures are so blotched with lichen it looks as though they've been struck by some rampant disease. The structure of this substantial setpiece, made in the 1580s, is relatively complex, like that at Plougastel-Daoulas for which it served as something of a model. One of the calvary arches has a font in it. The statue of St Pol of Léon stands on a kind of altar under the main classical arch. And a stairway leads to the top of the platform.

From the Annunciation scene, the Virgin depicted with the symbolic lily of purity, to the monster swallowing sinners destined for hell, the detail and expressions of the carvings are engrossing and more full of life than on any other Breton calvary. In the depiction of the Last Supper, for example, several of the apostles peer round from behind Christ's shoulder to be able to see what's going on at the table – and there awaits the roast. In fact most of the apostles appear distinctly more interested in the thought of a good feast than in religious matters.

The ossuary has been turned into a shop selling wooden statues among other things. Its retable is dedicated to Ste Anne. The other unusual building tacked on to the main church with its rounded little roofs is the 17th-century sacristy. The church itself, essentially Flamboyant Gothic in style, has had other features added to it. The south porch, built at the start of the 17th century, fuses late Gothic and Renaissance styles. Elaborate carving continues as a theme within the church. The richly wrought organ, an early example of the art dating from 1677, sticks out on stilts. The baptismal baldaquin, from the same period, rests on twisting Baroque pillars.

St-Thégonnec

St-Thégonnec boasts the most grandiose of the Léon's *enclos paroissiaux*, which is rivalled in Brittany only by the one at Pleyben in Cornouaille (*see* p.279). Its elements were commissioned in the second half of the 16th century and the early 17th. Famous for its calvary, St-Thégonnec's was one of the last major ones made, dating from 1610. The saint Thégonnec is said to have sailed across the sea to Ireland to become bishop of Armagh later in life. Here he is presented with an ox and a deer below him. Several Breton saints are closely associated with oxen, ploughing and the fertility of the soil.

Set in the centre of the village, the *enclos* isn't particularly well situated, although its cluster of architectural elements is quite imposing. You enter via a chunky Renaissance gateway, constructed in 1587 by the builders of the Château de Kerjean (*see* p.242). This gateway reads like a lesson in Renaissance motifs, with its niches, shells, orbs and ornate scrolls, all topped by lanterns. A depiction of the Annunciation has been added into the corners.

The **calvary** outside is relatively simple compared with that at Guimiliau, with just one layer of scenes below the crosses. The story of Christ is limited pretty well to the time from his arrest to his resurrection. The costumes show some fashions of the time, the rounded hats standing out. In certain scenes of the way of the cross, several of the guards show off bulging codpieces. Their barbaric cruelty is shown in their monstrously grinning faces.

On to the **church** itself. The end belltower of 1563 is the only remnant of an earlier, Gothic-style church. The other much more imposing tower went up in the first part of the 17th century, apparently to try to compete with the great Renaissance tower that had recently been erected at Pleyben. The elaborate riot of carving inside was badly damaged by a disastrous fire in the late 1990s, but a good deal has been restored.

Into the Monts d'Arrée

Other Bretons were long suspicious of the people of the isolated Monts d'Arrée, an eerie ridge of hills east inland from the Rade de Brest. In centuries past, this area was considered a kind of no-man's-land between the county of the Léon to the north and Cornouaille to the south. You may read tales of Monts d'Arrée priests in times past performing exorcisms. Or you may hear of religious festivals that turned into pagan rituals. Even the locals claimed that the gates to hell lay hidden within the forbidding peat bog of Yeun Elez. But nowadays the hills, and especially their southern slopes, seem particularly appealing and peaceful, with some of the prettiest chapels in Brittany scattered along their slopes.

Along the Northern Side of the Monts d'Arrée

Sizun continues the theme of the *enclos paroissiaux* of the previous touring section, only this *enclos* has no proper calvary. But the very substantial triumphal gateway by which you enter the religious enclosure somewhat makes up for it, with a simple crucifixion scene added on top. The splendid ossuary dates from the 1580s, like that gateway. It offers the cheering sight of the apostles under their Renaissance niches, neatly separated by channelled pilasters. The curious caryatids and atlantes carved between the windows below further reflect the Renaissance influence that inspired the sculptors here. The church of St-Sullian itself dates almost entirely from the 16th and 17th centuries, except for the steeple tower and porch, added for show in the 18th century. The interior is very noticeably more sober than the rich churches to the north.

The **Maison de la Rivière, de l'Eau et de la Pêche** (*open daily July and Aug 10–7, June and Sept 10–12 and 2–5.30; at other times, call t 02 98 68 86 33*) in the Vergraon mill just northwest of Sizun informs the public about the waters of the Monts d'Arrée.

A handful of kilometres southeast of Sizun lies the **Drennec reservoir**, formed when a dam was built across the river Elorn here in 1982. The **Maison du Lac**, a modern centre, is an annexe of the Maison de la Rivière. It can tell you something about the creation of the lake, about trout farming, and about the now-rare Breton salmon. The **Menez Kador**, or Tuchen Gador, in the background to the south is just about the highest peak in Brittany, at 384 metres.

Along the D764 between Sizun and Commana, the **Moulins de Kerouat** (*open July and Aug daily 11–7; June Mon–Fri 10–6, Sat and Sun 2–6; mid-Mar–May, Sept and Oct Mon–Fri 10–6, Sun 2–6*), or watermills of Kerouat, are now home to a charming museum on the traditions of the rural community in these parts.

Now a quiet village on its hilltop, with the Roc Trévézel peak in the background, **Commana** has a fairly elaborate *enclos paroissial* – proof that not all the parishes in the Monts d'Arrée were eternally poverty-stricken. The impressive spire went up in 1592. Inside the church, the most famous piece of ornate decoration is the Ste Anne retable of 1682. Two large statues, one of the Virgin, one of Ste Anne, are shown seated in a riot of Breton-Baroque decoration.

Head up to the dinosaur's back of the **Roc Trévézel**. Just a short walk along this rugged crest might tempt you into trying a longer hike along the 40-kilometre **Chemin des Crêtes**, which takes you through heather and myrtle tracks, past sharp slices of slate schist sticking viciously out of the ground. From up on the heights of the Monts d'Arrée, views open out to the north on to the steeples and patchwork of fields of the Léon. To the south, the Montagne St-Michel-de-Brasparts looks satisfyingly rotund and impressively barren, with just a small chapel placed at the top. The St-Michel reservoir and disused Brennilis nuclear power station lie below. The Roc'h Trédudon stands out to the east.

Along the Southern Side of the Monts d'Arrée

Scrignac, southeast of the Rochers du Cragou, is home to the **Maison de la Faune Sauvage et de la Chasse**, presenting the flora and fauna of the Monts d'Arrée, as well as hunting. **Berrien** is regarded as something of a capital of Breton wrestling – an international week of **Celtic wrestling** takes place every second year around Easter.

Huelgoat and its Giant Boulders

Some have said that it is due to a show of strength by the Celtic giant god Gawr that the narrow, secretive valley at Huelgoat became so strewn with giant granite boulders. Others have blamed a grumpy Gargantua for throwing down these rocks in a fit of pique at being served bad Breton gruel. And another story blames a war of projectiles between the villages north and south of Huelgoat, Berrien and Plouyé for the chaos – their war catapults weren't strong enough to hurl these vast cannonballs the full 12 kilometres. The boulders lie roughly at the start of the valley of the river Argent ('Silver') as it comes down from Huelgoat's lake. The pretty little town is set by this lake, which was only created in the 18th century to help exploit a silver-bearing lead mine down below in the valley. The enormous mossy rocks date back to the mists of time. There is of course a natural explanation for them – where the granite was more thickly grained it took longer to erode and these tougher boulders were thus left in strange contorted shapes along the river bank.

Visit the picturesque **Moulin du Chaos** by the bridge first. From the mill you can then follow the *sentier pittoresque* into the dappled valley. You can descend into the **Grotte du Diable** ('Devil's Grotto') with the aid of little rungs in the rock. Another secretive little low path takes you to the **Ménage de la Vierge**, where certain rocks are supposed to have been carved into household shapes catering to the Virgin's needs; you're supposed to be able to make out the Virgin's bed, the cradle for Christ and a cauldron. The **Roche Tremblante** is an enormous boulder that even a child can get to move. There's also an outdoor theatre and a crêperie down in this wacky valley.

Celtic men from the Iron Age appear to have gathered around Huelgoat. You might fancy a walk further out of town to the **Camp d'Artus**, one of the few vestiges of the pre-Roman Armorican tribes that you can see in Brittany. Later, legend claimed that this was one of King Arthur's camps.

Tourist Information

Office de Tourisme du Pays de Landivisiau, des Enclos et des Monts d'Arrée, 14 Avenue Foch, 29400 Landivisiau, t 02 98 68 33 33, www.ot-paysdelandivisiau.com.

Pays d'Accueil Touristique du Centre Finistère, 13 Rue de l'Eglise, 29190 Pleyben, t 02 98 26 60 25, pays.du.centre.finistere@wanadoo.fr. Covers the southern section.

Sizun: 3 Rue de l'Argoat, t 02 98 68 88 40.
Huelgoat: Moulin du Chaos, t 02 98 99 72 32.
Brasparts: Place des Monts d'Arrée, t 02 98 81 47 06, www.yeun-elez.com.

Market Days

Sizun: 1st Friday of the month.
Huelgoat: 1st and 3rd Thursdays of the month.
St-Rivoal: 1st day of the month in April, July, Aug and Sept.

Where to Stay and Eat

This is a good area for an unpretentious, inexpensive rural holiday.

Plounéour-Ménez ✉ 29410

Le Roc'h Trédudon, 11 Place de l'Eglise, t 02 98 78 01 16 (inexpensive). An unassuming hotel and restaurant popular with walkers.

Commana ✉ 29450

M. and Mme Lancien, Kerverous, t 02 98 78 92 87 (inexpensive). A B&B in a very pretty 18th-century weaver's cottage.

Scrignac ✉ 29640

Hôtel Lesénéchal, t 02 98 78 23 13 (inexpensive). Very simple rooms and quite elaborate cuisine (moderate) with a good reputation.

Trédudon-le-Moine, northwest of Berrien ✉ 29690

Ferme-auberge de Porz Kloz, t 02 98 99 61 65 (inexpensive–moderate). A converted farmhouse set in picturesque moorlands in the Monts d'Arrée, with very pretty and comfortable studio rooms in peaceful surrounds. You need to book in advance for both rooms and meals.

Huelgoat ✉ 29690

**Hôtel du Lac, 12 Rue de Brest, t 02 98 99 71 14 (inexpensive). A reasonable budget option that looks out prettily over the lake of Huelgoat.

Crêperie des Myrtilles, 26 Place Aristide Briand, t 02 98 99 72 66 (inexpensive). A crêperie in a beautiful house in the centre of town, with Breton furniture.

Brennilis ✉ 29690

Auberge du Youdig, t 02 98 99 62 36, www.youdig.fr (inexpensive). A place offering B&B accommodation and typical Breton meals, and housing an eccentric museum with a reconstructed local village.

La Feuillée ✉ 29690

Auberge de la Crêpe, t 02 98 99 68 68 (inexpensive). A typical Breton stop for a bite to eat, in the pretty village itself.

Brasparts ✉ 29190

Domaine de Rugornou Vras, t 02 98 81 46 27 (inexpensive). A very good-value B&B option in a detached stone building that is well placed for walks. Meals are available by advance reservation.

Garz ar Bik, t 02 98 81 47 14 (inexpensive). Comfortable B&B rooms in a traditional house, plus table d'hôte.

St-Herbot

St-Herbot, south of Brennilis, has a gem of a Breton church standing proudly in its small wooded valley. It is in need of a bit of love and attention, but the decoration is possibly unsurpassed in charm in Brittany. A massive rectangle of a tower dominates the building. This is one of those Breton country churches where you wonder where the community it was built for has gone to. It was apparently made to serve a priory belonging to the Carmelite order at Rennes. The mighty tower is decorated in elegant Flamboyant Gothic style, with pinnacles, thin elongated openwork arches and a Gothic balustrade around the top, all set against a backdrop of trees.

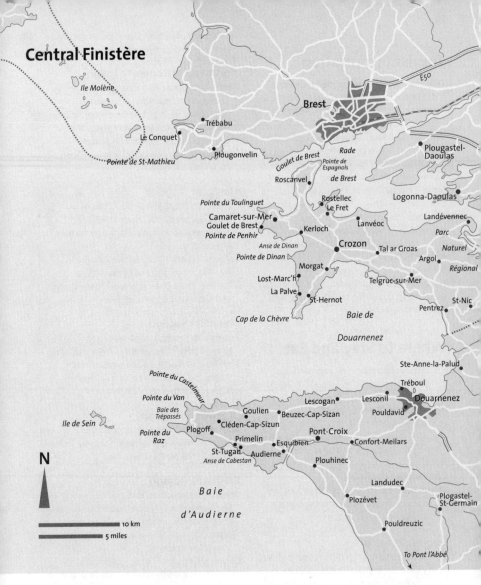

Central Finistère

Ile Molène

Trébabu

Le Conquet

Pointe de St-Mathieu

Plougonvelin

Brest

Rade

Goulet de Brest

Pointe de Espagnols

de Brest

Roscanvel

Rostellec

Le Fret

Pointe du Toulinguet

Camaret-sur-Mer

Goulet de Brest

Pointe de Penhir

Kerloch

Lanvéoc

Anse de Dinan

Pointe de Dinan

Morgat

Lost-Marc'h

La Palve

St-Hernot

Cap de la Chèvre

Plougastel-Daoulas

Logonna-Daoulas

Landévennec

Parc

Crozon

Tal ar Groas

Naturel

Argol

Régional

Telgruc-sur-Mer

St-Nic

Pentrez

Baie de

Douarnenez

Ste-Anne-la-Palud

Tréboul

Pointe du Castelmeur

Pointe du Van

Baie des
Trépassés

Ile de Sein

Pointe du
Raz

Plogoff

Goulien

Cléden-Cap-Sizun

Primelin

St-Tugan

Anse de Cabestan

Audierne

Lescogan

Beuzec-Cap-Sizan

Pont-Croix

Esquibien

Lesconil

Pouldavid

Douarnenez

Confort-Meilars

Plouhinec

N

Baie

d'Audierne

Landudec

Plozévet

Plogastel-St-Germain

Pouldreuzic

To Pont l'Abbé

10 km

5 miles

E50

The calvary outside the church stands out as one of the most characterful and memorable in the whole of Brittany. Its big block of Kersanton stone was carved in 1571. The crucified Christ has been given a caricature of a large Jewish nose. His ribs stick out painfully from his emaciated body. An angel hovers insect-like above him, while two robed figures collect drops of his blood, busily but somewhat indifferently. A statue of St Herbot stands over one of the two porches leading inside the church. He was venerated as a protector of cattle and horses. In times past, local farmers would cut locks off the tails of their beasts and come and present them to St Herbot on one of the church altars, seeking protection for their cattle. Both of the porch entrances are wonderfully embellished. The granite-floored church interior is

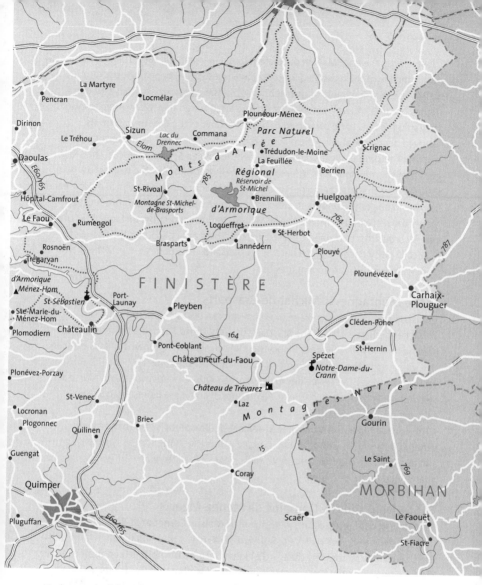

utterly wonderful, with a semi-abandoned yet strongly spiritual feel. The choir is
lit by a beautiful rose window and by a main window that is filled with some
splendid 16th-century stained glass.

Loqueffret and Lannédern

Loqueffret's Gothic church and its calvary are coloured with bright lichens, orange
on the church roof and green on the calvary. The simple cross has two remarkably
acrobatic angels holding up one of its branches. Go round the outside of the church
to appreciate further exterior stone carvings. One figure sticks out like a merry sailor
peering out to sea.

Just nearby, the little **Maison du Recteur** (*open July and Aug Tues–Sun 10–12 and 2–6*) recalls the life of the old-styled Breton village priest, often of peasant background, as well as the rag merchants of the Monts d'Arrée, the *pilhaoueriens*. These itinerant figures became known as storytellers in Brittany, though they were often despised. They sold the rags to be converted to paper in some of the Breton watermills.

Carved deer frolic all over the place in the *enclos paroissial* of **Lannédern**. One is stuck on the simple calvary, being ridden by the cowled St Edern himself. The story goes that this religious man offered refuge in his hermitage in the woods to a terrified deer that was being pursued by hunters. The church and village of Lannédern now lie on one of the brightest, prettiest and most open of slopes of the southern Monts d'Arrée, with the Montagne St-Michel-de-Brasparts in the distance. The whole *enclos paroissial* is photogenic in the extreme. The ossuary includes the figure of a comically puffy-cheeked angel between a skull and cross bones. *L'Ankou*, the Breton Grim Reaper, puts in an appearance too.

To the Montagne-St-Michel-de-Brasparts

Brasparts is the modest village by which you can best go up to the Montagne St-Michel-de-Brasparts. On the Brasparts ossuary, *l'Ankou* appears twice, in one image holding an arrow, in the other his scythe. The calvary is best known for its Pietà scene.

Heading up to the rugged, rounded hilltop of the Montagne St-Michel-de-Brasparts, you might stop at the **Ferme des Artisans** (*open April–Dec daily 10–7; Jan–March Sat, Sun and public and school hols 1–7*). All manner of crafts are represented in the exhibition spaces here.

The circular hill of the **Montagne St-Michel-de-Brasparts** is said to have been venerated by the pre-Roman inhabitants of Armorica, its roundness symbolizing the sun god Belenos. The 17th-century chapel on top of it, battered by the winds, has been abandoned to the elements.

To St-Rivoal and the Domaine de Menez-Meur

Set in unspoilt Breton countryside, the little **Maison Cornec at St-Rivoal** (*open July and Aug daily 11–8; June daily 2–6; Sept Sun–Fri 2–6*) is a traditional village farm that has been subtly restored by the Parc Régional Naturel d'Armorique and turned into a little museum on rural life in centuries past. The farmhouse dates from 1702; the name of the first occupant, Y. Cornec, is inscribed over the door.

The **Domaine de Menez Meur** (*open May–Sept daily 10–6; Feb–April and Oct–Dec Wed, Sun and public hols 1–5*) is the Monts d'Arrée's animal park, incorporating the **Maison du Cheval**, the latter explaining the history of Breton horses. The Domaine lies due west of St-Rivoal. From the car park, a beautiful old Breton *talus* track, with beeches planted on the moss-covered earth walls, leads to the farmyard with its explanatory panels on Breton horses. On certain days you can take a ride around the park on a Breton horse-drawn cart. In the neatly separated fields, you can go in search not just of Breton horses, but also of tiny Ouessant sheep, wild boar and wolves, among the animals most strongly associated with Brittany. Endangered types of Breton cattle and several species of deer are also kept here.

Up the Aulne Valley

Ignoring the Aulne estuary covered in the section on the Crozon peninsula (see p.282), this route takes you along the winding banks of the Aulne river, past rustic chapels, from Châteaulin to Carhaix-Plouguer. This area is reputed for its river fishing. The hill range of the Montagnes Noires or 'Black Mountains' stretches along the river's south bank, from the Ménez-Hom looming over the Baie de Douarnenez to the meeting of Breton *départements* of the Finistère, the Côtes d'Armor and Morbihan.

St-Sébastien-en-St-Ségal

The **chapel of St-Sébastien-en-St-Ségal** sits quietly above a meander in the Aulne, northwest from Châteaulin. It was built in the mid-16th century, apparently to help in the Christian fight to ward off the plague. On the monumental gateway, St Sebastian, a saint often associated with the dreaded epidemic, is being shot at from close range by archers. Close to the gateway, the calvary, in darker Kersanton stone, lies just outside the enclosure wall. The chapel's interior seems rather empty and sorry in the main, but the choir end is abuzz with carved activity. Incredibly sickly-sweet, and typically Breton-Baroque, it may be the work of one Jean Cevaër, from around 1700. Look out for the Nativity scene, in which one of the shepherds has brought along his Breton bagpipes. A separate set of panels tells the hilarious story of the Virgin Mary's miraculous flying house doing its tour of Europe, carried by angels.

To Châteaulin

Heading east along the Aulne valley from St-Sébastien-en-St-Ségal, the road curves round past the crescent of houses of **Port-Launay**, following a meander in the Aulne. From Port-Launay you soon arrive at the appealingly picturesque but untouristy small town of **Châteaulin**, with its substantial quayside houses on either side of the river. A row of bridges connects the two banks. In season, you can see locals fishing on the boulders out in the water. A **passe à poissons** was installed by the river so that you can go and view what fish are going up and down the Aulne.

Do venture up the left bank of the river at Châteaulin to the **Chapelle Notre-Dame**, a lovely Breton chapel set by some old village houses and the meagre ruins of Châteaulin's château. In fact the chapel was built to serve the lords of this fort. The very primitive calvary, dating from the late 15th century, carries a carving of the Last Judgement on one side, a rare scene to see on Breton crosses.

Pleyben

Unlike Châteaulin, Pleyben suffers from being a little too popular in high summer. Though less attractive than Châteaulin, it has possibly the grandest of all the Breton *enclos paroissiaux*, and the parish seems to have got involved in a rivalry of religious show with St-Thégonnec, the other major Breton *enclos paroissial*, up in the Léon.

The **calvary** is the most famous feature of this *enclos*. It looks like a massive triumphal arch set well forward from the entrance to the church. Because the architectural base is so much taller than that of most of the other Breton calvaries, it makes the sculpted scenes that much harder to look at in detail. On two levels, episodes in Christ's life unfold below the crosses. Some of the figures were carved in the mid 16th century, more in the mid 17th, the latter by one Ozanne of Brest – look at how Christ changes in character. Generally, all the work is of a particularly high order as Breton sculpture goes.

The ossuary, one of the oldest in Brittany, dating from the mid 16th century, now houses a tiny museum. The sacristy, with its typical period roundedness, was added for further show in 1719. The church itself is dedicated to St Germain l'Auxerrois – not a local saint but a national one. Two competing towers rise from the edifice. The choir is lit by a refined 16th-century stained-glass window once more illustrating Christ's Passion, the trees curiously shaped like vases.

Pleyben's other claim to fame is its Breton butter biscuits, the *galettes de Pleyben*.

Domaine and Château de Trévarez

Open July and Aug daily 11–6.30; April–June and Sept daily 1–6; rest of year Wed, Sat, Sun and school and public hols 2–5.30. Closed until Oct 2005.

Close to Laz, this *château rose* is actually more ruddy orange than pink, the brick structure sticking out like a sore thumb on the slopes of the Montagnes Noires. It is quite rare to see brick at all in western Brittany, let alone in such a sumptuous dwelling. The château only dates from the late 19th to early 20th century, built in mock Loire Renaissance style for an ambitious Breton, the Marquis de Kerjégu, president of the Conseil Général du Finistère and a member of the French parliament. For a long time, the château lay partially ruined after the Second World War, but the Conseil Général du Finistère bought it in 1968 and it has now been fully restored.

The history of the Trévarez estate is a colourful one, and Canadians may be interested in certain local lordly connections with their country. One Troïlus de Mesgouez, Marquis de la Roche, was viceroy of Newfoundland in the 1570s. The views north over the Aulne valley are stunning. The place serves as the setting for an annual gathering of Breton writers, the Salon des Romanciers de Bretagne, held in mid-August and open to the public. In fact all manner of exhibitions and festivals take place here across the year, many centring on the large grounds and their special plants; Trévarez is well known for its different seasonal collections, of camellias, azaleas, rhododendrons, hydrangeas and fuchsias in particular.

Châteauneuf-du-Faou to Carhaix

Châteauneuf-du-Faou, a little town north of Trévarez, looks down on another meander of the Aulne and across to the Montagnes Noires to the south. The painter Paul Sérusier, so closely associated with the Pont-Aven School (*see* p.335), came and settled here for much of his life. In 1919 he decorated the little chapel that contains the baptismal font in the town church.

It's quite some walk along the Aulne towpath from Châteauneuf-du-Faou eastwards to the **Chapelle du Moustoir**, but the way is rather beautiful and well worth the effort. The chapel has been saved from ruin by a passionate local group

Getting Around

Carhaix-Plouguer has a **railway** station (t 02 98 93 00 01) and is roughly 2hrs from Rennes by train, or 4hrs 30mins from Paris. Châteaulin also has a railway station (t 02 98 86 00 52), on the north–south Brest to Quimper line.

A local **bus** service links Châteaulin with Carhaix-Plouguer. A bus route also links Carhaix-Plouguer with Morlaix to the north and Pleyben with Quimper to the south.

Tourist Information

Pays d'Accueil Touristique du Centre Finistère, 13 Rue de l'Eglise, 29190 Pleyben, t 02 98 26 60 25.
Châteaulin: Quai Cosmao, t 02 98 86 02 11, *www.chateaulin.fr.*
Pleyben: Place Charles de Gaulle, t 02 98 26 71 05.
Châteauneuf-du-Faou: Place Ar Segal, t 02 98 81 79 30, *www.chateauneuf-du-faou.fr.*
Carhaix-Plouguer: Rue Brizeux, t 02 98 93 04 42, *www.ville-carhaix.com.*

Market Days

Châteaulin: Thursday.
Pleyben: Saturday and 2nd Tuesday of the month.
Châteauneuf-du-Faou: 1st, 3rd and 5th Wednesdays of the month.
Spézet: last Friday of the month.
Carhaix-Plouguer: Saturday.

Where to Stay and Eat

Port-Launay ✉ 29150

★★Au Bon Accueil, Route de Brest, t 02 98 86 15 77, *www.inet-bretagne.fr/ent/bonaccueil/* (*inexpensive*). A large and cheerful family hotel by the Aulne river, with 45 ensuite rooms across 2 buildings, a restaurant, a garden, mini-golf and more.

Châteaulin ✉ 29150

★★Le Chrismas, 33 Grand-Rue, t 02 98 86 01 24 (*inexpensive*). A classic French hotel run by the same family for several generations.

Pont-Coblant, south of Pleyben ✉ 29190

Le Poisson Blanc, t 02 98 73 34 76 (*inexpensive–moderate*). A nicely located restaurant by the Aulne.

Pleyben ✉ 29190

La Blanche Hermine, 1 Place du Général de Gaulle, t 02 98 26 61 29 (*moderate*). Traditional Breton food. *Closed Wed exc July and Aug, Mon and Tues eves in winter.*
Crêperie de l'Enclos, 51 Place Charles de Gaulle, t 02 98 26 38 68 (*inexpensive*). Good crêpes.

Châteauneuf-du-Faou ✉ 29520

★★Relais de Cornouaille, 9 Rue Paul Sérusier, t 02 98 81 75 36 (*inexpensive*). A traditional French provincial hotel. The restaurant (*moderate*) is popular with locals.
Crêperie Le Petit Rozell, 6 Rue de la Mairie, t 02 98 73 25 49 (*inexpensive*). A crêpe joint with rustic décor.

Spézet ✉ 29540

Hôtel Argoat, Route de Châteauneuf, t 02 98 93 80 23 (*inexpensive*). Basic but cheerful rooms.

Carhaix-Plouguer ✉ 29270

★★Noz Vad, 12 Boulevard de la République, t 02 98 99 12 12, *www.nozvad.com* (*inexpensive–moderate*). A modern place with traditional Breton touches.
Mme Le Moal, Port de Carhaix, t 02 98 99 53 50 (*inexpensive*). A B&B 15km south town, with a view of the Canal de Nantes à Brest. Meals can be arranged.
La Rotonde, Place des Droits de l'Homme, t 02 98 93 30 41 (*inexpensive*). Traditional Breton meat dishes served in an old townhouse.
Crêperie Ty Gwechall, 25 Rue Victor Massé, t 02 98 93 17 00 (*inexpensive*). An option with plenty of Breton charm.

that has turned the surrounds into what rather resembles a suburban flower garden. The place can look as colourfully gaudy on the outside as Breton retables often look on the inside of Breton chapels. In contrast, the restored interior proves pleasantly simple.

Spézet is a colourful little village, deeply proud of its Breton culture; it organizes a festival of the Breton language every Whitsun. The **chapel of Notre-Dame du Crann**, slightly hidden by trees off a road south of Spézet, is renowned for its rare 16th-century Renaissance stained-glass windows. The windows tell the stories of Christ, the Virgin, and the man who became the patron saint of blacksmiths and goldsmiths, Eloi.

The roads south from Spézet lead over the highest hills of the Montagnes Noires to Gourin in the Morbihan, capital of these 'mountains' (see p.355).

Carhaix-Plouguer has known more exciting days. It may have been a Gallo-Roman town of some importance, called Vorgium; it became the legendary capital of the evil chieftain Comorre in the Dark Ages; it was intimately linked with the legend of Tristan and the second Yseut, she of the white hands; and later still, in medieval times, it was the capital of the county of Poher. It still has a couple of pretty old streets, notably Rue Brizeux. The **Maison du Sénéchal**, with its carved timbers, contains the tourist office and the little local history museum. The real local hero is 18th-century Théophile-Malo Corret, alias La Tour d'Auvergne, an honourable man deeply passionate about both the French Revolution and Breton grammar.

The Crozon Peninsula

Nowhere in Brittany does the coast look more unrelentingly sensational than along the alarmingly beautiful cliffs of the Presqu'île de Crozon. These are specially protected as part of the the Parc Régional d'Armorique. At the mouth of the Aulne river, the ruins and museum of the abbey of Landévennec are the major cultural attraction on the peninsula. Camaret-sur-Mer and Morgat are the main resorts.

From Le Faou on to the Crozon Peninsula

Le Faou is the northern gateway on to the Crozon peninsula, a sweet old village set back in a typical Breton river estuary. The slate-covered sides of the 16th-century houses in the centre show that this community once knew a certain prosperity from its port activity. At one period, timber used to be brought down from the forests to the east to be shipped over to Brest for the building of the great wooden naval vessels of the Ancien Régime. An exceptionally pretty corniche road leads you from Le Faou to the **Pont de Térénez**, a bridge spanning the Aulne. From the bridge you can admire the most gorgeous wooded river valley.

Abbaye de Landévennec

Open July–mid-Sept daily 10–7; May, June and 15–30 Sept Sun–Fri 2–6; Oct–March Sun and public hols 2–6.

Rather impressively, in 1985 the abbey of Landévennec celebrated its 1,500th Christian anniversary. A Gallo-Roman religious edifice may even have preceded the Dark Ages Breton one that was so feted in 1985. However, the mysterious Celtic

Christian foundation is the most intriguing of Landévennec's chain of religious establishments. The memory of it centres around stories of the life of Gwennolé, or Guénolé, who was one of the great Breton saints of the Dark Ages (*see* box, below). Guénolé and Landévennec are also intimately associated with the powerful Breton legends of Gradlon, King of Cornouaille, and of the fabulously opulent and immoral town of Ys, which is said to be lost somewhere under the waters of the bay of Douarnenez (*see* p.294).

The abbey ruins open to visitors are a bit of a mess, and certainly a bit of a let-down if you don't know the deeply significant historical background to this important Breton spiritual centre. Archaeological digs have been going on here for many years, and the funky modern museum next to the ruins displays some of the finds.

A History of the Abbey of Landévennec

As already explained, almost nothing concrete is known about Guénolé's Celtic Christian monastery. However, some evidence exists of Landévennec in the 9th century. The Carolingian kingdom to the east of Brittany was making sure that the Breton Celtic Church fell into line with the mainstream Catholic Church. But a certain veneration of the old Celtic Church and its religious leaders certainly continued at Landévennec. This was quite possibly the last place where Celtic Christianity kept a foothold on the European continent. Roman Catholicism was triumphing though, with seemingly little forceful resistance in Brittany.

With St-Sauveur in Redon, this abbey became the main centre for spiritual and literary endeavour in Brittany. Some weird and wonderful illuminated manuscripts were prepared at Landévennec in this period. The most famous depict the Evangelists,

St Guénolé

'Bold White' might be a translation for the name Guénolé. The stories about his life derive from the hagiographies devoted to him, notably the work by a Landévennec monk named Clément, who was writing around AD 860 – that is, some three centuries after Guénolé is reckoned to have lived. Guénolé is described by Clément not as an immigrant to Armorica, but as the son of immigrants. Guénolé's father, Fracan, was already a man of some standing, cousin of the Breton chieftain Catovius, but his mother, the purely named Gwenn-Alba ('White White'), had higher ambitions for her son. Guénolé was sent as a boy to St Budoc's monastic school on the island of Lavret near Bréhat (*see* p.197) to prepare for his future. Having learnt to work miracles, Guénolé headed off to perform them in western Brittany. He first stopped on the Ile Tibidy. Then, driven on by a vision, he crossed the sea to Landévennec (without getting his feet wet, of course). He was followed by 11 disciples. On the site of some Gallo-Roman ruins, they set about building a Christian monastery.

A cult grew up around St Guénolé after his death. He was supposed to be able to assist with problems of fertility and to help babies to grow strong and walk. This was in addition to his powers for curing neuralgia and warts. His cult spread far: three parishes in Cornwall are named after him, and the name of Gwenolé also crops up at Winchester and Exeter.

but with strange anthropomorphic heads. Some have said that these were inspired by Egyptian or Middle Eastern models. These manuscript treasures are now in the hands of the New York Public Library, but copies of them are visible around the museum.

Vikings brought this period of prosperity to a swift end. A calendar kept in Copenhagen notes how the abbey of Landévennec fell prey to the pillaging Norsemen in 913. The monks fled east, spreading the cult of St Guénolé. Some of their manuscripts were also scattered far and wide. It seems that the Anglo-Saxon King Athelstan received one from Jean de Landévennec in person, along with some relics, to thank him for the help that he gave Alain Barbetorte in reconquering Brittany from the Vikings. The abbot Jean returned to see to the rebuilding of the abbey. Duke Alain contributed lucrative lands.

Getting Around

Public transport on the Crozon peninsula consists of **bus** services from Brest to Camaret-sur-Mer and from Quimper to Camaret-sur-Mer. Buses go via Argol, Telgruc-sur-Mer, Tal ar Groaz, Lanvéoc and Crozon.

Tourist Information

Pays du Ménez-Hom Atlantique, B.P. 45, 29160 Crozon, **t** 02 98 26 17 18.
Le Faou: t 02 98 81 06 85.
Landévennec: 02 98 27 72 65 (village hall).
Camaret-sur-Mer: Quai Kléber, **t** 02 98 27 93 60, *www.camaret-sur-mer.com*.
Crozon/Morgat: Boulevard de Pralognan-la-Vanoise, **t** 02 98 27 07 92, *ot.crozon.morgat@wanadoo.fr*.
Telgruc-sur-Mer: t 02 98 27 78 06.
Argol: t 02 98 27 75 30.

Market Days

Le Faou: last Saturday of the month.
Camaret-sur-Mer: 3rd Tuesday of the month, plus every day in high season.
Crozon: 2nd and 4th Wednesdays of the month.
Telgruc-sur-Mer: Tuesday and Friday.

Where to Stay and Eat

Le Faou ✉ 29580
★★★**La Vieille Renommée**, 11 Place de la Mairie, **t** 02 98 81 90 31 (*moderate*). A well-reputed option with some spacious rooms.
Crêperie Ty Bihan, 9 Place de la Mairie, **t** 02 98 81 05 44 (*inexpensive*). A lively crêpe house.

Rosnoën ✉ 29580
Ferme Apicole de Térénez, Route de Crozon, **t** 02 98 81 06 90 (*inexpensive*). B&B accommodation in a beautiful place that both produces honey and has a little *écomusée* on the subject. *Table d'hôte* is available on reservation.
Ferme-auberge du Seillou, Le Seillou, **t** 02 98 81 92 21 (*inexpensive*). A pretty stone farm with a few bright B&B rooms. Advance reservations are essential.
L'Ermitage, along the road to the Térénez bridge, **t** 02 98 81 93 61 (*moderate*). Fish and *grills du jour* served on a covered terrace facing on to the Aulne, with lovely views.
Vivier du Térénez, shortly before L'Ermitage, **t** 02 98 81 93 61 (*inexpensive*). A kind of lakeside *poissonnerie* where you can sample the daily catch marinated, smoked or filleted, on a little terrace by the water.

Landévennec ✉ 29560
Le St-Patrick, by the church, **t** 02 98 27 70 83 (*inexpensive*). A basic little hotel with a bright, almost Mediterranean air.

Le Fret ✉ 29160
★★**Hostellerie de la Mer**, **t** 02 98 27 61 90 (*inexpensive–moderate*). A lively, well-kept hotel on the shore, with a good restaurant (*moderate–expensive*) attached.

Camaret-sur-Mer ✉ 29570
★★★**Thalassa**, Quai du Styvel, **t** 02 98 27 86 44, *www.hotel-thalassa.com* (*inexpensive–expensive*). A modern hotel that gives directly on to the *sillon*. It has comfortable rooms, some with balconies overlooking the

The Romanesque reconstruction of Landévennec lasted throughout the 11th and 12th centuries, which were seemingly periods of relative prosperity. But during the 14th century, few parts of Brittany would be spared the effects of warring, and Landévennec was once again largely ruined. A dark period seems to have ensued. Jehan du Vieux Chastel ordered the abbey's rebuilding early in the 16th century. He also commissioned the statue of St-Guénolé that you can see on a visit here. Jehan du Vieux Chastel became the last abbot of Landévennec elected by the Church rather than by French royalty.

The abbey fell into decline through the 16th century, but the establishment of the Congregation of St-Maur (a Benedictine reforming order) at Landévennec in 1632 was to lead to a renewed lease of life. The monk Brother Robert Plouvier was called upon

sea, plus a heated seawater pool, a sauna, a gym and a jacuzzi. *Closed Dec–Easter.*

**Hôtel de France, 19 Quai Toudouze, t 02 98 27 93 06 (*inexpensive–moderate*). A hotel on the waterfront, with a first-floor dining room (*moderate*) with a view.

**Le Styvel, Quai du Styvel, t 02 98 27 92 74, *hotelstyvel@wanadoo.fr.* (*inexpensive*). A small, traditional-style family hotel with a good restaurant (*moderate*) and a number of rooms with sea views.

**Hôtel Vauban, 4 Quai du Styvel, t 02 98 27 91 36 (*inexpensive*). A place with good views and a garden.

La Voilerie, 7 Quai Toudouze, t 02 98 27 99 55 (*moderate*). A very good fish restaurant.

Crêperie Rocamadour, 11 Quai Kléber, t 02 98 27 93 17 (*inexpensive*). A crêpe house looking out on to the port.

Plage du Goulien ✉ 29160

Crêperie Parc Yan Aod, t 02 98 27 13 34 (*inexpensive*). A crêperie in a big house overlooking a beach west of Crozon.

Lost Marc'h ✉ 29160

Crêperie de Lost Marc'h, 3km west of Morgat, t 02 98 27 28 97 (*inexpensive*). A wonderfully located crêperie on the west coast of the Crozon peninsula, overlooking a wild bay.

Morgat ✉ 29160

***Grand Hôtel de la Mer, 17 Rue d'Ys, t 02 98 27 02 09, *thierry.regnier@vvf-vacances.fr* (*inexpensive–moderate*). A big hotel dating back to the Belle Epoque. Located between the beach of Morgat and a wooded park, it was refurbished in the 1990s and has a wide

array of facilities, including a tennis court. *Closed Oct–March.*

*Hôtel Julia, 43 Rue de Tréflez, t 02 98 27 05 89 (*inexpensive*). A bright, white hotel with some quite pretty rooms and a garden. *Closed Oct–March.*

Hôtel de la Baie, on the port, t 02 98 27 07 51 (*inexpensive*). A simple but charming choice.

Les Echoppes, 24 Quai Kador, Morgat, t 02 98 26 12 63 (*moderate*). Daily-changing fish menus. *Closed Sun eve, Mon lunch and Oct–March.*

La Flambée, 22 Quai Kador, t 02 98 27 12 24 (*inexpensive*). A crêperie with a first-floor dining room that looks out over the delightful bay.

Crozon ✉ 29160

**Le Clos St Yves, 61 Rue Alsace-Lorraine, t 02 98 27 00 10 (*inexpensive*). One of the oldest hotels in the area, with rooms furnished with old-style Breton pieces.

Le Mutin Gourmand, Place de l'Eglise, t 02 98 27 06 51 (*moderate–expensive*). A popular place offering fine cuisine with exotic touches, using only home-grown ingredients. *Closed Mon lunch, plus Sun eve and Tues lunch in low season.*

Crêperie du Menez Gorre, 86 Rue de Poulpatré, t 02 98 27 19 66 (*inexpensive*). A good choice in a pleasant 19th-century stone house on the eastern edge of town.

Tal ar Groas ✉ 29160

Crêperie Maëligwenn, Tal ar Groaz, t 02 98 26 18 02 (*inexpensive*). A crêperie worth seeking out.

as an architect to rebuild the abbey between the years 1650 and 1655. But the power of the Jansenists in Brittany from late in the 17th century was to lead once again to a period of decline.

In the late 19th century, one Comte de Chalus seems to have fallen for the ruined Landévennec and decided to devote his life to restoring the place, albeit to his tastes. He it was who had the palm trees planted around the ruins, giving them a vaguely exotic air. He also apparently enjoyed wandering around the property dressed up as a monk. Taking Landévennec rather more seriously, a group of Benedictine monks bought the place from the Comte de Chalus's heirs in 1950, built the separate modern abbey, and encouraged restoration and research work on the ruins.

The Ruins and the Museum

The **ruins** you can walk around are basically those of the early medieval church, its plan in good part inspired by the model of the influential abbey of St-Benoît-sur-Loire, near Orléans. The bases and capitals of the columns at the entrance to this church were decorated with typical Romanesque motifs. The nave of seven bays had cruciform pillars to hold up the ceiling. The wide transept was followed by a choir with an ambulatory and three rounded ends. Two chapels stood next to the south transept. One is still known as King Gradlon's Tomb, but it only dates from the 12th century, while the remains of frescoes are from the 16th and 17th centuries. The other chapel was where the tomb of St Guénolé was housed for a time, its walls one of the oldest vestiges of Landévennec, dating from Carolingian times. The south transept of the Romanesque ruins leads out to where the abbey cloisters stood.

The air-conditioned **museum** opened in 1990, displaying finds going back beyond the Breton Dark Ages and well beyond the confines of the abbey. Statuettes and an amphora are signs of Gallo-Roman settlements around the Rade de Brest. Models and plans give an impression of what successive monasteries at Landévennec looked like.

You can attend services at the **new abbey**, built of sturdy granite. There's a monastic shop as well, which helps fund the monastery. The small village of **Landévennec** is charming, so well protected from the worst of the Atlantic weather that Mediterranean plants thrive here.

You can walk a stretch of coastal path westwards from Landévennec, but after that a large portion of the north shore of the Crozon peninsula is reserved for the French military. A little way inland, by Les Quatre Chemins, signs lead you to the **Musée du Cidre**, basically a glorified farm shop with a makeshift cider museum tacked on.

The North Shore of the Crozon Peninsula

The little old ports of **Le Fret** and **Rostellec** to the west of military Lanvéoc look quite innocent with their old fishermen's cottages, but they lie at the foot of the submarine base of the Ile Longue. West of the Ile Longue you can head up and round the coast road of the large **peninsula of Roscanvel**. The top of this peninsula forms the south bank of the Goulet de Brest. The **Pointe des Espagnols**, the most northerly outpost, guards the Goulet. It was occupied by Spanish soldiers at the end of the 16th century, during the French Wars of Religion, hence the name.

You finally emerge from the military landscape around the **Plage de Trez Rouz**, the Red Beach. The rocks do have rather orange tinges, but the beach was named after the blood of English and Dutch sailors, whose bodies were washed ashore here after the naval battle outside Camaret in 1694.

Camaret-sur-Mer

The extraordinary natural feature of Camaret-sur-Mer, its pebbly jetty or *sillon*, curves out into the well-protected bay of Camaret. Along this flat spit of land, the wooden skeletons of several large abandoned fishing boats add a melancholic but picturesque note to the scene. Modern yachts have replaced these redundant fishing vessels, although there is still a small fishing fleet based at Camaret. The community long made a living from sardine fishing. But, after the sardines moved elsewhere at the beginning of the century, the fishermen also moved on, to rock lobster catching. These sailors became known (as did similar men in certain other Breton ports) as *mauritaniens*, because of their frequent rock lobster trips to Mauritanian waters. However, disputes over territorial fishing rights up and down the western Atlantic were destined to bring about an end to this trade. You should enquire at the tourist office about the possibility of going out on a **boat trip** around Camaret, with fishing lessons included.

The **Chapelle Notre-Dame de Rocamadour** on the *sillon* lost the top of its steeple to an English cannonball in an epic naval battle between French and Anglo-Dutch vessels in 1694. The church's light-coloured stone mimics marble, with its swirling traces of colour. Inside, three ex voto models of boats hang from the nave crossbeam. The choir window has been blocked up, but candles often throw a flickering light over the interior.

The **Tour Vauban** (*open daily July and Aug 10–6; Sept, Oct and April–June daily 3–6; Nov–March Sat and Sun 3–6*) is an eccentric piece of architecture that's worth having a closer look at. Louis XIV's famed military architect Sébastien de Vauban apparently ordered those deeply pigmented, striking walls. As a port, the bay of Camaret clearly had enormous potential, offering an obvious safe haven and an outer harbour for Brest, hence Vauban's interest in the place. He came to see to its elaborate fortification in 1689. The orangey-red tower rises out of an orange-shaped segment of lower fortifications. The sea used to provide a moat for the defences. Vauban's military and engineering genius and achievements are recalled in the modest museum situated inside the tower.

North of the *sillon*, the **beach of Corréjou**, part pebbly, part sandy, stretches along to the unspoilt **Pointe du Gouin**, which you can walk round.

The Western Headlands of the Crozon Peninsula

The many headlands of the fully exposed western coast of the Crozon peninsula vie with each other in drama. Through the suburban streets that lie to the west of Camaret-sur-Mer, the road takes you to the **Pointe du Toulinguet**. After the protected Anse de Camaret, suddenly you are exposed to the vastness of the Atlantic ocean. On the Rade de Brest side, you can look down on to some weirdly shaped rock formations, one pierced by a natural arch, others topped by pinnacles. The Pointe du Toulinguet is sensational and rather less well known than the major headlands to the south – an advantage in high summer.

Past the disconsolate neolithic **Alignements de Lagatjar**, some messy former Nazi fortifications provide spaces for a bird and seashell museum, the **Musée Ornithologique et des Coquillages**, and for a museum devoted to the Second World War Battle of the Atlantic, the **Musée Mémorial International de la Bataille de l'Atlantique** (*call t 02 98 27 92 58 for opening times*). French, US, British and European flags fly over this museum in such a fitting location. An anchor memorial outside the museum pays homage to the 45,000 Allied merchant navy sailors who lost their lives between 1939 and 1945 in the vital actions to keep supply convoys going between Britain and North America in the Second World War. The success of the Allies against the Nazis depended to a great degree on keeping this transatlantic link open. Some 30,000 German submariners would die in this atrocious Atlantic conflict – their average age was just 20.

The Pointe du Toulinguet is breathtaking enough, but the **Pointe de Penhir** eclipses it. The most sensational natural element to this headland is the **Tas de Pois**, a series of massive lumps of rocks ricocheting out to sea. A huge cross of Lorraine also marks out the headland. This huge cement memorial commemorates the efforts of Breton fighters in the Second World War.

The coastal path leading from the Pointe de Penhir right down to the Cap de la Chèvre takes you along a gloriously rugged coast. First comes the great **Plage de Veyrach**, followed by further smaller sandy creeks below the next few headlands. Follow the coastal path round to Kerloc'h and the **Anse de Dinan**. This bay changes dramatically with the tides. At low tide, a tremendous, enormous sandy beach is uncovered across the bay. The sea has carved grottoes into the geologically colourful cliffsides. Looking into the distance to the south, you can see why the **Pointe de Dinan** is also known as the Château de Dinan – although there is no man-made castle, the rocks have formed what looks like a massive fort, complete with a drawbridge of an arch of rock in front of it.

The territory stretching down from the Pointe de Dinan to the Cap de la Chèvre is especially wild, with the odd old Breton hamlet popping up along the way. A series of untamed beaches succeed one another. The **Plage de Lost Marc'h** is certainly lost, situated far down a sandy track surrounded by heath. Swimming is supposed to be forbidden here, but that doesn't stop surfers from coming out, and naturism is permitted on the beach. The headland above the beach was the site of an Iron Age fort, and you can still clearly make out the trenches built to defend the promontory. To the south, the **beach of La Palue** is more substantial, but has the same dangers and sense of drama.

Inland from La Palue, you come to the sleepy old village of **St-Hernot**, with its little **Musée des Minéraux** (*open July–Sept daily 10–7; June daily 10–12.30 and 2–7; Oct–May Sun–Fri 10–12 and 2–5.30*). It's rare to go into a museum and discover that you can be more illuminated by turning off the lights than leaving them on – the highlight of this little geological museum is the room full of fluorescent rocks.

The views suddenly open up on to the enormous, more tranquil Baie de Douarnenez once you reach **Cap de la Chèvre**, the most southerly Crozon headland. On clear days, the Ménez-Hom hill rises like a mountain at the back of the huge bay. Back on the 'Goat's Cape' (*see* box below), the naval watchtower rather spoils the immediate natural surroundings. Looking out to the Atlantic, an alarming war memorial to naval air pilots shows the tail of an aeroplane sticking out of a hole in the ground.

Morgat and Crozon

Tucked away from the pounding ocean, **Morgat** offers a still better-protected beach resort than Camaret-sur-Mer, with a long stretch of sand reaching round its fabulous bay. A big marina was built here behind the embracing arm of a jetty, while a small fishing fleet still operates from the town. Morgat has been popular with holidaymakers since the end of the 19th century, as you can see from some of the old villas.

There are grottoes you can visit on both sides of town. Some to the east of the resort can only be reached by boat. The most spectacular cave, the **Grotte de l'Autel**, is often described as a 'cathedral of the sea' with its natural 'altarpiece' and the rich decoration of its naturally coloured rocks.

The town of **Crozon** above Morgat serves as a shopping centre but is not inspiring. The one cultural thing you might like to see is the retable in the church. It so teems with carved figures that it is known as the 'retable of the 10,000 martyrs'. The packed panels retell the story of soldiers in Emperor Hadrian's Roman army, persecuted for converting to Christianity following what they considered a divinely inspired victory. Breton art doesn't get much more cartoon-like than this.

East of Morgat the coast along the north side of the **bay of Douarnenez** is restfully beautiful. It starts to resemble an Emile Bernard painting here and there (*see* p.335), the big *cloisonnée* blocks of colours of the fields sloping down to the deep blue water, where families build low stone walls on the pebbly beach to stake out their territory. Steep roads lead down to the sensational **Plage de l'Aber**.

Dahut and the Keys to the City of Ys

The splendid, debauched, drowned, legendary city of Ys is supposed by tradition to lie somewhere out in the bay of Douarnenez. A place name close by the Cap de la Chèvre, Poul-Dahut ('Dahut's Hole'), recalls the evil daughter of King Gradlon of Cornouaille, whose unbridled desires and callous murdering led both to the creation and the destruction of this fabulous godless city. In the story, Dahut, having seduced and killed countless lovers on Ys, falls for a fiery-bearded stranger who refuses to tell her his name. Such is her all-consuming passion for him that she accepts his challenge to prove her love by stealing the keys to Ys's protective sea gates from her sleeping father. It is only once she has delivered the keys to the stranger that she is overcome with a fearful foreboding of where her evil has finally led her. As the storm gathers force to wipe out Ys, she follows the stranger to the top of her castle. But by the time she arrives he has disappeared, leaving only the trace of a goat's hoof, the sign of the devil. Ys's fate is sealed. Read the fuller story on p.294.

The Eastern Bay of Douarnenez

The area around the Ménez-Hom and the strip of coastal land along the eastern side of the bay of Douarnenez make up an extraordinarily beautiful, rural part of Brittany, known by the rather unattractive name of Porzay. The area is absolutely steeped in Breton legends. The two main tourist attractions beyond the long stretches of beach are the splendid old towns of Locronan and Douarnenez.

Ménez-Hom

From the top of the Ménez-Hom hill you get views all round the Finistère on good days. The folds of the Montagnes Noires stretch to the east, while a patchwork of fields descends west to the sea. Some say that a sun god was worshipped on the Ménez-Hom in prehistoric times. Legend claims that an ancient tumulus hidden on the north side of the 'mountain' is the tomb of King Marc'h, forbidden from being buried in a cemetery because of his bad conduct. Nowadays, the Ménez-Hom hilltop looks slightly undignified in its balding state, with what look like the scrappy remnants of a green-rinse grass toupee clinging to its bare, rounded pate.

To Trégarvan

North of the Ménez-Hom, a little-used road takes you towards the Aulne river and the lost village of Trégarvan. Before you arrive, set along a country road, you'll find an isolated old rural Breton school that has been turned into a museum, the **Musée de l'Ecole Rurale** (*open daily July and Aug 10.30–7, June 1.30–7, Sept 2–6*). There's not even a village here, just the school with its walled playground, the old classrooms recreated as they might have been at the start of the 20th century. This rural museum may evoke a feeling of nostalgia or innocence, but the place does remind visitors of the fact that it was in schools that the Breton language was so effectively banned in the past, the schoolteachers enforcing the policy of the central French government. Some Breton children were deliberately made to feel ashamed of speaking their mother tongue, between the two World Wars in particular.

Continue along the gorgeous road to **Trégarvan** and its church, set on a lovely slope above the Aulne. A curious carving of the Pietà stands in the cemetery through which you have to walk to get to the church, in the Gothic interior of which an old clock ticks like a slow heartbeat.

Ste-Marie-du-Ménez-Hom

Coming down the southern side of the Ménez-Hom, you arrive at the village of Ste-Marie-du-Ménez-Hom. Its **chapel** looks surprisingly rich for such a small and remote hillside village. In fact, Ste-Marie-du-Ménez-Hom lay at a crossroads where an important regional fair was held four times a year. Over one period, a tax was put on all purchases made at these fairs to raise money to construct the chapel. Most of the building dates from the late 16th century, but you enter the *enclos paroissial* under

> ### St Anne, Mother of Mary and Princess of Cornouaille
> Among the most wildly implausible of Breton legends is the one that claims that Anne, mother of the Virgin Mary, was originally a princess of Cornouaille. The story goes that she was flown away from this corner of Brittany by angels who wanted to rescue her from her first husband, who had been mistreating her. She was supposedly taken to Judaea, where she remarried and went on to give birth to the mother of Christ. She returned to Brittany to live out her old age. Jesus, that kind boy, is supposed to have paid a visit to his distant grandmother, creating the spring of Ste-Anne-la-Palud for her. This absurd tale may stem from storytellers playing on the Breton word for a moor or marsh, *ana*.

a pompous 18th-century gateway given a Baroque top that looks rather like a Napoleonic hat. Statues of the Virgin and of St Hervé adorn the gateway. The calvary, dating back to 1544, has been restored. Inside the church, the most exuberant of richly carved retables runs across the whole length of the choir end.

The Coast from Pentrez-Plage to Ste-Anne-la-Palud

A league of beach runs down from the village of **Pentrez-Plage**. As at Trez-Bellec to the north, just the camp sites detract from the beauty of the place. The scattering of chapels close to the coast have some lovely wood carvings: the **Chapelle St-Jean** with its decorative stringbeams, and the **church of St-Nicaise** with the grotesque figures in its porch (as well as some restored 16th-century stained glass). Most ornate of the lot is the **Chapelle St-Côme et St-Damien**, with its monsters seemingly trying to swallow the crossbeams, and miserable figures holding their hands to their stomachs on the rafters. The **Pointe de Talagrip** is one of the best spots from which to appreciate the full sweep of the bay. Further chapels lie along the way south to Ste-Anne-la-Palud.

After the colourful Celtic adaptation of the Biblical story (*see* box above), the 19th-century church of **Ste-Anne-la-Palud** looks disappointingly drab in its present form, lost by the dunes. Inside stands a 16th-century painted granite statue of the 'Breton princess'. She has been greatly venerated over the centuries, and the *pardon* of Ste-Anne-la-Palud, on the last Sunday in August, remains one of the most popular in Brittany. Countless tourists join in the religious procession through the dunes. But Ste-Anne-la-Palud is more generally admired through the rest of the year for its fine long sands and the turquoise waters caught within the claws of its bay. Fields slope gently down to the strand. The currents are dangerous on the southern end of the beach, but you can enjoy the walk to the **Pointe de Tréfeunteuc**.

Douarnenez

Douarnenez is a fishing town both practical and poetic, deeply immersed in Breton legend, culture and class warfare. The river estuary is marked by Tristan's island, while out in the bay that carries the town's name, the ruins of the glorious legendary city of Ys (*see* p.294) are supposed to lie under the waves.

Getting Around

The **bus** service running from Quimper to Camaret-sur-Mer passes through Plogonnec, Locronan, Plonévez-Porzay, Plomodiern and St-Nic. There's another bus route linking Quimper with Douarnenez.

Tourist Information

Pays du Ménez-Hom Atlantique,
B.P. 45, 29160 Crozon, t 02 98 26 17 18.
St-Nic/Pentrez: t 02 98 26 55 15
(or village hall, **t** 02 98 26 50 36).
Plonévez-Porzay: t 02 98 92 53 57,
www.tourisme-porzay.com.
Douarnenez: 2 Rue du Docteur Mével, **t** 02 98 92 13 35, *www.douarnenez-tourisme.com.*
Locronan: Place de la Mairie, **t** 02 98 91 70 14 (high season); **t** 02 98 51 80 80 (out of season), *www.locronan.org.*

Market Days

Douarnenez: Monday, Wednesday and Friday.

Where to Stay and Eat

Ste-Anne-la-Palud ✉ 29550
★★★★**Hôtel de la Plage, t** 02 98 92 50 12, *www.plage.com* (*very expensive–luxury*). The only hotel giving onto the beach of Ste-Anne-la-Palud. The sea views from the restaurant and from some of the bedrooms are glorious. The cuisine includes Breton seafood at its most refined. In summer you can easily feel a part of the beach crowds, or you can stay aloof from them in the peace of the hotel grounds, which have their own swimming pool. There's also a tennis court. *Closed Nov–April.*

Plonévez-Porzay ✉ 29550
★★**Manoir du Moëllien, t** 02 98 92 50 40, *manmoel@aol.com* (*moderate–expensive*). A characterful manor with a terrace. The guest rooms are in outbuildings. *Closed mid-Nov–mid-March.*

Locronan ✉ 29180
★★**Le Prieuré**, 11 Rue du Prieuré, **t** 02 98 91 70 890 (*inexpensive–moderate*). A hotel by the western car parks outside the village. During the day, the tourist crowds traipse past it, and there is a large dining room with a front conservatory section to receive the hordes. *Closed mid-Nov–mid-March.*
Au Fer à Cheval, Place de l'Eglise, **t** 02 98 91 70 74 (*inexpensive–moderate*). A good French restaurant in the heart of the village.
Crêperie A R Geben, Rue du Prieuré, **t** 02 98 91 76 29 (*inexpensive*). A crêperie with a good reputation.
Crêperie Le Temps Passé, t 02 98 91 87 29 (*inexpensive*). A recommended place to come for your crêpes.

History

Fish gut went into making the pungent garum sardine paste that was considered such an important ingredient in cookery across the Roman Empire. The traces of numerous garum-making tanks have been found along the Douarnenez coast. Garum must have brought some prosperity to merchants here in the 2nd and 3rd centuries AD. By the end of the 3rd century, troubles across the Empire caused the rapid collapse of the trade. After this busy period of commercial activity, Douarnenez's history then enters the land of legends. The tale of the Ville d'Ys is one of the most famous and tragic in Brittany (*see* p.294).

In the Middle Ages, the fishing harbour became part of the estates of the dukes of Brittany. Its fortunes seem to have waxed and waned over the course of the centuries. And the morals of the people of the area appear to have greatly worried the Church from time to time; in the 17th century the Breton evangelizer Michel Le Nobletz (*see* p.247) settled in town for a time, presumably hoping to convert some of the debauched inhabitants.

Restaurant-Crêperie La Pierre de Lune,
Place des Charrettes, **t** 02 98 91 82 20
(*inexpensive*). A fabulously located option
with a pretty little garden, serving meats
cooked on a stone.

Ty Coz, Place de l'Eglise, **t** 02 98 91 70 79
(*inexpensive*). The loveliest of the handful of
beautiful crêperies on this square.

Douarnenez ✉ 29100

★★★Hôtel-Restaurant Le Clos de Valombreuse,
7 Rue Estienne d'Orves, **t** 02 98 92 63 64
(*moderate–expensive*). An imposing
residence in private gardens with a
swimming pool, 20m from the beach.

★★Auberge de Kervéoc'h, Route de Kervéoc'h,
t 02 98 92 07 58, *www.auberge-kerveoch.com*
(*inexpensive–moderate*). A converted country
farmhouse with a good reputation for its
peaceful guest rooms and for its food,
which is served in a large, rustic dining room
(*moderate–expensive*).

★★Hôtel de France, 4 Rue Jean Jaurès, **t** 02 98
92 00 02, *hotel.de.france.dz@wanadoo.fr.*
(*inexpensive*). A good option in the centre of
town, with comfortable rooms, spacious
bathrooms, a courtyard with private parking,
and its own little club/ballroom, Le Caveau,
catering for local weddings and parties. The
food in the **Le Doyen** restaurant downstairs
(*expensive*) is reliably good.

Chambres d'hôtes Rose Marine, 17 Rue
d'Estiennes d'Orves, **t** 02 98 92 85 08,
www.rosemarine.fr.fm (*inexpensive*).
A fine-looking 19th-century house with a
courtyard, offering B&B.

Le Kériolet, 29 Rue Croas-Talud, **t** 02 98 92 16 89
(*inexpensive*). A newly renovated option
with some bedrooms with a view of the
bay, and a recommended restaurant
(*inexpensive–moderate*).

Manoir de Kervent, near Pouldavid , **t** 02 98 92
04 90 (*inexpensive*). A few B&B rooms in a
charming, ivy-covered, modern-style large
family house just in the countryside on the
outskirts of Douarnenez towards Pont-Croix.

Chez Fanch, 49 Rue Anatole France,
t 02 98 92 31 77 (*inexpensive–expensive*).
A restaurant offering good seafood dishes.
Closed Fri eve.

La Crêperie au Goûter Breton, 36 Rue Jean
Jaurès, **t** 02 98 92 02 74 (*inexpensive*).
A funky and informal place refreshingly free
of Celtic overplay. The pancakes are similarly
original in style, and there is a garden
terrace out the back.

Tréboul ✉ 29100

★★Ty Mad, at Tréboul, **t** 02 98 74 00 53,
(*inexpensive–moderate*). A delightful hotel
situated in the quiet lanes up from the
Plage St-Jean, close to a lovely Tréboul
chapel. A tranquil place with a little garden,
it has been renovated since Kit Wood and
Max Jacob (*see* p.296) stayed here in 1929.
Closed Nov–March.

It was in the mid 19th century that the traditional fishing port began to modernize
dramatically. The first fish-canning factory opened in 1851. Workers flocked to
Douarnenez and were apparently housed in almost as cramped conditions as the fish
they were tinning. This fish-canning town became a bastion of coastal working-class
militancy after the First World War. In 1921, the citizens elected the first ever French
Communist mayor. Three years later they voted for a woman to join their municipal
council, but she was refused the appointment by French law. In 1924 to 1925 the
Douarnenez workers took on the employers in one of the first epic union battles in
the country. During the Second World War, Douarnenez became an important
recruitment centre for the French Résistance.

Publishing is one of the new small-scale industries to have grown up in
Douarnenez recently. Two excellent magazines devoted to Breton culture,
Chasse-Marée and *Armen*, are produced here. The place has also inspired a cartoon
series in Breton. For visitors today, though, the most obvious recent initiative has been
the port museum.

The Legend of the Ville d'Ys

The precise location of the legendary Ville d'Ys is, as you might imagine, disputed, but over the course of the centuries some of the inhabitants of Douarnenez have claimed to have seen vestiges of the city 'where the poorest were richer than kings', lying under the waters near the fishing harbour. What's more, the curious fragment of an old ramp at Le Ris, now leading nowhere, has been imaginatively viewed as the road that King Gradlon had constructed from Quimper in order to serve the ostentatious new city.

King Gradlon had Ys built to satisfy the unbridled desires of his wild daughter Dahut, who is also sometimes referred to as Ahès. Dahut's mother died at sea while giving birth to her; her grieving father was anxious to indulge her every whim. And as she grew up in Quimper, she became exceptionally beautiful, to the point that 'no one could resist the sparkle or wishes of those eyes'. No one except Corentin, that is, bishop of Quimper, who warned Gradlon of Dahut's immodest clothing, her frivolous conversation, her mocking attitude towards clergymen, and her refusal to go to church. Corentin tried to show Gradlon that his blind paternal love could lead to disaster.

Dahut, meanwhile, was becoming frustrated by a Quimper that had lost its sense of fun in favour of the joyless strictness of its religious orders. She argued powerfully, and even asked her father whether he wasn't the prisoner of the Church, for Christianity, she said, was stifling her. She also felt an overwhelming desire to live next to the ocean on which she had been born. Gradlon asked his daughter how he could make her feel better, and she said that he could oblige by building her a new city by the sea.

Gradlon told Dahut that her hopes were based in pure fantasy, but in secret he called his architects together and ordered the building of a city so splendid, he said, that even the ocean would be surprised. When it was complete, Dahut went to reign in the churchless city of Ys. The city became increasingly debauched and wicked, however, and Dahut and its inhabitants were punished by a wrathful God. In the terrible foaming, wave-lashing finale to the tale, King Gradlon managed to escape from the calamity of the drowning city on his stallion Morvark, who was powerful and nimble enough to run over the waves. But then the doting king tried to save his daughter too. The weight of her evil dragged the horse down and it looked as though all would be drowned. Then the monk Guénolé arrived at the last minute to save Gradlon from the engulfing waves. He reassured the Cornouaille king that God had pardoned him for his blindness because of the churches he had founded, including Landévennec (*see* p.282).

But Christianity was unforgiving in its final judgement on Dahut. Guénolé told Gradlon that he must push her from the horse. The holy man had to give the wavering king a helping hand to throw off his diabolical daughter. Dahut fell from the horse to be swallowed up by the waves and torn apart by the rocks. Miraculously, the storm abated. King Gradlon made it onto land thanks to Morvark and was left to consider the tragedy from the rocks (*see* also pp.289 and 299).

Musée du Bateau at Port-Rhu

Open daily March–15 June and 16 Sept–7 Nov 10–12; 16 June–15 Sept 10–7.

At this boat museum, you go round looking at real, not model, boats. The theme is the traditional working boat. A whole stretch of the river bank at Port-Rhu has been turned into a museum. Some of the vessels are moored to the quays; others have found shelter inside a large converted canning factory. A wide variety of old fishing and transport boats is displayed inside. There are boats from Brittany and boats from Britain and Ireland, but some of the most striking exhibits come from further afield, such as the flamboyantly shaped Portuguese marsh boat with its amusing paintings, or the Vietnamese paddy field boat, which resembles a very large basket. The old Douarnenez fishing industry is also recalled. Three larger vessels are moored outside. The *Anna Rosa*, the oldest, from 1892, was made from Norwegian pine. The *Northdown* worked as a Thames barge and then a pleasure boat. The *St Dennis* is a Cornish steam tug that served as a fire-ship. You can walk up and down and in and out of some of these boats. A few maritime craft shops have set up along the quay beside them. Douarnenez hosts regular gatherings of old sailing boats. For those special occasions, the bay of Douarnenez takes on an even more picturesque look, with the tanned brown sails of the past flitting across the waters.

Port de Rosmeur

Colourful houses look down on to Rosmeur, Douarnenez's working port, east of Port-Rhu. This counts among the dozen largest fishing ports in France. Enormous refrigerated lorries come to carry away a portion of the fresh haul. Vast quantities of fish are still canned in the Rosmeur quarter. Rosmeur is so atmospheric that it is fascinating to walk around, even if it can't be said to be conventionally beautiful. Just to the west of the newest fishing port, central Douarnenez offers the surprise of its own little beach, the Plage des Dames. The Port de Rosmeur is where you should come to catch the *Vedettes de Rosmeur* for tours of the bay.

Tréboul

Tréboul is home to the Douarnenez yachting harbour, west of Port-Rhu. Some façades as brightly coloured as those at Rosmeur look down on this marina. But while Douarnenez has big, lumbering buildings, Tréboul has retained its secretive winding lanes. A gorgeously located seaside cemetery slopes down towards the bay; this is a good point from which to set out on a walk west through Tréboul. Above the intimate St-Jean beach, you can go up to the little chapel by the Hôtel Ty Mad. A bust of the 20th-century Quimper poet and artist Max Jacob stands behind the chapel. He stayed at the Hôtel Ty Mad with his English artist friend Christopher Wood in 1930 (*see* boxes p.293 and p.296).

From Tréboul harbour you can go out on a tour of the Baie de Douarnenez on a former sardine boat – an excellent way to appreciate the natural beauty of the bay. The coast west from Tréboul is covered in the Cap Sizun section (*see* p.306); this touring section now heads towards Quimper via Locronan and lesser-known villages.

An Englishman Inspired

Christopher, better known as Kit, Wood, a golden boy of British 20th-century painting, fell in love with the area surrounding Douarnenez, and with Tréboul in particular, when he came to stay here in 1929 and 1930. His tragically brief life has been pieced together by Sebastian Faulks in his biographical book, *The Fatal Englishman: Three Short Lives.*

Bisexual, a drug addict, madly seeking inspiration, Wood killed himself at an early age. But he left some wonderful images of Douarnenez, where he had formed a firm friendship with the brilliant intellectual artistic figure from Quimper, Max Jacob, who wrote movingly about the young English artist after the latter's death.

Locronan

If Douarnenez was for so long grimly working class, you just have to take one look at Locronan's central square to see how upmarket this place was in centuries past. The substantial granite homes of Locronan's sail merchants surround the Place de l'Eglise. They date mostly from the 18th century, with their solid dormer windows sticking out of their silvery-grey slate roofs. Locronan's sail cloth became well known long before these houses went up.

Tourism dictates life in Locronan. Virtually all the houses have been turned into restaurants, crêperies or boutiques. The tourist invasion is the price Locronan pays for being one of the most picturesque of all Breton villages. Film director Roman Polanski came here to film his version of Thomas Hardy's *Tess of the d'Urbervilles.* Nastassja Kinski, playing the role of tragic Tess, was even sent to mull over the tomb of Ronan in the church. Ronan, a saint who came to Armorica from Ireland in the Dark Ages, ironically moved down to Cornouaille from Léon to try to find a little peace and quiet here for contemplation (*see* box opposite).

Ronan's Church

... a masterpiece of humidity, with its large silvery patches of lichen decorating the walls like the clouds of eternity.
François-René de Chateaubriand

The focal point of the town, and of its history and its ceremonies, the slightly unstable-looking old church just about offers an escape from Locronan's commercialism. The building is a graceful piece of granite architecture dating from the 15th century. It was funded by Breton dukes, who came here on pilgrimage to pray to Ronan for fertility. Lovely Flamboyant Gothic tracery rails run above the main entrance gable, along the top of the church tower and down the sides.

A cavernous entrance porch leads into the church under the stocky main tower, Ronan looking over those who come to worship. But generally these days you have to enter the church via the side chapel, which was commissioned by Duchess Anne of Brittany early in the 16th century – she too came to pray for fertility here. This side chapel has been cleaned of its cloudy lichens; its pale beige exterior looks quite out of keeping with the grittier greys around the square. The tomb effigy of Ronan lies inside the chapel. It was carved from deeply grey Kersanton granite in the 15th century. An elaborate carved and painted pulpit illustrates scenes from the legend of Ronan. The main church window depicts Christ's Passion, with most of the work dating back to the late 15th century.

On the lower end of the square, the Compagnie des Indes (the French equivalent of the East Indies Company) kept offices at Locronan. Nearby, you can head down the steep **Rue Moal**, lined with delightful old houses and offering beautiful views on to the countryside. The way leads to the chapel of **Notre-Dame de Bonne Nouvelle**. A fine Breton fountain and washplace lie by this chapel.

From the upper end of the main square, **Rue St-Maurice** leads steeply up the hillside. Once you're past the cottages, spectacular views open up across the countryside to the sea. Up here, the **La Tour Maurice gallery** is worth visiting just for its splendid location. Further up the hill, a large building houses the **Conservatoire de l'Affiche en Bretagne** (*check opening hours at the tourist office*), a Breton poster museum.

Ronan Refutes the Evil Kéban

...we saw lying at his side the fearful does and the savage wild boars.

La Légende de la ville d'Ys

So pestered was Ronan (also known as Renan) by miracle-seekers in the Léon area of northern Finistère that he began to fear for his sanity and decided to move south in order to get away from the crowds. He settled in the deep forest of Névet that lies behind the bay of Douarnenez. Adopting the life of a hermit, he lived there in harmony with the natural world, taming the wilder animal passions of the creatures of the woods.

However, a deranged woman from the area accused him of a heinous crime. One day, Kéban (or Kében) went to the court of King Gradlon in Quimper screaming for justice against Ronan. She claimed that he had come to her cottage, transformed himself into a wolf, and then carried away her little daughter to devour her in the forest. And there was more: she also accused Ronan of taking her husband from her by witchcraft to live with him, leaving her to fend for herself with her child. She had been reduced to living off berries and grass. And she claimed still further that Ronan had mocked the authority of King Gradlon.

The chieftain decided to have Ronan face a primitive kind of trial. He had him bound to a tree and set his two mastiffs on him. The bloodthirsty dogs came bounding up to devour him. But as Ronan made the sign of the cross, they stopped in their tracks. Convinced of Ronan's innocence by this miracle, Gradlon apologized to the hermit and asked him what he wished for by way of reparation. Ronan asked that Kéban be forgiven. The saintly man also went on to reveal that Kéban had hidden her daughter in a chest in her cottage. A crowd ran there and found that the poor little girl had suffocated inside the chest. But the story was to have a happy ending: Ronan resuscitated the girl.

Churches and Chapels North of Quimper

Pretty **Plogonnec** southeast of Locronan has a church with some marvellous stained-glass windows. These depict memorable scenes, not just of the Crucifixion, but also of the Apocalypse, with some frightfully active purple and green demons. In the Resurrection window, Breton saints surround Christ, a couple riding stags, another shoeing a horse, yet another sailing along in his galleon.

The pain of crucifixion has bent the legs of the two thieves crucified with Christ into almost acrobatically impossible poses on the very worn calvary of **Guengat**, which lies to the southwest of Plogonnec. Enter the church through the Gothic porch and a much more gruesome and painful crucifixion awaits you, portrayed in the exceptional 16th-century stained glass of the choir windows. Look out too for an amazing gilded processional cross dating from 1584, the figures on it quite naïvely portrayed for such a piece. Much cruder Breton art still is packed into the stringbeams, where among the cider-barrel and milk-churning scenes you can also make out a number of carved animals.

A couple of rare Breton **triangular-based calvaries** can be seen by the very peaceful rural chapels at **St-Venec** and at **Quilinen**, both west of Briec. Whereas most of the Breton calvaries balance horizontal scenes with the verticality of the crosses, on these all the figures and forms emphasize ascension.

Quimper

*In Quimper castle lived Gradlon, King of Cornouaille, in great mourning,
in great sadness.*

La Légende de la ville d'Ys

The capital of the old Breton county of Cornouaille, Quimper has lost its castle, but the legendary King Gradlon still rides sadly through the city, up between the splendid twin spires of the cathedral. Those joyous soaring spires tower over Quimper's old town, which is not in the least melancholic, but a lively, cheerful place.

A row of bridges spans the Odet river flowing through the centre of town. Kemper (which is the Breton word for Quimper) actually means confluence; the Steir joins the Odet here. In artistic and cultural terms, Quimper is best known abroad for its pottery, with its characteristic naïve decoration of Breton figures, but it is also home to two excellent museums.

Some Quimper History and Some Quimper Legend

Settlements around Quimper have been dated back as far as the late Iron Age. Pottery-making was already underway then. Known as Aquilonia under the Romans, the Gallo-Roman Quimper, although not the centre of one of the five Armorican *civitates*, did boast some important public buildings. A port developed too.

Legend then claims that Quimper became the seat of power of King Gradlon of Cornouaille some time during the Dark Ages. The story goes that he appointed Corentin, a holy hermit who he encountered while out hunting one day, bishop of Quimper (*see* box below). The city is still devoted to Corentin, who is regarded as one of the major saintly figures in the founding of Brittany after the fall of the Roman Empire. Whatever the legend, Quimper became the seat of one of the first bishoprics of the Brittany that succeeded Armorica in the Dark Ages. In 849, Quimper was one of the five Breton bishoprics where the great Nomenoë had the previous Frankish appointees sacked for corruption and appointed his own men, chosen from the Breton race. Anaweten then became bishop of Quimper.

King Gradlon and Bishop Corentin

The stories of the legendary chieftain Gradlon probably combine memories of a certain number of local Breton leaders with pure fantasy to make for a moving and entertaining morality tale.

Gradlon is the builder of the tragic, godless city of Ys for his daughter. The painful Gradlon stories retold in Charles Guyot's *La Légende de la Ville d'Ys* indicate the influence on the Breton imagination of battles with Scandinavians and of a powerful Church leading a crusade against pagan beliefs, sexual freedom and materialism. At the beginning of Guyot's version, Gradlon lies wailing in his Quimper castle. His deep cries sound like the agonized howling of a dying wolf or the love-sick barking of a rutting stag. He is grieving for Malgven, the formidable Queen of the North with whom he fell in love as he was besieging her castle. She had asked Gradlon to kill her odious husband and then the two had escaped from Scandinavia. Lost at sea, they enjoyed a long period of passion. One stormy night Malgven gave birth to their daughter Dahut on the ship, but then died. Dahut grew up in Quimper confused and capricious. One day, hunting in the forest, Gradlon encountered a hermit, Corentin, who soothed his troubled soul and conjured up a miraculous feast out of fish and sacred water – only half a fish to avoid destroying one of God's creatures, for the fish could rejuvenate itself endlessly. Gradlon was so impressed he made Corentin Bishop of Quimper, and under him, to Dahut's chagrin, the nature of Quimper changed to a city ruled over by the clergy. *See p.294 for the rest of the story.*

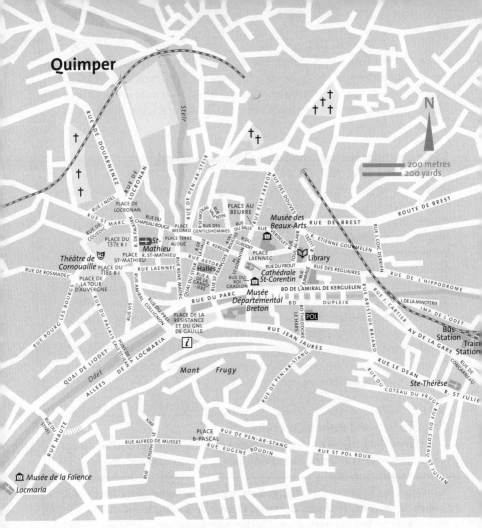

Quimper

In the early Middle Ages, the main settlement here on the Odet was named in honour of the Virgin and was known as Locmaria. Pottery flourished as a trade, and gradually the area around the confluence of the Odet and the Steir gained in importance. The 13th century saw the start of the building of Quimper cathedral, the raising of town ramparts and the establishment of a Franciscan monastery. The bishop ruled within the city walls, the duke of Brittany outside them. Quimper cathedral counted among the seven cathedrals to be visited on the medieval pilgrimage around Brittany, the *Tro Breizh*. In the Breton War of Succession in the mid 14th century, Charles de Blois took Quimper and his soldiers pillaged it.

The prosperity of some of the Quimper merchants of the 15th and 16th centuries can still be witnessed along such streets as the Rue Kéréon leading to the cathedral. The major Breton family of the Rohans left their mark on the town, constructing the 16th-century portion of the bishops' palace. In the Wars of Religion that scarred the second half of the 16th century, Quimper was split between Catholics and

Protestants. The merchants supported the Huguenot cause, but the clergy and the people took the side of the ultra-Catholic Ligue. After several bloody switches in power, eventually the Catholics had to give in to the peace-seeking King Henri IV, whose troops bombarded the city from the Frugy hillside.

At the Revolution, the city was briefly dechristianized and rather pompously renamed Montagne-sur-Odet, which really exaggerates the size of the Frugy hill in the centre of town. The cathedral was badly damaged in the upheaval. With the creation of the French *départements*, Quimper struggled with Landerneau to become the administrative capital of the newly formed Finistère, and won.

Quimper seems not to have fared too badly in the course of the 19th century, especially during the second half, even if large portions of the old town ramparts were brought down and the Odet was canalized. Among the trades to flourish were the modern potteries and the makers of *crêpes dentelles*, light Breton biscuits. In the second half of the century, Quimper's cathedral was embellished with those magnificent twin spires, the work of Joseph Bigot, who built other significant works in town. The equestrian statue of Gradlon on top of the cathedral also dates from that time.

The most interesting cultural figure to emerge from Quimper in the 20th century was the artist Max Jacob. After brilliant studies in his home town, Jacob went up to Paris to live a Bohemian existence. You can see some of his works of art at the Quimper fine arts museum.

The city's potteries encouraged a host of Breton artists, and their offerings can be viewed at the pottery museum rather than in the fine arts one. More 20th-century art has been commissioned for the cathedral.

Cathédrale St-Corentin

You can admire the west front of the cathedral from the large cobbled square in front of it. Excavation has shown that a substantial early medieval graveyard lies under the cobbles. The Cathédrale St-Corentin is mainly Gothic, begun in the middle of the medieval period. But it is a surprise to many that those wonderful spires were only added in the 19th century. They look genuinely Gothic. Between them, you can make out quite easily the tragic figure of King Gradlon as he rides along, his horse's head bowed. Down below, a grand Gothic arch with rows of angels in the archivolts leads into the building. The lion above this entrance carries the Breton banner that was the symbol of the De Montfortist side, which won the Breton War of Succession in the 14th century.

The nave, like the towers on which the twin spires were built, is 15th-century, while the choir is in great part 13th-century. But despite the time difference and the disconcerting deviation in line from nave to choir, this remains an impressively harmonious religious building inside. The stone was scrubbed clean during 1990s restoration work. However, much of the interior lost its original decorative features to the Revolution, and a lot of the interior design dates only from the 19th or 20th centuries. Some 15th-century stained glass has survived in the nave and in the choir, up in the taller windows, representing religious leaders and lords with their guardian

Getting Around

Quimper is easily reached from Paris by TGV fast train. You can also fly from Paris to Pluguffan airport just outside Quimper (t 02 98 94 30 30).

Contact the *gare routière* for details of bus routes, t 02 98 90 88 89.

Tourist Information

Quimper: Place de la Résistance, t 02 98 53 04 05, *www.quimper-tourisme.com*.

Market Days

Markets are held in various parts of town on Wednesday, Friday, Saturday and Sunday.

Festivals

The **Festival de Cornouaille** is a major annual Breton festival, one of the best in Brittany, held every year the third or fourth week in July.

Where to Stay

Quimper ✉ 29000

Most of Quimper's hotels are modern, but there are a couple of peaceful options close to the historic centre.

★★**Le Dupleix**, 34 Boulevard Dupleix, t 02 98 90 53 35, *www.hotel-dupleix.com* (*moderate–expensive*). A modern building with the advantage of some spacious rooms looking out over the Odet river and onto the cathedral spires.

★★★**Gradlon**, 30 Rue de Brest, t 02 98 95 04 39, *www.hotel-gradlon.com* (*moderate*). Prettily decorated rooms and a courtyard near the Musée des Beaux-Arts.

★★**Hôtel Mascotte**, 6 Boulevard Théodore Le Hars, t 02 98 53 37 37, *mascotte-quimper@hotel-sofibra* (*moderate*). A very central, well-kept hotel.

For cheaper options try by the railway station, close to the historic centre:

Le Derby, 13 Avenue de la Gare, t 02 98 52 06 91 (*inexpensive*). A well-run budget hotel.

Hotel de la Gare, 17 Avenue de la Gare, t 02 98 90 00 81, *hoteldelagarequimper@free.fr* (*inexpensive*). A pleasant choice with rooms giving on to an inner courtyard.

Hôtel TGV, 4 Rue de Concarneau, t 02 98 90 54 00 (*inexpensive*). A decent affordable option.

Logis du Stang, Allée de Stang-Youen, 10mins southeast of old Quimper, t 02 98 52 00 55, *www.logis-du-stang.com* (*inexpensive*). A charming B&B next to the Cornouaillian 19th-century hosts' house, with family rooms.

Auberge de Jeunesse, 6 Avenue des Oiseaux, t 02 98 64 97 97, *www.fuaj.org* (*inexpensive*). A youth hostel 3km from the station.

saints. A few 15th-century bishops' tombs also made it through the destruction. A further pre-Revolutionary piece of art to look out for in the nave is the 17th-century pulpit with scenes representing the life of St Corentin.

The building of the choir began in 1239. The work lasted through to around 1300, although the Gothic stone vaulting and the stained-glass windows would be added in the 15th century. A whole series of 19th-century murals covers every inch of the lancet-shaped walls in the choir side chapels. Most of them depict Breton scenes in sickly pre-Raphaelite style.

Musée Départemental Breton

Open June–Sept daily 9–6; Oct–May Tue–Sat 9–12 and 2–5, Sun 2–5.

This is the ethnographic museum of the Finistère. Its grand home since the early part of the century has been the former bishops' palace, which is glued on to the cathedral. You are left to tour through the rambling rooms at whim. There are some wonderful exhibits on display. One of the best, a stunning but simply designed gold

Eating Out

La Fleur de Sel, 1 Quai Neuf, **t** 02 98 55 04 71 (*moderate–expensive*). Light fish dishes served on the opposite bank from the pottery area of Locmaria, south of the centre down the Odet, with a view of the river. *Closed early May.*

Le Jardin de l'Odet, 39 Boulevard de l'Amiral de Kerguélen, **t** 02 98 95 76 76 (*moderate–expensive*). Tasty fare presented in an amusing dining room with the feel of an ocean liner, by the Odet and the cathedral. *Closed Sat eve and Sun.*

L'Ambroisie, 49 Rue Elie Fréron, **t** 02 98 95 00 02 (*moderate*). A restaurant with a friendly 1950s feel and cuisine with inventive touches. *Closed June–July, Sun eve and Mon.*

Café de l'Epée, 14 Rue du Parc, **t** 02 98 95 28 97 (*moderate*). A brasserie well known as a meeting place for artists and politicians, who appreciate the good seafood.

Erwan, 1–3 Rue Aristide Briand, **t** 02 98 90 14 14 (*moderate*). A place just by the cathedral, specializing in traditional recipes. *Closed Sat lunch and Sun.*

Crêperie des Artistes , 11 Rue le Déan, **t** 02 98 53 06 06 (*inexpensive*). Very pretty décor and quick, cheap food.

Crêperie du Sallé, 6 Rue du Sallé/Place au Beurre, **t** 02 98 95 95 80 (*inexpensive*). One of the best of the many crêperies in town, with tables spilling out on to the pretty little square in summer. Inside, Breton furniture and tablecloths give the place ambiance in any season. *Closed Sun and Mon.*

Crêperie St-Marc, 2 bis Rue St Marc, up from the Eglise St-Mathieu, **t** 02 98 55 53 28 (*inexpensive*). A decent crêpe house with Breton decoration. *Closed Sun in high season.*

Le Saint-Cô, 20 Rue du Frout, behind the cathedral, **t** 02 98 95 11 47 (*inexpensive*). A favourite among students, with grilled meats a speciality.

Au Vieux Quimper, 20 Rue Verdelet, **t** 02 98 95 31 34 (*inexpensive*). A good option where you can watch the *crêpières* at work and enjoy the Breton décor. Cider comes on tap. *Closed 2wks June.*

Near the Château de Lanniron south of the pottery quarter lie two good restaurants and a cheaper option:

Les Acacias, 88 Boulevard Creac'h Gwen, **t** 02 98 52 15 20 (*moderate–expensive*). Refined seasonal cooking. *Closed Sat lunch, Sun and Mon eve.*

La Ferme de l'Odet, Boulevard Creac'h Gwen, **t** 02 98 10 11 10 (*moderate–expensive*). A former farm with a very pleasant terrace. *Closed Sat eve, Sun and Mon lunch.*

L'Orangerie, grounds of former bishops' palace **t** 02 98 57 93 63 (*moderate*). A more basic choice in a grand building in lovely surrounds. *Open Tues and Wed lunch, and Thurs–Sat.*

chain, turns out to be one of the very oldest – a Celtic piece dating back to many centuries before Christ. Certain archaeological fragments recall the Gallo-Roman period, including a stele (or column) seemingly representing four gods. With nothing much to show from the Dark Ages, the displays move swiftly on to early medieval carved capitals and tomb effigies. The collection of later painted statues of saints stands out.

The steps up the enormous spiral staircase lead past some extravagant religious items and the sword of Guy-Eder de Beaumanoir, better known as the lord De la Fontenelle, who caused such terror in Brittany during the French Wars of Religion. Upstairs, fine collections of Breton costumes, furniture and pottery take up the rooms – the costume collection is particularly colourful. From the beginning of the 19th century to the period between the two World Wars, the embroidery that was used to decorate Cornouaille festive garments became increasingly elaborate. You can also see how some contemporary designers have adapted traditional Breton styles to modern fashions.

Musée des Beaux-Arts

Open July and Aug daily 10–7; Sept and April–June daily 10–12 and 2–6;
Oct–March Mon and Wed–Sat 10–12 and 2–6, Sun 2–6.

The building housing Quimper's fine arts museum stands out in the square situated to the north of the cathedral, the Place Laënnec. This museum was built in 1864 in order to present the substantial collection that had been donated to the town by Jean-Marie de Silguy. The architecture was designed by Joseph Bigot. Behind the 19th-century façade lie very modern, well-lit museum rooms. Representative works of European art dating from the 14th century to the present are displayed in the various galleries. De Silguy was also particularly interested in fine Flemish painting from the late 16th century to the early 18th century and French art from the 18th and 19th centuries.

The curators of the new museum early set about acquiring additional works inspired by Brittany, and have done so ever since. Several of the ground-floor rooms by the entrance concentrate on Breton-inspired art and Breton artists. One of the most impressive works is by Boudin, *Le Port de Quimper*, painted in 1857. The Pont-Aven School (*see* p.335) is represented by some striking works by Paul Sérusier, showing Bretons with Asiatic features, by Charles Filiger and by Emile Bernard. One of the most famous depictions of a Breton religious procession is the highly realistic canvas by Alfred Guillou showing beautifully attired women arriving by boat for the *pardon* of Ste-Anne-de Fouesnant. Charles Cottet painted several deeply melancholic and dark pictures that convey how tough Breton life could be before the First World War. Breton legend isn't forgotten either, Evariste Luminais depicting the end of the city of Ys. Sculptures by René Quillivic convey contrasting sides to Breton women, one piece representing a startling group of Bigoudènes smoking pipes, another a young Breton girl making lace.

One of the rooms is devoted to Max Jacob, who was born next to the Hôtel de l'Epée. His paintings depicting Brittany tend to be caricatural. Other works in the room show what Jacob looked like, and depict of his famous friends. One of the portraits is by Picasso. Although close as young men, the two drifted apart. Christopher Wood's portrait of Jacob shows a wizened, wise-looking old man, his monocle firmly in place.

Old Shopping Quarters

The most remarkable street in Quimper, with the poshest boutiques and the finest old houses, some timberframe, some slate covered, is the wonderful **Rue Kéréon** (Kéréon is the Breton word for cobblers). To the south of Rue Kéréon, the wacky architecture of the modern covered market or **Halles**, rebuilt after a fire in 1979, draws shoppers in large numbers. A little way further west you come to the **Place Terre-au-Duc** and the **Place Médard**, with more old houses built close to the Steir river. This was where the western limit lay of the old medieval town. A watchtower remains. Beyond, the spire of the 19th-century **church of St-Mathieu** stands out, with more old lanes around it.

Locmaria and the Pottery Quarter

The pottery corner of Quimper lies in the shadow of the big Romanesque church of **Locmaria** on the opposite bank of the Odet river.

Musée de la Faïence

Open mid-April–Oct Mon–Sat 10–6.

This modern museum is housed in a converted late-18th-century pottery factory situated right by the Odet river. It recounts the story of Quimper pottery from the late 17th century onwards. The first important potter to set up in Quimper at the end of the 17th century came from southern France. Jean-Baptiste Bousquet started working in Locmaria in the 1690s and produced Provençal-style work. One of his granddaughters married one Pierre Bellevaux, a potter hailing from Nevers on the Loire. Bellevaux changed the decoration to the typical Nevers patterns, which were inherited from Renaissance Italy. Another marriage, that of a daughter of Bellevaux to Pierre Clément Caussy, the latter a potter from Rouen, led to a further shift in style in the mid 18th century.

During the second half of the 18th century, the styles of Nevers and Rouen were merged to give a distinctive look to Quimper designs, the Rouen themes of flowers and birds executed with the bright colours and broad brush strokes of Nevers. Towards the end of the 18th century, further potters were to establish their own companies, Eloury-Porquier-Beau (using the initials PB) was created in 1772, and Henriot (abbreviated to HR) a couple of decades later in 1791. They mainly produced glazed or earthenware crockery.

The new style of adding Breton rural figures appeared in the mid 19th century with the 'Petit Breton', a caricatural Breton wearing traditional baggy pants, bright breeches and a waistcoast, and sporting a black Breton hat. This quaint, if rather patronizing, vision of a Breton caught on, and has been the success of Quimper pottery ever since.

From the 1920s, a number of Breton artists formed the association of 'Seven Brothers' (the name playing on the long tradition of the seven founding saints of Dark Age Brittany) to revive Breton crafts at the same time as taking into account new, more experimental trends.

HB Henriot Faïenceries de Quimper

Open Mon–Thur 9–11.15 and 1.30–4.15, Fri 9–11.15 and 1.30–3; call t 08 00 62 65 10 for times of tours.

You can visit these workshops to see how the traditional Quimper pottery is still made and decorated. This is one of the few major French potteries still painting designs entirely by hand, without using transfers. Each piece is unique and signed by the artist who executed it. The tours are extremely popular and the guides speak good English. After the tour, many people visit the shop with its large selection of Quimper pottery and seconds.

The Cap Sizun and the Ile de Sein

A stunning, precipitous coastal path leads west from Douarnenez to two of the most famous headlands in France, the Pointe du Van and the Pointe du Raz. The French feel they can find their Land's End here. Audierne, the major town of the Cap Sizun, looks the archetypal Breton fishing port. It is from here that boats leave for the tiny island of Sein, seemingly always on the verge of being submerged by the sea. Celtic druids apparently thought they could leave from here for the afterlife.

The Coast from Douarnenez to the Pointe du Van

You have to walk along the coastal path to appreciate the beauty of the Baie de Douarnenez from this side. Starting from Tréboul west of Douarnenez, the path takes you past the dramatic **headlands of Leydé and the Jument**. The bracken grows high in summer, here and there obstructing the narrow track. The Baie de Douarnenez is often spotted with sails. Inland from the Pointe de Leydé, **Lesconil** has preserved a quite impressive neolithic gallery chamber.

Continuing along the coastal path towards the Pointe du Millier, a short way inland you might take a look at the **Moulin de Keriolet**, with its metallic wheel still in place, and a little exhibition on local watermills inside. The **Pointe du Millier** is a well-known viewing point along the coast, its lighthouse still in operation. Below, to the west, you can find one of the rare sandy beaches along this unspoilt stretch of coast. Remnants of a neolithic settlement lie scattered around **Lescogan** inland from the Pointe du Millier, including the Menhir de Kerlafin, the gallery chamber of Kerbalanec and a dolmen. Heading on past **Lillouren**, you'll see a large block of stone by a mill that is said to be the stone boat in which St Conogan, Dark Ages religious immigrant from across the Channel, arrived.

Back at the coast, past another beach, the Plage de Pors Péron, and the Pointe de Trénaouret, you come to the **Pointe de Beuzec** or **Castel Coz** ('Old Castle'), with the traces of its Iron Age defences. The **Fête des Bruyères** or Heather Festival, celebrating Breton music, dance and ceremony, takes place at **Beuzec-Cap-Sizun** on the second Sunday of August. The way continues dramatically until you reach the area of the **bird reserve of Cap Sizun** (*open daily 15 April–June 10–12 and 2–6, July and Aug 10–6*).

Past the reserve, the shore looks much more savage and unforgiving, although a small number of yachts can draw into the tiny harbour below the **Pointe de Penharn** with its monumental rock formations. Spectacular views open out from the **Pointe de Brézellec** to the west, while a little further on, the **Pointe de Castel Meur**, site of another Iron Age defence, looks particularly scary.

La Pointe du Van

At the treeless **Pointe du Van** ('van' means headland or promontory in Breton, so the French name rather labours the point), tourist cars are herded into car parks sensitively surrounded by low stone walls. Walking across the heath to the end of the headland, among the scrub you can see the remains of much older stone walls, a sign, amazingly, that this land was once cultivated, divided into small protected plots. The little **chapel of St-They** on the slope to one side of the promontory was restored not too long ago. The spirit of the saint supposedly used to get the bells to ring to warn ships away from this lethal coast. That didn't stop many being wrecked. You get spectacular views of other headlands from here, including the more famous and much more touristy Pointe du Raz nearby.

La Pointe du Raz and the Bay of the Dead

The road between the headlands leads you down and across the **Baie des Trépassés**, the Bay of the Dead. Legends of death have piled up here like so many bits of wreckage after a ship goes down. The name is seemingly derived from a misinterpretation of the Breton *aon*, meaning 'river', for the Breton *anaon*, meaning the deceased. Some versions of old tales say that dead Celtic druids were transported from here to be laid to rest on the island of Sein; this bay may have been considered a point of departure for the afterlife. In more recent times, it was said that the sounds of sailors lost at sea gathered here. With its hotel, large car park, beach and grottoes to go and see at low tide, the bay doesn't feel as frightening today as the legends make it sound.

Arriving at **La Pointe du Raz**, it can feel at times as if you're caught in the weekend queues for a big city hypermarket. You have to pay to park here, unlike at the Pointe du Van. In the 1990s, much was done to try to protect this overpopular, tourist-worn site. A hotel was demolished, much to the chagrin of its owner, and the tourist boutiques moved to new, more discreet buildings. At the visitor centre you can find out about the local history, while a video tells the story of the city of Ys (*see* p.294).

As you walk to the end of the wild promontory, the landscape still looks lunar for the moment, polished clean by visitors' feet. One unfortunate monument that has not been removed is a white statue of the Virgin, the vulgar Catholic **Notre-Dame des Naufragés** (Our Lady of the Shipwrecked), a work by Cyprian Godebski inaugurated at the *pardon* in 1904. A fair number of visitors clamber out quite far on to the tortuous rocks that tail off into the ocean. One particularly rough chasm on this headland, where the sea boils down below, is known as the **Gouffre de Plogoff**. The name is a reminder of the pathological evil of Dahut, daughter of King Gradlon, in the legend of Ys. Each night she chose a new partner. After making love, she had her latest lover suffocated with a silk mask and had the body discarded in the Gouffre de Plogoff.

On good days you can see north to the Pointe de St-Mathieu in the Léon and south to the Pointe de Penmarc'h at the end of the vast bay of Audierne. Straight out to the west, the **Phare de la Vieille** and the **Phare de la Plate** count among the best-known lighthouses in France. You may be able to make out the island of Sein too, floating like a mirage in the distance.

The Southern Coast of the Cap Sizun

To appreciate the southern coast of the Cap Sizun, you need to take the coastal path again. The road to Audierne runs parallel to the coast. It passes through the village of **Plogoff**, with Cléden- Cap-Sizun just to the north. The churches here have

Getting Around

Ask at tourist offices about **bus** services from Douarnenez and Quimper to get around this area by public transport.

Boats leave from Ste-Evette beach to the west of Audierne for the island of Sein.

Tourist Information

Association Ouest Cornouaille Promotion, BP 52 041, 29123 Pont-l'Abbé, **t** 02 98 82 30 30, *www.ouest-cornouaille.com*.
Audierne: Place de la Liberté, **t** 02 98 70 12 20, *ot-audierne@wanadoo.fr*.
Pont-Croix: Place de l'Eglise, **t** 02 98 70 40 38, or out of season **t** 02 98 70 40 66.

Market Days

Plogoff: Friday.
Cléden-Cap-Sizun: 4th Thursday of the month.
Audierne: Saturday.
Pont-Croix: 1st, 3rd and 5th Thursdays of the month.

Where to Stay and Eat

Plogoff ✉ 29770

★★La Baie des Trépassés, **t** 02 98 70 61 34, *hoteldelabaie@aol.com* (*inexpensive–moderate*). A large modern hotel overrun during the day by the Pointe du Raz hordes.
★★Kermoor, Plage du Loch, Route de la Pointe du Raz, **t** 02 98 70 62 06, *www.hotel.kermoor.com* (*inexpensive–moderate*). Probably the best of the bunch of hotels near the Pointe du Raz. The owner-chef can cook up a storm. Half-board is obligatory mid-July–Sept.
Ferme de Kerguidy Izella, 5km from the Pointe du Raz, **t** 02 98 70 35 60 (*inexpensive*). B&B accommodation in a characterful Breton building. The guest rooms are in modern style.
Relais de l'Ile de Sein, **t** 02 98 70 60 67 (*inexpensive–expensive*). A simple place to eat, with the added bonus of fine views. *Closed Wed in low season.*
Crêperie du Cap, **t** 02 98 70 60 52 (*inexpensive*). A crêperie that has been run by the same family for 3 generations. *Closed Mon–Fri exc school hols.*

Cléden-Cap-Sizun ✉ 29770

L'Etrave, Route de la Pointe du Van, **t** 02 98 70 66 87 (*moderate–expensive*). A basic-looking restaurant with sea views, known above all for its excellent but expensive lobster dishes. *Closed Oct–March.*

Esquibien ✉ 29770

★Le Cabestan, 1 Rue Laennec, **t** 02 98 70 08 82 (*inexpensive*). A quite comfortable hotel with a pleasant garden.

Audierne ✉ 29770

★★★Le Goyen, Place Jean Simon, **t** 02 98 70 08 88 (*moderate–expensive*). A hotel with a smart front conservatory from which you can lap up the atmosphere of the port. The rooms, in both modern and traditional styles, are extremely comfortable, while the restaurant (*expensive–luxury*) serves some of the finest seafood dishes in Brittany, though it's very strange to see waiters wearing black tie to serve breakfast in this kind of location. *Closed Dec–March.*
★★Au Roi Gradlon, 3 Avenue Manu Brusq, **t** 02 98 70 04 51, *www.auroigradlon.com* (*inexpensive–moderate*). A hotel right next to the beach, with sea views from the rooms (many of which have balconies) and the seafood restaurant (*moderate*).
★★Hôtel de la Plage, 21 Boulevard Emmanuel Brusq, **t** 02 98 75 04 69 (*inexpensive–moderate*). A sunny seafront hotel. *Closed Oct–April.*

Pont-Croix

★★Hotel-Restaurant Ty-Evan, 18 Rue du Docteur Neïs, **t** 02 98 70 58 58 (*inexpensive*). A hotel in the heart of this 13th-century village, by the town hall and overlooking the Goyen river, offering a warm welcome and meals in the garden in summer. Half-board is required in Aug. *Closed Jan–mid-March.*

Ile de Sein ✉ 29990

Contact the Audierne tourist office about other places to stay on the island. There are several places to eat in the village.
★★Hôtel Ar Men, Route du Phare, **t** 02 98 70 90 77, *hotel.armen@wanadoo.fr* (*inexpensive*). A charming hotel, the last before America!

ships sculpted in stone on the walls. Plogoff is the village renowned for its successful protests in the 1970s against the outrageously insensitive French government plan to build a nuclear power station nearby. *Des Pierres contre des fusils* (*Stones Versus Guns*) was the name of a well-known film made of the almost epic environmental battle.

At Primelin, you might branch off to stop and look at the delightful Flamboyant Gothic **Chapelle St-Tugen**. This substantial 16th-century chapel stands in a traditional Breton parish enclosure, the entrance to it making a memorable picture; the accolade arch of the gateway echoed in the porch entrance. The porch holds statues of the apostles and of St Tugen. Tugen was one of the best-known healing saints from the Breton Dark Ages, brother, according to some sources, of the great Irish saint Brigid. The story goes that he tried in vain to put a stop to his sister's unbridled pleasure-seeking. In frustration, Tugen cried out that it would be easier to stop a rabid dog from biting than getting a wanton girl to give up her evil ways; God supposedly consoled the man by giving him the power to cure rabies. At the St-Tugen *pardons* keys were sold that believers were meant to throw at a mad dog if it approached them. The eccentric interior is richly decorated with all manner of quirky Breton craftsmanship.

Southwest of St-Tugen, seek out the tracks to the beautiful beach in the **Anse du Cabestan**, one of the few stretches of sand along the south coast of the Cap Sizun before Audierne. The coastal path becomes rocky again from the old fortifications of the Penn an Enez on the eastern end of the Anse du Cabestan to the Pointe de Lervily. Round the corner and you come in view of the lovely string of beaches of **Ste-Evette**.

Audierne

Audierne still feels like a busy fishing port. Safely anchored up the Goyen estuary, its west bank is lined with former shipping merchants' houses. Audierne boasts the largest lobster tanks in Europe, which you can visit, and from which you can buy all manner of crustaceans. The port front has its fair share of seafood restaurants and actually supplies restaurants all around France with shellfish.

The **Aquarium La Pointe du Raz** on Rue du Goyen (*open daily May–15 Sept 10–7, 16 Sept–April 2–5*) heads the list of attractions in the town. You might also like to pay a visit to the small furniture museum situated by the quays. Head up into the old town and you can get lost in the charming maze of steep old streets. Squeezed in among them, Audierne's old church has a ship carved in stone over its entrance, appropriately enough.

Ile de Sein

Qui voit Sein voit sa fin.
(If you see Sein you see your end.)

It seems a miracle that this island hasn't been swallowed up by the ocean. The highest point on this southwestern outpost of Brittany doesn't even manage to reach 10 metres above sea level. Treacherous reefs spread out from Sein, hence the

Getting There

Boats for Sein depart from Ste-Evette beach, southwest of Audierne. The Compagnie Penn Ar Bed, t 02 98 70 70 70 (tickets from the Quai Jean Jaurès in Audierne) runs a service every day except Wed throughout the year. The *Vedette Biniou II*, t 02 98 70 21 15 (*April–Oct*) or t 02 98 70 13 78, offers alternatives in summer. The boat journey lasts around 1hr.

grisly rhyme on p.309, warning sailors against straying this way. A pair of imposing lighthouses mark the island's tips. More than 10 kilometres to the west of Sein, the lighthouse of **Ar Men** ('The Rock') is one of the most famous symbols of Brittany to French people.

Beyond the single village with its ugly church and little museum commemorating in particular the heroic action of the islanders in the Second World War, there is very little to visit on Sein. The place is about as barren as Brittany gets, almost ceaselessly windswept, and you can wander round to most parts of the island in a half-day. But it has a compelling atmosphere; and there are a number of restaurants and bars to take refuge in on bad days.

Mythology and History of the Ile de Sein

Sein has featured large in Breton mythology. Strange stories still survive about nine virgin Celtic priestesses or druidesses who lived totally isolated on Sein, the guardians of a Celtic oracle, endowed with frightening supernatural powers. These Senes were supposed to be able to whip up storms, metamorphose into terrifying beasts, cure terrible diseases, and tell the future. They would only use their oracular powers for sailors who came specifically to the island to consult them. Neolithic inhabitants had come to Sein millennia before. Just one or two monuments remain from that period.

The Senes play a part in versions of the legend of the city of Ys. The debauched and godless Dahut, daughter of King Gradlon, comes to consult them, distraught at the building of a church in her beloved irreligious town on the ocean. To counteract this encroachment of Christianity, she entreats the Senes to come to her aid. Together they chant Dahut's wishes, including one for a castle that will utterly dominate the church. *Korrigans*, Breton pagan fairies, are sent out to accomplish its construction in just one night. These *korrigans*, invisible to mortal men, will look after the protection of Ys. However, despite their superhuman powers, the Senes see that the arrival of the God from the Orient will bring about their end. They lament that 'the Senes will die one by one, and with the death of the last one the old gods of Armorica will die'. The history of Sein indicates that old pagan ways were not so easily eradicated here and Christianity not so simply espoused.

Two powerful Breton saints are connected with the history of the place, Guénolé and Corentin. St Guénolé is said to have brought Christianity to the island in the time of Dark Ages immigration from Britain. St Corentin, associated with the town of Quimper, is also said to have spent time here. No trace has been found of the monastery that may have been established around the late 5th or early 6th century, although it is said that vestiges were still visible in the 18th century.

When Sein Made Up One Quarter of France

While the rest of France capitulated so meekly to the Nazis in 1940, the men of the Ile de Sein made the most of their isolated position to take up General Charles de Gaulle's call to join him across the Channel and go and fight for a free France. A large number of the adult population of able and fit men, approximately 150 in number, took to their boats on hearing De Gaulle's message and immediately headed for England.

'So the island of Sein makes up a quarter of France, does it?', De Gaulle is claimed to have wryly remarked as he inspected the first batch of French arrivals in Britain. Several thousand further Frenchmen got away to Britain from Sein in the ensuing weeks. Some 30 Sénans died in the Second World War.

The island is referred to as Sedhun on the 11th-century cartulary of the abbey of Landévennec. Its name changes time and again in written sources, but the fear that it instilled in sailors remained unaltered down the centuries. The small number of Sénans, as inhabitants of Sein are known, gained a filthy reputation as wreckers. The redemptive Christian story goes that the islanders basically had to be reconverted during the 17th century.

Even this tiny island was to some extent affected by the colonial wars of the 17th and 18th centuries – when colonial fighting abated, apparently the locals remained reluctant to help any British men washed up on their shores. The island was often under threat from the seas. In 1756, after a tidal wave crashed over Sein, the royal governor of Brittany, the Duc d'Aiguillon, offered the Sénans money to move to the mainland. They refused, but did agree to the building of a jetty.

The island has been engulfed a fair number of times since then by a raging sea. The most dramatic incident occurred in 1868, when the islanders took refuge in the highest attics. Such was the feeling of desperation that Sein's priest is supposed to have offered everyone the last rites. A similar rush to take cover under the village roofs occurred on a couple of further occasions in the 19th century and again in 1919. The second half of the 19th century was the time of the construction of many of the great Sein lighthouses.

Tour of the Ile de Sein

You feel you can take in the whole of Sein in one easy glance as you arrive by sea. Without the slightest hint of a hill, practically the whole of the island spreads out in front of you. And there are no trees for anything or anyone to hide from the wind. A very long cement jetty reaches round like an embracing arm to protect the harbour. The port-cum-village occupies the centre of the island. Narrow isthmuses on either side lead to scrub-covered tips.

The **village** itself does have its secretive side, with its very narrow, crooked streets. They are supposed to be just wide enough to roll a barrel along. The favoured mode of transport in fact appears to be the wheelbarrow – there are no cars. Up by the church, the two menhirs facing each other like slightly irascible but close friends are comically known as the *Pregourien*, 'the Chatters'. The **church**, in neo-Romanesque style, dates from the late 19th century but is dedicated to the Celtic Christian Guénolé. Inside, it contains some quite interesting postwar stained-glass windows. On the northern end of the village, the **Kador** ('Seat') rock is traditionally associated with those powerful pagan priestesses of Sein, the Senes.

Heading southeast of the village, you can walk along the wide sweep of sand and stones still protected by the arm of the jetty. The isthmus itself can be a tricky place to negotiate with its great number of rockpools. The southern tip of the island is totally uninhabited. A whole network of stone walls that have been swallowed up by scrub makes the terrain fairly difficult to cross. You feel like you are walking over a ruined settlement.

The more common path taken by visitors is the concrete one out of the village to the **lighthouse** on the western end of Sein. Before you arrive there, a very small and inconsequential chapel tries its best to hide in the undergrowth. It is dedicated to St Corentin. So too is the lighthouse, the Phare St-Corentin – the one substantial building on the island, with its soaring tower.

Pont-Croix and Around

Back on the mainland and up the Goyen river from Audierne, cobbled little streets as treacherously steep as alpine slopes lead up from the river bank to the historic town of Pont-Croix that sits on its height. You'd do best to don mountain boots to make it up the Grande or the Petite Rue Chère, which are lined by minute old cottages. The site of Pont-Croix is fit for a castle. And in fact a fort did used to stand here, marking the frontier between the Cap Sizun and the Pays Bigouden to the south. This was the seat of power of a lordly Cornouaille family during medieval times. The port back down at the foot of the town would once have been bustling with activity. In fact Pont-Croix was the proud capital of the Cap Sizun, before the Goyen began to silt up.

The story of Pont-Croix's medieval wealth is written in the stones and finery of the **Eglise Notre-Dame de Roscudon**, a Breton church that was influenced by English architecture. The edifice dates back in fair part to the 13th century. A whole string of other religious buildings followed this style, forming what became known as the Pont-Croix school of architecture. The two main outer features of the church are a towering spire and a sensational Flamboyant Gothic porch, which was added on to an otherwise reasonably sober building. Inside the church, tightly ranked semicircular arches in the Romanesque style hold up the dark nave. Only in the choir do lighter Gothic pointed arches take over. The west façade and the sacristy both date from the 18th century.

To the east of Pont-Croix, at **Confort-Meilars**, the outdoor calvary looks fairly grandiose, but the niches for the apostles stand empty. The most exciting curiosity of this church is its chime wheel, with 12 bells, each playing a different note. It is said to have been a gift from Alain de Rosmadec and Jeanne de Chastel to thank the Virgin for getting their mute child to speak.

The Pays Bigouden

The Pays Bigouden occupies one of the wildest parts of the whole Breton peninsula. Pont-l'Abbé is its capital, where a uniquely tall *coiffe* was traditionally worn. This towering headdress of the women of the area, surely one of the most architectural manifestations of fashion in the world, is such a powerful image that it has become something of a symbol for the whole of Brittany to many outsiders.

An immense, gently curving but inhospitable beach runs down the Baie d'Audierne on the western side of the Pays Bigouden. The chapel of Tronoën, which boasts the most famous calvary in Brittany, looks over at the barren scene. Despite the sinister rocks of the area, a whole string of fishing ports line the southern shore of the Pays Bigouden. Their forces combined, they make up one of the biggest fishing fleets in all France. Between these ports, the beaches are particularly appreciated by windsurfers.

The Bay of Audierne

The predominant feature of the Bay of Audierne is the great sweep of its sands disappearing into the distance. Sea spray often obscures the view of the entire curve, while the Atlantic waves thunder in incessantly. On the northern end of the bay there is a rough, rocky stretch of coastline before you arrive at the immense beach. The Pays Bigouden starts by **Pors-Poulhan**, where René Quillivic's statue of a Bigoudène girl blushes orange with lichen at her prominent role marking the frontier with the Cap Sizun.

The coast road sticks close to the rocks as you head south past the **Menhir des Droits de l'Homme**, at the beach of Canté. This neolithic menhir stands close to the spot out to sea where the ship *Les Droits de l'Homme* was hounded, holed and sunk by two English frigates in 1797. A French fleet of 45 vessels, carrying some 16,000 troops, had set off from Brest in December 1796. It was heading to Ireland to try to start an insurrection there against the British. But three consecutive storms scattered the ships, which never even made it to Ireland. As the French fleet headed back to Brest, the British navy attacked. *Les Droits de l'Homme* went down with some 600 men. One Englishman who survived the battle and made it to shore, only to be imprisoned by the French, was Major Pipon from Jersey. In 1840, he returned to the scene of the terrible event and asked for memorial words to be engraved on the menhir to remember the men who had died in the tragedy.

The **Chapelle de Penhors** adds a picturesque religious note to the village of Penhors by which it stands, looking out over the bay. Like many other chapels in the area, its architecture follows the Pont-Croix style.

Inland from Penhors, **Pouldreuzic** is known above all as the location for Pierre Jakez Hélias's famous book (*see* box p.314), but the popular Breton crêpe-making machines by Krampouz are also manufactured and sold here, as is the popular pork Pâté Hénaff, and good cider.

The Bitch of the World and the Horse of Pride

As I'm too poor to buy any other kind of horse, at least the horse of pride will always have a place in my stable.

The subtitle to *Le Cheval d'orgueil*, a deeply evocative autobiographical book by Pierre Jakez Hélias, reads *Mémoires d'un Breton du Pays Bigouden*. Originally written in Breton and then translated into French by the author, it has become the most read 20th-century book on Brittany and even been turned into a French film. It tells the story of a Bigouden community centred around Pouldreuzic and how its people lived in the first half of the 20th century.

Most of the locals' lives were dominated by the *chienne du monde* (the bitch of the world) – poverty. In an area and a time where a horse remained the sign of a wealthy man, the poor were still tied to their overlords, their employers and the clergy, in an almost feudal, medieval manner. After a hard day working for the master, they would sometimes get together by moonlight to clear by hand a piece of meagre earth to cultivate for themselves. Children slept in *lits-clos* on bedding stuffed with seaweed. The cottage floors were of beaten earth: 'Each head of a family had his own recipe for preparing his floor, just as each wife had hers for preparing her stew,' Hélias explains.

Despite the harshness of life for most in the parish, the rituals, the pleasures and the comedy of everyday events, conversations and ceremonies fill the pages. The Bigoudens' comments on life can be coarse and subtle at the same time. Pettiness, rivalry and superstition go hand in hand with heartfelt love and intelligence.

One of the Longest Beaches in Brittany

South of Penhors, one of the longest beaches in Brittany curves gently round the bay of Audierne down to St-Guénolé. This is also one of the wildest strands in the province, backed by a curious bank of ancient pebbles. The odd Nazi blockhouse has toppled down to deface the sands. Going back in time, it was along this coast that the wrecks from the Pointe de Penmarc'h tended to be blown ashore. The poor people of the region would comb the beaches to recuperate remnants. They long had a reputation as wreckers, deliberately trying to get ships to go astray on their shore. Behind the beach, many of the old houses were built without any openings on the Atlantic side, to give no opportunities to the ocean's draughts to enter.

Southeast out of the village of Plovan, the **chapel of Languidou** lay in ruins long before the war. It was built in the 13th century, in the style of the school of Pont-Croix, and was an early flowering of Gothic architecture in Brittany. In fact, some art historians now say that this was the church where the so-called school of Point-Croix style began. The place will appeal to romantics, with its delicate ruins. The most notable remnant here is the rose window, emptied of its glass but with its lacy Gothic stone tracery practically intact.

The sandy and marshy lands that lie behind the great beach have an unkempt look about them, with the rare lines of trees contorted by the winds. But birds love the place, and a bird observatory has been set up at the end of the track beyond Trunvel.

However, the best place to go to learn about the natural environment of the bay is the **Maison de la Baie** (*t* 02 98 82 61 76) lost in the countryside to the south of Tréguennec. The barren coastal strip stretching westwards of this village is marked by a long stretch of wall that looks as though it might have formed a massive section of Nazi defences, a substantial chunk of Atlantic wall. The abandoned site is eerily atmospheric. In fact, this was a factory where the Germans had the beach pebbles sorted 24 hours a day by virtual slave labour, to then have them transported for construction work in Brest, Lorient and elsewhere. The Plovan pebbles continued to be exploited for building purposes through until the late 1960s, and the protective band of them has been irreparably depleted.

Of the many rural chapels that are lost in the small valleys and plots just inland of here, do seek out the dollsized **Chapelle de St-Vio** for its sheer comical charm.

Tronoën, the Little 'Cathedral of the Dunes' and its Calvary

Its Breton steeple standing out of the melancholy countryside like a lichen-rusted trident, Tronoën possesses the most famous calvary in Brittany, and one of the oldest, the exposed stone figures eaten away by the winds. The calvary dates from around 1450. The two-level sculpted friezes tell many stories from Christ's life and Passion.

The Tronoën sculptures count among the most expressive of any on the Breton calvaries. The bold little compositions have great force. Perhaps the best-known panel shows the Virgin after Jesus's birth. Here, rather than religious decorum completely denying the physicality of the act, Mary is depicted naked-breasted in bed. Other striking scenes stand out in the Passion: Jesus blindfolded as he is beaten; Pilate, in what slightly resembles a pirate's hat, washing his hands; Christ carrying his cross that sticks out above the other friezes, while the two thieves follow him with their lighter burdens; the Virgin, almost as rigid as an Egyptian mummy in her grief, being supported by the women surrounding her. Three crosses rise like bent masts from the rectangular base of the calvary. At the foot of the central cross, the Pietà scene has a particular tenderness to it as two figures reach up to draw back the Virgin's veil. The faces here look swollen, the Virgin grim. A much more refined countenance has been carved in skilful low relief on St Veronica's veil – that of a deeply pensive Christ, portrayed as a wise man with flowing locks.

A fair number of small statues of Venus have been discovered in digs around the chapel, pointing to the existence of a Gallo-Roman sacred site here. Also close to Tronoën, archaeological excavations at St-Urnel unearthed a huge burial ground from AD 500 to 1100, containing more than 5,000 tombs. Nowadays it comes as a surprise to see that a good portion of the land behind the bay of Audierne, once considered unsuitable for growing anything, is being cultivated – an area once seemingly washed out by the sea air is now set ablaze, in season, with tulips and other colourful flowers.

On the southern end of the Baie d'Audierne, the slashed piles of rocks of the dramatic spit of the **Pointe de la Torche** are lashed most of the year by large crashing waves, but these assailants are reduced to nothing more than cascading foam by the

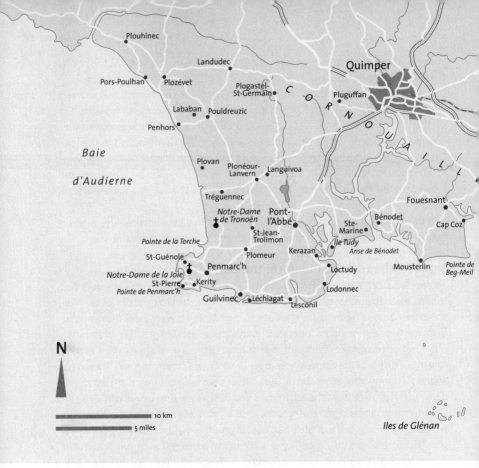

N

10 km
5 miles

Iles de Glénan

encounter. It's an exhilarating walk to the tip of the point. A discreet dolmen and German concrete bunkers mark the crowning points of the headland. One of the Nazi posts has been turned into an information centre. The first world windsurfing championships were held here in 1983 and several others have taken place here since. The beautiful **beach of Pors Carn** curves round to the bleak port of St-Guénolé.

The Fishing Ports of the Southern Pays Bigouden

The big four ports of St-Guénolé/Penmarc'h, Guilvinec/Léchiagat, Lesconil and Loctudy are what are termed *ports de pêche artisanale*, or craft fishing ports, to distinguish their activity from *pêche industrielle*. Together they form the largest centre for this type of fishing in the whole of France. The harbour streets of these towns that live so largely by seafood smell pungent, the screech of greedy gulls often filling the air. The people of the area have been busy fishing and sea trading since medieval times. Canning grew up as an important industry in the second half of the 19th century. Working conditions in the canneries led to furious strikes in 1926–27, but this industry has now pretty well died out in the area.

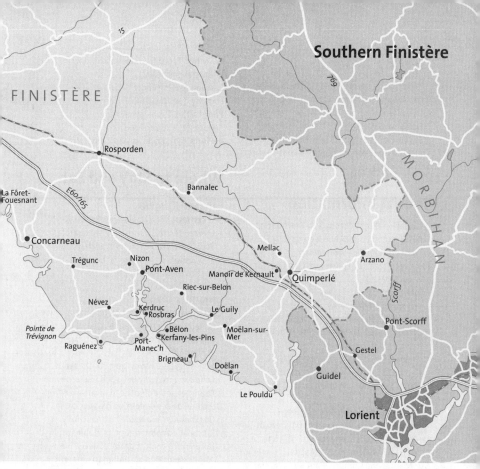

St-Guénolé and Penmarc'h

Eterne God, that thurgh thy purveiaunce
Ledest the world by certein governaunce,
In ydel, as men seyn, ye nothyng make.
But, Lord, thise grisly feendly rokkes blake,
That semen rather a foul confusioun
Of werk than any fair creacioun
Of swich a parfit wys God and a stable,
Why han ye wroght this werk unresonable?

The noble lady Dorigen bemoaning the danger of the Pointe de Penmarc'h's rocks in Chaucer's 'Franklin's Tale' from *The Canterbury Tales*

St-Guénolé, the main port of the greater parish of Penmarc'h, is more than a little grim, with its evil-looking rocks, but compelling in a sinister kind of way. On the northern side of the port, not many of the owners of the scattered houses have even bothered to paint their houses white as is traditional in Brittany, but have left them grely exposed to the briny winds that quickly turn everything grubby here. On the

Getting Around

The only means of public transport in the Pays Bigouden is **buses**. Services around the area radiate out from Pont-l'Abbé, making it possible, if slow, to get to the ports, resorts and some of the chapels in the countryside. There is a good service between Pont-l'Abbé and Quimper.

Tourist Information

Association Ouest Cornouaille Promotion, B.P. 41, 29120 Pont-l'Abbé, t 02 98 82 30 30, *ouest.cornouaille@wanadoo.fr*.

Plozévet: Place de l'Eglise, t 02 98 91 45 15, *www.plozevet.org*.

Pouldreuzic: Salle Per-Jakes Hélias, t 02 98 54 49 90. *wwwpouldreuzic.org*.

St-Guénolé and Penmarc'h: Place du Maréchal Davout, B.P. 47, St-Pierre, 29760 Penmarc'h, t 02 98 58 81 44, *www.penmarch.fr*.

Guilvinec: 62 Rue de la Marine, t 02 98 58 29 29, *www.leguilvinec.com*.

Loctudy: Place de la Mairie, t 02 98 87 53 78, *www.loctudy.fr*.

Pont-l'Abbé: Place de la République, t 02 98 82 37 99, *www.ot-pontlabbe29.fr*.

Ile-Tudy: 1 Rue des Roitelets, t 02 98 56 30 14, or t 02 98 56 42 57 out of season.

Ste-Marine and Combrit: Pont de Cornouaille, 29120 Ste-Marine, t 02 98 56 48 41, or t 02 98 56 41 74 out of season, *www.ville-de-combrit.fr*.

Market Days

Plozévet: 1st Monday of the month.
St-Guénolé: Friday.

Guilvinec: Tuesday, and Sunday in July and Aug.
Léchiagat: Saturday.
Lesconil: Wednesday.
Loctudy: Tuesday.
Pont-l'Abbé: Thursday (all day), Place de la République.
Ile-Tudy: Monday in July and Aug.

Where to Stay and Eat

Lababan ✉ 29710

★★★Ker Ansquer, t 02 98 54 41 83, *www. keransquer.com (inexpensive–moderate)*. Very comfortable rooms in a small neo-Breton-style manor a few km to the northwest of Pouldreuzic.

Landudec ✉ 29710

Château de Guilguiffin, t 02 98 91 52 11, *www. guilguiffin.com (expensive)*. One of the most enchanting 18th-century Breton castles, converted into holiday flats but with a few luxurious B&B rooms, just southeast of Landudec, midway between Audierne and Quimper. *Table d'hôte* can be arranged.

Domaine de Lesvaniel, t 02 98 91 55 05 *(inexpensive–moderate)*. A beautifully landscaped combination of stables and hotel in the middle of the countryside, with rooms decorated according to different themes. There's a library and a salon where they serve crêpes and other traditional food.

Penhors ✉ 29710

★★Breiz Armor, t 02 98 51 52 53, *www. breiz-armor.fr (inexpensive–moderate)*. A surprising modern complex next to the

northern side of town, still overlooking the beach of Pors Carn and the Pointe de la Torche, the all too obvious fenced-off France Télécom compound is where the phone cable linking France to North America heads off on its immensely long journey under the Atlantic. You might visit the old-fashioned **Musée Préhistorique Finistérien** (*open 10–12 and 2–6 Wed–Mon June–Sept, Wed–Sun Oct–May*) nearby. Menhirs, dolmens, steles and a gallery chamber have been gathered at the entrance. Inside the museum, exhibits from down the millennia are displayed in an archaic fashion.

The port of St-Guénolé is at the technological forefront of the fishing industry, however, with computerized auctioning of the catch. It is possible to go walking on the savage rocks that protect the port, but beware – the Rocher du Préfet is named after the head of a French *département* who was swept out to sea with his family.

beach of Penhors. All 23 rooms have views onto several kilometres of unspoilt coast. M. Ségalen, who runs the hotel with his wife, is also the head cook, preparing fine seafood.

Plonéour-Lanvern ✉ 29720
Manoir de Kerhuel, at Kerhuel, **t** 02 98 82 60 57, *perso.wanadoo.fr/manoir-kerhuel* (*moderate*). A quite luxurious hotel set in a splendid Breton manor in its own grounds, with a pool, tennis court and various treatments. *Closed Dec–March exc Christmas–New Year.*

St-Guénolé ✉ 29760
★★★Le Sterenn, Rue de la Joie, Penmarc'h, **t** 02 98 58 60 36, *www.le-sterenn.com* (*moderate*). A place right on the coast, with fine views of the rocks and reefs. Many of the pleasant modern rooms share the view. The seafood platters and fresh fish are excellent. *Closed Nov–March.*
★★★L'Ocean, **t** 02 98 58 71 71 (*inexpensive–moderate*). A recently renovated little hotel with a swimming pool. *Closed Dec–March.*
★★Hôtel de la Mer, **t** 02 98 58 62 22 (*inexpensive*). Rooms in a typical Breton port house, with rustic furniture; some have good views on to the rocks. The cuisine (*moderate*) is of a high standard and traditionally French.
★★Les Ondines, Rue Pasteur, **t** 02 98 58 74 95, *www.lesondines.com* (*inexpensive*). An appealing holiday hotel. *Closed Dec–March.*

Kerity ✉ 29760
Le Doris, **t** 02 98 58 60 92 (*inexpensive*). A bit of an institution in the port of Kerity, popular for its seafood. There are a few B&B rooms with sea views above the restaurant.

Guilvinec-Léchiagat ✉ 29730
★★Hôtel du Centre, 16 Rue du Général de Gaulle, Guilvinec, **t** 02 98 58 10 44 (*inexpensive*). A classic, traditional French hotel just a short walk away from the port.
★★Hôtel du Port, 53 Avenue du Port, Léchiagat, **t** 02 98 58 10 10 (*inexpensive*). A hotel with a popular quayside restaurant specializing in grilled langoustines. It's a good place to stay if you fancy going on a day's fishing expedition aboard *La Torche*.
Le Chandelier, 16 Rue de la Marine, Guilvinec, **t** 02 98 58 91 00 (*moderate–expensive*). Inventive nouvelle cuisine dishes in an old fisherman's cottage. *Closed Mon, and Tues and Sun eves in low season.*

Plomeur ✉ 29120
Chaumière de Keraluic, **t** 02 98 82 10 22 (*inexpensive*). High-quality B&B rooms in a renovated thatched cottage close to St-Jean-Trolimon. *Table d'hôte* is available.
Crêperie Men-Lann-Du, Route de Penmarc'h, **t** 02 98 82 01 06 (*inexpensive*). A popular place serving good crêpes in a simple old Breton farmhouse that has kept its traditional beaten-earth floor.

Lesconil ✉ 29740
★★Hôtel de la Plage, Rue Joliot Curie, **t** 02 98 87 80 05 (*inexpensive*). A good-value place to stay, with views onto this pretty port.

Loctudy ✉ 29750
★★Hôtel de Bretagne, 19 Rue du Port, **t** 02 98 87 40 21, *hoteldebretagne@msn.com* (*inexpensive*). A very comfortable and charming hotel for its price.

As you head south along the coast from the port of St-Guénolé, a memorable rockscape opens out in front of you. Rocks stretch out to sea like a shower of meteorites scattered over the waters. On top of many of them stand small beacons, reminiscent of candles. The **Chapelle Notre-Dame de la Joie** is the 15th-century chapel that was seemingly built among the reefs here. A stone boat is carved on one gable. The name of the edifice, Our Lady of Joy, may seem ironic given the treacherous setting but this is the church where sailors came to pray in thanks to the Virgin Mary for sparing their lives on dangerous sea journeys. It also served as the house in which materials salvaged from wrecks were stored. Not surprisingly, with so many local people depending on the risky work of fishing for their livelihood, the church gathered a deeply devoted following, its *pardon* of 15 August becoming one of the

Le Relais de Lodonnec, 3 Rue des Tulipes, Plage de Lodonnec, 2km south of Loctudy, **t** 02 98 87 55 34 (*inexpensive–expensive*). A restaurant in an old granite fisherman's cottage, serving flavoursome seafood dishes. *Closed Mon in July and Aug; Tues eve and Wed in low season.*

Pont-l'Abbé ✉ 29120

★★Hôtel de Bretagne, 24 Place de la République, **t** 02 98 87 17 22 (*inexpensive*). A well-kept hotel with an old Breton feel, dating from the 18th century and located in the centre of town. There is a good restaurant attached.

★★Hotel la Tour d'Auvergne, 22 Place Gambetta, **t** 02 98 87 00 47, *www.tourdauvergne.fr* (*inexpensive*). A hotel that was recently taken over by a Franco-Irish team; renovation of the rooms is imminent. The cuisine is varied and excellent.

La Bodega, Rue du Lycée (*inexpensive*). An appealing place for soft-option tucker. A sort of a Tex-Mex/brasserie hybrid, it offers a cheap French *menu du jour* (the kind that comes with big fries), served up in bright and pleasant dining room with a garden terrace. It's a great place for kids, with friendly service.

Crêperie Courot, Rue du Lycée, **t** 02 98 87 02 61, (*inexpensive*). A highly recommended eaterie where you can count on a warm welcome. Toys are provided for children. *Closed part of Sept.*

Ile-Tudy ✉ 29980

★★Hotel Euromer, 6 Avenue Téven, **t** 02 98 51 97 00 (*inexpensive*). A large, well-run hotel in the modern part of Ile-Tudy. It may be on the characterless side, but the rooms are quite comfortable and it is only about 150m from the beach. There's a restaurant attached, and you can sometimes eat by the swimming pool.

Modern Hôtel, 9 Place de la Cale, **t** 02 98 56 43 34 (*inexpensive*). A misleadingly named hotel (it's traditional rather than modern) in a lovely location right by the harbour, in the older part of Ile Tudy. The guest rooms are basic and don't have soundproofing, but the restaurant is a very pleasant place in which to eat.

Ste-Marine ✉ 29120

Hôtel-Restaurant de Sainte-Marine, 19 Rue du Bac, **t** 02 98 56 34 79, *www.hotelsaintemarine.com* (*moderate*). A hotel situated close to the old village chapel, with all guest rooms and the restaurant overlooking the delightful harbour. It's a little favourite among various French celebrities.

L'Agape, 52 Route de la Plage, **t** 02 98 56 32 70 (*expensive*). The restaurant with the most established reputation in Ste-Marine, situated not by the ports but very close to the beaches. *Closed Sun eve, Mon and Tues lunch in low season.*

Café de la Cale (*inexpensive*). A wonderfully located café.

Crêperie La Misaine, **t** 02 98 51 90 45 (*inexpensive*). A very cheerful place to eat by the port.

Café du Port/Brasserie de la Mer, **t** 02 98 56 44 36 (*inexpensive*). A pleasant café and brasserie where you can enjoy live jazz on certain summer evenings.

---

most important events in the entire calendar of the Pays Bigouden. A famous old Breton song, the 'Gwerz Penmarc'h', tells a chilling story, though, cursing the people of the Pointe de Penmarc'h for lighting fires in their church in order to mislead sailors and wreck their ships.

Dwarfing the diminutive port and chapel of **St-Pierre** (the latter was employed as a lighthouse before the central one was constructed), the grandiose **Phare d'Eckmühl** (*open daily 1 April–30 Sept 10.30–12.30 and 2–7, 1 Oct–31 March 2.30–5.30*), wearing its crown of a lantern, serves as a landmark for several kilometres around. Its beam can apparently reach more than 60 kilometres out to sea. Visitors can climb almost to the top of its 65 metres. The life-saving centre below it has clearly had a major role to play in times past – it went by the disconcerting name of the

Société Centrale des Naufragés (the 'Central Company for the Shipwrecked'). An old life-saving boat has been preserved at the port, where there's now also a centre for maritime discovery.

Penmarc'h and the Church of St-Nonna

Coming on to the southern side of the Pays Bigouden round from the Phare d'Eckmühl, you stumble upon the small port of **Kerity**. Its present appearance belies its much grander past. This area was cosmopolitan in its heyday in the 16th century; Kerity was then the largest port in the Pays Bigouden, serving the whole Penmarc'h area, and one of the most important in Brittany. Ships coming up from Bordeaux laden with wine would frequently stop here on the way to England and Flanders. Apparently, in 1534, out of 808 Breton ships that stopped off at the port of Arnemuiden near Antwerp, 270 were from the Penmarc'h region.

Just inland, **Penmarc'h's church of St-Nonna** stands out by its grand dimensions, rising high above the town's little houses. In contrast with the generally minute chapels of the area, St-Nonna is on an impressive scale. It was built early in the 16th century, when Penmarc'h was a thriving town thanks to Kerity's trade. The church was dedicated to St Nonna, a man, not a woman, and not to be confused with Ste Nonna, mother of St David (*see* p.266). St Nonna is supposed to have become bishop of Armagh in the 6th century. The bulky west tower of the church was never completed, but you can see several ships sculpted in its stone – a sign of the shipping merchants' donations. Inside, the spaces supported by towering, wide Gothic arches seem cavernous in comparison with all the tiny chapels of the Pays Bigouden.

To see a few exceptional contemporary stained-glass windows in a Breton chapel, head for the **Chapelle de la Madeleine**, just northwest of Penmarc'h, clad in palest grey stone. Inside, the flaming semi-abstract religious figures by the artist Jean Bazaine flow with energy and emotion.

From Guilvinec to Loctudy

Guilvinec and **Léchiagat**, facing each other across a river estuary, have joined forces to form one very lively, workmanlike port. Guilvinec's harbour seems the busiest place to be after 4pm on weekdays in the Pays Bigouden, when the fishing boats return. TThere is also the Centre for the Discovery and Interpretation of Fishing at Sea, **Haliotika** (*open 15 March–15 Oct and school hols Mon–Fri 2.30–7, Sat and Sun 3–6.30*), which covers the contemporary realities of the maritime fishing profession through imaginative presentations, and is especially worth visiting for the tour of the fishmarket. The maze of lanes in both Guilvinec and Léchiagat have all the atmosphere you would expect of Breton ports.

A series of long beaches, separated by rocky outcrops and backed by tallish sand dunes, runs to **Lesconil**, a popular little fishing port that doubles as a small resort. Lesconil's old fishermen's houses are kept immaculately whitewashed. The coast that leads east from Lesconil to Loctudy presents a more complex mix of rocks and beaches, the sand particularly white, especially in contrast with the black algae that come to die on the strands.

Potatoes brought the port of **Loctudy** to life in the 19th century. Edouard Le Normant des Varannes, a proprietor of the Château de Kérazan just inland from the town, began growing spuds successfully in the 1830s. He persuaded his farmer neighbours to follow suit and set up an export business from Loctudy to Britain. Then sea-bathing became fashionable in the middle of the century, and rich families from Quimper and Pont-l'Abbé started building along Loctudy's coast and river estuary. Loctudy has been a relatively chic little resort since then. Its fishing port and yachting harbour stand out on the western end of the Pont-l'Abbé river estuary. Loctudy has the biggest market for live langoustines in France. In high summer, cruise boats from here can take you up the Odet or out to the Glénan islands.

The **church of St-Tudy**, somewhat notorious for its carving of a male erection, lies just up from Loctudy's port, surrounded by its sandy graveyard into which the tombstones seem to be sinking. You can admire a pre-Christian stele in front of the church, like a finely cut menhir. The Christian Church has had to put its own mark on it in the shape of a cross. The church is described in Breton art books as one of the finest examples of Romanesque architecture in Brittany, but it has actually been given a classical 18th-century façade. Once inside, the Romanesque dominates. The capitals are carved with intriguing Celtic-style patterns that you can see reproduced on the traditional embroidered Bigouden jackets. The erection turns out to be a little affair, carved at the base of a column in the choir.

Outside Loctudy, the **Manoir de Kérazan** (*open daily Easter–15 June and Sept 2–6, 16 June–Aug 10.30–7*) is a fine Breton house dating from the 16th and 18th centuries. The eccentric shapes of its slate-covered roofs give it immediate appeal, and it is well surrounded by typical Breton hydrangeas. The Manoir's last private owner, Joseph Astor, left it to the Institut de France on condition that it be turned in part into a museum, in part into a school of embroidery for young Bigoudènes. The last pupils left during the 1960s, but the museum survives. The place is filled with paintings by well-known names of the Breton art scene, including Maurice Denis, Charles Cottet and Auguste Goy.

Also situated between Loctudy and Pont-l'Abbé, the **Maison du Pays Bigouden** (*open Mon–Sat Easter–31 May 10–12 and 2–5, June–Sept 10–12.30 and 2–6.30; last tour 30mins before closing*) at the Ferme de Kervazégan contains a pretty collection of Bigouden rural furniture.

Pont-l'Abbé

Pont-l'Abbé stretches out from the river now named after it. It grew up around the place where an abbot of Loctudy decided to build a bridge, hence the name. Subsequently the barons of the bridge became powerful lords in the region and from the 12th century had a castle on the river. But it never proved a very successful stronghold, its occupants failing to put up much of a fight as it changed hands time and again, until the town finally bought the castle in 1836. Pont-l'Abbé long benefited from an inland port, as the quays show, but this area no longer plays centre stage.

A Tour of Pont-l'Abbé

The **castle**, Pont-l'Abbé's major building, nowadays houses the town hall, the tourist office and the **Musée Bigouden**, the main historical and cultural museum in the Pays Bigouden. The castle overlooks a 'a big sad lake', as the 19th-century writer Guy de Maupassant described it. This was much cleaned up in the 1980s, and a quite un-Breton-looking modern cultural centre, the Triskell, was put up on one side. Otherwise, Pont-l'Abbé has a strongly Breton feel. In fact, for Guy de Maupassant this was one of the most Breton towns of Breton-speaking Brittany. Some fine granite buildings line Pont-l'Abbé's main streets, as do whitewashed fronts, doors and windows bordered with granite blocks. Even early in the 21st century you can still see the odd old Bigoudène wandering around town in her towering *coiffe* (see box p.324), although most of the traditional costume-wearing Bigoudènes have now sadly passed away.

Not far east of the castle stand Pont-l'Abbé's two interesting churches. On the far side of the water, the shell of the **church of Lambour**, one of a series of decapitated churches in the Pays Bigouden (see box below), has been lovingly scrubbed clean.

A Premature Revolution, a Peasants' Code and Decapitated Churches

The countryside around Pont-l'Abbé became the centre of a determined Breton revolt against the impositions of French royalty in 1675. That was the year in which King Louis XIV's chief minister Jean-Baptiste Colbert tried to force through new taxes on tobacco, pewter and, most notoriously, on all legal acts, which from that time on would have to be made on specially stamped paper. These harsh measures were drawn up to pay for a hugely costly war with Holland.

Popular wrath at these new taxes gave rise to unrest throughout France, but the reaction proved particularly violent among peasants in the Pays Bigouden. Several noble houses were attacked, the archives of Pont-l'Abbé's baron were stolen and burned, and the local lord of Cosquer was hanged from one of his trees. The populace even held control of the Pays Bigouden for a brief period.

On 2 July the chapel of Notre-Dame-de-Tréminou near Plomeur, a short distance to the southwest of Pont-l'Abbé, became the rallying point of the uprising. Fourteen parishes from Douarnenez to Concarneau were represented at the meeting, which drew up a Code Paysan, or Peasants' Code. This famously listed a number of demands for profound and well-reasoned political change, for example the abolition of forced labour for overlords, the right of marriage between nobles and commoners, and the abolition of excessive, unfair taxes. The members of this revolt wore the *bonnedou ru* or *bonnet rouge*.

The Révolte des Bonnets Rouges was violently put down by the troops of the Duc de Chaulnes, who was then royal governor of Brittany. Not only were many Bigoudens hanged or sent to the galleys, but half a dozen parishes in the area also had their church towers decapitated. You can still see three of these decapitated towers at Lambour in Pont-l'Abbé, and at Languivoa and Lanvern a little way to the north.

The Tallest *Coiffe* in Brittany

Legend has it that the towering Bigoudène *coiffe* grew to its extraordinary height as a sign of protest at the churches that were decapitated in the region after the revolt of the Bonnets Rouges in 1675 (*see* box p.323). This is a purely mythical, if highly attractive, story. In fact, the *coiffe* edged gradually skywards from the middle of the 19th century and reached its dizzying height of more than 30cm around 1935. The sight is all the more amazing to visitors today as it is now so very rare – the Bigoudène *coiffe* is just about the only Breton headdress to have been worn regularly by any group of Breton women through to the turn of the century.

The *coiffe*'s origins can apparently be traced back to the medieval hats that were worn by the nobility. In time, the fashion for an elegant headpiece moved down through the social classes. Rivalry between neighbouring Breton *pays*, pride, and a desire for show all seem to have played their part in creating the huge Bigoudène *coiffe*. So too did the machine manufacture of lace, making extravagance easier. The *coiffe* consists of a tube of patterned lace, closed at the top and fixed with a curved comb and a piece of velvet onto the wearer's hair, which has been gathered up over a little bonnet. Another piece of lace closes the back of the *coiffe*. Finally, two broad lace ribbons are tied together under the left ear and allowed to trail down over the costume.

After the war, many women opted for shorter hair, and fashions from Paris caught on increasingly in the province. The tradition of the *coiffe* became not merely a chore, but also unfashionable, viewed as backward by a good number of Breton town dwellers. But for those women who were brought up in the tradition of wearing a *coiffe* every day, it proved hard to abandon the custom. More than that, many women in the Bigouden countryside who had always worn it would have felt uncomfortable, perhaps even a little ashamed, to be seen by others, as the expression put it, *en cheveux* ('in their hair').

On the opposite bank stands **Notre-Dame-des-Carmes**. The Baron Hervé IV asked the Carmelites to found an order to help to instruct the townspeople, so giving rise to this substantial church in the early 15th century. Its most admirable features are its two rose windows with their fine Gothic tracery. The eccentric slate-covered tower only dates back to the 19th century. Notre-Dame-des-Carmes, like the Triskell, organizes a series of annual **summer concerts** that attracts internationally respected musicians.

The **towpath** south along the riverbank from Notre-Dame-des-Carmes offers beautiful, peaceful walks towards the river's estuary. Back in the centre of town, the **Halles** or covered market, here in sturdy granite, stands to one side of the vast central square, the **Place de la République**, the enormous car park in the middle making way for the Thursday market. The smaller tree-shaded **Place Gambetta** is then dedicated to a tempting food market.

Pont-l'Abbé is at its most lively for the **Fête des Brodeuses**, the major folk festival of the Pays Bigouden, held each year on the second Sunday in July. You can find traditional Breton costumes and ceramics on sale in several shops in town.

To Ile-Tudy

On the way east from Pont-l'Abbé to Ile-Tudy, you pass a small botanical garden, the **Parc Botanique de Cornouaille**, with its seasonal collections of camellias, magnolias, azaleas, rhododendrons, maples, roses, and so on.

Adorable **Ile-Tudy** is not quite an island but a thin spit of land connected to the mainland by a sandy causeway. The wide estuary of the Pont-l'Abbé river lies on one side, the bay of Bénodet on the other. Tudy, a saint of the Dark Ages, is said to have founded his hermitage in this tranquil setting before moving to Loctudy 'on the continent' across the water. For a long time only fishermen and their wives lived here, their houses huddled together in the narrow, picturesque lanes. A great stretch of beach heads round to Ste-Marine.

Ste-Marine

The crescent of shaded Breton houses around the tiny port of Ste-Marine have almost all been converted into restaurants and cafés in order to make the most of this extremely beautiful location on the Odet estuary. Ste-Marine's diminutive 16th-century chapel has so far resisted being turned into an eating place, although its stringbeams are appropriately enough carved with fish. South of Ste-Marine's port lies the **Pointe de Combrit** and its spectacularly flat horizons. Out to sea, the slabs of rock are the Iles des Glénans. Just set back from the point, hiding in very cowardly fashion in a dip, lurks a coastal **fortification** dating back to the mid-19th-century reign of Emperor Napoleon III. So well hidden from sight, it is in immaculate condition and now serves as a local art gallery. It is only in recent decades that it has been possible to cross the great span of the modern bridge of Cornouaille to Bénodet; prior to that, travellers had to take the little ferry across the Odet.

From Bénodet to Concarneau: The Pays Fouesnantais

After the wild shores and the gritty fishing ports of so much of the Pays Bigouden, the part of the Finistère coast that stretches east from Bénodet is much gentler. Bénodet has long been one of the most genteel of Breton resorts, its yacht harbour popular with sailors from north of the Channel. Following the long swathes of beaches to either side of the Pointe de Mousterlin, one sweet resort succeeds the next, making the most of the protected beaches around the Baie de la Forêt. The countryside of this Pays Fouesnantais produces some of the finest Breton cherries and some of the best Breton cider.

Bénodet

Bénodet is Ste-Marine's much bigger brother, across on the eastern bank of the Odet. The two resorts are exceptionally beautiful. They are joined by the Pont de Cornouaille, a bridge that offers a spectacular view over the Odet estuary and Bénodet's marina, lying well in from the sea. Many regattas start out from this beautiful harbour. Before the Bénodet quays were built, it is said that when the tide was very high, the waves would wash up into the port-side church, which is dedicated to Thomas à Becket. Dating back in part to the 13th century, the building with its Breton steeple was enlarged in the 16th century and restored in the 19th.

Tourist cruising boats leave from the quays in front of the church. They either go up the Odet to Quimper or head out to sea to the tiny islands of Les Glénans. Both trips are wonderful. Contact Les Vedettes de l'Odet, **t** 02 98 57 00 58, for information. The **Odet cruise** takes you along the twisting river with its rocky banks and creeks. From time to time, pastures and lawns open out, leading to smart châteaux and manors. Up in the town centre, the **Musée du Bord de Mer** (*open June–Sept*) recounts the story of how Bénodet became a premier seaside resort and yachting destination.

South of Bénodet's ports lies its main curving beach, with its concrete promenade, its changing rooms, its hotels and its casino. Go round the wooded tip of the Pointe de Bénodet and out to sea you can make out what look like giant stepping stones on the horizon. These are the islands of the tiny Glénan archipelago. East round the point, you come to Bénodet's adjoining village of Le Letty, looking across a seawater lagoon known rather grandiosely as La Mer Blanche ('White Sea').

Glénan Islands

Bénodet is just one resort from which you can take a boat out to the Glénans, which lie some 20 kilometres from the shore and are well known for their sailing and diving schools, and for the numerous old wrecks. You can only land on the **Ile St-Nicolas**, with its couple of bars. If you're not diving, just walk round the magical island, or forget the world on one of its lovely beaches. La Chambre, the waters encircled by the close-knit archipelago, has been called the prettiest lagoon in Brittany. The plant Narcisse des Glénans, said to be unique in the world, was supposedly brought to Les Glénans by the ancient Phoenicians. You can only see it flowering in late spring.

The Pays Fouesnantais

Two long, flat stretches of beach curve away from the **Pointe de Mousterlin**, one of the best places from which to view the Glénan islands. Mousterlin itself doesn't have a real centre but has grown into a rambling maze of holiday homes. The point ends with a jetty and little rocks heading out to the Glénans. To the west, the beach reaches almost all the way back to Bénodet. The narrow spit of land cuts off the shallow Mer Blanche from the ocean. In summer, some wade across the Mer Blanche as a short cut to Mousterlin's western beach. The more westerly section is popular with nudists and gays. The beach east from the Pointe de Mousterlin stretches round to the very popular resort of Beg-Meil. A curious marshland lies behind the beach on the eastern side, attracting a great deal of bird life.

Beg-Meil, in contrast to Mousterlin, has a well-established identity and lots of hotels and restaurants. The writer Marcel Proust and the actress Sarah Bernhardt counted among the more illustrious early visitors to the resort. Here the fishermen

Getting Around

Concarneau has a **railway** station, t 02 98 97 00 66; you can connect with the rapid TGV line to Paris at nearby Rosporden or Quimper.

For information on local **bus** services, contact the local tourist offices.

Tourist Information

Bénodet: 51 Avenue de la Plage, t 02 98 57 00 14, *www.benodet.fr*.
Fouesnant: t 02 98 56 00 93, *www.ot-fouesnant.fr*.
La Forêt-Fouesnant: t 02 98 56 94 09, *www.foret-fouesnant-tourisme.com*.
Concarneau: Quai d'Aiguillon, t 02 98 97 01 44, *www.tourismeconcarneau.fr*.

Market Days

Bénodet: Monday.
Fouesnant: Friday.
La Forêt-Fouesnant: Sunday.
Concarneau: Monday and Friday.

Where to Stay and Eat

Bénodet ✉ 29950

There are lots of quite posh 3-star hotels in this chic resort, hence its popularity among British tourists.

★★★Ker Moor, t 02 98 57 04 48, and **Kastel Moor,** t 02 98 57 05 01 (*expensive*). Sister hotels about 200m from each other, with a fine swimming pool, a tennis court, and a good restaurant.

★★★Gwel-Kaer, 3 Avenue de la Plage, t 02 98 57 04 03 (*moderate–expensive*). A place close to the beach, with many rooms with terraces.

★★★Le Grand Hotel Abbatiale, t 02 98 57 05 11, *abbatiale.benodet@wanadoo.fr* (*moderate*).

A hotel at the centre of the action on the port. The rooms are soberly decorated, and there's a restaurant.

★★Les Bains de Mer, 11 Rue de Kerguélen, t 02 98 57 03 41, *www.lesbainsdemer.com* (*inexpensive–moderate*). A modern, very friendly hotel in the centre, with a swimming pool. You can choose simple or more elaborate food. *Closed Dec–Feb.*

Restaurant du Centre, 56 Avenue de la Plage, t 02 98 57 00 38 (*inexpensive–moderate*). A classic French restaurant with authentic seafood platters, plus pizzas in summer. *Closed Oct–March, and Tues Sept–July.*

Brasserie Tri Martolod, Z.A. de Keranguyon, t 02 98 66 20 22 (*inexpensive*). A mini-brewery where you can stock up on unpasteurized, unfiltered, traditionally fermented beer and see how it is made. *Closed Sun.*

Crêperie La Boulange, 11 Rue de l'Eglise, t 02 98 57 17 71 (*inexpensive*). The best-known crêperie in town.

Pointe de Mousterlin ✉ 29170

★★★Hôtel de la Pointe de Mousterlin, t 02 98 56 04 12, *www.mousterlinhotel.com* (*moderate–expensive*). A hotel very close to the large beaches of Mousterlin, with rooms in both the old part and the modern wing, some with balconies looking out to sea. Little luxuries you can enjoy include a jacuzzi, a sauna, a small gym and tennis courts. *Closed Feb and March.*

Fouesnant ✉ 29170

★★Auberge du Bon Cidre, 37 Rue de Cornouaille, t 02 98 56 00 16, *www.aubergeduboncidre. com* (*inexpensive*). A well-run and cheap family option.

★★L'Orée du Bois, 4 Rue de Kergoadic, t 02 98 56 00 06, *www.hotel-oree-du-bois.fr.st* (*inexpensive*). A sweet, low-priced little family hotel.

continue to sell fish and langoustines *Vente Directe* straight from the sea every evening, from a kiosk right next to the tourist office at the port. The beaches situated on the western side of Beg-Meil offer expansive views out to sea, while those on the eastern side hide away in shaded creeks giving on to the Baie de la Fôret. Make sure that you don't miss the astonishing **Cap Coz**, a pine-shaded resort with the safest of beaches and enchanting views from its thin spit of land stretching across the back of the bay.

Pointe du Cap Coz

**Hôtel de la Pointe du Cap Coz,
t 02 98 56 01 63, *www.hotel-capcoz.com*
(*moderate*). A hotel situated on a wonderful
spit of land overlooking a delightful Breton
bay. It has been run by the same family
since 1919.

La Forêt-Fouesnant ✉ 29940

****Manoir du Stang, t 02 98 56 97 37
stang@chateauxhotels.com (*inexpensive*).
An immaculate Breton manor dating
from the 15th and 18th centuries, hidden in
its own chunk of wooded valley, with a
tennis court. The rooms are wonderfully
comfortable and filled with old-fashioned
furniture. *Closed Sept–March.*

Concarneau ✉ 29900

Ville Close

Le Penfret, 40 Route de Vauban,
t 02 98 50 70 55 (*moderate*). A restaurant
inside a fine old granite building in the
heart of the Ville Close, with a terrace and a
16th-century spiral staircase. Although it's
on the busiest street, it has remained
authentic and still offers reasonable value.
Closed Oct–Jan.

Les Remparts, 31 Rue Théophile Louarn, t 02 98
50 65 66 (*inexpensive*). A tranquil spot with a
good choice of crêpes, a flowery façade and
a terrace. *Closed Nov–April.*

New Town

***De L'Océan, Plage des Sables Blancs,
t 02 98 50 53 50, *www.hotel-ocean.com*
(*moderate–expensive*). The only 3-star
hotel in town, with a swimming pool
among its attractions.

**L'Hôtel Kermoor, Plage des Sables Blancs,
t 02 98 97 02 96, *kermoor@lespiedsdansleau.*
com (*moderate*). A hotel with a beautiful

interior, carefully decorated rooms offering
a high degree of comfort, a *salle* and a
stylish terrace that overlooks the beach of
Les Sables Blancs. Visitors can listen to radio
traffic from passing ships while relaxing in
the lounge.

**Le Port, 11 Avenue P. Guéguin, t 02 98 97 31 52
(*inexpensive*). A good option for those
wishing to stay much closer to the fishing
port itself.

*Modern, 5 Rue du Lin, t 02 98 97 03 36,
(*inexpensive*). A calm, well-run family hotel
just behind the port.

Citotel de France et d'Europe,
Avenue de la Gare, t 02 98 97 00 64,
www.hotel-france-europe.com (*inexpensive*).
A modern, efficient and welcoming choice
situated in the centre of town, 300m from
the Ville Close and not far from the harbour.

Auberge de Jeunesse, Place de la Croix,
t 02 98 97 03 47, *www.fuaj.org* (*inexpensive*).
A youth hostel set in a large house by
Concarneau's rocks.

La Coquille, 1 Rue du Moros, by the fishing
harbour, t 02 98 97 08 52 (*moderate–very
expensive*). An excellent seafood restaurant
with a very pleasant terrace overlooking the
port for sunny days, and a dining room
decorated with Breton paintings for less
clement weather. *Closed Sun eve, Mon and
2wks May.*

Le Buccin, 1 Rue Duguay Trouin, t 02 98 50 54 22
(*moderate–expensive*). A place serving good
seafood, including iced gazpacho and fish
cotriade. *Closed low season Sun and Thurs
eves, Mon lunch in season.*

Chez Armande, 15 bis Avenue du Docteur
Nicolas, t 02 98 97 00 76 (*moderate*).
A simple restaurant opposite the marina,
with wood panelling and a tank where you
can choose your seafood.

L'Escale, 19 Quai Carnot (*inexpensive*).
An authentic fishermen's haunt.

Coming to Fouesnant and La Forêt-Fouesnant, you arrive in a land of cherry trees
and apple orchards. **Fouesnant**, with its cheerful old centre, is synonymous with
good cider in Brittany. It also has a quite impressive modern indoor pool, should the
weather let you down, and a Romanesque church of some repute. Built in the late
11th and early 12th centuries and since restored, it looks surprisingly light inside, given
its period. Outside, the calvary and the sacristy with its little roof in the shape of an
upturned hull were both added in the 17th century.

La Forêt-Fouesnant climbs delightfully up the slope from a densely wooded valley. Outside the Flamboyant Gothic chapel that you will see on the way up the hillside, the simple calvary is surrounded by an outdoor preaching pulpit, its four corners marked by Gothic pinnacles.

Down from La Forêt-Fouesnant, the impressive hidden marina of **Port-La-Forêt** was built in the 1970s.

Concarneau

The Ville Close may have become the tourist heart of Concarneau – the small walled island is extremely safely located in the mouth of the Moros river estuary and only remains attached to the mainland by a bridge – but the fishing harbour that lies behind it is the local heart of the place. Concarneau ranks as one of the three largest fishing ports in the whole of France for live catches brought in, and the biggest tuna port in the country.

Between 1870 and 1950, Concarneau became one of the major Breton centres to attract artists. When the sardine banks suddenly moved on from their familiar waters in 1905, it was the artists who had come regularly to Concarneau from outside Brittany who in large part helped to start up charitable works to assist the desperately impoverished community.

The Ville Close

The old town of Concarneau, measuring a mere 100 metres by 350 metres, was fortified as early as the 14th century. The Ville Close's island offering such a good obvious natural defence, it also became an obvious point to attack. English troops took it for the De Montfortist side during the Breton War of Succession, but Du Guesclin eventually wrested it from them. The sturdy ramparts that you can now walk round were largely remodelled for Duke Pierre II of Brittany in the mid 15th century, much added to in the mid 16th century, then altered by Vauban in the late 17th century. Vauban most notably chopped off the tops of the towers along the ramparts, to make artillery platforms.

You arrive on the island close to the comical clock tower, which was only built at the beginning of the 20th century. Through the triangular fortifications, you come almost immediately to the fishing museum. First you might go for a stroll up on the **ramparts** (*small fee*), or along the main street, crammed with tourist shops and places to eat. The main centre of the Ville Close is the **Place St-Guénolé** with its monumental fountain, a turtle, an otter and a crocodile among the animals carved on it.

Musée de la Pêche

Open daily July and Aug 9.30–8, Sept–June 10–12 and 2–6.

The history of fish canning is an extremely important one in Concarneau, which explains why a rusty-topped mid-19th-century tin is reverentially included among the other much larger and more impressive exhibits at this museum.

Numerous large models of fishing boats, and even whole boats, are on display in the buildings that made up the former arsenal of the Ville Close. The 15th-century chapel of the rosary has also been incorporated into the museum, having served as the meeting place for the town council before the Revolution, and as a co-operative for fishing captains after it.

The museum spreads its net wide; you can get an introduction to the international history of fishing and fishing techniques down the centuries. Aquaria present the variety of marine fauna to be found off the Breton coast. You can even climb on board the *Hémérica*, a 34-metre trawler moored outside the ramparts.

Concarneau's Ports, Festivals and Other Attractions

To see real fishermen at work and to take in the smell as well as the sight of the most recent catch, you need to get up early to go to the **Concarneau criée** for the extremely lively sale of the catch brought in to port during the night. During the summer, the tourist office arranges guided tours.

Concarneau's best-known traditional festival, the **Fête des Filets Bleus**, named after the blue nets employed in sardine fishing, gathers together Breton musicians and dancers in large numbers. The festival takes place on the second to last Sunday in August. The **Festival International de la Baie**, held during the first week of August, features a range of music and dance from across the continents. The **Salon du Livre Maritime de Concarneau**, at Easter, is a celebration of books about the sea.

The **Marinarium** (*open daily Easter–Sept 10–12 and 2–6.30*), on the southern point of Concarneau, beyond the yacht harbour, is a bit old fashioned. But this marine research centre, part of that august French academic institution the Collège de France, can teach visitors a fascinating thing or two about life in the ocean. Above town, the **Château de Keriolet** (*open June–mid Sept daily 10.30–1 and 2–6*) at **Beuzec-Conq** makes for an eccentric visit, with its neo-Gothic architecture and its links with Russian prince Felix Youssoupov, the castle's one-time owner and assassin of Rasputin.

From Concarneau to Le Pouldu via Pont-Aven

Between Concarneau and Pont-Aven there's a slightly wilder stretch of coast leading down to the Pointe de Trévignon, then you follow a string of well-protected narrow estuaries known as *avens*. The village of Pont-Aven is anything but secretive, becoming a tourist black spot in high summer, for which you can blame the painter Paul Gauguin. The pays homage to the innovative, daring circle of artists of the so-called Pont-Aven School he led, and virtually every house has been turned into an art gallery.

The Coast from Concarneau to Pont-Aven

From the rocky **Pointe de la Jument**, long, exposed stretches of beaches and dunes extend south. The **Pointe de Trévignon** seems a curiously rough and uninviting spot to have established a little port, but it remains an active harbour. A cement sea wall offers it protection. The crenellated fort on the point has a Scottish air.

East of Trévignon, you come to the coast of the *avens*. Gorgeous sandy creeks replace the great stretches of beaches to the west. Some adorable hamlets lie in the countryside behind. First, the coast road follows the beaches to **Raguenèz and its island**. Walking out to the latter is a popular activity here at low tide. The **Anse de Rospico** along from Raguenèz looks like the perfect pirate's sandy cove. Inland, the hamlet of **Kerascoët** comes under siege from photographers in summer because of its splendid little granite and thatched cottages. Some of the buildings are made with walls of standing blocks of granite. These *pierres debout*, or *mein zao* in Breton, were used both in the local architecture and as field divides in times past, and you may come across other remnants of them in the area around Névez and Trégunc.

Back along the coast, east of Rospico, the little resort of **Port-Manec'h** serves as a good introduction to the typical harbours of the *avens* of southern Brittany, located at the western end of the mouths of the Aven and Bélon rivers. The wooded slopes give the harbour a warm feel. The way north leads to a delightful little estuary port, **Kerdruc**. The waterside scenes are typical of the twin harbours you'll find along these tidal rivers around Pont-Aven.

Pont-Aven

Paul Gauguin is God in Pont-Aven. A bit of an absent God, mind you – you'll see few genuine works of his in this quaint Breton village, as most of the canvases he painted in the area have flown far away across the globe. You may be lucky and be able to view one or two in the museum – though it has few great works of its own in its permanent collection, it does attract back some of the originals for the excellent temporary exhibitions that it puts on. Pilgrims come to worship in great number this site of the Nativity of a New Art (*see* pp.335–336) .

A century after Gauguin and Emile Bernard brought a radically new look to French art, the **Musée de Pont-Aven** (*open daily July and Aug 10–7, mid-Feb–June and Sept–Nov 10–12.30 and 2–6.30*) was opened. It has grown astonishingly quickly, developing its own collection from nothing. A short video rapidly presents the outlines to the story of the Pont-Aven School. Old photos give some idea of the atmosphere of the village in the late 19th century. Gauguin changes rapidly from a fresh-faced young man to a hardened character. Paul Sérusier stands out because of his wacky haircuts.

The works of art on display include some interesting engravings and some excellent zincographs by Gauguin, and such fascinating peripheral pieces as a painted studio door and the sign from the Pension Gloanec, where many of the artists stayed. Despite the increasingly interesting acquisitions for the permanent collection, the museum's highlights are its temporary exhibitions.

A Tour of Pont-Aven

This is a village that has attracted its fair share of poets, as well as painters. On the central square, you can see a plaque in English on the Ajoncs d'Or hotel recalling the passage of expansive writer Ernest Dawson in the late 19th century. Dawson, you

Getting Around

Quimperlé and Rosporden both have **train** stations on the fast TGV line running from Paris to Quimper.

Otherwise, you need to use the **bus** services to get around the area.

Tourist Information

Pays des Portes de Cornouaille,
  1 Rue Nationale, 29380 Bannalec,
  t 02 98 39 47 00.
Trégunc: 16 Rue de Pont-Aven, t 02 98 50 22 05, www.tregunc.com.
Névez: 18 Place de l'Eglise, t 02 98 06 87 90, www.nevez.com.
Pont-Aven: 5 Place de l'Hôtel de Ville,
  t 02 98 06 04 70, www.pontaven.com.
Riec-sur-Belon: Place de l'Eglise, t 02 98 06 97 65, ot-riec.sur.belon@wanadoo.fr.
Moëlan-sur-Mer: Rue des Moulins,
  t 02 98 39 67 28, www.moelan-sur-mer.fr.
Le Pouldu: Boulevard des Plages,
  t 02 98 39 93 42.
Quimperlé: Rue du Bourgneuf, t 02 98 96 04 32, www.quimperletourisme.com.

Market Days

Trégunc: Wednesday, plus Sunday
  in July and Aug.
Névez: Saturday.
Pont-Aven: Tuesday.
Riec-sur-Bélon: Wednesday and Saturday.
Moëlan-sur-Mer: Tuesday.
Quimperlé: Friday.

Where to Stay and Eat

Trégunc ✉ 29910
★★★Les Grandes Roches, Rue des Grandes Roches, t 02 98 97 62 97, www.hotel-lesgrandesroches. com (*moderate–expensive*). A very peaceful, pleasant old Breton house in a large park. Some of the cosy rooms have fireplaces.
Château de Kerminaouët, t 02 98 50 19 68, www. kerminaouet.com (*moderate–expensive*). A B&B in a family château.
Le Menhir, 17 Rue de Concarneau,
  t 02 98 97 62 35 (*inexpensive*). A rustic inn offering hearty fare.

Raguenèz ✉ 29920
★★Le Men Du, Rue des Iles, Raguenèz-Plage, t 02 98 06 84 22 (*moderate–expensive*). A small, modern hotel in its own garden close to the beach, with practical rooms with sea views. *Closed Nov–March.*
★★Chez Pierre, t 02 98 06 81 06 (*inexpensive– moderate*). A very popular hotel close to the road and the beach, with a dining room (*moderate*) that is often packed in summer.

Kerdruc ✉ 29920
Pen Ker Dagorn, Chemin des Vieux Fours, t 02 98 06 85 01 (*inexpensive*). A delightful B&B 200m from the port of Kerdruc, set in an exuberant garden and offering spacious, comfortable rooms.
Auberge de l'Aven, t 02 98 06 78 51 (*moderate*). A gorgeous portside inn reputed both for its cuisine and its lovely terrace. Studio accommodation is also available.

read, was the 'author of Cynara and other beautiful poems', but he is now largely forgotten, we fear. Art galleries and souvenir shops line the principal streets of the village. The paintings on sale vary widely in quality; many works are derivative of the original Pont-Aven School, while others take contrasts in colours to gaudy extremes. Pont-Aven is almost as celebrated in Brittany for its buttery biscuits as for its art; the tins often come decorated with tempting copies of Gaugin works. For some truly splendid photos and posters of Brittany, visit the Plisson photography gallery. Ask at the tourist office about artistic activities in and around Pont-Aven.

The Breton poet who was most inspired by the place was Xavier Grall, a fiery postwar writer who is portrayed as a wild-eyed figure in a sculpted bust of him set among the little bridges of the village north of the main bridge. Follow the Promenade Xavier Grall, which takes you up past many little wash-houses and former

Névez ✉ 29920

Yveline Gour Laduen, Kerambris, Port-Manech, **t** 02 98 06 83 82 (*inexpensive*). A B&B in a 16th-century building.

Pont-Aven ✉ 29930

Moulin de Rosmadec, Venelle de Rosmadec, **t** 02 98 06 00 22 (*moderate*). A converted 15th-century mill in the centre of the village, surrounded by water, so set somewhat apart from the tourist hordes, and beautifully shaded by its riverside trees. It has a small number of sober, smart but sweet rooms and serves excellent seafood (*expensive*).

★★★Roz Aven, 11 Quai Théodore Botrel, **t** 02 98 06 13 06, *www.hotelrozaven.free.fr* (*inexpensive–moderate*). A hotel spread across 3 characterful buildings by the port, including the most beautiful of thatched houses. Many rooms overlook the port.

Hôtel Les Mimosas, 22 Square Botrel, **t** 02 98 06 00 30 (*inexpensive*). A peacefully located, no-smoking choice at the southern end of the quays.

Café des Arts, 11 Rue du Général de Gaulle, **t** 02 98 06 07 12 (*inexpensive–moderate*). A relaxed, atmospheric bar-brasserie in the centre, with good-quality, varied cuisine, occasional live music and wine by the glass.

Restaurant Le Tahiti, 21 Rue Belle-Angèle, **t** 02 98 06 15 93 (*inexpensive–moderate*). A charming restaurant run by a French-Tahitian husband-wife team, serving up delightful, exotic South Pacific dishes in a colourfully decorated dining room. *Closed Mon, Tues and Wed outside hols.*

Crêperie Aux Vieux, 1 Place de l'Eglise, Nizom, **t** 02 89 09 11 10 (*inexpensive*). A reasonable budget option.

Le Talisman, 4 Rue Paul Sérusier, **t** 02 98 06 02 58 (*inexpensive*). A decent crêperie with a very pleasant atmosphere and a nice terrace. *Closed June.*

St-André ✉ 29930

La Taupinière, Route de Concarneau, **t** 02 98 06 03 12 (*expensive–very expensive*). A very well-reputed restaurant offering extremely carefully prepared Breton fare, even if in an unremarkable house, situated about 4km to the west of Port-Aven. Diners are able to watch the talented chef and his team at work. *Closed Mon and Tues, and end Sept–Oct.*

Riec-sur-Belon ✉ 29340

★★★Domaine de Keristinec (at the Pont du Guily on the road towards Moëlan, 3km south of Riec-sur-Belon), **t** 02 98 06 42 98, *www. hotelbelon.online.fr* (*moderate–expensive*). Some of the smartest, largest rooms in the area, set in the converted buildings of a 19th-century farm dominating the surrounding countryside. The dining room overlooks the Belon river.

Le Châtel, 1km east of Pont-Aven, **t** 02 98 06 00 04 (*inexpensive*). Farm buildings converted to provide charming little B&B rooms in rustic style.

Ty Coz, towards Rosbras, **t** 02 98 06 92 07 (*inexpensive*). The most charming Breton crêperie imaginable, in a thatched cottage.

---

mills. It used to be said that there were as many watermills as houses in Pont-Aven. Some of the mill wheels still turn. The path north leads past wonderful big natural stepping stones in the water to the Promenade du Bois d'Amour. Picturesque spots in this 'Wood of Love' inspired many an artist from the Pont-Aven School, but this route now has something of a neglected air. By Pont-Aven's bright port, another acclaimed Breton poet, Auguste Brizeux, is recalled in a memorial.

The Breton crooner of the early part of the 20th century, Théodore Botrel, is buried at Pont-Aven too. Botrel helped to get the local **folklore festival of Les Fleurs d'Ajonc** (Gorse Flowers) off the ground. You can continue walking some way south down the estuary. While the river only serves for yachts nowadays, in times past, flour, cereals, oysters, wine and salt were transported up and down this beautiful working waterway.

Port-Belon ✉ 29340

Chez Jacky, t 02 98 06 90 32 (*moderate–expensive*). A touristy, pricey restaurant in a large house in this wonderful little port, serving some of the best seafood along the coast. *Closed Sun eve and Mon.*

Crêperie du Belon, t 02 98 71 12 14 (*inexpensive*). A crêpe house with a view.

Moëlan-sur-Mer ✉ 29350

★★★★**Manoir de Kertalg**, t 02 98 39 77 77 (*expensive–very expensive*). A property with large private grounds where you can fish in the river or walk through the woods. Rooms look out on to the 15th-century manor and the Belon estuary. *Closed 16 Nov–14 April.*

★★★**Les Moulins du Duc**, t 02 98 96 52 52, *www.hotel-moulins-du-duc.com* (*expensive–very expensive*). Enchanting, characterful rooms in little Breton cottages and buildings along the river. The grounds also boast a swimming pool and lakes, and you can fish and hunt here at certain times of year. The restaurant (*expensive*) takes up the mill. *Closed Nov–Feb exc Christmas and New Year.*

★★**Hôtel Kerfany**, Blorimond-en-Moëlan, t 02 98 71 00 46 (*inexpensive*). Peaceful rooms in a big new Breton house.

Le Pouldu ✉ 29121

Hôtel du Pouldu, port, t 02 98 39 90 66 (*inexpensive*). A simple family-run hotel.

★★**Le Panoramique**, Route de la Plage de Kérou, t 02 98 39 93 49 (*inexpensive*). A small, charming hotel west of Le Pouldu, with quite basic rooms.

Quimperlé ✉ 29300

La Maison d'Hippolyte, 2 Quai Surcouf, t 02 98 39 09 11 (*inexpensive*). Delightful B&B accommodation by the pretty river Isole. The building also hosts changing exhibitions of contemporary Breton painting and photography, of which the owner is an enthusiast.

Le Bistro de la Tour, 2 Rue Dom Morice, t 02 98 39 29 58 (*moderate–expensive*). The best restaurant in town, offering classic dishes with experimental touches. The dining room looks like an antique dealer's shop. *Closed Sat lunch, Sun eve and Mon.*

Le Relais du Roch, Route du Pouldu, t 02 98 96 12 97 (*moderate*). Gastronomic French cuisine in a modern Breton house in the most bucolic of settings just outside town. *Closed Sun eve, Mon and Wed lunch.*

Crêperie des Archers, 6 Rue Dom Morice, t 02 98 39 09 54 (*inexpensive*). A favourite with the locals.

Crêperie du Pont Fleuri, 5 Rue Ellé, t 02 98 96 19 35 (*inexpensive*). Crêpes served in a pretty dining room.

Crêperie Ty Gwechal, 4 Rue Mellac, t 02 98 96 30 63 (*inexpensive*). A restored 17th-century house in which you can enjoy a wide selection of crêpes.

Arzano ✉ 29300

Château de Kerlarec, t 02 99 71 75 06 (*moderate*). Refined B&B accommodation in a grand 19th-century white villa. *Table d'hôte* meals are available on request. There's a tennis court and an art gallery.

Up to the Yellow Christ

The Christ figure in one of Gauguin's most famous works, *Le Christ Jaune*, is still being crucified above Pont-Aven. A trip to the **Chapelle de Trémalo** takes you a short way north out of the village to view it. On the way up, you see how tightly packed the houses are in the little valley below. A beautiful tree-lined lane leads to the chapel with its roofs trailing down to the ground. This is a typical Breton Gothic building. Inside, the carvings on the stringbeams look like illustrations for a children's book. A Goldilocks lookalike is terrorized by a wolf of a monster; a green-spotted dog holds on to its bone, a man on to his fish. There are interesting free-standing statues to look at too, including a refined, mature portrayal of the Virgin and her mother, Ste Anne. But visitors come in particular to admire the 17th-century yellow Christ. He looks thinner and much more resigned than in Gauguin's famed painting of 1889, now in Buffalo, USA.

On to the Green Christ at Nizon

The Nizon church and calvary are located just to the northwest of Pont-Aven. The 16th-century calvary looks shockingly new because it has been restored – its figures now appear as though they're made of tightly moulded, solidified granular sand. The crucified Christ here inspired a *Green Christ* by Gauguin. Inside, the collection of wooden statues is interesting. However, the most extraordinary of all the figures around this church lies outside at the fountain – the most primitive of stone Virgins in Brittany.

River Estuaries from Pont-Aven to Le Pouldu

A series of *avens* indent the coast between Pont-Aven and Le Pouldu. Down the east side of the Aven from Pont-Aven, seek out **Rosbras**, opposite the port of Kerdruc. This is a paradise of a *port de plaisance* or yacht harbour, quietly set among wooded banks. The slopes are lightly built up, some houses in stone, some painted white. The name of **Belon**, a village a short and winding way east of Rosbras, is linked with fine oysters

The Pont-Aven School of Art, 1886 to 1896

European art took a great leap forward in the little Breton village of Pont-Aven during the 1880s, although in many ways it was a deliberate leap backwards too. Gone was the academic painters' obsession with perspective. Gone was the imperative that a painting should jolly well look like nature. And away went the obsession with accurate detail.

It is true that during the 1870s the Impressionist movement had already got rid of many rules of traditional academic painting. But the artists who gathered together at Pont-Aven around Paul Gauguin and Emile Bernard from 1886 on moved away from the feathery-looking touches of Impressionism too, and from the tenderness and movement that Impressionist techniques were so adept at conveying.

Gauguin, Bernard and their followers painted big bold blocks of colour on to their canvases. Horizons were flattened out and forms greatly simplified. When the pictures of the so-called Pont-Aven painters were depicting such scenes as Breton festivals that would have been full of movement in real life, they generally turned the occasions into frozen images on the canvas. People were transformed into statues. Haystacks and trees became boulders in the landscape. These painters often exploited shockingly bright colours that exaggerated or provocatively contradicted the much more muted tones seen in the natural world. The seeds of abstract art lay in these works.

Paul Gauguin and Emile Bernard, the artists jointly at the forefront of this new movement, settled in Pont-Aven for large periods in the second half of the 1880s. During the preceding decades, Pont-Aven had already become well known to artists hailing from far and wide. For example, a colony of American painters had fallen for the place well before Gauguin and Bernard. But these and the others were in the main part attracted by the quaint Breton countryside and costumes that they could portray, more interested in rendering the conventional aesthetic beauty of Brittany that can be tasted in the bars and restaurants of the area. Belon's crescent of houses looks over to a miniature château. The walk south takes you down to the **Pointe de Penquernéo**, where the Belon and the Aven meet.

It's an awkward drive round from the west to the east side of the Belon river. The walking track takes you past countless oyster beds. On the east bank, **Port-Belon** has a little chapel overlooking the creek. The Vedettes Aven Belon (**t** 02 98 71 14 59) organize boat tours around the Belon and Aven estuaries.

Going by road, it can be surprisingly difficult to find the way to **Brigneau**, another delightful pocket-sized port east along the coast from Kerfany. Continuing east, **Merrien** and **Doëlan** are two further absolutely adorable *aven* ports. The former is tiny; the latter is slightly more substantial, with little lighthouses marking the estuary. You can take boats to the island of Groix from here at certain times of year.

Steep-sided **Le Pouldu** has lost some of its old charm to modern buildings. Despite all the construction, however, the slopes lead down to a pretty port and some lovely beaches. Le Pouldu drew its fair share of artists, including Gauguin,

---

than in devising a new aesthetic. Emile Bernard should rightfully be regarded as the instigator of the new style in western European art. He is often credited with bringing in *Cloisonnisme*. The word *cloison* is French for partition, and Bernard in particular partitioned off the blocks of colour in his canvases with thick lines, just like *cloisonné* enamel work. Even if Bernard only adopted this technique for a short while, reverting in time to more classical forms, some of the results of his *cloisonniste* period match Gauguin's works in their intensity and power. The style of the Pont-Aven School was also officially described as Synthetism – painting's answer to the literary movement of Symbolism.

The Pont-Aven painters lived extremely close together, sharing their ideas and enthusiasms. Many of these artists stayed at the Pension Gloanec, which was run by Marie-Jeanne Gloanec. Gloanec is portrayed as a kind of mother figure for the movement, spoiling her artistic children with her warmth and good food. You can see photographs of her surrounded by a posse of artists in the museum.

The majority of the Pont-Aven School artists were French but not Breton. Several came from abroad. Paul Sérusier and Maurice Denis are two other crucial figures in the Pont-Aven School. Gauguin's tips to the young Sérusier make some of the most memorable quotes, showing the aims of this new artistic movement. *Ne copiez pas trop la nature, mais rêvez devant elle* ('Don't copy nature too much, but dream in front of it'). Charles Filiger, Armand Seguin and Emile Jourdan count among other important Pont-Aven artists.

Certain striking elements in the Breton landscape may have encouraged the *cloisonnistes*: the natural blocks of boulders against the sea, naïve church art, local costumes. There's no more obvious example of how the Pont-Aven School was inspired by Brittany than Gauguin's *Le Christ Jaune*, the jaundiced crucified body a pretty close copy of the naïve but bold yellow Christ that you can still see hanging in the Trémalo chapel just above the village.

Champions of Breton Culture

Two famous figures in Breton culture are buried in Quimperlé. The first is one of the best-known Breton *bombarde* or oboe players, Mathurin. The other is Théodore Hersart de La Villemarqué. Born in Quimperlé, La Villemarqué became just about the most important figure in the revival of Breton culture in the 19th century. He had left his native Brittany to go to Paris, where he met Le Gonidec, who was preparing a Breton grammar. The latter's enthusiasm seems to have encouraged La Villemarqué's interest in Breton culture. He returned full of nostalgia to western Brittany and went round zealously collecting oral Breton stories and songs. Such influential postwar artists as the Breton singer Alan Stivell have drawn great inspiration from this repository of Breton stories.

late in the 19th century. The mural paintings that you can view at **La Maison de Marie Henry** (*open for guided tours July and Aug daily 10.30–7; April–Sept Wed–Sun 3–6*) are an amusing fake.

Quimperlé

Quimperlé is a typical historic Breton town built around a port down a deep, navigable river estuary. A pretty road leads up to it from the coast through the woods of the Forêt de Carnoët. But far prettier is the hiking path up the Laïta river. At Quimperlé, the Laïta is formed by the confluence of the Isole and Ellé rivers.

There may have been a Gallo-Roman settlement here, on the border between the territories of the Osismi and the Veneti tribes. Moving on to the period of emigration from Britain in the Dark Ages, the town claims links with a Welshman, Guntiern, prince of Cambria (the medieval Latin name for Wales). The story goes that during the 6th century he fled here, having killed his nephew, and became a hermit. Vikings came and destroyed the settlement that grew around this hermitage in the 10th century. Quimperlé then developed around the abbey of Ste-Croix, founded in 1029. The monastery brought the place its relative prosperity. The town spread up the hillside, where the church of Notre-Dame de l'Assomption et St-Michel was begun in the 13th century. Quimperlé inevitably became embroiled in the Breton War of Succession. It became a stronghold for the De Montfort side, backed by the English. The Breton leader of the French troops, Du Guesclin, took the place in 1371.

The **Eglise Ste-Croix**, which is Quimperlé's main monument, was built on the round model of the famed church of the Holy Sepulchre in Jerusalem. The church lies on an island between the Isole and Ellé just before the two rivers meet. Although it dates back to the late 11th century, it was heavily restored during the 19th century. Three side apses and the entrance porch added on to the circle give the church the shape of a Greek cross.

Although much of the decoration is not original, this remains an extraordinary church. First, as soon as you've entered the building, glance back at the refined sculptures behind you. Many of the figures look as though they are peering down on to a procession passing below them. You can then walk all the way round the ambulatory. A bridge leads up to the main altar. Underneath, you can go down to the dark crypt with its column capitals decorated with stylized carving, and with its two tomb effigies. Outside the church, some of Quimperlé's old streets have remarkable timberframe houses.

A few kilometres to the northwest of Quimperlé, the severe **Manoir de Kernault** (*open high season daily 10.30–12.30 and 2–7; rest of year school hols, public hols and Sun 2–6*) outside Mellac was splendidly restored during the 1990s by the *département* of the Finistère. As well as learning about the ways in which such a manor and its farm evolved down the centuries, you can also appreciate different aspects of Breton culture presented in the regular exhibitions held inside.

Morbihan

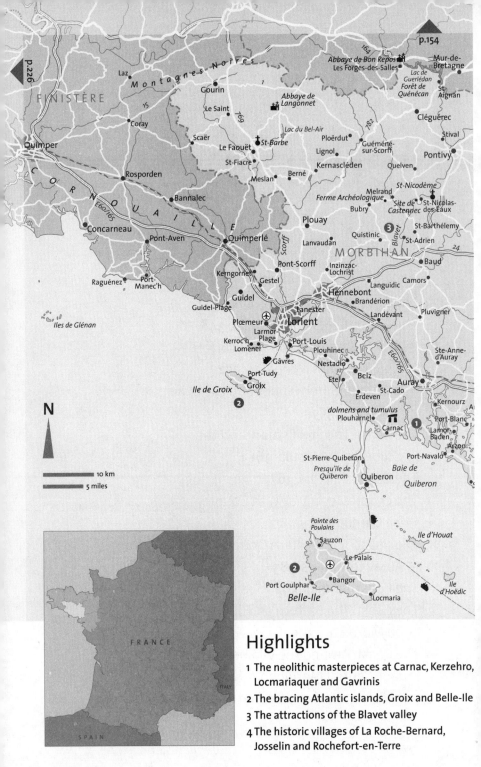

p.226

p.154

Highlights

1 The neolithic masterpieces at Carnac, Kerzehro, Locmariaquer and Gavrinis
2 The bracing Atlantic islands, Groix and Belle-Ile
3 The attractions of the Blavet valley
4 The historic villages of La Roche-Bernard, Josselin and Rochefort-en-Terre

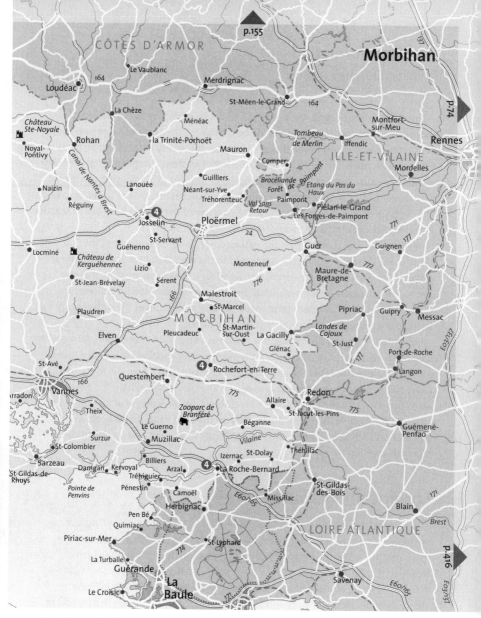

p.155

Morbihan

p.74

CÔTES D'ARMOR

Le Vaublanc
164
Merdrignac
Loudéac
La Chèze
St-Méen-le-Grand   164
Montfort-sur-Meu

Château
Ste-Noyale
Méneac
Iffendic
Rennes
Rohan
la Trinité-Porhoët
Tombeau
de Merlin
Noyal-Pontivy
Mauron
ILLE-ET-VILAINE
Comper
Mordelles
Naizin
Guilliers
Brocéliande
Forêt
de
Paimpont
Etang du Pas du
Haux
Réguiny
Lanouée
Néant-sur-Yve
Tréhorenteuc
Paimpont
Piélan-le-Grand
Val Sans
Retour
Les Forges-de-Paimpont
Josselin
Ploërmel
St-Servant
24
Guer
Guignen
Locminé
Guéhenno
Château de
Kerguéhennec
Lizio
Monteneuf
Maure-de-Bretagne
St-Jean-Brévelay
Sérent
MORBIHAN
Malestroit
Pipriac
Guipry
Messac
Plaudren
St-Marcel
Elven
Pleucadeuc
St-Martin-sur-Oust
La Gacilly
Landes de
Cojoux
St-Just
St-Avé
Glénac
Port-de-Roche
Questembert
Rochefort-en-Terre
Langon
Vannes
rradon
Theix
Zooparc de
Branféré
Allaire
Redon
Surzur
Le Guerno
Béganne
St-Jacut-les-Pins
Guémené-Penfao
St-Colombier
Muzillac
Vilaine
Sarzeau
Billiers
Izernac
St-Dolay
Théhillac
St-Gildas-de-Rhuys
Damgan
Kervoyal
Tréhiguier
Arzal
La Roche-Bernard
Pointe de
Penvins
Pénestin
Camoël
St-Gildas-des-Bois
Blain
Pen Bé
Herbignac
Missillac
Piriac-sur-Mer
Quimiac
St-Lyphard
LOIRE ATLANTIQUE
La Turballe
Brest
Guérande
La
Baule
Savenay
Le Croisic

p.416

Mor bihan, which means 'little sea' in Breton, boasts some of the most blissfully varied of all seascapes in Brittany. The little sea after which the *département* is named is the Golfe du Morbihan. Most of the tiny islands in the gulf are private, but you can visit three: Ile aux Moines and Ile d'Arz, which attract the summer hordes, and the secretive third, Gavrinis, which conceals the finest neolithic tomb in Brittany. To the French, the name Morbihan also means megaliths, as this is where the many thousands of menhirs of Carnac stand in their long rows. But a visit to lesser-known neolithic remains at Locmariaquer, Kerzehro or Arzon can be just as rewarding.

Tourist Information

Comité Départemental du Tourisme (CDT) du Morbihan,

PIBS, Allée Nicolas Leblanc, BP408, 56010 Vannes Cedex, t 02 97 54 06 56, *www.morbihan.com*.

The marks of the Second World War are particularly obvious in the western Morbihan, where military Lorient could be considered the Morbihan's answer to Brest. It isn't exclusively naval, though – it is one of the very biggest fishing ports in France, and it hosts the great annual gathering of western European Celts. The spiky citadel of nearby Port-Louis guards memories of Brittany's colonial past, while north from Lorient, you can seek out atmospheric old churches around Le Faouët, or take in the plethora of delightful sights along the gorgeous Blavet valley. Back out to sea, the island of Groix has remained wonderfully unpretentious.

Heading east from Lorient past the extraordinary indented estuary of the Etel, you come to the Quiberon peninsula, connected to the mainland by a dramatic, thin strip of sand. The lively port of Quiberon, renowned for its seawater treatment centre, serves the extremely popular islands of Belle-Ile, Houat and Hoëdic. Belle-Ile, which Claude Monet and Sarah Bernhardt made popular at the turn of the 19th century, has become chic enough to charge almost Parisian prices.

Two of the Morbihan's major historic towns lie at the back of the Golfe: Auray, with its picture-postcard port, and Vannes, the *département's* appealing capital. Close to Auray, Ste-Anne d'Auray is the largest pilgrimage site in Brittany. The Morbihan coast comes to a very pretty end around the Vilaine estuary, where the best place to appreciate the beauty of the precipitous Vilaine valley is at historic little La Roche-Bernard. Further inland, a journey up the Oust valley to lively old towns and villages such as Rochefort-en-Terre, La Gacilly, Malestroit and Josselin proves highly rewarding.

Lorient and Around

Although the western Morbihan is dominated by the oddly compelling but grizzly-grey military and fishing port of Lorient, you don't feel its presence on the most western stretch of the Morbihan coast between Guidel-Plage and Larmor-Plage. Lorient, one of France's great colonial ports, was destroyed during the Second World War, but its string of modern harbours have their own attractions. To learn more about Lorient's colonial history and former grandeur, and its estuary, head round to nearby Port-Louis.

From the Laïta to Lorient

The **Laïta** river, which heads down from the town of Quimperlé, forms the beautiful border between the Finistère and the Morbihan. You can wander along its shaded wooded banks. In summer however, most of the attention is focused around the well-protected Laïta estuary at **Guidel-Plage**. The coastal strip heading southeast looks quite wild, and provides a good stretch for windsurfers.

As you continue down the coast road to the typical little port of **Kerroc'h**, the island of Groix comes more closely into focus. Past the tip of the Pointe du Talut, the equally small port the other side is **Lomener**, by a part of the coast that is popular with the Lorientais.

The Centre Nautique de Kerguelen is a highly reputed school for learning water sports and diving, set behind the sandy beaches on the western side of **Larmor-Plage**. In the centre of town, the unusual design of the well-scrubbed church stands out. The interior contains some rich carvings, most notably the painted apostles in the north porch. Apparently, in centuries past the tradition was for naval vessels leaving the Rade de Lorient, heading off to war, to fire cannon shots as they passed this church. The priest was supposed to respond in nationalist religious manner by ringing the bells and raising the French flag on the spire. At Larmor-Plage's northern end, smart yachts moor at the chic modern sailing harbour of **Kernével**. Since 1997, the dreadful **Keroman former Nazi submarine base** has been open to visitors – an engrossing and awful sight across the Le Ter river estuary.

Getting Around

There's a small **airport** in the vicinity of Lorient, Lann-Bihoué-en-Ploemeur, from which there are flights to Waterford and Galloway by Aer Arann, t 02 97 87 21 50, *www.aerarann.ie.*

Lorient is easily reached by TGV fast **trains** from Paris.

You can reach the ports along the coast by **bus** from Lorient.

Tourist Information

Guidel: t 02 97 65 01 74 (summer only).
Guidel-Plage: t 02 97 32 82 75, *www.guidel56.com.*
Larmor-Plage:
Rue des 4 Frères Leroy Quéret,
t 02 97 84 26 24, or Avenue Général de Gaulle, t 02 97 33 70 02 (summer only).
Lorient: Maison de la Mer, Quai de Rohan, t 02 97 21 07 84, *www.lorient-tourisme.com.* The **Lorient Passe-Partout** ticket is a bargain; it allows visitors a return trip to the island of Groix and entrance to the museum there, a return trip to Port-Louis and entrance to its museum, plus 3 days of free local transport. Enquire at the tourist office.
Port-Louis: 47 Grande Rue, t 02 97 82 52 93, *mairie.villeport.louis@wanadoo.fr.*

Market Days

Guidel: Wednesday and Sunday.
Larmor-Plage: Sunday.
Lorient: Wednesday and Saturday.
Port-Louis: Saturday.

Where to Stay and Eat

Kergornet ✉ 56530

For a traditional Breton house near Guidel-Plages, try one of these B&Bs:
Mme Bissonet, t 02 97 05 00 89 (*inexpensive*).
M Le Couric, t 02 97 05 00 44 (*inexpensive*).

Larmor-Plage ✉ 56260

**Les Mouettes, Anse de Kerguelen, t 02 97 65 50 30 (*moderate*). Comfortable, modern, cheerful rooms behind the dunes on the western edge of the town. The hotel has side-on views along the beaches and a large terrace looking directly on to the sea.

Lorient ✉ 56100

This is a useful place to spend the night for those taking early ferries to the island of Groix.
**Victor Hugo, 36 Rue Lazare Carnot, t 02 97 21 16 24, *www.contact-hotel.com* (*expensive*). An option right near the yacht harbour, and a short walk from the landing stage for boats to the island of Groix. It's clean and comfortable, if overpriced for its category.

Lorient

There may be a campaign to return this town's name to L'Orient or 'The Orient', but there's no reviving its once-opulent colonial look. Built from scratch in the second half of the 17th century to serve as one of France's main colonial ports, the original L'Orient became the base of the Compagnie des Indes, France's equivalent to the British East India Company, and grew wealthy on lucrative trading. When the colonial trade dried up, it became a major naval harbour, and after the First World War a large-scale fishing port was added. In the Second World War, Allied bombers, desperately trying to hit the extraordinarily important Nazi U-Boat installations of Keroman, wiped out the civilian parts of the town instead. By the end of the war, 80 per cent or more of the town's buildings had been left in ruins.

To add to the bare postwar architecture of Lorient, the air often stinks of fish – this is the second largest fishing port in France. Lorient also looks alarmingly military in parts. Up to the mid 1990s, some 40,000 people here were employed by the navy or

***Hôtel Mercure**, 31 Place Jules Ferry, t 02 97 21 35 73, *ho873@accor.hotels.com* (*moderate*). The only 3-star hotel in town, offering a taste of typical post-war Lorient architecture. It is comfortable and close to the Bassin à Flot yacht harbour.

***Rex Hotel**, 28 Cours de Chazelles, t 02 97 64 25 60 (*inexpensive–moderate*). A newly refurbished hotel close to the railway station.

***Le Square**, 5 Place Jules Ferry, t 02 97 21 06 36 (*inexpensive*). A reasonable option, but you should try to avoid getting a noisy first-floor room.

Auberge de Jeunesse, 41 Rue Victor Schoelcher, Rives du Ter, t 02 97 37 11 65, *www.fuaj.org* (*inexpensive*). A youth hostel located outside the town by the Le Ter river. It's noisy but comfortable.

L'Amphitryon, 127 Rue du Colonel Muller, Route de Quimperlé, t 02 97 83 34 04 (*expensive–very expensive*). A smallish and rather exclusive restaurant serving refined cuisine, and boasting the best reputation in town. Outside the centre of Lorient at Keryado. *Closed 2nd half May and Sept.*

Le Jardin Gourmand, 46 Rue Jules Simon, t 02 97 64 1724 (*moderate–expensive*). A good-value restaurant, one of the best in Lorient, serving fresh and creative cuisine. Guests can dine in the garden during the summer months.

Le Pic, 2 Boulevard Maréchal Franchet d'Esperey, t 02 97 21 18 29 (*moderate–expensive*). A restaurant with a relaxed atmosphere, serving fresh Lorient seafood. Tables are set out on the street during the summer months. *Closed Sun and Mon eves, and 2nd half Aug.*

Bar-Restaurant La Liberté, 26 Rue Poissonnière, t 02 97 21 07 05 (*inexpensive–moderate*). A crowded spot that offers a good lunch. *Closed eves.*

Le Marrakesh, 18 Rue Maréchal Foch, t 02 97 21 91 41 (*inexpensive–moderate*). Robust Moroccan dishes served in wholehearted portions within a refined setting, complete with mosaic tiles and a fountain.

Le Bistrot du Yachtman, 14 Rue Poissonnière, t 02 97 21 31 91 (*inexpensive*). A place close to the Bassin à Flot, serving up good-value classic dishes.

Port-Louis ✉ 56290

Le Commerce, 1 Place du Marché, t 02 97 82 46 05 (*inexpensive–moderate*). A well-kept hotel with good food, on a pleasant, shady square. Half-board is required in July and August.

Avel Vor, 25 Rue de Locmalo, t 02 97 82 47 59 (*moderate–expensive*). Elaborate seafood dishes served in a curious bourgeois dining room overlooking the inland Mer de Gâvres. *Closed Sun eve, Mon, Tues eve, and out of season.*

by industries connected with it in the area. The town has suffered badly not just from cuts in the French military budget, but also from cuts to fishing quotas, causing unemployment and despair in parts. Yet this is a town that will appeal to those of you who appreciate a bit of urban grit mixed in with your beach holiday, and once a year it also plays host to the largest and merriest international gathering of Celts in Brittany, which fills the streets and squares around the Bassin à Flots, the swanky sailing harbour.

A Tour of Lorient's Ports

A tour along Lorient's quays brings you into contact with the distinct and separate lives of its various ports. To fully appreciate the extensive **Port de Pêche**, or fishing harbour, at its bustling loudest and best, you should really go there first, at the crack of dawn, in order to see the streaming quantities of fish that are being auctioned. The tourist office organizes early-bird tours. If you prefer to avoid the pleasure of an early alarm call, start your visit of Lorient's ports at the **Bassin à Flot** harbour in the heart of town. On its north bank, along the **Quai des Indes**, go and view the vast murals at the Art Nouveau **Chambre de Commerce** for a rare glimpse of Lorient as a colonial port.

Further along the quay stand some of the few remaining stocky granite houses that were constructed for rich merchants during the 18th century. On the southern side of the Bassin à Flot, the **Quai de Rohan** shows off its slick modern development of shops and bars, which look down on the beautiful boats that are kept in the centre of town. Lorient has actually become a port of call for some of the most glamorous yachting races in France. **La Thalassa** at the quayside (*open July and Aug daily 9–7; Sept–June Mon–Fri 9–12.30 and 2–6, Sat and Sun 9–12.30*) is located on the veteran *Fremer* trawler. One of the *espaces découvertes* series of museums that have been opened around the Morbihan, this presents experiences at sea from four different perspectives, those of captain, seamn, fisherman and oceanographer, each with a deck of the boat devoted to it. It makes for fascinating viewing, with good use of interactive displays.

Quai de Rohan leads out to the **Boulevard de l'Estacade**, where you'll find the car park as well as the **Gare Maritime** for trips out to the island of Groix. Beyond this, an interesting wedge of a modern building, the **Club Nautique**, has a lively bar open to all. From the tip of the Estacade, you may see the rare container ship or tanker carefully parking at the Port de Commerce, while up the Scorff, one of several rivers flowing into the Rade de Lorient, the naval vessels come into view. You can drive along the **Port de Commerce** quays, though huge petrol and grain storage tanks predominate here.

Coming back into the centre of town from the fishing port, stop at the circular **Halles Merville**, a covered market. You then arrive at the western end of the **Jardins Jules Ferry**, the central town gardens. The grid of streets that lie to the north are quite vibrant, and **Rue du Port** the busiest shopping artery. Little palm trees grow along the **Rue de Liège**, giving it an exotic touch. Head up to the **Place Alsace-Lorraine**, one of

> ### Festival Interceltique
> Lorient, which architecturally has had its links with the past so brutally cut off, has become the proud rallying point for Brittany's most important annual display of Celtic culture, the **Festival Interceltique**. The sound of bagpipes fills the air as Breton, Irish, Welsh, Scottish, Manx, Galician and Asturian people unite to celebrate their Celtic roots and to organize serious meetings on the defence of Celtic culture, and even political action. Information is available from 2 Rue Paul Bert, **t** 02 97 21 24 29.

the rare spots in Lorient where you can see stone among the building materials. It's only appropriate that the town's central church has a tower sticking into the sky like a stylized fish bone.

The former **Nazi submarine pens of Keroman** are the subject of guided tours organized by the tourist office (*5 June–1 Sept*). The trawler the **Victor Pleven** (*open daily July and Aug 9–7*), situated at the submarine base, concentrates on the everyday-life-at-sea angle, with tours of the living quarters conducted by real-life former sailors, plus the usual multimedia props.

Round the Rade de Lorient to Port-Louis and Gâvres

The town's ramparts, and the thick stone layers of the fortifications of the citadel within, give **Port-Louis** all the historical atmosphere that Lorient so lacks. Its main attraction, the colonial museum, lies admirably well protected deep inside the citadel. It brings to the fore not just the significant link between the Rade de Lorient and France's colonies, but also the wider story of the French colonial adventure of the Ancien Régime. One gateway in the town's ramparts also takes you out to a fine beach.

The construction of the citadel was embarked upon by Spaniards called upon during the French Wars of Religion to support the ultra-Catholic cause. Early in the 17th century, Cardinal Richelieu convinced King Louis XIII of the great potential strategic importance of the Rade de Lorient. The citadel was then named Port-Louis in his honour. Under King Louis XIV, the place became the base for the Compagnie des Indes Orientales from 1664. Its role as a major colonial port was shortlived, however, when virgin marshland on the opposite bank of the Blavet was chosen to develop a larger purpose-built port for the developing colonial trade – L'Orient.

The citadel contains the **Musée Nationale de la Marine** (*open June–Sept daily 10–6; April and May Wed–Sun 10–6; Oct–March Wed–Sun 10–12 and 2–6*), which is especially good on sea rescue through the ages and on marine archaeology along the route to the Indies. More significantly, it also houses **The Musée de la Compagnie des Indes**, where the story of France's 17th- and 18th-century colonies and trading posts, and the bitter battle over them with the Dutch and the British, unfolds in a series of galleries ordered chronologically or geographically. Copies of maps and documents, and fine objects in glass cabinets, give visitors a visual notion of how colonial trade developed and what products were brought back to France. Highlights include a collection of porcelain of the Compagnie des Indes, the odd piece of period furniture, and printed calico imported from the East.

Head straight for the shipbuilding, navigation and crew rooms rather than following the order suggested in the museum leaflet (particularly if you're with children), to delight in the models there, including those of several huge ships built in L'Orient in the 18th century. They spark off the imagination, and make you think about what life must have been like on board. This section also contains a good, large world map indicating the destinations for which these ships were bound. As some of the names of French colonial trading posts may not be familiar to English-speaking visitors, and as many of the detailed maps in the other rooms do not set their precise location in a wider geographical context, it is well worth taking a careful look at this map.

After visiting the ships' models, it's best to follow the rooms chronologically. Taking in the complex developments in France's colonial companies, explained in some detail on densely packed, didactic panels, is a bit of a daunting task. Basically, a series of floundering companies succeeded one another after King Henri IV's administration gave letters patent for the creation of an Indies trading company in 1604. The museum focuses in particular on the minister Colbert and the colonial trade he helped set in motion in the 1660s under King Louis XIV. In that period, the Sun King allowed Colbert to make a concerted effort to establish a French naval fleet to rival that of the Dutch and the English. In 1664, the Compagnie des Indes Orientales, or Compagnie Colbert, was created and given special-to-exclusive trading rights with Africa, the Americas and the East.

How Raging European Romance Still Beats Black Slavery

You would have thought a room in the Musée de la Compagnie des Indes could have been devoted to the slave trade from which the companies, Lorient, Brittany and France so benefited. Instead, you must look for slavery in the subtext; for instance, in an engraving showing King Louis XIV dressed up a Roman, directing the disembarkation of goods, with chained slaves prostrate at his feet. Or pay close attention to the prominence given to the sentimental nonsense of the story of *Paul et Virginie* in the room focusing on the Ile de France and the Ile Bourbon. The book, telling the tragic love story of a European couple on the islands, was a runaway success on publication in 1787: its continuation of Rousseau's notion of the 'noble savage' and the exoticism of the tropical setting made it irresisitible to a wide readership. All sorts of memorabilia was produced on the back of the tale, and one of the many pieces here shows maroon slaves carrying gilded Paul and Virginie, and their dog, on a golden clock.

As regards the slave issue, 156 slave-trading expeditions were recorded as departing from L'Orient in the 18th century – a slightly smaller number than was recorded from St-Malo, and a tenth of the vast number that set sail from Nantes. Soon after *Paul et Virginie* was published, slavery was briefly banned during the French Revolution, but Napoleon, a great admirer of the novel, reinstated it soon after.

After the collapse of the major Compagnie des Indes, splinter companies were formed to exploit specific territories again until John Law, an infamous Scotsman who settled in France, saw to their reuniting in 1719 as the Compagnie Perpétuelle des Indes. This more ambitious and successful Compagnie des Indes exercised sovereignty over its trading posts, dispensing justice, minting coinage, and making treaties. It also saw to the colonization of the Ile de France and the Ile Bourbon (now Mauritius and La Réunion). The Compagnie des Indes's resources were drained by the Austrian War of Succession through the mid 1740s, followed by the crippling Seven Years' War from 1756 to 1763, before it lost its privileges and died with the Revolution. The room covering the French colonial companies from 1719 to 1769 contains some comical colonial titbits and copies of illustrations of L'Orient in its heyday. Separate rooms are dedicated to India, China and Africa, among other areas.

To Gâvres

At **Riantec**, the little **Maison de l'Ile de Kerner** (*open July and Aug daily 10–7; Sept–June Mon 2–6, Tue–Sun 10–12.30 and 2–6*) overlooking the *petite mer* of Gâvres is another *espace de découverte* showcasing the area's ecosystem. The displays here are beautifully executed, with terracotta reproductions of native birds made by a local craftsman. The place has a very harmonious atmosphere, with a wave-based soundtrack. Accompanied nature trails are offered from the house in the summer.

The sign to the military spit of Gâvres, *Vue Imprenable* ('Unbeatable View'), reads with unintentional irony. This absurdly thin finger of land is a mixture of ugliness and beauty, scarred by the military yet for all that one of the most atmospheric places along the generally splendid Morbihan coast. Be warned that this is an army shooting ground, though panels indicate that you can visit the unspoilt beaches on certain days. The views along this great stretch of 'virgin' military coastal territory and out to Groix are spectacular.

You can follow little signs through **Gâvres'** labyrinth of little streets to reach the **Tumulus du Goërem**, a neolithic burial site now indecorously squeezed between two townhouses. The explanatory panel describes it as 'the most beautiful example preserved of a megalithic sepulture with a right-angled corridor', but to say that this neglected site has been preserved is a bit on the cheeky side. Bring a torch if you're feeling daring enough to venture inside. The relatively elaborate funeral chamber at the end dates from 3000 BC and is split into four cells by partial divides of stone. You need to be thin as a cat to squeeze through the last. Just beyond this tumulus lies a beach that looks out onto Larmor-Plage, on the other side of the opening to the Rade de Lorient.

The Island of Groix

Once you arrive on Groix, which lies just beyond the mouth of the Rade de Lorient, you feel decades away from the modern town. Here gulls and rabbits rule, and in the summer season the island is scented with honeysuckle.

Getting There

Boats for Groix leave from Lorient. The crossing lasts around 45mins, as it takes some time to get out of the busy Rade de Lorient. Contact the Compagnie Morbihannaise et Nantaise de Navigation for info on regular services and to reserve tickets, **t** 02 97 64 77 64. The Ecomusée can arrange half-day trips on a Groix fishing boat, **t** 02 97 86 84 60.

Places for **cars** on the boats are extremely limited, so book well ahead, or better still, leave the car at the Lorient Gare Maritime car park (free) and hire bikes on the quay at Groix (they aren't allowed on the coastal paths).

Tourist Information

Quai de Port-Tudy, **t** 02 97 86 54 96 (summer only), *www.groix.fr*.

Where to Stay and Eat

Groix ✉ 56590

Port-Tudy

★★Hôtel Escale, quay, **t** 02 97 86 80 04 (*inexpensive*). A loud, cheerful option, with rooms with lovely views on to the harbour.

★★La Jetée, quay, **t** 02 97 86 80 82, *lawrence. tonnerre@freasbee.fr* (*inexpensive*). Nicely presented rooms and a snack bar.

★★Ty Mad, **t** 02 97 86 80 19, *www.tymad.com* (*inexpensive*). A hotel up the slope from the port, with views down on to it.

Les Courreaux, **t** 02 97 86 82 66 (*moderate–expensive*). A recommended restaurant. *Closed Jan–March, Mon, and Tues lunch.*

Groix (Le Bourg/St-Tudy)

Les Cormorans, Rue du Chalutier les Deux Anges, **t** 02 97 86 57 67 (*moderate*). Good-quality B&B accommodation.

La Dame de Nage, 13 Rue de Bellevue, **t** 02 97 86 55 90 (*moderate*). A decent B&B.

★★La Marine, 7 Rue du Général de Gaulle, **t** 02 97 86 80 05, *www.hoteldelamarine.com* (*inexpensive–moderate*). A charming hotel with a front courtyard shaded by a mighty yew. The restaurant has lots of shell decorations on its old stone walls and is a good place to try rod-caught sea bass, plentiful around Groix.

La Grek, 3 Place du Leurhé, **t** 02 97 86 89 85, *grek@infonie.fr* (*inexpensive*). A pleasing café-au-lait-coloured B&B (Grek is a Breton nickname for the people of Groix, meaning coffee-drinker) set in a little square in the main village.

Auberge de Jeunesse, **t** 02 97 86 81 38, *www.fuaj.org* (*inexpensive*). A youth hostel beautifully situated east along the coast from Port-Tudy. Guests must arrive between 9 and 11.30am or 7 and 8pm.

Chez Paule, 6 Rue Port Mélite, **t** 02 97 86 80 73 (*inexpensive*). A family-run crêperie on the market square, marked out by hydrangeas in pretty blue box-tubs, with a lovely stone floor and a little fireplace. There are both traditional and more adventurous crêpes, including one filled with smoked pollock.

Locqueltas

La Criste Marine, **t** 02 97 86 83 04 (*moderate*). Monique Poupée's cottage, covered with climbing plants and facing right onto the ocean. You can take your breakfast on a terrace with a sea view.

Groix seems like a sanctuary of human innocence after military Lorient and Gâvres. The most noticeable things about its hamlets are their wash-places... although islanders did use to nickname these 'the courts', implying that the gossip could be harsh. Ties with mainland Brittany and Breton culture have traditionally been strong here, but the geology of the island sets it apart from the mainland. The diversity of its rocks makes it a geologist's dream – to such an extent that Groix has had to protect itself against rock pillagers. The island has a couple of well-known beaches, including the **Plage des Grands Sables**, with its sands tinted red because of the local powdered garnet that blows over it. A couple of days on Groix should enable you to discover many of its hidden corners.

History

You can learn a great deal on the island's history from a visit to the Ecomusée at the port. A certain number of megaliths, both menhirs and dolmens, shows that neolithic people settled here. Port-Tudy, the main port from the 10th century, carries the name of a Breton saint associated with the southern Finistère and Ile Tudy and Loctudy. No trace remains of the most famous archaeological find made on Groix – a Viking burial mound containing the remains of a mature man, a child, a dog and other animals, all burnt in a Viking boat. Arms, utensils and decorative objects were also found in this cache, which was shipped off to the Musée des Antiquités Nationales outside Paris.

Groix was divided into two parts under different ownership in medieval times, the more prosperous east known as the Primiture, and the slightly harsher west called the Piwisi. The two sections were brought under joint ownership by the powerful Breton family, the Rohans, in 1384. Maritime activities became increasingly important down the centuries. By the Ancien Régime, the great majority of the men of the island would go out to sea, either in fishing or with the naval fleet, leaving the women to tend the soil. The Dutch and the British, fighting for control of the seas and new colonies in the second half of the 17th century, troubled Groix on several occasions. But it was only in the mid 18th century that the French military built serious fortifications on the island to protect it from invasion.

The islanders remain proud of their fishing past, much as it has dwindled so drastically. Sardine-fishing formed the backbone of the catch until the mid 19th century, when more advanced boats made long-haul trips possible. Between 1870 and 1940, Port-Tudy was one of France's biggest tuna-fishing ports. In fact, the first fishermen's school in France was founded here in 1895, as the captains of Groix were held in particularly high esteem on the mainland. But between the wars, the island's fishing fleet collapsed, and during the Second World War the people of Groix experienced German occupation with some intensity. One fort, Surville, served as a detention camp, while the Bourg briefly contained a camp for Jewish prisoners.

A Tour of Groix

The Groisillons, the 2,500 or so people of Groix, still divide the island into the Primitures to the east and the Piwisis to the west. The east is much more populated, and the people on that side have traditionally been wealthier. After all, the eastern side of the island benefits from much better climatic conditions – even the vegetables ripen earlier, they say...

Port-Tudy and the Ecomusée

The novelist Henri Queffélec wrote of the tuna dundees at **Port-Tudy** standing 'touching each other like animals squashed together in a livestock truck'. The description gives you some idea of the claustrophobic crush of boats that would have greeted you in the last century. Now yachts and passenger ferries take up much more of the picturesque harbour.

It is fitting enough that the **Ecomusée** (*open daily 9.30–12.30 and 3–7; for slight out-of-season variations, call* **t** *02 97 86 84 60*) should have taken over a former Groix canning factory. Footprint trails painted on the floor of the museum lead you past cabinets explaining the prehistory, history and traditions of Groix. Large models show how the local fishing boats became streamlined through time. The toughness of the fishing trade is well brought out, and the section on sailmaking is a reminder of the days when Port-Tudy would have been lined with sailmakers, ships' carpenters, chandlers and painters, all long gone. One of the worst storms in the island's history occurred in September 1930, when six boats were wrecked and many people died. Reference is made to this disaster here and in several other spots around Groix. The museum also pays homage to a Breton poet born on Groix, Jean-Pierre Calloc'h.

Northwestwards from Le Bourg

Up the hill from the port, the main settlement of the island is known to the locals as **Le Bourg**, although it is sometimes called St-Tudy and maps mark it as 'Groix'. Le Bourg has a quiet charm, and the weather vane of the church takes the form of a tuna, appropriately enough.

Port Lay lies a short distance northwest of Le Bourg. Down from the flowery upper village, this pretty and well-protected little port is tucked into a narrow inlet. Port Lay was the site of the fishermen's school where so many Groix sailors were once trained. Inland and up from Port Lay, between Kermario and Clavezic, you can go in search of the **Grand Menhir**, a tall, eroded schist monolith now submerged in scrub. Not that long ago it was still prominent enough to be used by sailors as a seamark.

West along the coast from Port Lay, the main reservoir for the island lies behind **Port Mélin**, where a statue honours poet Calloc'h, known in Breton as Bleimor, killed fighting for France in the First World War. Further on, you can walk almost to the rocky tip of the island, at **Pen Men**, though this is classified as a nature reserve. As well as a good number of birds and a profusion of honeysuckle in season, it is home to the rare *glaucophane bleu*, a type of rock, which makes it a protected geological area.

Down the Southern Coast

Starting down the southern coast, you go past the sites of the **Trou du Tonnerre** and the **Grotte aux Moutons**, on past a prehistoric camp and a stretch inland where several megaliths lie low in the undergrowth. The typical hamlet of **Kerlard** stands close by. Continuing along the coast you come to **Port St-Nicolas**, the most makeshift port imaginable, where small boats are tied to two rocks with ropes. Groix has a reputation for excellent sea diving, and this is one spot from which to explore. Sights include the wreck of the U-boat *U171*, lost with all hands in 1942. (For diving around Groix, contact Subagrec, **t** 02 97 86 59 79 or **t** 06 75 50 219 27.) The dolmen nearest the port is where legend says that the Breton Grim Reaper, *l'Ankou*, sets out at night to collect those about to die on the island.

The **Trou de l'Enfer** is the major tourist attraction of Groix after the beaches, a great hole formed in one of the cliffs. From here, on clear days you can see the length of the south side of the island, the lighthouses at opposite ends both coming into view.

To the west of Locmaria, at **Les Saisies**, natural black jetties of rock stretch into the sea, and if you're lucky you can find a deserted tiny patch of sand for yourself among the rocks. **Locmaria** can offer you a more generous beach. The village itself has a simple-structured church, **Notre Dame de Placemance**, and the wash place looks particularly well kept. The area from Locmaria to the southern tip of the island, the **Pointe des Chats** ('Cats' Point'), has the greatest geological interest on Groix. The *millefeuille* effects of the schist rocks, with their occasional veins of quartz, count among the mineralogical wonders that draw geologists to the island.

The Beaches on the Eastern Coast

The eastern coast is the place to go to find the island's curious beaches. You come to some of the small **red sand beaches** of Groix here. A very light powdering of garnet dust, dried-red in colour, streaks the shore. These beaches were not always so small – a holiday village and restaurant were built above the spacious sands before they shifted swiftly north. The main beach on the island, the **Plage des Grands Sables**, is constantly on the move. Year by year it seems to want to get closer to Port-Tudy. A delightful stretch of coastal path leads west from the beach back to the harbour, passing by the typical old hamlet of **Le Méné**, which is a good place to see the traditional architecture of Groix.

From Lorient up the Scorff to Northwestern Morbihan

The next two sections go inland up the two main rivers that spill into the Rade de Lorient, the Scorff and the Blavet. The trip up the Scorff is of particular interest if you would like to see several exceptional Breton chapels, clustered around Le Faouët.

Around Pont-Scorff

The D769 is the main road up from Lorient to northwestern Morbihan, but you can take more rural routes up the Scorff valley, sticking quite close to the river. **Pont-Scorff** has a thriving artistic community that welcomes visitors, and offers a circuit tour of artisans' studios (ask at the tourist office) to see them at work on a range of materials, centring on the **Cour des Métiers d'Art** on Rue de Polignac (*open July and Aug Tues–Sat 10–12 and 2–7, Sun 2–7; Sept–June Wed 2–6, Thurs–Sat 10–12 and 2–6, Sun 2.30–6*). The **zoo** to the south of town might appeal to children. A Grande Randonnée walking route keeps to the river along a particularly beautiful stretch here.

The **Odyssaum** (*open July and Aug daily 9–7; Sept–June Tues–Fri 2–6, Sat–Mon 9–12.30 and 2–6*) is another *espace découverte* – an eco-museum exploring the lifecycles of the river Scorff's wild salmon. The exhibition, which follows the surprising 'odyssey' the fish go through in their lives, is beautifully located in a renovated mill, the Moulin des Princes. In the summer, staff put on salmon-themed open-air theatre productions and organize a season of cookery displays where restaurant chefs of local repute come and show off their skills with salmon.

Kernascléden

The village of **Kernascléden** to the north of Plouay may look rather colourless on the outside, but its chapel contains a splendid display of 15th-century frescoes. This is one of the many Morbihan religious buildings to have been constructed with some of the wealth of the Rohan family. It went up between 1420 and 1464, and the style is Breton Flamboyant Gothic, of course.

You should go to the depiction of hell in the southern transept first, which looks like a diabolical funfair in full swing. The damned start their painful voyage downwards by being impaled on the viciously sharp branches of a barren tree. Monstrous devils then come to pluck the condemned captives from the tree, to be cooked in three great cauldrons, while further damned men are placed in a barrel to be churned round.

Getting Around

There are limited **bus** services into this area. One line goes from Lorient to Gourin, which is also on a route between Carhaix-Plouguer and Rosporden in the Finistère.

Tourist Information

Pays d'Accueil du Roi Morvan, Mairie, 56770 Plouay, t 02 97 34 81 52, *www.paysroimorvan. com*. General information on the area.
Le Faouët: 1 Rue de Quimper, t 02 97 23 23 23, *www.paysroimorvan.com*.
Gourin: 24 Rue de la Libération, t 02 97 23 66 33, *www.paysroimorvan.com*.
Guémené-sur-Scorff: Mairie, t 02 97 39 33 47; Rue Bisson in season, *www.paysroimorvan.com*.
Pont-Scorff: t 02 97 32 50 27, *www.pont-scorff.com*.

Market Days

Le Faouët: 1st and 3rd Wednesdays of month.
Gourin: Monday.
Guémené-sur-Scorff: Thursday.

Where to Stay and Eat

Le Faouët ✉ 56320

★★La Croix d'Or, 9 Place Bellanger, t 02 97 23 07 33 (*inexpensive*). A hotel overlooking the main square, once frequented by artists. The carefully prepared food (*moderate–expensive*) is rather better than the dullish but adequate rooms.

Crêperie Sarrasine, 1 Rue du Château, t 02 97 23 06 05 (*inexpensive*). A pretty, rustic setting for excellent-value crêpes. *Closed Mon in low season.*
Ferme-auberge de Kerizac, towards Le Scaër, t 02 97 34 44 57, *cyrillelemeur@wanadoo.fr* (*inexpensive*). A barn deep in the countryside outside town, where you can eat farm-reared meat. Rooms are sometimes available.

Berné and Meslan ✉ 56240

Mme Brigardis, Marta, Berné, t 02 97 34 28 58 (*inexpensive*). Characterful B&B rooms just south of Le Faouët.
Mme Jambou, Roscalet, Meslan, t 02 97 34 24 13 (*inexpensive*). A picturesque B&B option on a former farm.

Le Croisty

Tavarn Ar Roue Morvan, 4 Rue de la Mairie, along the D132 northeast out of Le Faouët, t 02 97 51 60 44 (*inexpensive*). A place that puts on evenings of Breton food and music.

Guémené-sur-Scorff ✉ 56160

★★Le Bretagne, 18 Rue J Pérès, t 02 97 51 20 08 (*inexpensive*). A newly modernized traditional hotel with cheap menus. *Closed last 2wks Sept.*
Crêperie des Rohan, 24 Rue Bisson, t 02 97 39 35 14 (*inexpensive*). A bright, clean place on the main street, popular with locals.
Crêperie d'Ingrid Broussot, t 02 97 39 46 64 (*inexpensive*). A splendid country crêperie (head west on the D131, branch north onto the D128 between Lignol and Ploërdut, and take the turning for Kermaquer).

More elevating scenes have been painted on the choir. Immediately above the arches you can make out the events of Christ's Passion, though some of the stone shows through. The finer art fans out above, the different scenes divided into segments by the ribs of the Gothic vaulting. The paintings here, refined and in fascinating detail, illustrate the life of the Virgin and the baby Jesus. This is accomplished art, possibly done by someone from outside Brittany. Large painted figures of angels with peacock-style wings make music in the north transept. With their tambourines and viols, they are apparently singing an Agnus and a Sanctus, as musicians have managed to make out from the notes and lyrics on the scrolled parchments.

To Le Faouët via St-Fiacre

The D782 from Kernascléden leads east to Guémené-sur-Scorff and west to Le Faouët. Heading west, this corner of the Morbihan historically formed part of the Breton county of Cornouaille before the Revolution. Before arriving at Le Faouët, make sure to stop at the church of **St-Fiacre**, a fine example of typical Breton architecture, awkward and appealing at the same time. Inside, the chapel was commissioned for the Boutteville family, who appear to have wanted to rival the work ordered by the Rohans at Kernascléden.

Once inside the church, you will most probably be attracted like a child to the colours of the **jubé**, or rood screen. Its carver, Olivier Le Loergan, composed a fantastic multicoloured piece of Breton art, with the wood seeming almost as light as lace. Christ is depicted on his cross as an emaciated, aged figure, his placid suffering in contrast to the clear pain of the two robbers being crucified with him. Below, a deeply sad Mary shows her years, while the more stoical heads of saints are raised upwards. The original stained glass, which was made in the mid 16th century, shows scenes from the life of St Fiacre. Christ is represented in the main apse window, the 'Roman' soldiers who guard him wearing 16th-century armour. Other notable details in the chapel include the lord's exclusive gallery in the apse and a statue of the Virgin and Child.

Le Faouët

The great sloping roofs of the covered market dominate the large central square of Le Faouët, indicating that the town, now a drowsy place, once held extremely important fairs. A **fine arts museum** (*open April and 11 June–2 Oct daily 10–12 and 2.30–6.30*) occupies the former Ursuline convent, built off one corner of the square in the mid 17th century. The institutionalized interior setting for the paintings has none of the charm of the unspoilt chapels around Le Faouët. The museum holds a smallish permanent collection with works by the artists who formed something of a colony here in the early 20th century, but each year it puts on a more substantial exhibition, often of local interest. Germain David-Nillet is perhaps the painter most strongly associated with Le Faouët. He gave some indication of this quiet corner's popularity with artists when he remarked in 1911 that: 'Here we are...invaded by painters. There are eleven of them working at the chapel of St-Fiacre.' It comes as no surprise then, that lots of the works in the permanent exhibition depict the beautiful local chapels.

The Chapel of Ste-Barbe and Beyond

The chapel of Ste-Barbe just north of Le Faouët was another of the artists' favourite spots, and from the hilltop above you can still look out onto unspoilt inland Brittany. It was used as a location for the film *Marion du Faouët*, which retold the story of a local 18th-century highwaywoman who imposed her own sense of justice on Cornouaille, robbing the rich to feed the poor. The chapel was built from 1483, in Flamboyant Gothic style. The story goes that Jean de Toulbodou was out hunting when lightning struck the rocks above him, causing large blocks to break off and tumble down around him. He escaped unscathed – miraculously he felt, vowing to erect a chapel on the very spot where he had been saved.Tall twin Gothic accoladed doorways make for a noble entrance. Among the statues stands one representation of Ste Barbe. On the left-hand side, carved panels decorate a little gallery attached to the wall. But the most beautiful feature of the interior is the French Renaissance stained-glass windows from around 1520, showing scenes of Ste Barbe's life and of the legend of the lord of Toulbodou. You can walk down the steep side of the valley from the chapel to the early 18th-century fountain, where young women used to throw pins in the water to see if they crossed – a superstitious manner of testing whether they would be blessed with a good marriage.

East at **Priziac**, explore typical inland Breton countryside at the **Parc Aquanature Le Stérou** (*open April–Oct daily 11–7*), where you can go walking, fishing or on a horse and carriage ride, as well as appreciating the large herd of deer reared here.

To Gourin and Guémené-sur-Scorff

The main D769 road north from Le Faouët leads to **Gourin**, the crêpe capital of Brittany, lost in the very northwestern corner of the Morbihan, and deep in the Breton interior. Gourin also calls itself the capital of the Montagnes Noires (a chain of central Breton hills rather than mountains), on whose southern side the town lies. The **Fête de la Crêpe** takes place on the third weekend in July, in the grounds of the **Château de Tronjoly** a short walk from the centre of town. The festival, which includes a crêpe-making competition and traditional Breton dancing and music, promotes the tradition of the hand-made crêpe, despite the fact that Gourin is also the largest industrial producer of crêpes in Brittany. Regular art exhibitions by contemporary (often local) artists are also held in the outbuildings of the château.

The D1 road east links Gourin with **Guémené-sur-Scorff**, the reputation of which rests on *andouilles*, a speciality of salted pigs' intestines stuffed in concentric circles into a casing of cow's stomach, considered a delicacy in the region. Here in this quiet town, with its pleasing sloping main street of old stone houses and the vestige of a Rohan castle, the town butchers fight it out for supremacy in the *andouille* market.

Inland from Lorient up the Blavet to Pontivy

The Blavet river flows through an exceptionally beautiful Breton valley. Between the relatively lively towns of Hennebont and Pontivy you can go in search of a clutch of sights that have been extremely well done up in the last few years.

Hennebont

Hennebont is the most northerly of four semi-detached towns strung along the Rade de Lorient. Southwest of it, Lanester, Lorient and Ploemeur stretch out in a fairly unbroken ugly urban chain. Hennebont, though not the most obvious of tourist stops, can claim to be the most traditionally pretty of these four towns, with sections of its old ramparts still standing. Two impressive towers along these walls house the interesting local history museum, the **Musée des Tours Broërec'h** (*open June–Sept daily 10.30–12.30 and 1.30–6.30*). A traditional Breton church towers over the centre and draws visitors inside. Thursday is Hennebont's market day, a big event in the western Morbihan.

Getting Around

Hennebont has a station on the line from Paris to Quimper via Rennes, but virtually no TGVs stop there. Pontivy also has a **railway** station, on the line crossing central Brittany north to south, from St-Brieuc to Vannes.

There's a **bus** service up the Blavet valley from Lorient to St-Brieuc, stopping at Hennebont, Languidic, Baud and Pontivy.

Tourist Information

Pays d'Accueil de la Vallée du Blavet, 4 Rue de Botkermarrec, B.P. 43, 56150 Baud, t 02 97 51 09 37. General information on the area.
Hennebont: 9 Place du Maréchal Foch, t 02 97 36 24 52, www.hennebont.com.
Baud: Place Mathurin Martin, t 02 97 51 02 29.
Pontivy: 61 Rue du Général de Gaulle, t 02 97 25 04 10, http://www.bfi.fr/pontivy/.

Market Days

Hennebont: Thursday.
Baud: Saturday.
Pontivy: Monday.

Where to Stay and Eat

Hennebont ✉ 56700

★★★★Château de Locguénolé, Route de Port-Louis, Kervignac, a few km south of Hennebont, t 02 97 76 76 76, www. chateau-de-locguenole.com (*expensive–luxury*). Part of the luxurious Relais & Châteaux chain, with a tennis court, heated swimming pool and highly reputed cuisine, set in 120 hectares of grounds sloping down to the Blavet. The guest rooms are in the château and the adjacent manor.
Hôtel-Restaurant du Centre, 44 Rue du Maréchal Joffre, t 02 97 36 21 44 (*inexpensive*). Simple, renovated rooms set in the centre of town. The elaborate cooking is considered by locals to be some of the best in town; specialities include gravadlax and salmon *millefeuille*. Half-board is obligatory in July and Aug.
L'Orchis, 25 Quai du Port-Louis, t 02 97 65 02 89 (*moderate*). Good-value traditional regional food in a modern setting with river views.
Crêperie St-Michel, t 02 97 85 02 88 (*inexpensive*). A simple choice run by very friendly young people. *Closed Sun, Mon and 10 days in June and Sept.*

Inzinzac-Lochrist ✉ 56650

Le Ty Mat, at Penquesten, t 02 97 36 89 26, http://pro.wanadoo.fr/ty-mat (*inexpensive–moderate*). A little manor with large B&B rooms on the edge of woods.
Auberge de Jeunesse, Ferme du Gorée (bus I or H from Hennebont), t 02 97 36 08 08, www. fuaj.org (*inexpensive*). A youth hostel well situated on a farm, with cooking facilities.

Languidic ✉ 56440

Ferme-auberge de Lann-Menhir, t 02 97 65 80 00 (*inexpensive*). A simple option a few km northeast of Hennebont off the N24. The décor is not its strong point, but the farmers treat you to a feast of a meal.

Quistinic ✉ 56310

Crêperie Au Coin Tranquille, St Trugdual, t 02 97 39 70 76 (*inexpensive*). A typical Breton crêperie in a quiet spot. *Closed Mon–Fri exc school hols.*

If you are interested in horses, visit the **Haras National d'Hennebont** (*open July and Aug Mon–Fri 9–7, Sat and Sun 2–6, Sept–May Mon–Fri 9–12.30 and 2–6, Sat and Sun 2–6*). This stud farm is a short way outside the historic centre, in formal grounds that belonged to a Cistercian nunnery. The château-like main building has a ground floor with stabling space, where you can admire many traditional sturdy Breton horses, as well as a collection of rather lighter-looking carriages. The tour also includes a visit to the farrier's, the saddlery and the massive feed room. The latter was converted into one of the *espaces découvertes* in the Lorient area, with the result that visitors can now enjoy an attractively presented, sizeable exhibition on the history of the horse and horse-breeding as an industry. Temporary art exhibitions are also hosted here.

Melrand ✉ 56310

La Tourelle, Place de l'Eglise, **t** 02 97 39 51 13 (*inexpensive*). A very simple hotel and restaurant in a pleasant old village house.

Baud ✉ 56150

Auberge du Cheval Blanc, 16 Rue de Pontivy, **t 02 97 51 00 85 (*inexpensive*). An old-fashioned provincial hotel in a stone house in the centre.
La Chenaie, Talnay, St-Barthélemy, **t** 02 97 27 14 73 (*inexpensive*). A British-owned place with a heated swimming pool.
Robics, Kersommer, **t** 02 97 51 08 02 (*inexpensive*). Comfy B&B rooms on a farm.

Camors ✉ 56330

Hotel-Restaurant Ar Brug, opposite the church, **t** 02 97 39 18 94 (*inexpensive*). A cheap and cheerful, newly renovated option.

Plumeliau ✉ 59630

Paul Vessier, 29 Rue de Kervernen, **t** 02 97 51 94 73 (*inexpensive*). Good B&B rooms in 15 acres.

St-Nicolas-des-Eaux ✉ 56930

Le Vieux Moulin, Rue des Combats Kervenen, **t 02 97 51 81 09 (*inexpensive*). A reasonably priced hotel on the edge of the Blavet.
Maison Magique, Allée du Vieux Blavet, **t** 02 97 51 86 02 (*inexpensive*). An eccentric B&B, with hosts who may treat you to a magic show.
Bar-Hôtel-Restaurant de la Vallée, **t** 02 97 51 81 04 (*inexpensive*). A basic hotel with a swimming pool and mini-golf.

Quelven ✉ 56310

Auberge de Quelven, **t 02 97 27 77 50 (*inexpensive*). Appealing, comfy rooms with views over the church green in a quiet village.

Pontivy ✉ 56300

Hôtel de l'Europe, **t 02 97 25 11 14 (*inexpensive*). A 19th-century hotel offering rooms with a period feel, a wood-panelled interior, and animal-head carvings sticking out of its façade.
La Pommeraie, 17 Quai du Couvent, **t** 02 97 25 60 09 (*moderate–expensive*) A restaurant offering unusual cuisine near the old town, run by a young couple. *Closed Sun and Mon, April, and end Aug–Sept.*
Le Martray, Rue du Pont, just off Place du Martray, **t** 02 97 25 68 64 (*moderate*). Good-quality traditional cuisine in the centre of town. *Closed Tues and Wed.*
La Petite Marmite, Rue des Puits, **t** 02 97 27 94 71 (*moderate*). A popular place in a cosy timberframe building, specializing in hearty meat and fish dishes served *en cocotte* (clay stew-pots).

Ploërmel ✉ 56800

Le Thy 19, Rue de la Gare, **t** 02 97 74 05 21 (*inexpensive*). Seven bedrooms each embodying the style of an artist, from Gustave Klimt to Edward Hopper. The Van Gogh bedroom mimics his famous interior. The rooms are surprisingly subtle and well appointed, and there is a very bohemian 'cabaret' and café.

Noyal-Pontivy ✉ 56920

1703 Restaurant, next to the church, **t** 02 97 38 25 89 (*inexpensive*). The place to come for a classic, good-value *menu ouvrier*, or workman's meal. Make sure you blag your way into the locals' side at lunchtime to enjoy a simple, good-quality, multiple-course lunch.

Another *espace découverte* was set up in nearby **Brandérion** in order to pay homage to the world of weaving. **La Tisserie** (*open July and Aug daily 10–12.30 and 2–6; rest of year, call* **t** *02 97 32 90 27*) offers a small and meticulously presented tour of Brittany's weaving history, but it also puts the craft in its wider, global context. There are temporary exhibitions in the summer months and off-season classes on how to weave with an ancient loom.

The Hennebont tourist office organizes day trips in summer from Hennebont's port, down the Blavet estuary, and out to and around the island of Groix. The industrial side of Hennebont lies to the north of the old town up the Blavet at Inzinzac-Lochrist. Ironworks used to cover some two and a half kilometres along the river bank here, and several large industrial buildings are still standing. Here, the woman behind the **Ecomusée Industriel** (*open Mon–Fri 10–12 and 2–6, Sat and Sun 2–6*) has made such a success of the subject that she has been made an honorary museographer for her efforts. In the **Musée des Métallurgistes** you can learn through panels, plans and tools how the ironworks developed.

Up the Blavet to Poul-Fétan by Quistinic

The absurdly picturesque thatched village of **Poul-Fétan** lies above the Blavet by Quistinic. But Poul-Fétan is not absolutely perfect – you have to pay to get into it, and it isn't always open. The hamlet had been virtually abandoned when the local municipality decided to buy it in 1977 and turn it into a showpiece village for the benefit of tourists. The restoration work is perhaps too immaculate for some tastes. The dozen houses, mainly dating from the 16th century, are regularly re-thatched, and blue irises are left to grow along their crests. Enthusiasts dressed in Breton period costume bring life to some of the cottages on many weekends of the year, with displays of old-fashioned spinning, and millet-making and butter-churning among the culinary activities.

Baud and Postcards in Old Baths

The main reason to visit Baud is to study old Breton postcards at the **Cartopole** or **Conservatoire Régional de la Carte Postale** (*open June–Sept daily 9.30–12.30 and 2–7, Oct–May Wed, Thurs, Sat and Sun 2–5.30*). Located in the town's former public baths, or *bains-douches*, this modern exhibition space has been extremely well conceived, and its enormous collection of postcards helps to create a rich and diverse visual documentary on the development of Brittany and Breton culture over the past century or so. There are a few hundred postcards on CD-ROM, which allows you to magnify images of old Breton festivals and weddings, or of the ports in a time when fishing boats still had sails. English-speaking visitors are offered audioguides for the whole exhibition.

Baud is also known for the peculiar **Vénus de Quinipily** statue situated just to the south of it by the Evel, which is a tributary of the Blavet. Gustave Flaubert, on his tour of Brittany, wrote of the statue having a 'a sensuality both barbarous and refined'. This naked Breton colossus, reaching more than two metres in height, may date back to Gallo-Roman times.

Melrand's Ferme Archéologique and Lann Gouh Verlan

Open Mon–Fri 11–5, Sat and Sun 11–6; double check in winter on t 02 97 39 57 89.

Wander up the Blavet valley west of Baud, perhaps going via the pretty roads through St-Adrien or St-Barthélémy, then head onto the western side of the river to see **Melrand's Ferme Archéologique**, next to the well-disguised **ruins of Lann Gouh Verlan**, old Melrand. At the beginning of the 20th century, the low moss- and grass-covered humps that form the remaining vestiges of village walls were thought to date back to the Gallo-Roman period. It is now known that these are in fact the remains of an early medieval settlement from around AD 1000. The reconstructions of early medieval houses share an extremely thatched look, the roofs almost reaching to the ground. *Maisons mixtes* were the norm, with animals sharing the living quarters with families. You should find a fire warming the interior of one of the houses even in summer, as it is thought that fire not only provided warmth, light and cooking facilities but was also used to fumigate the house.

To the Church of St-Nicodème via the Site de Castennec

East of Melrand, back by the Blavet, head on via the beautiful hilltop **Site de Castennec**, caught in a tight meander of the river. Just west, **St-Gildas's chapel** at the foot of a large rock overlooking the valley is where the christianizing Breton who founded the abbey of St-Gildas (*see* p.402) supposedly died as a hermit in 570.

The church of **St-Nicodème** lies on the other side of the river, east of the hillside village of St-Nicolas-des-Eaux. Approaching it through surrounding fields, all that you can make out of the church is the top of its ornate steeple, rising sharply out of the rolling countryside. This church was built in Flamboyant Gothic style in 1537. Within, a large sculpted scene of the Resurrection greets you, only Christ appears to have disappeared from it. Further carved wooden figures attract your attention around the church, including angels and musicians along the string-pieces. An elaborate fountain stands outside the church.

Quelven

A startlingly substantial church towers over the lovely granite village of **Quelven**, west of the Blavet (from St-Nicodème, go up the D1, then onto the D2 to get there). **Notre-Dame de Quelven** is a huge Gothic building more suitable in size for a large town. The edifice went up at the end of the 15th century. An amazing thin pencil of a Gothic tower was stuck on to the main one. Big dragon gargoyles, carved dogs and semi-human creatures cling to the outside of the building, while the curvaceously roofed outdoor pulpit with its double staircase was added in 1738.

The statuary within this church is wonderful. At the back of the nave, a large-scale scene shows a Little Red Riding Hood of a Virgin looking on as an emaciated St George on a thin white horse clinically lances the dragon. In another extraordinary animal scene, a muzzled wolf accompanies a holy man – this is the traditional representation of the Breton St Hervé (*see* p.34). The most famous statue of the whole collection is the cross-eyed Virgin of Quelven.

To Pontivy or Napoléonville

The area around Pontivy is extremely rich in chapels and churches, with several used as settings for temporary art exhibitions. The way to the **Art dans les chapelles** sites is well indicated.

Pontivy has a straight-lined Napoleonic town tacked on to a winding medieval one, and a château with two of the fattest, squattest towers that you're ever likely to see on a French castle. The **Château de Pontivy** (*open July and Aug daily 10.30–6.30; Sept–June Wed–Sat 10–12 and 2–6*) was one of a string of defences belonging to the mighty Rohan family. In fact, from 1396, Pontivy served as the capital of the Rohans' viscounty. Several châteaux have stood in this town; the stocky outer forms that you see now were built between 1479 and 1485. In summer, temporary exhibitions are held inside.

The streets of the **old town** meander in a gentle fashion down towards the Blavet from the castle and the adjacent former religious quarter; this part of town includes the long and thin Place Leperdit, which is home to a nice mix of old houses. The Rue du Fil, a narrow, curving old shopping street with some beamed houses, takes you down to Place du Martray, the old heart of town, which is somewhat cruelly cut through by the Rue Nile, a long, straight shopping street that dates back to the Napoleonic experiment in town planning. Pontivy was in fact briefly rebaptized **Napoléonville** when Napoleon's government decided to exploit it's central position in Brittany and its waterways in order to build a new administrative town to the south of the old town.

The Chapelle Ste-Noyale

The **Chapelle Ste-Noyale**, a handful of kilometres northeast of Pontivy, may lie close to a wide, dull plain made uglier by a vast grain silo complex; but the mass of wall paintings in this chapel, which tell the terrible legend of Ste Noyale – twice – are absorbing. The first set of scenes of Ste Noyale's life decorates the separate oratory. In the transept and choir of the chapel itself, you're likely to get a cricked neck trying to decipher the panoply of martyred female saints painted on the ceiling. Luckily, in high season, a guide can provide some enlightenment.

Ste Noyale Arrives on Tree Leaves

Noyale, otherwise known as Nolwenn, was carried across the Channel to Brittany on tree leaves, so the legend poetically has it. Of royal lineage, Noyale had given away all her material possessions to the poor and decided to cross the waters in search of a hermitage. She arrived in Armorica in the 6th century, accompanied by her former wet-nurse. Captured by a tyrant of a chieftain, Nizall by name, she refused to give in to his carnal desires, and in retaliation he had her decapitated in front of him. Unperturbed, she headed off, her head in her hand. She found a rock on which to pray, and where she planted her baton an ash tree rose up. Noyale then shed three drops of blood that turned into a fountain before wandering into the wilderness to finally die.

The Etel Estuary and the Quiberon Peninsula

Dividing the Lorient military area to the west from the area of the Morbihan's major megaliths and holiday resorts to the east, the Etel estuary is the least known of the Morbihan's series of enormous river mouths. It is extraordinarily beautiful in parts, often tranquil, with very few modern additions.

A precariously narrow strip of land, a *tombolo* of sand, is all that connects the Quiberon peninsula to the mainland. In the distant past, the land mass of Quiberon has been cut off, creating an island, and this may happen again in the future. The eastern side of the whole peninsula is wonderfully protected from the battering Atlantic waves, while the rocky shoreline to the west is often at their mercy, forming a quite spectacular and dangerous stretch of the Breton coast, known unreassuringly as the Côte Sauvage, or the Wild Coast. Quiberon itself is a highly popular resort looking out to Belle-Ile.

The Etel Estuary and Erdeven's Beaches

You could start out by going to take a look at the **mouth of the Etel** with its sand bar just out to sea, then head for the unspoilt Plouhinec side. You'll be struck by the beauty of the **wild beach** that runs westwards from here, the sand deeply golden, with curious red ladders growing out of it. This beach still forms part of the long military shooting ground that goes as far as Gâvres to the west. Signs announcing *Servitude militaire* remind you of the fact, but this area is actually open to the public.

Start heading up the western side of the Etel estuary. The skeletons of two large boats lie decaying opposite the workaday port of Etel town, symbols of the estuary's loss of its traditional trade. Just south of the D781 main road, take a narrow winding track to the small, secretive **Port du Vieux Passage**. Next, join the D9 northwards up the estuary, then turn off for **Nestadio**. The beautiful road takes you across marshland into pine woods, past lovely old stone houses, and on to a dead end with a little whitewashed chapel. Opposite Nestadio, the beautiful village of St-Cado looks so close across the water, but following the itinerary set out below, it could take hours to reach.

The northern end of the Etel inland sea has some charming chapels, notably those of **Kergoh**, **Locmaria** and **Legevin**. Negotiating the tip of the Etel ria, with the busy N165 dual carriageway rushing past, you can descend the eastern side of the estuary. Take a quick look at the village of **Langonbrac'h**, then cross the N165 for the **Jardin du Château de Kerambarh** (*open May–Oct*) towards Landaul, with a whole range of gardens inspired by different periods. Then head back for the Etel water's edge. The **Pointe du Verdon** reaches deep into the centre of the ria, views opening out onto a confusion of further spits of land. On the way to the point, keep your eyes peeled for the Kegil Berhed or **Quenouille de Brigitte**, a neolithic menhir that, in the christianizing tale, turned into Ste Brigitte's spinning distaff. Follow the long branch of water to **Locoal-Mendon**, from where you can explore the beautiful scorpion's tail of land to the west.

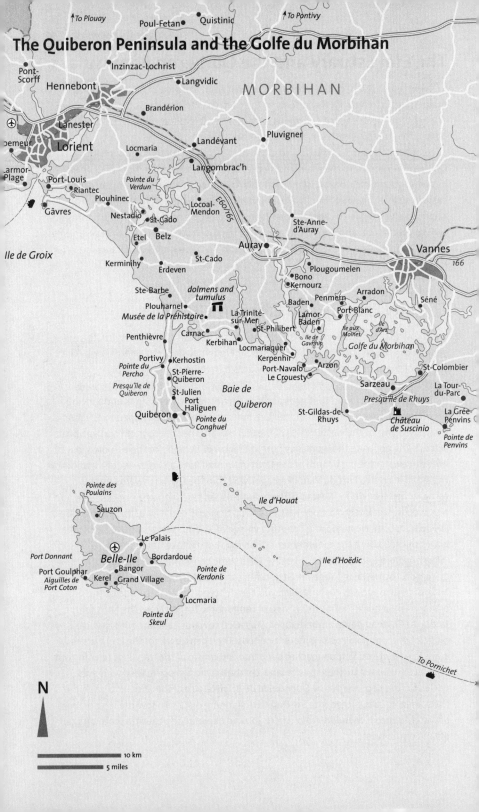

The Quiberon Peninsula and the Golfe du Morbihan

↑ To Plouay
↑ To Pontivy

Poul-Fetan • • Quistinic

Inzinzac-Lochrist

M O R B I H A N

• Langvidic

Pont-
Scorff
Hennebont

Brandérion

Lanester

Lorient

Locmaria

Landévant

Pluvigner

Langombrac'h

Pointe du
Verdun

Armor-
Plage
Port-Louis
• Riantec
Plouhinec

Locoal-
Mendon

Ste-Anne-
d'Auray

Gâvres

Nestadio
St-Cado
Belz

St-Cado

Auray

Vannes

166

Ile de Groix

Etel

Kerminihy

Erdeven

St-Cado

Plougoumelen

Bono
Kernourz

Arradon

Séné

Ste-Barbe

dolmens and
tumulus

Penmern

Port-Blanc

Plouharnel

Baden

Lamor-
Baden

Musée de la Préhistoire

La Trinité-
sur-Mer

St-Philibert

Ile
d'Arz

Penthièvre

Carnac

Kerbihan

Ile de
Gavrinis

Golfe du Morbihan

Portivy

Kerhostin

Locmariaquer

Ile aux
Moines

Pointe du
Percho

St-Pierre-
Quiberon

Kerpenhir

Presqu'île de
Quiberon

St-Julien

Baie de

Port-Navalo
Le Crouesty

Arzon

St-Colombier

Quiberon

Port
Haliguen

Quiberon

La Tour-
du-Parc

Pointe du
Conghuel

St-Gildas-de-
Rhuys

Sarzeau

Presqu'île de Rhuys

La Grée-
Pénvins

Château
de Suscinio

Pointe de
Penvins

Ile d'Houat

Pointe des
Poulains

Sauzon

Le Palais

Ile d'Hoëdic

Port Donnant

Belle-Ile

Bordardoué

Port Goulphar
Aiguilles de
Port Coton

Bangor
Kerel
Grand Village

Pointe de
Kerdonis

Locmaria

Pointe du
Skeul

To Pornichet

N

10 km
5 miles

St Cado Has a Cat Killed for His Causeway

Cado is a Breton saint of the Dark Ages who is said to have come across from Glamorgan in Wales to convert the local people. The story goes that once he had chosen the site where he was going to settle, he first had to chase the snakes from the land. He began building an island monastery but realized that he didn't have the funds he needed to make the causeway to attach the island to the mainland. Satan came and offered to construct the causeway for him in exchange for the first life that crossed it. Cado managed to get a black cat to cross it first, thus sparing any human life.

In later times, St Cado became associated with miraculous cures for the deaf, and visitors would come to the saint's stone 'bed' in the church and put their bad ear to the hole in it – their ear was pronounced better when they could hear the waters lapping below the church.

St-Cado and Etel

Continue south for Belz and look for signs to the historic village of St-Cado. A scattering of tiny islands marks the estuary here. One, connected to the village by an old stone bridge, will draw your attention with its extraordinary huddle of houses. This is old St-Cado, and you are not allowed to take cars across. The main point of interest on this island is the old church, with its Romanesque elements. The working port of **Etel** to the south has known better days, but the town has developed a small yachting harbour despite the obstacle of the sand bar, which makes coming in and out of the estuary awkward.

Pretty Unspoilt Beaches Below Erdeven

Erdeven, with its neolithic alignments of Kerzehro, is reserved for the section of mega megaliths (*see* p.375). But to the south of it, wide stretches of low, now mainly uncultivated dunes separate the old villages from the sea. The bulky, stern farms in the dunes did once live off the coastal land, as the many old stone walls still separating the plots of land around them indicate.

The most westerly beach along this stretch, located close to the Barre d'Etel, is that of **Kerminihy**, a golden stretch that is favoured by nudists, while **La Roche Seiche beach** follows Kerminihy to the east. The two lovely rocky islands standing a little way out to sea endow this stretch with its particular character.

Although the village of **Kerhillio** has come out in a rash of modern developments, the **beach** lies well away from the buildings, and its beautifully curving bay looks out on to two lighthouses. The sea can be wild along here, attracting windsurfers and even surfers.

Two Museums South of Plouharnel and Quiberon's Sandy Spit

The spit of sand connecting the Quiberon peninsula to the mainland starts just below **Plouharnel**. Two curious little museums stand out at the entrance on to this spit, the loudly self-advertising Galion, and the inward-looking Musée de la

Chouannerie. The **Galion** (*open daily July and Aug 9.30–7, Easter–June and Sept 10–12 and 2–6*), a startling, firmly beached modern copy of an 18th-century vessel, contains a ridiculous number of seashells for you to admire, while the **Musée de la Chouannerie** (*open April–Sept daily 10–12 and 2–6*) took over a genuine Second World War Nazi bunker. This museum commemorates an anti-Revolutionary uprising in these parts (*see* **History**, p.19). Copies of portraits of the anti-Revolutionary leaders, models, weapons and short texts explain the importance of the Chouannerie in Brittany, particularly in this area.

Getting Around

In summer, the railway service from Auray down to Quiberon comes to life. **Trains** serve Plouharnel, Les Sables Blancs, Penthièvre, L'Isthme, Kerhostin and St-Pierre-Quiberon along the sandy *tombolo*.

In high summer, the roads around the peninsula clog up with **cars**, and the whole spit can turn into an enormous traffic jam.

Book well in advance for **boat** trips out to the islands of Belle-Ile from the port of Quiberon. Also, if you are heading to Quiberon to take the ferry, make sure you get there several hours beforehand.

Tourist Information

Etel: Place des Thoniers, t 02 97 55 23 80, *syndicat.initiative-etel@wanadoo.fr*.

Erdeven: 7 Rue de l'Abbé Le Barth, t 02 97 55 64 60, *www.ot-erdeven.fr*.

Quiberon: 14 Rue de Verdun, t 02 97 50 07 84, *www.quiberon.com*.

Market Days

Etel: Tuesday.
Quiberon: Saturday.

Where to Stay and Eat

Plouhinec ✉ 56680

★★Hôtel de Kerlon, Kerlon, t 02 97 36 77 03, *www.auberge-de-kerlon.com* (*inexpensive*). A friendly, comfortable hotel in a converted farm in the countryside. The owners rear their own fowl and lambs. Half-board is required in July and Aug.

La Roquaille, t 02 97 36 76 23 (*inexpensive*). Bargain meals.

Pluvigner ✉ 56330

Gérard et Nelly Greves, Chaumière de Kerreo, t 02 97 50 90 48 (*inexpensive*). A classic Breton thatched cottage, owned by a former cookery teacher, offering B&B.

Locoal-Mendon ✉ 56550

Le Relais de Port Kerio, t 02 97 24 67 57 (*inexpensive*). A 15th-century manor in the countryside, with an impressive fireplace in the dining room.

Belz ✉ 56410

★★Le Relais de Kergou, 1km out of the village towards Auray, t 02 97 55 35 61 (*inexpensive*). A pleasant little hotel with a garden and reasonable cooking.

Crêperie de Ty Baron, t 02 97 55 46 39 (*inexpensive*). Tasty crêpes served in a pretty Breton farmhouse.

Etel ✉ 56410

★★Le Trianon, 14 Rue du Général Leclerc, t 02 97 55 32 41, *www.hotel-le-trianon.com* (*inexpensive–moderate*). Comfortable rooms and a smart dining room.

L'Amirauté, 9 Rue Amiral Schewerer, t 02 97 55 48 59, *www.amiraute-etel.com* (*inexpensive*). A good hotel in the home of former commander of the liner *France*, with a minimum 2-night stay.

Crêperie La Pourleth, 4 Rue Alphonse Rio, t 02 97 55 51 64 (*inexpensive*). A pretty little crêperie.

Le Bistrot à Thon, Ruelle des Quais, t 02 97 55 32 50 (*inexpensive*). A bar-cum-restaurant with a repertoire of 50 tuna recipes. *Closed lunch, 10 days June, and Sun and Mon out of season.*

Kerhostin ✉ 56510

La Chaloupe, t 02 97 30 91 54, *chaloupe.ker@ freesbee.fr* (*inexpensive*). Simple, pretty rooms.

Past these two museums, as you go south down the **sandy spit** connecting the mainland to the Quiberon peninsula, turn to the left in order to reach the flat beaches by the bay, which are colonized here by campers. The first couple of turnings on the right take you to what might be called specialist beaches, where the rough waters attract surfers in large numbers, and the nudist beach and dunes attract gay men in droves. Follow the beaches down the sandy spit; at low tide the sand-yachts come out on the Plage de Penthièvre to make the most of the wider stretches of sand.

St-Pierre-Quiberon ✉ 56510

***La Plage**, 25 Quai d'Orange, **t** 02 97 30 92 10, *hotel.plage@wanadoo.fr* (*inexpensive*). Many rooms in this modern hotel have balconies looking onto the bay.

St-Pierre, 34 Route de Quiberon, B.P. 3, **t** 02 97 50 26 90, *www.hotel-st-pierre.com* (*inexpensive*). Another well-kept hotel.

Crêperie Le Floch, 4 Avenue des Druides (*inexpensive*). Unfussy and serves some of the best crêpes on the peninsula, so it's busy (no reservations possible).

Quiberon ✉ 56170

****Sofitel Thalassa**, Pointe du Goulvars, B.P. 170, **t** 02 97 50 20 00, *www.thalassa.com* (*moderate–luxury*). A very large and uninspiring-looking hotel well known for its modern seawater treatments. It lies east of the town, right by a beach, and it has its own swimming pool, tennis court, sauna, gym and restaurant (*expensive*).

***Bellevue**, Rue de Tiviec, B.P. 37, **t** 02 97 50 16 28, *www.bellevuequiberon.com* (*moderate–expensive*). A comfortable and peaceful modern hotel set back just behind the beach, with a lovely swimming pool in its garden. *Closed Oct–March.*

La Petite Sirène, 15 Boulevard René Cassin, **t** 02 97 50 17 34 (*moderate*). A reasonably priced option next to the seawater treatment centre, with a restaurant where you can enjoy fresh, good-value food.

*Hôtel de l'Océan**, 7 Quai de l'Océan, **t** 02 97 50 07 58 (*inexpensive*). A budget option with pretty views on to the fishing harbour.

La Chaloupe, 10 Rue Hoche, **t** 02 97 30 95 76 (*inexpensive*). Decent place, offering cheap rooms and good food, a little off the beaten track between St Pierre and Penthièvre. *Restaurant closed Sun out of season.*

Auberge de Jeunesse, 45 Rue du Roch-Priol, **t** 02 97 50 15 54, *www.fuaj.org* (*inexpensive*). The local youth hostel.

La Chaumine, 36 Place du Manémeur, in Manémeur village, **t** 02 97 50 17 67 (*moderate–expensive*). A restaurant in a fisherman's cottage, with good traditional cuisine. *Closed Sun eve and Mon.*

Le Verger de la Mer, Boulevard du Goulvars, **t** 02 97 50 29 12 (*moderate–expensive*). A charming place offering good classic fare. *Closed Tues eve and Wed.*

La Criée, 11 Quai de l'Océan, **t** 02 97 30 53 09 (*moderate*). One of the best seafood restaurants here, with reasonable prices.

Le Vivier, Beg er Goalennec, **t** 02 97 50 12 60 (*inexpensive–moderate*). A great place to eat good-value platters of mussels or langoustines, on the most spectacular of the Côte Sauvage headlands to the northwest of Quiberon, with splendid views. It gets packed out, so book. *Closed Dec–end Feb.*

La Crêperie du Manoir, 2 Rue du Puits, **t** 02 97 50 13 86 (*inexpensive*). Classy crêpes served in a beautiful 18th-century house with a walled garden for the summer months. The *crêpe bretonne* (cooked apple with cider ice-cream) is recommended.

Port-Haliguen ✉ 56170

***Europa**, Boulevard de la Teignouse, **t** 02 97 50 25 00, *europa.hotel@wanadoo.fr* (*moderate–expensive*). A hotel dominating a little bay. Inside, it is comfortable, with a covered swimming pool, jacuzzis and a reputable restaurant. *Open March–Nov.*

Le Relax, 27 Boulevard Castero, **t** 02 97 50 12 84 (*moderate*). A dining room overlooking the sea, with relatively simple but good food.

La Crêperie du Vieux Port, 44 Rue Surcouf, **t** 02 97 50 01 56 (*inexpensive*). A stylish crêperie.

The Quiberon Peninsula

Once past the **Fort de Penthièvre** military installations, with a big panel reminding passers-by that some 60 Resistance fighters were shot here in the Second World War, look out for the turning to Portivy and the **Côte Sauvage**. The name of **Portivy** conveys well the diminutive size of this port, protected from the worst of the waves by its northerly position on the peninsula, and by the small sea wall defending its boats. The village huddles cosily around the harbour, and the pretty Chapelle Notre-Dame de Lotivy remains one of the few interesting religious buildings on the peninsula.

Once you turn the **Pointe du Percho**, the Côte Sauvage rocks start in earnest. Belle-Ile comes increasingly clearly into focus as you head down the coast road, which is lined by quite barren coastal land, the grasses mown by the salt winds. You can spot some menhirs down this wild side of the peninsula. Car parks near the **Port du Rhu** and the **Port Bara** give good opportunities to view dramatic parts of the Côte Sauvage, but note that the waters here are only for the experienced surfer. The most spectacular views along this coast can be had from the **Beg er Goalennec headland**, as you near the southern end of the peninsula and the town of Quiberon.

Quiberon Town

On the western point of town, Beg er Lann, the turreted mansion also known as the Château Turpeau, or even the Château de la Mer, stands out as a symbol of the grand tourists who used to come here at the start of the century to enjoy the sea air, the seawater, and the views on to Belle-Ile.

Beyond the popular beaches and the thalassotherapy centre, another big tourist attraction is the town's fish-canning factories, one of which, La Belle Iloise, continues to can fish in the old-fashioned way. The **Grande Plage**, the main arc of sand on the seafront, turns into one of the busiest family beaches in Brittany in the summer, while past the point of Beg er Vil you come to the area dominated by Quiberon's **thalassotherapy centre** and the adjoining hotels. Apparently, more than 50,000 people a year come here to follow one of the seawater treatments. Beyond this area, the **Pointe du Conguel** is the curious southerly headland that throws itself into the water.

The Eastern Side of the Presqu'île de Quiberon

This eastern side of the peninsula seems a gale apart from the wild western side. The beaches are much more protected and look across to the coast around Carnac and the Golfe du Morbihan. This is an excellent place for children to learn to sail or windsurf. There isn't a coastal road to follow except the short stretch to Port-Haliguen.

Port-Haliguen has been converted from a fishing port into the peninsula's main yachting harbour. It was the site of a terrible Chouan battle after the landing here in 1795 of a royalist Catholic army of emigrés, come to take on the Revolutionary forces. The much-feared Republican leader General Hoche, having got wind of the invasion plans, was waiting for them when they arrived. A monument recalls the fateful event. The persecuted Jewish army officer Alfred Dreyfus also landed here in 1899, returning from his period of imprisonment on Devil's Island off French Guyana (*see* Rennes, p.93). Continuing north from Port-Haliguen, you come to the discreet resort of **St-Pierre-Quiberon**, where finds of Celtic pottery and Gallo-Roman coins show that this delightfully protected harbour has long been appreciated. North still, mesmerizing stretches of sand are uncovered at low tide, reaching across the bay to the western side of the resort of Carnac. (*See* p.373 for details on the famous Anglo-French colonial naval battle of Quiberon Bay.)

Belle-Ile

I draw renewed artistic strength from Belle-Ile's invigorating and restful skies.
Sarah Bernhardt, one of France's most famous actresses

Bernhardt loved this island so much she bought a disused fort and built a house for her daughter on it. She fell for Belle-Ile aged 50 and apparently would be carried onto the beach by sailors. The Impressionist Claude Monet found inspiration here, painting scenes taken from the savage southern shore. By contrast, a small number of Acadians, French settlers in North America, were forcibly repatriated here after Britain had removed them from the New World in the colonial wars of the 18th century. Since the age of popular tourism, many Parisians have 'discovered' Belle-Ile.

Belle-Ile is the largest island off the Breton coast, and although the mainland remains within view, the Bellilois have somewhat distanced themselves from the Breton region and Breton culture, proud of their own independence and energy. Unlike the other Breton islands, Belle-Ile is not so easy to acquaint yourself with in a day. Around 20 kilometres long and almost 10 kilometres across in parts, it has a spectacular coastal path, reserved for walkers. The walks are magnificent and offer small beaches at regular intervals on which to relax.

History

Geologically, Belle-Ile is made up of schist, the region's second most important stone. Quartzite and micaschists add sparkle to the coast, and a couple of neolithic menhirs in schist still stand on the island, nicknamed Jean and Jeanne. The great 2nd-century Greek cartographer Ptolemy noted Belle-Ile down as the island of Vindilis, but with the Breton immigration in the Dark Ages, the place changed its name to Guédel. No self-respecting Breton island would be complete without a tale of saintly men arriving to save it from ungodly wickedness, and in this case it was a band of monks from Bangor, hence the name given to one of the villages on Belle-Ile.

In the course of time, the island would become known by the Latin Bella Insula, changing ownership several times, from the Vikings and the counts of Cornouaille to the duke of Brittany Geoffrey I, who took hold of it at the start of the 11th century. Control over the everyday running of the island, however, then lay in the hands of monks either attached to Quimperlé or Redon for five and more centuries. As naval conflicts broke out across western Europe, Belle-Ile became more strategically important; this caused Pope Nicholas V in 1454 to proclaim that all the pirates who were regularly ransacking the vulnerable island would be excommunicated.

Getting There and Around

The usual way to get to Belle-Ile is by **boat** from Quiberon, taking about 40mins. Contact the Société Morbihannaise et Nantaise de Navigation at the *gare maritime* of Quiberon, **t** 02 97 31 80 01 or **t** 02 97 50 06 90. In summer, ferries also operate between Vannes, Sauzon, La Turballe and Pornichet.

The boats have a limited number of spaces for **cars**, but they're expensive and you have to book ages in advance. Parking is a nightmare in Quiberon, so it's wise to leave the car in one of the paying car parks around the town.

Because of the expense of taking cars, most visitors hire **bicycles** or **mopeds** to get around. If you decide to bike, try to stick to the cycle routes to avoid accidents. **Motorbikes** are available from some hotels in winter.

Car Verts runs a **bus** tour service round the island, but exploring it yourself gives you access to some of the island's most beautiful beaches not on the route.

Tourist Information

Quai Bonnelle, B.P. 30, 56360 Le Palais, **t** 02 97 31 81 93, *www.belle-ile.com*.

Market Days

Le Palais: every day in summer; otherwise Tuesday and Friday.

Where to Stay and Eat

Belle-Ile ✉ 56360

Le Palais

★★Le Vauban, 1 Rue des Remparts, **t** 02 97 31 45 42, *www.hotelvauban.com* (*moderate*). A hotel looking down on to the port from the opposite side to the citadel, away from the quayside crowds. It has very neat rooms with lovely views out to sea but is expensive for a 2-star. Excellent fresh seafood (*very expensive*) is available with advance booking. *Closed mid-Oct–mid-Feb.*

★★De Bretagne, Quai de l'Acadie, **t** 02 97 31 80 14 (*moderate*). An old-fashioned hotel with some rooms with a sea view.

Hôtel Le Galion, **t** 02 97 31 81 71 (*inexpensive–expensive*). A newly refurbished hotel in the best buccaneering style in the town centre.

★★L'Atlantique, Quai de l'Acadie, **t** 02 97 31 80 11, *www.hotel-atlantique.com* (*inexpensive–moderate*). An option right by the port, with extremely comfortable rooms, some with sea views. It has a restaurant, algae baths and a sauna.

La Frégate, Quai de l'Acadie, **t** 02 97 31 54 16 (*inexpensive*). A bargain choice with sea views. *Closed Dec–Feb.*

Auberge de Jeunesse, Haute-Boulogne, **t** 02 97 31 81 33, *www.fuaj.org* (*inexpensive*). A popular youth hostel serving good food as well as offering diving and kite-flying courses. There are strict rules and it's quite difficult to access (it's behind the Citadelle). Book well in advance.

La Saline, **t** 02 97 31 84 70 (*moderate*). A traditional restaurant worth seeking out, located slightly inland along the quays. *Closed Mon in low season.*

Café Atlantique (*inexpensive*). A pleasant harbourside place to eat a tourist-orientated *plat du jour* with a view over the port.

Outside Le Palais

★★★Le Clos Fleuri, Route de Sauzon, **t** 02 97 31 45 45 (*moderate*). A peaceful hotel about 500m from the port, offering free bike hire to guests. Rooms are spacious and comfortable, some with little terraces.

Fortifications at Le Palais, the island's capital, were constructed in the mid 16th century, but a couple of decades later, in 1572, English troops caused havoc on the island for three weeks. The Duc de Retz (of the Gondi family) then took over the running of Belle-Isle, as its name was then written, from the monks, followed by Nicolas Fouquet, all-too-successful director of finances for King Louis XIV. In 1674, it was the turn of the Dutch to lay waste to Belle-Ile, after which the French royal authorities called upon the great military architect Sebastien de Vauban to put up some serious defences around the island.

Annick Paulic, Port Halan, t 02 97 31 85 20 (*inexpensive*). Sweet B&B rooms in a pretty, whitewashed hamlet on the southern outskirts of Le Palais.

Sauzon

Hostellerie La Touline, Rue du Port Vihan, t 02 97 31 69 69 (*moderate*). One of the oldest houses on the island, a short distance from the lighthouse. The garden has a good view of the port.

**Les Tamaris, 11 Allée des Peupliers, t 02 97 31 65 09 (*inexpensive–moderate*). Quite comfortable rooms in a modern house.

Le Contre Quai, Rue St-Nicolas, t 02 97 31 60 60 (*inexpensive*). A hotel-restaurant with a simple rustic look but highly regarded cuisine (*expensive*). *Closed Nov–Feb.*

Hôtel du Phare, Quai Guerveur, t 02 97 31 60 36 (*inexpensive*). A well-located option with a red roof. The rooms are rather old fashioned but there's a pleasant terrace.

Le Roz Avel, Rue du Lieutenant Riou, t 02 97 31 61 48 (*moderate–expensive*). Very tasty dishes, including Belle-Ile lamb. There are tables outside for warmer days.

Crêperie Les Embruns, t 02 97 31 64 78 (*inexpensive*). An extremely pink and popular crêpe house. *Closed Wed, and Jan and Feb.*

Port Goulphar

****Castel Clara, t 02 97 31 84 21, *castelclara@ relaischateaux.com* (*expensive–luxury*). The modern architecture of this large hotel on the rough, south side of the island comes as a shock on Belle-Ile, and the prices will blow you away. It offers a thalassotherapy and beauty centre, and excellent seafood cuisine. You can appreciate the rugged coast from the rooms and the restaurant, but you can't swim in the sea, so a heated seawater pool is provided, as are 2 tennis courts.

***Manoir de Goulphar, t 02 97 31 80 10, *www. manoir-de-goulphar.fr* (*expensive–luxury*). A hotel almost matching the Castel Clara for outrageous prices. Guests have use of the Castel Clara facilities.

**Le Grand Large, t 02 97 31 80 92, *www.hotelgrandlarge.com* (*moderate*). A reasonably priced option.

Le Petit Cosquet

***Désirade, t 02 97 31 70 70, *www.hotel-la-desirade.com* (*moderate*). A charming cluster of little houses around a swimming pool, located inland near the little airport. The chef-owner runs the well-established restaurant across the road.

Bangor

Crêperie Chez Renée, t 02 97 31 52 87 (*inexpensive*). The best-known crêperie on the island, set in a delightful, typical Bellilois house with a garden. *Closed Mon.*

Houat ✉ 56170

***La Sirène, Route du Port, t 02 97 30 66 73 (*expensive*). A cheerful hotel on the outskirts of the village, with a bare-breasted mermaid painted on the outside. Half-board is obligatory. *Closed Oct–Easter.*

*Hôtel des Iles, Le Bourg, t 02 97 30 68 02 (*inexpensive*). A budget option set just back from the shore, with views over the sea to the Breton coast.

L'Ezenn Bar-Hôtel, on the way to the Plage de Treac'h Er Goured, t 02 97 30 69 73 (*inexpensive*). Excellent-value rooms.

Mme Le Gurun, t 02 97 30 68 74 (*inexpensive*). Basic, bargain-priced B&B rooms.

Hoëdic ✉ 56170

Les Cardinaux, Le Bourg, t 02 97 52 37 27, (*inexpensive–moderate*). A simple hotel.

In 1719, Nicolas Fouquet's great-grandson officially ceded Belle-Ile to the French Crown, but incessant warring between France and Britain in the 18th century led to Britain again taking over the island in 1761, destroying many of its chapels. The Treaty of Paris in 1763 saw Belle-Ile returned to France in exchange for Minorca! Further pawns in the colonial conflicts, a group of 78 Acadian families from North America were packed off to live on Belle-Ile in 1763, after they had languished for some time in a number of British ports as forgotten prisoners. A few decades before the Revolution, the families of Belle-Ile, including the recent Acadian immigrants, became the proprietors of their island. Since the Second World War, strong ties have been re-formed between the Belle-Ile Acadians and their New World relatives; the Acadian flag, a French *tricolore* with a yellow star of Mary, flies over Le Palais's citadel.

People harp on about Belle-Ile's artistically inspiring 19th-century past, but during that time the island fort continued to serve as a prison of note. The list of Belle-Ile's most famous 19th-century detainees reads like a summary of social upheaval against the status quo. The anti-Revolutionary Chouan, Georges Cadoudal, was held here, as was anti-slavery campaigner Toussaint Louverture. Napoleon III's administration decided to fortify the island on a grand scale in the mid 19th century, and many of the Second Empire forts survive in a good state of repair. Even the beaches on the protected, northeastern side of the island (the *dedans* or 'inside', as the locals call this coast facing the Breton mainland) were fortified. For the ordinary population of Belle-Ile, the 19th century was the time when fishing brought increased prosperity.

In the First World War, German prisoners of war were interned on the island, though roles were reversed in the Second World War when Belle-Ile was heavily occupied by the Nazis. Unfortunately, Belle-Ile was one of the last German-occupied territories to surrender to the Allies, in May 1945. Since then, Belle-Ile has attracted a mixed crowd, many outsiders falling for the charms of the place, many Bellilois heading off to the continent to seek their fortune. One of the best-known painters to settle here was the Australian John Peter Russell, who brought many English-speaking artists in his wake.

A Tour of Belle-Ile

The island is divided into four parishes, Le Palais, Sauzon, Bangor and Locmaria. This tour starts at Le Palais, where the boats arrive, then heads northwest to Sarah Bernhardt's wildly beloved Pointe des Poulains beyond Sauzon, before following the Côte Sauvage southeast to the village of Locmaria, on the eastern end of Belle-Ile. The north coast stretching back up to Le Palais has some of the best beaches.

A remarkable and intensely rewarding voyage of discovery is in store for those who follow the coastal path right round the island, which can be done in four to six days, depending on how fast you want to (or are able to) go. Do not be fooled by the apparent flatness of the island: there are plenty of ups and downs. A good pair of walking boots is essential. The tourist office can provide you with an excellent guide and advice on where to stay, in the form of either *gite d'étapes, chambres d'hôtes* or hotels. Accommodation is limited, so be sure to make your enquiries and reservations early. A certain amount of advance planning is required, but it's worth it to experience one of Brittany's finest stretches of coastline. Motorcycles and mountain bikes are banned from the coastal path.

Le Palais

The capital of the island is dominated by the star-shaped structures of the citadel designed by Sébastien de Vauban. As you approach the town by sea, you get a very good view of the citadel and its barracks. A wealthy couple purchased the property during the 1960s and have been seeing to its gradual restoration ever since then. Most of the quaysides of Le Palais lie on the opposite side of the estuary from the citadel.

The Vauban Citadel

Open daily Easter–Sept 9–7, Oct–April 9.30–12 and 2–5.

Fortification upon fortification have succeeded one another on the site of Le Palais's citadel. Monks were given a castle here in the Middle Ages, then the Duc de Rohan saw to the building of another one. A larger fort went up slowly under the Gondis, and then Vauban came towards the end of the 17th century and put his stamp on the place. Thanks to restoration work, the grander sections of the citadel have now been spruced up. The museum inside covers the history of Belle-Ile from the time of the Ancien Régime in particular. The first room concentrates on the 16th to 18th centuries, the second on the 19th and 20th. There are lots of copies of engravings and portraits, and a rather confusing clutter of diverse objects. The battle of Quiberon Bay (*see* p.373) doesn't go unmentioned here, and homage is paid to some of the most successful 19th-century military men from the island.

To Sauzon and Sarah Bernhardt's Point

Sauzon has a good deep river harbour, which gave its inhabitants a natural advantage in fishing. Nowadays, the people of Sauzon welcome tourists, and have opened a string of restaurants and cafés in the colourful houses along the quays.

The dramatic rocks of the **Pointe des Poulains**, or Foals' Headland, mark the northwest corner of the island. The place might be rechristened Sarah Bernhardt Point, given the fuss made over her stays; she bought an old military fort on the site and used to hold sumptuous parties there. However, in the Second World War the Nazis destroyed her house, as its red roof risked drawing attention from the enemy.

The West Coast to Port-Donnant

The **Grotte de l'Apothicairerie**, south past the island's ornithological reserve, although signalled on many tourist maps, can no longer be visited as it is too dangerous and there is no way anyone could hear your cries of distress if you fell. The rock surfaces around here are intriguing; their mother of pearl colours and rough texture make you feel like you're walking on a giant oyster shell. Continuing southwards along the main central road down the island, you pass the two menhirs **Jean** and **Jeanne** (to the south of the road), said to be star-crossed lovers turned to stone by displeased druids. The petrified pair are only supposed to be able to meet up again once a year, on New Year's Eve.

Port-Donnant, on the coast below Jean and Jeanne, draws the young of the island in droves to practise their greatest passion, bodyboarding. Port-Donnant isn't a port with houses, but a beach of wide golden sands with a big dune behind, covered with wild roses in season – in Brittany, the word port or *pors* can simply mean a slightly sheltered place where fishermen might once have pulled their boats onto the beach.

The Grand Phare and Monet's Aiguilles de Port Coton

The **great lighthouse** (*open high summer daily 10.30–12 and 2–5.30*) is unmissable at 47 metres in height. In fact, on really clear days you can view vast stretches of the south Breton coast from it. When you visit Carnac you are told with disgust that many of the menhirs of the Petit Menec alignment were transported here to help create firm foundations for this colossus.

Port Coton with its **aiguilles** (needles) of rock is the site most associated with Claude Monet's work on Belle-Ile, which depicted some of the island's raging, violent, churning storms. You should be able to find beautifully illustrated books of Monet's works around the island, and other art volumes on the diversity of painters who have been inspired by Belle-Ile, including the Australian John Peter Russell. A distinctly uninspired luxury hotel complex dominates the deep creek of **Port Goulphar** just southeast of the Aiguilles.

Bangor to Locmaria and the South Coast

The village of Bangor lies inland, but our focus is on the beautiful stretch of coast to the south of it. Various rocks lie just out to sea, and after passing **Port Kérel**, which boasts what is claimed to be the warmest beach on Belle-Ile, you can view the Ile de Bangor. Between the **Pointe du Grand Village** and the **Pointe de St-Marc** are little beaches (one for nudists) to stop and rest on, although they're hard to reach. Walking these clifftops is a sublime experience, and you mustn't miss the exquisitely shaded cove of the Plage d'Herlin, again only accessible on foot. The final stretch of coast along this side of the island takes you to its most southerly point, the **Pointe du Skeul**, also known as the Pointe de l'Echelle. The track then turns up the east coast to Port Blanc and Port Maria.

You now find yourself in the eastern parish of **Locmaria**. This village is home to a dazzlingly whitewashed little church that boasts a squat, curving slate steeple. Inside, you will see two boat ex votos hanging from the roof, and a Madonna stretching her gaze up to the sky, said to be the work of a follower of the sentimental Spanish painter Bartolomé Esteban Murillo. Locmaria appears to be a quietly charming place, but other island dwellers long suspected the villagers of indulging in magic practices.

To the north of Locmaria, the **Pointe de Kerdonis** with its little lighthouse marks the most easterly point of the island; from here you get the best views on to the neighbouring islands of Houat and Hoëdic.

The Northern Beaches to Le Palais

Heading up along the coast that looks to the mainland is the biggest beach on the island, **Les Grands Sables**, the fortifications of which form a theatrical backdrop to this splendid and popular curve of sand. Above lies the pretty hamlet of **Samzun**. A couple of other particularly lovely fortified beaches lie along the coast back up to Le Palais, **Port York** and the **Plage de Bordardoué**, separated from each other by the Pointe du Gros Rocher.

The Islands of Houat and Hoëdic

'Duck' and 'duckling' are the Breton names for these two joyous little islands south of Quiberon, but actually it's seagulls whose strident screams fill the air. In the major tourist season, these islands do suffer a daily summer invasion, but go outside July and August and you shouldn't unduly interrupt the islanders' life. Belle-Ile may be beautiful, but Houat and Hoëdic, reached by ferry from Quiberon, are more magical.

Houat

The boat trip from Quiberon to Houat (pronounced like an astonished Frenchman trying to say 'What?') passes through cormorant waters and by a string of curious uninhabited rocks before arriving at the port – a grand word for the landing quay with its single building. The island is a langoustine-shaped rock, measuring around five kilometres at its longest. If you wish to head straight for the beautiful beaches, they lie around the outstretched 'pincers' on the eastern end. But the island has two other special attractions: an enjoyable, modern museum telling of the heroic role of plankton in the world's creation, and its coastal path, especially round the western parts of the island.

First, the village of **Port St-Gildas** (above the landing quay) looks as brightly whitewashed as a Spanish *pueblo blanco*, only here the little houses are roofed with slate. Two squares lie side by side: the tiny church square, the serious administrative and spiritual capital of the island; and the business square, with its *boulangerie*, newsagent-cum-gift shop and bar. Inside the church, with its picturesque stone tower, a large ex voto of a ship hangs from the new honey-coloured wood ceiling while a statue of Joan of Arc shows a little of her armoured leg.

The Battle of Quiberon Bay

Between 1756 and 1763, Britain and France were locked in the Seven Years War over colonies and commerce. In 1759, a British naval fleet led by Admiral Hawke rushed to the west coast of Brittany, waiting there to take on the French fleet sheltering in the Rade de Brest. The British were caught napping and the French admiral, Conflans, slipped out with his fleet onto the open seas round the south Breton coast. But Admiral Hawke's men-of-war were soon snapping at the heels of the French ships, racing past the Quiberon peninsula and Belle-Ile, and catching up with them. In one of the most devastating defeats in European naval history, the British managed to wipe out a great portion of the French fleet. It went down in British history as the celebrated battle of Quiberon Bay, but in France the disaster became known as the Bataille des Cardinaux, because the reefs off Hoëdic are called the Petits Cardinaux and Grands Cardinaux.

The colonial consequences were far reaching, and France found its powers on the seas severely depleted. The British navy had established its superiority in this utterly crushing victory; in 1763, the Treaty of Paris ended the Seven Years War, and France was forced to cede major portions of its colonies to Britain.

You can take the road out by the end of the church to the gorgeous **eastern beaches**. The gentle arc of sand that curves towards the mainland is one of the finest in the whole of Brittany, with lovely views and a place from which you can restfully watch the boating activity around the landing stage. Heading across the rougher dunes, you come to the island's biggest beach, with views out to Hoëdic.

The walk from the village to the **Eclosarium** (*open daily July and Aug 10–6, Easter–June and Sept 10–12 and 2–5*) isn't particularly charming, but you do pass in front of a football pitch where the island's finest standing menhir has been comically left as a permanent spectator on the sidelines. The lovely museum tells the island's local history alongside that of plankton.

Going at a steady pace you can walk round the **coastal path** from the Eclosarium, via the western tip and back to the port, in three to four hours. It's never far from one side of the island to the other – around 500 metres – and if you get tired of the coastal path, you can take the central track. From the Eclosarium, head down towards the coast, an Avalon-like isle beckoning out to sea. Resist, turn right on to the southern coastal path and you soon leave any sign of human civilization or habitation behind. You're just left with beautiful landscapes and seascapes, and gull-garrisoned points.

It takes roughly an hour to reach the glorious **western tips** of Houat with their ruddy-coloured rocks and gull islands at either end. Go up to the fortified northwest point to appreciate the panorama. The northern coastal path can be overgrown, but eventually you reach the first isolated house along the northwest coast. Further along, the second house announces the start of the village back close to the port.

Hoëdic

Hoëdic, shaped a bit like a whelk, lies south of the langoustine contours of Houat. It is smaller still, two and a half kilometres long, barely a kilometre at its widest, and surrounded by reefs. Sandy coves alternate with rocky points along its secretive coastline. Finds of extraordinarily old civilization have been found on this granite isle (*see* the Musée de la Préhistoire Miln-Le Rouzic in Carnac, p.378), and though most of the remains were taken away, you can still search out the island's menhir and dolmen.

The **Port d'Argol** at which you arrive was constructed in 1973, as the older Port de la Croix is only accessible at high tide. The new port lies by the Pointe du Vieux Château, and its coarse grass, scattered with thistles, suits the little frogs that proliferate on the island. French soldiers posted here in centuries past apparently used to complain about these critters jumping into their cooking pots and pockets. The village church is dedicated to St Goustan, a 10th-century pirate who turned preacher after a shipwreck.

Mega Megalith Country via Carnac

The most famous concentration of neolithic monuments in the western world is crammed into the short stretch of the Morbihan coast from Erdeven to Gavrinis, passing via Carnac and Locmariaquer. Such is the density of stone alignments and burial tumuli here that local authorities seem at a loss as to what to do with them all.

Getting Around

Buses are the only form of public transport serving the area.

Tourist Information

Erdeven: 7 Rue de l'Abbé Le Barth, B.P. 27,
t 02 97 55 64 60, www.ot-erdeven.fr.
Carnac: 74 Avenue des Druides, B.P. 65,
t 02 97 52 13 52, www.carnac.fr.
La Trinité-sur-Mer: Môle Loïc Caradec, B.P. 56,
t 02 97 55 72 21, www.ot-trinite-sur-mer.com.
Locmariaquer: Place de la Mairie, t 02 97 57 33 05,
ot.locmariaquer@wanadoo.fr.

Market Days

Erdeven: Saturday.
Carnac: Wednesday and Sunday.
La Trinité-sur-Mer: Tuesday and Friday.
Locmariaquer: Tuesday and Saturday.

Where to Stay and Eat

Carnac-Plage ✉ 56340

Carnac-Plage is a place that really comes alive during the summer holidays, when it attracts more than its fair share of upmarket holidaymakers.

****Le Diana**, 21 Boulevard de la Plage,
t 02 97 52 05 38, www.lediana.com
(expensive–luxury). The most luxurious of the modern seafront hotels at Carnac-Plage, with scenic views, a heated swimming pool and a tennis court among its attractions. Closed Dec–March.

****Novotel**, t 02 97 52 53 00, thalasso-carnac@wanadoo.fr, and **Ibis**, t 02 97 52 54 00, Avenue de l'Atlantique (expensive–very expensive). Out-of-place, slightly pretentious, large twin establishments overlooking a lake on the western side of Carnac-Plage. They offer specialist thalassotherapy treatments and a swimming pool.

****Le Bateau Ivre**, 70 Boulevard de la Plage,
t 02 97 52 19 55, www.hotel-le-bateau-ivre.com (moderate–expensive). Extremely comfortable rooms on the eastern edge of the resort, many with private balconies overlooking the sea. There's also a heated swimming pool in the walled garden and a chi-chi restaurant.

Les Rochers, 6 Boulevard de la Base Nautique,
t 02 97 52 10 09 (inexpensive–moderate). The cheapest option along Carnac beach, with delightful balconies, and some rooms with window bays. Closed Oct–March.

Carnac Old Town ✉ 56340

Carnac Old Town, more traditionally Breton in style than Carnac-Plage, is quite elegant.

****Lann Roz**, 36 Avenue de la Poste, B.P. 126,
t 02 97 52 10 48 (inexpensive–moderate). A very pretty townhouse with a garden right in the old centre, with flowers everywhere and excellent cuisine.

****Le Tumulus**, 31 Rue du Tumulus,
t 02 97 52 08 21, www.hotel-tumulus.com (inexpensive–moderate). A place that is set apart from the other hotels, near to the Tumulus St-Michel. Attractions include good views over the surrounding area and a swimming pool.

Megaliths Around Erdeven

The little town of **Erdeven** (the name derives from the Breton for dunes) is a quiet place with a few simple restaurants and a hotel. It's often ignored, but major megaliths are scattered south out of town along the main D781. It's possible not just to drive by the **alignments of Kerzehro**; you can even drive right *through* a section of them.

These alignments are impressive. You can count 10 rows at the thickest part, heading off diagonally from the road. The whole megalithic ensemble proves more extensive upon closer view; it apparently still contains more than 1,000 standing stones, stretching over some two kilometres. Still more impressive than the alignments themselves are the **géants de Kerzehro**, massive granite blocks, one of which has a side worn into a weird fantastical face, like a fossilized, monstrous

★★Chez Nous, 5 Place de la Chapelle, t 02 97 52 07 28 (*inexpensive*). A very characterful budget option.

★★Le Râtelier, 4 Chemin du Douët, t 02 97 52 05 04, *www.le-ratelier.com* (*inexpensive*). A wonderful ivy-covered hotel down a quiet side street, with quite experimental cuisine.

Le Passe-Mauve, 1 Rue du Tumulus, t 02 97 52 04 14 (*moderate–expensive*). A chic setting for good seafood.

Crêperie Chez Marie, by the church, t 02 97 52 83 05 (*inexpensive*). An excellent crêpe house. *Closed Dec–March*.

Outskirts of Carnac

★★Les Ajoncs d'Or, Kerbachique, between Carnac and Plouharnel, t 02 97 52 32 02, *www.lesajoncsdor.com* (*inexpensive–moderate*). A characterful old stone family house in a beautifully tended, walled, shaded garden.

La Calypso, down by the Pô, t 02 97 52 06 14 (*moderate–expensive*). A restaurant with a fine reputation, in an old whitewashed house close to the superb sandscapes of the estuary. *Closed Sun eve and Mon*.

La Trinité-sur-Mer ✉ 56470

L'Azimut, 1 Rue du Men-Du, t 02 97 300 17 00, *www.charme-gastronomie.com* (*moderate–expensive*). Six rooms and a restaurant with a splendid terrace overlooking the port, and excellent food at reasonable prices.

★★L'Ostréa, Cours des Quais, t 02 97 55 73 23, *www.hotel-ostrea.com* (*inexpensive–moderate*). A small number of rooms looking onto the port, perched above a simpler bar where you can come to enjoy good, copious

seafood platters (*moderate–expensive*). *Closed Dec and Jan*.

La Maison du Latz, north of La Trinité, Latz, t 02 97 55 80 91, *www.stiren-ar-mor.fr.st* (*inexpensive*). A typical whitewashed modern Breton house with views over the Crac'h river, offering B&B.

A string of tempting restaurants overlook the yacht-packed port.

St-Philibert ✉ 56470

Lann Kermané, t 02 97 55 03 75 (*moderate*). Charming little B&B rooms within a Breton stone house.

★★Les Algues Brunes, Route des Plages, t 02 97 55 08 78 (*inexpensive–moderate*). A calm retreat, well shaded by pine trees and quite cheap for this area. The cool garden slopes down towards the river estuary, and some of the rooms have balconies.

Locmariaquer ✉ 56740

★★★Les Trois Fontaines, Route d'Auray, t 02 97 57 42 70, *hot3f@aol.com* (*moderate–expensive*). The most comfortable hotel in town.

Le Menhir, 7 Rue Wilson, t 02 97 57 31 41, *le.menhir@wanadoo.fr* (*moderate*). A good-value, pleasant hotel-cum-bar. *Closed Oct–April*.

★★L'Escale, 2 Place Dariorigum, t 02 97 57 32 51 (*inexpensive*). An unpretentious hotel beautifully situated close to the church, on the waterfront. You'll be very lucky if you get one of the rooms with a mesmerizing view onto the Golfe du Morbihan. There's a wonderful covered terrace you can eat out on in summer. *Closed Oct–March*.

---

whale-man. A ring of stones appears to encircle the giants. Continue on past them, then follow the signs for the Mané-Bras, on the **Grand Arc megaliths walk** signposted around Erdeven. You can do the eight-kilometre track either on foot or by mountain bike, though it's quite a distance to the **Mané-Bras dolmen**, unusual for having a chamber with four separate cells off the central corridor.

The Crucuno and Mané-Groh Dolmens

Two more picturesquely situated dolmens lie southeast of the Kerzehro alignments – look out for a turning north off the D781 road to Plouharnel. The Dolmen de Crucuno and the equally comical-sounding Dolmen de Mané-Groh are both well signposted. The **Dolmen de Crucuno**, which dates from around 4000 BC, has been left bizarrely exposed in the middle of a hamlet. The **Dolmen de Mané-Groh** lies some 500 metres further inland, past a stone cross carved with a primitive figure of Christ. This dolmen is photogenically set among small oaks and pines, though originally it would have been covered by a tumulus, and most of the pines are fairly recent. The Mané-Groh dolmen, constructed some time between 4000 BC and 3500 BC, is practically identical to that of Mané-Bras, with its fairly sophisticated chamber divided into four cells, each still covered by the top stones. A *sentier des mégalithes*, a country track leading to other neolithic sites, heads off from here.

Ste-Barbe, a hamlet more than a village (just off the D781 northwest of Plouharnel), feels particularly appealing. It is a place of small delights, with a view down towards the unkempt moors and dunes leading to the sea. A road from the village takes you to the stunning beach below Ste-Barbe. The dunes are only spoilt by a few wartime constructions, but no modern developments have been allowed.

Carnac

Carnac, the neolithic capital of the western world, doesn't just boast one great prehistoric site; it contains a dense but scattered concentration of varied edifices, tumuli, dolmens laid bare, and, most famously, four great alignments of standing stones, Le Ménec, Kermario, Kerlescan and Le Petit Ménec. To give you an idea of the number of megalithic monuments packed into the area, the local map shows four tumuli, at least 16 dolmens and half a dozen separate menhirs beyond the thousands gathered in rows in the alignments.

An Introduction to the Neolithic Civilization Around Carnac

The monumentality of neolithic civilization's activities here, and our inability to penetrate the mysteries of those times, make the megaliths suitable objects of passion. Actually, more and more fragments of reliable information on this society are being pieced together by serious archaeological surveys, making the study of this civilization increasingly lively. For much of the 19th century, most people considered these megaliths to date back to Celtic Iron Age times – that is, to the millennium before Christ. But research and modern dating techniques have shown that some of the monuments in this area go back to 4500 BC and maybe beyond, almost a couple of thousand years before the great pyramids of Egypt. This means that neolithic civilization lasted and evolved over many thousands of years.

Much of the neolithic study around Carnac has concentrated on the deaths of neolithic people and their burial rituals, because that is all that remains as evidence. But you shouldn't forget that these people did have a life, beliefs and communities. The extent of their achievements in this Carnac area, their buildings, their finely wrought tools, and the forms they engraved on stones show that theirs was certainly in many ways a complex civilization.

Beyond visiting the monuments, you may want to see the prehistory museum and La Maison des Mégalithes at Carnac to help you appreciate the subject. The main site at Locmariaquer also has an informative display, and Vannes has a prehistory museum.

But Carnac doesn't only attract millions of visitors every year because of its neolithic riches. The place has a delightful old upper town with a remarkable church dedicated to that saintly protector of cattle, St Cornély. And it has a beach resort, vibrant, chic and expensive. From the pine-scented woods among which so many of the dolmens hide to the mesmerizing, wide open sands of the Pô oyster bay to the west, the whole area is exceptionally beautiful. To reduce confusion, note that there are effectively three Carnacs: neolithic Carnac; Carnac-Ville or Carnac-Bourg, the town; and Carnac-Plage, the modern seaside resort.

Neolithic Carnac

You can go walking among the staggering neolithic alignments of Carnac, but note that between April and September possibilities are limited, and you need to book in advance. To learn specifically about the alignments, head for La Maison des Mégalithes. The Musée de la Préhistoire covers the neolithic period more widely.

Musée de la Préhistoire Miln-Le Rouzic

Open June–Sept Mon–Fri 10–6, Sat and Sun 10–12.30 and 2–6;
Oct–May Wed–Mon 10–12 and 2–5.

Discoveries about the prehistoric societies around Carnac are advancing so fast that this museum has trouble keeping up to date. But then many of the biggest questions still remain unanswered. For a long time neolithic sites were thought, quite wrongly, to be Celtic in origin. Their serious study from the 19th century onwards led slowly to the debunking of this theory, along with more extreme myths that the stones were erected by giants, or by the Breton equivalent of fairies, the *korrigans* (*see* p.31). Excavations of the Carnac area by serious-minded archaeologists go back to the 1820s, and this museum is named after two of the most passionate archaeologists to have researched here and made important finds, Scotsman James Miln and his helper Zacharie Le Rouzic.

Although this museum is relatively recent, it's an old-fashioned, hard slog round the rooms if you stick to the serious task and read the panels covered with dense text. The displays, while containing a large number of interesting artefacts, are sometimes pretty hard to decipher. Borrow the English text from the reception desk, as the explanations there are more succinct than on the panels, even if the translation is amateurish.

A brisk introductory slide show first rushes you through millions of years. It talks of humankind's ancestors traced back to at least 7 million years ago, their presence in France estimated to go back 1.8 million years. As recently as 1977, remains of a community dating back to around 450,000 BC were discovered in St-Colomban, just west of Carnac-Plage. The first signs of burials by human ancestors found to date go back to roughly 100,000 BC; and from the period of the Ice Age, as far back as 35,000 BC, some artistic traces have been found around Europe hinting at the preoccupations and creativity of certain prehistoric people. The vast period of many millions of years in which primitive humans developed, going up to around 12,000 BC, is referred to as the Palaeolithic era. It is subdivided into Lower, Middle and Upper periods, and then into further smaller periods.

The last Ice Age, the Würm, ended around 10,000 BC and led to the slow thawing of Europe. The period roughly from 12,000 to 3000 BC is referred to as the Mesolithic era, which witnessed great progress in the production of miniature tools. One of the first showcases displays the reconstruction of a mesolithic grave from the island of Hoëdic. Buried among kitchen debris, one figure wears a long shell necklace and is decorated with antlers. The end of the Mesolithic age merged with the start of the Neolithic, said to go from some time in the 5th millennium BC to around the close of the 3rd. The most important change that neolithic culture brought was the shift from a hunter-gathering way of living to one where agriculture and cattle-rearing were mastered.

A number of neolithic sites from the Morbihan were decorated with engraved stones, which may well indicate some of the society's major concerns, but they are hard to interpret exactly. The recurrence in the engravings of axes and horns might show the importance of felling and of cattle. Other symbols are not as easy to explain, though some may be concerned with leadership and female fertility.

This Carnac museum is one of the most important repositories of neolithic artefacts in the world, found in and around burial sites of the area. Neolithic graves are well represented by a whole corridor lined with carved tombstones. For whom exactly the great tumuli of Carnac were built is not known, but the panels talk of a powerful élite emerging in neolithic society in these parts, who brought in extremely important changes in technical skills and culture, such as developing pottery and weaving. After you have walked through the corridor of engraved tombstones, you come to a lighter, more appealingly presented room with a useful model of the Carnac alignments. Neolithic daily life is evoked here, although some of the fantastically polished axes are clearly rare, rather than everyday, pieces.

The rooms on the first floor move you more quickly through the subsequent ages, with a useful comparative table of world civilizations. The upper displays also include bizarre curiosities such as a neolithic canoe and healing beads. Apparently such stones, known as *gollgad paternerem* or *grains de pierre*, were still used in the Breton countryside in the last century. Further sections upstairs dwell on the Celts (with some coins and even one or two ornaments on display), and on Gallo-Roman Brittany. The distinction is then clearly made between prehistoric Celts and Dark Age Bretons.

The Carnac Alignments

Open July, Aug and French school hols April–Sept only by visite-conférence;
in July and Aug, when there is 1 visit a day in English, call t 02 97 52 29 81
to book; other months call t 02 97 52 89 99 for times and bookings.
Oct–March visitors are free to wander around sections of the alignments.

The Carnac alignments were probably erected around 3000 BC and may have taken 500,000 to one million days in total to construct, according to the archaeologist Charles T. LeRoux. Four alignments run in a row northeastwards from the top of

Carnac-Ville, their four curves spanning around four kilometres; altogether, they still include many thousands of standing stones. The individual blocks are very diverse in shape and size and tend to be much rougher in look than the caringly shaped menhirs. You should know that many stones have gone missing and that a good number had fallen down before being set back upright by archaeologists.

These deeply complex monuments are unique in the world (although there are other lesser alignments in Brittany and elsewhere). Two related theories can be plausibly linked to them: first, that they marked out a religious site; second, that they relate to astronomical calculations and the seasons. The alignments might have been connected with funeral rites and imaginings of an afterworld, especially given the density of tombs scattered in the vicinity.

The **Alignements du Ménec**, the most southwesterly of Carnac's four alignments, count the largest number of stones left. More than 1,000 still stand in up to a dozen rows, a cromlech formed on either end. To make out the 70 or so rocks in Le Ménec's western cromlech you need to search around homes on Carnac's outskirts – these neolithic wonders haven't always been treated with respect. Things get extremely chaotic in summer around the **Alignements de Kermario**, the most impressive of the four lots of alignments. These are of roughly the same dimensions as those of Le Ménec, the standing stones roughly as numerous, the lines stretching over a kilometre. But the Kermario alignments have suffered greater indignities; the enclosure of menhirs that once finished off the western end was destroyed some time ago. But then imagine that in 1874 only around 200 of the stones were still standing; hundreds have been put back up since that time.

The largest and most impressive stones of this rough crescent of 10 rows can be viewed in the southwesterly corner of Kermario. One fallen stone is supposed to be engraved with serpentine forms at its base. In the middle of these alignments, by the woods, you can sometimes climb the watchtower for reasonable views to east and west. From up on the tower the rows look almost like rough stone stitching across the ground, and their great length along the undulating terrain becomes clearer.

Just before you arrive at the Kerlescan alignments, a tree-shaded path (with only a bit of space in which to park) leads into the woods and towards the **Grand Quadrilatère du Manio** and the **Géant du Manio**. It's a fair walk into the countryside to see these two, but this only adds to their mystery. The big menhir looks, in shape, very much like the polished axes so beloved of neolithic civilization. And those looking for worship of the fertile phallus in the neolithic should be relatively satisfied with this menhir's shape too. It is said that in past centuries, infertile women would come to this spot to rub themselves against the stone in the hope that it might bring on conception.

The **Kerlescan alignments** only consist of around 240 standing stones now, and many of them are quite small. But you should be able to make out some 13 parallel rows of them, extending over roughly 400 metres. There's also a dolmen on the eastern side. Many visitors miss the **Petit Ménec alignments** east of the D186 road, but eight rows still stand there, despite the number of stones sadly depleted by a raid to build the foundations for the lighthouse on Belle-Ile.

For further explanations on the alignments and their conservation, together with an audio-visual display in French, consider a visit to the **Maison des Mégalithes** (*open daily July and Aug 10–10, May and June 10–7, Sept–April 10–5.15*) a short drive away.

In Search of Some of Carnac's Scattered Neolithic Tombs

The most impressive burial mound left in the area is the **Tumulus St-Michel** (*closed for restoration*) on the eastern edge of Carnac-Ville. Though the bracken and the chapel on top can obscure the fact that this is an artificial hillock, this is a massive piece of neolithic architecture. The tumulus conceals a series of tombs, probably dating from around 6,000 years ago. The burial chambers were covered with a layer of stones about eight metres thick; then a dome of sea mud was applied to seal the mound before a further 80 centimetres or more of stones were piled on top. The whole construction is 120 metres long, 58 metres wide and 10 metres high; originally it stood higher still.

The **Kercado tumulus** lies just south of the Carnac alignments, between Kermario and Le Manio, on the south side of the alignments road. It stands in the grounds of a château that remains better hidden than many a neolithic monument. To reach the property, you need to go down a delightful wide driveway, the pastures either side enclosed by low stone walls. Once you've picked up the explanatory text, it's a short walk to the tumulus, which is some five metres high and marked by a little menhir topping its mound.

The entrance to the burial corridor has one of the most comical touches of any neolithic site – a light switch. Turn it on, then you can advance, squatting, through the corridor to the nearly square chamber. The great table stone of the ceiling is engraved with a double axe, and some shield shapes or stylized mother goddesses can also be made out. This tumulus has been dated from before 4000 BC, though the text claims it dates as far back as between 4800 BC and 4500 BC. Around 150 beads were discovered here; they can now be seen in the Carnac prehistory museum. A rough ring of old stones surrounds the tumulus.

Carnac-Ville

Carnac town has its own Christian-era stone structure that proves quite amazing – the **church of St-Cornély**, with an exterior polychrome statue representing the saint Cornély, protector of horned cattle. The church otherwise looks sternly Breton on the exterior, except for the addition of an extravagant 17th-century baldaquin-porch, the top tied together with ribbons of granite. Within you'll find a riot of decoration. The ceiling paintings, added in the 18th century, portray four cycles, depicting the life of Christ, the life of John the Baptist, the Mysteries of the Rosary, and the life of St Cornély. Other extraordinary features in this church include ornate altarpieces with decorative paintings, and rich pieces in the church treasury.

A Tour of the Carnac Coast from the Pô to the Plage du Men-Du

This beautiful coastal trip completely ignores the megaliths and the old town of Carnac, concentrating on the oyster beds of the Pô, moving round to the old village of St-Colomban, and then going along by the beaches in front of Carnac-Plage.

At low tide, the flat sands of the **Pô estuary** lead your gaze to the low peninsula of Quiberon, and flat-bottomed oyster boats lie like beached creatures on the firm bed, though the scene quickly changes with the rising waters. Follow the coast down to the peninsula of **St-Colomban**. Beyond the cross you pass en route, a large old Breton fountain has been cleaned up; one section was reserved for the village women to do their washing, the other for cattle to drink at. The road takes you up to the village of substantial old stone houses, huddled around the rustic Flamboyant Gothic church that you can visit in summer. The walk all the way round the coastal edge of the St-Colomban peninsula, via the Pointe St-Colomban and the Pointe Ty Bihas, is uplifting.

Pine-backed beaches, with their lifeguards' ladders planted in the sands, follow along the southern side of **Carnac-Plage**. Here, the Carnac yacht club tucks into the artificial harbour on the western end of the resort's extensive main beach, a gentle and genteel curve of sand. Numerous posh hotels mix with the villas looking out to sea at the little islands of Houat and Hoëdic.

The beach resort turns into a hive of activity in summer, with all manner of bars and restaurants in the shaded streets just behind the beach. Carnac-Plage is bound to the east by the Pointe Churchill. The other side of this spit, residential quarters overlook further beaches, and in the middle of the bay, the Ile de Stuhan is joined to the mainland at low tide by a *tombolo*, or spit of sand.

The Peninsulas of La Trinité-sur-Mer and St-Philibert

You cross two thin peninsulas to get from Carnac to another of the neolithic high points of Brittany, Locmariaquer. On the way, you might be tempted to explore La Trinité-sur-Mer and St-Philibert, separated by the river Crac'h's estuary.

The name of **La Trinité-sur-Mer** means yachts to a French person, and this port attracts the finest yachters in the country. It also has a certain notoriety as the home of extreme right-wing politician Jean-Marie Le Pen. Through spring and summer, the place seems to be in a permanent state of regatta, packed with state-of-the-art yachts. The long street that parallels the vast estuary marina is lined with alluring cafés, restaurants and boutiques, many of the last specializing in sea gear. Look out also for spectacular Breton photos and posters at the Plisson gallery. The harbourside remains vibrant for much of the year. Up among the quaint, quieter lanes of the slopeside old town, the main church contains paintings depicting La Trinité's quay in times gone by. At the back of the estuary, oyster boats busy themselves with harvesting.

Down the peninsula via Kerbihan are some excellent beaches. The **Pointe de Kerbihan** juts out into the bay of Quiberon. From here you can watch yachts sailing in and out of La Trinité and the Crac'h estuary on regatta days. Up from La Trinité, follow the typical ria banks of the Crac'h and catch the arresting views north of the bridge of Kerisper. The bridge takes you to the **St-Philibert peninsula**, a pine-covered spit sheltered from the hordes. A coast road goes down the edge of the river Crac'h then up the other, mud-edged side of the peninsula to **St-Philibert**, a quiet, old-fashioned village with a tiny **mariners' chapel** and typical old fountain overlooking another oyster river estuary.

Locmariaquer's Neolithic Peninsula

At the western entrance to the wonderful Golfe du Morbihan, Locmariaquer's peninsula is one of France's most famous megalithic sites after Carnac. Like Carnac, Locmariaquer is also a sprawling, highly popular summer resort.

The Grand Menhir Brisé, Tumulus Er-Grah and Table des Marchands

Open daily May–Sept 10–7, Oct–April 10–12.30 and 2–5.15.

Exciting neolithic discoveries were made when this group of three vast-scale monuments was excavated in the late 1980s and early 1990s. Since then, they have been fenced in together to form one tourist site. You enter via the Centre d'Informations Archéologiques. The connection between the great menhir and the two tumuli remains unclear, but what the massive scale of these architectural achievements would seem to show is that this site held enormous importance for neolithic people.

Weighing in at some 350 tonnes, the **Grand Menhir Brisé** must have been awe-inspiring when it stood upright, some 18 metres in height. Even looking at it now, prostrate and split into four sections on the ground, you wonder how engineers could have organized the lifting into place of such a mammoth piece of stone. This huge granite block would have been planted around two to three metres deep in the ground, some time between 5000 BC and 4000 BC. Its stone was not excavated at Locmariaquer, and experts are convinced that it was brought from around 10 to 15 kilometres away, from the Rhuys peninsula on the other side of the Golfe du Morbihan.

In 1989, it was discovered that the menhir did not always stand alone, as the excavations revealed the roots of an alignment stretching out from it. What happened to those menhirs and in particular to the Grand Menhir Brisé? Until the recent digs, it was said the great menhir fell as a result of an earthquake or of a lightning strike. Now it is thought that all these menhirs were uprooted by neolithic inhabitants, who cut the Grand Menhir into pieces. It seems that later neolithic people were willing to put the massive fragments to other building uses, though how they might have split up the Grand Menhir so neatly is not known.

It may be that both of the large tumuli close to the Grand Menhir date from a second phase of occupation, roughly between 4000 and 3500 BC. The **Er-Grah tumulus**, sometimes referred to as the Er-Vinglé tumulus, has been only vaguely estimated to have been built around 4000 BC. Much reduced from its original height, it consists of a tomb on its northern end, covered by part of an enormous trapezoid barrow stretching a long way southwards. This massive man-made mound was not actually built all in one go. The single tomb was built, then covered by a larger one, around 40 metres in length, which sealed the tomb off from the outside world. Later, the building was much extended to north and south, creating a stepped tumulus some 170 metres long and between 15 and 30 metres wide. Excavations carried out under the tumulus revealed neolithic hearths and ditches below it, as well as the remains of two heads of cattle, perhaps sacrificed on the spot. These signs of earlier occupation have helped advance the theory that the tumulus was part of a second period of construction here.

The **Table des Marchands**, possibly constructed between 3700 and 3500 BC, looked like a vast table when it was still an uncovered dolmen in the last century. During this time, it featured in countless period representations of neolithic Brittany. However, after archaeological research carried out during the 1930s, it was covered up once again with a mass of stones to form a cairn similar to the one that would have been constructed over it originally. Further signs of an earlier settlement have now been found under this cairn, and the roof slab of the dolmen itself was demonstrated to have been taken from an older, broken menhir on this site. At the Table des Marchands, you can see a small part of the carving of a bull on the roof slab of the dolmen, as well as an axe and two buckles. Staggeringly, the other half of this engraving has been found some way off, in the dolmen on the island of Gavrinis (*see* p.390). However, the most remarkable carving here covers the ogival end stone, decorated with four rows of almost symmetrically positioned crooks; this recurring symbol inside Morbihan neolithic tombs has often been read as a sign of power or authority.

Around Locmariaquer

Locmariaquer is overwhelmed by its neolithic vestiges, with the result that it virtually ignores all but its three most famous monuments. However, another reputed neolithic burial chamber lies in the northern outskirts of the village, just off the D781. The **Mané-Lud** is difficult to find and to park near, but the big covering stones for this tomb are visible on the rise of the tumulus, and a few stairs can take you down into it. Light comes in through the cracks in the covering stones and some engravings can be made out. You might also go in search of the nearby **Mané Retual**, a dolmen with axes engraved on the massive covering stone, upheld by some 40 supporting pieces. South of the village, towards Kerpenhir, the tumulus of **Mané-er-Hroëck** yielded a substantial treasure of axe heads and beads when it was opened up in 1863.

Locmariaquer itself has sprawled down this western side of the Golfe du Morbihan. The 11th-century church of **Notre-Dame de Kerdro** still contains some Romanesque carved capitals. The views onto the calm, flat inland gulf, dotted with headlands and islands, are totally enchanting, and the many oyster boats reveal how a fair number of the locals make their living. You can visit oyster beds here from June to September (*book via the tourist office on* **t** *02 97 57 33 05*).

On the beach south of Locmariaquer, looking out on to the bay of Quiberon and the ocean, stands the dolmen of **Les Pierres Plates**. Several of the stones in this tumulus have interesting carvings, including embossed shields said to be representations of the mother god, and an illustration of what may be a stylized boat with oars that indicates that these neolithic men could have been mariners. The **Pointe de Kerpenhir** at the southeastern tip of the Locmariaquer peninsula marks the western entrance to the Golfe du Morbihan. North of town, the huge **La Trinitaine** Breton biscuit factory has a shop selling a wide variety of Breton specialities.

The Western Golfe du Morbihan from Auray to Vannes

The river of Auray runs down into the western side of the magical Golfe du Morbihan, past the historic town of Auray and the prettiest picture postcard of an inland Breton port below it, St-Goustan. Ste-Anne d'Auray, a short way north, is one of the most venerated places in Brittany, and includes the major memorial to the Breton victims of the First World War. Take the road down the east bank of the Auray river, via the port of Bono and the neolithic tombs of Kernourz, then dozens of little roads lead down to the coastal path along the Golfe du Morbihan. Brittany doesn't get much more serenely beautiful than this. Private gardens slope down almost to the water's edge. From this track, you can watch boats weave their way through the gulf's confusion of wooded islands. The cairn of Gavrinis, on one of the islands, and the best of all the Breton neolithic sites, can only be reached by boat.

Auray

The port of St-Goustan, down in Auray's steep valley, outshines the upper town. But through the Middle Ages the hill dominating the Loch river was of great importance in this part of Brittany. The major event in Auray's history took place in 1364, when the battle that sealed the Breton War of Succession took place outside the town.

The battle of Auray, fought in the marshlands of Kerzo, brought an end to one of the most terrible wars Brittany has known. Charles de Blois and his troops, pitted against Jean de Montfort and his army, had adopted a poor position overlooked by De Montfort's men, but he decided to attack, against the better judgement of his great commander, Bertrand Du Guesclin. The De Blois side was massacred, Charles dying in the battle, while Du Guesclin was captured. Jean de Montfort apparently rued the death of his cousin Charles and saw to it that De Blois was given a grand funeral. The area of Auray, however, was left to suffer the consequences of pillaging armies. Jean de Montfort assumed the title of Duke Jean IV of Brittany after this battle, and built a church on the site of the decisive victory, which later became the Chartreuse d'Auray. Most of this monastery's buildings still standing date from the 17th and 18th centuries.

During the Ancien Régime, Auray merchants prospered from fishing and trade. You can see the results of their successes both in the upper town and in the gorgeously restored port of St-Goustan. In 1776, bad weather forced Benjamin Franklin to land in this safe harbour, while on his way to discuss with King Louis XVI how France might assist in the American War of Independence against Britain.

The memory of the anti-Revolutionary royalist and Catholic Chouannerie also lingers at Auray. One of Brittany's most determined anti-Revolutionary and anti-Napoleonic figures, Georges Cadoudal, was born in the Kerléano district in 1771. He spent his short life battling ceaselessly for the restoration of the French monarchy, and in 1795 he played an important part in the failed attempted invasion by royalist émigrés via the Quiberon peninsula. Cadoudal survived, but 950 émigrés and Chouans who were

Getting Around

Auray has a **railway** station on the rapid TGV line linking Paris with Quimper.

Otherwise, **buses** from Auray or Vannes serve this area.

Details on going out on the Golfe du Morbihan are given on p.391.

Tourist Information

Auray: 20 Rue du Lait, B.P. 403, t 02 97 24 09 75, *www.auray-tourisme.com*.
Ste-Anne-d'Auray: 1 Rue de Vannes,
t 02 97 57 69 16 (*summer only*); rest of year contact the Mairie, t 02 97 57 63 91, *tourisme.steanne@wanadoo.fr*.
Larmor-Baden: 24 Quai Pen Lannic,
t 02 97 58 01 26.
Ile aux Moines: Le Port, t 02 97 26 32 45 (*Easter–Sept only*).
Arradon: t 02 97 44 01 56, *www.arradon.com*.

Market Days

Auray: Monday.
Larmor-Baden: Sunday.
Arradon: Friday.

Where to Stay and Eat

Auray ✉ 56400

The port of St-Goustan is packed with restaurants with riverside terraces. The upper town is very pleasant too.
★★Hôtel du Loch, 2 Rue Guhur, t 02 97 56 48 33, *www.hotel-du-loch.com* (*inexpensive*). A comfortable option a little out of town to the north. *Closed Wed and Tues low season*.

★Le Marin, 1 Place du Rolland, t 02 97 24 14 58, *www.saint-goustan.net* (*inexpensive–moderate*). An unpretentious hotel at the port of St-Goustan. Canoes are available for guest use.
L'Abbaye, Place St-Sauveur, t 02 97 24 10 85 (*inexpensive–moderate*). A characterful Breton option among the restaurants at the port, serving good crêpes.
L'Eglantine, Place St-Sauveur, t 02 97 56 46 55 (*inexpensive–moderate*). A rather conservative-looking place with excellent seafood and pictures of royalist Chouan leaders on the walls. *Closed Wed.*
Crêperie La Frégate, 11 Rue du Petit Port, t 02 97 50 71 95 (*inexpensive*). A decent budget option. *Closed Thurs.*
Crêperie Quintin, Rue du Père Eternel (*inexpensive*). A very cheap option in the upper town, with a rustic Breton dining room giving on to the main square.
Crêperie-Restaurant Capucine, 6 Rue St-Sauveur, t 02 97 56 35 53 (*inexpensive*). A simple family-run crêperie-restaurant with a snug pocket of a dining room and a small, colourful terrace.
Le Relais Franklin, 8 Quai Franklin, t 02 97 24 82 54 (*inexpensive*). The place where Franklin stayed when he landed here, now a charming crêperie.

Ste-Anne-d'Auray ✉ 56400

★★La Croix Blanche, 25 Rue de Vannes, t 02 97 57 64 44 (*inexpensive*). A hotel characterized by pleasant rooms, a garden and an agreeable dining room serving decent food.
★L'Auberge, 56 Route de Vannes, t 02 97 57 61 55 (*inexpensive*). A number of basic guest

captured during the disastrous landing were brought to a place outside Auray since known as the Champ des Martyrs. There, they were shot dead by the Republicans. At the Chartreuse d'Auray, a mausoleum in white marble in the funerary chapel was commissioned in the 19th century to commemorate the event. Another 19th-century chapel at the Champ des Martyrs itself also marks the massacre.

In 1796, at the tender age of 25, Cadoudal was made lieutenant-general of the royalist army in the *département* of the Morbihan, but after a fierce battle in 1800 he signed a treaty with the enemy. Soon, however, he was off to Britain to rally troops there. He then became involved in a plot to bring about Napoleon's downfall, but was caught and sentenced to death.

rooms and a beamed dining room full of Breton paraphernalia, offering elaborate seafood cuisine.

Bono ✉ 56400

★★★Hostellerie Abbatiale, Manoir de Kerdréan, t 02 97 57 84 00, *www.abbatiale.com* (*moderate–expensive*). A Breton manor with a great deal of style, offering comfortable rooms, a swimming pool, a tennis court and a golf course.

Le Vieux Pont, 23 Rue Pasteur, t 02 97 57 87 71 (*inexpensive*). A bar-cum-crêperie that is about as simple as they come, but with the advantage of being set on the delightful little port.

Les Rahed Koët, at Plougoumelen a few km northwest of Le Bono, t 02 97 56 34 96, (*inexpensive–moderate*). An extremely reasonably priced restaurant located within a thatched farmhouse. *Closed Mon and Tues out of season.*

Toul Broc'h ✉ 56870

★★★Le Gavrinis, 2km east of Baden, t 02 97 57 00 82, *www.gavrinis.com* (*moderate*). A very cheerful hotel with flowers galore, some bright, modern guest rooms and its own garden. The cuisine (*moderate–expensive*) is superb.

Larmor-Baden ✉ 56870

★★Auberge Parc Fetan, 17 Rue du Berder, t 02 97 57 04 38 (*moderate*). A handy option for the ferry.

Ile aux Moines ✉ 56780

Le San Francisco, Le Port, B.P. 7, t 02 97 26 31 52, *www.ileauxmoines.com*

(*inexpensive–moderate*). A hotel set in a former Franciscan convent, offering much sought-after cosy rooms and 2 dining rooms with good views.

Le Clos, Rue Neuve, Le Lério, t 02 97 26 34 29 (*inexpensive–moderate*). A B&B that just about sums up the character of the island, set in a rustic old fisherman's cottage with a delightful garden.

Les Embruns, Le Bourg, t 02 97 26 30 86 (*moderate*). An appealing restaurant run by an islander who first made a successful career as a chef on the mainland. *Closed Wed and 2wks Oct.*

Penmern ✉ 56870

Pilitrinic, Penmern-Bois-Bas, t 02 97 57 06 85 (*inexpensive–moderate*). A restaurant that soaks up the gulf's atmosphere, accessed via a pine-scented road on to a little-known peninsula located to the north of Port-Blanc. Try the excellent seafood outside when the weather permits.

Arradon ✉ 56610

★★Les Vénètes, La Pointe d'Arradon, t 02 97 44 85 85, *www.lesvenetes.fr* (*expensive–very expensive*). A modern hotel enjoying a truly splendid location overlooking the gulf.

St-Avé ✉ 56890

Le Pressoir, 7 Rue de l'Hôpital, t 02 97 60 87 63 (*moderate–expensive*). A thoughtful gastronomic haunt just to the northeast of Vannes, converted from the bistrot of a small railway station by the chef-proprietor. *Closed Mon and Tues, 2wks March and Oct, and 1 wk July*

Touring Auray

The lively **upper town** of Auray has retained a good number of grand houses, constructed both in timberframe and granite, and boasts the substantial church of **St-Gildas**. The architecture of the latter is a typically Breton hotch-potch of styles, with Gothic, Renaissance and Baroque features all rolled into one.

The stylish 19th-century Hôtel de Ville occupies the centre of Auray's main square, the Place de la République, while the Rue Barré leading off the square is the main shopping artery. The Commanderie du St-Esprit, with its enormous Gothic arches, recalls medieval Auray.

However, the unmissable part of the town is the port of **St-Goustan** in the valley. Tourist success means that almost every house here has been turned into a restaurant. Number 8 along the quay is where Benjamin Franklin stayed in 1776, now a crêperie (*see* p.386). It's a steep little climb to the two **churches** lying almost next to each other above the port. The first, still mainly covered with ugly plaster on the outside, pays homage to Lourdes tackiness with a Virgin in a grotto, lit by naked light bulbs. The second church, St-Goustan, with its slate helmet, contains vivid tales from the New Testament told in the 19th-century stained glass in the apse.

On the river, you'll find the little **Musée La Goélette** in the schooner that is permanently moored by the towpath; its displays recall the sailor's life at the start of the 20th century.

A Pilgrimage to Ste-Anne d'Auray

C'est un peu le Lourdes breton. (It's a bit like a Breton Lourdes.)
Le Guide du Routard

A handful of kilometres north of Auray, Ste-Anne d'Auray is one of the holiest places in Brittany for most Breton Catholics today. In fact, it has probably become the most venerated spot in the whole province, eclipsing the traditional seven cathedral stops along the Tro Breizh pilgrimage route. It helps that the biggest memorial to the Bretons who died in the First World War was also built here.

The story of Ste-Anne d'Auray begins in 1623. That year one Yves Nicolazic, a local peasant, witnessed the recurring apparition of a woman dressed all in white, coming to him carrying a candle. She turned out to be none other than Anne, mother of the Virgin Mary, considered the patron saint of Brittany. She eventually explained to him on the evening of 25 July 1624 that a chapel dedicated to her had once stood in one of the fields where he worked, though it had been destroyed in the year 701. She asked him to tell his priest that she wished for a chapel to be rebuilt in her honour. At first the peasant was dismissed as mad, but in March 1625 the apparition told him to go and dig in a precise place. Nicolazic went with some friends and there unearthed a statue of Ste Anne, supposedly dating – guess what – from 701. After such a 'miracle', the Breton Church built a chapel on the spot. The 17th-century structure was replaced between 1866 and 1877 by the enormous neo-Renaissance church you now see.

You might go and wander round the **First World War memorial enclosure** before looking inside the church. The enclosure commemorating the Bretons who died in the First World War is one of the most moving places in Brittany, with the names of tens of thousands of war dead engraved on the walls. Some sources claim that almost a quarter of a million Bretons died in the First World War – an enormous percentage of the population.

Close to the enclosure, people can go and pray at the simple little oratory to Ste Anne, containing a dignified Breton statue showing mother and daughter reading. Further on, a special area commemorates Pope John Paul II's visit in 1996, in particular with the *dallage de la foi* ('paving stones of faith'). There's also a museum of Breton dolls in costume, adding a lighter note to this sobering site.

Near the church, the 19th-century Scala Sancta, or Holy Staircase, stands out. The most fanatical pilgrims climb these stairs on their knees. Yet the **basilique**, as the church is called, dominates the spacious religious compound. The imposing structure was built to plans by Edouard Deperthes, who is best known for designing the Paris Hôtel de Ville with Théodore Ballu. The bulky church tower is topped by an enormous statue, not the Ste Anne discovered by Nicolazic.

Inside, the stained-glass windows tell the life of Ste Anne and the miraculous local story. Nicolazic is portrayed as a clueless simpleton. (His body rests in the first right-hand side chapel.) The Church's persecution by the Revolution also features, along with the Breton determination to stick to the faith. The statue of Ste Anne that Nicolazic 'unearthed' was actually burned by rabid Republicans. There is much else to see in the basilica, however, including an altar to the Virgin incorporating five 15th-century alabaster panels depicting Christ's Passion, and the main altar donated by Pope Pius IX. On the south side, the Maison de Nicolazic is the house where Ste Anne supposedly appeared to the Breton peasant. The *pardon* of Ste-Anne d'Auray draws tens of thousands of people every year on 25 and 26 July.

A few kilometres to the west of Ste-Anne d'Auray you can visit the **Ecomusée de St-Degan-en-Brech**, with various displays demonstrating how Breton country people lived in the past.

Bono and the Megaliths of Kernourz

Back to the south of Auray town and just east of the Auray river, **Ste-Avoye** by the Bono valley has not just the attraction of its thatched houses but also a Renaissance chapel boasting a sculpted 16th-century rood screen, which shows the apostles on one side and a depiction of saintly Breton lawyer, St Yves (*see* p.208), as well as the virtues, on the other side.

The port of **Bono** is tucked away on the steep slopes where the Bono meets the Auray river. This inland harbour rivals the port of St-Goustan for quaintness, but is much less touristy. Among the southern outskirts of Bono is one of the most beautiful but least well-known megalithic sites in Brittany, **Kernourz**. The series of tumuli here are delightfully located in the shade of pine trees that appear to bow inwards to pay homage to the central tomb. Some of these neolithic burial chambers may date from around 3000 BC; you can make out further prehistoric ones from the first millennium BC, described as Iron Age *tombelles*.

Below Baden, the views along the peninsulas of Le Blaire and Locmiquel give out on to the Golfe du Morbihan. Head along the narrow **Pointe de Toulvern**, a spit of land colonized by oyster farmers.

To Larmor-Baden and the Island Tumulus of Gavrinis

On the western side of Larmor-Baden a road leads down to the delightful **Pointe de Berchis** and **Le Paludo**, but signs spelling out *baignade interdite* ('bathing forbidden') warn people off swimming. **Larmor-Baden**, a quite popular small-scale resort with gorgeous views, is the port from which to get a ferry out to the island and cairn of Gavrinis.

Ile de Gavrinis

*For boat trips (which run roughly every 30mins daily Easter–Sept 10–11.30
and 2–5, Oct–5 Nov 2–5), call t 02 97 57 19 38. Reserve ahead as numbers are
extremely limited.*

Having to take a little boat to get to Gavrinis, heading out past the beautiful
scenery of pine-covered islands, certainly adds to the excitement of going to see
France's most artistic neolithic monument. The island of Gavrinis is privately owned,
but the tumulus situated on the southern end, roughly reckoned to date from the 4th
millennium BC, is open to the public.

The wealth of decorative designs engraved on the stones of the corridor and the
burial chamber distinguish the Gavrinis monument from all the other neolithic sites
in Brittany. Many of these neolithic engravings, which were probably executed with
pieces of quartzite, look rather like magnified fingerprints. It has been claimed that
they represent a mother goddess linking the world of the living with the world of the
dead. Axe-heads stand out too, as do some crooks that could be symbols of authority.
Serpentine shapes writhe below, while other designs resemble birds' feathers. The
tomb's entrance apparently lines up to coincide with the winter solstice.

Located just a short distance away from the island of Gavrinis, the much smaller
island of Er Lannic boasts a cromlech in a figure of eight half submerged by the sea.
You can make out the shape of the stones – a clear sign of how much the oceans
have risen since neolithic times, at which point experts believe that this area would
have been a large marsh.

The Golfe du Morbihan

There are a little over 40 islands in this massive, inland saltwater sea, helping to
create one of Brittany's most exquisite landscapes; your gaze is ceaselessly distracted
as you turn the tip of one island to find another two or three waiting for you. All but
two of the islands are privately owned, the Ile aux Moines and the Ile d'Arz.

Measuring some 25 kilometres north to south from Vannes to Port-Navalo and
around 20 kilometres from east to west, the Golfe du Morbihan has some of the
strongest currents in Europe at its narrow opening to the ocean between
Locmariaquer and Port-Navalo. As a result, the coastline behind this opening changes
substantially as the tide goes in and out; in the west, however, around the main two
islands, you feel the effects of the tides much less than in the east. In summer,
crisscrossing vessels churn the waters in all directions and the traditional fishing and
oyster boats are greatly outnumbered by yachts, motor boats, canoes and sailboards.

Port-Blanc

East of Lamor-Baden, the next peninsula is that of Port-Blanc. Boats leave from here
for tours of the gulf or trips out to the Ile aux Moines or Ile d'Arz. The Ile aux Moines,
the most important island in the gulf, is a stone's throw from the mainland.

Getting There

The main Golfe du Morbihan port is the Gare Maritime de Vannes. Contact Navix Atlantique, **t** 02 97 46 60 00, or the Compagnie des Iles, **t** 02 97 46 18 19, for ferry information. These companies also operate services from Locmariaquer, Port-Navalo and, in summer, Auray and Bono. The simplest way to get onto the Ile aux Moines is to take the very short and regular ferry from Port-Blanc.

Ask at local tourist offices about hiring a motorboat or sailing boat to cruise around the gulf. At the port of Arradon, Le Blan Marine, **t** 02 97 44 06 90, offers such possibilities, or for a flight over the gulf you can try the Aéroclub de Vannes-Meucon, **t** 02 97 60 73 08. Romantics might appreciate a trip on a *sinagot*, an old-fashioned gulf boat, departing from Séné. Contact Vannes tourist office for full details, **t** 02 97 47 24 24, *www.tourisme-vannes.com*,.

Ile aux Moines

Called the Monks' Island in French, this place apparently never saw any monks as inhabitants – they simply managed the place from a distance and exacted their dues. Nowadays, the **port** quays crawl with tourists throughout the summer. Apart from the crowds, Ile aux Moines is a little Breton paradise, with creeks and beaches, fishermen's cottages and luxuriant walled gardens. Bicycles provide the easiest way of discovering the island, but they can't take the coastal path that hugs the shores. Pick up a free map from the tourist office on the port quay before you set out to discover the place.

The north end of the island is the most crowded part. Many of the slightly grander 19th-century houses were built for Vannes ships' captains, who made up the 'aristocracy' of the island. It's a fair walk from the port to the island's most northerly tip, complete with its 19th-century calvary. You go through the busy centre of **Le Bourg**, as the main village is named, where there is a selection of restaurants and bars. Down from the northern tip, you'll find the church of Locmiquel, a cheerful whitewashed 19th-century building. Along the eastern arm of the island, the views open up onto the Ile d'Arz. Here is the late-18th-century Château du Guéric, built for the Du Bodan family.

Head southwards from Le Bourg and the crowds quickly thin. Sloe bushes proliferate and you get lovely views across the gulf. Around a kilometre from the *bourg* you come to **Kergonan**, a kind of second village. The neolithic **cromlech** known as Er Anke has been broken up by houses built in the midst of it, but in its entirety it would apparently have been the largest cromlech discovered in France. As you reach the southern tip of Ile aux Moines, a solitary dolmen, Pen Hap, lies fully exposed on a bare patch of ground. An impressive top slab covers the main burial chamber. The very southern tip of the island, Pen Nioul, is private property, but it's worth cycling up as far as you can go to enjoy the views. Make for a couple of slithers of beaches just to the east, where you can take a breather and watch the yachts gliding around the gulf.

Ile d'Arz

Arz is much flatter, less wooded and less popular than Ile aux Moines, and not quite as accessible. When you're dropped off on Arz, there's just a single jetty and a few isolated modern buildings to greet you, one with a booth where you can pick up a free map of the island. A sturdy 17th-century restored windmill also marks this northern **Pointe de Beluré**. It may be worthwhile to hire a bicycle by the jetty as it's quite a walk to the main centre.

The village (again, Le Bourg) lies in the middle of the island, its belt of houses spanning the island's girth. Arz measures around three kilometres in length, and its thin strips of beach fill up with families in summer. **Le Bourg** is delightful; the lanes have a nice open feel to them. The church is topped by a typical slate-helmeted Romanesque spire, and the edifice, dedicated to Our Lady, dates back in good part to the 12th century. The southern end of the island, **Pen Liouse**, has the vestiges of several neolithic dolmens, while from the eastern shore of Arz you get views on to the quieter half of the gulf. **Pennéro**, on the eastern side of the island has some particularly smart old houses.

From Port-Blanc to Arradon

There is only one way to appreciate the full beauty of the north coast of the Golfe du Morbihan from Port-Blanc to Arradon – walk the fabulous **coastal path**. The views of the pine-covered islands out in the gulf accompany you all the way past Arradon and the peninsula to the east of it. You then pass the wonderful properties of **Penboch** and **Raguédas**, Penboch standing out with the top-heavy pyramidal steeple on its church. At **Kerguen** you arrive opposite the tiny Chapelle de St-Antoine on the tip of the Ile du Petit Bois. Towards Vannes you come to a pretty faded pink house on the water's edge; the owners are not allowed to change the colour as the property is marked on navigational maps. North from here hides the town of Vannes.

Vannes

A croissant of cafés curves out from the gateway leading from Vannes's yachting harbour into the old town on its hill; this row of cafés offers an excellent place from which to contemplate how to spend a day or two in and around this city. Behind you, through that religious-looking gateway into town, you have the old paved streets leading to the cathedral on its sloping ground, the museums of Vannes (which include an important archaeological museum and a fine arts one), the bourgeois shops in splendid timberframe buildings, and the medieval ramparts. In front of you, the quays lead to the glorious Golfe du Morbihan, beside which you'll find a batch of small, fun, modern museums.

History

Vannes has a superb naturally protected port, as it lies hidden at the back of the vast inland sea of the Golfe du Morbihan. Historians have speculated that this might have been the main location of the settlement of the Venetes, the reputed Celtic tribe of the region when the Romans attacked. A Gallo-Roman settlement called Darioritum certainly grew up northeast of medieval Vannes, where remnants of a forum and a fortified castrum have been found.

Getting There

Vannes's **railway** station is on the TGV line linking Paris to Quimper, and also at the end of the line crossing central Brittany north to south from St-Brieuc to Vannes. The station lies well north of the historic centre.

Well to the south of town, Vannes's Gare Maritime is the principal port from which **ferries** leave for the islands of the Golfe du Morbihan (*see* p.391 for further details).

Tourist Information

1 Rue Thiers, **t** 02 97 47 24 34, *www.tourisme-vannes.com*.

Market Days

Wednesday and Saturday.

Where to Stay

Vannes ✉ **56000**

★★★**Le Roof**, Presqu'île de Conleau, **t** 02 97 63 47 47, *leroof@club-internet.fr* (*expensive*). The most exclusive hotel in Vannes, located 5mins to the south of the centre and offering wonderful views on to the Golfe du Morbihan.

★★★**La Marébaudière**, 4 Rue Aristide Briand, **t** 02 97 47 34 29, *www.marebaudiere.com* (*moderate*). Part of the Comfort chain set east of the Préfecture, with slightly more character than other hotels in the centre.

★★★**Le Manche Océan**, 31 Rue du Lieutenant Colonel Maury, **t** 02 97 47 26 46, *www. manche-ocean.com* (*inexpensive–moderate*). A slightly dull but good-value choice.

★★**Hôtel Le Bretagne** 34/36 Rue du Mené, **t** 02 97 47 20 21, *hotel.le.bretagne@wanadoo.fr* (*inexpensive*). A friendly, family-run place with small clean rooms.

★★**Marina**, 4 Place Gambetta, **t** 02 97 47 22 81, *lemarina@aol.com* (*inexpensive*). Pleasant rooms affording views over the lively port.

★★**Au Relais du Golfe**, 10 Place du Général de Gaulle, **t** 02 97 47 14 74 (*inexpensive*). A hotel situated above a locals' bar close to the Préfecture.

Le Richemont, 24 Place de la Gare, **t** 02 97 42 61 41 (*inexpensive*). A well-furbished railway hotel with a restaurant fusing Mediterranean and Breton cuisine.

Eating Out

Ask at the tourist office about the possibility of taking an evening dinner cruise around the Golfe du Morbihan.

With the collapse of the Roman Empire, the Armorican peninsula would gradually turn into Brittany. Franks from the east advanced this far, while at approximately the same period, immigrants from Britain were arriving in western Armorica. In fact, Saint Patern, one of the seven Christian founding fathers of the province, who were thought to have come over from Wales, appears to have made Vannes into his spiritual centre.

Around the middle of the 6th century, a Breton chief, Waroc'h, took control of the Vannetais by force. The great historian of the period, Gregory of Tours, details some of the brutal violence involved in the campaign, and one Bishop Regalis rued the fact that his people were put under what he called the 'Breton yoke'.

A still more powerful figure than Waroc'h in Breton history, Nomenoë, rose through Charlemagne's ranks in the early 9th century and was made Comte de Vannes. Charlemagne's successor, Louis le Pieux, conferred on him the title of *missus* to Brittany in 826. Once Louis had died, Nomenoë embarked on his project to make Brittany a power independent from the Carolingians, extending the Breton frontiers. Within 10 years he had succeeded, uniting the Bretons under him. For a short time at the start of this new Breton region, Vannes became capital of Brittany.

Regis Mahé, Place de la Gare, t 02 97 42 61 41 (*expensive–very expensive*). The most highly regarded restaurant in town, situated close to the railway station and mixing Provençal and Breton fare. *Closed Sun, Mon and 2wks Nov and June.*

Arnaud Lorgeoux - Le Pavé des Halles, 17 Rue des Halles, t 02 97 47 15 96 (*moderate–very expensive*). A charming restaurant in an old Vannes house. The eponymous chef has a reputation among locals for imaginative cooking using really fresh ingredients.

Roscanvec, Rue des Halles, t 02 97 47 15 96 (*moderate–expensive*). A place offering *haute cuisine* of good repute, including surprising dishes such as turbot in a honey crust with sweet pepper confit. *Closed Sun eve and Mon in low season.*

La Table des Gourmets, 6 Rue Alexandre Le Pontois, t 02 97 47 52 44 (*moderate–expensive*). Tasty gastronomic Breton fare such as marinated sardines with chilled tomato mousse, plus views on to the ramparts from outside Vannes's walls. *Closed end June and low season Mon lunch, Wed and Sun eves.*

La Nappe Monde, Rue des Halles, t 02 97 47 21 94 (*inexpensive–moderate*). A relatively informal place for grills, salads and pizzas.

Breizh Caffé, 13 Rue des Halles, t 02 97 54 37 41 (*inexpensive*). A restaurant in an old, beamed house on an atmospheric street, serving fresh, simple Breton produce.

Bistrot du Pont Vert, at the Golfe end of the Avenue du Maréchal de Lattre de Tassigny t 02 97 40 80 13 (*inexpensive*). A good-value place situated on the tree-lined road following the port out to the sea, and extremely popular with local workers. The unpretentious but copious lunches include a *moules-frites* special on a Friday.

Crêperie La Cave St Gwenaël, 23 Rue St-Guenhaël, t 02 97 47 47 94 (*inexpensive*). A long-established crêperie situated in one of the oldest and most beautiful houses in Vannes, on the south side of the cathedral. *Closed Sun and Mon.*

Crêperie La Taupinière, Place des Lices, t 02 97 42 57 82 (*inexpensive*). A sweet crêperie; you'll see why it's called the mole's house when you enter. *Closed Mon.*

La Saladière, 36 Rue du Port, t 02 97 42 52 10 (*inexpensive*). A low-cost option located just down from the tourist office. As the name suggests, the speciality here is salads. Large and lovely, they come with a wealth of meat and fish ingredients. A good value 3-course *menu rapide* is available at lunchtime. *Closed Sun and Wed eves.*

Scant remnants from the earlier Middle Ages in Vannes include parts of the oldest gateways into town, sections of La Cohue opposite the cathedral, and vestiges of the Romanesque cathedral built after the Vikings left. La Cohue was a centre of activity, housing a covered market and the law courts. In the Breton War of Succession in the mid 14th century, Vannes was bitterly fought over by the opposing sides, its people forced to switch allegiance with head-spinning frequency. The city was occupied by English troops backing the De Montfort side for some time; when the De Montfortists won, Duke Jean IV of Brittany had the fortifications extended in the late 1300s.

Duke Jean V of Brittany established Vannes as one of the centres of his duchy in the early 15th century. A few of the fine half-timbered houses characteristic of the centre date as far back as this, as does the massive Tour du Connétable along the ramparts, the lodgings for the head of the ducal army, as well as Vannes's imposing cathedral. The citizens had continued to support the cult of St Patern down the centuries, much to the annoyance of the Church of Rome, which did not recognize such Breton saints. A brilliant Spanish Catholic propagandist, Vincent Ferrier, was shipped in to bring a bit of Roman Catholic religious and moral discipline and fervour to the people, quickly spreading a new piety and stricter morality across the region from 1418 to 1419.

Brittany came much more directly under the control of the French monarchy once Anne de Bretagne had been forced into the French royal family late in the 15th century. However, it still held meetings of its own Estates, which gathered on several occasions at Vannes, and its own Parlement. Brittany's Act of Union with France of 13 August 1532, 'the perpetual union of the land and duchy of Brittany with the kingdom and crown of France', was signed in the city.

In the French Wars of Religion in the second half of the 16th century, Spanish troops in support of the ultra-Catholic side came briefly to occupy the town and Vannes lost the ducal administrative importance it had known during the 15th century. In 1675, prosperity returned to the town, however. King Louis XIV's administration punished the Rennes Parlement for what it saw as its part in the violent tax riots known as the Révolte du Papier Timbré, and the Breton Parlement was moved to Vannes for 15 years. During the Revolution, support in Vannes was mainly for the royalist, conservative, Catholic side; this caused the Revolutionaries in Paris to send the ruthless Republican General Hoche to do his persuasive worst in the region, notably to counter the Quiberon peninsula landing of émigrés in 1795.

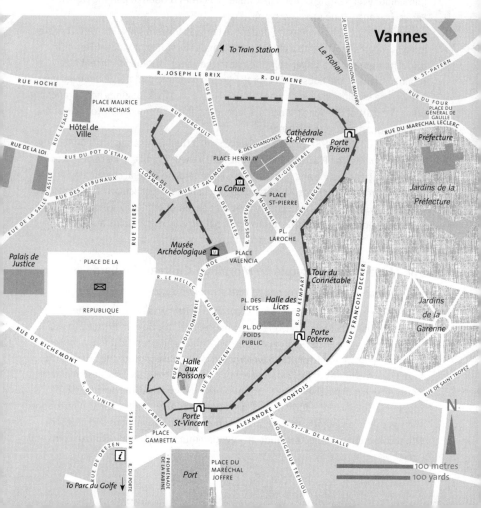

This conservative centre stagnated somewhat in the 20th century, and the neglected port even began to stink. But things have changed a good deal in the last 40 years or so, with merchant ships replaced by yachts, a vibrant cultural scene coming to the fore, and university students and posh shops bringing a new lease of life to Vannes.

A Tour of the Town

Looking out from **Place Gambetta**, that croissant of a 19th-century square by the yachting harbour, you can see the long, straight, narrow channel of water and the modern shaded quays leading out to the Golfe du Morbihan, restored in the mid 1970s. The work completely transformed this neglected part of town. You may spot the *Corbeau des mers* on display close to the Place Gambetta; this langoustine-fishing boat has been declared an historic monument, as it counted among the fleet of small boats in which the loyal Frenchmen of the island of Sein sailed off to Britain immediately on hearing Général de Gaulle's call from London to join the French Resistance on 26 June 1940 (*see* p.311).

Head into the old town passing under the **Porte St-Vincent**. This 18th-century gate looks like a great portal into a church; on it stands the statue of Vincent Ferrier, a colourful figure with a finger pointing out to the water. The **Rue St-Vincent** has retained many of the houses built for the Breton parliamentarians who moved here in 1675; the Revolution's henchman General Hoche also took lodgings here. Branching off at the start of the Rue St-Vincent, a lane leads almost immediately to the Halle aux Poissons, the covered fishmarket.

Continue up the Rue St-Vincent and you come to the first in a series of connecting, sloping squares. The **Place du Poids Public** lies to the left, and the **Place des Lices** takes you up the incline and joins with the **Place Laroche**. Several characterful buildings from different periods stand out, including the particularly striking Hôtel de Francheville, with its 17th-century turret made out of tender tufa limestone. The 1900 neo-Moorish building, decorated with patterns in yellow bricks and green ermine tails, transforms itself into a food market on certain days of the week.

The Musée Archéologique du Morbihan-Château-Gaillard

Open June–Sept daily 10–6; rest of year school hols 1.30–6.

The Château-Gaillard is a very smart townhouse that was built during the 15th century for Jean de Malestroit, one-time chancellor to the duke of Brittany. In 1912 it was bought by the Société Polymathique of Vannes, which turned it into a museum concentrating on prehistory. Now well known, it contains many of the finest finds from the excavations of Morbihan's neolithic sites: polished axes the design and finish of which make them look like admirable, modern works of craftsmanship; rougher jewellery, in the form of necklaces, pendants and bangles, some in rare stone such as callaïs, a kind of turquoise; and fragments of tools, weapons and pottery. Other collections of objects include an Egyptian mummy, and Gallo-Roman coins and colourful rings. Upstairs, you stumble upon a room full of unintentionally comical 17th-century painted panels, the Cabinet des Pères du Désert. Medieval religious objects, tapestries and other ornate objects from Vannes's past lie on display in the room beyond it.

The Cathedral Quarter

The **Cathédrale St-Pierre** (*open daily summer 8–7, rest of year 8–12 and 2–7; treasury open May–Oct Mon–Sat 10.30–6, Nov–April school hols and by request*) perches uncomfortably on the great slope of Vannes's hill, which gives its architecture some originality. It is hemmed in by old streets on all sides, however, so you can't get any grand perspectives. But take a walk all the way round the outside and you can appreciate its architectural features, which originate from the 12th to the 19th centuries. Head down the south side first, where the very pretty timberframe façades of houses on the **Rue St-Guenhaël** may distract you more than the religious building. Several features stand out along the north side of the cathedral, on the **Rue des Chanoines**: a crudely carved little calvary, the vestiges of a cloister, and a classically ordered round side chapel from 1537, which holds Vincent Ferrier's remains. The interior of the cathedral is remarkably wide and sombre, with a Gothic tracery balustrade running along above the low-pointed Gothic arches and an elaborate old organ with a clock incorporated in the middle of it. Behind the sobriety of the main part of the cathedral, the wildly carved chapel at the east end comes as a shock; the place is a rococo orgy of decoration, where stone fruit pours out of a cornucopia above the figures of the Virgin and Baby Jesus.

La Cohue

Open daily 15 June–Sept 10–6, rest of year 1.30–6.

Opposite the main entrance to the cathedral, on Place St-Pierre, the Act of Union between Brittany and France was signed in 1532 behind the thick walls of La Cohue. This building has served several purposes in its lifetime; in medieval times the covered market was held under its arches, while the local court met above. Occasionally, the Estates of Brittany gathered here, and now La Cohue contains a collection of museums.

Delacroix's *Crucifixion* is the most famous work in the collection of the intelligently presented **Musée des Beaux-Arts**, or fine arts museum. It's not one of the 19th-century prodigy's best pieces, however, showing an over-busty Mary Magdalene in the Rubens mould. Painted wooden statues of Breton saints have been gathered around the enormous canvas. One room features Breton landscapes by Jean Frélaut (1879–1954), including a view of Vannes in a darkly grey but attractive light, with a tall ship at the very gates of the town. There are also displays of work by Jean-François Boucher (1853–1937), a Parisian who captured the spirit of local markets and processions. Jules Noël, best known as a master of Breton seascapes, also features here. The museum has acquired a collection of royal portraits by Louis Michel Van Loo, showing King Louis XV, his wife and their two children.

The massive chambers downstairs hold exhibitions from the museum's fine collections of engravings as well as contemporary art exhibitions. Separate rooms are given over to an exhibition on the Golfe du Morbihan, the **Musée du Golfe et de la Mer**, which covers the history and ethnography of the beautiful inland sea.

From the Place Henri IV to the Hôtel de Ville

The square diagonally north of the cathedral and La Cohue, the **Place Henri IV**, looks particularly striking with its amazingly colourful display of timberframe houses. Off it, the **Rue St-Salomon** is one of the major shopping arteries in Vannes and leads out to some of the grand 19th-century buildings on the western edge of the old town and the upper part of the **Rue Thiers**. The **Hôtel de Ville**, or town hall, counts among the grandiose buildings on this street that leads back down to the tourist office and port.

From the Place Brûlée to the Ramparts

From the other, choir end of the cathedral, the enchanting **Place Brûlée**, surrounded by chic shops, leads down to the imposing **Porte Prison**, one of the best-preserved medieval gates into town. It once served as a prison, and narrowly avoided annihilation at the turn of the 19th century. The streets radiating out beyond it contain a lively lively array of boutiques, bars and restaurants behind yet more colourful timberframe façades. The **church of St Patern** stands out on **Rue St-Patern** in this quarter, while the imposing **Préfecture** dominating **Rue du Maréchal Leclerc** is backed by smart gardens.

The **ramparts** to the south have been well looked after. The ditch below these formidable walls is planted with immaculate formal flowerbeds. Several towers add to the attractiveness of the scene, the most impressive being the Tour du Connétable, while the Tour du Bourreau (Executioner's Tower) was where the town hangman lived.

As you head back down to the port you pass the grand 19th-century Château de l'Hermine. Law students study within, but it was on this site that Pierre de Bretagne, later Duke Jean V of Brittany, was born. Very humble by comparison and almost at the feet of the château, the little roofed structure from the 17th century was the town wash-house. Climb the hillside opposite this stretch of ramparts to get a better view of it from the height, among more well-tended gardens, the **Jardins de la Garenne**.

The Tourist Attractions of the Parc du Golfe

The shaded quayside walk out from Place Gambetta and along the **Promenade de la Rabine** leads to the commercial port and the site from which you can take a boat out onto the Golfe du Morbihan. A trio of modern tourist attractions have set up shop here, with accompanying car parks. The least unsuccessful building holds a good **aquarium** (*call* t *02 97 40 67 40 for opening times*), with pools containing sharks, turtles, dangerous fish such as stone fish and the electric eel, and the less threatening polka-dot-marked fish known affectionately as the Grace Kelly. At the **Papillonneraie** (*open Easter–Oct; call* t *02 97 46 01 02 for opening times*) you can learn about the stages in a butterfly's life. The architecture is uninspiring, but the interior houses a humid tropical zone full of bright flowers, with butterflies flying around your face. The **Palais des Automates** (*open mid-Feb–mid-Nov; call* t *02 97 40 40 39 for opening times*) is a mechanical toy museum.

The Eastern and Southern Golfe du Morbihan

The eastern shore of the Golfe proves more difficult to explore than the rest. What's more, a large portion of the eastern waters of the gulf is given over to oyster farming and to a bird reserve, and is greatly affected by the tides. Large expanses of mud are revealed as the water recedes. The gulf remains as beautiful as ever, though, and the best way to see it is once again by foot. The Presqu'île de Rhuys is the long spit of land that forms the protective southern barrier to the whole Golfe du Morbihan.

From Vannes Down the Eastern Side of the Golfe du Morbihan

South from Vannes via built-up Séné, signs lead to the **Réserve Ornithologique de Falguérec**, a 400-hectare bird reserve covering former salt pans. A secretive peninsula heads back in the direction of Arradon, and here you will be rewarded by superb views onto the gulf at the **Pointe de Moustérian**, or, on the western tip of the peninsula, at **Port-Anna**. This delightful miniature port in a creek looking across to Conleau is home to a *sinagot*, a traditional oyster boat with a ruddy sail. A little east, past **Theix**, the **Château du Plessis-Josso** (*open July and Aug for daily afternoon guided tours*) presents a pleasing image of a defensive medieval manor and some interesting interiors.

The D780 main road hogs the first stretch of the eastern side of the Golfe du Morbihan. For a glimpse of a grand Ancien Régime home in these parts, make for the **Château de Kerlévenan** (*open July–mid Sept daily 2–5*), where you can go on a guided tour of the grounds with their follies. Among the beautiful spots to stop at along the north bank to the tip of the Rhuys peninsula, the port of **Le Logeo** stands out.

The Tip of the Presqu'île de Rhuys: Port-Navalo and Le Crouesty

The end of the Rhuys peninsula has become quite heavily built up with holiday blocks and suffers the consequences of massive overpopularity in summer. Arzon is the town by the point, but visitors focus on its two protected ports in their separate little inlets: the older **Port-Navalo**, the fishing fleet of which was well known back in the 18th century; and the more suburban-looking **Le Crouesty**, which has become a packed yachting harbour, the buildings around it resembling a modern shopping precinct.

Two of the best places from which to appreciate the natural beauty of the tip of the Rhuys peninsula are its two neolithic tumuli. Standing on their heights, you can get extensive views onto the gulf and the ocean.

Le Petit Mont and the Butte de César

The **Petit Mont** (*open daily June–Sept 2.30–6.30; rest of year check with tourist office for opening times*), the more westerly of the two tumuli, is one of the most memorable and substantial neolithic sites that you can visit in Brittany. It also has the dubious distinction of having served as a large Nazi bunker. As you arrive at Le Petit Mont you are greeted by the surprising, saddening and yet also slightly comical sight of sections of German blockhouse cement appearing out of the dry stone sides of the tumulus. More respectful digs carried out during the 1980s have allowed for an interesting visit within, and the tombs contain some well-preserved engraved stones.

Tourist Information

Sarzeau: Rue du Général de Gaulle,
  t 02 97 41 82 37, *www.ville-sarzeau.com*.
Arzon: Place des Huniers, B.P. 47,
  t 02 97 53 81 63, *www.crouesty.com*.
Damgan: Place du Presbytère, t 02 97 41 11 32,
  www.damgan.org. There are free Breton
  dancing lessons in Damgan town centre
  should you feel so inclined.

Market Days

Sarzeau: Thursday.
Arzon: Tuesday.
Le Crouesty: Monday in summer.
Port-Navalo: Friday in summer.
St-Gildas-de-Rhuys: Sunday, plus daily in
  July and August.

Where to Stay and Eat

St-Colombier ✉ 56370
Le Tournepierre, 4km east of Sarzeau,
  t 02 97 26 42 19 (*moderate–expensive*).
  An excellent restaurant serving tasty
  cuisine in a village on the edge of the Golfe
  du Morbihan.

Le Crouesty ✉ 56640
★★★★Miramar, t 02 97 67 68 00, *www.
  miramar-crouesty-com* (*luxury*). A fake liner
  anchored in an artificial round pond by the
  sea, with a piano bar, a heated seawater
  pool, a tennis court, a sauna, a gym, a
  thalassotherapy centre and a beauty salon.

Port-Navalo ✉ 56640
Hôtel Glann Ar Mor, 27 Rue des Fontaines,
  t 02 97 53 88 30, *www.glannarmor@fr*
  (*inexpensive*). Recently renovated rooms and
  a restaurant.
Le Grand Largue, 1 Rue du Phare, t 02 97 53 71 58
  (*moderate–expensive*). Great views, carefully
  cooked seafood such as lobster in a coral
  sauce. *Closed Mon and Tues in low season*.

Damgan ✉ 56750
This is mainly a residential and camping
resort, with a couple of hotels.
★★L'Albatros, 1 Boulevard de l'Océan, t 02 97 41
  16 85, *www.hotel-albatros-damgan.com*
  (*inexpensive–moderate*). A hotel with many
  rooms with excellent sea views, though the
  decent restaurant looks on to the car park.
  Half-board is obligatory in summer.
Hôtel de la Plage, t 02 97 41 10 07,
  www.hoteldelaplage-damgan.com
  (*inexpensive*). A budget option with rooms
  with little balconies and a *saladerie*-cum-bar
  where you can eat cheaply.

Kervoyal
Crêperie L'Ecurie, t 02 97 41 03 29 (*inexpensive*).
  A cheerful crêpe house situated at the
  eastern end of Damgan's bay, with terrace
  tables set out in front of two houses in the
  middle of the village's main street.
Sally MacLennan, Grande-Rue, t 02 97 41 05 29
  (*inexpensive*). An Irish 'pub' where, apart
  from Guinness, you can work through a
  selection of Belgian beers. Occasional music
  concerts are hosted here. *Closed lunch*.

This tumulus evolved in several stages. The first cairn has been dated to around 4500 BC and it seems that it was built on a pre-megalithic mound from around 5000 BC. No tomb was discovered in the first cairn, which may have been a cenotaph. The second cairn, which holds a dolmen and dates from around 4000 BC, was built onto the south side of the first. In a third stage of building, around 3000 BC, two further dolmens were added on the eastern side of the mound, though one of these two was destroyed by the German meddling.

The **Butte de César** or **Tumiac tumulus** just outside Arzon along the D780 is much less interesting than Le Petit Mont. The way this circular tumulus was excavated makes it impossible to see the fascinating engraved stones it contains, though precious finds were made here and transferred to the local museums. Traditionally, it is said that this tumulus was where Caesar may have watched the fatal naval battle that brought about the downfall of the Celtic Veneti tribe (*see* box opposite). Recent research has

Caesar's Account of How the Romans Thrashed the Veneti

Caesar's explanation of the Roman naval campaign and battle with the Veneti in 56 BC counts as one of the most informative and evocative pieces on Armorica to have come down to us from ancient history.

Caesar had conquered Gaul in 57 BC, and the local Celtic tribe, the Venetes or Veneti, were the first to foolishly revolt in defiance of Caesar's troops. The great Roman commander led the campaign against them himself and, having written of the Veneti's strength, described how his army managed to defeat them through luck as much as good judgement. The unfortunate Veneti were becalmed in their excellent sailing vessels. The Romans caught and massacred the seamen and Caesar sold the rest of the population as slaves.

Read the famous passage in Caesar's *Conquest of Gaul* to get a fuller picture of this extraordinary event.

shown that it is unlikely that he could have seen much from here, though Gallo-Roman fragments found at Le Petit Mont indicate that the site may have become a sanctuary where the Roman victory was remembered and celebrated.

The Atlantic Side of the Presqu'île de Rhuys

St-Gildas-de-Rhuys

After the succession of beaches east of Arzon, you come to St-Gildas-de-Rhuys. The church of **St-Gildas-de-Rhuys** appears none too welcoming from the outside, but its Romanesque apse and extravagant 17th-century stone retable must have filled medieval pilgrims with awe. It is dedicated to Gildas, one of the most influential British religious figures in Armorica's conversion to Brittany (*see* box, p.402).

The Château de Suscinio

Open daily June–Sept 10–7, April–May 10–12 and 2–7;
rest of year call t 02 97 41 91 91.

It's really rather extraordinary to see a medieval castle plonked by itself on a beach like this. Actually, the attraction of Suscinio (which lies some way to the east of St-Gildas) for the medieval dukes of Brittany was hunting, as the lands of the peninsula were covered with forests during the Middle Ages. An Act of 1218 mentions a castle here, but little is left of that early construction. However, massive walls and towers aplenty do survive from the 14th-century building campaigns.

In the second half of the 15th century, the château fell into decline, though the dowager duchess Isabel of Scotland, the widow of duke François I, did stay on at Suscinio from 1450 to 1487. In 1488, the Breton Duke François II gave the property to Jean de Châlon, Prince of Orange, and though the Duke of Mercoeur did maintain the fortifications throughout the French Wars of Religion, the Château de Suscinio was then neglected by its absent owners, the powerful Conti family. After a long period of

Gildas, a Zealous Celtic Christian Traveller and Writer

Gildas, who may have been born by the Clyde at the start of the 6th century, became one of the most influential figures in the 6th-century Celtic Church. He went off to become a monk at Llaniltud in south Wales, and also built strong ties with many notable Irish monks of the period, visiting Ireland and writing to various Irish monasteries. He is credited with composing *De Excidio Britanniae*, a work deeply critical of the secular rulers and clerics of the British Isles, in around 540. He blamed them for their lack of moral fibre, claiming that this was responsible for the success of the Anglo-Saxons' supremacy.

Gildas is thought to have gone to live for a time on the island of Flat Holm in the Bristol Channel, though he spent his latter years in Brittany. Breton tradition says he settled on the island of Houat, then at St-Gildas-de-Rhuys around 536, where he founded a religious community of note. One legend has it that he encountered the devil when he arrived here, disguised as a terrifying serpent. The saintly man made the serpent swallow a ball of wool in which he had hidden a needle. The needle perforated the serpent's intestine and the triumphant Gildas attached the agonized creature to his horse and dragged it to the sea to drown.

neglect, at the Revolution a Lorient property speculator took large quantities of stone away from the château to sell on to builders, hence the much-damaged building you now see. The *département* of the Morbihan bought the château ruins in 1965 and has been slowly mending them. The heavily restored apartments give an indication of the sumptousness of Breton ducal life in the Middle Ages. The medieval flooring display stands out, with its richly varied patterns of tiles that lay hidden for centuries just outside the castle walls. They originally decorated a chapel, destroyed around 1350.

A little way inland, the old stone **Manoir de Kerguet** may have been the château commander's home. It now contains the **Musée Régional des Petits Commerces et des Métiers** (*open July and Aug daily 10–12 and 2–7, Sept–June Mon–Sat 2–7*), run by a compulsive collector who has crammed it with displays of traditional items, from *coiffes* and clogs to old school desks.

The Atlantic pounds the long stretches of beach at Suscinio and Penvins. The Presqu'île de Rhuys officially comes to an end at **Le Tour-du-Parc**, where the area's former salt pans have been turned into a mass of modern oyster farms. On the eastern side of the Penerf river, the six-kilometre stretch of sandy beach along the bay of **Damgan** is appealing, despite the uninspiring housing that forms the backdrop.

Around the Vilaine Estuary

The beautiful section of the Vilaine valley from Rennes to Redon is described in the Ille-et-Vilaine chapter, but the river ends in style in the Morbihan. Don't miss the fine riverside village of La Roche-Bernard. Several other charming tourist sights lie close by. Beyond Tréhiguier, the Morbihan coast comes to a dramatic end with the golden cliffs of Pénestin.

North of the Vilaine's Mouth

The **Pointe de Penn Lann** just south of Billiers marks the northern entrance to the beautiful Vilaine estuary, often referred to as La Vilaine Maritime. There's a lighthouse at the headland, while a little port nestles in the northern tip of the point.

Slightly inland, close to Muzillac and by the emerald-green waters of a lovely lake, the **Etang de Pen-Mur**, you will find the **Moulin de Pen-Mur** (*open daily in holiday season 10–12.30 and 2–6.30; otherwise Sat, Sun and public and school hols, call* **t** *02 97 41 43 79 for times*), a restored old watermill. The three *papetiers* here use cloth to make paper, and on the half-hour guided tour they show you how.

The **Zooparc de Branféré** (*open daily May–Aug 10–7.30, April and Sept 10–6.30, Oct, Nov and Feb–April 2–5.30*) is clearly marked from Le Guerno, to the northeast of Muzillac. The lovely lawns running down from the 19th-century manor house are often covered with scores of hopping maras, hare-like creatures that originated in Patogonia and have slightly marsupial manners. The Buddhist creator of Branféré, Paul Jourde, and his wife, Hélène, were passionate zoological collectors, and Hélène, a well-known painter, featured many of their animals on her atmospheric canvases. The Fondation de France has run and developed this highly regarded zoo along the lines of its creators since they died. It has 2,000 animals in its 60 hectares, plus a children's farm.

South of the Vilaine's Mouth

The **Barrage d'Arzal** is a funky modern dam across the Vilaine estuary, behind which lies a large **yachting harbour**. The best way to appreciate the beauty of the Vilaine valley east of the dam is to take a cruise up it. In the dam itself, you can go down to an **observation room** with a glass wall that allows you to see fish migrating up- or downstream according to the season.

The area of Pénestin is associated with *la mytiliculture*, and the comical lighthouse at **Tréhiguier** has been turned into a bright little **museum** (*open daily July and Aug 10.30–12.30 and 3–6, Easter weekend and June and Sept 3–6*) explaining this cultivation of mussels, as well as cockles – the Vilaine estuary is in fact the largest site for cockles in France. There are clear explanatory panels in English and French. The place can even help you sort out your netted dogwhelks from your piddocks, should you be having problems with them.

The dramatic **Pénestin peninsula beach** is backed by impressively high cliffs, not made of rock but of hardened, ochre-coloured sand, eroded into an arc by the elements. At sunset, the cliffs light up a lustrous golden colour, and you can well understand how the place got its nickname of *La Mine d'Or*, 'the Gold Mine'.

Up the Vilaine to La Roche-Bernard

Tucked out of sight of the N165 rushing past high over the Vilaine, La Roche-Bernard's narrow streets tumble prettily down very steep hillsides to the river. Up in the flatter part of the village, a number of good restaurants congregate around the series of adjoining little squares with their atmospheric façades.

Tourist Information

Pays d'Accueil Touristique de Vilaine,
Place de la République, 35600 Redon,
t 02 99 72 72 11. For general information
on this area.
Muzillac: Place de l'Hôtel de Ville,
t 02 97 41 53 04, ot-pays-de-muzillac@
worldonline.fr.
Questembert: 15 Rue des Halles,
t 02 97 26 56 00, www.questembert.com.
Pénestin: Allée du Grand Pré, B.P. 7,
t 02 99 90 37 74, www.penestin.com.
La Roche-Bernard: 41 Place du Docteur Cornudet,
t 02 99 90 67 98.

Market Days

Muzillac: Friday.
Questembert: Monday.
Pénestin: Wednesday and Sunday.
La Roche-Bernard: Thursday.

Where to Stay and Eat

Billiers ✉ 56190

★★★★Domaine de Rochevilaine,
Pointe de Penn Lann, t 02 97 41 61 61,
www.domainederochevilaine.com
(expensive–luxury). A very exclusive hotel
with a swimming pool and well-tended
gardens, on a Breton headland that it has
bagged all to itself. You can enjoy splendid
seafood dishes in the dining room with its
panoramic views.

Questembert ✉ 56230

★★★★Le Bretagne, 13 Rue St-Michel,
t 02 97 26 11 12, www.paineaulebretagne.com
(very expensive–luxury). A hotel that is
outrageous in every way – in the extravagant
décor behind the sober ivy-covered front, in
the superlative food, and in the prices.

Tréhiguier

La Visnonia, t 02 99 90 31 58 (moderate–
expensive). A place named after the ancient
word for the Vilaine, with a simple bar for
local fishermen and a lively restaurant
overlooking the quayside by the river
mouth. Come here to taste good, simple
fresh seafood, proffered in generous
quantities. Crêpes are also served.
Closed Sun eve and Mon.

Pénestin ✉ 56760

★★★Hôtel Loscolo, Pointe de Loscolo, around
3km south of Pénestin, t 02 99 90 31 90
(moderate). Practical modern rooms with
views onto a wildish section of the Pénestin
coast and direct access to a beach. The food
is good. Closed Nov–April.

The **Maison des Basses-Fosses**, containing the **Musée de la Vilaine Maritime** (open
daily mid-June–mid-Sept 10.30–12.30 and 2.30–6.30; rest of year call t 02 99 90 83 37),
demonstrates the dramatic geography of the village. From the upper entrance the
place seems like an elegant, low 16th-century house, but look at it from down by the
river and you'll realize its back descends five floors to the water. The stormy history of
La Roche-Bernard is retold inside. Going by the evidence of the name, a Viking founded
a settlement here during the 10th-century raids – the Viking term Bern-Hart means
'strong as a bear'. Since then, several castles built for the early medieval lords of La
Roche-Bernard have been destroyed. In the Breton War of Succession, the local baron
backed the losing side and lost his house. Subsequent barons of La Roche-Bernard then
moved to the splendid Château de la Bretesche, built in the 14th century near Missillac,
some way southeast of the village. From 1558, La Roche-Bernard became one of the
most important enclaves of the Huguenots in ultra-Catholic Brittany.

Due to its protected location along the deep Vilaine river, ideal for shipbuilding, the
place developed a major construction yard in the Ancien Régime, and built the first
three-deck French ship, *La Couronne*, ready for service in 1638. In 1644, the queen of

Relais International de la Jeunesse, by the Plage de la Mine d'Or, **t** 02 99 90 30 22, *www.fuaj.org* (*inexpensive*). A delightful youth hostel situated in a thatched house by the beach.

La Roche-Bernard ✉ 56130

★★★Auberge Bretonne, 2 Place Du Guesclin, **t** 02 99 90 60 28, *jacques.thorel@ wanadoo.fr* (*moderate–expensive*).
An inn in the upper village, with attractive rooms and the reputation for containing one of the best restaurants in Brittany, with a stupendous wine list. *Closed Thurs and lunch Mon, Tues and Fri.*
★★Auberge des Deux Magots, 1 Place du Bouffay, **t** 02 99 90 60 75 (*inexpensive–moderate*).
A place in the upper village, distinguished by the two sculpted monkeys emerging from its walls. The rooms are comfortable in the old-fashioned French manner, as is the popular dining room.
Le P'tit Marin, Quai de la Douane, **t** 02 99 90 79 41 (*moderate–expensive*).
A crêperie-cum-*moulerie* down by the river, with an extensive menu of creative crêpe dishes of a good standard.
Les Copains d'à Bord, moored alongside Quai Saint Antoine (*inexpensive*).
A boat-restaurant offering ordinary food in a friendly setting.

Crêperie Madame Gatin, 14 Rue de la Saulnerie, **t** 02 99 90 63 60 (*inexpensive*).
An atmospheric crêperie in an historic house in the upper village. *Closed Mon eve–Thurs exc school hols.*

Around La Roche-Bernard ✉ 56130

There are a couple of recommended addresses just to the east of La Roche-Bernard, off the D34:
★★★Domaine de Bodeuc just north of Izernac, **t** 02 99 90 89 63, *www.hotelbodeuc.com* (*expensive*). A smart 19th-century country home set in its own lovely garden, offering a high degree of comfort. There's a heated swimming pool and a billiards table.
★★★Manoir du Rodoir, near Nivillac, **t** 02 99 90 82 68 (*moderate*).
Accommodation in an old converted ironworks surrounded by woods.

Théhillac ✉ 56130

Brossiers' B&B, St Michel, Route de Sévérac, east along the Vilaine valley towards Redon, **t** 02 99 90 24 16 (*inexpensive*). An option well worth seeking out, owned by keen Breton dancers – Madame might even get out her accordion to play a few songs. The rooms in this almost bright-orange schist house are very comfortable. *Table d'hôte* dinners are available by arrangement.

England, Catholic Henrietta-Maria, daughter of King Henri IV of France and wife of Charles I of England, came briefly to the Maison des Basses-Fosses, having fled the civil war across the Channel. But much of this beautifully presented museum focuses on the life of the ordinary people of La Roche-Bernard and especially on traditional types of fishing along the Vilaine, with models, nets and ephemera. Particular attention is also paid to the bridges built here since the 19th century in order to span the wide chasm of the Vilaine valley. Local customs are evoked in the collections under the eaves.

Central Morbihan Around Josselin

This section takes you into the Morbihan countryside to the northeast of Vannes, around Josselin, one of the grandest little inland towns of southern Brittany. The castle was once the main seat of power of the mighty Breton Rohan family; its enormous walls rise like a sheer cliff from the Oust river. Josselin is also a boating town, as the Oust here doubles as the Canal de Nantes à Brest.

The Domaine de Kerguéhennec and its Centre d'Art Contemporain

Open Mon–Sat mid-June–mid-Sept 10–7, mid-Sept–mid-June 10–6.

The wonderful contemporary art centre at the Château de Kerguéhennec lies some 10 kilometres to the east of Locminé, which is itself almost 30 kilometres north up the D767 from Vannes. Brittany, a region that thrives on tradition, is not generally thought of as making many concessions to contemporary art. Here, though, the directors have gone for an uncompromising display placed defiantly in that traditional image of French Ancien Régime conservatism – an 18th-century château designed by Olivier Delourme. The château itself is a well-ordered classical piece of architecture. You can go in search of the permanent collection of discreetly or not so discreetly outrageous sculptures scattered around the park. You can pick up a little map at the entrance to the grounds detailing their locations. The château and its stables are used for temporary exhibitions of provocative new art, while a further outbuilding has been converted into a very fashionable and extremely comfortable café-cum-library.

Around Kerguéhennec

Some 10 kilometres north of Kerguéhennec, by the rather messy public lake at Réguiny, stands a curious war museum, the **Musée Les Sanglots Longs** (*open May–Sept daily 10–7; rest of year Wed–Mon 2–6*), which recalls the importance of the wireless during the Second World War and for the French Résistance. The museum's curious name recalls the coded message that announced the imminence of D-Day, 'Les sanglots longs des violons d'automne blessent mon coeur d'une langeur monotone', the first verse of Paul Verlaine's beautiful, melancholy poem *Chanson d'Automne*.

Tourist Information

Locminé: 30 Rue du Général de Gaulle, summer t 02 97 60 09 90, otherwise t 02 97 60 00 37.
Josselin: Place de la Congrégation, t 02 97 22 36 43.

Market Days

Locminé: Thursday.
Josselin: Saturday.

Where to Stay and Eat

Josselin ✉ 56120

The bed and breakfast options in this town are a better bet than the hotels.

Other eating options to the ones listed below include a large number of crêperies in the centre of town.

**Hôtel de France, Place Notre-Dame, t 02 97 22 23 06 (*inexpensive*). The best hotel, on a delightful little square in the centre of town, with quite comfortable rooms and a restaurant serving traditional fare (*moderate–inexpensive*).

La Carrière, 8 Rue de la Carrière, t 02 97 22 22 62 (*inexpensive*). A refined townhouse not far from the château, with a pretty garden. The bedrooms have charm and the reception rooms are elegant.

Le Manoir du Val aux Houx, 2km south of Josselin towards St-Servant, t 02 97 22 24 32 (*inexpensive*). A typical 17th-century Breton manor done up by the owner.

M. & Mme Eschech, 61 Rue Glatinier, t 02 97 73 94 72 (*inexpensive*). A good-value B&B.

Café de France, central square (*inexpensive*). A brasserie with daily-changing menus offering the likes of cod mash gratin with fried bread.

Guéhenno lies along the D778, about 10 kilometres east of Kerguéhennec and some 10 kilometres southeast of Josselin. The small attraction of this sleepy village is the 16th-century **Guéhenno calvary**, which is unique in the Morbihan region.

Josselin

One of the sturdiest castles in Brittany, built on a solid outcrop of rock, dominates the river Oust at Josselin. This is one of the rare great feudal Breton châteaux to still be owned by descendants of a great feudal Breton family, the Rohans. The town is also associated with Olivier IV de Clisson, one of the most power-hungry, violent and successful lords in Brittany in the Middle Ages.

History

The early medieval story starts with Guéthenoc, lord of Porhoët, the area in which Josselin lies. He was supposedly attracted to this site above the Oust in AD 1000 by a statue of a Virgin found in the brambles here. His son was named Josselin, and would give his name to the new settlement. The lords of Porhoët continued to rule Josselin until they sided against Henri Plantagenet of Anjou, alias King Henry II of England, who in 1168 destroyed much of Josselin and its castle.

The area round Josselin became a major battle zone in the Breton War of Succession. In 1351 the fort was commanded by Jean de Beaumanoir, supporter of Charles de Blois, who was backed by the French monarch. At neighbouring Ploërmel, the De Montfortist Bretons were supported by English troops under Robert Bemborough, or Bembro. On 26 March, Beaumanoir successfully took on Bembro, halfway between Josselin and Ploërmel, in an epic chivalric clash that took the form of a select battle between the 30 best knights from the opposing sides. The famed 14th-century chronicler Froissart gave a highly memorable if made-up account of the spectacularly violent encounter.

In the medieval period of incessant warring between French and English royals, the Breton dukes would often switch allegiance according to their best interests. The lords at Josselin would, by contrast, most often remain loyal to the French king. One man who become lord of Josselin in 1370 did, however, change sides, notoriously. Olivier IV de Clisson, from a noble family whose lands lay just south of the Loire, was brought up at the English court – his father had been killed by order of the French king. Nursing this grievance, when Olivier returned to Brittany in the course of the Breton War of Succession he took the side of the English-backed Jean de Montfort. A brilliant military man, Olivier helped win the battle of Auray for De Montfort in 1364 (*see* p.385), enabling Jean de Montfort to become Duke Jean IV of Brittany.

But Olivier was an opportunist; he soon saw what he could gain from serving the French and switched sides. By 1380, he would even succeed the famed Bertrand Du Guesclin as Connétable de France. Olivier, who had bought the lordships of Josselin and neighbouring Ploërmel in 1370, proceeded to challenge the ducal power of Jean IV. In this time, he had Josselin mightily fortified on the outside, erecting 13 towers along the castle's ramparts, only a few of which remain standing today.

Olivier de Clisson had taken Marguerite de Rohan as his second wife. He died in 1407 and his great estates were left to his daughter Béatrice, who had been married to Alain VIII de Rohan, allowing the Rohans to become lords of Josselin – a position they had held in the past. Peace between the lords of Josselin and the dukes of Brittany would be shortlived, as Alain IX's son Jean II de Rohan married into the ducal line and fought for power with his brother-in-law, soon to become Duke François II de Bretagne. Jean II de Rohan had to flee to the French court for a while, while Duke François II had a part of Josselin castle brought down in 1488. Time was fast running out, though, for the dukes of Brittany. François II died and his daughter, the young Anne de Bretagne, succeeded him. The French king Charles VIII imposed his authority in Brittany and took Anne as his bride. Jean II de Rohan played an important part in brokering this crucial wedding, which has been viewed ever since as fateful in the history of Brittany. Jean II was granted all manner of privileges; it enabled him to finance the lavish new decoration of the inner façade of the château.

Later, in the course of the French Wars of Religion during the second half of the 16th century, the Rohans famously supported the Reformation and the Château de Josselin became a Protestant stronghold. In the course of the first half of the next century, the centralizing, Catholicizing state imposed its will under Cardinal Richelieu's instructions. The Josselin castle keep was brought tumbling down, as were most of the outer towers. For the remainder of the Ancien Régime, life for the Rohan lords centred around the French court in the Ile de France.

Château de Josselin

Open July and Aug daily 10–6; June and Sept daily 2–6; April, May and Oct Wed, Sat, Sun and school hols 2–6.

The formidable walls and three of the many towers built for Olivier de Clisson rise almost sheer from the river bank. By contrast, approaching the castle from the town side, it is hard to get any sense of the extent of the fortifications. The chapel to one side of the gateway scarcely hints at the major military building beyond; it is actually devoted to seasonal art exhibitions.

Through the gateway, you are greeted by a fabulous riot of decoration on the inner façade. Late Gothic adornment was often exuberant, but this is late Gothic gone wild. How much of it is entirely original is hard to say, but the variety of motifs is staggering. Symbolism runs all over the building, along the roof balustrade, with its lozenges (a device adopted by the Rohans), its stylized ermine tails paying homage to the duchy, and its capital 'A's recognizing Anne de Bretagne. Coats of arms decorate the dormers, while monstrous dragons and beasts carved in stone rush round the masonry.

The tour inside is quite short, covering five extravagantly decorated rooms along the main floor. The craftsmanship, from floor to ceiling, is a fine example of revivalist art. Some elaborate portraits and pieces of furniture also stand out. The late-19th-century stables were converted by the present duchess into a **Musée de la Poupée** (you can visit this separately from the castle, but if you buy a joint ticket it makes each visit cheaper), with an extensive collection of antique dolls.

The Church of Our Lady of the Bramble Patch

An effigy of the Virgin Mary said to have been 'miraculously' found in a bramble patch led to the creation of this church around 1000 AD. Beasts adorn the church of **Notre-Dame du Roncier** (Our Lady of the Bramble Patch) as well as the château; they include a pair of rabbits being chased down the façade by a pair of dogs above the main west entrance, and a crude, hairy-bodied gargoyle, which sticks out obscenely from one side of the façade.

Although the look of the church is late Gothic, the building actually consists of an amalgam of pieces from different periods. In fact, the belltower and the soaring steeple date from as recently as the early 20th century. You can climb the church tower to get fine views onto the town. On the right-hand side of the choir, the 14th-century Chapelle Ste-Marguerite was built to hold the tomb of Olivier de Clisson and his second wife. To the left, the Chapelle Notre-Dame-du-Roncier has many features that recall the story of the discovery of the miraculous statue of the Virgin. Three children who suffered from a condition referred to as 'barking epilepsy' were said to have been cured here in 1728. Since that time, the Josselin *pardon*, which takes place on 8 September every year, has drawn many epileptics and their families in search of a miracle.

From Josselin Down the Oust to Redon

The Oust river runs down from Josselin to Redon, where it joins up with the Vilaine. It doubles as the Canal de Nantes à Brest for this particular stretch, and several delightful historic small towns and villages stand on or near the river banks. St-Marcel may be less attractive, but it has a fascinating museum on Brittany and the Second World War.

Lizio

Lizio, a village of solid old granite houses located approximately 20 kilometres to the south of Josselin, has gained a bit of a reputation for its prettiness. The **Ecomusée de la Ferme et des Vieux Métiers** that is based here recalls the traditional trades of the past with its vast collection of objects. At the **Musée Merveilleux d'un Poète Ferrailleur** eccentricity reigns, including in an amusing collection of mechanical scenes constructed from scrap objects. The modern **Insectarium** (*open April–Sept Mon–Fri 10–12.30 and 1.30–6.30, Sat and Sun 1.30–6.30; Oct–March daily 1.30–6.30*) catalogues the lives and loves of insects and is a good option for children.

An unmissable event of the Lizio summer calendar is the **Festival des Artisans d'Art** held in the second week of August each year. The village streets are given up to the exhibitions and stalls of more than 150 artisans and artists. At lunch and dinner, there is a communal feast; the highlight of the festival is the free *bal populaire*. In the neighbourhood, the Manoir de Guermahia produces seriously good Breton beer, or *cervoise*.

Tourist Information

Pays Touristique de l'Oust à Brocéliande,
   Centre d'Activités de Ronsouze,
   56800 Ploërmel, t 02 97 73 33 33.
Malestroit: 17 Place du Bouffay, t 02 97 75 14 57
   www.malestroit.com.
Rochefort-en-Terre: Place des Halles,
   t 02 97 43 33 57 (summer),
   t 02 97 43 32 81 (winter),
   ot.rochefortenterre@wanadoo.fr
La Gacilly: Le Bout du Pont, t 02 99 08 21 75.

Market Days

Malestroit: Thursday.
Rochefort-en-Terre: Saturday in July
   and August.
La Gacilly: Saturday.

Where to Stay and Eat

Malestroit ✉ 56140

Le Canotier, Place du Docteur Queinnec,
   t 02 97 75 08 69 (moderate). The best
   place in town to eat, offering a variety of
   good-quality regional dishes. Closed Sun eve
   and Mon.
Crêperie La Riveraine, 35 Faubourg de la
   Madeleine, t 02 97 75 22 22 (inexpensive).
   A decent and well-run budget option that
   lies close to the ruins of the 12th-century
   church of La Madeleine.

Rochefort-en-Terre ✉ 56220

Château de Talhouët, outside Rochefort
   (head briefly north towards Pleucadeuc
   then west for Talhouët), t 02 97 43 34 72,
   www.chateaudetalhouet.com
   (expensive–very expensive). A stunning
   manor-sized château surrounded by
   greenery, with extremely comfortable
   rooms and luxurious bathrooms. Dinner is
   available if reserved in advance.
Hôtel Le Pelican, Place des Halles,
   t 02 97 43 38 48 (inexpensive). A small logis
   set in 16th- and 18th-century buildings.
Hôtel-Restaurant à la Bonne Table à Molac,
   3 Place de l'Eglise, t 02 97 45 71 88
   (inexpensive). An old coaching inn that is
   much appreciated locally for its food
   (inexpensive–moderate). Closed Fri and Sun
   eves in winter.

St-Martin-sur-Oust ✉ 56200

Auberge du Château de Castellan, a couple of
   km outside the village (signposted), t 02 99
   91 51 69, www.chateaudecastellan.com
   (inexpensive–moderate). A handful of light,
   spacious B&B rooms set in the grounds of a
   grand 18th-century building. Table d'hôte
   meals are available.

La Gacilly

★★Hôtel de France, 15 Rue Montauban, t 02 99
   08 11 15, www.hoteldefrancelagacilly.com
   (inexpensive). A reasonable option.

Malestroit

Returning to the Oust, continue downstream to Malestroit, which is a favourite
stop among those cruising along the Canal de Nantes à Brest. The heart of the place
somehow lacks soul, although it was once home to three different religious orders,
and in medieval times it had the distinction of being capital of one of the nine
baronies of Brittany. In fact, in the Breton Wars of Religion an important treaty was
signed here. The town celebrated its millennium in 1987.

The church of **St-Gilles** remains very much the centrepiece of Malestroit. It was
built in a curious mix of a dried-blood-red blocks and light stone that looks as
though it may have been shipped up from the Loire. A few vestiges of the original
12th-century structure have survived on the choir end, and above the main porch
entrance, the Romanesque-looking symbols of the evangelists stand out, notably the
bull (representing Luke's gospel) with its sharp horns, and the lion (representing
Mark's), with a man appearing to put his hand into the beast's mouth.

Off the church square, the **Place du Bouffay** and several of the houses here carry charming carved figures, including an animal playing bagpipes and a pig spinning. A little museum recalls the importance of inland navigation in these parts.

Some way northeast of Malestroit at **Monteneuf** (along the D776 to Guer), the fine array of megaliths of **Les Pierres Droites** is one of the most important of inland Brittany.

St-Marcel Musée de la Résistance

Open 15 June–15 Sept daily 10–7; rest of year Wed–Mon 10–12 and 2–6.

This is a complex, moving museum on the Second World War, set a few kilometres west of Malestroit. Once you've penetrated into the dark, bunker-like rooms you fast become engrossed in the mass of detail and pain accumulated here. It would take a whole morning to do any justice to this museum. The best way to begin is by watching the film, which expains the importance of this location in the Second World War, with interesting accompanying footage. Basically, the area was very well suited for parachute expeditions by the Allies and the French Resistance, with places to land and woods in which to hide men and weapons. Already in 1943, it was used for one landing, but the more important battle fought here in 1944 is recalled in great detail.

Rochefort-en-Terre

The re-cobbled streets have added even more of an historical feel to this utterly beautiful old village steeped in Breton history. But in summer you'll probably find the tourists as numerous as the cobblestones, and packed as close together.

History of the Rocheforts and the Château

The first lord of Rochefort goes back to the start of the 12th century, when his territories seem to have been split off from the massive Elven lordship of Argoët. The first castle was built on a spur of rock that overlooks what was once a significant trade route, and that was possibly settled by much older civilizations. It looks down over the Gueuzon valley and across to the Landes de Lanvaux, a great length of rocky moorland that stretches east–west across much of central Morbihan.

Below the castle a community developed, and a priory was founded on the family wealth. But the Rochefort lords would by no means limit themselves to local issues. In the 14th century, Thébaud III de Rochefort gained the fief of Ancenis by the Loire through marriage, and became a *chevalier banneret* in the king of France's service. He died in 1374 and left an heiress who married Jean II de Rieux, who took on the name of Rochefort so that the family became the Rieux-Rocheforts. The family grew increasingly powerful in Breton politics and French affairs, playing a major role in the Hundred Years War.

Jean IV de Rieux-Rochefort probably eclipses all the family in terms of his importance. He was appointed tutor to the young Duchess Anne de Bretagne by her father François II de Bretagne shortly before the duke passed away in 1488. Jean IV had fought alongside the duke against King Charles VIII of France at the battle of St-Aubin-du-Cormier earlier in that year, in a defeat that spelled the end of Breton ducal autonomy. Though Charles VIII had Jean IV's properties destroyed, including the castles of Rochefort-en-Terre, Rieux and Elven, Jean IV later received the sum of 100,000 gold *écus* from the French Crown for his part in organizing Anne de Bretagne's marriage to Charles VIII, leaving him the money needed to reconstruct his castles.

Jean IV's granddaughter Claude married into the great Huguenot family of the Colignys. During the bitter, mad French Wars of Religion, the Catholic side burned down the castle. Descendants of François de Coligny, who was the brother of a famous Protestant admiral, held on to Rochefort-en-Terre, until they sold it off in 1658 to Vincent Exupère de Larlan, the president of the Breton Parlement and a counsellor to King Louis XIV. The Larlans rebuilt a castle here, and their wealth overflowed into the village below. At the Revolution, the family fled, and the castle was eventually destroyed by the Revolutionary government because it was a symbol of the old order.

After this, deprived of the influence of any mighty, lordly family, Rochefort-en-Terre lost much of its prosperity. But the village pulled through thanks to its sheer beauty. A colony of artists came and fell in love with the place at the end of the 19th century, decorating the doors of Anastasie Lecadre's inn very prettily, as you can see in the museum by the castle. An American artist, Alfred Klots, arrived at the start of the 20th century; he liked the place so much he bought what remained of the château and built a fantasy home comprised of sections of fine old houses collected from around the region. The composite reconstruction is extremely well done and the château has now been sold to the *département* of the Morbihan.

The Castle and Museum

Open July and Aug daily 10–6.30; June and Sept daily 2–6.30; April and May Sat, Sun and public hols 2–7.

Having climbed the village slope, you penetrate the old **château** fortifications by the former gateway and enter an utterly enchanting courtyard. Only the 14th-century well is an original feature, though. The few rooms you can visit in the château have been described as being in the 'Americano-Hispanic-Italiano-Breton' style... The rooms in the **museum** by the side of the castle have been more carefully and thematically arranged. Temporary art exhibitions are held here, but at all times you can see the painted panels taken from Anastasie Lecadre's hotel and other works of the school of painters who came to Rochefort-en-Terre. Further rooms are devoted to typical Breton furnishings and Breton *coiffes*.

The Village and the Church of Notre-Dame de la Tronchaye

Down in the village of Rochefort-en-Terre, the **church of Notre-Dame de la Tronchaye**, rather than being a focal point as you might expect, was placed to one side, down a slope. You have to approach this grand church via its north façade, which is built of granite as well as the local schist. During the Viking invasions, so the story goes, a statue of the Virgin was concealed in a tree trunk (hence the name 'Tronchaye') in order to save it from destruction. Its secret location was only rediscovered by a shepherdess a couple of hundred years later. To celebrate the find, it was decided to build the church on the same spot. This 12th-century edifice was subsequently added to.

Among the carvings that you will see around the Flamboyant Gothic tracery windows along the church's north façade, look out for what appears to be a lumberjack trying to carry home a whole tree trunk. Inside, across the nave's ceiling, the stringbeams have been carved with creatures and men, as well as family coats of arms. The finest statue here, the black-stained figure of the Virgin, heavily robed, can be found on the gallery at the west end; it was originally part of a rood screen. To one side, the multicoloured sheep in the stained-glass window, representing the scene of the shepherdess' discovery of the statue, rather steal the show.

The main attraction for visitors to Rochefort-en-Terre is the **principal village street**, which is packed with craft shops, and the picturesque Place du Puits. If you've always wanted an engraved bellows, this is the certainly the place to come, as one boutique sells nothing else. Amidst all the quaint beauty, look out for a rude gargoyle of a man bearing his bottom at passers-by.

A short way south of Rochefort-en-Terre, outside **Malansac**, the **Parc de Préhistoire de Bretagne** (*open April–Oct*) attracts visitors with impressively sized models of dinosaurs but also covers human evolution in Brittany.

La Gacilly

The village of La Gacilly is about 20 kilometres northeast of Rochefort-en-Terre along the D777 road, passing via St-Martin-sur-Oust. The place doesn't have the same beauty as Rochefort-en-Terre, it's true, but it is prettily situated on the slopes of the Aff, a tributary of the Oust. Yves Rocher, the Breton cosmetics magnate, hails from here. He apparently built the foundations of his glamorous empire on haemorrhoid cream, made according to a recipe that was handed down to him by his grandmother. You can visit the **Yves Rocher cosmetics factory** at the bottom of the village.

Above the factory, the old houses have been taken over by a **craftspeople**, encouraged to settle here over the course of the last 30 years or so. You can usually watch several of them at work on any given day, with the most popular probably being the blacksmith and the costume makers of Claymore. The latter are a couple who create all kinds of extravagant historical costumes, so if you've ever yearned for a Viking helmet, a Celtic cape or a chain-mail suit, you can order them here.

Not so long ago, a joint project between Yves Rocher and the Muséum National d'Histoire Naturelle brought the the the **Végétarium**, or museum of the vegetable, to the village (*open Feb, March and 21 Oct–31 Dec Sat and Sun 2–6; April–11 June and 12 Sept–15 Oct and school hols Tues–Sun 2–6; 12 June–10 Sept daily 10.30–7*). Way better than it sounds and a good bet for kids, it consists of an enjoyable exploration of the world of plants.

You can also go on a pleasant cruise on the Aff from La Gacilly to view the **Marais de Glénac**, a marshland around the Aff to the south, with reedy expanses looking on to the rocks opposite.

Further south, a few kilometres from Redon, the area around **L'Ile aux Pies** counts as one of the prettiest spots along the whole Oust valley.

Loire Atlantique

11

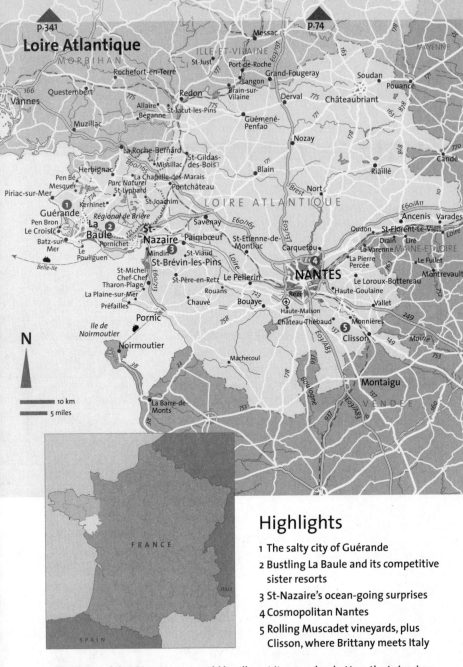

Highlights

1 The salty city of Guérande

2 Bustling La Baule and its competitive sister resorts

3 St-Nazaire's ocean-going surprises

4 Cosmopolitan Nantes

5 Rolling Muscadet vineyards, plus Clisson, where Brittany meets Italy

The name of the *département* could hardly put it more clearly. Here the Loire river finally reaches the Atlantic, after its 1,000-kilometre journey from southeastern France. The massive tidal estuary of this, France's greatest river, stretches some 50 kilometres and more from Nantes to St-Nazaire, the latter with its great serpent of a bridge spanning the enormous river mouth.

Nantes should count as by far the largest Breton city, being one of the largest towns in France. But in administrative fact, Nantes and the Loire Atlantique no longer form part of Brittany. In a stroke of questionable regional reorganization in the 1960s, this southern section of Brittany was shifted into the Pays de la Loire region. Although many Nantais may feel indifferent to questions of regional identity – the town is large enough to feel self-confident and independent – many other inhabitants of the Loire Atlantique do retain a sense of belonging to Brittany, particularly those north of the Loire. However, most of the Loire Atlantique was never traditionally a Breton-speaking area. The Dark Ages immigration from Britain appears to have left few marks on the area, certainly to go by the few Breton place names in the *département*. This chapter focuses on the most Breton areas of the *département*.

Before the Act of Union that formally joined Brittany to France in 1532, Nantes did serve for a long time as capital of the fiercely independent duchy of Brittany in the late Middle Ages. The massive Château des Ducs de Bretagne still stands in the city, while the cathedral contains the tomb of the last Breton duke. After the union, Nantes emerged as the capital of the French slave trade.

Old châteaux and château ruins across the Loire Atlantique still recall the Breton frontiers of medieval times. West of St-Nazaire, the granite ramparts of Guérande stand guard above the coastal salt pans. East of Nantes along the Loire, Ancenis served as one of Brittany's frontier towns next to Anjou. So too did Châteaubriant to the north of Ancenis, and Clisson to the south of it.

The magnificent Loire estuary divides the *département* in two. The look changes from north to south of the river. To the north, the architecture reflects the Breton allegiances, with typical whitewashed, granite or schist houses. This northern Loire Atlantique is very quietly rural, with plentiful rivers and woods. As you reach the Loire river, suddenly features associated with southern France start to emerge. Orange-tiled roofs begin to replace the slate ones, and vines appear.

Moving to the Loire Atlantique coast, along the stretch north of the Loire, you still feel strongly in Brittany, with a string of pretty port resorts around Guérande. But the most popular of all the Loire Atlantique's resorts, La Baule, doesn't look in the least Breton, with cloned blocks of apartments looking on to the massive beach. Two strongly contrasting marshes lie either side of Guérande and La Baule. To the west, the salty white Marais Salants are supplied by ocean waters. To the east, the waterways running through the black peat bogs of the Brière were traditionally replenished by the flood waters of the Loire. The Brière is Brittany's second regional natural park after the Parc d'Armorique in the Finistère. The Loire Atlantique's coast south of the Loire feels much less Breton than the coast to the north of the great river mouth, though Pornic, with its rocky coves and megaliths, might be considered a last outpost of Brittany.

Tourist Information

Comité Départemental du Tourisme de Loire Atlantique,

2 Allée Baco, BP 20502,
44001 Nantes, Cedex 1,
t 02 51 72 95 30, *www.cdt44.com*.

Northern Loire Atlantique

The band of land running across the northern Loire Atlantique is one of the least touristy parts of Brittany. It has a pretty, rural tranquillity. Rivers, lakes, patches of forest and undulating fields lead to provincial Châteaubriant, significant among a chain of defences that marked the eastern frontier of the region in medieval times.

Châteaubriant

To the gastronomic world, the name of this town is synonymous with the finest of steaks. To the French, the name also evokes the country's most famous Romantic writer, François René de Chateaubriand; note the difference in spelling. Actually it was one Brient who gave this place its name. He was a Breton lord called upon to fortify these parts in the 11th century, in the aftermath of Viking incursions. He had a fortress erected on the promontory above the Chère river. This fortress gave way to mighty medieval defences, some of which still stand. A succession of important families held sway at Châteaubriant through the centuries.

The barony came into the hands of the Dinan family later. Françoise de Dinan, who inherited it in the late medieval period, served the young Breton duchess, Anne de Bretagne, as governess. In 1488 the troops of the French king Charles VIII, whom Anne de Bretagne would marry, destroyed much of this Breton frontier town. When Brittany was annexed to the French kingdom by King François I in 1532, Châteaubriant played a small part in the proceedings, the king staying here a while. Jean de Laval, the lord of the castle, had been made governor of Brittany, while his wife, Françoise de Foix, had earlier served as the French king's mistress.

Châteaubriant's Château

Open for guided tours 15 June–15 Sept Mon and Weds–Sat 11, 2.30 and 4.30, Sun 2.30 and 4.30. Free access to park daily April–Sept 7.30–8, Oct–March 7.30–6.

This château, though relatively unknown and with little to show inside its chambers, offers an enchanting confusion of styles, with examples of good and bad building. Passing under the towering gateway, you enter the outer courtyard. In front stands the 13th- to 14th-century keep, still imposing though now too dangerous to visit. Although the Renaissance castle grabs your attention to the right, you are first shown round the substantial ruins of the medieval fortifications. You can walk along a small portion of the ramparts. The area by the medieval chapel is particularly attractive: look out for the variety of colours of the schist stone above the chapel doorway. The great feature of the architectural decoration of this château is the way that beautiful blue schist has been used to pick out architectural details.

Go through to the Renaissance château and you can admire a whole colonnade of blue schist columns. They are of a rare beauty, contrasting with the brick building above them. Jean de Laval had this arcade and the end pavilion with its loggias built in the 1530s. This was relatively soon after Renaissance styles had been brought back

Getting Around

Châteaubriant is at the end of a minor **train** line from Rennes.

For information regarding the meagre **bus** services operating from Châteaubriant, call **t** 02 40 28 10 26.

Tourist Information

Pays Touristique de Châteaubriant et des Marches de Bretagne, 21 Rue Basse, 44110 Châteaubriant, **t** 02 40 81 40 82. **Châteaubriant**: 22 Rue du Couéré, **t** 02 40 28 20 90, *www.tourisme-chateaubriant.fr.st*.

Market Days

Châteaubriant: Wednesday morning.

Where to Stay and Eat

Châteaubriant ✉ 44110

You'll find some old-fashioned French establishments in this rural town.

★★★Hostellerie de la Ferrière, Route de Nantes, **t** 02 40 28 00 28 (*moderate*). The most exclusive accommodation in these parts, situated out in the countryside 2km to the south of Châteaubriant off the D178 road. It's a charming, mid-sized château, dating from the 18th and 19th centuries.

★★★Auberge Bretonne, 23 Place de la Motte, **t** 02 40 81 03 05 (*inexpensive–moderate*). The smarter-looking of the hotels in town, with some modern touches. Its restaurant battles it out with Le Poêlon d'Or (*see below*) to produce the finest Châteaubriant steak in town.

★★★Hôtel Le Châteaubriant, 30 Rue du 11 Novembre, **t** 02 40 28 14 14 (*inexpensive*). A hotel built entirely in local schist, with a practical courtyard-cum-car park in front and old-style, eccentric rooms, some with a bit of charm and the odd comic touch. The front rooms look out on to an attractive shop selling *articles funéraires*!

La Boissière B&B, Soudan, **t** 02 40 28 60 00 (*inexpensive*). An ideal starting point for walks, set deep in the forest to the east of Châteaubriant. A sound night's sleep is guaranteed in its shuttered cottage rooms, and there are family rooms, a swimming pool, a television room, and other facilities, plus carefully prepared meals available by advance reservation.

Le Poêlon d'Or, 30 bis Rue du 11 Novembre, **t** 02 40 81 43 33 (*moderate–expensive*). The restaurant next to Le Châteaubriant hotel, slightly cluttered and with fussy décor, but serving elaborate and refined cuisine. The Châteaubriant special is richly dressed *en croûte* and in foie gras. Or try the 'catch of the day' with herbs and fresh pasta. *Closed Mon and Sun eves and 2–3 weeks Aug.*

Au Vieux Castel, 25 Rue Pasteur, **t** 02 40 81 12 51 (*inexpensive–moderate*). Another good place in which to sample the luxurious Châteaubriant local steak, a straightforward restaurant with a terrace.

Le Bilig, opposite St-Nicholas church, **t** 02 40 81 48 49 (*moderate*). Excellent crêpes. *Closed Mon and Sun eves.*

from Italy to France. But this work is not so much pure Renaissance architecture as poor Renaissance. While Jean de Laval may have wished to be fashionable, his masons weren't up to the task. Look out for details where they got the symmetry, so vital to the harmony of Renaissance architecture, slightly wrong.

The other Renaissance wing is less eccentric, with *lucarnes* (dormer windows) typical of Loire châteaux. Blue schist again adds greatly to the decorative effects. Further lovely blue columns contrast with the Loire-white stone as you take the staircase up to the exhibition hall, done up for temporary, often contemporary, art shows. You can wander round a few more rooms. Blue schist provides the material for the noble-looking fireplaces. The library is signalled by the frescoed frieze of books around its walls, and a separate staircase leads to the so-called room of Françoise de Foix, an early-17th-century extravaganza of a suite, restored to its original beautiful vulgarity.

The Coast from La Vilaine to La Baule

This is major Breton beach-tourist territory.

From Pen Bé to Pen Bron

The most northerly stretch of the Loire Atlantique's coast is known above all for its oysters. Go to the headland of **Pen Bé** for a first taste of the Loire Atlantique's shores and seafood. This marks the northern entrance to the Mès estuary, clogged with oyster beds and saltpans as it heads inland. Another excellent place to see how oysters are treated and sold is the *port ostréicole* of **Kercabellec**, opposite Pen Bé.

Once you've rounded the spit of land that protects the southern entrance to the Mès estuary, you come to the popular resort of **Quimiac**, its stretches of beaches packed out in summer. The spectacular coast road to Piriac-sur-Mer passes just above a series of small cliffs and creeks where more intrepid families go scrambling down the sides of the low sharp black rocks in search of precious private corners of sand.

Piriac-sur-Mer has the feel of a traditional Breton port and resort. The Phoenicians are supposed to have come trading here way before the Romans arrived in Gaul. Close to the Pointe du Castelli, from which sea views open out, the 6th-century Breton chief Waroc'h may have built one of his most southerly fortifications. In the 19th century, writers such as Flaubert, Zola and Daudet discovered the port. **La Turballe**, a short distance south along the rugged coast road, is grittier, with a large working harbour. The port took off in the 19th century, tinned sardines its speciality. It has grown into the largest fishing port in the Loire Atlantique and one of the biggest in Brittany. Climb on to the roof of the large, ugly fishmarket to visit the **Maison de la Pêche**.

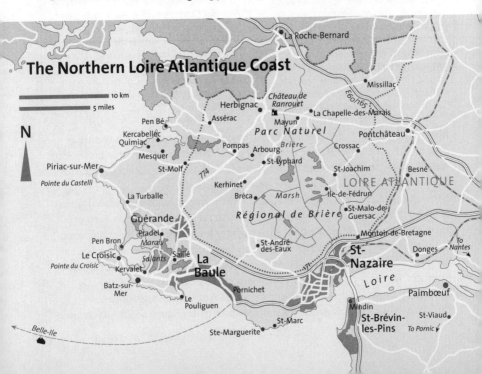

The Northern Loire Atlantique Coast

Tourist Information

St-Molf: Rue du Pays Blanc,
t 02 40 62 58 99, *tourisme.st.molf@ wanadoo.fr*.

Mesquer-Quimiac: Avenue de la Plage,
t 02 40 42 64 37, *www.mesquer-quimiac.fr*.

Piriac-sur-Mer: 7 Rue des Cap-Horniers,
t 02 40 23 51 42, *www.piriac.net*.

La Turballe: Place du Général de Gaulle,
t 02 40 23 32 01, *http://otsi.la.turballe.free.fr*.

Guérande: 1 Place du Marché aux Bois,
t 02 40 24 96 71, *www.guerande.fr*.

La Baule: 8 Place de la Victoire,
t 02 40 24 34 44, *www.labaule.fr*.

Pornichet: 3 Boulevard de la République,
t 02 40 61 33 33, *www.pornichet.org*.

Le Pouliguen: Port Sterwitz, t 02 40 42 31 05,
www.lepouliguen.fr.

Batz-sur-Mer: 25 Rue de la Plage,
02 40 23 92 36, *www.mairie-batzsurmer.fr*.

Le Croisic: Place du 18 Juin 1940,
t 02 40 23 00 70, *www.ot-lecroisic.com*.

Market Days

St-Molf: Sun in July and Aug.
Mesquer-Quimiac: large Tue and Fri markets
  between 15 June and 15 Sept.
Piriac-sur-Mer: Mon, Wed and Sat
  15 June–15 Sept; rest of year Tue
  morning only.
La Turballe: fishmarket generally Mon–Sat.
Guérande: Wed am and Sat am, plus Sun at
  Pradel in July and Aug.
La Baule: a superb covered market every
  morning April–Sept, plus various other
  markets held on Mon, Tue, Thur and
  Sat mornings.
Pornichet: fishmarket generally Mon–Sat,
  plus Wed and Sat morning markets.
Le Pouliguen: large markets Tue, Fri and Sun.
Batz-sur-Mer: Mon am year round,
  plus Fri am in summer.
Le Croisic: Thur and Sat mornings in the
  covered market, plus Tues am and local
  produce market Fri am in July and Aug.

Where to Stay and Eat

Mesquer ✉ 44420
Clos de Botelo, 249 Rue des Cap Horniers,
t 02 40 42 50 20 (*inexpensive*). A pleasant
B&B looking out over the Mesquer marshes.

Piriac-sur-Mer ✉ 44420
**La Poste, in the centre of the old harbour,
t 02 40 23 50 90 (*inexpensive*). A sweet,
nicely located option. *Closed Dec–March*
Hôtel de la Pointe, 1 Quai de Verdun, t 02 40 23
50 04 (*inexpensive*). A basic hotel overlooking
the port. Half-board is required in July and Aug.

La Turballe ✉ 44420
Manoir des Quatres Saisons, 744 Boulevard
de Lauvernac, on the D333 (in the direction
of Piriac), t 02 40 11 76 16 (*inexpensive–
moderate*). An old Breton manor with a
swimming pool.
Terminus, 18 Quai St-Paul, t 02 40 23 30 29
(*moderate*). A pleasant seafood bistrot.
Closed Sun eve and Mon.

Guérande ✉ 44350
There's a plethora of crêperies and cafés
catering for the tourist hordes.
B&B Le Tricot, 8 Rue du Tricot, t 02 40 24 90 72
(*moderate*). A château offering 2 large and
'untouched' rooms to guests in summer,
with a serene courtyard.
**Les Remparts, 14–15 Boulevard du Nord,
t 02 40 24 90 69 (*inexpensive*). Comfortable,
traditional rooms and good food
(*moderate–expensive*).
**Roc Maria, 1 Rue des Halles, t 02 40 24 90 51
(*inexpensive*). A charming old house, with a
crêperie attached.
**Les Voyageurs, Place du 8 Mai, t 02 40 24 90
13 (*inexpensive*). A reliable, traditional French
hotel with a restaurant (*moderate*).
La Collégiale, 63 Faubourg Bizienne, t 02 40 24
97 29 (*moderate–expensive*). A rather OTT if
well-reputed restaurant.

A long stretch of beach known as **La Grande Falaise** reaches down to the headland
of **Pen Bron**. Windsurfers congregate in large numbers here, while the unspoilt
southern end attracts nudists. The long spit of land of Pen Bron protects the salt
marshes of Guérande behind.

La Baule ✉ 44500

Budget accommodation doesn't really exist here (the cheapest hotels are by the railway station, less than 1km from the beach), but there are lots of smart hotels.

★★★★Hermitage, 5 Esplanade Lucien Barrière, t 02 40 11 46 46, *www.lucienbarriere.com* (*luxury*). An enormous, impeccable hotel with more than 200 rooms – what the French call a 'palace'. **Les Evens** is its more luxurious restaurant, with extremely inventive cuisine; the **Eden Beach** is cheaper, more relaxed and more popular with customers from outside the hotel. There's also a casino, a heated seawater swimming pool, beauty treatments and gym facilities.

★★★★Castel Marie-Louise, 1 Avenue Andrieu, t 02 40 11 48 38, *www.castel-marie-louise.com* (*very expensive–luxury*). A neo-Gothic mansion with a large garden in the heart of La Baule. The rooms are extraordinarily comfortable. The restaurant (*expensive*) giving on to the garden offers cuisine full of interesting touches, and you can take cookery courses here in low season. There's a tennis court in the grounds.

★★★★Royal Thalasso, 6 Avenue Pierre Loti, t 02 40 11 48 48, *www.lucienbarriere.com* (*very expensive–luxury*). A major luxury hotel, with a luxury seawater treatment centre attached. The cuisine (*expensive*) is luxurious.

★★★Majestic, 14 Esplanade Lucien Barrière, t 02 40 60 24 86, *hotel-le-majestic@wanadoo.fr* (*very expensive–luxury*). Luminous modern rooms with excellent sea views.

★★★Le St-Christophe, Place Notre-Dame, t 02 40 62 40 00, *www.stchristophe.com* (*very expensive–luxury*). Three family villas joined to form a very comfortable hotel with a relaxed family feel, providing a good example of the town's early-20th-century architecture. The food (*moderate*) is good and the dining room stylish, with a charming host. The seafront is about 100m away.

★★★Bellevue Plage, 27 Boulevard de l'Océan, t 02 40 60 28 55, *www.hotel-bellevue-plage.fr* (*expensive*). One of the grander sea-view 3-stars, with a good reputation locally.

★★★La Concorde, 1 bis Avenue de la Concorde, t 02 40 60 23 09, *www.hotel-la-concorde. com* (*moderate–expensive*). A hotel looking out on to the La Baule beach, with comfy rooms and a garden but no restaurant.

★★Hôtel Marini, 22 Avenue G Clemenceau, t 02 40 60 23 29, *www.lemarinihotel.com* (*inexpensive–moderate*). Rooms with sea views.

★★La Palmeraie, 7 Allée des Cormorans, t 02 40 60 24 41, *www.hotel-lapalmeraie-labaule. com* (*inexpensive–moderate*). A hotel with a lovely flower garden shaded by pines.

★★Hôtel Riviera, 16 Avenue des Lilas, t 02 40 60 28 97, *www.hotel-riviera.com* (*inexpensive–moderate*). A tranquilly located choice towards Le Pouliguen, with some rooms with sea views.

Hostellerie du Bois, 65 Avenue Lajarrige, t 02 40 60 24 78, *www.hostellerie-du-bois. com* (*inexpensive–moderate*). A place steps from the beach, with a garden full of flowers and souvenirs of southeast Asia. *Closed Dec–mid-March*.

★★Le Lutétia and the **Rossini Restaurant**, 13 Avenue des Evens, t 02 40 60 25 81 (*inexpensive*). Among the best 2-stars in town, smart and set on one of the chic streets behind the beach. It has an elegant and highly regarded restaurant serving refined cooking (*moderate–expensive*).

Ferme du Grand Clos, 52 Avenue du Maréchal de Lattre de Tassigny, t 02 40 60 03 30 (*expensive*). A high-priced crêperie with a good reputation. (There are cheaper alternatives.) *Closed Tues and Wed Sept–June*.

La Marcanderie, 5 Avenue d'Agen, t 02 40 24 03 12 (*moderate–expensive*). The best-known seafood place in town, with pretty décor. You need to book ahead for 4 or more people.

Le Maréchal, 277 Avenue du Maréchal de Lattre de Tassigny, t 02 40 24 51 14 (*moderate–expensive*). A rustic-looking place serving good seafood. *Closed Sun eve, Mon lunch and Wed Sept–June*.

Guérande

The name Guérande derives from the Breton language: it means 'White Land'. Salt was long a precious commodity, particularly vital for preserving food in the times before the refrigerator. Guérande's wealth in the Middle Ages was largely built on the

Pornichet ✉ 44380

****Sud Bretagne**, 42 Boulevard de la République, t 02 40 11 65 00, www. hotelsudbretagne.com (expensive–very expensive). A romantic choice situated in an old villa and run by the same family since 1920. The place has two swimming pools, one of them covered and heated, and a restaurant (moderate).

**Le Régent, 150 Boulevard des Océanides, t 02 40 61 05 68, www.le-regent.fr (moderate). The best of the cheaper seafront options, with a pleasant terrace.

**Villa Flornoy, 7 Avenue Flornoy, t 02 40 11 60 00, www.villa-flornoy.com (moderate). A comfortable choice close to the beach.

**Normandy, 120 Avenue de Mazy, t 02 40 61 03 08 (inexpensive–moderate). A hotel in a shining timbered building in the heart of town. Closed Oct–Jan.

Le Bistrot du Pêcheur, Boulevard de la République, t 02 40 61 25 30 (moderate). Recommended by readers.

Le Sunset Beach, 138 Boulevard des Océanides, t 02 40 61 29 29 (moderate). An haute cuisine restaurant with a good reputation. Closed Thurs.

Le Bidule, 122 Avenue de Mazy, t 02 40 61 03 54 (inexpensive). A wine bar that has retained some of its 1930s character. Closed Sun eve and Mon low season.

Le Pouliguen ✉ 44510

Le Garde Côte, 1 Jetée du Port, t 02 40 42 31 20 (moderate). A dining room on the beach, done out like a boat and offering an unbeatable view on to the port and the bay of La Baule.

Batz-sur-Mer ✉ 44740

L'Atlantide, in the little bay of Port St-Michel, t 02 40 23 92 20 (moderate–expensive). The restaurant with the best reputation for seafood dishes in the area. The dining room has excellent views.

L'Ecume de Mer, Route de la Grande Côte, t 02 40 23 91 40 (moderate–expensive). Sensational sea views to accompany fresh seafood. Closed Sun eve, Mon and Tues Sept–June.

Fleur de Sel, in Kervalet village, t 02 40 23 90 73 (inexpensive). One of the best crêperies in the area, where you can also enjoy kig ha farz, a Breton meat stew.

Le Temps Perdu, t 02 40 23 81 64 (inexpensive). A crêperie in typical Breton style. Closed Sun and Thurs eves, and Mon Sept–June.

Le Croisic ✉ 44490

***L'Océan, Port Lin, t 02 40 62 90 03 (moderate–expensive). A hotel superbly located above the ocean, with charming rooms and an excellent seafood restaurant, with sea bass in Guérande sea salt among the specialities.

**Le Castel Moor, Avenue du Castouillet, t 02 40 23 24 18, www.castel-moor.com (inexpensive–moderate). A good mid-budget option.

Pluche's, 43 Rue de la Ville d'Ys, t 02 40 23 12 30 (inexpensive). B&B rooms in a typical modern Breton home, with sea views.

La Bouillabaisse, 12 Quai de la Petite Chambre, t 02 40 23 06 74 (moderate–expensive). A good seafood option.

Le Bot, 6 Rue de la Marine (inexpensive). A very Breton, very popular place where the crêpes are made in front of you.

Le Transat, 4 Quai du Port Ciguet, t 02 40 15 75 60 (inexpensive). Good Breton seafood and galettes. Closed Wed Sept–June.

St-Marc-sur-Mer ✉ 44600

***La Plage, 37 Rue du Commandant Charcot, t 02 40 91 99 01, www.hotel-de-la-plage-44.com (moderate–expensive). A film star of a little hotel – it featured in one of the most famous comedies in French cinema, Jacques Tati's Les Vacances de Monsieur Hulot. The restaurant serves local seafood dishes, and has a terrace for summer dining, and there's also a relaxing bar. Closed Jan.

precious white crystals, and the place maintained a thriving port at the foot of its slopes through the medieval period to export its salt. Solid granite ramparts surround Guérande's wealthy streets with their fine granite houses. This was clearly a Breton town of some importance, especially before Brittany's union with France.

When a separate Breton state was created in the mid 9th century, the town very briefly became home to a bishopric, Bishop Gislard backed by the Breton chief Nomenoë in opposition to the Frankish bishop of Nantes. After the Vikings had spread terror in the region, a Romanesque church was built in town, vestiges of which remain in the Collégiale St-Aubin, the impressive main church situated in the centre of town. Inevitably Guérande was fought over by opposing sides during the 14th-century Breton War of Succession. The inhabitants lent their support to Jean de Montfort, backed by the English, but early in the conflict the enemy came and pillaged the place, massacring many. By the treaty of 1381, Jean IV of Brittany's position as duke was recognized by the French monarchy. Guérande could celebrate in 1386 when the duke decided to get married to Jeanne de Navarre at the church of Saillé just outside town.

Subsequent dukes had the fortifications adapted to the warfare of the 15th century, and the ramparts with the four gateways and 11 towers you can still see today date mainly from that period. The collegiate church was also enlarged in fashionable Flamboyant Gothic style.

Guérande's Culinary Saltpans

The seawater that enters the Guérande marshes is carefully regulated by a system of canals and gates. The salt harvest goes on through the summer. When the time is right, the gates are opened to allow the water into the *vasières*, the pools that supply the *salines*, the network of smaller pools. In the *vasières*, some of the water evaporates and the salt settles. The salt water can then go through an intermediary set of pools, the *corbiers*, before heading down the extremely gentle slopes to the *salines* themselves. These *salines* are divided up into three kinds of pools. The water goes through the *fares*, then the *adernes*, then into the *oeillets*. Slate divides regulate the flow. More and more water evaporates at each stage. The wind and the sun help in this process of creating increasingly saline waters. It is in the *oeillets*, rectangular basins around seven by ten metres, that the salt is farmed.

The salt farmers are known as *paludiers*. They use special implements to harvest two types of salt, going about their business barefoot. Around 100 of them still work in the saltpans. Of the two types of salt they gather, the *fleur de sel* is much the finer. This salt collects in crystals on the surface of the pools. How much can be harvested depends on how clement the weather is. These surface crystals are skimmed off the top of the salt pools with a special implement known as a *lousse*. The *fleur de sel* has a particularly sparkling white colour, as it never enters into contact with the murkier bottom of the salt pools. It is especially rich in magnesium and other elements. The crystals of the *gros sel* settle on the bottom of the pools.

The salt, once gathered, is piled high on the banks of the pools and left to drain overnight on small round patches of land known as *ladures*. Then it is transported by wheelbarrow to the *trémets*, the sides of the *salines*, where it is left in pyramids before being taken to the *salorges*, the salt houses. Here it is dried and stocked for a year, then sieved and sorted before it goes on sale. The farmers do not use any chemical treatments or add anything; all Guérande salt is regarded as particularly pure.

Guérande's port began to silt up more and more. In the centuries that followed, the harbours at Le Croisic and Le Pouliguen grew at Guérande's expense. However, the grand townhouses from the 17th and 18th centuries show that Guérande merchants knew how to defend their interests. Salt continued to bring prosperity until the Revolution. The place fared less well in the 19th century, increasingly isolated, bypassed by industrialization along the Loire estuary.

The most impressive entrance into town is the **Porte St-Michel**, built in the second half of the 15th century. It looks more like a portion of castle than a mere gateway, and it did serve as home to the town governors in centuries past. It is now the town **museum** (*open daily April–Sept 10–12.30 and 2.30–7, Oct 10–12 and 2–6*). The various displays are devoted to local history and different local themes. Pieces of typical old Guérande furniture, painted in ox-blood red, stand out, as do the the mannequins dressed in local costumes, and the flowers made from shells. You can walk out on to a portion of the ramparts from here.

The streets of Guérande are packed with craft shops, gift shops and restaurants. In summer you have to fight your way through the tourist hordes to reach the **Collégiale St-Aubin**. This sombre mix of Gothic and Romanesque architecture turns out to have been heavily restored in the 19th century. Inside, the column capitals teem with Romanesque carvings. Much of the stained glass with its amazing blue backgrounds dates from the 19th century. Among the many fine pieces of art inside the church, the tomb effigy of Tristan Carné and his wife are quite remarkable. The man served as *maître d'hôtel* to Anne de Bretagne and her second royal husband, Louis XII. The magnificence of Carné's tomb proves his was no lowly post at the time, but one of the most privileged positions at court. Excellent organ concerts are held in the church.

The Marais Salants or Pays Blanc

The dour landscape of the salt marshes below Guérande and the eccentric geometry of the saltpans are worth exploring. The Marais Salants of Guérande-Batz and the Mès estuary combined cover some 1,700 hectares. The inland sea that supplies the Guérande and Batz marshes is known as Le Traict. The mounds of salt piled high on the sides of the saltpans make quite a sight. And in the holiday season, many salt farmers leave bags of Guérande salt outside their homes for visitors to buy.

The best way to appreciate the salt marshes and the work of its *paludiers* is to go on a guided walking tour. These are run from **La Maison du Sel** at **Pradel** (*open daily 10–1 and 3–7; daily guided walking tours 15 June–15 Sept at 10.30, 3.30 and 5.30*). At this Maison you will also find an exhibition on the flora and fauna of the Marais Salants. The **Maison du Paludier** at Saillé offers similar small attractions.

La Baule, Pornichet and Le Pouliguen

Charming kitsch and nine kilometres of unbroken fine sand count among the attractions of **La Baule**, one of Brittany's most upmarket, popular and busy resorts. When you first arrive on the **waterfront** of the splendid south-facing sandy bay, the row of countless postwar apartment blocks disappearing round into the distance makes quite an impression.

You don't come to La Baule for history or museums. In fact, the place seems to be a museum-free zone. In the 19th century, property developers planted a large number of pines to keep the dunes in place along this coast. After that, the way was open to build a resort. By the 1920s, La Baule had an international reputation as one of France's grand seaside towns. The splendid station from the 1930s, renovated in 1990 with the arrival of the TGV, is a listed historic building. The luxury sea treatment market finds an easy home here; there are now three thalassotherapy centres in the Baie de la Baule alone.

Head inland to see some of the earlier **La Baule villas**. Fantasy reigns. Set behind neat fences and hedges, deeply shaded by pines, these holiday homes were built in a variety of mock styles, not all in the best possible taste. Normandy beamed houses, Basque-type chalets, modern thatched homes, the odd Arabic folly and many other styles vie with each other for your attention. L'Allée Cavalière is one of the best streets along which to admire La Baule's pre-war architecture; the name of this street derives from the narrow horse track going down the centre of the road. The **Parc des Dryades** public gardens at the eastern end are very well tended, full of flowers and rare trees.

Pornichet is the loud easterly extension of La Baule with its own thalassotherapy centre, casino and railway station to match. Head east and things quieten down at more traditional **Ste-Marguerite** and **St-Marc**, around which the coast becomes rockier. The latter little resort was made famous by Jacques Tati's classic film, *Les Vacances de Monsieur Hulot*. A beautifully shot film, *Presque Rien*, directed by Sébastien Lifschitz in 1999, presents another memorable view of this stretch of coast. It depicts what turns out to be much more than an ordinary holiday romance; instead, it's an extremely sensitive, thought-provoking young gay love story.

To the west of La Baule, **Le Pouliguen** stands slightly aloof, a more old-fashioned resort. It too has a marina, while its fishing port has been revived. The old village has kept some of its winding fishermen's lanes.

Le Croisic Peninsula and Batz-sur-Mer

In summer this peninsula is blighted by traffic; the rocky south coast road unfortunately counts as a favourite drive for holidaymakers from La Baule. This **Côte Sauvage** is bordered by small cliffs that diminish in size as you head west. Breton legend ascribes the grottoes along here to the Breton fairies, the *korrigans*.

Batz-sur-Mer, straddling the peninsula, has an old Breton feel to it with its cluster of whitewashed houses. Apparently, Breton continued to be spoken here up until the last century, and you can still buy Breton clogs at the Maison du Sabot. The church that dominates the centre of town is dedicated to a revered Breton saint of the Dark Ages, St Guénolé (*see* p.283). Climb the narrowing stairs to the top of the steeple and you can get the most magnificent views on to the Guérande-Batz salt marshes and the whole of the Le Croisic peninsula. The **Batz Musée des Marais Salants** (*open June–Sept and school hols daily 10–12 and 3–7; rest of year Sat and Sun 3–7*) is one of the oldest traditional local museums in France. It was started in 1887 by Adèle Pichon, a nun who was the daughter of a local *paludier* (*see* box p.424), who realized that the old, local ways of life would rapidly disappear with the arrival of tourism in the region.

The **Grand Blockhaus** (*open Wed–Mon April–mid Nov 10–7, school hols and Feb 10–6*), the biggest German bunker in Hitler's Atlantic Wall, at 2,000 square metres, was concealed between the villas at Batz-sur-Mer during the war. Today it houses a Second World War museum on the St Nazaire pocket, which was the last area to be liberated in France. Inside you can see dormitories, the weapons room, the radio post and various displays

.The port of **Le Croisic** stands sheltered on the north shore of the peninsula. It looks out across the inland sea of Le Traict to the salt flats of Guérande. Only a narrow channel of water allows the boats into its harbour. Like Batz-sur-Mer, Le Croisic has retained its historic Breton feel. The port has even kept some of its 16th-century buildings. The Flamboyant Gothic granite church of Notre-Dame-de-Pitié was consecrated in 1507. Roughly from that time, the Le Croisic fleet went off to fish for cod and whales off North America. Corsairs also set sail from here. Briefly rechristened Port Liberté during the Revolution, Le Croisic became one of the first successful Breton tourist destinations in the mid 19th century. The old fish auctioning hall from the late 19th century stands on the Place Boston. The modern fish auctioning hall went up on the Mont Lénigo, an artificial hillock built from ballast that the ships left at Le Croisic in times past as they loaded up with salt.

Beyond the port and the seafront restaurants and boutiques, the ultramodern **Océarium** (*open daily July and Aug 10–7, Sept–Dec and Feb–June 10–12 and 2–7*) is the major tourist attraction here. This starfish of an aquarium was set down amid the town's rampant modern suburbs. Its most impressive feature is a transparent-sided tunnel through which visitors can walk, looking at sharks, groupers and rays swimming around them. The southern hemisphere penguins were actually brought here from London Zoo.

The Brière, St-Nazaire and the Loire Estuary

Given that the Brière is the second largest marsh in France after the Camargue, it's no surprise to discover that there aren't many roads through it. The natural park stretches north to south from below La Roche-Bernard on the Vilaine to the outskirts of St-Nazaire on the Loire. From southwest to northwest it extends from outside Guérande up to Missillac. Its marshy heart is crisscrossed by a network of canals (*curées*) linking some of the many lakes (*piardes* or *copis*). St-Joachim, diminutive capital of the Brière, lies roughly in the centre of the marshes, along the only main road through them, the D50.

The Brière is an important natural site, in particular for migrating birds. The whole park covers 40,000 hectares, the marshland at the heart of it some 7,000 hectares, giving the birds plenty of space in which to find a peaceful place to rest in the extensive reed beds. The best way to discover the Brière is definitely in a punt, with a local Briéron guide. There are also various nature trails to follow and local museums that explain more about the Brière and Briéron ways. The Brière has added attraction of the greatest density of thatched houses left standing in France.

Getting Around

St-Nazaire has a **railway station**. For **bus** transport around the area from St-Nazaire, call **t** 02 40 11 53 00.

The Brière regional natural park lies within a quadrangle of **roads**: the N165, the D774, the N171 and the D773. There are just 2 main roads that serve the Brière proper: the D47 runs round the western edge of the marshes from Herbignac to St-Nazaire; and the D50 cuts through the centre of the marshes from La Chapelle-des-Marais to Montoir-de-Bretagne, the latter just east of St-Nazaire.

Tourist Information

La Chapelle-des-Marais: 38 Rue de la Brière, **t** 02 40 66 85 01.
Herbignac: Mairie, Place du Général Argence, **t** 02 40 88 90 01.
St-Lyphard: Place de l'Eglise, **t** 02 40 91 41 34, *www.saint-lyphard.com*.
St-André-des-Eaux: 1 ter Rue de la Chapelle, **t** 02 40 91 53 53, *www.standredeseaux.com*.
St-Nazaire: Place François Blancho, **t** 02 40 22 40 65, *www.saint-nazaire-tourisme.com*.

Market Days

Herbignac-Missillac: Wednesday morning.
Kerhinet: late June–early September, all day Thursday
St-Joachim: Saturday morning.
St-Malo-de-Guersac: Thursday morning.
St-Nazaire: Tuesday–Sunday.

Where to Stay and Eat

Herbignac ✉ 44410

Château Coëtcaret, off the D47, 4km south of Herbignac towards St-Lyphard, **t** 02 40 91 41 20, *coetcaret@free.fr* (*moderate*). A smart little 19th-century manor on a large estate of some 200 hectares. Its B&B rooms are calm and comfortable.
M.& Mme Fresne, 12 Rue Jean de Rieux, Marlais, 6km from Herbignac, **t** 02 40 91 40 83, *j.h.fresne@wanadoo.fr* (*inexpensive*). A B&B in a typical *longère*.

Pompas ✉ 44410

La Chaumière des Marrcais, Route de Guérande, **t** 02 40 91 32 36 (*moderate–expensive*). A typical Briéron thatched cottage, with a good reputation for gutsy dishes such as duck with oysters and asparagus. *Closed Mon eve, and Tue Sept–June*.

Missillac ✉ 44780

★★★★**Hôtel de la Bretesche**, **t** 02 51 76 86 96, *www.bretesche.com* (*expensive–luxury*). One of the finest establishments in Brittany, a few km north of the Brière. You arrive to see a Gothic château reflected in a beautiful lake – the hotel occupies the buildings around the castle's former farm courtyard. The rooms have been impeccably done up. **Le Green**, the restaurant (*expensive*), which also counts as one of the finest in the area, looks out on to the lake and the château, while the stable stalls have been converted into a wonderful bar. The grounds behind

History of La Brière

As ever in Brittany, the odd vestige of neolithic civilization remains around the Brière, for example the **Dolmen de la Barbière** at Crossac, or the **Dolmen de Kerbourg** at St-Lyphard. The people of the Brière, the Briérons, have long been independent. As far back as the 15th century, the Breton duke François II granted them the right to exploit the main section of the marshes, the Grande Brière Mottière. It was, exceptionally, declared an indivisible possession of the community. The Briéron independence was only radically altered with the growth of St-Nazaire in the first half of the 20th century. The Brière became increasingly neglected as many of the locals left their subsistence living to go and work in the major shipbuilding yards, and the traditional marshland activities of reed-cutting and peat-extraction quickly dwindled. The regional natural park of the Brière was created in 1970 to try to protect the natural environment.

the castle have been turned into one of the finest golf courses in France. There's also a tennis court and a swimming pool.

St-Lyphard ✉ 44410

★★Hôtel Les Chaumières du Lac, Route d'Herbignac, t 02 40 91 32 32 (*moderate*). A modern cluster of upmarket, purpose-built thatched cottages. The restaurant, **Les Typhas** (*expensive*), serves refined food. *Closed March, Sun eve, and Mon Sept–June.*

Auberge de Kerbourg, t 02 40 61 95 15, (*expensive–very expensive*). Perhaps the most memorable Briéron setting in which to eat. The cuisine is extremely refined and inventive, featuring dishes such as pigs' ears and pistachios, and sometimes uses produce from the beautifully tended garden behind the thatched restaurant. *Closed Tues lunch, Sun eve and Mon.*

Auberge du Nézil, on the D47, t 02 40 91 41 41 (*moderate–expensive*). A modern rendering of the Briéron thatched cottage. The cuisine is in the classic French tradition.

Kerhinet ✉ 44410

★★L'Auberge de Kerhinet, t 02 40 61 91 46 (*inexpensive*). Thatched houses in the most touristy spot of the Brière; if you manage to book one of the 7 rooms you will at least have the possibility of appreciating the village when the tourist hordes have gone home. The place, which has a great deal of atmosphere, serves local food (*moderate*), including eels and frogs' legs. *Closed Tues and Wed.*

Ile de Fédrun ✉ 44720

Auberge du Parc, la Mare aux Oiseaux, t 02 40 88 53 01 (*inexpensive–moderate*). An inn that is well known in the area, with a restaurant (*moderate*) where you can come to enjoy original presentations of classic *produits de terroir*.

Besné ✉ 44160

Les Pierres Blanches B&B , t 02 40 01 32 51 (*inexpensive*). A typically modern Breton house with a well-kept garden, clearly marked from Besné on the eastern edge of the Brière. You'll get a very warm welcome from your hosts. The guest rooms are comfortable if unremarkable.

St-André-des-Eaux ✉ 44117

Auberge du Haut-Marland, t 02 40 01 29 00 (*moderate–expensive*). A place that is renowned for its gourmet cuisine, with a highly picturesque location on the banks of the marshes. *Closed Sun and Thurs eves, and Mon.*

Savernay ✉ 44260

Le Chêne Vert, 10 Place de Hôtel de Ville, t 02 80 56 99 60, *chenevert.savernay@ wanadoo.fr* (*inexpensive*). A hotel-restaurant popular with the locals.

St-Nazaire ✉ 44613

Korali Hotel, Place de la Gare, t 02 50 01 89 89 (*inexpensive–moderate*). A modern hotel where you are guaranteed a warm welcome by the friendly staff.

Northern Brière

If you're arriving in the Brière from the main N165 dual carriageway, take the Missillac exit for a look at the magnificent **Château de la Bretesche**, a castle built for the barons of La Roche-Bernard from the late 14th century, a splendid Gothic vision reflected in its lake. The château is now divided into private flats, but you can pay a small fee to wander round the grounds.

La Chapelle-des-Marais, southwest of Missillac, brings you to the Brière proper. Its tourist office is the main one serving the park. The **Maison des Traditions** (*ask at tourist office for opening times*) presents some of the old professions of the Brière. **Mayun**, just south of La Chapelle-des-Marais, has preserved a fair number of its thatched cottages. The place was long known for its basket-weaving, and a few locals continue the tradition. For families seeking diversion, the **Chaumière des**

Marionnettes (*open April–Oct and school hols Mon–Fri pm; call* **t** *02 40 53 22 40 for times*) is an Aladdin's cave, or cottage, of hand-crafted puppets. They also run workshops, for children and adults, where you can make your own.

The nearby **Miellerie de la Brière** is housed in an interesting interpretation of a futuristic-looking *chaumière*. Here you can get an insight into all aspects of honey and the ecology of bees. West of Mayun, the ruins of the medieval **Château du Ranrouet** still impress.

Western Brière

Off the D51 from Mayun to St-Lyphard, the **Port des Fossés Blancs** is one of the places where you can take a boat out on the waterways of the Brière. The authorities recommend Alexandre David and Christophe Cotté, **t** 06 62 28 50 93 or **t** 06 68 11 84 61. Those of you interested in gardening might like to visit the small **Jardins du Marais** (*open 15 May–15 Sept daily 4–8*), an experimental and ornamental kitchen garden. On the north side of St-Lyphard, off the D47, at the **Port des Prises du Coin**, there is a beautiful area for walking. In **St-Lyphard**, the church tower may not be inspiring architecturally, but you can climb it (for a small fee) to get the best of views down on to the Brière. The prettiest thatched villages in the park lie close to St-Lyphard. **Arbourg**, just west of it, has a typical huddle of lovely Briéron thatched cottages.

A string of absolutely delightful thatched villages lie south of St-Lyphard off the main D47. **Kerhinet** is by far the best known. The park authorities have taken this traditional village under their wing and made it into the main showcase of the Brière. Cars are banned, craftspeople encouraged, and flowerpots proliferate. The **Musée du Chaume** (*open 8 April–Sept daily 2–6*) explains the principal features of the traditional Briéron home (*chaume* means thatch in French.) Nearby, you'll find the **Brasserie de la Brière** (*open daily 9–12 and 2–7; closed Sun in low season*), where you get the chance to taste, and buy, some fine 'local' beers – blonde, amber, white and organic – brewed in massive copper vats.

To the east of Kerhinet, **Bréca** is another Brière port from which you can take a punt out on the waterways. Nicolas Legal, **t** 02 40 91 48 09, Yannick Thual, **t** 02 40 91 32 02, and Claudette Deniaud, **t** 02 40 91 33 97, have all signed the park charter. As well as organizing punt outings, they can also all offer alternative trips in horse-drawn carriages. Nicolas Legal can arrange English guided tours in the tourist season.

St-André-des-Eaux lies in the southwestern corner of the park. Duck enthusiasts should head east out of St-André for **Ker Anas**, the 'duck village' (*open daily July and Aug 10–7, April–June and Sept 2.30–5.30; for other times of year, call* **t** *02 40 01 27 48*). You can follow the kilometre-long nature trail around various lakes where some 90 different species from around the world live.

Southeastern Brière

The real heart of the Brière marsh is the group of semi-islands around **St-Joachim** north of St-Nazaire. **Ile de Fédrun** is where the tourist action is concentrated. It is an excellent place to go on a guided punt trip out on the Brière waterways. The people recommended by the park authorities are Gisèle Aoustin, **t** 02 40 91 61 28, and

Philippe Garoux, **t** 02 40 88 41 81. Frédéric Guillou, **t** 02 40 91 66 53, has not signed the charter but is also recommended. **La Maison de la Mariée** (*open April–Sept Tue–Sun 9–12 and 2–7*) recalls the local 19th-century tradition of making false orange-blossom crowns for French brides.

Rozé, just south of St-Joachim, was once one of the most important traditional ports in the Brière. Here you will find **La Maison de l'Eclusier** (*open daily 8 April–8 May and June–Sept 10.30–1 and 2.30–6.30*), a former lock-keeper's house done up by the park authorities. The displays present the geology and history of the Brière and include models of the traditional Briéron boats. The place also introduces the natural life of the Brière, most notably in the form of a video on the local flora and fauna. But often a better way to appreciate the last is by going to the **Parc Animalier** (*open daily April–Sept 9–6; guided tours July and Aug at 10, 3 and 5, June and Sept at 10 and 3*) to see the natural environment of the Brière for yourself.

St-Nazaire

Hard-hit by war bombs, hard-hit by the decline of shipbuilding in western Europe, traditionally hard-hit by guidebooks, St-Nazaire does in fact have plenty of character. And it has cleverly turned its attentions to tourism in recent years. Its famed shipbuilding yards were developed from the 1860s on, at first in association with the Scottish company of John Scott. Penhoët, in the east of town, was chosen as the site for the shipyards. The vessel *L'Impératrice Eugénie* was the first to be built there, during the French Second Empire. St-Nazaire became one of the major European ports to operate transatlantic services. Many people sailed off from here to seek a new life in the Americas. During the First World War, thousands of North American soldiers arrived here before being sent out to the front.

The supposedly glorious shipbuilding period came between the two world wars. The most famous of France's massive ocean liners were built here, the *Paris*, the *Ile-de-France*, the *Champlain* and, most impressive of the lot, the misleadingly named *Normandie*, launched in 1932. But this was also a time of major world economic recession. The shipyard workers suffered terribly from the cyclical nature of their work, and in 1933 went on an important hunger march to Nantes.

Notoriously, when the Nazis occupied France, they turned St-Nazaire into one of their most important submarine bases. St-Nazaire was also the only French Atlantic port large enough to take German battleships. The town became a crucial target for the British air force to wipe out. Operation Chariot in 1942 wrought much damage, with 600 British commandoes on HMS *Cambelltown* wrecking the docks, closing it to German battleships. There is a monument to them on Boulevard Verdun. Several of the major St-Nazaire ocean liners were destroyed in the war. While most of France was liberated in the summer of 1944, St-Nazaire was one of the pockets of territory that the Nazis defended right through to May 1945. By then, the town lay in ruins. It was rapidly reconstructed along a grid plan in the 1950s, and naval and aeronautical construction took off again.

Escal' Atlantic

Open July and Aug daily 9.30–7.30, nocturnal visits Tues and Sat;
April–June, Sept and Oct daily 9.30–12.30 and 1.30–6;
Feb, March, Nov and Dec Wed–Sun 10–12.30 and 2–6.

Inside a massive hangar at the former German submarine base, this 'floating city' is quite unlike most sea museums. Dispensing with the tradition of inhabiting a crabby old authentic vessel, this is an entirely re-created *paquebot* or ocean liner, made with the aid of top architects and theatre set-designers. The project was 17 years in the planning; the appearance of the film *Titanic* around the time of its opening was a pleasing coincidence.

Every conceivable part of a liner is represented, including the hair salon, the emigrants' quarters and the engine room, and everywhere are bits of movie footage (excerpts from the classics of the ocean liner's golden age) on porthole screens. You get a fascinating idea of the cabins of each era, including the 1860s Jules Verne model, complete with *vomitoire*. The set design is at its most impressive inside the bar and dining room.

Your tour should end inside the cinema, where more multimedia japes will have you swaying (forcibly) in your seats. If you're not feeling involved enough, the journey back to the real world requires the donning of a life jacket and a slightly hair-raising proximity to water – you have been warned.

The Ecomusée and the *Espadon* Submarine

Open same hrs as Escal' Atlantic.

The older town museum and submarine make for quite an engrossing visit, too. Outside, a moving sculptural group, *A l'Abolition de l'Esclavage*, which was put up in 1991 by the sculptor J-C. Mayo, recalls the slave trade that brought such wealth to the Loire estuary in the 18th century (*see* p.438) and remembers the importance of the abolition of slavery.

The Ecomusée tells the prehistory and history of St-Nazaire, while the guided tour around the *Espadon* makes for a quite memorable experience. The submarine lies in the water in a heavily fortified concrete lock built by the Nazis in 1943. It was donated to the town in 1986, having served the French navy for 25 years. Built in Le Havre in 1957, the *Espadon* became the first French submarine to cross the North Pole under the ice fields, in 1964. Some 60 sailors lived in it for up to 45 days at a time – just a half-hour visit can make you feel claustrophobic. If you're lucky the guided tour will be given by a man who did his military service on a submarine.

You might consider proceeding to one of the port's 'working' museums (*open summer season and school hols daily, 4–6 visits a day, and low season by reservation; call t 0810 888 444 for reservations and information on all the port's sites*). The **Chantiers de l'Atlantique** offer you the chance to explore the actual construction of the ocean liners by stepping aboard the *Alstom*. More industrial terrain is explored at **Aérospatiale**, essentially a massive aircraft factory, where you can see St-Nazaire's technological industry in action .

From the Centre to the Sea

In the centre of town, a slick **shopping centre** has been built to mimic some of the forms of an ocean liner. You could go in search of the **Place du Dolmen**, too, actually boasting a neolithic menhir and *lech* as well as the table of stone.

West of the centre, St-Nazaire has a long **seafront** that turns its back on the docks and looks out to the ocean. It is an interesting stretch of coast. Along Boulevard Président Wilson, some 19th-century villas survived the bombs. Further west is a string of beaches that are comfortably wide at low tide. Curious *carrelets*, square fishing nets left suspended in the air while not in action, add a picturesque note, as do the lighthouses. Some of the best beaches in Brittany lie just to the west (*see* p.426).

To the south of the Loire estuary, the flat **beaches** are more typical of the Vendéen coast. To reach them you have to cross St-Nazaire's splendid serpent of a bridge, which provides a spectacular ending to the Loire.

Nantes

We would go to the Pommeraye Arcade to buy Chinese shades, Turkish sandals or Nile baskets, to take our time examining all the knick-knacks brought back here from overseas, to touch them with our own hands: the gods, the shoes, the parasols, the lanterns, the splendid, futile, colourful objects that make us dream of other worlds, useless frivolities which we take so seriously.

Gustave Flaubert

The cosmopolitan city that Flaubert conjured up still exists within the postwar urban sprawl of Nantes. Nantes has an ocean feel to it – even if the Atlantic lies some 50 kilometres away, and most of the shipping trade that brought the place such riches in the Ancien Régime moved out towards the sea a long time ago. And despite the destruction of Second World War bombs, large portions of historic Nantes have survived, including the massive castle of the late medieval dukes of Brittany, the medieval cathedral where the last Breton duke was buried, and the grand streets and squares that the young Jules Verne would have known in his childhood.

The centre of Nantes shines brightly now. It's a delightful, vibrant, inspiring place, teeming with students in term time. However, a huge historical shadow casts its darkness over the place. The vast 18th-century wealth of the merchants of Nantes was built on the triangular slave trade. Clusters of ornate 18th-century townhouses are the most obvious legacy. The finest are typically decorated with *mascarons*, appropriately grotesque stylized masks. To date, the slave-trading part of Nantes' past appears to have been almost totally ignored in the town museums, of which there are many. The best ones include the Musée des Beaux-Arts and the Musée Thomas Dobrée. It's somewhat ironic, given the city's forgetfulness about those slaving expeditions, that Nantes is best known in French history for a famous edict of tolerance, signed here by King Henri IV of France in 1598 at the end of the terrible French Wars of Religion.

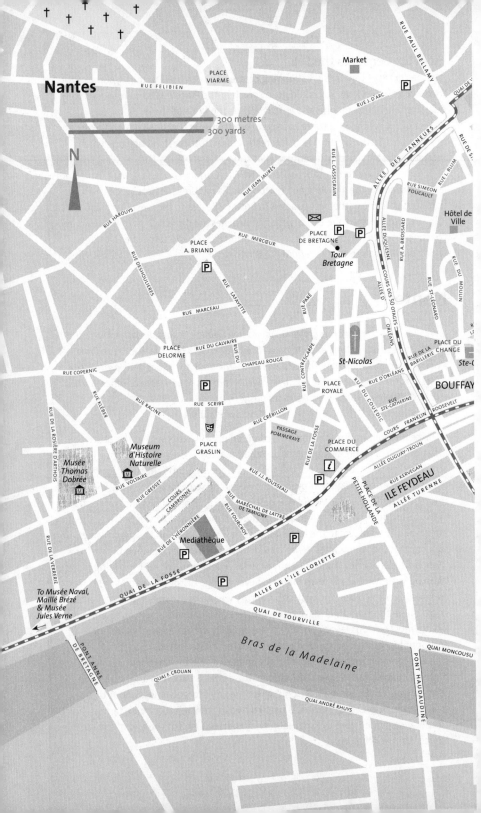

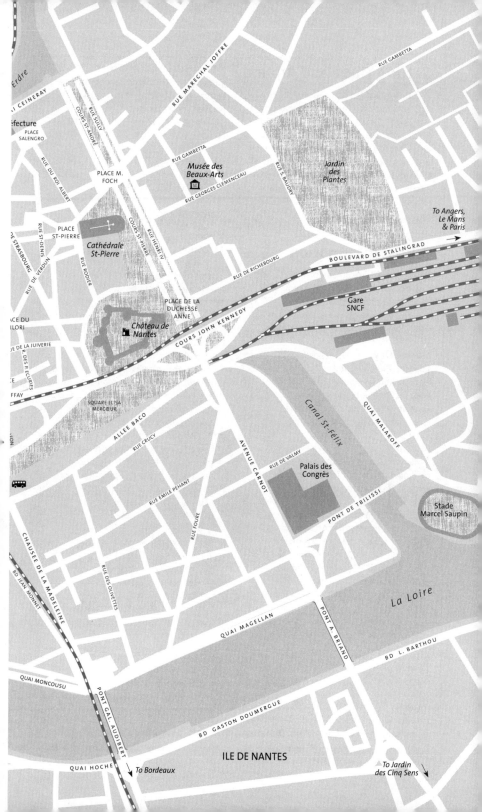

Getting There and Around

Nantes-Atlantique southeast of the city (t 02 40 84 80 00) is an international airport receiving flights from London Gatwick. You can also fly to Nantes from Paris, but the super-fast TGV train is really more convenient as it amazingly takes you from one centre of town to the other in a mere 2hrs.

Tram lines crisscross the centre of town, complementing the bus service (call t 02 40 29 39 39 for information on both).

Tourist Information

Tourist office: Place du Commerce, t 02 40 20 60 00, www.nantes-tourisme.com. Allo Visit Nantes, t 08 92 68 25 11 (code 003-003), gives a guided tour of the city via your mobile phone (15mins).

Market Days

Talensac: Tuesday–Sunday.
Place du Bouffay: Food market Tues–Sun.
Place du Commerce: Flower market, daily.
Place de la Petite Hollande: Saturday.
Place Viarme: Flea market, Saturday.

Festivals

Many of Nantes' festivals have a distinctly cosmopolitan flavour. La Folle Journée, first weekend in February, concentrates on honouring the works of one or a school of composers. There is a big carnival every March. Le Printemps des Arts celebrates Baroque music and dance in venues across the region in April, May and June. The Festival International d'Eté features traditional folk music, dance and theatre from across the globe. It takes place the first week in July. Nantes l'Eté involves a whole programme of free cultural events, concerts and street entertainment throughout July and August.

All manner of boats and jazz musicians gather in Nantes for the Rendez-Vous de l'Erdre, the last weekend in August or first weekend in September.

The Festival des Trois Continents focuses on films from Africa, Asia and South America every November.

Where to Stay

Nantes ✉ 44000

Moderate

***L'Astoria, 11 Rue de Richebourg, t 02 40 74 39 90, hotelastoriananantes@wanadoo.fr. Large rooms reached by the fanciest of staircases behind a pre-war façade.

***L'Hôtel, 6 Rue Henri IV, t 02 40 29 30 31. A modern block right opposite the château, with neat, good-value, comfortable if slightly characterless rooms.

***Hôtel de France, 24 Rue Crébillon, t 02 40 73 57 91. The smartest of the old-style hotels in town, with quite cosy rooms.

***Le Jules Verne, 3 Rue du Couëdic, t 02 40 35 74 50. A member of the reliable Best Western chain, in the heart of Nantes.

***La Pérouse, 3 Allée Duquesne, t 02 40 89 75 00, www.hotel-laperouse.fr. The most exciting hotel in Nantes, built in an ultra-modern style by architects Barto & Barto, with walls at gravity-defying angles. It is well located, close to the main shopping and restaurant quarters.

Inexpensive

**Cholet, 10 Rue Gresset, t 02 40 73 31 04, hotelcholet@wanadoo.fr. Pleasant and good-value rooms close to the theatre.

**Les Colonies, 5 Rue du Chapeau Rouge, t 02 40 48 79 76, www.hoteldescolonies.fr. Quiet rooms close to the central pedestrian area of Nantes.

History

The Gaulish tribe of the Namnetes had a port at the spot where the Erdre river joins the Loire. The Gaulish Pictones seem to have favoured the south bank. Few signs remain of Gallo-Roman Nantes, however. Christianity came early to the place, with its usual tale of cruel martyrdom. Donatien and Rogatien were the children of Aurlien, a Gallo-Roman governor of the town in the late Roman Empire, who converted to the

*Fourcroy, 11 Rue Fourcroy, t 02 40 44 68 00. A basic option in a posh part of town.

*St-Daniel, 4 Rue du Bouffay, off Place du Bouffay, t 02 40 47 41 25. An extremely well-located and good-value hotel for central Nantes.

Auberge de Jeunesse, Cité Universitaire Internationale, 2 Place Manu, t 02 40 20 57 25. The youth hostel, situated north out of the centre. You will need to present your youth hostelling card.

Eating Out

Central Nantes has a much wider choice of restaurants than hotels. In summer, restaurant terraces are built out into the streets, many of them covered with green baize like fake lawns.

Expensive–Very Expensive

L'Atlantide, 16 Quai Ernest-Renaud, at the end of the Quai de la Fosse, t 02 40 73 23 23. Michelin-starred Nantes cuisine from a chef who returned to his roots after inspirational travels. There's a roof-top view over Nantes and the Erdre. *Closed July and Aug Sat lunch and Sun.*

Moderate–Expensive

Auberge du Château, 5 Place de la Duchesse Anne, t 02 40 74 31 85. A warm, intimate little restaurant opposite the massive castle, with classic Nantes food. *Closed 8–23 Aug.*

Le Chiwawa, 17 Rue Voltaire, t 02 40 69 01 65. Cosy dining rooms on a typically elegant Nantes square, plus a summer terrace. The cuisine is inventive. *Closed Sat lunch and Sun.*

L'Esquinade, 7 Rue St-Denis (near the cathedral), t 02 40 48 17 22. Traditional Loire gourmet cuisine, including *menus du marché* and a speciality of sea bass cooked in potato skins. *Closed Sun and Mon.*

Le Galion – Les Boucaniers, 28 Rue Kervégan, t 02 40 47 68 83. Good French food in an atmospheric 18th-century building, with a restaurant in one half and a more informal buffet in the other, the latter serving *rapide* versions of the same food for a fraction of the price. *Closed Sat lunch, and Sun and Mon eves.*

Lou Pescadou, 8 Allée Baco, t 02 40 35 29 50. A very popular place offering tasty fish dishes. Book ahead. *Closed Mon eve, Sat lunch, Sun and 3wks Aug.*

Moderate

Le Carnivore, 7 Allée des Tanneurs, t 02 40 47 87 00. A brasserie for traditional meat lovers, though bison and ostrich meat also feature on the menu.

La Poissonnerie, 4 Rue Léon Maître, t 02 49 47 79 50. A good fish restaurant with a light, nautical look and an aquarium. *Closed Sat lunch, Sun and Mon.*

Inexpensive

La Baguett', 19 Rue Paul Bellamy, t 02 40 48 15 20. Almost a pastiche of a traditional Breton crêperie, near the Talensac market.

Chez l'Huître, 5 Rue des Petites Ecuries, t 02 51 82 02 02. A tiny brasserie with fresh and fast seafood specialities served by an eccentric host. There's a little terrace and humorous blackboard drawings.

La Cigale, 4 Place Graslin, t 02 51 84 94 94. A classic French brasserie that is worth visiting for its extravagant Art Nouveau décor alone, set on one of Nantes' most elegant squares.

Ile Verte, 3 Rue Siméon Foucault, t 02 40 48 01 26. French vegetarian food.

Pommier Laprugne, 3 Allée de l'Ile Gloriette, t 02 40 47 78 08. A crêperie offering some interesting fillings. *Closed Mon and Wed eves, Sat lunch and Sun.*

new faith. Donatien had already been baptized, Rogatien had not, by the time the persecutors hounded them down at the very start of the 4th century. The imprisoned Rogatien is said to have uttered the tender words: 'If my brother, who is baptized, will deign to kiss me, his kiss will serve as a baptism for me.' The two were viciously tortured before having their heads cut off in 304. Christianity soon got the upper hand, however, the bishops of Nantes becoming powerful figures.

During much of the Dark Ages, the county of Nantes was fought over by Franks and Bretons. In Merovingian times, this county formed a part of the Frankish Marches. **Nomenoë**, appointed leader of Brittany by one Frankish king, made his successful bid for Breton independence under another. He conquered Nantes and its territories. But soon the Vikings sailed up the Loire to wreak havoc.

In the **Breton War of Succession** in the mid 14th century, the city switched hands several times between the Penthièvres and the De Montforts. Nantes competed with Rennes as ducal capital through the later Middle Ages; under the De Montfort dukes, it got the upper hand. In the chaotic, war-torn, superstition-riddled first half of the 15th century, **Gilles de Rais**, or **de Retz**, became one of the most notorious Frenchmen of his age. He owned various estates to the south of Nantes and along the Loire, and became a major figure at the French court under King Charles VII, where he is supposed to have sported a blue beard. Having fought alongside Joan of Arc, he was later accused of raping and murdering scores of boys in his castles, using them in satanic rituals. He may have been framed, but was certainly hanged and then burnt in Nantes, in 1440.

Under **Duke François II**, who was to be the last duke of Brittany, Nantes thrived as capital of the province. A prestigious university was inaugurated here in 1460, with the papacy's blessing. Duke François II's famed daughter, Duchess **Anne de Bretagne**, was born at the Château de Nantes (*see* p.441) in 1477. Nantes would remain a city close to her heart for all her life – and after it was over. She married two French kings in a row; the first, Charles VIII, she was wedded to at the Château de Langeais up the Loire; the second, Louis XII, she married in the chapel of the Château de Nantes in 1499. Anne died at another château on the Loire, Blois, in 1514. While most of her mortal remains were taken to the French royal resting place of the abbey of St-Denis, outside Paris, she specifically asked for her heart to be returned to Nantes to be buried. Anne's daughter Claude de France was married to King François I, who arranged Brittany's official union with France in 1532.

During the **French Wars of Religion** in the second half of the 16th century, Nantes fell under the control of the ultra-Catholic governor of Brittany, Philippe-Emmanuel de Lorraine, **Duc de Mercœur**, but at the end of the torments the 1598 **Edict of Nantes** worked out by King Henri IV famously granted some freedom of worship for Protestants in France. At the close of the 17th century, King Louis XIV revoked the edict, rekindling the persecution of the Huguenots. In between times, Nantes was rapidly growing into one of the major French colonial ports.

Nantes and the Triangular Slave Trade

The most prosperous times for Nantes came with the acquisition of France's Caribbean colonies. By 1633, Guadeloupe and Martinique were in French hands. With the 1697 Treaty of Ryswick, France gained the western half of Santo Domingo (present-day Haiti), which became the most lucrative of all of France's colonies. Before long, Nantes was possibly the largest centre in Europe for the triangular slave trade, outstripping all others in the 18th century. The first leg of the journey took the ships from Nantes to the east African coast. Goods such as guns, powder, alcohol, jewellery, trinkets and cloth were exchanged with the local slave traders for the human cargo that filled the vessels on the second leg of the journey. Many slaves died on these appalling, degrading journeys; survivors were sold to the colonial plantation owners of the Caribbean in exchange for the precious goods other slaves were busily helping to produce, notably sugar, coffee, cotton and indigo. On the third and final leg of the triangular journey, these luxuries were brought back to Europe.

Between 1715 and 1775, the return to port of 787 slave ships was registered in Nantes – half the number recorded for the whole of France. However, the sailing ships grew too large to travel right up to the city's quays. Much of the merchandise imported and exported was loaded and unloaded at Paimbœuf, west along the Loire. New industries developed in and around Nantes on the back of the Caribbean imports. Sugar was refined here to be sold across Europe. Cotton was turned into printed calico, known in French as *indiennes*, much of which went back to Africa to be bartered for more slaves.

Black African slaves became a common sight in wealthy Nantes households. Hugh Thomas, in his fascinating book *The Slave Trade*, describes the casual attitude some of the rich merchants had towards their human chattels: 'Slave merchants, living in their fine townhouses ... would give such "négrillons" or "négrittes" to members of their household as tips. In 1754, an ordnance provided that colonials could bring into France only one black apiece. But that rule was often forgotten.' From the end of the 17th century to the end of the 18th, Nantes' population doubled, from 40,000 to 80,000. The successful merchants, putting their sickening wealth to aesthetic use, built their grand townhouses (known as *hôtels particuliers* in French) in the Louis XV and Louis XVI styles. A concentration of fine mansions went up on the Ile Feydeau, then still an island, and many survive, even if branches of the Loire river around it have disappeared underground. Before the Revolution, in the second half of the 18th century, new town planning on a large scale was carried out across the centre of Nantes by the architect Jean-Baptiste Ceineray. Grand streets, squares and perspectives were added to the city. The architect Mathurin Crucy was also influential around the time of the Revolution.

Revolution and Nantes After Slavery

The Revolution banned the slave trade. When the slaves of Santo Domingo rose up in revolt in 1791, the Nantes shipowners wrote in protest to the king. The terrifying Carrier was sent to Nantes by the Committee of Public Safety; his mission was to make some of the pig-headed royalists of the city wed the cause of the Revolution. The so-called 'republican marriages' were cruel mock ceremonies: the un-Revolutionary offenders were tied in pairs and bundled on to a boat with a hole in the bottom. The boat sank and the 'couples' drowned in the Loire. François-Athanase Charette, a nobleman from the Loire Atlantique and one of the main leaders of the anti-Revolutionary, pro-Catholic and royalist Vendée uprising, led a desperate attack on Nantes in 1793. But it failed. Jacques Cathelineau, another hero of the anti-Revolutionary cause, was mortally wounded in the battle. Charette was eventually executed in Nantes in 1796.

Napoleon reintroduced slavery under pressure from colonial interests. It would be finally abolished in France in 1848, which was an absolute catastrophe for many Nantes merchants.

Turner came to paint here and along the Loire in 1828, the year that Jules Verne was born in Nantes. Rather less glamorously, the modern techniques of canning fish were developed in town at this time. Canning became a big industry in Brittany as a consequence, and played an important part in employment as well as culinary culture. In spite of the end of the slave trade, Nantes' prosperity didn't entirely drain away, as you can see for example in the mid-19th-century shopping arcade of the Passage Pommeraye. Trams started operating in the town as early as 1874 and have recently been revived.

Aristide Briand, one of the major French political figures of the early 20th century, came from Nantes. He became general secretary of the French Socialist Party in 1901 and framed the extremely important bill separating the Church from the French State in 1905. In the turbulent times at the start of the 20th century, he also served as prime minister no fewer than 11 times.

After the First World War, as part of the German war reparations, most of the seven channels of the Loire that had flowed through the city centre for so long were filled in by German workers. Briand continued to be a major political figure in France. With Jean Jaurès he founded the left-wing newspaper *L'Humanité*. From 1925 to 1932, he served as French foreign minister and worked hard for reconciliation and disarmament, proposing a form of United States of Europe. In 1926 he and German foreign minister Gustav Stresemann were even awarded the Nobel Peace Prize. Unfortunately their efforts would prove fruitless, although Briand can be considered one of the forefathers of the European Union.

The Allied bombing raids on Nazi-occupied Nantes that took place during the Second World War have left their scars. The wide modern road artery through the centre, known as the Cour des 50 Otages, commemorates the execution of 50 French hostages in 1942.

Postwar, several figures from the French art world have paid homage to Nantes, including the much-respected film-maker Jacques Demy, whose movie *Lola* was shot here, and the writer Julien Gracq, whose work *La Forme d'une ville* is devoted to the city. The university, closed at the Revolution, was reinstated in 1962, and hi-tech industries have settled here. As to the Caribbean connection, sugar still arrives here in large quantities, in part to make some of France's best-known biscuits, produced by the local firm Lu, familiar to all French children. Interestingly, the biscuit industry originally grew up to cater for the shipping expeditions.

A Tour of Nantes

Nantes is one of those cities that does not have an obvious heart, but there are several quarters that are worth exploring. The most obvious place to start is with the massive château.

Château de Nantes (Château des Ducs de Bretagne)

Courtyard and ramparts open July and Aug daily 10–7; rest of year Wed–Mon 2–6.

This château is massive, forbidding and an architectural mess, to put it mildly. The thick dark outer walls enclose some slightly more graceful, whiter wings. A deep broad dry **moat**, where many Nantais now take their dogs for a walk, separates the ramparts and their seven artillery towers from the surrounding boulevards, but originally the Loire lapped at the château's walls. What you see today, known as the Château des Ducs de Bretagne, was in fact built in the main for the last duke of Brittany and his daughter, although their forebears did have a castle on the spot.

This castle might be regarded as the most westerly of the châteaux of the Loire. It might also be described as the least harmonious of them all. On entering the huge **inner courtyard**, it's hard to know where to focus your attention, what with the irregular shape of the site, the diversity of buildings from down the centuries, and the miserable alley of trees that goes nowhere in particular. The **two main wings** show reasonably well the change from French late Gothic architecture to French Renaissance forms so characteristic of the Loire châteaux of the late 15th and early 16th centuries. The soaring vertical lines, the slight lack of symmetry in the windows, and the ornate *lucarnes*, or dormer windows, fit the bill. In the corner between the two main wings rises the **Tower of the Golden Crown**, lightened by Renaissance loggias high up. The name of the tower refers to the elaborate covering on top of the well in front. This crown in wrought iron was once gilded and was meant to represent the crown of the kings of Brittany of the Dark Ages.

The **Petit Gouvernement** is the small 16th-century building added for King François I and covered with restored French Renaissance detail, such as the shells in the dormers and the slate inlaid in the chimneys. The large rectangular building stranded in the inner courtyard is the 18th-century **Bâtiment du Harnachement**. This is the architectural equivalent of a sore thumb, but it reminds you of the fact that the château served as an army camp from the beginning of the 18th century to the start of the 20th. In between, in 1800, the military managed to blow up a whole section of the castle by accident, including the chapel. You can climb some of the ramparts, but the views of the roads and modern town are disappointing.

The château housed several museums. Now work is underway to create one single much grander museum of the history of Nantes, but this will not be completed until 2008. It even promises to cover the slave trade. In the meantime, temporary **exhibitions** will be held in the swishly restored Harnachement.

To the Cathedral of St-Pierre

From the château you might like to take the **Rue Rodier** (named after the man who planned the castle for Duke François II) straight up to the front of the cathedral on the Place St-Pierre. Or if you prefer something a little grander, opt for the wide, mid-18th-century boulevard of the **Cours St-Pierre**, running up from the Place de la Duchesse Anne to the choir end of the cathedral. This *cours* is of Parisian proportions and elegance. It takes you to the imposing **Place Maréchal Foch**, where a column commemorating King Louis XVI stands in the centre. The big building on the north side was where Napoleon stayed on a visit to Nantes in 1808. The **Hôtel Montaudoin**, built for an infamously wealthy Nantes slave-trading family, stands out, the family arms proudly showing. The grand **Cours St-André**, the extension northwards of the Cours St-Pierre, leads to the **Erdre boat station**. Clashing with the careful classical planning of the rest of the Place St-Pierre, the massive **Porte St-Pierre** is a remnant of Nantes' 15th-century town walls, built on much earlier Gallo-Roman vestiges.

While the exterior of the bulky, squat **Cathédrale St-Pierre** looks rather grey, the inside is superbly white. This is the cleanest cathedral you're likely to see, and one of the emptiest. The interior had to be restored and cleaned after a terrible fire in 1972. Some of the uncluttered monuments appear even whiter than the Loire limestone used in the building of this cathedral. Work began on it in 1434, financed by Jean V Duc de Bretagne and the bishop Jean de Malestroit. It was built on the site of the previous Romanesque cathedral, and possibly of Bishop Félix's 6th-century church. Only the Romanesque crypt under the present choir was kept from the previous structures. The 15th-century architects were Guillaume de Dommartin-sur-Yèvre and Mathelin Rodier. The work proved laborious and lengthy, but the façade was completed before the end of the 15th century and the towers added by 1508. The nave and the aisles slowly went up in the 16th century, worship in the building only starting in 1577.

The major artistic interest within consists of the **tomb of François II Duc de Bretagne** and his two wives. This moving work is generally said to have been executed in the Tours workshops of sculptor Michel Colombe between 1502 and 1507, though an Italian artist of great ability may have carried out some of the work. The two main effigies represent the duke and his second wife, Marguerite de Foix, mother of Anne de Bretagne. The large corner statues show personifications of Justice (thought to be a portrait of Anne de Bretagne), Fortitude, Temperance and Prudence, the last with its double-faced head, the one of a young woman, the other of an old man. This grand and beautiful tomb was commissioned by Anne de Bretagne, who asked for her heart to be placed in it after her death; her wish was granted. Another remarkably fine tomb in the cathedral dates from the 19th century. It was made by Paul Dubois in 1879, in honour of the formidably moustached military commander General Lamoricière. A Nantais by birth, he was celebrated for his role in the French taking of Algeria, and in particular for his capturing of the Algerian leader Abd-el-Kader. Almost all of the cathedral's original stained-glass windows have been destroyed by explosions and fire. Some striking modern ones have replaced them.

The Rue du Roi Albert leads north from the cathedral square up to the **Préfecture**. This is Ceineray's classical masterpiece in the town, built from 1763. On the cathedral side, the arms of France have been sculpted in the pediment. On the side of the Erdre river, the arms of Brittany feature.

The best way to appreciate the beautiful **Erdre river** is on a cruise. The **Gare Fluviale de l'Erdre** from which boats depart lies on the west bank of the river, near the Ile de Versailles. Contact Bateaux Nantais, t 02 40 14 51 14, for cruises on slick modern boats. The company operates a variety of tours, including meals and cabaret performances, child-orientated cruises and floodlit tours past the Erdre's chateaux.

Musée des Beaux-Arts

Open Mon, Wed, Thurs and Sat 10–6, Fri 10–8, Sun 11–6.

The splendid Nantes fine arts museum is situated on the other side of the Cours St-Pierre from the cathedral. Allegorical statues on the façade represent the arts; architecture, with temple and measuring rod in hands, is represented over the main entrance. The museum building is a beautiful, cleanly planned work by the architect Xavier Josso, built in 1900 for the elevating educational purposes of the French Third Republic. The founding collection was actually donated to the town a century earlier, in 1801, or the Year IX as it was known under the Consulate; this was one of a total of 15 major provincial museums that were established around France after the Revolution.

Some of the works came from war booty. Another large haul arrived in 1810 from the collections of the Cacault brothers and their lovely Italianate villa in Clisson, which lies to the southeast of Nantes (*see* p.452). The brothers had been away on a wild art-shopping spree in Italy in the late 18th century. Further generous 19th-century donations and the 20th-century legacy of the French industrialist Gildas Fardel added to the riches on display. If you want a crash course in the history of western art from 13th-century religious works to present-day conceptual projects, this is as fine a place as any to come. The 19th- and 20th-century collections are exceptionally good.

There are so many masterpieces in the museum that it just isn't possible to single them all out here. Among the highlights, of the three famous De La Tours held by the museum are two showing his archetypal candlelit effects cast on waxen faces and figures. The best pieces from the 18th century include a typical Watteau inspired by *commedia dell'arte – Arlequin, Empereur de la Lune –* several Greuzes, and a whole series of portraits of rich families by Tournières. Gros' work *Le Combat de Nazareth* was an early 19th-century piece that had a profound effect on Delacroix and has been viewed as a precursor of the Romantic movement. The same room contains two exceptional sculptures, one by Canova of Pope Clement XIII; the other, by Ceracchi, of Washington.

Courbet's *Les Cribleuses de blé* counts as one of the most famous works of the second half of the 19th century in the museum. There is a fair representation of wildly over-the-top, sickly French Romanticism to revolt you, too. You might view with some irony, given Nantes' history, *L'Esclave blanche* ('The White Slave') by Lecomte du Nouy. *Le Sorcier Noir* by Herbert Ward shows a typical European vision of the black man as witch. On the ground floor, while Monet takes you off to Venice and the otherwordly visions of his *Nymphéas*, Emile Bernard's *Le Gaulage des pommes* depicts a forceful Breton landscape in the style of the Pont-Aven School. Local artist Metzinger gives a Pointilliste interpretation of the Château de Clisson. A whole room is devoted to Kandinsky's abstract work, while Chagall's *Le Cheval Rouge* is a typical piece by that great artist. Raymond Hains, a well-known conceptual artist, pays homage to the thriving Nantes biscuit industry with a bar code.

The pretty **Jardin des Plantes** lies at the eastern end of Rue Georges Clemenceau.

The Bouffay Quarter

Make your way back to the very centre of historic Nantes; west of the castle lies the Bouffay quarter. The tightly packed network of old streets makes this the liveliest and most charming part of old Nantes. The area is mainly pedestrian. Several street names recall the medieval activities along them, but only a few timberframe houses remain from the 15th and 16th centuries. In the Ancien Régime, grander townhouses were built here in what became the lawyers' quarter in particular. Nowadays, this is a neighbourhood of chic boutiques, restaurants and apartments.

Wandering around you will come across several little squares. The **Place du Pilori** served for executions and other public punishments until the Place du Bouffay took over that role. **Place du Bouffay** now plays host to a lively and smelly daily fishmarket. The former town belfry has been affixed to the **church of Ste-Croix** in Place Ste-Croix nearby. The church is a quirky mix of architectural styles. Angels trumpet out the Christian message from the top of the belfry.

North of **Rue de la Marne** and **Rue de la Barillerie**, the main shopping arteries, several further elegant streets lead to the town hall, for instance those leading north from the **Place du Change**, once the hub of historic Nantes. The **Hôtel de Ville** (town hall) is a mix of 17th-century mansions and modernity.

Ile Feydeau

On the opposite side of the Allées from Place du Bouffay, the Ile Feydeau was once an exclusive residential island on the Loire. It is now sadly isolated by wide roads. This is where some of the very grandest Nantes shipowners had their townhouses and offices from the mid 18th century on. You can only really get a good impression of their wealth by wandering along the **Rue Kervégan**. The finest features on the façades are the grotesque Baroque masks, or *mascarons*, carved above the windows, each one showing a different grimacing face.

Squares and Museums West of the Cours des 50 Otages

To the west of the broad curving Cours des 50 Otages lie many elegant squares and streets from the late 18th and early 19th centuries. More chic shops line many of the streets. The Rue d'Orléans leads to **Place Royale**. This sober-sided square was planned by the architect Mathurin Crucy. Personifications of certain of the Loire's tributary rivers adorn the granite fountain in this square. Just to the northeast of Place Royale lie the **Place Fournier** and the **Basilique St-Nicolas**. The latter is a neo-Gothic church from the mid 19th century, its soaring spire reaching 85 metres in height. A fair way further north rises the much taller **Tour Bretagne**, Nantes' isolated central skyscraper, visible from afar as you approach the city. A modern shopping precinct surrounds it.

South of the Place Royale, a wonderful array of cafés lines up opposite the **Bourse** on **Place du Commerce**. The Bourse, or exchange building, with its impressive row of monumental Ionic columns, was again planned by Crucy and completed in 1812. A few of the original statues of famous Breton sailors (some notorious corsairs in fact) remain in place. The Loire used to flow by here and the quay was reserved for the Nantais wine trade. Now it's the domain of the beautiful, trendy student set.

The **Passage Pommeraye**, Nantes' most elegant shopping arcade, heads up to Rue Crébillon from Rue de la Fosse. You won't find Passage Pommeraye as exotic as Flaubert did in his day, but the mid-19th-century sweeps of stairs have a kitsch romance to them. **Rue Crébillon** links Place Royale with the more serious **Place Graslin** to the west. This square was again planned by Crucy. It's dominated by the **theatre**, which saw its first performance in 1788. Statues of muses stand on top of the Corinthian columns. The **Cours Cambronne**, off the southwest corner of Place Graslin, could hardly be more refined.

Musée Thomas Dobrée and Manoir de la Touche

Open Tues–Sat 10–12 and 1.30–5.30, Sat and Sun 2.30–5.30.

The golden reliquary for the heart of Anne de Bretagne stands on public display in the Musée Thomas Dobrée. Little can the last duchess of Brittany have imagined that it would one day be on view for all to see. It's the most striking piece of fine craftsmanship in a museum crammed with the finest stonework, woodwork and enamel work. Thomas Dobrée was a dedicated collector through the 19th century, the son of an extremely wealthy industrialist and shipowner. Among other objects, he amassed sculptures, paintings, furniture, art objects, and manuscripts and letters from royals, nobles and literary figures in an obsessive manner.

He decided to build a grand house in which to install these collections, next to the Manoir de la Touche, and even oversaw much of the construction work on the building, with its neo-Romanesque look. It was built in brown-bear coloured stone, with figures of carved bears added on to the corners. Dobrée also had the Manoir de la Touche restored. The manor had been constructed for Bishop Jean de Malestroit as his country retreat outside the city walls at the start of the 15th century. It later served as a Huguenot hospital in the Wars of Religion and from 1695 until the Revolution as a religious refuge for Irish priests who had been driven out of their country.

The museum contains religious sculptures of great beauty. You can observe close up several huge statues originally made for Nantes' cathedral front, carved in Loire tufa, and a collection of Romanesque capitals with weird grotesque faces. A magnificent length of wooden stringbeam shows a bizarre mix of particularly graceful faces and crudely gesturing figures. Among the exquisite medieval church ceremonial objects on display, the collection of enamelled *pyxides* from the Limousin stands out, plus various encrusted altar crosses.

The **Manoir de la Touche** contains a mixed bag of collections. The ground floor is devoted to Nantes at the time of the Revolution. Upstairs are archaeological finds from around the Loire Atlantique, including some interesting Bronze Age, Celtic, Gallo-Roman and Merovingian pieces.

Jules Verne's Museum and Other Specialist Museums in Nantes

Nantes has at least another half-dozen smaller museums. The **Muséum d'Histoire Naturelle** (*open Wed–Mon 10–6*), situated to the east of the Musée Thomas Dobrée on Rue Voltaire, is Nantes' respected natural history museum. Nearby, down on the quays with the modern Médiathèque, the **Musée de l'Imprimerie** (*24 Quai de la Fosse; open Mon–Sat 10–12 and 2–5.30, plus Oct–April Sun 2–5*) explores the development of printing in the region through an impressive collection of old printing presses. Looking further west along the Quai de la Fosse, it's hard to miss the **Maillé Brézé** (*open June–Sept daily 2–6; Oct–May Wed, Sat and Sun and school hols 2–5*), a decommissioned naval squadron escort vessel converted into a museum.

Head westwards to reach the Ste-Anne quarter on its hill, where you'll find a further cluster of sights. The little **Musée Jules Verne** (*3 Rue de l'Hermitage, t 02 40 69 72 52; open Mon and Wed–Sat 10–12 and 2–6, Sun 2–6*) pays its respects to the great French visionary 19th-century science-fiction writer from Nantes with old editions, posters and topical displays. It was redecorated to modern effect not so long ago. Jules Verne was the author of such worldwide classics as *Around the World in Eighty Days*, *Journey to the Centre of the Earth* and *Twenty Thousand Leagues Under the Sea*. You can easily imagine what an inspiration cosmopolitan Nantes must have been to him, even if it hardly features in his writing. Americans might also particularly enjoy his *De la terre à la lune* (*From the Earth to the Moon Direct in 97 Hours 20 Minutes*), a hilarious story about Americans competing to becoming the first men on the moon – in the 19th century! It seems appropriate enough that the **Planétarium** (*8 Rue des Acadiens, t 02 40 73 99 23; showings Mon–Fri 10.30, 2.15 and 3.45, Sun 3 and 4.30*) should stand close by.

The **Musée des Compagnons du Devoir**, in the Manoir de la Hautière in the same area (*14 Rue Guillon Verne, t 02 40 69 30 55; open Sat 2–6*), presents masterpieces by French master craftspeople.

Some distance to the north of it, by the Parc de Procé, the **Musée de la Poste** (*10 Boulevard Auguste Pageot; open Mon–Fri 8.30–6, Sat 8.30–12*) is dedicated to the French postal services through the centuries. The **Parc de Procé** is another of what the French call 'English gardens' – that is, not as formal as a French garden. This one has collections of rhododendrons, fuchsias, dahlias and magnolias.

South Across the Loire

On the Ile de Nantes, a hard-working island located just to the south of the historic city, you might sniff out the **Jardin des Cinq Sens**, a garden that plays on the five senses with its different-textured paths and its musical fountain. Head around the western tip of the island and you come to an astonishing industrial landscape of hills of scrap metal.

Cross south from the Ile de Beaulieu to reach **Rezé**, which had a Gallo-Roman settlement like Nantes but which is known nowadays for its modern architecture. The most famous piece in town is **Le Corbusier**'s bold experiment in new urban living, the *unité d'habitation de grandeur conforme*, or **Cité Radieuse**, rising on its stilts. It was built in the mid 1950s to provide a new concept in council housing and has been restored in the meantime. The striking curve of Rezé's modern town hall was conceived by Alessandro Anselmi.

East from Nantes

Along the Loire to the Old Breton Border

Turner found inspiration along this stretch of the Loire, though it is not particularly well known. By contrast with the generally flat, dull and in parts heavily industrial estuary banks from Nantes to the mouth of the Loire, east of the former Breton capital the Loire Valley becomes more dramatic.

You can enjoy some dreamy glimpses of the Loire from around **Le Cellier**, near which the **Château de Clermont** boasts the finest views of all. This mid-17th-century castle built in brick, an archetypal Louis XIII construction, was once owned by one of France's most famous comedians, Louis de Funès. There is an impressive panorama of the Loire from the vantage point of the **abbey of St-Méen** at **St-Cléen** too, as well as a towpath edging the river all the way to Nantes. A many-sided keep rises high above the village of **Oudon**, a landmark along this stretch of the Loire. It formed part of a medieval castle built here for the Malestroit family under Duke Jean IV of Brittany. You can climb the tower at certain times of year to appreciate the superb views.

Ancenis is most appealing for its huge traditional market, which brings a good deal of life to its renovated heart. Here, you can try the local roast pork delicacy, *rillaud*, or buy some works of the local poet, who looks as if he's had a stall here for almost as long as the market has existed. In medieval times, this was an important Breton frontier post. The castle grew to substantial proportions in that period, although it has long lain in ruins. For centuries, boats passing this way paid tolls to cross the frontier between Brittany and Anjou. As well as the Maison des Vins, wine-lovers who like to browse a cellar or two would be expertly advised to visit the Épicerie-Cave of Jean-Pierre Bournigault near the market square on Rue de l'Abbé-Fresneau.

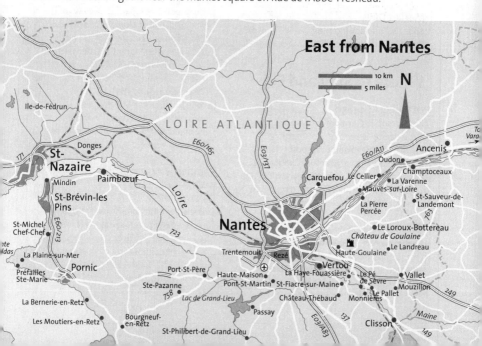

Palais Briau

Grounds open 2–6 April–Oct daily; house open 2–6 April–July, Sept and Oct Sat and public hols, Aug daily.

Close to Varade, this sumptuous brick and limestone château of the 19th century has been open to the public since its relatively recent restoration. François Briau, a model of a 19th-century engineer, commissioned the construction. He had made his fortune planning the railway lines from Tours to Nantes and from Nantes to Pornic. But he had also worked in Italy. When he returned to the Loire, he decided to build his own *palazzo* along Italianate lines. The architect Edouard Moll planned the stocky building in 1854, following Palladian models. Inside, money was lavished on the stucco decoration, the elaborate wall coverings, the odd fresco and the monumental staircase. A tour of the beautifully proportioned interiors gives an excellent feel for life at the cutting edge of design and engineering in the Second Empire.

Getting Around

Ancenis has a **railway** station at which fast TGVs from Paris to Nantes sometimes stop.

Tourist Information

Oudon: Rue du Pont Levis, **t** 02 40 83 80 04, *www.ville-oudon.fr.*
Ancenis: Place du Millénaire, **t** 02 40 83 07 44, *office.tourisme.ancenis@wanadoo.fr.*
Varades: 182 Rue du Maréchal Foch, **t** 02 40 83 41 88, *si.varades@wanadoo.fr.*

Market Days

Ancenis: Thursday morning.
Varades: Saturday morning.

Where to Stay and Eat

Le Cellier ✉ 44850

Restaurant de Clermont, t 02 40 68 19 90 (*moderate–expensive*). A sumptuous place to eat, providing the best way to appreciate the 17th-century Château de Clermont and its sensational location high above the Loire's north bank. *Closed eves exc for groups.*

Oudon ✉ 44521

L'Hôtel du Port, 10 Place du Port, **t** 02 40 83 80 64 (*inexpensive*). A charming place tucked into the rock below the ruins of Oudon castle. The dining room is decorated with some interesting paintings and the bar has delightful murals of local scenes.

Ancenis ✉ 44150

Domaines du Maître des Forges, Étang de la Provostière, Riaillé, 21km from Ancenis on the D14, **t** 02 40 97 88 38, *www.domainedesforges.com* (*inexpensive*). A magnificent *maison de maître*, a relic from a 17th-century ironworks, with beautifully restored B&B rooms. There are also *gîtes.*
Les Terrasses de Bel Air, Bel Air, along the N23 towards Angers, **t** 02 40 83 02 87 (*moderate–expensive*). Top-notch Loire Valley food accompanied by views of the river itself. *Closed Mon, Sat and Sun lunch.*
La Charbonnière, t 02 40 83 25 17 (*inexpensive–expensive*). A restaurant perched over the river, with lots of glass windows and terrace seating, offering good local river fish dishes. *Closed Sun eve and Wed.*
La Toile à Beurre, Rue St-Pierre, **t** 02 40 98 89 64 (*moderate*). A good traditional restaurant by the church in the centre of town. *Closed Sun and Mon.*

Varades ✉ 44370

Palais Briau, t 02 40 83 45 00 (*moderate–expensive*). A grand B&B.
Closerie des Roses, on the river's edge, **t** 02 40 98 33 30 (*moderate–expensive*). Seasonal takes on river specialities by a young chef, plus a carte of local wines. *Closed Tues eve, Wed, Sun eve, and Tue and Wed in July and Aug.*

Ancenis Wines

The cliffs of the Loire begin to rise to some height around Mauves-sur-Loire. Vineyards slope down to the river, producing Coteaux d'Ancenis ('slopes of Ancenis') wines. The wide local range includes VDQS wines made from Cabernet, Gamay, Pinot or Gros Plant. The Coteaux d'Ancenis Malvoisie VDQS is a rare sweet white made from either Pinot Beurot or Pinot Gris. The one wine given the added distinction of its own *appellation* in this area is the Coteaux de la Loire Muscadet.

Ancenis has a *Maison des Vins*, **t** 02 40 96 14 92, where you can learn about, taste and buy local wines. It also hosts blindfolded wine-tasting competitions where anyone willing and foolish enough can pit their taste-buds against the knowledge of the locals. You can organize vineyard visits from there. One recommendation is the **Domaine des Génaudières**, belonging to Brigitte Augustin (*open Mon–Sat 8–12.30 and 2.30–7*) and idyllically located on the hillside overlooking the Loire.

After visiting the house, you can wander freely through the terraced grounds, which are being slowly restored. You can also go in search of the meagre ruins of a medieval fort that was destroyed in 1599. This fort of Varades long guarded the north bank of the Loire.

The pretty village of **Varades** stands on the slope of the Loire's bank. On a round trip, head back to Nantes by crossing the Loire to the dramatically sited small town of **St-Florent-le-Vieil**, then follow the splendid **south bank** to the city. The Loire in these parts is covered further in the separate *Cadogan Guide to the Loire*.

Muscadet Country from Nantes to Clisson

The undulating, vine-covered countryside producing the well-known Muscadet de Sèvre et Maine *appellation* wines fans out from the southeastern suburbs of Nantes to the border with Anjou. You can visit wineries and the wine museum in this area, the latter also paying tribute to that passionate medieval theologian and lover, Pierre Abélard, who was born around here. Don't miss the little town of Clisson, which seems to think that it's Italian. You can follow the **Loire Valley Wine Route** (rather long-windedly known as La Route Touristique des Vignobles en Val de Loire in French) through this area and across to the coast at **Pornic**.

Le Musée du Vignoble Nantais at Le Pallet

Open Mon–Fri July and Aug 11–6, March–June and Sept–Nov 1–6.

For those of you accustomed to traditional, unreformed French local history museums, which tend to be chaotic and dusty, sometimes charming, sometimes dismal affairs, this newfangled building and approach will come as something of a shock. The museum is startlingly slick, with an office-smart reception area, video rooms, exhibits placed neatly under glass, and a lawn as a roof. It offers a good introduction to those uninitiated in the pleasures of *dégustation*, especially since staff serve up samples of each region's *médailles d'or* for your delectation.

The origins of the Nantais wines go back as far as Gallo-Roman times, and monks and noblemen carried on viticulture through medieval times. Muscadet benefited greatly when the Breton coastal resorts nearby took off in the early days of the 20th century. Tourists grew accustomed to drinking the zingy, refreshing white wine with their seafood, and the fashion soon spread to Paris.

The Pays Nantais produces three main types of wine nowadays: Muscadet, which is made from that memorably named Melon de Bourgogne variety; Gros Plant, which is generally considered its poorer cousin, from a grape variety with an even more visual name, the Folle Blanche (the 'Mad White One'); and the Coteaux d'Ancenis (from further north along the Loire).

This being a museum devoted to Pierre Abélard as well as to the Pays Nantais vineyards, there's an interesting video presenting the history of the lives of Abélard and Héloïse, while one room contains a diversity of engravings that were inspired by their famously tormented love story.

Getting Around

There's a **railway** line down through the Muscadet de Sèvre et Maine area to Clisson, or ask at tourist offices about **bus** services between Nantes and Clisson.

Tourist Information

Vertou: Place Beauverger, **t** 02 40 34 12 22, *www.vertou.fr*.
Le Loroux-Bottereau: 12 Place Rosmadec, **t** 02 40 03 79 76, *otsi.loroux@free.fr*.
Le Pallet: Mairie, **t** 02 40 80 40 24.
Vallet: 1 Place Charles de Gaulle, **t** 02 40 36 35 87, *www.cc-vallet.fr*.
Clisson: Place du Minage, **t** 02 40 54 02 95, *www.clisson.com*.

Market Days

Vertou: Saturday and Sunday.
Le Loroux-Bottereau: Sunday.
Vallet: Sunday.
Clisson: Friday.

Where to Stay and Eat

Les Sorinières ✉ 44840

★★★★**Abbaye de Villeneuve**, Route de la Roche-sur-Yon, **t** 02 40 04 40 25, *www.abbayede villeneuve.com* (*moderate–very expensive*). There is something slightly wicked about staying in this former Cistercian abbey, built in the 18th century but now converted into a top-class luxury hotel, a short way south of Nantes and Rezé. There's also something hedonistic about eating in the former monks' library. The grounds have a pool.

Vertou ✉ 44850

★★**Hôtel de la Haute Forêt**, Boulevard de l'Europe, **t** 02 40 34 01 74 (*inexpensive*). A simple, family-run place in a charming little town. Staff can give you recommendations of vineyards to visit, and you can take a cruise on the Sèvre from nearby.
L'Ecluse, 9 Quai de la Chaussée des Moines, **t** 02 40 34 40 70 (*moderate–expensive*). A restaurant by a picturesque lake, specializing in frogs' legs in a Muscadet sauce. Other tempting choices include lobster with a caviar of aubergine. *Closed Sun eve and 3wks from 15 Aug*.

La Haye-Fouassière ✉ 44690

Le Cep de Vigne, Place de la Gare, **t** 02 40 36 93 90 (*moderate–expensive*). Classic French cuisine and Loire wines. *Closed Sun eve, Wed and 2wks July*.

St-Fiacre-sur-Maine ✉ 44690

Le Fiacre, 1 Rue des Echicheurs, **t** 02 40 54 83 92 (*inexpensive*). A buzzing bistrot-cum-bar where you'll eat with locals. The patron is passionate about Muscadet, and has a list of more than 100 producers' wines.

Muscadet Vineyards

A good place to start touring the Muscadet vineyards is the **Maison des Vins de Nantes** at La Haye-Fouassière (*open Sept–June Mon–Fri 8.30–12.30 and 2–5.45; July and Aug Sat and Sun 10.30–12.30 and 2.30–6*), overlooking hectare upon hectare of vines. If you wish to visit a winery, it's always wise to telephone in advance to see if you can fix a time.

If you're looking for a spectacular property, you're well advised to try the **Château du Coing** (*t 02 40 54 81 15*), close to St-Fiacre-sur-Maine. The vineyards lie on some of the prettiest slopes in the Muscadet region. The place, a true château, has some impressive cellars where you can sample the wines. The winemaker is Véronique Günther Chéreau, a member of a well-known Muscadet-making family.

Another good Muscadet vineyard to see is the **Château de la Galissonnière**, close to Le Pallet (*t 02 40 80 42 03*), which is is well known and well used to receiving foreign visitors.

Château-Thébaud ✉ 44690

Gérard & Annick Bousseau, Domaine de La Pénissière, **t** 02 40 06 51 22 (*inexpensive*). A working wine estate that's situated in the heart of the Muscadet, affording fine views over the vineyards. The smart B&B accommodation is inside an atmospheric old house. Private fishing trips can be arranged from here.

Chez Valentine Barjolle, **t** 02 40 03 81 35 (*inexpensive*). A good, competitively priced B&B option.

Monnières ✉ 44690

Château de Plessis-Brézot, **t** 02 40 54 63 24, *a.calonne@online.fr* (*moderate–expensive*). A reputed wine domaine and luxury B&B choice within a little 17th-century property situated above the Sèvre Nantaise river. Guests can enjoy the use of its private swimming pool.

Le Pallet ✉ 44330

Château de la Sébinière, **t** 02 40 80 49 25, *www.chateausebiniere.com* (*moderate*). Outstanding B&B accommodation in a lovely 18th-century home. The comfort and elegance of the three *chambres* (and their exquisite ensuite bathrooms, some of which have lovely views on to the rear rose garden) are exemplary. The place is run by genuinely charming hosts who offer their guests a *petit-déjeuner gourmand* that is not to be missed.

Vallet ✉ 44330

Don Quichotte, 35 Route de Clisson, **t 02 40 33 99 67 (*inexpensive*). Simple rooms and a restaurant (*moderate*) where you can try such regional specialities as hot oysters in Muscadet, located close to a windmill. *Closed Sun and Fri eves.*

Hôtel de la Gare, **t 02 40 33 92 55 (*inexpensive*). A peaceful hotel by vineyards. **Les Voyageurs**, 2 Route de Clisson, **t** 02 40 33 92 38 (*inexpensive*). A friendly cheapie.

Le Landreau ✉ 44430

Auberge du Vignoble, Place de l'Eglise, **t** 02 40 06 42 94 (*inexpensive*). A very appealing, rustic-looking, good-value inn with hearty country cooking. *Closed Mon.*

Clisson ✉ 44190

La Bonne Auberge, 1 Rue Olivier de Clisson, **t** 02 40 54 01 90 (*moderate–expensive*). A stylish gastronomic restaurant well located in the centre of this pretty town. *Closed Mon, Tues and Wed lunch, Sun eve and 3wks Aug.*

Restaurant de la Vallée, 1 Rue de la Vallée, **t** 02 40 54 36 23 (*moderate*). A good fish restaurant delightfully located over the river, with a summer dining terrace.

Le Croque-Mitaine, 56 Rue des Halles, **t** 02 40 54 34 84 (*inexpensive–moderate*). A good place to take the family for potato pancakes, steaks at modest prices and a view of the château.

To help you discover lesser-known wine estates, you might seek out an excellent little book called *Découvertes en terroir du Muscadet*, published by Ouest-France for the wine and tourism authorities of the Loire Atlantique.

The Château de Goulaine

Open 15 June–15 Sept Wed–Mon 2–6;
Easter–15 June and 15 Sept–Oct Sat, Sun and public hols 2–6.

This château is both a reputed Muscadet-producing estate and an historic castle that you can visit. It is located just east of Haute-Goulaine, relatively close to the southeastern suburbs of Nantes. An old square schist tower is reflected in the moat, known as the **Tour des Archives**.

The history of the family of Goulaine goes back almost 1,000 years. The strong vertical lines of the main façade leading to decorated Loire *lucarnes* look archetypal Loire Valley stuff. Inside the château, you only see a small number of rooms, but they are sumptuously decorated. The tour includes a visit to the butterfly house. You also get the opportunity to buy the estate's wine.

Clisson

Clisson is the town where Brittany and Italy meet. The darkly romantic feudal ruins of its château dominate the slopes of the valley where the Moine joins the Sèvre Nantaise. The vestiges look classically French. Several medieval lords of Clisson became feared warlords. In the 13th century, when Olivier I de Clisson returned from crusading, he is believed to have ordered the start of work on a castle based on the model of the fort of Caesarea in the Holy Land. Some of his successors became famously embroiled in the Breton War of Succession in the mid 14th century. The Clissons supported the English-backed Jean de Montfort against the French king's candidate, Charles de Blois. The awkward Olivier III de Clisson was duped into accepting an invitation to Paris from the first French Valois king, Philippe VI. The Valois had the courtesy to have his guest's head chopped off, sending it back to Nantes by way of example.

Olivier IV de Clisson was brought up by his mother with an understandable hatred of the French and was sent for a time to the English court to be educated with Jean de Montfort the younger. Once of age, Olivier IV joined the fighting, taking part in the decisive battle of Auray, in which Charles de Blois was killed and Bertrand Du Guesclin captured. But after the De Montfort victory, Olivier IV was deeply disappointed by his rewards. He fell out with Duke Jean IV de Montfort and joined the French army. Ironically, he became so successful that he succeeded the Breton Du Guesclin as Constable of France, or head of the French army, gaining the honoured title of Boucher des Anglais ('Butcher of the English'). In the course of his life, he amassed substantial territories in Brittany, for example the Château de Josselin and its estates.

You can visit the ruins of the **Château de Clisson** (*open Oct–March 9.30–12 and 2–6 Tue–Sun*), an impressive carcass of a castle. Much of it was built in the 13th century. Important additions were made to the western side in the 15th century for the last duke of Brittany, François II, trying desperately to strengthen his region's frontier castles in response to pressure from the French king Louis XI. In the times of the Wars of Religion, further defensive bastions were built, adding to the château's great bulk. But Jean-Baptiste Kléber, a Revolutionary leader against the Vendéen uprising, had the château burned down in 1793 in revenge for his defeat at Torfou. Many walls still stand among the rubble, and much restoration work has been carried out, but it's hard to make out the rooms and the place remains dramatically open to the skies. For the most part, the architecture looks almost as thin as a stage set.

In fact, most of the town of Clisson was also devastated by the Revolutionary troops. The town that arose afterwards, from 1798, was inspired by artistic, wealthy local brothers Pierre and François Cacault of Nantes, and their friend, sculptor Frédéric Lemot, who had spent a great deal of time in Italy. They deliberately decided to build Roman-style homes that influenced the whole new town.

The slope northwest from the château is worth wandering along. The *halles*, or covered market, have a vast and breathtaking wooden timber frame that has survived from the 15th century. In the first week of December, local *viticulteurs* gather here for the *nouvel an du Muscadet*, celebrating the new year's produce with tastings. There is also regional food, outdoor dining and a free concert. In the first weekend of August, the town hosts a medieval festival with a feast in the *halles* and traditional *fest noz* ball.

The church of **Notre-Dame** is a fine example of Clisson's Italianate style, a campanile rising next to the colonnaded apse, a couple of umbrella pines framing the church. It is best seen from the river.

La Garenne Lemot

Park open daily April–Sept 9–8, Oct–March 9.30–6.30;
Maison du Jardinier open Mon 2–7, Tue–Sun 10–12 and 2–7;
villa open Tue–Sun during exhibitions.

This Italianate villa situated on the other side of the river is a delight. Ironically, it was anti-republican riots in Rome that forced Frédéric Lemot to return to France. He bought La Garenne ('The Warren' – of the castle) in 1805. Lemot was a sculptor. His most famous works are of royalty; he executed the casting of the equestrian statue of Henri IV on Paris's Pont-Neuf. He kept his great love of Italy through his life.

The **Maison du Jardinier** near the entrance to the estate was built in rustic Italian style. It houses a very well-presented permanent exhibition, 'Clisson ou le Retour d'Italie'. This focuses not just on La Garenne Lemot but also more widely on the Italian influence on French artistic circles in the second half of the 18th century. The whole place makes for a charming excursion into Italy. The **villa** is reached by a garden lined with statues. The front courtyard is formed by a semi-circle of columns. The villa is light and graceful inside, with an elegant polished stone stairway decorated with deep relief friezes. The house contains Lemot's prize-winning sculpture of the Judgement of Solomon and also hosts temporary exhibitions. The grounds offer a treasure hunt of **follies**. You can go in search of the fake antique columns and tomb, or the temple of Vesta, or simply enjoy the picturesque river walk.

To the Southern Loire Atlantique Coast

Here you enter Bluebeard country, the Pays de Retz. Arriving from the west, once you've made your way around the enormous lake of Grand-Lieu, you soon come to a string of coastal resorts. They feel much more southern than those to the north of the Loire, with the exception of Pornic.

Via the Lac de Grand-Lieu

Heading southwest from Nantes towards the coast, you pass by the enormous but well-hidden and slowly dwindling **Lac de Grand-Lieu**. If you go north of the lake, the road takes you past the **Safari Africain**, a game park by Port-St-Père that you can tour in your car. Head down the eastern side of the lake and you could make a detour to **Passay**, a sleepy little port with fine views on to the lake itself. **La Maison des Pêcheurs** presents the life of the local fishermen. An observatory has been posted in this strategic position to help visitors spot the rich bird life of the area.

St-Philbert-de-Grand-Lieu, south of the lake, has very sound Christian credentials and the distinction of a well-preserved Carolingian church. It is very rare to find such an edifice, dating in good part from the 9th and 10th centuries, that has survived down the centuries. St Philibert was a zealous 7th-century religious man who founded numerous monasteries in France, most famously those of Jumièges in Normandy and Noirmoutier, the latter, to the south, in the Vendée. He was buried at the monastery on the island of Noirmoutier.

Muscadet is produced all around the lake of Grand-Lieu. To the west of it, you come into Bluebeard country. The frightening figure of Gilles de Retz (*see* p.438) had one of his most important castles at Machecoul, now a sad ruin. At **Bourgneuf-en-Retz** nearby, the old-fashioned local history museum recalls the more innocent country ways of the area in centuries past.

The whole coast of the Pays de Retz, known poetically in the tourist literature as the **Côte de Jade**, doesn't feel particularly Breton. The big resorts of **St-Michel-Chef-Chef** and **St-Brévin-les-Pins** are hugely popular and very lively. But they look like part of the long, flat Vendée strands. However, the southern stretch of the Côte de Jade around Pornic can justifiably claim to possess the last of the Breton rocks.

Pornic

If Pornic was good enough for Lenin it should do everyone else nicely. The Russian revolutionary stayed some time in this utterly delightful bourgeois retreat, the most southerly historic Breton port.

At the back of the estuary lies the **old fishing port**. You can go on boat trips out to sea from here. The south quay leads you into the smart residential areas of Gourmalon. On the north side, the Quai Leray is at the centre of the action. The western end of it leads to the schist castle of Gilles de Retz, a medieval fort somehow transformed in the 19th century into a pleasure villa. It is privately owned. Up above

Getting Around

An SNCF **rail** service links Nantes with Préfailles almost at the westernmost tip of the Pays de Retz. There are stops along the coast at Bourgneuf-en-Retz, Les Moutiers-en-Retz, La Bernerie-en-Retz, Pornic and Ste-Marie-sur-Mer.

Tourist Information

Pornic: Place de la Gare, t 02 40 82 04 40, *www.ot-pornic.fr*.

Market Days
Pornic: Thursday and Sunday.

Where to Stay and Eat

Pont-St-Martin ✉ 44860
Château du Plessis-Atlantique, t 02 40 26 81 72 (*expensive–very expensive*). An historic house with 3 luxury B&B bedrooms, situated close to Nantes-Atlantique airport and closer still to the Loire vineyards.

Ste-Pazanne ✉ 44680
La Plauderie, 1 Rue du Verdelet, t 02 40 02 45 08 (*moderate*). An elegant address away from the noisy coast, with delightful B&B rooms, a garden by the village church, and a very kind welcome.

La Bernerie-en-Retz ✉ 44760
★★★Domaine du Château de la Gressière, Rue de la Noue Fleurie, t 02 51 74 60 06, *www.lagressiere.com* (*inexpensive–expensive*). Stylish rooms in a property overlooking the coast, with a tennis court.

Pornic ✉ 44210
★★★L'Hôtel Alliance, Plage de la Source, t 02 40 82 21 21, *www.thalassopornic.com* (*expensive–very expenive*). A posh hotel attached to the Pornic thalassotherapy centre, on the sea on the south side of town.
★★Beau Soleil, 70 Quai Leray, t 02 40 82 34 58 (*inexpensive–moderate*). A modern wedge of a building on the quay just north of the castle, in the centre of the action. It has bright, sparkling, neat and clean rooms looking out over to the chic villas of Gourmalon to the south. It's a delightful place, brilliantly situated.
★★Le Relais St-Gilles, 7 Rue de Fernand Mun, t 02 40 82 02 25, *www.relaisstgilles.com* (*inexpensive–moderate*). A pleasant option in the upper old village, away from the quayside bustle and without estuary views.
Beau Rivage, Plage de la Birochère, t 02 40 82 03 08 (*moderate–very expensive*). A superb location for superb seafood cuisine. *Closed Mon, and Wed and Sun eves in low season.*

Préfailles ✉ 44770
★★La Flottille, Pointe St-Gildas, t 02 40 21 61 18, *www.laflottille.com* (*moderate*). A traditional-looking seaside hotel, with a restaurant with a terrace and a bar/crêperie. There's also a covered pool and a sauna.

La Plaine-sur-Mer ✉ 44770
★★★Anne de Bretagne, 163 Boulevard de la Tara, Port de la Gravette, just north of the Pointe St-Gildas, t 02 40 21 54 72, *www.annedebretagne.com* (*moderate–expensive*). An extremely comfortable modern seaside hotel in front of the Loire's mouth. The cooking is excellent and there's a pool and a tennis court in the garden.

the Quai Leray and the castle, the old village and its picturesque network of lanes are sometimes somewhat quieter than the quays, although there are plenty of seaside boutiques up here. Pornic has its own **pottery works**. To visit, ask at the tourist office.

An unmissable walk takes you from the busy Quai Leray out to the **Port de Plaisance de Noëveillard**. A boardwalk circles the ramparts of the castle. You then follow a schist path past some of the grandest of Pornic's houses, each built in different style. The first, an Italianate villa from the Ancien Régime, went up for a St-Malo shipping magnate at a time when rumour had it that a great new harbour was going to be built in southern Brittany, subsidized by the royal government. In fact, several

Malouins bought into Pornic through marriage and property, but the great project was never realized. The path leads to the *port de plaisance*, pleasure boats packed like sardines, with more than 1,000 berths. One end is reserved for the dwindling number of traditional fishing boats; some 45 still make a living from the waters off Pornic. Their most profitable catch is of *civelles*, the baby eels that are so highly prized in some countries that they fetch astronomical prices. Virtually all the catch is snapped up by Japanese and Spanish buyers for up to €200 a kilo.

Beautiful coastal paths leave Pornic in either direction. You may come across the odd neolithic remain or Nazi blockhouse. The most famous neolithic monument in Pornic is the **Tumulus des Mousseaux** to the north, a cairn from around 3500 BC, but the **Tumulus de la Joselière** along the southern coastal path retains far more atmosphere.

Ever-present in the distance lies Noirmoutier, a mirage of an island with gorgeous beaches. A boat service links Pornic and Noirmoutier.

Language

Use *monsieur, madame* or *mademoiselle* when speaking to everyone (and never *garçon* in restaurants!), from your first *bonjour* to your last *au revoir*.

For Food vocabulary, *see* p.50.

Pronunciation

Vowels

a/à/â between *a* in 'bat' and 'part'
é/er/ez at end of word as *a* in 'plate' but a bit shorter
e/è/ê as *e* in 'bet'
e at end of word not pronounced
e at end of syllable or in one-syllable word
pronounced weakly, like *er* in 'mother'
i as *ee* in 'bee'
o as *o* in 'pot'
ô as *o* in 'go'
u/û between *oo* in 'boot' and *ee* in 'bee'

Vowel Combinations

ai as *a* in 'plate'
aî as *e* in 'bet'
ail as *i* in 'kite'
au/eau as *o* in 'go'
ei as *e* in 'bet'
eu/œu as *er* in 'mother'
oi between *wa* in 'swam' and *wu* in 'swum'
oy as 'why'
ui as *wee* in 'twee'

Nasal Vowels

Vowels followed by an **n** or **m** have a nasal sound.
an/en as *o* in 'pot' + nasal sound
ain/ein/in as *a* in 'bat' + nasal sound
on as *aw* in 'paw' + nasal sound
un as *u* in 'nut' + nasal sound

Consonants

Many French consonants are pronounced as in English, but there are some exceptions:

c followed by *e, i* or *y*, and *ç* as *s* in 'sit'
c followed by *a, o, u* as *c* in 'cat'
g followed by *e, i* or *y* as *s* in 'pleasure'
g followed by *a, o, u* as *g* in 'good'
gn as *ni* in 'opinion'
j as *s* in 'pleasure'
ll as *y* in 'yes'
qu as *k* in 'kite'
s between vowels as *z* in 'zebra'
s otherwise as *s* in 'sit'
w except in English words as *v* in 'vest'
x at end of word as *s* in 'sit'
x otherwise as *x* in 'six'

Stress

The stress usually falls on the last syllable except when the word ends with an unaccented *e*.

Useful Phrases

hello *bonjour*
good evening *bonsoir*
good night *bonne nuit*
goodbye *au revoir*
please *s'il vous plaît*
thank you (very much) *merci (beaucoup)*
yes *oui*
no *non*
good *bon (bonne)*
bad *mauvais*
excuse me *pardon, excusez-moi*
Can you help me? *Pourriez-vous m'aider?*
My name is... *Je m'appelle...*
What is your name?
   Comment t'appelles-tu? (informal),
   Comment vous appelez-vous? (formal)
How are you? *Comment allez-vous?*
Fine *Ça va bien*
I don't understand *Je ne comprend pas*
I don't know *Je ne sais pas*
Speak more slowly
   Pourriez-vous parler plus lentement?

How do you say ... in French?
Comment dit-on ... en français?
Help! *Au secours!*

WC *les toilettes*
men *hommes*
ladies *dames* or *femmes*

doctor *le médecin*
hospital *un hôpital*
emergency room *la salle des urgences*
police station *le commissariat de police*
No Smoking *Défense de fumer*

Shopping and Sightseeing

Do you have...? *Est-ce que vous avez...?*
I would like... *J'aimerais...*
Where is/are...? *Où est/sont...*
How much is it? *C'est combien?*
It's too expensive *C'est trop cher*

entrance *l'entrée*
exit *la sortie*
open *ouvert*
closed *fermé*
push *poussez*
pull *tirez*

bank *une banque*
money *l'argent*
traveller's cheque *un chèque de voyage*
post office *la poste*
stamp *un timbre*
phone card *une télécarte*
postcard *une carte postale*
public phone *une cabine téléphonique*
Do you have any change?
Avez-vous de la monnaie?
shop *un magasin*
central food market *les halles*
tobacconist *un tabac*
pharmacy *une pharmacie*
aspirin *l'aspirine*
condoms *les préservatifs*
insect repellent *l'anti-insecte*
sun cream *la crème solaire*
tampons *les tampons hygiéniques*

beach *la plage*
booking/box office *le bureau de location*
church *l'église*

museum *le musée*
sea *la mer*
theatre *le théâtre*

Accommodation

Do you have a room?
Avez-vous une chambre?
Can I look at the room?
Puis-je voir la chambre?
How much is the room per day/week?
C'est combien la chambre par jour/semaine?
single room *une chambre pour une personne*
twin room *une chambre à deux lits*
double room
une chambre pour deux personnes
... with a shower/bath
... avec douche/salle de bains
... for one night/one week
... pour une nuit/une semaine

bed *un lit*
blanket *une couverture*
cot (child's bed) *un lit d'enfant*
pillow *un oreiller*
soap *du savon*
towel *une serviette*

Directions

Where is...? *Où se trouve...?*
left *à gauche*
right *à droite*
straight on *tout droit*
here *ici*
there *là*
close *proche*
far *loin*
forwards *en avant*
backwards *en arrière*
up *en haut*
down *en bas*
corner *le coin*
square *la place*
street *la rue*

Transport

I want to go to... *Je voudrais aller à...*
How can I get to...? *Comment puis-je aller à..?*
When is the next...? *Quel est le prochain...?*

What time does it leave (arrive)?
A quelle heure part-il (arrive-t-il)?
From where does it leave? *D'où part-il?*
Do you stop at... ? *Passez-vous par... ?*
How long does the trip take?
Combien de temps dure le voyage?
A (single/return) ticket to...
un aller or aller simple/aller et retour) pour...
How much is the fare?
Combien coûte le billet?
Have a good trip! *Bon voyage!*

airport *l'aéroport*
aeroplane *l'avion*
berth *la couchette*
bicycle *la bicyclette/le vélo*
mountain bike *le vélo tout terrain, le VTT*
bus *l'autobus*
bus stop *l'arrêt d'autobus*
car *la voiture*
coach *l'autocar*
coach station *la gare routière*
flight *le vol*
on foot *à pied*
port *le port*
railway station *la gare*
ship *le bateau*
subway *le métro*
taxi *le taxi*
train *le train*

delayed *en retard*
on time *à l'heure*
platform *le quai*
date-stamp machine *le composteur*
timetable *l'horaire*
left-luggage locker *la consigne automatique*
ticket office *le guichet*
ticket *le billet*
customs *la douane*
seat *la place*

Driving

breakdown *la panne*
car *la voiture*
danger *le danger*
driver *le chauffeur*
entrance *l'entrée*
exit *la sortie*
give way/yield *céder le passage*
hire *louer*

(international) driving licence
un permis de conduire (international)
motorbike/moped
la moto/le vélomoteur
no parking *stationnement interdit*
petrol (unleaded) *l'essence (sans plomb)*
road *la route*
roadworks *les travaux*
This doesn't work
Ça ne marche pas
Is the road good?
Est-ce que la route est bonne?

Numbers

one *un*
two *deux*
three *trois*
four *quatre*
five *cinq*
six *six*
seven *sept*
eight *huit*
nine *neuf*
ten *dix*

eleven *onze*
twelve *douze*
thirteen *treize*
fourteen *quatorze*
fifteen *quinze*
sixteen *seize*
seventeen *dix-sept*
eighteen *dix-huit*
nineteen *dix-neuf*

twenty *vingt*
twenty-one *vingt et un*
twenty-two *vingt-deux*
thirty *trente*
forty *quarante*
fifty *cinquante*
sixty *soixante*
seventy *soixante-dix*
seventy-one *soixante et onze*
eighty *quatre-vingts*
eighty-one *quatre-vingt-un*
ninety *quatre-vingt-dix*

one hundred *cent*
two hundred *deux cents*
one thousand *mille*

Months

January *janvier*
February *février*
March *mars*
April *avril*
May *mai*
June *juin*
July *juillet*
August *août*
September *septembre*
October *octobre*
November *novembre*
December *décembre*

Days

Monday *lundi*
Tuesday *mardi*
Wednesday *mercredi*
Thursday *jeudi*
Friday *vendredi*
Saturday *samedi*
Sunday *dimanche*

Time

What time is it? *Quelle heure est-il?*
It's 2 o'clock (am/pm) *Il est deux heures (du matin/de l'après-midi)*
... half past 2 *...deux heures et demie*
... a quarter past 2 *...deux heures et quart*
... a quarter to 3 *...trois heures moins le quart*
it is early *il est tôt*
it is late *il est tard*

month *un mois*
week *une semaine*
day *un jour/une journée*
morning *le matin*
afternoon *l'après-midi*
evening *le soir*
night *la nuit*
today *aujourd'hui*
yesterday *hier*
tomorrow *demain*
day before yesterday *avant-hier*
day after tomorrow *après-demain*
soon *bientôt*

Glossary of Breton Words

You may recognize many of these words in western Brittany, but do note that Breton words beginning with a consonant often change the first consonant according to preceding article and case and if in the plural.

aber: river estuary
amzer fall: bad weather
amzer gaer: excellent weather
an: the (form used before words beginning with vowels and d, h, n or t)
ankou: sudden death, the Grim Reaper
aod: coast, strand
ar: the (form used before words beginning with most consonants)
arvor: coastal region
avel: wind
aven: river estuary
bag (bag pesketa): boat (fishing boat)
bagad: Breton band
banal: broom
bara: bread
ar bed: the earth
beg: headland
beuzec: boxwood
bez: tomb
bihan: small
bili: pebbles
biniou: bagpipes
bloavez mad: Happy New Year
bombarde: Breton oboe
bot: bush
braz: big
Breizh: Brittany
bro: region
brug: heather
bugel: child
buoc'h: cow
coat: woods
coz: old
cosquer: old village
croas: cross

de mad: hello
digemer mad: welcome
dol: table
douar: earth, ground
dour: water
drennec: bramble patch
du: black
enez: island
erenn: dune
faou: beech
fest noz: night festival
feunteun: fountain
frout: stream
Gallaou: French person
gast: [one of the most common Breton swearwords, literally meaning whore]
gast amzer: bloody awful weather
glaw (bezo glaw): rain (it is raining)
glaz: green or blue
gwele: bed
gwenn, guenn: white
gwern: marsh
gwez: trees
gwiler: hamlet, village
gwin: wine
gwreg: spouse
ha: and
hent: road
heol: sun
hir: long
huel: high
iliz: church
izel: the bottom, the lowest
kador: chair
karreg: rock or reef
kastell: castle
kenavo: goodbye
kenkiz (or quenquis): summer home
ker, quer, or **guer:** hamlet, village or town
ki: dog
killi (or quilly): hedged fields

konk (or **conq**): cove, creek:
kouer: peasant
krampouz: crêpes
kreiz: centre, middle
krogen: shell
lan: monastery, religious place
lann: moor or gorse
loc: hermitage, isolated place
lost: the end, tip or tail
louarn: fox
mad: good
mamm: mother
mamm goz: grandmother
marc'h: horse
men: rock
menez: rounded hill
mez: big
meur: large, important
mor: sea
moraer: seaman
mor braz: the big sea, i.e. the ocean
Mor Breizh: the Breton Sea or Channel
morzen: mermaid
nevez: new
nouz vad: good night
penty: cottage
penn: head, tip or start
pesk: fish
plou: parish
porz: cove, port
poul: pond, pool, creek
roc'h: crest, schist rock
roue: king

roz: mound, hillock
ruz: red
Saoz: English person
so or **zo**: is
stang: lake
ster: river or stream
tad: father
tad koz: grandfather
tal: opposite
taol: table (see also dol)
toul: place or hole
tref: part of a parish
ty: house
yer mat: cheers

Some Numbers in Breton

unan: one
daou: two
tri: three
pevar: four
pemp: five
c'hwec'h: six
seizh: seven
eizh: eight
nav: nine
dek: ten
ugent: twenty
tregant: thirty
daou-ugent: forty
hanter-kant: fifty
kant: one hundred

Further Reading

Breton Prehistory and History

Breton neolithic sites have inspired a large number of publications. In English, you might try Aubrey Burl's *Megalithic Brittany* (Thames & Hudson), a guide to the individual sites. The father and son team of A. Thom and A.S. Thom wrote *Megalithic Remains in Britain and Brittany* following their in-depth study to try to prove scientific hypotheses about the megaliths. Mark Patton's *Statements in Stone* (Routledge) has kept in touch with pretty recent serious archaeological discoveries. Giot's works on Breton prehistory are the most respected in French.

Moving on to history in Brittany, the obvious book to recommend in English is Michael Jones' and Patrick Galliou's *The Bretons* (Basil Blackwell). It concentrates on Brittany up to and including the Middle Ages, but is disappointing after that. Michael Jones also wrote *The Creation of Brittany* (Hambleden Press). In French, Skol Breizh has published a solid introduction to Breton history. Apart from looking at the obscure Breton saints' lives, you can get fascinating glimpses into specific periods of Armorican and Breton history in some famous texts, for instance Caesar's *Conquest of Gaul* (Penguin Classics), Gregory of Tours' *The History of the Franks* (Penguin Classics), Froissart's chronicles and the correspondence of Mme de Sévigné.

Breton Legends

Many different versions of Breton legends exist. These stories were, after all, handed down orally over many centuries. The writing down of legends is notoriously unreliable. The most famous 19th-century gathering of them was made by Théodore Hersart de La Villemarqué in his *Barzhaz Breizh*. Another famous 19th-century collection was made by Anatole Le Braz in *La Légende de la Mort*. Pierre-Jakes Hélias published several volumes gathering Breton legends.

For the stories of the legend of the drowned city of Ys the author relied in particular on Charles Guyot's *La Légende de la Ville d'Ys d'après les Anciens Textes*. The *Guide de la Bretagne Mystérieuse* is a popular reference work briefly outlining Breton legends according to place names.

Fiction by Bretons or Inspired by Brittany

Chateaubriand is one of the most famous of Breton and French authors. In his autobiographical Romantic monster, *Mémoires d'outre-tombe*, he relates his early life in Brittany. The great Honoré de Balzac, born east along the Loire, based much of *Les Chouans ou la Bretagne en 1799* in Fougères, while the action in Victor Hugo's *Quatre-Vingt-Treize* also takes place in good part in Brittany. Pierre Loti wrote a couple of late-19th-century classics set in Brittany, *Pêcheur d'Islande* and *Mon Frère Yves*. They still make tear-jerking reads. Stendhal and Flaubert both wrote about their tours of Brittany.

Moving to the 20th century, *Querelle de Brest* is Jean Genet's notorious, powerfully written tale of the naval and police underworld and homosexuality. Henri Queffélec wrote a series of more conventional novels on Brittany, worthy if patronizing. *Les Iles de la Miséricorde* tells the story of the sinking of the British liner *The Drummond Castle* in the Ouessant archipelago, while the *Recteur de l'Ile de Sein* recounts how the islanders were reconverted from their wayward beliefs. *Un Homme d'Ouessant* and *Ils Etaient Six Marins de Groix* are other Queffélec novels inspired by Breton islands. Colette's *Le Blé en Herbe* (*The Ripening*

Seed) is a delightful evocation of adolescent rites of passage set just east of St-Malo. Louis Guilloux is a Breton author who has written some gritty novels set in his home province, notably *Le Sang Noir*. The most famous book on traditional Breton communities written in the 20th century is Pierre-Jakez Hélias's autobiographical *Le Cheval d'orgueil* (*The Horse of Pride*).

Jack Kerouac went in search of his Breton roots in *Sartori in Paris*, while contemporary British author Joanne Harris set her 2003 novel *Holy Fools* on the half-island of Noirmoutier opposite Pornic. The cartoon adventures of Astérix cannot go unmentioned.

Breton Art History

V.-H. Debidour's book on Breton art history, *L'Art de Bretagne*, is enjoyable In English. Several works have been published on Paul Gauguin and the Pont-Aven School, for example *Gauguin and the Impressionists at Pont-Aven* by J. Le Paul, and *Gauguin and the School of Pont-Aven* by C. Boyle-Turner. You can read selected correspondence that was written by Gauguin when he was in Brittany in *The Search for Paradise: Letters* from *Brittany and the South Seas*, edited by B. Denvir (Collins & Brown).

Ouest-France publishes a plethora of specialized booklets on a massive range of Breton themes, from art and architecture to furniture, costumes and *coiffes*.

Newspapers and Magazines

Ouest-France, which is the regional newspaper boasting the largest circulation in France, is a heavyweight publication. *Le Télégramme* is popular throughout western Brittany. Two particularly attractive regular magazines on Brittany are published in Douarnenez: *Le Chasse-Marée* concentrates on the sea, while *Ar Men* covers Breton cultural matters more generally.

The English-language newspaper *French News* has a free *Brittany News* supplement with regular information on local events; see also *www.french-news.com*.

Index

Main page references are in **bold**. Page references to maps are in *italics*.

Brittany touring atlas

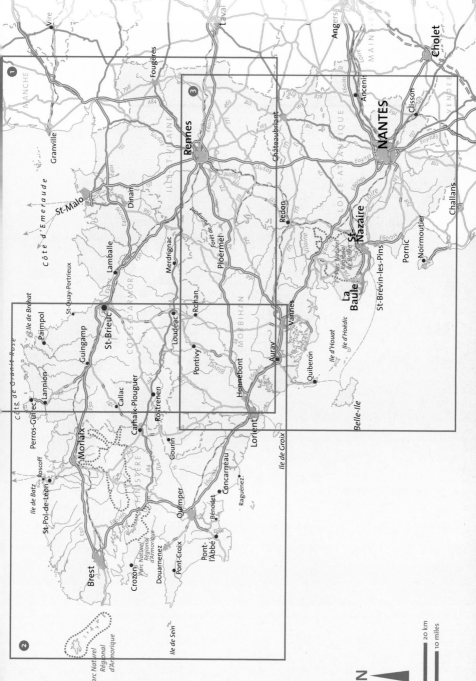

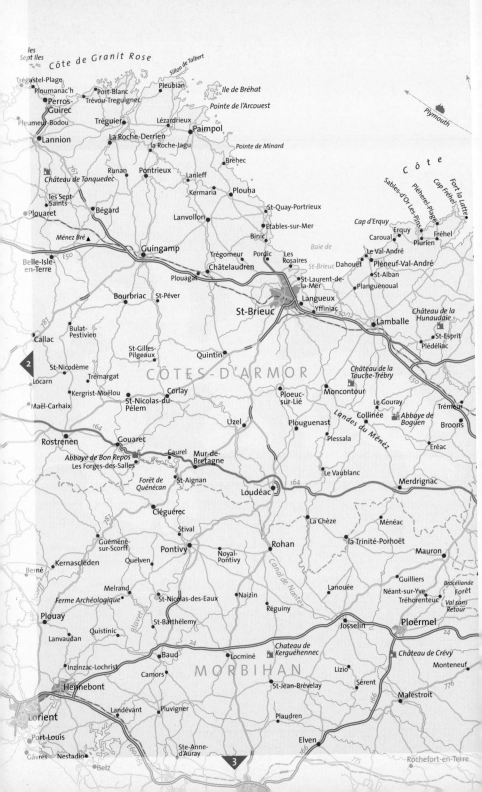

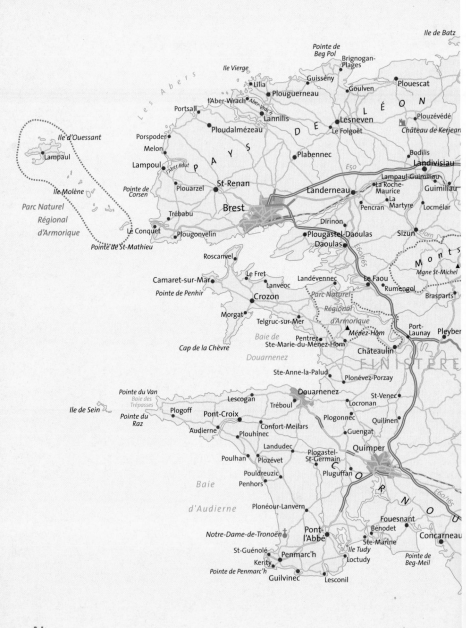

Cork/Rosslare

Plymouth

les Sept Iles

Côte de Granit Rose

Sillon de Talbert

Trégastel-Plage Ploumanac'h

Pleubian

Ile de Bréhat

Ile Grande

Port-Blanc

Pointe de l'Arcouest

Perros-Guirec

Trévou-Treguignec

Trébeurden

Pleumeur-Bodou

Tréguier

Lézardrieux

Paimpol

Baie de

le Yaude

Lannion

La Roche-Derrien

Pointe de Minard

Roscoff

Lannion

Locquémeau

la Roche-Jagu

Bréhec

St-Pol-de-Léon

Carantec

Locquirec

St-Michel-en-Grève

Rupan

Pontrieux

Lanleff

Kermaria

Plouha

Plouézoch

Lanmeur

Plestin-les-Grèves

Château de Tonquédec

St-Quay-Portrieux

Locquénolé

Château de Rosanbo

les Sept-Saints

Bégard

Lanvollon

Etables-sur-Mer

Taulé

Plouaret

Binic

Morlaix

Ménez Bré

Guingamp

Trégomeur

Pordic

St-Thé.gonnec

Châtelaudren

Les Rosaires

Plougonven

Belle-Isle-en-Terre

Plouagat

Plounéour-Ménez

Bourbriac

St-Péver

St-Brieuc

Parc Naturel

d'Arrée

Berrien

Scrignac

CÔTES-D'ARMOR

Régional

Bulat-Pestivien

St-Gilles-Pilgeaux

d'Armorique

Huelgoat

Callac

Quintin

St-Herbot

Locqueffret

St-Nicodème

Lannédern

Plouyé

Locarn

Trémargat

Corlay

Ploeuc-sur-Lié

Plounévézel

Carhaix-Plouguer

Kergrist-Moëlou

St-Nicolas-du-Pélem

Cléden-Poher

Maël-Carhaix

Uzel

Châteauneuf-du-Faou

St-Hernin

Rostrenen

Gouarec

Caurel

Mur-de-Bretagne

Laz

Notre-Dame-du-Crann

Abbaye de Bon Repos

Les Forges-des-Salles

St-Aignan

Loudéac

Château de Trévarez

Montagnes Noires

Forêt de Quénécan

Gourin

Le Saint

Abbaye de Langonnet

Cléguérec

Coray

Lac du Bel-Air

Stival

Rohan

Scaër

Le Faouët

St-Barbe

Guéméné-sur-Scorff

Pontivy

Noyal-Pontivy

Rosporden

St-Fiacre

Quelven

Meslan

Berné

Kernascléden

Réguiny

Bannalec

Melrand

St-Nicolas-des-Eaux

Naizin

AILLE

Ferme Archéologique

St-Barthélemy

Tregunc

Arzano

Plouay

Château de Kerguéhennec

Pont-Aven

Riec-sur-Belon

Quimperlé

Lanvaudan

Quistinic

Baud

Locminé

Névez

Kerdruc

Port-Manec'h

Moëlan-sur-Mer

Gestel

Pont-Scorff

Inzinzac-Lochrist

Camors

St-Jean-Brévelay

Raguénez

Guidel

Hennebont

MORBIHAN

Le Pouldu

Landévant

Pluvigner

Plaudren

Lorient

Larmor Plage

Port-Louis

Gâvres

Nestadio

Ste-Anne-d'Auray

Port Tudy

Belz

Auray

Vannes

Groix

Etel

St-Cado

Ile de Groix

Erdeven

Bono

Kernours

1

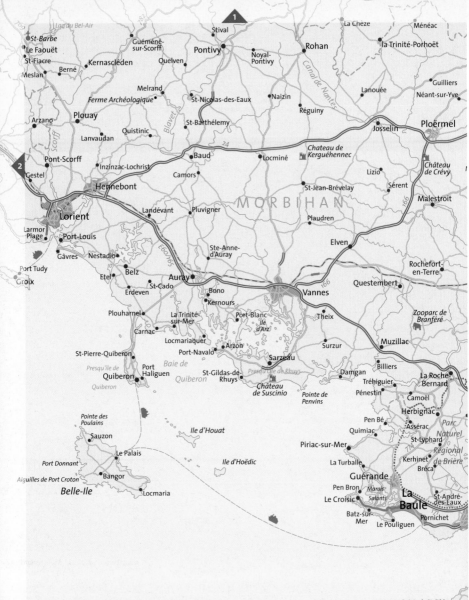

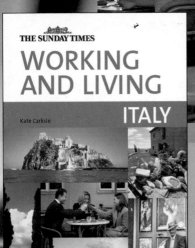

THE SUNDAY TIMES
WORKING AND LIVING
ITALY

Kate Carlisle

CADOGANguides

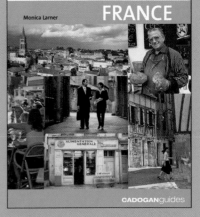

THE SUNDAY TIMES
WORKING AND LIVING
FRANCE

Monica Larner

CADOGANguides

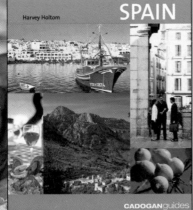

THE SUNDAY TIMES
WORKING AND LIVING
SPAIN

Harvey Holtom

CADOGANguides

Also available:

WORKING AND LIVING
PORTUGAL

CADOGANguides